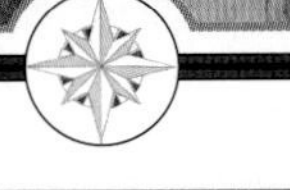

EYEWITNESS TRAVEL

FLORENCE & TUSCANY

MAIN CONTRIBUTOR: CHRISTOPHER CATLING

LONDON, NEW YORK,
MELBOURNE, MUNICH AND DELHI
www.dk.com

PROJECT EDITOR Shirin Patel
ART EDITOR Pippa Hurst
EDITORS Maggie Crowley,
Tom Fraser, Sasha Heseltine
DESIGNERS Claire Edwards,
Emma Hutton, Marisa Renzullo
MAP CO-ORDINATORS Simon Farbrother, David Pugh

CONTRIBUTORS
Anthony Brierley, Kerry Fisher,
Tim Jepson, Carolyn Pyrah

MAPS
Jan Clark, James Mills-Hicks
(Dorling Kindersley Cartography)

PHOTOGRAPHERS
Philip Enticknap,
John Heseltine, Kim Sayer

ILLUSTRATORS
Stephen Conlin, Donati Giudici Associati srl,
Richard Draper, Robbie Polley

Reproduced by Colourscan, Singapore
Printed and bound by South China Printing Co. Ltd., China

First published in Great Britain in 1994 by
Dorling Kindersley Limited
80 Strand, London WC2R 0RL

11 12 13 14 10 9 8 7 6 5 4 3 2

Reprinted with revisions 1994 (twice), 1996, 1997, 1999, 2000, 2001, 2002, 2003, 2004, 2005, 2006, 2007, 2008, 2009, 2011

A CIP CATALOGUE RECORD IS AVAILABLE FROM THE BRITISH LIBRARY.

ISBN 978-1-40535-878-1

FLOORS ARE REFERRED TO THROUGHOUT IN ACCORDANCE WITH EUROPEAN USAGE; IE THE "FIRST FLOOR" IS THE FLOOR ABOVE GROUND LEVEL

Front cover main image: the Duomo Cathedral, Florence

The information in this DK Eyewitness Travel Guide is checked regularly.

Every effort has been made to ensure that this book is as up-to-date as possible at the time of going to press. Some details, however, such as telephone numbers, opening hours, prices, gallery hanging arrangements and travel information are liable to change. The publishers cannot accept responsibility for any consequences arising from the use of this book, nor for any material on third party websites, and cannot guarantee that any website address in this book will be a suitable source of travel information. We value the views and suggestions of our readers very highly. Please write to: Publisher, DK Eyewitness Travel Guides, Dorling Kindersley, 80 Strand, London, WC2R 0RL, or email: travelguides@dk.com.

CONTENTS

Putto in Palazzo Vecchio

INTRODUCING FLORENCE AND TUSCANY

Flag from Siena's Palio

◁ **Detail from *The Procession of the Magi* by Gozzoli Benozzo (1420–1497), Palazzo Medici Riccardi**

A Tuscan country scene in the Crete

Cheese seller in Siena

Fresco in Santa Maria Novella

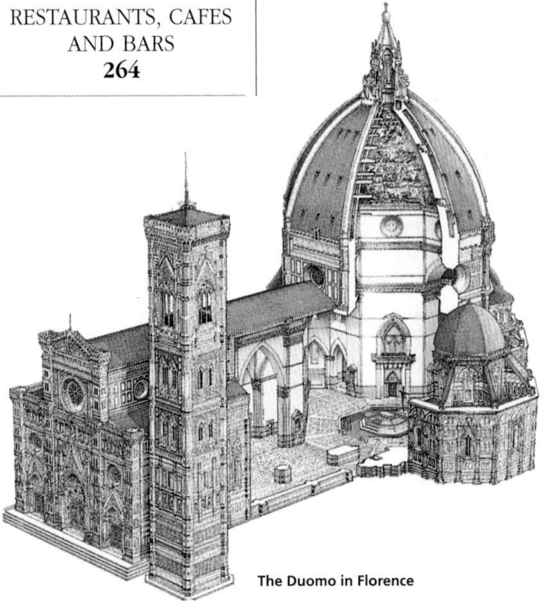
The Duomo in Florence

HOW TO USE THIS GUIDE

This guide helps you get the most from your stay in Florence and Tuscany. It provides both expert recommendations and detailed practical information. *Introducing Florence and Tuscany* maps the region and sets it in its historical and cultural context. *Florence Area by Area and Tuscany Area by Area* describe the important sights, with maps, pictures and detailed illustrations. Suggestions for food, drink, accommodation and shopping are in *Travellers' Needs*, and the *Survival Guide* has tips on everything from the Italian telephone system to getting to Tuscany and travelling around the region.

FLORENCE AREA BY AREA

The historic centre of the city has been divided into four sightseeing areas. Each has its own chapter, which opens with a list of the sights described. All the sights are numbered and plotted on an *Area Map*. The detailed information for each sight is presented in numerical order, making it easy to locate within the chapter.

All pages relating to Florence have red thumb tabs.

A locator map shows where you are in relation to other areas of the city centre.

Sights at a Glance lists the chapter's sights by category: Churches; Museums and Galleries; Historic Buildings, Streets and Piazzas.

1 Area Map

For easy reference, the sights are numbered and located on a map. The sights are also shown on the Florence Street Finder *on pages 140–47.*

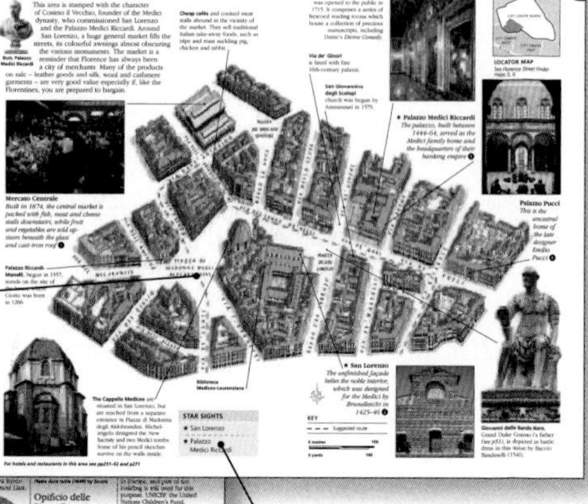

2 Street-by-Street Map

This gives a bird's eye view of the heart of each sightseeing area.

A suggested route for a walk covers the more interesting streets in the area.

Stars indicate the sights that no visitor should miss.

3 Detailed information on each sight

All the sights in Florence are described individually. Addresses, telephone numbers, opening hours and information on admission charges and wheelchair access are also provided.

1 Introduction
The landscape, history and character of each region is described here, showing how the area has developed over the centuries and what it offers to the visitor today.

TUSCANY AREA BY AREA

In this book, Tuscany has been divided into five regions, each of which has a separate chapter. The most interesting sights to visit have been numbered on a *Regional Map*.

Each area of Tuscany can be quickly identified by its colour coding.

2 Regional Map
This shows the road network and gives an illustrated overview of the whole region. All the sights are numbered and there are also useful tips on getting around the region by car, bus and train.

3 Detailed information on each sight
All the important towns and other places to visit are described individually. They are listed in order, following the numbering on the Regional Map. *Within each town or city, there is detailed information on important buildings and other sights.*

Stars indicate the best features and works of art.

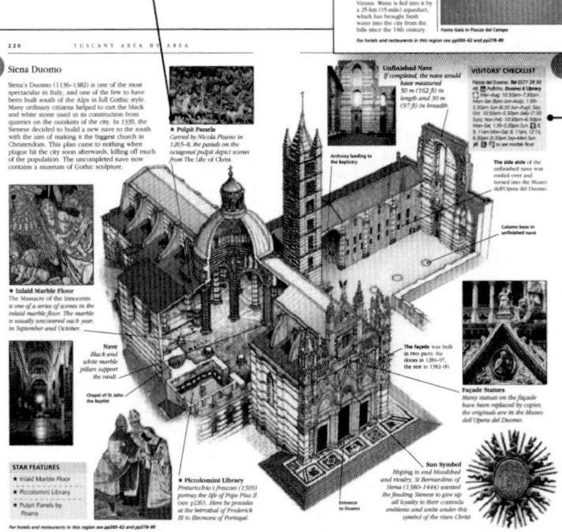

For all the top sights, a Visitors' Checklist provides the practical information you will need to plan your visit.

4 The top sights
These are given two or more full pages. Historic buildings are dissected to reveal their interiors; museums and galleries have colour-coded floorplans to help you locate the most interesting exhibits.

INTRODUCING FLORENCE AND TUSCANY

FOUR GREAT DAYS IN FLORENCE AND TUSCANY

There is something for just about everyone in Florence and Tuscany: from viewing some of the world's greatest Renaissance art to wandering around designer boutiques; and from exploring the surrounding countryside with its historic hilltowns, wine and charming restaurants to visiting one of the many spa towns. Each of these itineraries has a theme, but they can be tailored to suit your needs. Apart from the day of art in Florence, which can be done on foot, parts of the family day may be easier by bus or taxi while the other days do require a car. The price guides include the cost of travel, food and admission fees.

Shoes with style at the Ferragamo Shoe Museum, Florence

RENAISSANCE ART AND SHOPPING

- **The magnificent Duomo and Brunelleschi's dome**
- **Michelangelo's David**
- **Renaissance art in the Uffizi**
- **Stylish shoes and chic shops**

TWO ADULTS allow at least €130

Morning

Start the day at Brunelleschi's glorious church of **San Lorenzo** *(see pp90–91)*, with its unfinished, rough-hewn façade. The adjacent **Medici Tombs** *(see p91)*, designed by Michelangelo as a mausoleum for the Medici family, are gloomy yet impressive. Just a five-minute walk from here is the breath-taking **Duomo** *(see pp64–5)* with its vast dome also by Brunelleschi. Opposite it is the **Baptistry** with its ornate East Doors *(see p66)*, and the Campanile with fine views of the dome and the city below. Pause for a lively, cheap lunch at **Da Mario** *(see p270)*.

Afternoon

Stroll across to **Piazza della Signoria** *(see pp76–7)*, where a copy of Michelangelo's celebrated *David* stands outside the **Palazzo Vecchio** *(see pp78–9)*. The real one is in the **Galleria dell'Accademia** *(see p94–5)*. Just round the corner is the **Uffizi** *(see pp80–3)*, with its unrivalled collection of Renaissance art. At least half a day is needed to appreciate its wonderful treasures so you may wish to return another day to spend more time here. Head to the **Ponte Vecchio** *(see pp106–7)*, taking in the jeweller's shops and old workshops that line the bridge.

Afterwards walk to **Via de' Tornabuoni** *(see p105)* with its chic boutiques for a spot of shopping. For anyone interested in footwear, Ferragamo's Shoe Museum is also here. Finish with a chilled glass of *prosecco* at **Procacci** *(see p283)*.

A FAMILY DAY OUT IN FLORENCE

- **Gory waxworks**
- **View the Boboli Gardens**
- **Explore the Palazzo Vecchio**
- **Ride around town in a horse-drawn carriage**

FAMILY OF 4 allow at least €230

Morning

Go to the **Mercato Centrale** *(see p88)* and enjoy the colourful arrays of fruit and vegetables. Then, head over to the Oltrarno and the **Museo "La Specola"** *(see p119)*, an unusual zoological museum with a rather gory display of 18th-century anatomical waxworks (parental discretion may be required for young children).

The **Boboli Gardens** *(see pp124–5)* makes a great spot for a relaxing break or a run around. Unfortunately, picnics are not allowed here, so head for one of the many eateries near **Piazza di Santo Spirito** *(see p118)*. Lunch should be followed by a

A nightmarish scene at the Waxworks at La Specola

gelato (ice cream) from **Café Ricchi** *(see p272)* in the same square.

Afternoon

On a warm day, take the kids for a swim at the outdoor pool at **Bellariva** *(see p293)*, open Jun–mid-Sep. If cool, a visit to **Palazzo Vecchio** *(see p78)* is a good bet; tours of secret passages and other activities (also in English) geared to all ages are organized within the palazzo museum. End the day with a leisurely ride around the *centro storico* in one of the horse-drawn carriages that stand in Piazza Signoria, before going for a pizza.

MEDIEVAL HISTORY, ART AND CULTURE

- **A dramatic hilltown**
- **Siena's striped Duomo**
- **Sienese art in the Pinacoteca Nazionale**
- **An aperitivo in the Piazza del Campo**

TWO ADULTS allow at least €190

Morning

Arrive by car early in **San Gimignano** *(see pp212–15)*, arguably Tuscany's most famous hilltown. Must-see sights here are the 13th-century towers, the frescoes in the Collegiata church, and the art in the Museo Civico. You might like to buy a bottle of the local Vernaccia wine and have a coffee in Piazza della Cisterna before setting off to **Siena** *(see pp216–19)*.

Head straight for theatrical Piazza del Campo where the energetic can climb the Torre del Mangia, while others can visit the medieval state rooms in the Palazzo Pubblico. Don't miss Lorenzetti's frescoes of the *Allegory of Good and Bad Government*. Take a break for lunch at the **Osteria Le Logge** *(see p280)*.

Afternoon

Visit the striped Gothic **Duomo** *(see pp220–21)*, then pop into the **Pinacoteca Nazionale** *(see p219)* to see its 12th-15th century Sienese masters. Or you could wander the streets on the lookout for signs, which represent the 17 *contrade* (or districts), such as ceramic animal plaques and fountains. End the day with an *aperitivo* at one of the bars on Piazza del Campo.

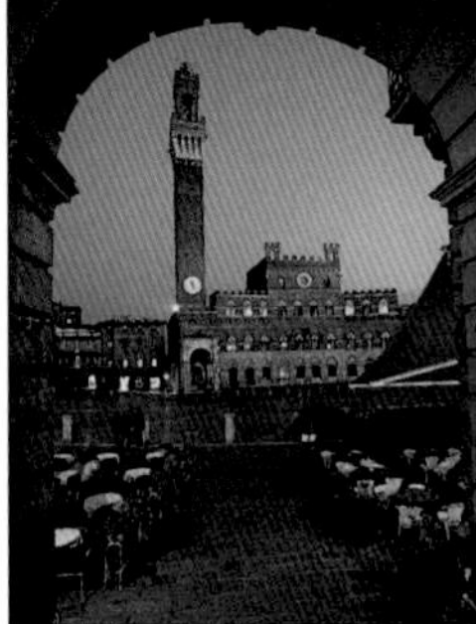

Archway view of Siena's Piazza del Campo at dusk

TUSCAN HILL TOWN TOUR

- **Montepulciano and its Vino Nobile wines**
- **A leisurely lunch in Pienza**
- **Frescoes in Sant'Anna**
- **A soak in the thermal pools at Bagno Vignoni**

TWO ADULTS allow at least €250

Morning

Drive to **Montepulciano** *(see p227)*, one of Tuscany's highest hilltop towns and famous for its Vino Nobile wines. Visit the Duomo and Sangallo's Temple of San Biagio just outside the town. About 5 km (3 miles)to the southeast, the tiny medieval village of **Monticchiello** *(see p209)*, set in an idyllic landscape, is a wonderful place to stop for a coffee break. Its 13th-century church is worth a visit too. Move on to **Pienza** *(see p226)*, Pope Pius II's ideal Renaissance town, where you will find charming cobbled streets and panoramic ramparts to explore. Buy some local *pecorino* (sheep's cheese) before lunching at **La Pergola** *(see p279)*.

Afternoon

From Pienza, the road winds through glorious countryside. Take a detour to the remote monastery of **Sant'Anna in Camprena** (where part of *The English Patient* was filmed) with its refectory frescoes by Sodoma *(see p226)*. Once you get to **San Quirico d'Orcia** *(see p225)*, visit the beautiful 12th-century Collegiata, with three Romanesque doorways carved in local travertine. There is also a pretty 16th-century Italianate garden, the Horti Leonini. Finish the day with a soak in the outdoor 37 °C (98.6 °F) pools at the Hotel Posta Marcucci in the medieval spa village of **Bagno Vignoni** *(see p226)*. You will find several good restaurants for dinner.

Tall cypress trees, in the timeless landcape of southern Tuscany

Putting Florence and Tuscany on the Map

Tuscany lies in Central Italy, bordered by the regions of Emilia-Romagna, Marche, Umbria and Lazio. Along with Elba, several islands in the Ligurian Sea also form part of Tuscany. A region of rolling hills, mountains and rugged coastlines, Tuscany covers an area of 22,992 sq km (8,875 sq miles), and has a population of more than 3.5 million. There are international airports at Pisa and Florence. Florence is about 2½ hours by train from Rome (1½ hours on Eurostar) and about 3 hours from Milan.

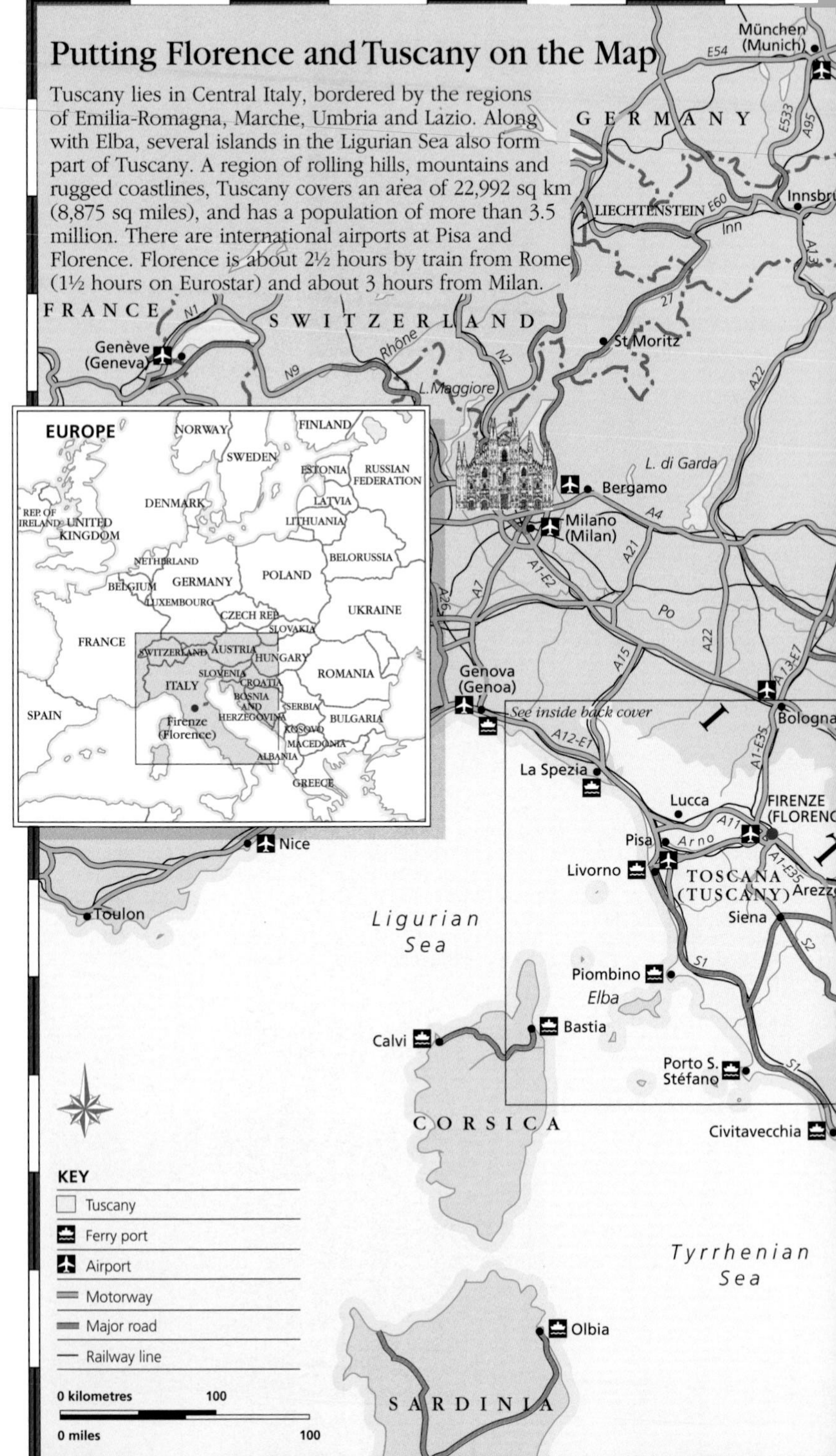

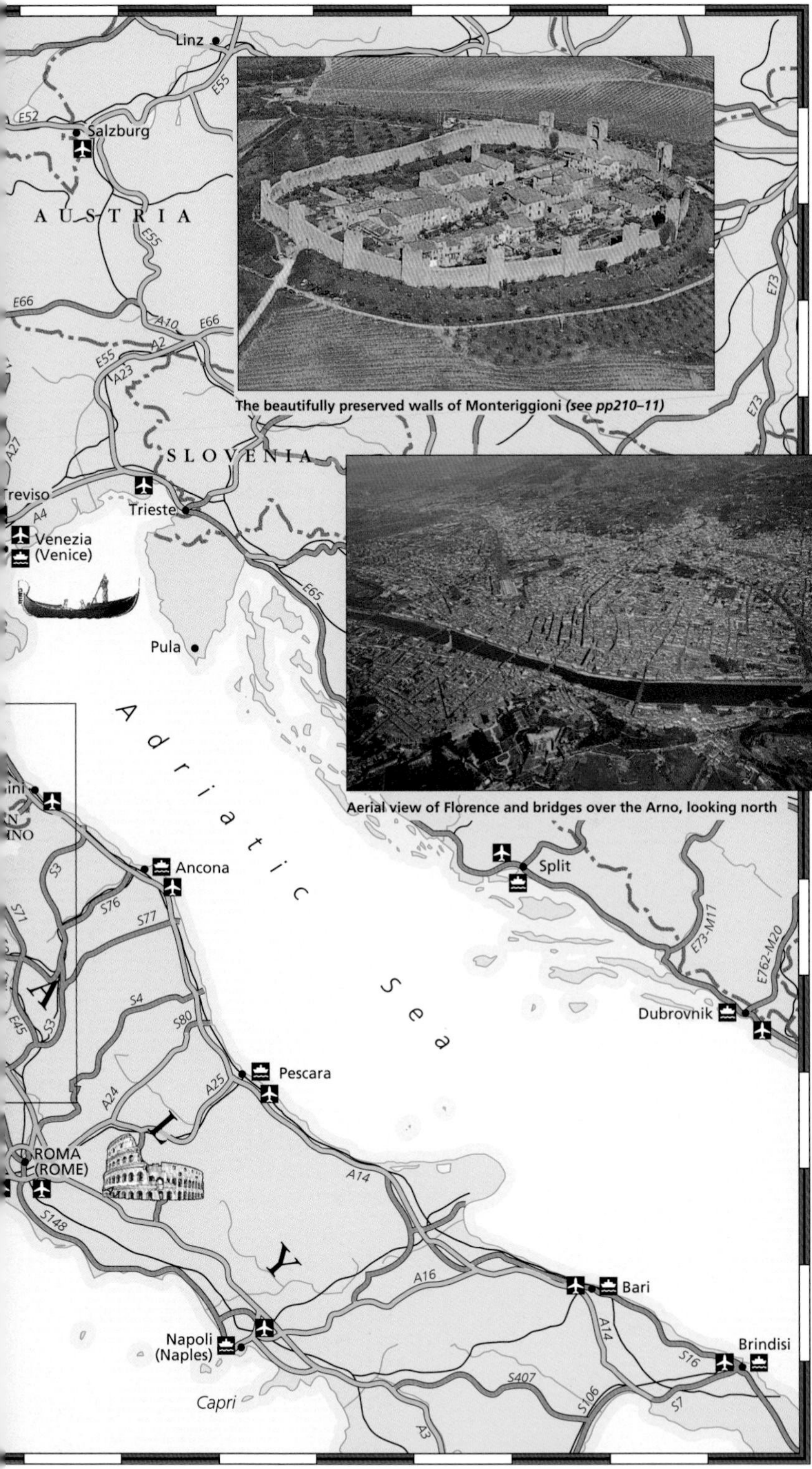

The beautifully preserved walls of Monteriggioni *(see pp210–11)*

Aerial view of Florence and bridges over the Arno, looking north

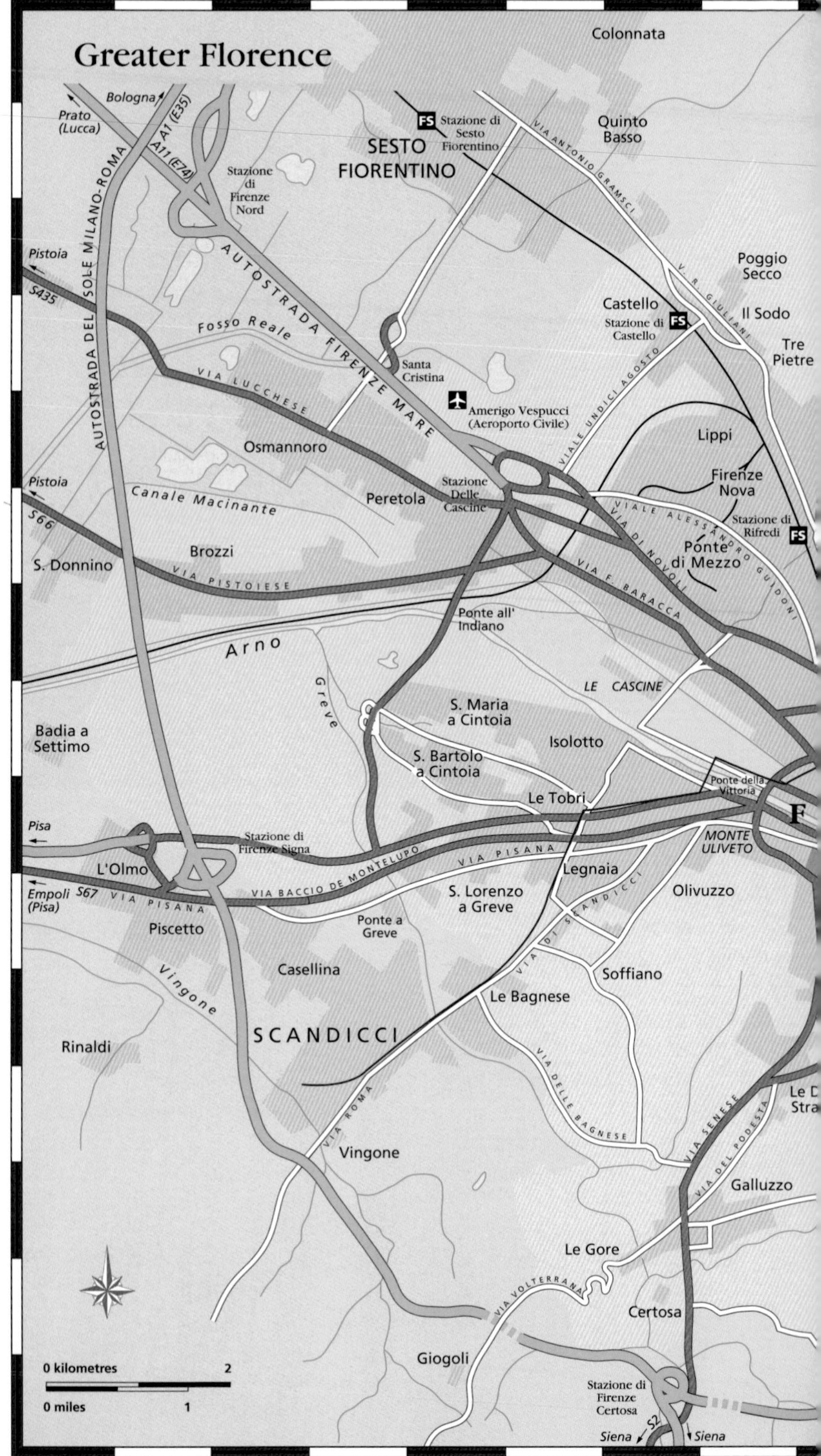
Greater Florence
Colonnata
Bologna
Prato (Lucca)
A1 (E35)
A11 (E74)
Stazione di Sesto Fiorentino
SESTO FIORENTINO
Quinto Basso
VIA ANTONIO GRAMSCI
Stazione di Firenze Nord
AUTOSTRADA DEL SOLE MILANO-ROMA
AUTOSTRADA FIRENZE MARE
Pistoia
S435
Poggio Secco
V. R. GIULIANI
Castello
Stazione di Castello
Il Sodo
Tre Pietre
Fosso Reale
VIA LUCCHESE
Santa Cristina
Amerigo Vespucci (Aeroporto Civile)
VIALE UNDICI AGOSTO
Lippi
Osmannoro
Firenze Nova
Pistoia
S66
Canale Macinante
Peretola
Stazione Delle Cascine
VIALE ALESSANDRO GUIDONI
Stazione di Rifredi
VIA DI NOVOLI
Ponte di Mezzo
Brozzi
S. Donnino
VIA PISTOIESE
VIA F. BARACCA
Ponte all' Indiano
Arno
LE CASCINE
Greve
S. Maria a Cintoia
Badia a Settimo
Isolotto
S. Bartolo a Cintoia
Ponte della Vittoria
Le Tobri
F
Pisa
Stazione di Firenze Signa
MONTE ULIVETO
VIA PISANA
L'Olmo
Legnaia
VIA BACCIO DE MONTELUPO
Empoli (Pisa)
S67
VIA PISANA
S. Lorenzo a Greve
VIA DI SCANDICCI
Olivuzzo
Piscetto
Ponte a Greve
Casellina
Soffiano
Vingone
Le Bagnese
SCANDICCI
Rinaldi
VIA DELLE BAGNESE
VIA ROMA
VIA SENESE
VIA DEL PODESTÀ
Vingone
Galluzzo
Le Gore
VIA VOLTERRANA
Certosa
Giogoli
0 kilometres 2
0 miles 1
Stazione di Firenze Certosa
S2
Siena
Siena

S65
Bologna
Faenza
S302
Via delle Masse
Via Bolognese
Pian di S. Bartolo
Mugnone
Via Faentina
Serpiolle
Terzolle
Trespiano
Pian di Mugnone
Via dei Bosconi
Monte Muscoli
Careggi
La Lastra
Fiesole
Via di Vincigliata
Le Panche
Ponte alla Badia
La Pietra
Lapo
Monte Ceceri
Mensola
S. Domenico
Via della Collina
Rifredi
Camerata
Maiano
Montebeni
V. d. Selva
Il Salviatino
Settignano
Piazza della Libertà
San Gervasio
Poggio Gherardo
Stazione di Campo di Marte
Campo di Marte
Coverciano
Ponte a Mensola
Stazione Centrale di Santa Maria Novella
Filarocca
Firenze
San Salvi
Pontassieve
Ponte alla Carraia
Madonnone
Via Aretina S67
Ponte Vecchio
Ponte alle Grazie
Varlungo
S. Iacopo al Girone
Ponte S. Niccolò
Ponte G. da Verrazzano
Via Generale dalla Chiesa
Ponte di Varlungo
Ricorboli
Via di Villamagna
Bobolino
Monte alle Croci
Gavinana
Nave a Rovezzano
Viale Europa
Rimaggio
Gamberaia
Bagno a Ripoli
Sorgane
Poggio Imperiale
Arcetri
Piazza Calda
Pian Dei Giullari
Ponte a Ema
Ema
Stazione di Firenze Sud
S. Piero a Ema
A1 (E35)
Autostrada del Sole Milano-Roma
Monte Cuccioli
Via dell'Antella
Monte Fattucchia
S. Gersole
Grassina
S222
Greve in Chianti

KEY

- Florence City Centre *See pp16–17*
- Built-up area
- Greater Florence
- Airport
- FS Railway station
- Motorway
- Major road
- Minor road
- Railway line
- Tram line

Florence City Centre

Florence's best sights are encompassed within such a compact area that the city seems to reveal its treasures at every step. The sights described in this book are grouped within four areas, each of which can be easily explored on foot. In the centre is the massive Duomo, providing a historical as well as geographical focus to the city. Santa Croce to the east and San Marco to the north, with Santa Maria Novella to the west and the Palazzo Pitti in Oltrarno, mark the outlying areas.

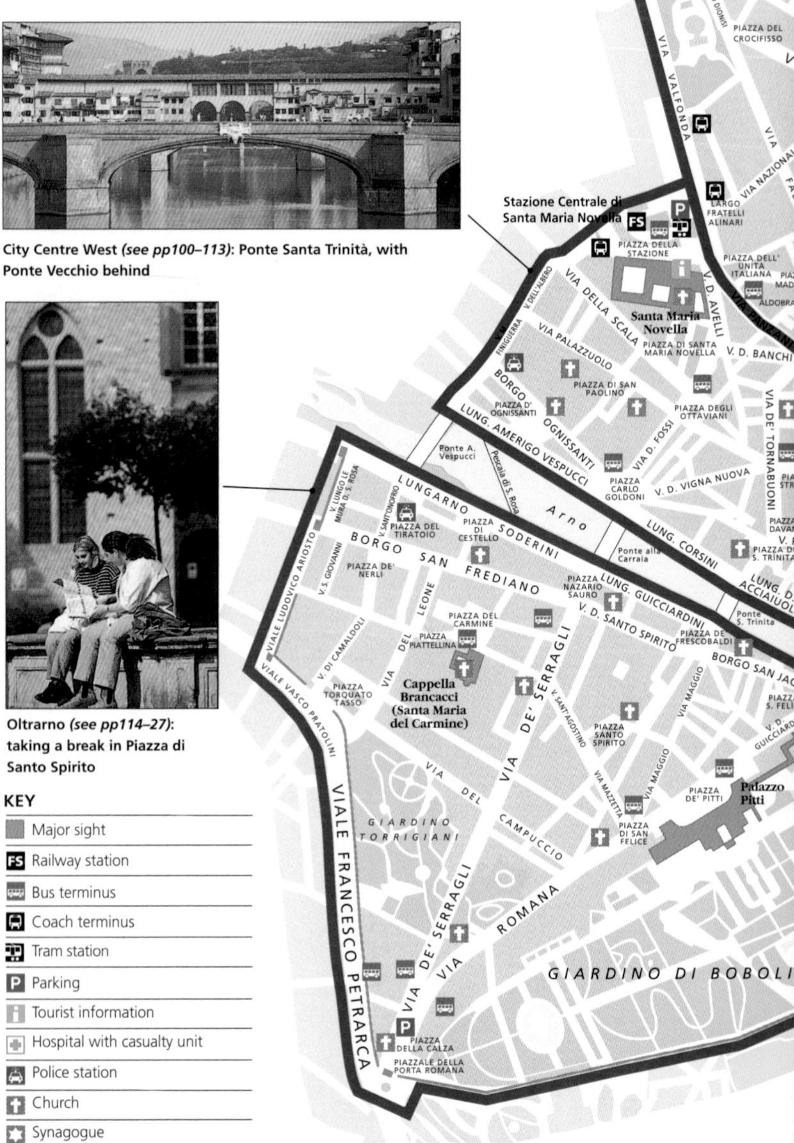

City Centre West *(see pp100–113)*: Ponte Santa Trinità, with Ponte Vecchio behind

Oltrarno *(see pp114–27)*: taking a break in Piazza di Santo Spirito

KEY

- Major sight
- Railway station
- Bus terminus
- Coach terminus
- Tram station
- Parking
- Tourist information
- Hospital with casualty unit
- Police station
- Church
- Synagogue

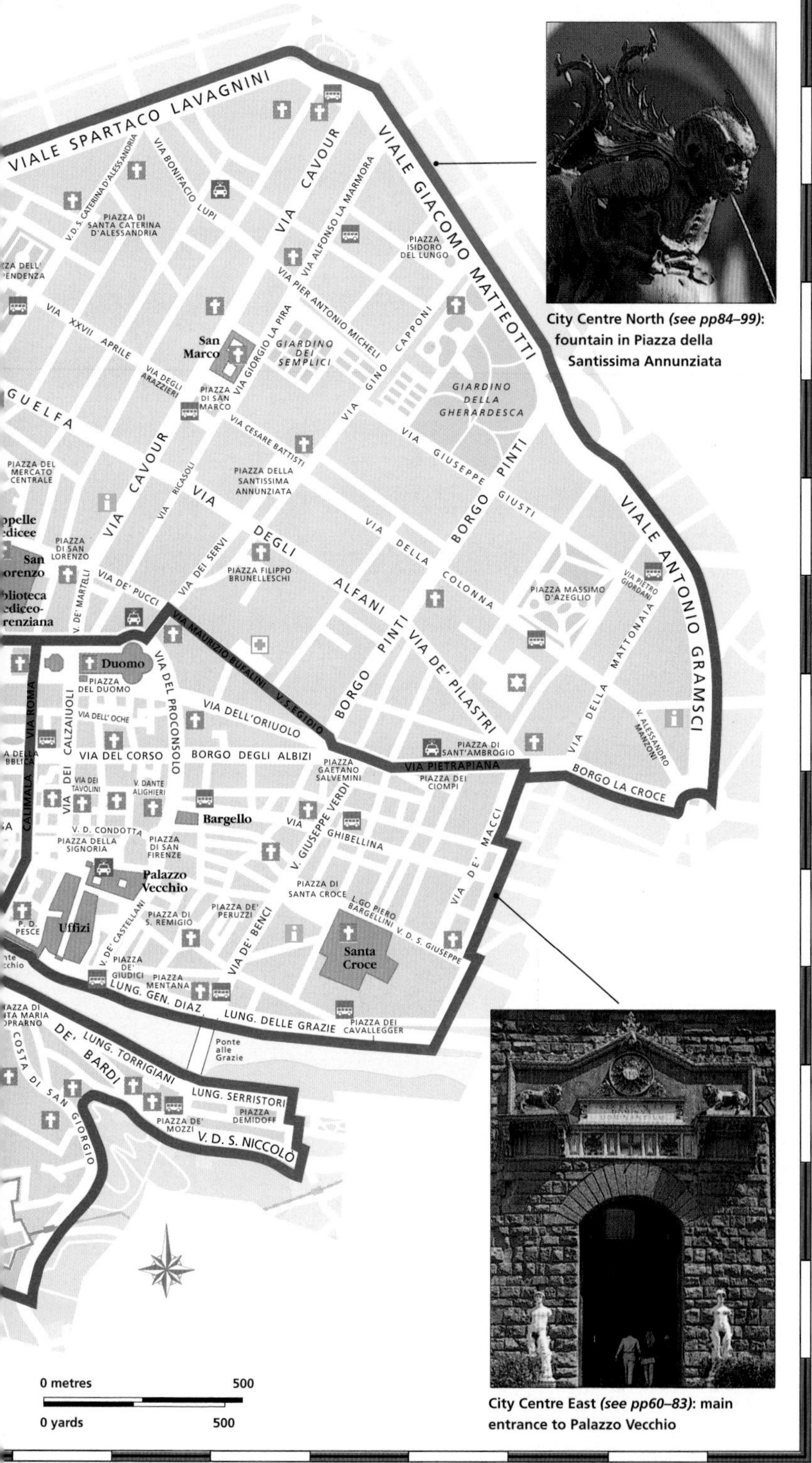

City Centre North *(see pp84–99)*: fountain in Piazza della Santissima Annunziata

City Centre East *(see pp60–83)*: main entrance to Palazzo Vecchio

A PORTRAIT OF TUSCANY

Tuscany is renowned throughout the world for its art, history and beautiful landscape. Here the past merges with the present to a remarkable degree, for its people pride themselves on their heritage. Independent and combative, for centuries they have preserved their surroundings and traditions, in which must lie much of Tuscany's eternal fascination for the outsider.

The people of Tuscany are fiercely proud of their ancestry, which they trace back to the Etruscans. Geneticists have even discovered gene segments that are uniquely Tuscan: there are strong similarities between the faces carved on Etruscan cremation urns *(see pp42–3)* and those of the people on the streets of modern Tuscany.

A classic Tuscan face captured by Botticelli

Florence and its surroundings were occupied by the Germans during World War II, and memories of the disgrace suffered under Fascism are still strong. As a result, people in this area have a fierce love of democracy and a strong sense of obligation to vote and participate in politics, even at grass-roots levels, through referendums on such issues as whether to ban traffic from the centre of Florence, for example. Florentines will, however, take the law into their own hands, as they did when they fought the police in 1990 to prevent the closure of San Lorenzo market.

The Tuscan love of home has resulted in a strong *campanilismo*: parochialism defined by the sound of the local church bell (in the campanile or belltower). Social anthropologists see in it a survival of medieval inter-city conflicts. It can be observed at many a Tuscan festival when, beneath the pageantry, there is a serious rivalry between a city's different quarters.

A timeless view and way of life: peaceful old age in Casole d'Elsa

◁ **Brilliant, medieval-style pageantry before Siena's Palio *(see p222)***

A rare sight today – farming with oxen near Pienza

Even the working day of many Tuscans echoes that of their ancestors centuries ago. For people who work out in the fields, the day begins at sunrise, as early as 4:30am in summer. Farm and vineyard labourers will have completed a day's work by noon, when they retire indoors to eat and rest.

Until the 1950s, most Tuscans were familiar with this pattern of life: the region still relied on a feudal system, *mezzadria*, whereby peasants working on the land without payment took a share of the crops as their reward. Today, agricultural produce remains an important ingredient in the Tuscan economy, but only 20 per cent of Tuscans now work in agriculture. Many farming families left the land in favour of a stable income and a shorter working day as factory hands. Town dwellers have a much easier way of life, but the old rhythms prevail: the *siesta* period is still observed, so that almost everything closes for a few hours in the afternoon. Wise travellers soon learn that it pays to follow the same pattern, rising early to join the café throng, before heading out to study ancient frescoes in peace. In the middle of Florence there are several lively early morning markets where you can buy fresh, local produce *(see p287)*. Bargain hunters and food-loving Tuscans frequent them, but by 2pm the stallholders will have packed up.

A cheese stall in Florence

Churches open at 8am, and, except on Sunday when mass is held, there will be few other people to disturb your thoughts if you stray into one. Today, very few Tuscans go regularly to church and Sunday is spent visiting friends, watching sport or enjoying

Clerics in conversation, Colle di Val d'Elsa

family lunch. After the burst of activity that marks the beginning of the day, Tuscan towns adopt a more sedate pace. New building is prohibited inside their walls, so that very many people of school or working age travel out, by bus or car, to schools, offices or factories in the suburbs, leaving the old centres to visitors.

The grape harvest in Chianti

Some of the larger towns, particularly Pisa, Lucca, Florence and Siena, have resisted this tide, determined not to become museum cities given over entirely to tourism. They have thriving service sectors, testimony to the same Tuscan flair for banking, insurance and accountancy that made the Medici family and the "Merchant of Prato" *(see p188)* some of the richest people in their time. It is, however, the lucky few who work in such beautiful towns. They practise as lawyers, architects, conservationists or designers and are often graduates of the renowned local universities: Pisa, Siena and Florence. For the great majority of Tuscans, however, the working day is spent in purpose-built suburbs, such as the one linking Prato to the Firenze Nuova (New Florence) suburbs west of the city. The Tuscan economy, however, still remains firmly rooted in craft traditions. Top designers from Milan use the textile factories of Prato and Florence for the execution of their designs. Gold-working is not confined to the Ponte Vecchio workshops in Florence – Arezzo produces jewellery which is sold throughout Europe.

The hour for relaxing in Cortona

THRIVING EXPORTS

Glass, marble and motorcycles are among Tuscany's most important industrial products, while its olive oil and wine are exported worldwide. This explains why Livorno, Tuscany's port, is the second busiest in Italy, while Pisa's Galileo Galilei airport is rapidly becoming a major air-freight distribution centre.

Individual Tuscan artistry can best be admired in the heart of any Tuscan town during the evening promenade – the *passeggiata*. One moment the streets are empty, the next they are filled with elegant people strolling and chatting. The skill of *fare bella figura* ("looking good") is so prized that visitors will be judged by the same standard. It is an opportunity for you to join in the inherently Tuscan aspiration to create a civilized world.

Italian chic, or *bella figura*

A Tuscan Town Square

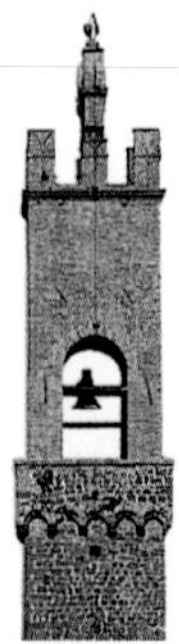

Town bell in the campanile

The main square or piazza of nearly every Tuscan town is the focus for much of the town's activities. Tt is here that the townsfolk gather around 6–7pm for the daily *passeggiata*, the traditional evening stroll, or to participate in local festivals and rallies. In most towns there are certain religious and civic buildings that are usually grouped around the piazza. Many of these buildings, you will notice, have standard features, such as the campanile, the *cortile* or the loggia, each of which fulfils a specific function. And often you will find that many of these buildings are still in use today, performing the same function for which they were originally built during the 13th–16th centuries.

Wellhead
Water was a valuable resource that was protected by strict laws to prevent pollution.

Cortile
The arcaded courtyard, or cortile, *of a palazzo served as an entrance hall shielded from the outside; it also provided a cool retreat.*

Marble or hard sandstone paving

A palazzo is any town house of stature. it is usually named after its owner.

There are three floors in most palazzi. public reception rooms were on the middle floor, the *piano nobile*.

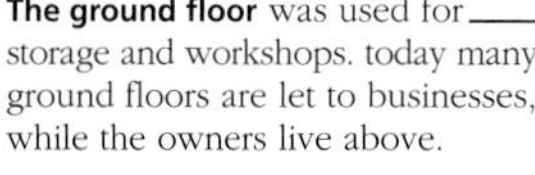

The ground floor was used for storage and workshops. today many ground floors are let to businesses, while the owners live above.

Baptismal font

The Baptistry, usually octagonal, was a separate building to the west of the church. After baptism, the infant was carried ceremoniously into the church for the first time.

Stemmae
Stone-carved coats-of-arms, belonging to citizens who served as councillors and magistrates, are often seen on public buildings.

Festival in the Piazza
The prestigious buildings of the main piazza often form an appropriate backdrop to costumed tournaments involving jousting, archery and horsemanship, recalling the medieval arts of war.

Loggia
Many loggias, built to provide shelter from the sun or rain, now harbour colourful street markets.

Fishtail battlements

The Palazzo del Comune (town hall) often houses the Museo Civico (town museum) and the Pinacoteca (art gallery).

Wide central nave, with narrower side aisles

Loggia or colonnade

The Duomo (from Latin *Domus Dei* or House of God) is the cathedral, the focal point of the piazza. A smaller parish church is called a *pieve*.

The campanile rose high so that the town bells could be heard far and wide. The bells were rung to announce public meetings or mass, to sound the curfew, or, when rung furiously *(a stormo)*, to warn of impending danger.

Side Chapel
Wealthy patrons paid for ornate tombs, paintings and frescoes in their own private chapels to commemorate their dead.

Understanding Architecture in Tuscany

Romanesque capital

The survival of so many fine Gothic and Renaissance buildings is part of Tuscany's immense appeal. Whole streets and squares, such as the Piazza dei Priori in Volterra *(see p167)* and the streets around the Mercato Nuovo in Florence, and even towns such as San Gimignano, have scarcely changed since the 16th century. Simple clues, such as the shape of arches, windows and doorways, reveal the style of the building and when it was built.

Gothic palazzi in Cortona

ROMANESQUE (5TH TO MID-13TH CENTURIES)

The Tuscan Romanesque style developed from late Roman architecture. Early Tuscan churches, such as Sant'Antimo *(see pp44–5)*, have round arches, Roman-style columns and arcades. Profuse surface decoration was introduced in the 12th century, resulting in the jewel-like church façades of Pisa and Lucca.

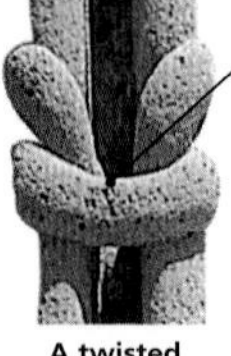

A twisted knot

Interlace and knots are typical motifs.

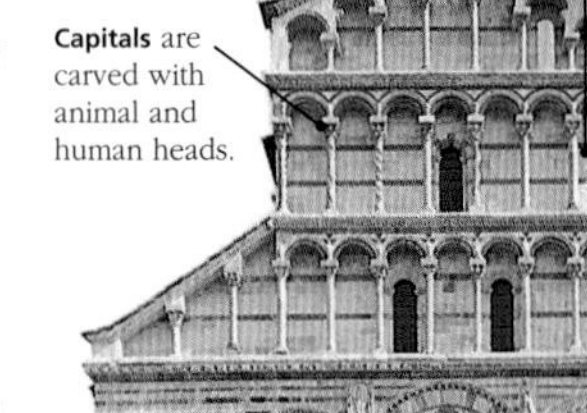

Gables often have three tiers of arcading.

Capitals are carved with animal and human heads.

The central portal is flanked by smaller side doors.

Pisa's San Paolo a Ripa d'Arno (see p161), *begun in 1210, has restrained geometric patterns on the lower façade and exuberant arcades above.*

Marble patterning on stonework

GOTHIC (13TH TO MID-15TH CENTURIES)

Pointed arches are the key feature of Gothic architecture. The style was introduced to Tuscany by French Cistercian monks who built the abbey of San Galgano in 1218 *(see p224)*. Siena then made this style her own, using it for the city's Duomo, palazzi and civic buildings such as Palazzo Pubblico *(see pp218–23)*.

Pinnacles, like miniature spires, bristle from the roofline.

Pointed gables

Gabled niches, sheltering statues of saints or Apostles, are a Gothic innovation.

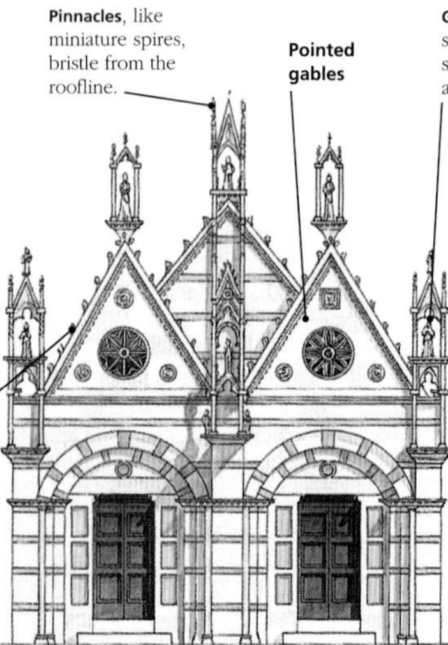

The crockets are shaped like leaves and flowers.

Santa Maria della Spina *(1230–1323), with its pointed gables and spikey pinnacles* (see p161), *is a typical example of Pisan Gothic architecture.*

St Luke, from Orsanmichele

RENAISSANCE (15TH AND 16TH CENTURIES)

Brunelleschi, the father of Renaissance architecture, was inspired by the purity and simplicity of Classical Roman buildings. This style is reflected in his first true Renaissance work, the loggia of the Spedale degli Innocenti in Florence (1419–24) *(see p95)*, with its elegant lines and simple arched bays. The style he created was adopted with enthusiasm by his fellow Florentines, who saw their city as the "new" Rome.

Arch with tear-drop keystone

Courtyard, Spedale degli Innocenti

Wedge-shaped masonry around semi-circular window arches is characteristic of Renaissance buildings.

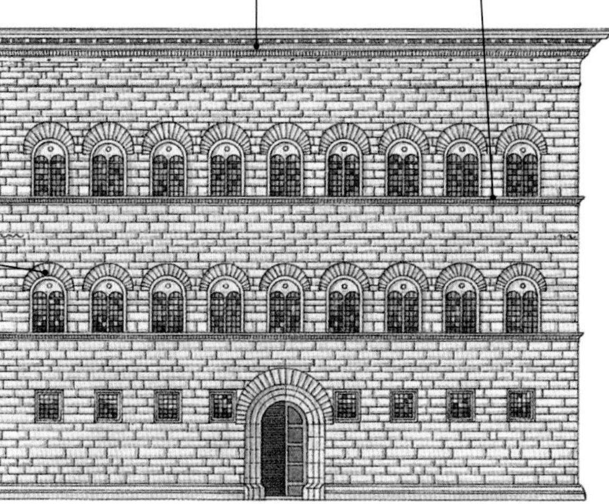

Classical cornices are moulded in Roman style.

String courses define each floor.

Palazzo Strozzi (see p105) *is typical of many Tuscan Renaissance buildings. The rusticated stonework gives an impression of strength and stability.*

BAROQUE (LATE-16TH AND 17TH CENTURIES)

The theatrical Baroque style, much favoured by the popes in Rome, largely passed Tuscany by. Although a few churches in Florence were given new façades in the 17th century, the Florentine version of the Baroque style is very Classical in spirit and not as bold or as exuberant as elsewhere in Italy.

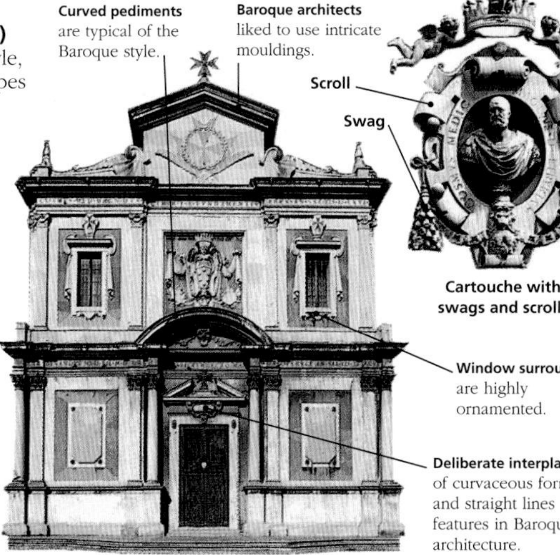

Curved pediments are typical of the Baroque style.

Baroque architects liked to use intricate mouldings.

Scroll

Swag

Cartouche with swags and scrolls

Window surrounds are highly ornamented.

Deliberate interplay of curvaceous forms and straight lines features in Baroque architecture.

Santo Stefano dei Cavalieri (see p156) *has columns and pilasters on its Baroque façade, which give the illusion of depth.*

Understanding Art in Tuscany

Tuscany was the scene of one of the most influential and sustained artistic revolutions in history. Its masterpieces record the transition from the stylized charm of medieval art to the Classical beauty and richness of the High Renaissance.

MEDIEVAL ART

Medieval art served as an aid to prayer and contemplation. The Virgin, patron saint of many Tuscan cities, including Siena, was often depicted as the Queen of Heaven, surrounded by adoring angels and saints.

Maestà *(1308–11)*
The stylized figures in this detail from Duccio's huge altarpiece for Siena cathedral are painted with great delicacy.

RENAISSANCE ART

The artistic revolution known as the Renaissance, which spread throughout Europe from the 15th century onwards, had its roots in Tuscany. Inspired by ancient Roman art, sculptors and painters brought about a "rebirth" of Classical ideals.

They were supported by wealthy and cultured patrons, themselves fascinated by the works of such Classical authors as Plato and Cicero. Nudes, landscapes, portraits, and scenes from mythology

The figures form a triangle, symbolizing the Holy Trinity. The viewer's eye is drawn upwards to the figures of Christ and God the Father at the apex.
The Virgin and St John are depicted as real people, rather than idealized figures.
Lorenzo Lenzi, Masaccio's patron, kneels opposite his wife.

The Trinity *(c.1427)*
Masaccio pioneered perspective in painting, using architectural illusion to create a three-dimensional effect (see p110).

TIMELINE OF GREAT TUSCAN ARTISTS

- **1245–1315** Giovanni Pisano
- **1260–1319** Duccio di Buoninsegna
- **1267–1337** Giotto di Bondone
- **1270–1348** Andrea Pisano
- **1374–1438** Jacopo della Quercia
- **1377–1455** Filippo Brunelleschi

1200 | 1250 | 1300 | 1350

- **1223–84** Nicola Pisano
- **1240–1302** Cimabue
- **1245–1302** Arnolfo di Cambio
- **1283–1344** Simone Martini
- **1319–47** Ambrogio Lorenzetti
- **1378–1455** Lorenzo Ghiberti
- **1386–1460** Donatello

☐ **Medieval Artists**

MANNERIST ART

Mannerist artists used "hot" colours, elongated forms and deliberately contorted poses, often within complicated, large-scale compositions.

The twisted pose and vivid colours of Michelangelo's *Holy Family (see p81)* established the key features of the style. Few artists could match the monumental scale of his work, but Bronzino, Pontormo and Rosso Fiorentino brought new life to traditional biblical subjects by their skilful and dramatic composition.

Statues of Roman gods reflect a direct debt to Classical art.

Writhing figures createa sense of dramatic tension.

Flesh and musculature are painted in subtle gradations of light and shade.

The Martyrdom of St Lawrence *(1569)*
With Mannerist bravura, Bronzino shows the human body in numerous poses (see p90).

and everyday life became legitimate subjects for art.

Rejecting the stylized art of the medieval era, Renaissance artists studied anatomy in order to portray the human body more realistically, and strove to develop innovations to please their patrons. They learned how to apply the mathematics of linear perspective to their art, to create the illusion of spatial depth. Painters set figures against recognizable landscapes or city backgrounds, and flattered their patrons by including them as onlookers or protagonists of the scene.

***La Maddalena* (1438), by Donatello**

The greatest Renaissance artists also added another dimension, that of psychological realism. It is evident in Donatello's sculpture *La Maddalena*, which vividly conveys the former prostitute's grief and penitence. Even when painting traditional subjects, they often tried to express the complexities of human character and emotion. The religious elements of the Virgin and Child theme gave way, for example, to an exploration of the mother-child relationship, as in the *Madonna and Child* (c.1455) by Fra Filippo Lippi *(see p82)*.

Pallas, symbolizing wisdom, tames the centaur, representing brute animal impulse.

Pallas and the Centaur
Botticelli's allegory (1485) typifies the Renaissance interest in pagan myth.

1400–82 Luca della Robbia
1401–28 Masaccio
1406–69 Fra Filippo Lippi
1410–92 Piero della Francesca
1449–94 Ghirlandaio
1452–1519 Leonardo
1457–1504 Filippino Lippi
1483–1520 Raphael
1486–1531 Andrea del Sarto
1511–92 Bartolomeo Ammannati
1524–1608 Giambologna

1400 | **1450** | **1500** | **1550**

1397–1475 Paolo Uccello
1396–1472 Michelozzo
c.1395–1455 Fra Angelico
1421–97 Benozzo Gozzoli
1435–88 Verrocchio
1445–1510 Botticelli
1494–1556 Jacopo Pontormo
1477–1549 Sodoma
1475–1564 Michelangelo
1511–74 Giorgio Vasari
1503–72 Agnolo Bronzino
1500–71 Benvenuto Cellini
1495–1540 Rosso Fiorentino

Renaissance Artists **Mannerist Artists**

Renaissance Frescoes

Frescoes decorate the walls of churches, public buildings and private palaces throughout Tuscany. Renaissance artists, in particular, favoured the medium of fresco painting for decorating new buildings. The word *fresco,* meaning "fresh", refers to the technique of painting on to a thin layer of damp, freshly laid plaster. Pigments are drawn into the plaster by surface tension and the colour becomes fixed as the plaster dries. The pigments react with the lime in the plaster to produce very strong, vivid colours. As the colours do not lie on the surface, restorers are able to remove the superficial soot and grime that have accumulated over the years to reveal the original, embedded colours *(see pp56–7).*

Chiaroscuro
This is a subtle method of contrasting light and dark for dramatic effect.

Jewel-like Colours
Artists used rare, costly minerals to create bright, striking pigments. The blue of Mary's robe in Piero della Francesca's Madonna del Parto *(c.1460)* (see p197) *is made from lapis lazuli.*

Earth colours such as reds and browns came from clay-based paints containing iron.

White pigment was used for important highlights because it reflects light.

Use of Sinopia
The outlines of the fresco were drawn on to the plaster undercoat using a red pigment called sinopia. *This layer was visible through the final plaster coat, guiding the artist as he painted in the details* (see p156).

The Giornato
Once the final plaster coat was applied, artists had to work quickly before it dried. This meant painting a small area of plaster each day (the giornato, *or daily portion). Joins between the sections were often concealed in borders, columns and frames.*

Masons left the bare wall surface uneven.

The bare wall was covered with coarse plaster, called *arriccio*, made of clay, hair, sand and lime.

The artist either sketched his design on to the *arriccio* using the pigment *sinopia*, and then painted directly on to the plaster, or he prepared a charcoal drawing on paper which was copied onto the wall.

The final fresco was painted on to a top coat of fine, lime-based plaster called *intonaco*.

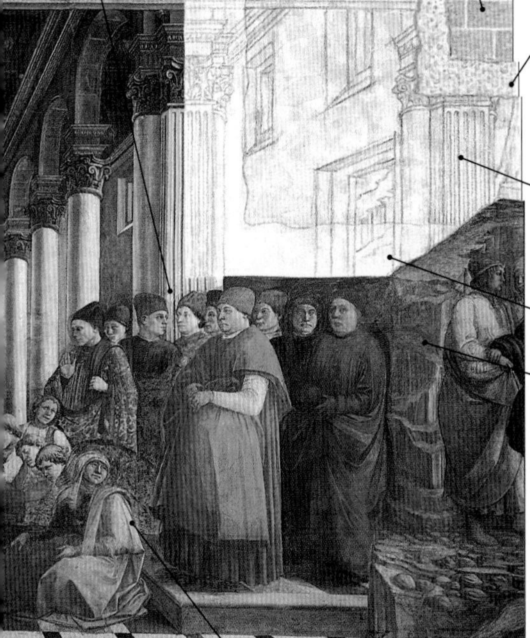

Workshops
The master artist worked in tandem with apprentices employed in his workshop. The master concentrated on important features, such as faces and expressive gestures.

Apprentices
While learning their trade, apprentices painted drapery, backgrounds and architectural details in the style of their master.

What to Buy in Tuscany

As a centre for high fashion and quality antiques, Florence is expensive but hard to beat. Bargains also abound, especially in leather goods and shoes. For food lovers there is a wide variety of wines, olive oils and preserves. Away from Florence, small farm estates in Tuscany sell their produce, such as honeys, liqueurs and wines, direct to the public, while many Tuscan towns have their own craft and food specialities. *(see also pp284–9).*

Desk tidy made of traditional hand-marbled paper

Marbled-paper notebook and box of pencils

Colourful Stationery
Marbled paper is a Florentine speciality. You can buy it in sheets and notebooks, or shaped into carnival masks and even birds and flowers.

Soap made to an ancient recipe

Flower-scented air freshener

Greetings Cards
Beautifully illustrated cards are sold at bookshops and museums.

Hand-made Perfumes and Toiletries
The products in Florentine pharmacies have often been made to ancient formulas by monks and nuns.

Alabaster figurine from Volterra

Terracotta and ceramic bowl

Hand-painted majolica

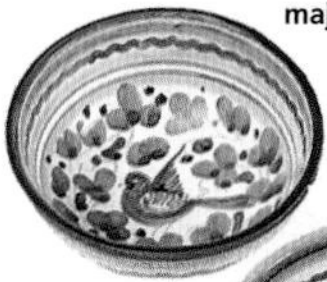

Reproductions of Renaissance ceramics

Ceramics and Reproductions
Tuscan potters produce highly decorative pieces, from modern originals (artistiche) *and Renaissance copies* (reproduzioni) *to attractive kitchenware. You can also buy copies of your favourite sculptures.*

Woven leatherwork handbag

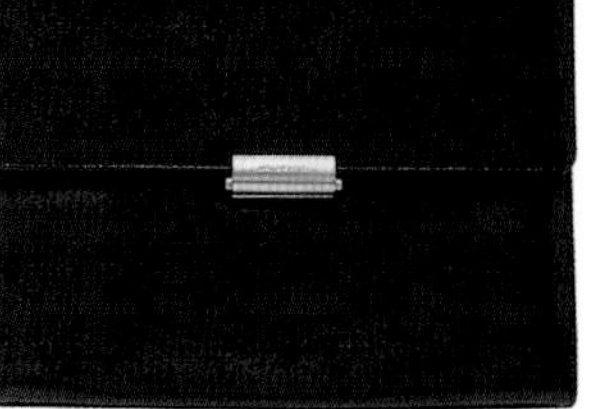

Elegant document case

Small coin purse

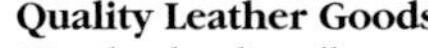

Quality Leather Goods

Fine leather handbags, wallets and jackets are all remarkably good value, but fake designer brands are also sold by street traders and market stalls.

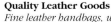

Belt with distinctive Gucci buckle

Hand-crafted men's footwear

Beautifully made lady's shoe

Fashionable Footwear

Even Hollywood filmstars come to Florence to buy shoes from boutiques such as Ferragamos.

Luxury charm bracelet

Designer silk scarf

Fashion Accessories

Florence has all the top names in fashion, including homegrown couturiers like Gucci.

Sunflower honey from Montalcino

Chocolate and biscuit cake

Red wine vinegar and fine olive oil

Tuscan Delicacies

Lovers of good food will want to visit an alimentari *(grocer's) to choose from the fascinating range of stock available. Tuscan products to sample and take back home include bottled antipasti, fruity olive oils, delicious honeys and a wide variety of confectionery.*

Artichoke hearts with peppers and olives

Sun-dried tomatoes in sunflower oil

Peppers preserved in olive oil

The Landscape of Tuscany

Tuscany is rich in wildlife, especially flowers and the insects that feed on them, including bees, crickets, cicadas and grasshoppers, whose song is heard during the summer months. For years Tuscan farmers were too poor to afford modern intensive agricultural methods, so the region was, until recently, still farmed by traditional methods. As a result, rural areas have remained relatively unspoiled, a safe haven for many species of flora and fauna – with the exception of the songbird, which has fallen victim to the Tuscan passion for hunting.

Cypress Trees
The flame-shaped cypress is often planted as a windbreak in fields and along roadsides.

The Crete
The clay landscape south of Siena is one of bare hillocks and ravines, denuded of topsoil by heavy rain.

Terracing
The steep hillsides are farmed by cutting terraces and holding the soil in place with stone walls.

Building on hilltops ensures a cooling wind in summer.

TUSCAN FARMLAND
A typical Tuscan farm will combine olive groves and vineyards with fields of maize and barley to feed the cattle and chickens.

Garfagnana Landscape
Much of this region is an unspoilt national park where deer, boar, martens and eagles are protected.

Viticulture
Many families make their own wine and every spare plot is planted with vines.

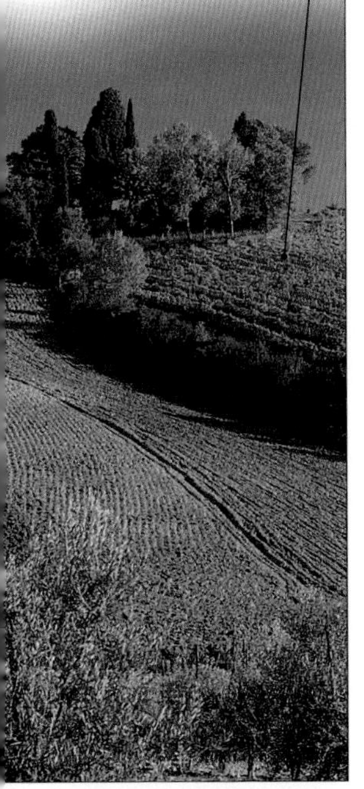

Olives
The olive tree with its silver-backed leaves is widely cultivated. Many farms sell home-produced olive oil.

TUSCAN WILDLIFE

The best time to see the Tuscan countryside is in May and June when all the flowers are in bloom. Autumn rains bring a second burst of flowering later in the year, and then cyclamen carpet the woodland floors. Even winter has its flowers, such as hellebores and snowdrops.

Animals, Birds and Insects

Hummingbird *hawk moths hover in front of brightly coloured flowers, feeding with their long tongues.*

Swifts perform *aerial acrobatics at dusk, flying high above the city rooftops and towers.*

The green lizard *feeds on grasshoppers and basks on walls in the sunlight.*

Wild boars *are abundant but very shy as they are hunted for their tasty meat.*

Wayside Flowers

The blue chicory *plant flowers all summer and is used as animal fodder.*

Pink, white and red *flowering mallows are a valuable food plant for bees.*

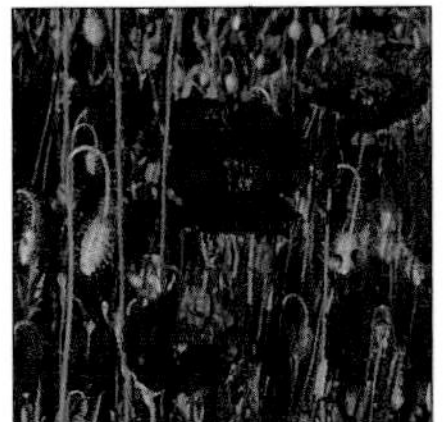

The blood-red poppy *often grows alongside bright white oxeye daisies.*

The almond-scented *bindweed attracts a variety of different insects.*

FLORENCE AND TUSCANY THROUGH THE YEAR

Tuscany is most beautiful in May when meadows and waysides are carpeted with the same bright flowers that Botticelli's Flora blithely scatters in *Primavera*, his celebration of spring *(see p82)*. Autumn is equally colourful, when the beech and chestnut woods turn a glorious blaze of seasonal red and gold.

A July harvest, medieval-style

The best months for escaping the heat and the crowds are May, September and October. Easter should be avoided, as also July and August, because of the long queues outside major museums. During August, when Tuscans head for the sea, you will find shops, bars and restaurants closed. To see traditional festivities like the Palio in Siena or Arezzo's Joust of the Saracen, you will need to book accommodation a year ahead, but there are many other local festivals to enjoy. For information, enquire at main tourist offices *(see p299)*.

SPRING

Tuscany begins to wake from winter as Easter approaches. The hillsides are vibrant with the soft green of new leaves and the scent of fresh growth. Even in the cities there is a sense of renewal as hanging baskets and window boxes are displayed outside from April onwards, and wisteria and iris bloom in the public gardens.

Instead of winter's heavy game dishes, asparagus, a speciality of the Lucca area, begins to feature on restaurant menus, along with tender young beans, usually served in lemon juice and oil.

Except at Easter time, the streets and main sights are rarely overcrowded, but the weather can be unpredictable and unseasonably wet.

A window box in bloom: the first sign of spring in Cortona

"Explosion of the Carriage" festival

MARCH

Carnevale *(four Sundays leading to Lent and Shrove Tuesday)*, Viareggio *(see p38)*.

Scoppio del Carro, or the Explosion of the Carriage *(Easter Sunday)*, Piazza del Duomo, Florence. An 18th-century gilded cart is pulled to the cathedral doors by white oxen, and a dove-shaped rocket swoops down a wire from above the High Altar inside to ignite fireworks in the cart. Ostensibly a celebration of the Resurrection, the ceremony has roots in pagan fertility rites. Many Tuscans still believe that a successful firework display means a good harvest.

Festa degli Aquiloni, or Kite Festival *(first Sunday after Easter)*, San Miniato *(see p163)*. Kite lovers perform aerial acrobatics on the Prato della Rocca, the grassy common above San Miniato.

APRIL

Sagra Musicale Lucchese, *(April–early July)* Lucca *(see pp178–9)*. This extensive festival of sacred music is held in the city's numerous Romanesque churches.

Mostra Mercato Internazionale dell'Artigianato, or Exhibition of Crafts *(last week)*, Fortezza da Basso, Florence. An important European exhibition of the work of artists and artisans.

MAY

Maggio Musicale, Florence. This is the city's major arts festival and it now lasts until late June, with concerts by the Orchestra Regionale Toscana, directed by Zubin Mehta, and other international performers. The festival has been extended to include dance (from classical ballet toa experimental work) and fringe events.

Festa del Grillo, or the Cricket Festival *(first Sunday after Ascension Thursday)*, Le Cascine, Florence. The huge park to the west of Florence, where Shelley wrote *Ode to the West Wind*, is the setting for this event, a celebration of the joys of spring. Stallholders used to sell live crickets, which were then released to bring good luck. These days the festival is celebrated with handmade crickets.

Balestro del Girifalco, or Falcon Contest *(first Sunday after 20 May)*, Massa Marittima *(see p39)*.

Sunshine Chart
Tuscany has been praised for its light, which has a clear golden quality most noticeable when the intensely sunny days of high summer begin to shorten. Spring and autumn days are still warm, with plenty of hours of sunshine to enjoy.

SUMMER

From June onwards, Tuscany's festive calendar becomes increasingly crowded. There are with scores of small town festivals, many of them taking place around Midsummer Day, the feast of John the Baptist, on 24 June. These provide an opportunity to sample local food and wine and join in the atmosphere, or to seek out some of the bigger set-piece festivals.

A glorious crop of sunflowers in high summer

JUNE

Calcio in Costume, or Football in Costume *(24 June and two other days in June)*, Florence *(see p38)*.
Estate Fiesolana, or Fiesole Summer *(mid-June to end August)*, Fiesole *(see p132)*. Festival of music, arts, drama, dance and film. Many events are staged in the amphitheatre.
Regata di San Ranieri *(17 June)*, Pisa *(see p156)*. Boat races in costume and processions of colourfully decorated boats on the river Arno. After dark, its bankside buildings are illuminated by tens of thousands of flaming torches.
Gioco del Ponte or Game of the Bridge *(last Sunday in June)*, Pisa. A ritual battle played out on a bridge *(see p38)*.

Celebrating a local saint's day on the streets of Siena

JULY

Corsa del Palio *(2 July and 16 August)*, Siena. Tuscany's most famous event *(see p222)*.
Pistoia Blues *(early July)*, Piazza del Duomo, Pistoia *(see pp186–7)*. Famous international festival of blues music, lasting for a week.
Settimana Musicale Senese *(dates vary)*, Siena *(see pp218–19)*. Throughout this "Musical Week", chamber music and classical concerts are performed in splendid settings, such as the Palazzo Chigi-Saraceni.

AUGUST

Festival Pucciniano *(late July–all August)*, Torre del Lago Puccini *(see p175)*. Performances of the composer's operas in an open-air theatre by the lake where he lived.

Italian ice cream, a feast for all ages

Rodeo della Rosa *(15 August)*, Alberese. Cowboys of the Maremma *(see pp236–7)* demonstrate cattle herding.
Cantiere Internazionale d'Arte *(late July–early August)*, Montepulciano *(see p227)*. Directed by the composer Hans Werner Henze, this is an important festival of new work by leading composers, dramatists and choreographers.
Festa della Bistecca *(15 August)*, Cortona *(see pp204–5)*. The Festival of the Beefsteak – a local speciality.
Il Baccanale *(penultimate Saturday)*, Montepulciano *(see p227)*. Feast of wine, food and song to celebrate the local Vino Nobile *(see p268)*.

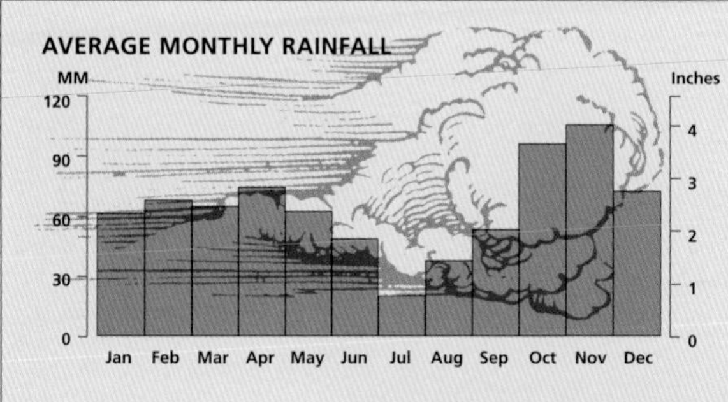

Rainfall Chart
Autumn is the wettest time in Tuscany, with heavy downpours which can last for days, especially late in the season. Late summer storms often bring relief from the heat. Winter and spring usually have fairly low rainfall.

AUTUMN

Autumn is the season of the *vendemmia*, the grape harvest. Visitors should watch for public notices of the many *sagre*, or festivals, that take place throughout the region. These are family-oriented events which typically feature a single local speciality which is in season, such as *funghi porcini* (porcini mushrooms). The first frosts will occur any time from the end of October, and at this point the great tracts of woodland all over Tuscany begin to turn brilliant shades of red and gold.

Autumn in the Val d'Orcia, in southern Tuscany

Grape-picking by hand in a Chianti vineyard

SEPTEMBER

Giostra del Saraceno or the Joust of the Saracen *(first Sunday)*, Arezzo *(see p39)*.
Festa della Rificolona *(7 September)*, Piazza della Santissima Annunziata, Florence. Children from all over the city carry candle-lit paper lanterns to honour the eve of the birth of the Virgin.
Palio della Balestra or Crossbow Festival *(second Sunday)*, Sansepolcro *(see pp196–7)*. Costume parades and flag throwing accompany a crossbow competition between Sansepolcro and the Umbrian town of Gubbio.
Luminara di Santa Croce *(13 September)*, Lucca *(see pp178–9)*. The city's famous relic, the *Volto Santo*, a wooden statue of Christ, is paraded around by torchlight.
Rassegna del Chianti Classico *(second week)*, Greve in Chianti. The biggest Tuscan celebration of local wines.
Mostra Mercato Internazionale dell'Antiquariato *(Sep–Oct, in odd-numbered years)*, Florence. A major biennial antiques fair.

OCTOBER

Amici della Musica *(Oct–Apr)*, Florence. The "Friends of Music" concert season begins.
Sagra del Tordo or Festival of the Thrush *(last Sunday)*, Montalcino *(see p39)*.

Participant in the Joust of the Saracen festival in Arezzo

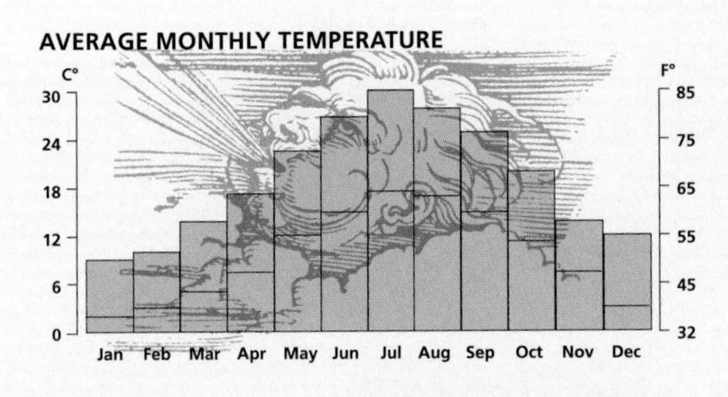

Temperature Chart
July is the hottest, driest month, with June and August only marginally less so. These are the least comfortable months for sightseeing. Choose late spring or early autumn for this, when you can also sit outside until late.

NOVEMBER

Festival dei Popoli *(Nov–Dec)*, venues throughout Florence show films in their original language with Italian subtitles.
Florence Queer Festival *(end Nov–early Dec)*. Film/arts festival celebrating gay lifestyles.

WINTER

This can be a good time to visit Florence and enjoy the city's museums and churches in tranquillity. It can be bitterly cold, but the skies are blue and the city is often bathed in golden sunlight, making this many photographers' favourite season. All over Tuscany, town squares are filled with the aroma of roasting chestnuts, and in December, the last of the olive crop is being harvested in the southernmost parts.

DECEMBER

Fiaccole di Natale, or Festival of Christmas Torches *(Christmas Eve)*, Abbadia di San Salvatore, near Montalcino *(see p224)*. Carols and torchlight processions in memory of the shepherds from the first Christmas Eve.

JANUARY

Capodanno. New Year's Day is celebrated with gusto all over Tuscany. There are firework displays, and volleys from hunters firing into the air, and from exploding firecrackers: all are part of a ritual to frighten away the ghosts and spirits of the old year and welcome in the new.

Roasting chestnuts, Montalcino

Pitti Immagine Uomo *(throughout January)*, Fortezza da Basso, Florence. At this prestigious fashion show, Italian designers and international couturiers gather to present their spring and summer collections for men. Children's collections (Pitti Bimbo) are sometimes presented in January too.

FEBRUARY

Carnevale *(Sundays before Lent, Shrove Tuesday)*, Viareggio *(see p175)*. A festive event renowned for its parades, competitions and amusing floats, often inspired by topical themes *(see p38)*.

There are many other opportunities to enjoy pre-Lent celebrations, such as the equally splendid carnival festivities that take place in San Gimignano and Arezzo.

PUBLIC HOLIDAYS

New Year's Day (1 Jan)
Epiphany (6 Jan)
Easter Sunday & Monday
Liberation Day (25 Apr)
Labour Day (1 May)
Republic Day (2 Jun)
Ferragosto (15 Aug)
All Saints' Day (1 Nov)
Immaculate Conception (8 Dec)
Christmas Day (25 Dec)
Santo Stefano (26 Dec)

Florence's Piazza di Santo Spirito in winter – serene and free of crowds

Festivals in Tuscany

Many Tuscan festivals celebrate battles and historical events that took place centuries ago; others have their origins in medieval tournaments. Yet they are not merely a pastiche of history, put on for the benefit of tourists. They are living festivals, mounted with an amazing degree of skill and commitment to authenticity and perfection. This can be seen in such details as the embroidery on the costumes worn by the participants and in the exhilarating displays of horsemanship, jousting or archery. Here is a selection of Tuscany's best.

Football in Costume at fever pitch

FLORENCE

Calcio in Costume, or Football in Costume (a festival held over three days in June), is a combination of football and rugby. Each of the four medieval quarters of the city (Santo Spirito, Santa Croce, San Giovanni and Santa Maria Novella) fields a team of 27 men. The games are usually held in Piazza Santa Croce, and always attract a lively crowd. There is fierce rivalry among the teams, and play can be quite violent. The final prize is a live cow. Before the game, the players and other characters in sumptuous 14th-century dress parade through the city.

The final often takes place on 24 June, the feast of John the Baptist, the patron saint of the city. These events are celebrated by a firework display, best seen from the north bank of the Arno, between Ponte Vecchio and Ponte alle Grazie, or from Fiesole.

WESTERN TUSCANY

The last Sunday in June is the occasion for the Gioco del Ponte, or Game of the Bridge, in Pisa *(see pp156–7)*. This battle, in Renaissance costume, takes place between the Pisans who live north of the river Arno and those who live south. Arranged into teams, they attempt to push a seven-tonne carriage over the historic Ponte di Mezzo (literally, the Middle Bridge), which divides the city. On the actual day, the river's banks are crowded with thousands of onlookers. This event probably has its roots in pre-Renaissance times, when there was no regular army and all citizens had to be trained and ready for war.

Some of the participants wear suits of antique armour which date from the 15th and 16th centuries, and their shields bear the colours of the city's different districts. This regalia is kept in the Museo Nazionale di San Matteo *(see p157)* when it is not in use.

Pisa's Game of the Bridge

NORTHERN TUSCANY

Carnevale (Carnival) in Viareggio *(see p175)*, on Shrove Tuesday and the four Sundays leading to it, is famous for its imaginative floats. These carry elaborate satirical models of politicians and other public figures. After courting controversy in recent years, however, this celebration is now more of a family event, but there is still an abundance of pointed visual jokes that can be appreciated by those in the know. The designers of the floats enjoy much flattery and prestige, and their creations remain on view all year. As elsewhere, the occasion is one of merrymaking, and it combines ancient pagan rituals and Christian values.

One of the spectacular floats from the Viareggio Carnival

Knights waiting to charge at the Joust of the Saracen in Arezzo

EASTERN TUSCANY

The Piazza Grande in Arezzo *(see pp198–9)* is the scene of the Giostra del Saracino, or Joust of the Saracen. Held on the first Sunday in September, this tournament dates back to the Crusades in the Middle Ages, when all Christendom dedicated itself to driving the North African Arabs (the Moors) out of Europe.

There are lively and colourful processions to precede the event, in which eight costumed knights charge towards a wooden effigy of the Saracen. The aim is to try to hit the Saracen's shield with lances and then avoid a cat-of-three-tails swinging back and unseating them. Each pair of knights represents one of Arezzo's four rival *contrade* (districts), and their supporters occupy a side each of Piazza Grande. They are quiet when their own *contrada* knights are jousting, but make as much noise as is possible to distract the opposition. The winner receives a gold lance.

Archery at the Festival of the Thrush in Montalcino

CENTRAL TUSCANY

The most important festival in this region is Siena's Palio *(see p222)*, but the Sagra del Tordo, or Festival of the Thrush, is also a great attraction. It takes place in Montalcino *(see pp224–5)* on the last Sunday in October. The 14th-century Fortezza (castle) is the setting for an archery contest which is fought in traditional costume by members of the town's four *contrade*. This is accompanied by considerable consumption of the local red Brunello wine and, much to the horror of many bird-lovers, of charcoal-grilled thrush.

The festival is essentially an excuse for gastronomic over-indulgence, and a celebration of its thriving local economy, which is based on olive oil and wine production. Brunello is widely regarded as one of the finest of Italian wines.

Visitors are welcome to participate, and more conventional specialities, such as *porchetta* (roast suckling pig), are available for those who prefer not to eat songbirds. Archery competitions are also held in Montalcino during August to mark the beginning of the hunting season.

SOUTHERN TUSCANY

Balestro del Girifalco, or the Falcon Contest, takes place in Massa Marittima *(see p234)* on the first Sunday after the feast of San Bernardino (20 May) and again on the second Sunday in August. It is preceded by a long procession through the town of people in dazzling Renaissance costume, accompanied by flag-waving and music. The contest itself is a test of ancient battle skills and the teams represent the town's three traditional historic divisions, which are known as *terzieri* or thirds. Marksmen come forward and try to shoot down a mechanical falcon, tethered on a wire, with their crossbows. Great precision is required to hit the target and the whole contest is imbued with intense *terzieri* rivalry.

Renaissance finery at the Falcon Contest in Massa Marittima

THE HISTORY OF FLORENCE AND TUSCANY

Tuscany is rich in historical monuments. Etruscan walls encircle many of the region's hilltop towns and the streets within are lined with medieval and Renaissance palazzi, town halls testifying to the ideals of democracy and self-government, and churches built on the ruins of ancient pagan temples. The countryside, too, is dotted with castles and fortified villages, symbols of the violence and intercommunal strife that tore Tuscany apart for so many years during the medieval period. Typical of these is the hilltop town of San Gimignano *(see pp212–15)*, with its defensive towers.

Some of the most imposing castles, such as the Fortezza Medicea in Arezzo *(see p198)*, bear the name of the Medici family. Their coat of arms, found all over Tuscany, is a reminder of the role they played in the region's history. They presided over the simultaneous birth of Humanism and the Renaissance and, later, when they were Grand Dukes of Tuscany, patronized eminent scientists and engineers such as Galileo. Tuscany has also played a part in wider events: Napoleon was exiled to Elba, and Florence served briefly as capital of the newly united Italy (1865–71).

The Marzocco lion, emblem of Florence

Much damage was done to Tuscany's art and monuments by World War II bombing and the floods of 1966. However, major restoration projects undertaken as a result have stimulated research into up-to-date scientific methods. In this way, Tuscany's artistic heritage continues to inspire contemporary life – something it has always done for the many creative people who live and work here and for its endless trail of admiring visitors.

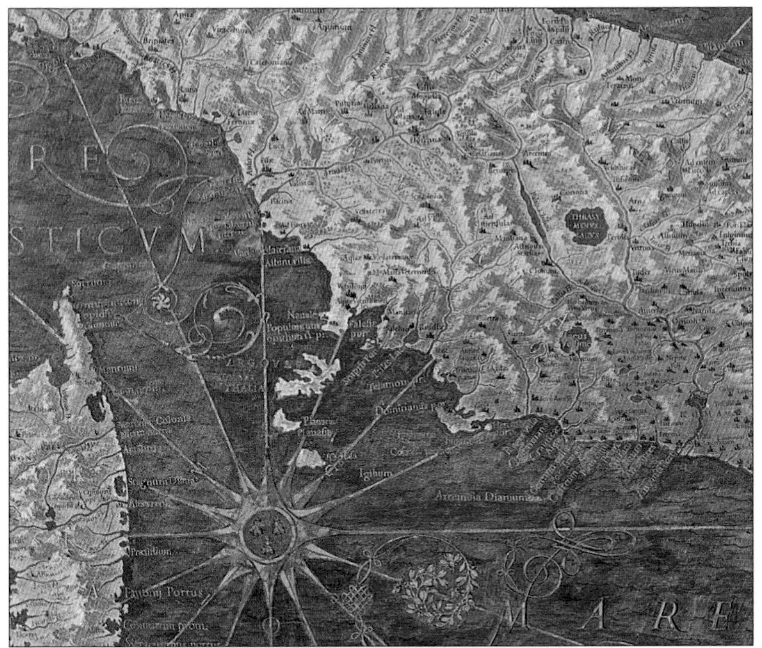

16th-century map of Italy, showing Pisa and the river Arno leading to Florence

◁ San Gimignano, held by its patron saint, and little changed since Taddeo di Bartolo (1362–1422) painted it

Etruscan and Roman Tuscany

Etruscan earrings worked in gold

The Etruscans migrated to Italy from Asia Minor around 900 BC, attracted to the area they called Etruria (now in Tuscany, Lazio and Umbria) by its mineral wealth. This they exploited to produce weapons, armour, tools and jewellery to trade with Greece. After a fierce war with Rome in 395 BC, the Etruscan civilization was eclipsed by Roman rule. Many aspects of Roman religion can be attributed to the Etruscans, including animal sacrifice and divination – reading the will of the gods in animal entrails or cloud patterns. Everyday Etruscan life and the preoccupation with the afterlife are reflected in detailed carved cremation urns and tombs like those at Volterra *(see pp166–7)*.

Bronze Chimera *(4th-century BC)*
The wounded chimera (part goat, lion and serpent) is a dramatic example of Etruscan bronze casting.

Athletic Games
Tomb paintings depicting chariot races, dancing and athletics suggest that the Etruscans had festivals similar to the Olympic Games of the ancient Greeks.

Wax writing tablets were used to keep household accounts.

A covered wagon carved on the urn shows the Etruscans were skilled at carpentry.

ETRUSCAN CREMATION URN
Much of what is known about the Etruscans comes from studying the contents of their tombs. This 1st-century BC terracotta cremation urn from Volterra is carved with scenes from Etruscan domestic life.

The relief depicts the last journey of the deceased into the underworld.

TIMELINE

9th century BC Earliest evidence of Etruscans on Elba

508 BC Lars Porsena, Etruscan ruler of Chiusi, leads an unsuccessful attack on Rome

474 BC Etruscans defeated in Asia Minor by their commercial rivals; trade with Greece suffers and Etruscan ports such as Populonia begin to decline

900 BC | 800 | 700 | 600 | 500 | 400 | 30

7th century BC Beginning of extensive maritime trade with Greece and the Near East

6th century BC Founding of the Dodecapolis, a confederation of the 12 most powerful Etruscan cities

Coin from Populonia

395 BC Rome captures Veii in Lazio, signalling the end of Etruscan independence

Circular Chandelier
Sixteen oil lamps decorate the rim of this bronze chandelier, made around 300 BC.

The family of the deceased watches the funeral cortège.

Statue of Venus
Under Roman rule, the Etruscans adopted new deities like Venus, goddess of beauty.

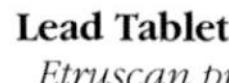

Lead Tablet
Etruscan priests recorded details of their prayers and religious rites on lead tablets. However, their language has not yet been fully deciphered, and many of their beliefs and traditions are not yet understood.

WHERE TO SEE ANCIENT TUSCANY

The famous bronzes of the *Chimera* and the *Orator* sare in Florence's Museo Archeologico *(see p99)*. Good museum collections are in Fiesole *(pp132–3)*, Volterra *(p166)*, Chiusi *(p228)*, Cortona *(p204)* and Grosseto *(p238)*. There are tombs at Vetulonia *(p238)* and Sovana *(p238)*, and the ruins of an Etruscan town have been excavated near Roselle *(p238)*.

Etruscan Rock-cut Tomb
The tombs in Sovana date from the 3rd century BC (p238).

Roman Theatre
The bath and theatre complex excavated in Volterra was built after Rome conquered the city in the 4th century BC (p167).

205 BC All Tuscany now under Roman control; the Etruscans forced to pay tribute in bronze, grain and iron

90 BC Etruscans granted Roman citizenship, marking the end of their existence as a distinct culture

AD 250 Christianity brought to Florence by Eastern merchants; St Minias martyred in the city

AD 313 Constantine grants official status to Christianity

200	100	AD 1	100	200	300	400

Bronze of a Roman Orator c. 300 BC

59 BC Florentia (Florence) founded as a town for retired Roman army veterans

20 BC Military colony of Saena (Siena) founded

AD 405 Flavius Stilicho defeats the Ostrogoths besieging Florence

Early Medieval Tuscany

Medieval carved stone lion

The church kept the flame of learning alive during the dark years when Tuscany was under attack from Teutonic tribes such as the Goths and Lombards. Charlemagne, responding to the pope's request for help, drove the Lombards out of Tuscany in the 8th century. He was crowned Holy Roman Emperor as his reward, but this was soon to spark off a long conflict between church and emperor about who should rule Italy.

Mosaic Madonna
A 12th-century mosaic of the Virgin from Cortona (see p204) *is typical of the Byzantine-influenced art of the early medieval period.*

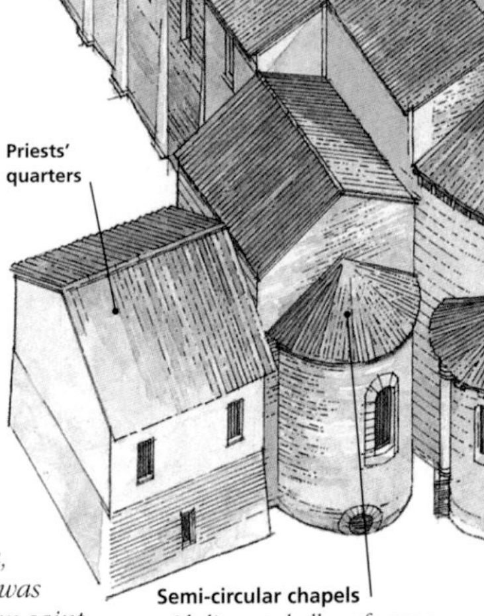
Early churches have simple wooden joists.
The capitals are carved with biblical scenes.
Priests' quarters
Semi-circular chapels with limpet-shell roofs are a typical feature of the period.

Knight on Horseback
This 11th-century carving from Sovana's cathedral symbolizes the conflict between pope and emperor over control of the church.

Chapel of Sant'Agata
Like most early churches in Tuscany, the 12th-century octagonal brick chapel in Pisa, with its pyramid-shaped roof, was built on the grave of a Christian saint martyred by the Romans (see p156).

TIMELINE

552 Totila the Goth attacks Florence

570 Lombards conquer northern Italy

Carts used by Charlemagne's army in battle

500 | 600 | 700 | 800

774 Charlemagne, King of the Franks, begins a campaign to subjugate the Lombards

800 Charlemagne crowned Holy Roman Emperor

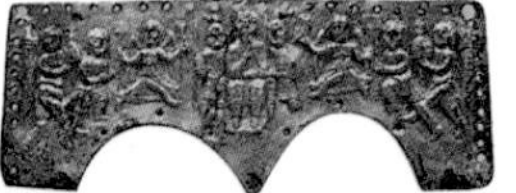

7th-century Lombardic gold crown in the Bargello Museum, Florence (see pp68–9)

The bells in the campanile were rung to call the village to church and prayer.

Countess Matilda
Matilda, the last of the Margraves, ruled Tuscany in the 11th century and built many churches in the area.

Baptismal Font
Scenes taken from the lives of Moses and Christ adorn the 12th-century font at San Frediano, Lucca (see pp178–9).

SANT'ANTIMO *(see p228)*

Founded, according to legend, by Charlemagne in 781, the shape of the church demonstrates the influence of the Roman *basilica* (law court) on the design of early churches; the altar occupies the position of the magistrate's chair.

The ambulatory ran behind the altar and was used for processions.

WHERE TO SEE EARLY MEDIEVAL TUSCANY

Well-preserved early medieval churches are found throughout Tuscany: in San Piero a Grado *(see p161)*; Barga *(p174)*; Lucca *(pp178–9)*; San Quirico d'Orcia *(p225)*; Massa Marittima *(p234)*; Sovana *(p238)*; San Miniato al Monte in Florence *(p130)*; and in Fiesole *(p132)*.

Castello di Romena
The 11th-century tower near Bibbiena was built by the Guidi family, who dominated the area.

Santi Apostoli in Florence
Founded in 786, the church includes columns from ancient Roman baths (p109).

900 | 1000 | 1100 | 1200

- **c.1025–30** Guido d'Arezzo invents a form of musical notation
- **1062** Pisa captures Sicily and becomes the foremost Mediterranean port
- **1063** Pisa cathedral begun
- **1115** Countess Matilda dies
- **1125** Florence captures and destroys Fiesole
- **1152** Frederick Barbarossa is crowned Holy Roman Emperor and invades Italy
- **1186** Siena cathedral begun

12th-century Tuscan School Crucifixion

Late Medieval Tuscany

During the 13th century Tuscany grew rich on textile manufacturing and trade. Commercial contact with the Arab world led the Pisan mathematician Fibonacci to introduce Arabic numerals to the West; a new understanding of geometry followed and Tuscan architects began to build ambitious new buildings. At the same time, Tuscan bankers developed the book-keeping principles that still underlie modern accountancy and banking practice. It was also an age of conflict. Cities and factions fought ruthlessly and incessantly to secure wealth and power.

Defensive towers protected the city.

Contented citizens had time for leisure.

Condottieri (mercenaries) were hired to settle conflicts.

Dante's Inferno
Dante (in blue) *was caught in the Guelph-Ghibelline conflict and was exiled from Florence in 1302. He took revenge in his poetry, describing his enemies' torments in Hell.*

Petrarch and Boccaccio
Petrarch and Boccaccio (top and bottom left), *like Dante, wrote in the Tuscan dialect, not Latin. Petrarch's sonnets and Boccaccio's tales were very popular.*

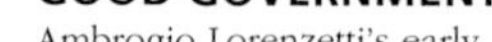

GOOD GOVERNMENT
Ambrogio Lorenzetti's early 14th-century allegorical fresco in Siena's Palazzo Pubblico *(see pp218–19)* shows thriving shops, fine buildings and dancing citizens, symbolizing the benefits of good government. Another fresco, *Bad Government*, shows rape, murder, robbery and ruin.

TIMELINE

1215 Start of conflict between Guelph supporters of the pope and Ghibelline supporters of the Holy Roman Emperor

1252 First gold florin minted

1260 Siena defeats Florence at Montaperti

1278 Campo Santo begun in Pisa

1200 | 1220 | 1240 | 1260 | 1280

1220 Frederick II of Germany is crowned Holy Roman Emperor and lays claim to Italy

1224 St Francis receives the "stigmata" (the wounds of Christ) at La Verna

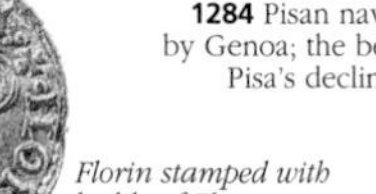

Florin stamped with the lily of Florence

1284 Pisan navy defeated by Genoa; the beginning of Pisa's decline as a port

Wool Traders' Emblem
Luca della Robbia's roundel depicts the Lamb of God, symbol of the Calimala (wool importers), whose trade guild was the most powerful in Florence.

A building boom resulted from increased prosperity.

St Francis (1181–1226)
From monasteries founded in Tuscany by St Francis, the Franciscans brought about a major religious revival in reaction to the excesses of the church.

Bankers in Siena
Tuscan banks provided loans to popes, monarchs and merchants. Many bankers were ruined when Edward III of England defaulted on his debts in 1342.

WHERE TO SEE LATE MEDIEVAL TUSCANY

San Gimignano's spectacular towers *(see pp212–15)* show what most Tuscan cities must have looked like during the Middle Ages. Siena has the best surviving late medieval town hall *(pp218–19)*, and Pisa's Leaning Tower, Duomo and Baptistry *(pp158–60)* reflect the willingness of architects of this period to experiment with new styles.

Medieval building techniques
Circular putlock holes show where medieval builders placed their scaffolding timbers.

Lucignano
Some of Tuscany's best-preserved medieval architecture, including several defensive towers, can be seen in Lucignano (p203).

1294 Work begins on Florence's cathedral

1300 Giovanni Pisano carves pulpit for Pisa's cathedral

1350 Pisa's Leaning Tower completed; Boccaccio begins writing *The Decameron*

1377 Sir John Hawkwood appointed Captain General of Florence

1300 | 1320 | 1340 | 1380

1302 Dante begins writing *The Divine Comedy*

1299 Work begins on Palazzo Vecchio in Florence

1345 Work begins on Florence's Ponte Vecchio

1348–93 Black Death carries off half the Tuscan population

Sir John Hawkwood, English mercenary

1374 Death of Petrarch

The Renaissance

Della Robbia roundel from the Cappella de' Pazzi (1430)

Under astute Medici leadership, Florence enjoyed a period of peace and prosperity. Rich bankers and merchants invested in fine palaces to replace their cramped tower houses, and paid for the adornment of churches. The result was an outpouring of art and architecture, remarkable for its break with the Gothic past and its conscious attempt to give "rebirth" to Classical values. The rediscovery of works by ancient philosophers like Cicero and Plato profoundly influenced the intellectual preoccupations of the day. Their ideas inspired the Humanists, who emphasized the role of knowledge and reason in human affairs.

Textile Market
The thriving Florentine textiles industry allowed the textile guilds and merchants like the dye importer Rucellai (see p104) *to become patrons of the arts.*

Terracotta roundels of babies in swaddling bands, added by Andrea della Robbia in 1487, reflect the building's function as an orphanage.

Classical arches illustrate the Florentine passion for ancient Roman architecture.

SPEDALE DEGLI INNOCENTI

The archetypal Renaissance building, Brunelleschi's colonnade (1419–26) for the *Spedale degli Innocenti (see p95)* is a masterpiece of restrained Classical design. Europe's first orphanage, the *Spedale* is also a major social monument.

Battle of San Romano *(1456)*
Florence hired condottieri *(mercenaries) to fight its battles. Its citizens were therefore free to concentrate on making the city wealthy. Uccello's striking depiction of the Florentine victory over Siena in 1432 is an early attempt to master perspective.*

TIMELINE

1400 | 1410 | 1420 | 1440

1402 Florence Baptistry doors competition *(see p66)*

1406 Pisa falls to Florence

1416 Donatello completes his *St George (see p67)*

1419 Work begins on the Spedale degli Innocenti

1425–7 Masaccio paints *The Life of St Peter* frescoes in Santa Maria del Carmine *(see pp126–7)*

1434 Cosimo il Vecchio returns from exile

1436 Brunelleschi completes dome for Florence cathedral *(see pp64–5)*. Work starts on San Marco *(see pp96–7)*

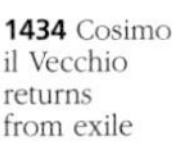

Cosimo il Vecchio

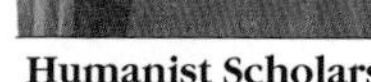

Humanist Scholars
By studying a broad range of subjects, from art to politics, the Humanists fostered the idea of Renaissance man, equally skilled in many activities.

Grey sandstone and white plaster contrasts radically with the rich surface ornamentation of late medieval architecture.

Classical Corinthian capital

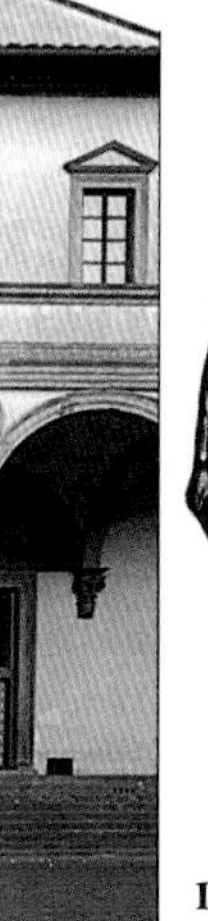

David *(1475)*
A favourite Florentine subject (see p77), *Verrocchio's bronze emphasizes David's youth and vulnerability.*

Pazzi Family Emblem
The wealthy Pazzi were disgraced after trying to assassinate Lorenzo the Magnificent and seize control of Florence in 1478.

WHERE TO SEE RENAISSANCE TUSCANY

Most of Florence was rebuilt during the Renaissance. Highlights include San Lorenzo *(see pp90–91)*, Masaccio's frescoes in the Brancacci Chapel *(pp126–7)*, many paintings in the Uffizi *(pp80–83)* and the sculptures at the Bargello *(pp68–9)*.

Pienza Duomo *(1459)*
Pope Pius II's plans for a model Renaissance city at Pienza (p226) *were never fully realized.*

San Marco Cloister *(1437)*
Cosimo il Vecchio paid for Michelozzo's cloister (pp96–7) *and used it as a retreat.*

1450 | 1460 | 1470 | 1480 | 1490

1454–66 Piero della Francesca's *The Legend of the True Cross (see pp200–1)*

1464 Death of Cosimo il Vecchio

1469 Lorenzo the Magnificent comes to power

1478 Pazzi conspiracy

1480 Botticelli's *Primavera*. The villa at Poggio a Caiano begun *(see p165)*

Lorenzo the Magnificent

1485 Botticelli's *The Birth of Venus*

1492 Death of Lorenzo the Magnificent

The Medici of Florence

The Medici family held power in Florence almost continuously from 1434 until 1743. Their rule began discreetly enough with Cosimo il Vecchio, son of a self-made man, Giovanni di Bicci. For years, Cosimo and his descendants directed policy with popular support, but without ever being voted into office. Later generations gained titles and power but ruled by force. Two were elected pope and, after the Republic *(see pp52–3)*, the decadent Alessandro took the title Duke of Florence. From him control passed to Cosimo I, who was crowned Grand Duke of Tuscany.

Medici coat of arms, San Lorenzo

Giovanni di Bicci
An astute merchant banker, he founded the Medici fortune.

Lorenzo the Magnificent
A poet and statesman, Lorenzo was the model Renaissance man. One of his greatest achievements was to negotiate peace among the cities of northern Italy.

Giovanni di Bicci (1360–1429)

① Cosimo il Vecchio (1389–1464)

② Piero the Gouty (1416–69)

③ Lorenzo the Magnificent (1449–92)

Giuliano (1453–78)

Giulio, Pope Clement VI (1478–1534)

④ Piero (1472–1503)

⑤ Giovanni, Pope Leo X (1475–1521)

⑦ Giuliano, Duke of Nemours (1479–1516)

⑧ Alessandro, Duke of Florenc (1511–37: parentage uncertain)

⑥ Lorenzo, Duke of Urbino (1492–1519)

Catherine, Duchess of Urbino *m* Henry II of France (1519–89)

Catherine of France
Catherine married Henri II of France in 1533. She is shown with two of her sons, who both became French kings: Charles IX and Henri III. Yet another son became Francis II of France.

Pope Leo X
Elected pope when only 38, Leo's corrupt plans to fund the rebuilding of St Peter's in Rome triggered a furious reaction that led to the birth of the Protestant movement.

MEDICI PATRONAGE

As one of the most powerful families in Florence, the Medici were responsible for commissioning some of the greatest works of the Renaissance. Many artists flattered their patrons by placing them prominently in the foreground of their paintings. In Botticelli's *Adoration of the Magi* (1475), the grey-haired king who is pictured kneeling at the feet of the Virgin is Cosimo il Vecchio. The kneeling figure in the white robe is his grandson, Giuliano. The young man holding a sword, on the far left of the painting, is thought to be a rather idealized portrait of Lorenzo the Magnificent, Cosimo's other grandson.

***Adoration of the Magi* (1475) by Botticelli**

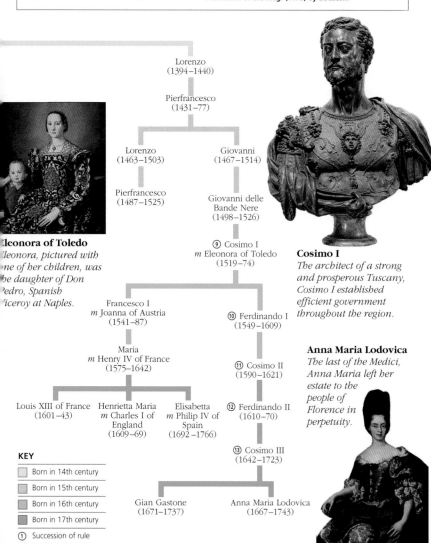

Lorenzo
(1394–1440)

Pierfrancesco
(1431–77)

Lorenzo
(1463–1503)

Pierfrancesco
(1487–1525)

Giovanni
(1467–1514)

Giovanni delle Bande Nere
(1498–1526)

⑨ Cosimo I
m Eleonora of Toledo
(1519–74)

Francesco I
m Joanna of Austria
(1541–87)

Maria
m Henry IV of France
(1575–1642)

Louis XIII of France
(1601–43)

Henrietta Maria
m Charles I of England
(1609–69)

Elisabetta
m Philip IV of Spain
(1692–1766)

⑩ Ferdinando I
(1549–1609)

⑪ Cosimo II
(1590–1621)

⑫ Ferdinando II
(1610–70)

⑬ Cosimo III
(1642–1723)

Gian Gastone
(1671–1737)

Anna Maria Lodovica
(1667–1743)

leonora of Toledo
leonora, pictured with ne of her children, was he daughter of Don edro, Spanish iceroy at Naples.

Cosimo I
The architect of a strong and prosperous Tuscany, Cosimo I established efficient government throughout the region.

Anna Maria Lodovica
The last of the Medici, Anna Maria left her estate to the people of Florence in perpetuity.

KEY

- Born in 14th century
- Born in 15th century
- Born in 16th century
- Born in 17th century
- ① Succession of rule

The Florentine Republic

Savonarola (1452–98)

In 1494, when Piero de' Medici abandoned Florence to the invading troops of Charles VIII of France, the city was declared a Republic. Under the leadership of the religious fundamentalist, Girolamo Savonarola, the people were encouraged to believe that God was their only ruler. After his execution in 1498, the Republic survived 32 years of constant attack. Finally, in 1530, the Medici Pope, Clement VII, and the Holy Roman Emperor, Charles V of Spain, combined forces and returned the city to Medici rule.

Palazzo Vecchio Frieze
The inscription, "Christ is King", on this Republican frieze implies that no mortal ruler has absolute power.

Present-day Boboli Gardens

Charles VIII Enters Siena
When the French invaded Tuscan cities in 1494, Savonarola claimed it was God's punishment for the Tuscan obsession with profane books and art. He ordered such objects burned in bonfires of "vanity".

Judith and Holofernes
Donatello's statue of the virtuous Judith slaying the tyrant Holofernes was placed in front of the Palazzo Vecchio in 1494 to symbolize the end of Medici rule.

THE SIEGE OF FLORENCE *(1529–30)*

Besieged by 40,000 papal and imperial troops, the citizens of Florence held out for ten months before starvation and disease led to their surrender. Vasari's fresco in the Palazzo Vecchio shows the full extent of the city's defences and the scale of the enemy assault.

TIMELINE

1494 Charles VIII attacks Florence. Savonarola seizes power from Medici family

1495

1498 Savonarola burnt at the stake

1502 Soderini elected first chancellor of the Republic

Chancellor Soderini

1504 Michelangelo completes *David* *(see p77)*

1505

1509 Pope Julius II begins driving the French from Italian soil

1510

1512 Florence besieged by Cardinal Giovanni de' Medici

1513 Giovanni de' Medici crowned Pope Leo X

Execution of Savonarola
Savonarola was an inspirational orator who commanded great popular support. His political enemies had him executed for heresy in 1498.

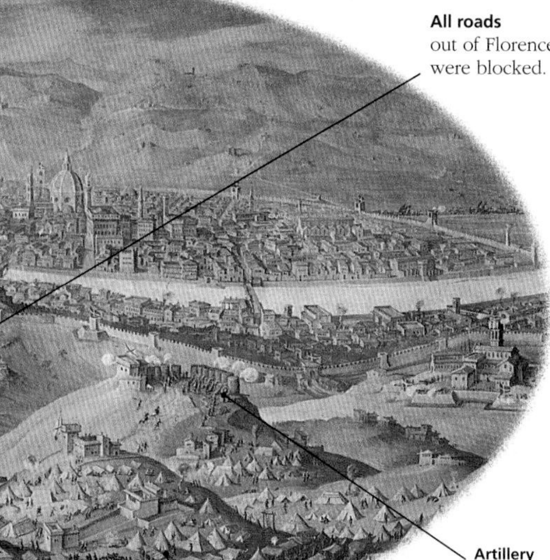

All roads out of Florence were blocked.

Artillery platform

Troops camped to the south.

Niccolò Machiavelli
The author of The Prince, *a treatise on the ruthless skills required to be a successful politician, was the last Republican chancellor.*

WHERE TO SEE REPUBLICAN TUSCANY

A plaque in Piazza della Signoria *(see pp76–7)* marks the spot where Savonarola was executed; his cell can be seen in San Marco *(pp96–7)*. Michelangelo's *David (p94)* symbolizes the victory of the youthful Republic over tyranny. The Republican council met in the Salone dei Cinquecento *(p76)*.

Tower of San Miniato
This was reinforced in 1530 as a gun platform (pp130–31)

Michelangelo's Sketches
During the siege of 1530, Michelangelo worked in the safety of the Cappelle Medicee (pp90–91).

Crystal casket belonging to Pope Clement VII

1527 Florentine Republic reconstituted when Rome is sacked by imperial troops

1531 Alessandro de' Medici becomes first Duke of Florence

15 | 1525 | 1530

1520 Michelangelo begins work on Medici tombs *(see p91)*

1521 Giulio de' Medici crowned Pope Clement VII and Medici rule restored in Florence

1530 Siege of Florence by combined forces of pope and emperor

1532 Posthumous publication of Machiavelli's *The Prince*

The Grand Duchy

Cosimo I was created Grand Duke of Tuscany in 1570, having forced Tuscany into a state of political unity for the first time. A period of prosperity followed, in spite of the corrupt and debauched nature of Cosimo's heirs. When the Medici line ended in 1737, the Grand Duchy was inherited by the Austrian Dukes of Lorraine. They were removed from power in 1860 during the Risorgimento, when the Italian people joined forces to overthrow their foreign rulers. From 1865–70, Florence was the nation's capital. With the final unification of Italy in 1870, however, the centre of power returned to Rome.

Leopoldo and Family
Leopoldo I, later Emperor Leopold II of Austria, introduced many reforms, including abolition of the death penalty

Livorno Harbour
Livorno became a free port in 1608: ships from every nation were granted equal docking rights, and the resulting influx of Jewish and Moorish refugees contributed to the city's prosperity.

The Church rejected Galileo's discoveries.

Galileo explains his theory of gravity.

The Old Market
Florence's Old Market was knocked down in 1865, when the city was briefly the Italian capital. In its place is the triumphal arch of the Piazza della Repubblica (see p112).

THE AGE OF SCIENCE

Galileo was one of several brilliant scientists who benefited from Medici patronage during the 17th century, making Tuscany a centre of scientific innovation. His experiments and astronomical observations laid the foundations for modern empirical science, but led to his persecution for contradicting the teachings of the Roman Catholic Church.

TIMELINE

1537 Cosimo I elected Duke of Florence

1558 Cellini's *Autobiography*

1570 Cosimo I granted the title: Grand Duke of Tuscany

1574 Francesco I succeeds Cosimo I

1577 Work begins on making Livorno Tuscany's main port

Emblem of the Medici dukes

1550 | 1600 | 1650

1609 Cosimo II succeeds Francesco I

1633 Galileo excommunicated

1642 Galileo dies under house arrest at Arcetri, near Florence

Helmet belonging to Cosimo III

The Grand Tour
It became fashionable for wealthy 18th-century European aristocrats to visit Tuscany. This detail from Zoffani's Tribuna *(1770) shows a tour of the Uffizi.*

Galileo conducted his experiments using specially designed equipment *(see p74)*.

Cosimo II gave refuge to Galileo after the Church accused him of heresy.

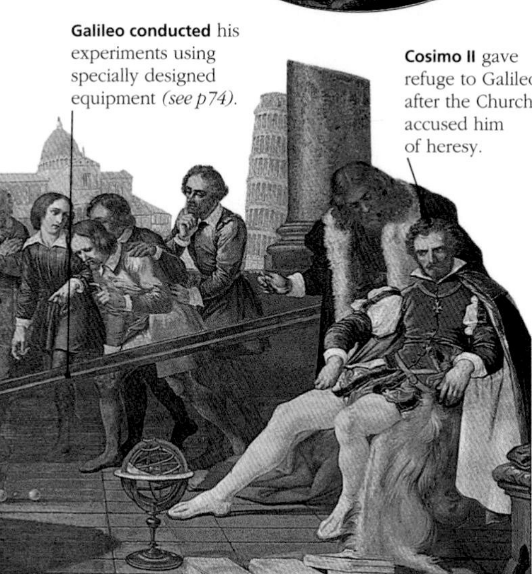

National Rule
Florence ran up huge debts while serving as the Italian capital. This cartoon shows a protest against the seat of power (the Palazzo Vecchio) being transferred to Rome.

WHERE TO SEE GRAND DUCHY TUSCANY

The Uffizi art collection *(see pp80–83)* was assembled by the Medici at this time, along with the collections in the Palazzo Pitti *(pp120–23)*, the building from which the Grand Dukes ruled Tuscany for over 300 years. The story of Galileo and his contemporaries is told in the Museo di Storia della Scienza in Florence *(p74)*. The frescoes of the Sala del Risorgimento, in the Palazzo Pubblico, Siena *(p218)*, depict the events that preceded the final unification of Italy.

Palazzo dei Cavalieri
Francavilla's statue of Cosimo I (1596) marks the entrance to Vasari's ornate Palazzo (p156).

Napoleon's Bathroom
Napoleon never used this bathroom (1790–99), built for him at the Palazzo Pitti (pp120–23).

1737 End of Medici dynasty; rule passes to Austrian House of Lorraine

1743 Death of Anna Maria Lodovica, last of the Medici

1750

1765 Grand Duke Leopoldo I introduces many social reforms

1796 Napoleon's first Italian campaign

1799 France defeats Austria: Tuscany ruled by Louis de Bourbon, then by Napoleon's sister, Elisa Baciocchi

1800

1814 Napoleon exiled to Elba

1815 Napoleon defeated at Waterloo

1822 Shelley drowns near Livorno

1840 Ruskin visits Florence

John Ruskin (1819–1900), who revived critical interest in the Renaissance

1850

1865 Florence chosen as capital of new Italian state

1871 Italian capital returns to Rome

The Modern Era

The 20th century has seen many threats to Florence's fragile artistic heritage. The city's historic bridges, except for the Ponte Vecchio, were destroyed during World War II, and worse was to come in 1966 from devastating floods. Traffic and pollution have also taken their toll, leading to tough environmental controls aimed at preserving the historic city centre. Fortunately, the city has energetically risen to these challenges. It continues to thrive both on its proud heritage as a tourist destination and as a living, working city with a robust commercial and industrial base.

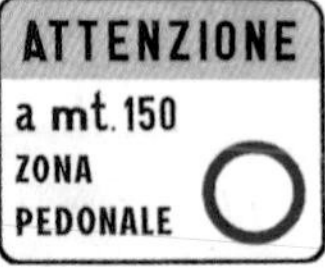

Traffic Control
In 1988 Florence banned cars from the city centre.

La Bohème *(1896)*
This popular opera by Puccini, Tuscany's greatest composer, often features in the region's music festivals (see p35).

Firenze Nuova
Florentine commerce and industry are moving to the suburb of "New Florence", leaving the city centre free for cultural and creative enterprises.

ART RESTORATION

Great pride is taken in Tuscany's artistic heritage, and modern scientific methods are used to analyse frescoes before restoration, such as *The Procession of the Magi (see p89).* These methods include computer-aided mapping of the pigments and plotting any structural damage.

TIMELINE

Domenico Tiburzi, folk hero and notorious Maremman bandit

1896 First performance of Puccini's *La Bohème*

1896 Domenico Tiburzi is caught and shot after 24 years on the run

1915 Italy enters World War I on the side of the Allies (France, Britain and Russia)

1922 Mussolini heads Italy's first Fascist government

1940 Italy enters World War II

1943 Fall of the Fascists

1944 Many historic structures in Tuscany are damaged by Allied bombing or retreating Nazis

1946 Italy becom a repub

1890 | 1900 | 1910 | 1920 | 1930 | 1940

The 1966 Floods
On 4 November, floodwater from the Arno rose to 6 m (19.5 ft) above street level. Many art treasures were ruined; some are still in restoration.

A scanned image lets restorers trace existing outlines and reconstruct damaged areas.

Commands for operating the computer program

Fashion
Many Florentine designers have become household names. These include Pucci, who invented the "Palazzo Pyjamas", Gucci, Ferragamo (see p284) *and, more recently, rising stars like Daelli and Coveri.*

Tourism
Florence and Tuscany have long been popular destinations for tourists (see p55). *Florence now receives some 5 million visitors each year.*

WHERE TO SEE MODERN FLORENCE

The shops of Via de' Tornabuoni and Via della Vigna Nuova *(see p105)* sell the best in Florentine fashion. Exhibitions of photographs at the Museo Alinari *(p104)* illustrate the city as it has developed during the 20th century. Cimabue's ruined *Crucifixion (p72)*, in the museum of Santa Croce, is displayed as a reminder of the 1966 floods.

Railway station *(1935)*
The Functionalist station is one of the city centre's few notable modern buildings (see p113).

San Giovanni Battista *(1964)*
Giovanni Michelucci's modern church stands near Amerigo Vespucci airport.

1966 Floods in Florence

1957–65 Italian industrial boom

Bomb damage at the Uffizi

1987 The Sorpasso: Italian economy outstrips that of France and the UK

1993 The Uffizi damaged in a terrorist explosion

1999 Italy joins the single European currency

2005 After a 26-year reign Pope John Paul II dies on 2 April. He is succeeded by Pope Benedict XVI on 19 April

2010 Line 1 of the tram system opens, linking Santa Maria Novella station with the Scandicci district

950 | 1960 | 1990 | 2000 | 2010 | 2020

Duomo and cityscape, Florence ▷

FLORENCE AREA BY AREA

CITY CENTRE EAST

The dominant building in this part of Florence is the magnificent Duomo, the first place most people will visit when they arrive in the city. Traffic is now banned in the Piazza del Duomo, which makes it easier to appreciate the immensity of this great building. It is, in fact, so large that a comprehensive view is impossible from such close quarters. As you wander the streets to the south you will continually catch glimpses of its multi-coloured marble cladding.

Duomo clock, decorated in 1443 by Paolo Uccello

The area's other major church, Santa Croce, containing the tombs and monuments of many great Florentines, sits at the centre of the traditional artisans' quarter. These streets have few prestigious palaces, but there is a lively and attractive sense of community. It is here that you will find characterful neighbourhood shops and restoration workshops where specialists continue to repair the many books and works of art damaged in the 1966 floods *(see pp56–7)*.

SIGHTS AT A GLANCE

Museums and Galleries

The Bargello pp68–9 6
Casa Buonarroti 10
Casa di Dante 4
Museo di Firenze com'era 8
Museo Horne 12
Museo dell'Opera del Duomo 2
Museo di Storia della Scienza 13
Palazzo Nonfinito 7
Palazzo Vecchio pp78–9 17
The Uffizi pp80–83 18

Churches

Badia Fiorentina 5
Duomo, Campanile and Baptistry pp64–5 1
Orsanmichele 3
Santa Croce pp72–3 11
Santo Stefano al Ponte 14

Historic Streets and Piazzas

Piazza della Signoria pp76–7 16

Shops

Erboristeria 15

Ice-Cream Parlours

Bar Vivoli Gelateria 9

PIAZZA DI SAN GIOVANNI
PIAZZA DEL DUOMO
VIA MAURIZIO BUFALINI
VIA DEL PROCONSOLO
VIA DELL'ORIUOLO
VIA ROMA
VIA DEI CALZAIUOLI
VIA DELL'OCHE
VIA DEL CORSO
BORGO DEGLI ALBIZI
PIAZZA GAETANO SALVEMINI
VIA PIETRAPIANA
CALIMALA
VIA DANTE ALIGHIERI
V. D. GIRALDI
VIA DE' PANDOLFINI
PIAZZA DEI CIOMPI
VIA DELL'ULIVO
VIA DEI CIMATORI
VIA GHIBELLINA
VIA GIUSEPPE VERDI
VIA MICHELANGELO BUONARROTI
VIA D. CONDOTTA
V. D. VIGNA VECCHIA
VIA DE' PEPI
VIA ALLEGRI
VIA DE' MACCI
PIAZZA DELLA SIGNORIA
PIAZZA DI SAN FIRENZE
VIA DELL'ANGUILLARA
V. D. BURELLA
V. D. LAVATOI
VIA TORTA
VIA DEL FICO
VIA D. PINZOCHERE
VIA S. CRISTOFANO
BORGO
VIA DELLE CONCE
V. POR S. MARIA
V. LAMBERTESCA
VIA D. NINNA
V. D. LEONI
BORGO DE' GRECI
PIAZZA DE' PERUZZI
PIAZZA DI SANTA CROCE
L. GO PIERO BARGELLINI
VIA DI SAN GIUSEPPE
PIAZZA DEL PESCE
P. LE DEGLI UFFIZI
V. DE' CASTELLANI
PIAZZA DI REMIGIO
VIA DE' NERI
VIA DE' BENCI
BORGO S. CROCE
VIA ANTONIO MAGLIABECHI
PIAZZA DE' GIUDICI
PIAZZA MENTANA
V. D. VAGELLAI
CORSO DEI TINTORI
Arno
LUNG. GEN. DIAZ
LUNG. DELLE GRAZIE
PIAZZA DEI CAVALLEGGERI

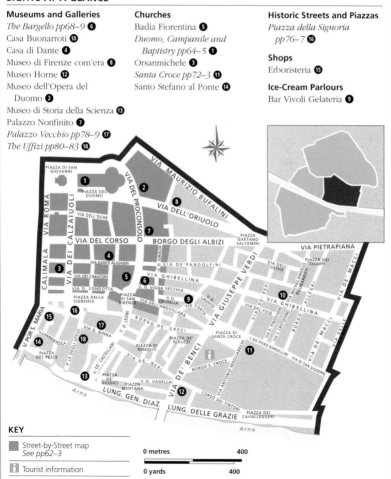

KEY

Street-by-Street map *See pp62–3*

Tourist information

0 metres 400
0 yards 400

Street-by-Street: Around the Duomo

Statue on Orsanmichele façade

Much of Florence was rebuilt during the Renaissance, but the eastern part of the city retains a distinctly medieval feel. With its confusing maze of tiny alleyways and hidden lanes, it would still be recognizable to Dante. His house, the Casa di Dante, still stands near the parish church where he first glimpsed his beloved, Beatrice Portinari *(see p70)*. He would also recognize the Bargello and, of course, the Baptistry. One of the oldest streets is the Borgo degli Albizi. Now lined with Renaissance palaces, it follows the line of the ancient Roman road to Rome.

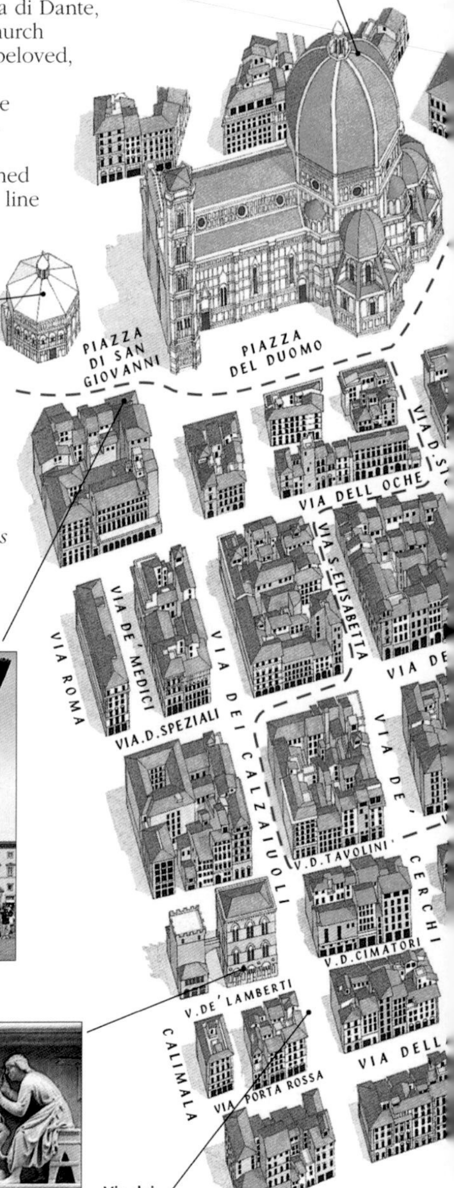

The dome, completed in 1436, was designed by Brunelleschi to dwarf even the great buildings of ancient Greece and Rome.

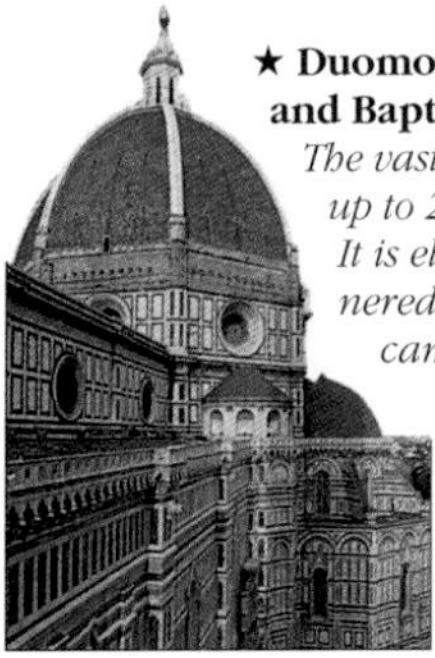

★ Duomo, Campanile and Baptistry

The vast Duomo holds up to 20,000 people. It is elegantly partnered by Giotto's campanile and the Baptistry, whose doors demonstrate the artistic ideas that led to the Renaissance ❶

The Loggia del Bigallo was built for the Misericordia by Alberto Arnoldi in 1358. During the 15th century, abandoned children were displayed here for three days. If, after this time, their parents had not claimed them, they were sent to foster homes.

★ Orsanmichele

The carvings on the walls of this Gothic church depict the activities and patron saints of the city's trade guilds, such as the Masons and Carpenters ❸

Via dei Calzaiuoli, lined with smart shops, is the focus of the *passeggiata*, the traditional evening stroll.

For hotels and restaurants in this area see pp250–51 and pp270–71

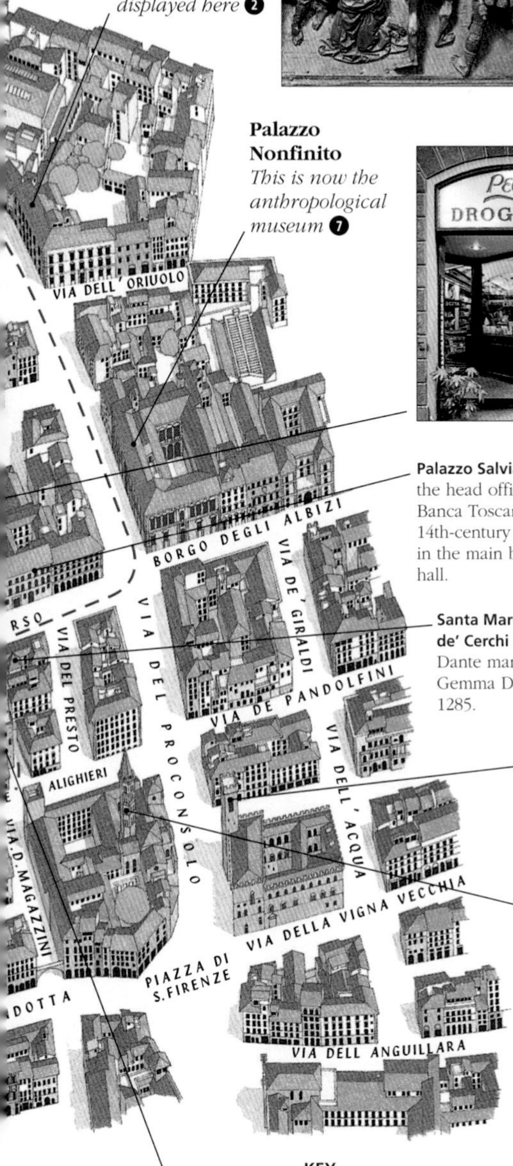

★ Museo dell'Opera del Duomo
Works removed from the Duomo, Campanile and Baptistry, like this panel by Verrocchio, are displayed here ❷

LOCATOR MAP
See Florence Street Finder map 6

Palazzo Nonfinito
This is now the anthropological museum ❼

Pegna, a mini-supermarket tucked away in the Via della Studio, sells a range of gourmet treats including chocolate, honey, wine, balsamic vinegar and olive oil *(see p285).*

Palazzo Salviati, now the head office of the Banca Toscana, has 14th-century frescoes in the main banking hall.

Santa Margherita de' Cerchi is where Dante married Gemma Donati in 1285.

VIA DELL' ORIUOLO
BORGO DEGLI ALBIZI
VIA DE' GIRALDI
VIA DEL PROCONSOLO
VIA DEL PRESTO
VIA DE PANDOLFINI
VIA DELL' ACQUA
ALIGHIERI
VIA D. MAGAZZINI
VIA DELLA VIGNA VECCHIA
PIAZZA DI S. FIRENZE
VIA DELL ANGUILLARA

★ The Bargello
The city's old prison is home to a rich collection of applied arts and sculpture, like this figure by Cellini (1500–71) ❻

Badia Fiorentina
The Badia's bell regulated daily life in medieval Florence ❺

Casa di Dante
This medieval house is a museum devoted to Dante's life and work ❹

KEY

– – – Suggested route

0 metres 100

0 yards 100

STAR SIGHTS

- ★ Duomo, Campanile and Baptistry
- ★ The Bargello
- ★ Museo dell'Opera del Duomo
- ★ Orsanmichele

Duomo, Campanile and Baptistry ❶

Set in the heart of Florence, Santa Maria del Fiore – the Duomo, or cathedral of Florence – dominates the city with its enormous dome. Its sheer size was typical of Florentine determination to lead in all things, and to this day, no other building stands taller in the city. The Baptistry with its celebrated doors *(see p66)* is one of Florence's oldest buildings, dating perhaps to the 4th century. In his capacity as city architect, Giotto designed the Campanile in 1334; it was completed in 1359, 22 years after his death.

The Campanile
At 85 m (276 ft), the Campanile is 6 m (20 ft) shorter than the dome. It is clad in white, green and pink Tuscan marble.

★ Baptistry Ceiling
Colourful 13th-century mosaics illustrating the Last Judgment are set above the large octagonal font where many famous Florentines, including Dante, were baptized.

Gothic windows

The Neo-Gothic marble façade echoes the style of Giotto's Campanile, but was only added in 1871–87.

Main entrance

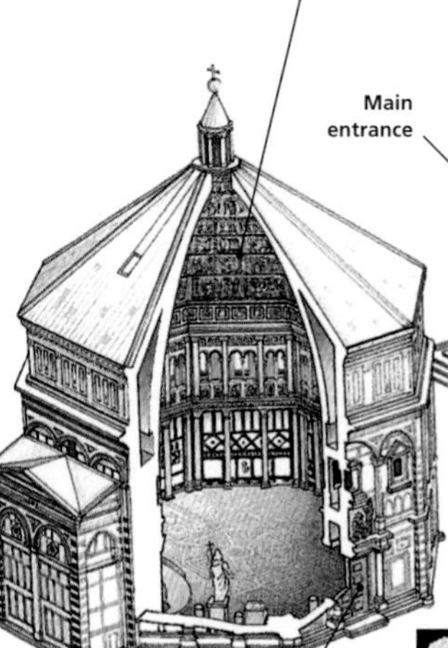

South Doors

The terracotta panels with bas-reliefs are by Andrea Pisano.

Steps to Santa Reparata
The crypt contains the remains of the 4th-century church of Santa Reparata, demolished in 1296 to make way for the cathedral.

STAR FEATURES

- ★ Brunelleschi's Dome
- ★ Baptistry Ceiling

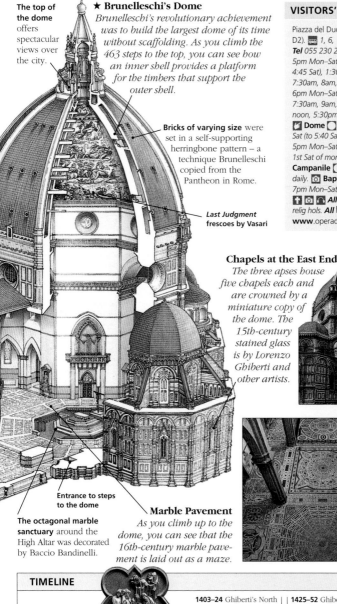

The top of the dome offers spectacular views over the city.

★ Brunelleschi's Dome
Brunelleschi's revolutionary achievement was to build the largest dome of its time without scaffolding. As you climb the 463 steps to the top, you can see how an inner shell provides a platform for the timbers that support the outer shell.

Bricks of varying size were set in a self-supporting herringbone pattern – a technique Brunelleschi copied from the Pantheon in Rome.

***Last Judgment* frescoes by Vasari**

VISITORS' CHECKLIST

Piazza del Duomo. **Map** 2 D5 (6 D2). *1, 6, 14, 17, 23.* **Duomo Tel** *055 230 28 85.* *10am–5pm Mon–Sat (to 3:30 Thu, to 4:45 Sat), 1:30–4:45pm Sun.* *7:30am, 8am, 8:30am, 9:30am, 6pm Mon–Sat; 5pm (English) Sat; 7:30am, 9am, 10am, 10:30am, noon, 5:30pm, 6pm Sun.* **Dome** *8:30am–7pm Mon–Sat (to 5:40 Sat).* **Crypt** *10am–5pm Mon–Sat (to 3:30 Thu and 1st Sat of month, to 4:45pm Sat).* **Campanile** *8:30am–7:30pm daily.* **Baptistry** *noon–7pm Mon–Sat, 8:30am–2pm Sun.* ***All*** *1 Jan, 15 Aug & relig hols.* ***All*** *(except Duomo).* **www**.operaduomo.firenze.it

Chapels at the East End
The three apses house five chapels each and are crowned by a miniature copy of the dome. The 15th-century stained glass is by Lorenzo Ghiberti and other artists.

Entrance to steps to the dome

The octagonal marble sanctuary around the High Altar was decorated by Baccio Bandinelli.

Marble Pavement
As you climb up to the dome, you can see that the 16th-century marble pavement is laid out as a maze.

TIMELINE

4th–5th centuries The Baptistry and Santa Reparata church built

Panel from South Doors

897 First documented record of the Baptistry

11th–13th centuries Baptistry re-clad in green and white marble

1209 Zodiac pavement laid in Baptistry

1271 *The Last Judgment* completed on Baptistry ceiling

1296 Arnolfo di Cambio begins the new cathedral on the site of Santa Reparata

1338 Andrea Pisano's South Doors added

1359 Giotto's Campanile completed

1403–24 Ghiberti's North Doors added

1425–52 Ghiberti's East Doors, the "Gate of Paradise", added

1436 Dome completed

1887 Long-delayed completion of the cathedral façade

400 | 600 | 800 | 1000 | 1200 | 1400 | 1600 | 1800

The East Doors of the Baptistry

Lorenzo Ghiberti

Lorenzo Ghiberti's celebrated doors were commissioned in 1401 to mark Florence's deliverance from the plague. Ghiberti was chosen after a competition involving seven leading artists, including Donatello and Brunelleschi. Ghiberti's and Brunelleschi's trial panels *(see p69)* are so different from Florentine Gothic art of the time that they are often regarded as the first products of the Renaissance.

Ghiberti's winning panel

The "Gate of Paradise"
Having spent 21 years on the North Doors, Ghiberti worked on the East Doors from 1424 to 1452. Michelangelo enthusiastically dubbed them the "Gate of Paradise". The original panels are in the Museo dell'Opera del Duomo; those on the Baptistry are copies.

The jagged rocks, symbolizing Abraham's pain, are carefully arranged to emphasize the sacrificial act.

Abraham and the Sacrifice of Isaac

Architecture is used to create the illusion of spatial depth. Ghiberti was a master of perspective.

Joseph Sold into Slavery and Recognized by his Brothers

KEY TO THE EAST DOORS

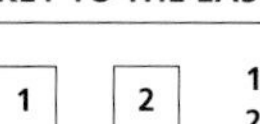

1	2
3	4
5	6
7	8
9	10

1 Adam and Eve are Expelled from Eden
2 Cain Murders his Brother, Abel
3 The Drunkenness of Noah and his Sacrifice
4 Abraham and the Sacrifice of Isaac
5 Esau and Jacob
6 Joseph Sold into Slavery
7 Moses Receives the Ten Commandments
8 The Fall of Jericho
9 The Battle with the Philistines
10 Solomon and the Queen of Sheba

Duomo, Campanile and Baptistry ❶

See pp64–5.

Museo dell'Opera del Duomo ❷

Piazza del Duomo 9. **Map** 2 D5 (6 E2). ***Tel*** *055 230 28 85.*
9am–7:30pm Mon–Sat; 9am–1:40pm Sun & public hols.
1 Jan, Easter Sun, 25 Dec.

The Museo dell'Opera del Duomo has been extensively remodelled to allow for a series of rooms dedicated to the history of the Duomo. Information about the renovation is available in English and Italian.

From the ticket booth, the main room is reached through open spaces containing Etruscan and Roman reliefs, carvings and sarcophagi.

The main ground floor room contains statues from the work-shop of Arnolfo di Cambio, which were once placed in the cathedral's niches. Some are by Arnolfo himself, including the Gothic *Madonna of the Glass Eyes*. Nearby visitors can see Nanni di Banco's *St Luke*, Bernardo Ciuffagni's *St Matthew* and, most striking of all, Donatello's *St John*. The three were carved between 1408 and 1415. A side room, added during the renovation, contains 14th–15th century religious paintings and a number of reliquaries, one of which includes the finger of San Giovanni.

Pulley used to build Brunelleschi's dome

Michelangelo's *Pietà* has pride of place on the staircase. The hooded figure of Nicodemus is widely believed to be a self-portrait. That Mary Magdalene is the inferior work of a pupil is strikingly obvious.

The first room on the upper floor is dominated by two choir lofts, dating to the 1430s, by Donatello and Luca della Robbia. Carved in crisp white marble and decorated with coloured glass and mosaic, both depict children playing musical instruments and dancing. But while della Robbia's figures seem innocent, Donatello's look like frenzied participants in some primitive ritual.

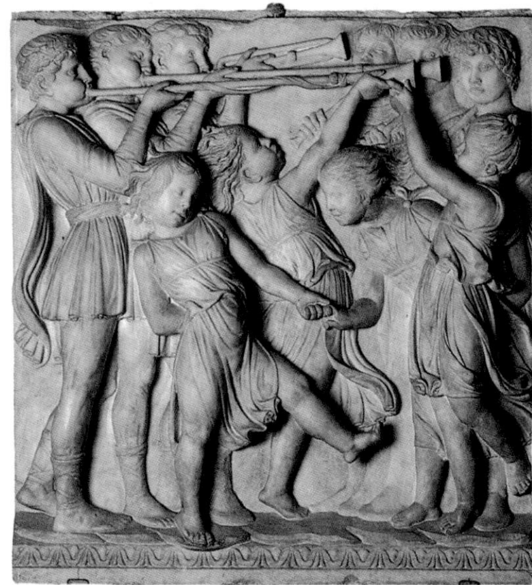

Carving from della Robbia's choir loft in the Museo dell'Opera del Duomo

Among a number of works by Donatello in this room are his statue of *La Maddalena* (1455) *(see p27)* and several Old Testament figures, including the prophet Abakuk (1423–5), affectionately known by Florentines as *lo zuccone* (marrow-head).

The room to the left contains an exhibition of the tablets which used to decorate the bell tower, some by Andrea Pisano and della Robbia.

Leaving this room, visitors descend to a lower level that houses examples of the tools used by Brunelleschi's workmen, and a copy of di Cambio's original cathedral façade. Visitors then descend to a courtyard, where one finds some of the original panels of doors of the baptistry, as well as the exit.

Orsanmichele ❸

Via dell'Arte della Lana. **Map** 3 C1 (6 D3). ***Tel*** *055 28 49 44.* *10am–5pm daily.*
First and last Mon of every month, 1 Jan, 1 May, 25 Dec.

The name is a corruption of *Orto di San Michele*, a former monastic garden. Orsanmichele was built in 1337 as a grain market, but was soon turned into a church. The open arcades became windows, and though these are now bricked in, the original Gothic tracery can still be seen. The outside walls have 14 niches, each holding a statue of the patron saint of one of Florence's major *Arti* (guilds).

The interior has two parallel naves. To the right is an extraordinary 1350s altar by Andrea Orcagna. It is covered in cherubs and carved reliefs and encrusted with coloured marble and glass. Close by is Bernardo Daddi's *Virgin and Child* (1348), its frame beautifully carved with angels.

St George on the façade of Orsanmichele

The Bargello ❻

Built in 1255 as the city's town hall, the Bargello is the oldest seat of government surviving in Florence. In the 16th century it was the residence of the chief of police and a prison: executions took place here until 1786. After extensive renovation, it became one of Italy's first national museums in 1865. The Bargello houses a superb collection of Florentine Renaissance sculpture, with rooms dedicated to the work of Michelangelo, Donatello, Verrocchio, Giambologna and Cellini, as well as a collection of Mannerist bronzes and examples from the decorative arts.

Mercury
Giambologna's famous 1564 bronze shows an athletic youth poised for flight.

GALLERY GUIDE

To the right of the entrance hall, the Michelangelo Room is presided over by his Bacchus *(1497). The courtyard staircase leads up to the Upper Loggia, filled with statues of birds by Giambologna. To the right is the Donatello Room, which contains the panels for the Baptistry doors competition of 1401. The Magdalen Chapel and Islamic Collection are also on the first floor. The Verrocchio Room, the Andrea and Giovanni della Robbia rooms, the Arms and Armour Collection and the Room of the Small Bronzes are on the second floor.*

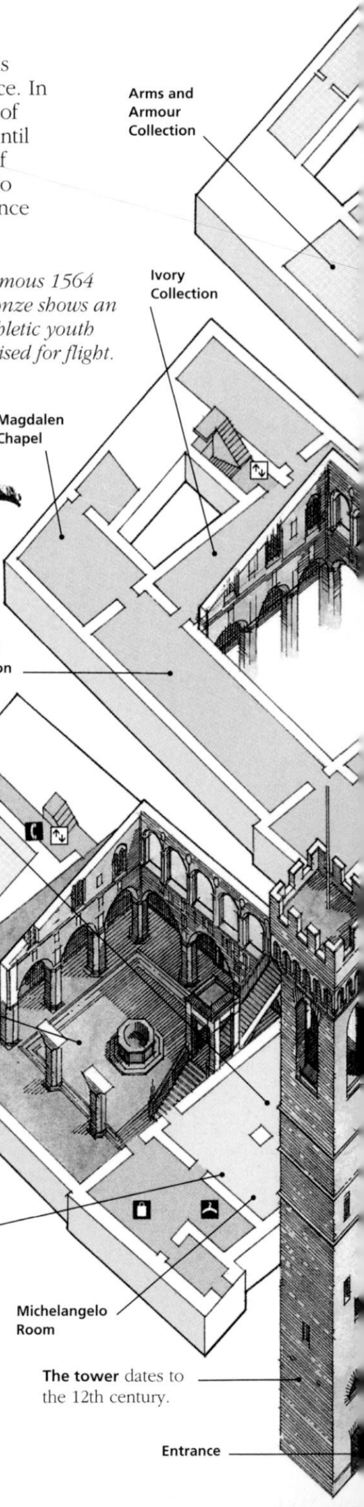

Arms and Armour Collection

Ivory Collection

Magdalen Chapel

Carrand Collection

The courtyard was once the place of execution.

★ Bacchus
The Roman god of wine with a small satyr was Michelangelo's first major work (1497). The modelling is Classical, but the unsteady, drunken posture mocks the poise of ancient works.

Michelangelo Room

The tower dates to the 12th century.

Entrance

KEY

- Ground floor
- First floor
- Second floor
- Temporary exhibitions
- Non-exhibition space

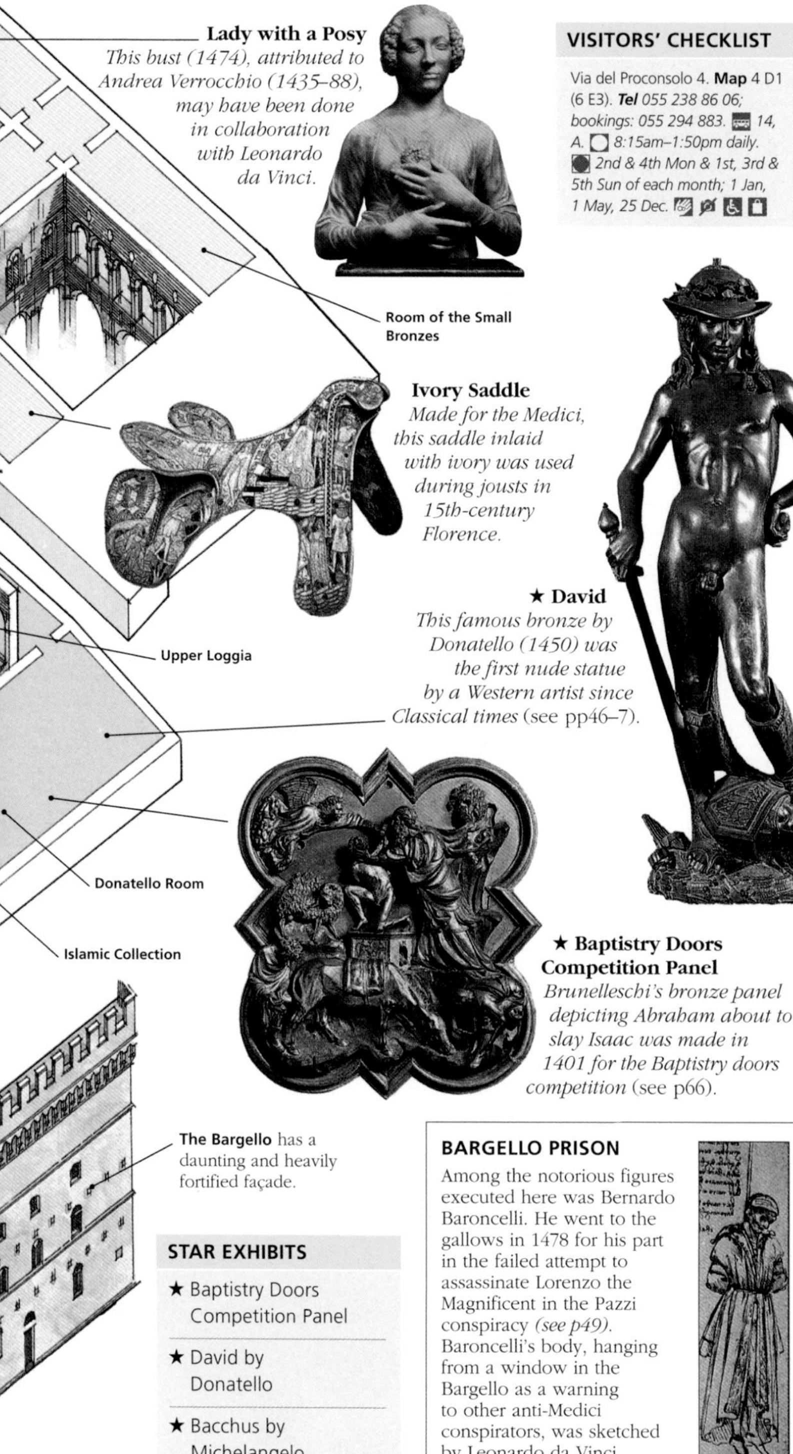

Lady with a Posy
This bust (1474), attributed to Andrea Verrocchio (1435–88), may have been done in collaboration with Leonardo da Vinci.

Ivory Saddle
Made for the Medici, this saddle inlaid with ivory was used during jousts in 15th-century Florence.

★ David
This famous bronze by Donatello (1450) was the first nude statue by a Western artist since Classical times (see pp46–7).

★ Baptistry Doors Competition Panel
Brunelleschi's bronze panel depicting Abraham about to slay Isaac was made in 1401 for the Baptistry doors competition (see p66).

The Bargello has a daunting and heavily fortified façade.

VISITORS' CHECKLIST

Via del Proconsolo 4. **Map** 4 D1 (6 E3). ***Tel*** *055 238 86 06; bookings: 055 294 883.* *14, A.* *8:15am–1:50pm daily.* *2nd & 4th Mon & 1st, 3rd & 5th Sun of each month; 1 Jan, 1 May, 25 Dec.*

STAR EXHIBITS

- ★ Baptistry Doors Competition Panel
- ★ David by Donatello
- ★ Bacchus by Michelangelo

BARGELLO PRISON

Among the notorious figures executed here was Bernardo Baroncelli. He went to the gallows in 1478 for his part in the failed attempt to assassinate Lorenzo the Magnificent in the Pazzi conspiracy *(see p49)*. Baroncelli's body, hanging from a window in the Bargello as a warning to other anti-Medici conspirators, was sketched by Leonardo da Vinci.

Casa di Dante ❹

Via Santa Margherita 1.
Map 4 D1 (6 E3).
Tel *055 21 94 16.*
10am–5pm Tue–Sun.
last Sun of the month.

It is uncertain whether the poet Dante Alighieri (1265–1321) was actually born here, but at least the house looks the part. In 1911, the remains of a 13th-century tower house were restored to give the building its rambling appearance.

Bust of Dante on the façade of Casa di Dante

Just a short stroll north of the house is the parish church of Santa Margherita de' Cerchi, built during the 11th century. It is here that Dante is said to have first caught sight of Beatrice Portinari, whom he idolized in his poetry. The church, which is often used for Baroque chamber music and organ recitals, contains a fine altarpiece by Neri di Bicci (1418–91).

Badia Fiorentina ❺

Via del Proconsolo. **Map** 4 D1 (6 E3). ***Tel*** *055 234 45 45.*
Church *8am–6pm Tue–Sat.*
Cloister *3–6pm Mon.*

The abbey, one of Florence's oldest churches, was founded in 978 by Willa, the widow of Count Uberto of Tuscany. Their son, Count Ugo, was buried inside the church in 1001. His splendid tomb was carved by Mino da Fiesole and dates from 1469–81. Mino also carved the altarpiece and, in the right transept, the tomb of Bernardo Giugni, the Florentine statesman, with its fine effigy of Justice.

Filippino Lippi's *The Virgin Appearing to St Bernard* (1485) also enlivens an otherwise drab and solemn interior. Its remarkable detail, particularly in the landscape, makes it one of the most artistically significant works of the 15th century.

The peaceful Chiostro degli Aranci ("cloister of the orange trees") is a little hard to find. Look for a door to the right of the altar. Sadly, the orange trees that the monks used to cultivate here are no longer present. The two-tier cloister, built by Rossellino in 1435–40, has a well-preserved fresco cycle showing scenes from the life of St Benedict. Dating from the 15th century, it was restored as recently as 1973. An early fresco by Bronzino (1503–72) can also be seen in the north walkway. Excellent views of the hexagonal campanile, which gets mentioned by Dante in the *Paradiso* section of *The Divine Comedy*, can be enjoyed from the cloister.

In the 14th century, a series of readings and lectures devoted to Dante's work were given at the Badia by the poet Boccaccio. In keeping with the spirit of these meetings, the abbey is today often used for talks and concerts.

***The Virgin Appearing to St Bernard* (1485) by Filippino Lippi**

The Bargello ❻

See pp68–9.

Palazzo Nonfinito ❼

Via del Proconsolo 12. **Map** 2 D5 (6 E2). ***Tel*** *055 239 64 49.*
9am–1pm Thu–Tue (to 5pm Sat).
1 Jan, 25 Apr, Easter Sun, 1 May, 24 Jun, 15 Aug, 8 Dec, 25–26 Dec, 31 Dec.

The Palazzo Nonfinito (Unfinished Palace) was begun by Buontalenti in 1593 and was still incomplete when it became Italy's first museum of anthropology and ethnology in 1869. The most striking architectural feature is an imposing inner courtyard usually attributed to Cigoli (1559–1613).

The museum's opening hours are severely restricted. However, it's worth setting aside some time to see the collection of art from Italy's former African colonies, and material carried away by Captain Cook, the 18th-century British explorer, on the last of his Pacific voyages.

19th-century copy of the *Pianta della Catena*, showing Florence's cityscape

Museo di Firenze com'era ❽

Via dell'Oriuolo 24. **Map** 2 D5 (6 F2). ***Tel*** *055 261 65 45.* *9am–2pm Mon–Wed, 9am–7pm Sat (last adm: 30 mins before closing).* *1 Jan, Easter Sun, 1 May, 15 Aug, 25 Dec.*

The museum traces the development of the city through drawings, plans and paintings. One of the most fascinating exhibits is the *Pianta della Catena*, a 19th-century copy of a woodcut made around 1470. The title refers to the chain-like border that surrounds the whole image, which shows Florence at the height of the Renaissance. Some buildings, for instance the Palazzo Pitti, can be seen.

The Palazzo Pitti features again in the delightful sequence of lunettes made by the Flemish artist Giusto Utens in 1599. They show all the Medici villas and gardens, with fascinating vignettes of rural life *(see pp121 and 165)*.

One room is devoted to a scheme devised by Giuseppe Poggi, the city architect involved in remodelling much of central Florence during its brief stint as the capital of Italy in 1865–71. If the scheme had been implemented, large parts of the centre would have been destroyed. The scheme was halted after an international outcry, but not before buildings had been cleared for the new Piazza della Repubblica *(see p112)* and the 14th-century walls had been torn down.

Bar Vivoli Gelateria ❾

Via Isola delle Stinche 7r. **Map** 4 D1 (6 F3). ***Tel*** *055 29 23 34.* *7:30am–1am Tue–Sat, 9:30am–1am Sun.* *three weeks in Jan & three weeks in Aug.* **www**.vivoli.it

Bar Vivoli Gelateria

This tiny ice-cream parlour attracts large crowds and long queues for its rich iced concoctions. Vivoli claims to make the "best ice cream in the world", and the walls of the bar are covered in press clippings from ice-cream connoisseurs that strongly support this view.

The bar stands at the heart of the colourful Santa Croce district, with its narrow alleys and tiny squares. Here, you will find small shops that serve the local community, rather than cater for tourists, and scores of little workshops where craftsmen make picture frames or mend furniture. Via Torta is typical of the area.

Casa Buonarroti ❿

Via Ghibellina 70. **Map** 4 E1. ***Tel*** *055 24 17 52.* *9:30am–2pm Wed–Mon.* *1 Jan, Easter Sun, 25 Apr, 1 May, 15 Aug, 25 Dec.*

Michelangelo (whose surname was Buonarroti) lived briefly in this group of three houses which he bought as an investment in 1508. Subsequent generations of his descendants added what they could to a significant collection of his works.

Among these is his earliest known work, the *Madonna della Scala*, a marble *tavoletta*, or rectangular relief, carved in 1490–92. There is also a relief from 1492, showing *The Battle of the Centaurs*, and the design, never used, for the façade of San Lorenzo, shown in a wooden model.

Santa Croce ⓫

The magnificent Gothic church of Santa Croce (1294) contains the tombs of many famous Florentines, including Michelangelo and Galileo. The spacious, airy interior is enhanced by the radiant frescoes of Giotto and his gifted pupil, Taddeo Gaddi, painted early in the 14th century. The Arnolfo and Brunelleschi Cloisters provide visitors with fine examples of Renaissance architectural precision, and a moment of peace and tranquillity during their tour. The rest of the monastic buildings ranged around the cloister form a museum of religious painting and sculpture.

The façade was reclad with coloured marble in 1863 paid for by an English benefactor, Francis Sloane.

Galileo's Tomb
Condemned by the church in 1633, Galileo was denied a Christian burial until 1737, when this tomb by Giulio Foggini was erected.

Lorenzo Ghiberti (1378–1455), creator of the magnificent doors of Florence's Baptistry, is buried here, along with his sons and assistants, Vittorio and Lorenzo.

Machiavelli *(see p53)* was buried here in 1527. His monument, by Innocenzo Spinazzi, was erected in 1787.

Ticket booth and entrance

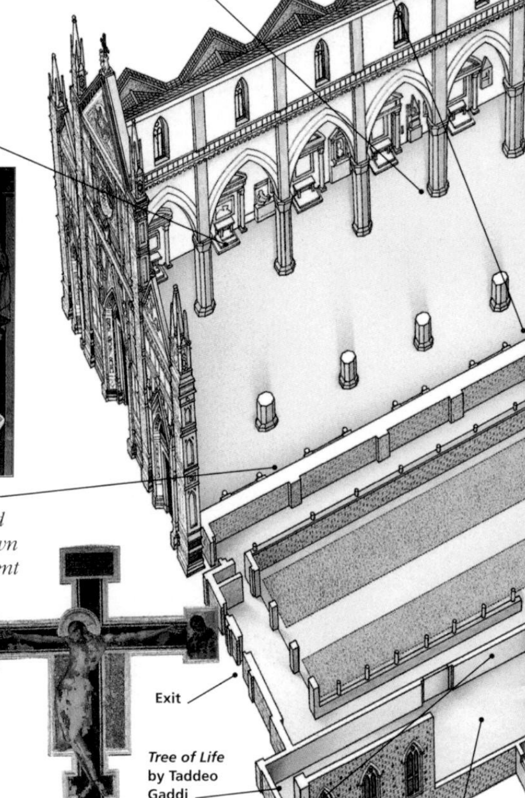

Michelangelo's Tomb
Michelangelo never completed the Pietà *he planned for his own tomb* (see p67). *This monument was designed in 1570 by Vasari. The figures are Painting, Architecture and Sculpture.*

Exit

***Tree of Life* by Taddeo Gaddi**

Refectory

★ Cimabue's Crucifixion
This ruined 13th-century masterpiece still expresses the grandeur of Cimabue's artistry.

STAR FEATURES

- ★ Cimabue's Crucifixion
- ★ Fresco by Gaddi in Baroncelli Chapel
- ★ Cappella de' Pazzi

Donatello's Crucifix (1425) is found in the Bardi di Vernio Chapel. The perfect balance in its form and its subtle play of light and shadow fill it with drama and realism. It is one of the most beautiful works of Florentine humanism.

In the Bardi and Peruzzi Chapels, Giotto's frescoes depict scenes from the lives of St Francis, St John the Baptist and St John the Evangelist.

VISITORS' CHECKLIST

Piazza di Santa Croce. **Map** 4 E1 (6 F4). ***Tel*** *055 24 46 19.* *C, 14, 23.* *9:30am–5pm daily (from 1pm Sun). Ticket office closes at 4:30pm. No visits during mass.* *8am, 9am (not Aug), 6pm Mon–Sat; 8am, 9:30am, 11am, noon, 6pm Sun and relig hols.*

The Neo-Gothic campanile was added in 1842, after the original was destroyed in 1512 by lightning.

★ Fresco by Gaddi in Baroncelli Chapel
This image of an angel appearing to sleeping shepherds (1338) was the first true night scene depicted in fresco.

Sacristy

Tomb of Leonardo Bruni
Rossellino's effigy (1447) of the great Humanist, depicted in serene old age, is a triumph of realistic portraiture.

This second cloister was designed by Brunelleschi, and offers a peaceful spot to absorb the atmosphere.

★ Cappella de' Pazzi
Brunelleschi designed this domed chapel in 1430. Delicate grey stonework frames white plaster inset with Luca della Robbia's terracotta roundels of the Apostles.

Museo Horne

Santa Croce ⓫

See pp72–3.

Museo Horne ⓬

Via de' Benci 6. **Map** 4 D1 (6 F4). ***Tel** 055 24 46 61. 9am–1pm Mon–Sat. 1 Jan, Easter Sun, Easter Mon, 25 Apr, 1 May, 15 Aug, 1 Nov, 25–26 Dec.*

The museum's small collection of paintings, sculpture and decorative arts was left to the city by Herbert Percy Horne (1844–1916), the English art historian. It is housed in a splendid example of a Renaissance *palazzino* (small town house), built in 1489 for the wealthy Alberti family.

The arrangement of rooms, with a working and storage area at ground level and grander apartments above, is typical of many Renaissance houses. The Alberti family, who grew wealthy from the city's thriving cloth trade, had wool-dyeing vats in the basement and drying racks in the courtyard.

Most of the museum's major artifacts, for instance a number of important 17th- and 18th-century drawings, are now housed in the Uffizi. However, the collection still boasts at least one major exhibit: Giotto's 13th-century *St Stephen* polyptych (an altarpiece with more than three panels). There is also a *Madonna and Child* attributed to Simone Martini (1283–1344) and *Madonna* by Bernardo Daddi (c.1312–48). The kitchen, which was built on the top floor to stop fumes passing through the entire house, now contains Horne's collection of Renaissance pots and cooking utensils.

Museo di Storia della Scienza ⓭

Piazza de' Giudici 1. **Map** 4 D1 (6 D4). ***Tel** 055 265 311. B, 23. winter: 9:30am–5pm Mon–Sat (to 1pm Tue), 10am–1pm second Sun of the month; summer: 9:30am–5pm Mon–Sat (to 1pm Tue & Sat). 1 Jan, 25 Apr, 1 May, 24 Jun, 15 Aug, 8, 25 & 26 Dec.*

This small museum is something of a shrine to the Pisa-born scientist Galileo Galilei (1564–1642). Exhibits include his telescopes and the lens he used to discover the largest moons of Jupiter.

The museum also features large-scale reconstructions of his experiments into motion, weight, velocity and acceleration. These are sometimes demonstrated by the attendants.

In memory of Galileo, in 1657 Florence founded the world's first-ever scientific institution, the Accademia del Cimento (Academy for Experimentation). Some of the academy's inventions, such as early thermometers, hygrometers and barometers

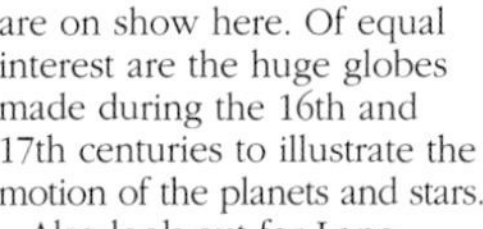

are on show here. Of equal interest are the huge globes made during the 16th and 17th centuries to illustrate the motion of the planets and stars.

Also look out for Lopo Homem's map of the world, dating to 1554, and the nautical instruments invented by Sir Robert Dudley, the Elizabethan marine engineer. He was employed by the Medici dukes to build the harbour at Livorno from 1607–21 *(see p162)*.

Galileo Galilei (1564–1642), court mathematician to the Medici

Santo Stefano al Ponte ⓮

Piazza Santo Stefano al Ponte. **Map** 3 C1 (6 D4). ***Tel** 055 22 58 43. Phone to check opening times.*

St Stephen "by the bridge", dating to 969, is so called because of its close proximity to the Ponte Vecchio.

Armillary sphere of 1564, used to map the stars and planets

MAPPING THE WORLD

The same preoccupation with space that made Florentine artists such masters of perspective also made them excellent navigators and mapmakers. Florentine cartographers based their maps on the observations and navigational records of early explorers. That is how America came to be named after the Florentine Amerigo Vespucci rather than Christopher Columbus. When Columbus returned from his transatlantic voyage, King Ferdinand of Spain hired Vespucci, an expert navigator, to check whether Columbus really had discovered a new route to the Indies. Vespucci was the first to realize that Columbus had discovered a new continent and he described his own voyage in a series of letters to Piero de' Medici. As soon as the letters were made public, Florentine cartographers rushed out revised maps of the world based on Vespucci's account. Out of loyalty to a fellow Florentine, they named the New World Amerigo, which was later corrupted to America.

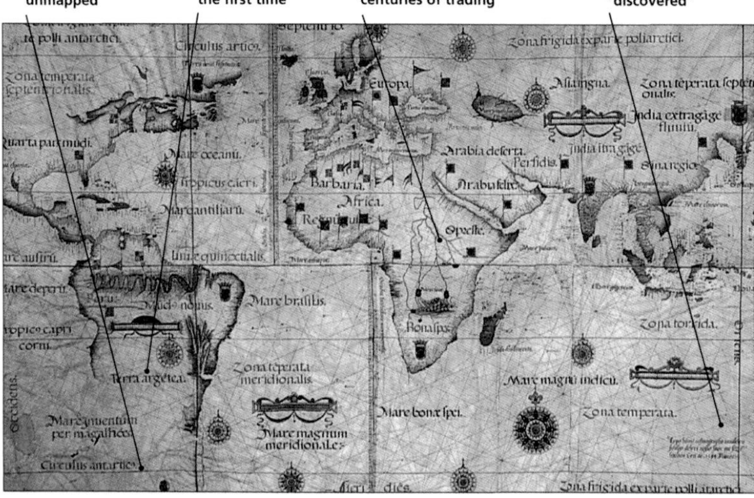

16th-century map by the Portuguese cartographer Lopo Homem, in the Museo di Storia della Scienza

The Romanesque façade, dating to 1233, is its most important architectural feature. Florentines, however, know the church better as a venue for some top-quality orchestral concerts.

Erboristeria ⓯

Spezieria–Erboristeria Palazzo Vecchio. Via Vacchereccia 9r. **Map** 3 C1 (6 D3). ***Tel*** *055 239 60 55.* *9am–7:30pm Mon–Sat, first & last Sun of month.* *1 Jan, 1 May, 25 & 26 Dec.*

This ancient herbalist's shop, known as Palazzo Vecchio, is hidden among the pavement cafés lining Via Vacchereccia, off Piazza della Signoria. It has a lovely frescoed interior. Several such shops in Florence sell a range of herbal soaps, pot pourri, cosmetics and fragrances made to ancient recipes by monks and nuns in various parts of Tuscany. Another *erboristeria* is just around the corner at Calimala 4r. Called the Erboristeria della Antica Farmacia del Cinghiale (Herbalist at the Old Boar Pharmacy), it takes its name from the famous bronze boar statue in the Mercato Nuovo opposite *(see p112).*

Piazza della Signoria ⓰

See pp76–7.

Palazzo Vecchio ⓱

See pp78–9.

The Uffizi ⓲

See pp80–83.

Arno façade of the Uffizi with the Vasari Corridor *(pp106–7)* above

Piazza della Signoria ⓰

The piazza is a unique outdoor sculpture gallery and, with the Palazzo Vecchio *(see pp78–9)*, has been at the heart of Florentine politics since the 14th century. Citizens gathered here when called to a *parlamento* (a public meeting) by the Palazzo's great bell. The statues, some copies, commemorate major events in the city's history. Many are linked to the rise and fall of the Florentine Republic *(pp52–53)*, during which the religious leader Girolamo Savonarola was burned at the stake here.

Campanile

Salone dei Cinquecento
This vast council chamber, built in 1495, is decorated with Vasari's frescoes on the history of Florence.

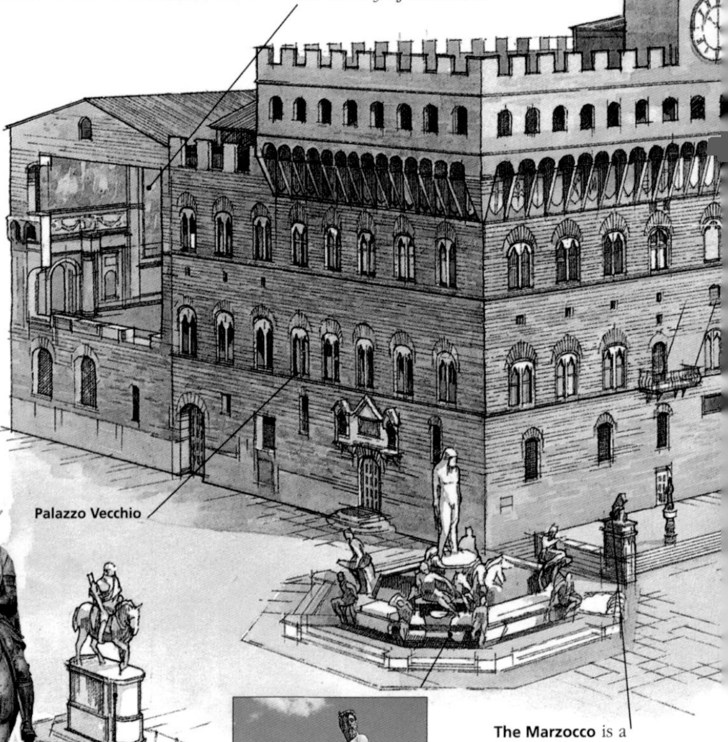

Palazzo Vecchio

The Marzocco is a copy. The original of Donatello's heraldic lion is in the Bargello.

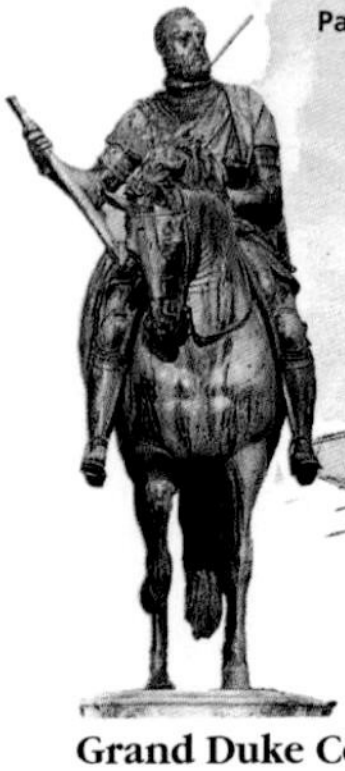

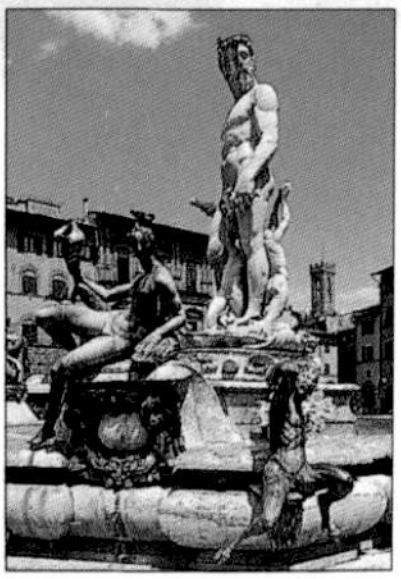

★ Neptune Fountain
Ammannati's Mannerist fountain (1575) of the Roman sea god surrounded by water nymphs commemorates Tuscan naval victories.

Grand Duke Cosimo I
Giambologna's equestrian statue (1595) celebrates the man who subjugated all Tuscany under his military rule (see pp54–5).

Pageantry
For centuries the piazza has been the city's venue for public rallies and festivities, as shown in this 18th-century engraving.

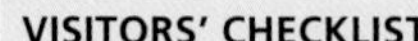

VISITORS' CHECKLIST

Map 4 D1 (6 D3).  *A, B. Pedestrian area.*

★ Perseus
Cellini's bronze statue (1554) of Perseus holding Medusa's head was meant to warn Cosimo I's enemies of their probable fate. The original of the base it rests on is in the Bargello.

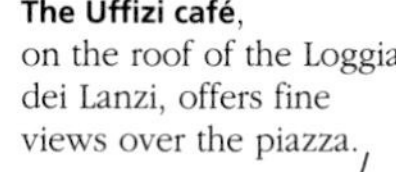

The Uffizi café, on the roof of the Loggia dei Lanzi, offers fine views over the piazza.

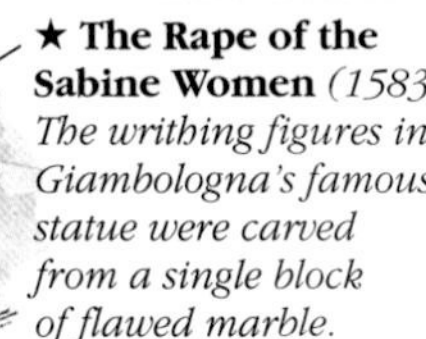

★ The Rape of the Sabine Women *(1583)*
The writhing figures in Giambologna's famous statue were carved from a single block of flawed marble.

***Hercules and Cacus* (1533) by Bandinelli**

The Loggia dei Lanzi (1382) is named after Cosimo I's bodyguards, the Lancers. Also known as Loggia di Orcagna, after the architect, it is lined with ancient Roman statues.

★ David
The original of Michelangelo's celebrated statue of David was moved from its initial location in the Piazza della Signoria into the Accademia in 1873 (see p94).

STAR FEATURES

- ★ David by Michelangelo
- ★ Neptune Fountain by Ammannati
- ★ The Rape of the Sabine Women by Giambologna
- ★ Perseus by Cellini

Palazzo Vecchio ⓱

The Palazzo Vecchio ("Old Palace") still fulfils its original role as Florence's town hall. It was completed in 1322 when a huge bell, used to call citizens to meetings or warn of fire, flood or enemy attack, was hauled to the top of the imposing belltower. The palazzo has retained its medieval appearance, but much of the interior was remodelled for Duke Cosimo I when he moved into the palace in 1540. Leonardo and Michelangelo were asked to redecorate the interior, but it was Vasari who finally undertook the work. His many frescoes (1563–5) glorify Cosimo and his creation of the Grand Duchy of Tuscany.

★ Sala dei Gigli (Room of the Lilies)
Gold fleurs-de-lis, emblems of Florence, cover the walls in between Ghirlandaio's frescoes (1485) of Roman statesmen.

PALACE GUIDE

A monumental staircase leads to the first-floor Salone dei Cinquecento, with its frescoed walls and marble statues. Above this is a suite of decorated rooms once used by the rulers of Florence. Parts of the Salone dei Cinquecinto, the Studiolo of Francesco I, the Treasury of Cosimo I and the staircase of the Duke of Athens are only accessible by tour. The tours follow the "secret routes" made for the rulers.

Heraldic Frieze
Shields on the façade symbolize episodes in Florentine history. The crossed keys represent Medici papal rule.

★ Cortile and Putto Fountain
A copy of Verrocchio's Putto Fountain was placed in the courtyard by Vasari in 1565.

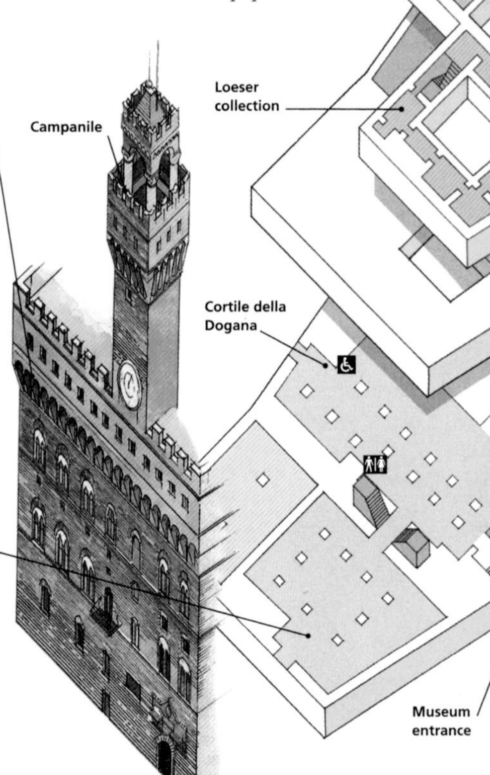

KEY TO FLOORPLAN

- Ground floor
- First floor
- Mezzanine floor
- Second floor
- Temporary exhibition space
- Non-exhibition space

For hotels and restaurants in this area see pp250–51 and pp270–71

Eleonora di Toledo's Rooms
Cosimo I's wife had a suite of rooms decorated with scenes of virtuous women. Penelope, wife of the Greek hero Odysseus, is shown waiting faithfully for her husband to return.

VISITORS' CHECKLIST

Piazza della Signoria. **Map** 4 D1 (6 D3). ***Tel*** *055 276 82 24.* *A, B.* *9am–7pm daily (to 2pm Thu). Last adm: 45 mins before closing. Some extended hours in summer.*
The Secret Routes
Mon–Fri. *1 Jan, Easter, 1 May, 15 Aug, 25 Dec.* *compulsory.*

The Map Room

The Quartiere degli Elementi contains Vasari's allegories of Earth, Fire, Air and Water.

Putto with Dolphin
Verrocchio's bronze fountain head (1470) is displayed in the Terrazzo di Giunone. The small room next door has fine views of San Miniato al Monte.

Pope Leo X's rooms

The Salone dei Cinquecento was a meeting place for the leaders of the Florentine Republic *(see pp52–3).*

Cappella di Eleonora
Egyptian soldiers in pursuit of Moses drown in the Red Sea, in the biblical frescoes (1540–45) by Bronzino in Eleonora di Toledo's chapel.

e Treasury Cosimo I

★ Victory by Michelangelo
Michelangelo's nephew presented this statue (1533–4), intended for the tomb of Pope Julius II, to Cosimo I in 1565, following the Duke's military triumph over Siena.

STAR FEATURES

★ Cortile and Putto Fountain

★ Victory by Michelangelo

★ Sala dei Gigli

The Uffizi ⓲

The Uffizi was built in 1560–80 as a suite of offices *(uffici)* for Duke Cosimo I's new administration *(see p50)*. The architect, Vasari, used iron reinforcement to create an almost continuous wall of glass on the upper storey. From 1581 Cosimo's heirs used this well-lit space to display the Medici family art treasures, creating what is now the oldest gallery in the world. A major expansion of the exhibition space is underway for 2013.

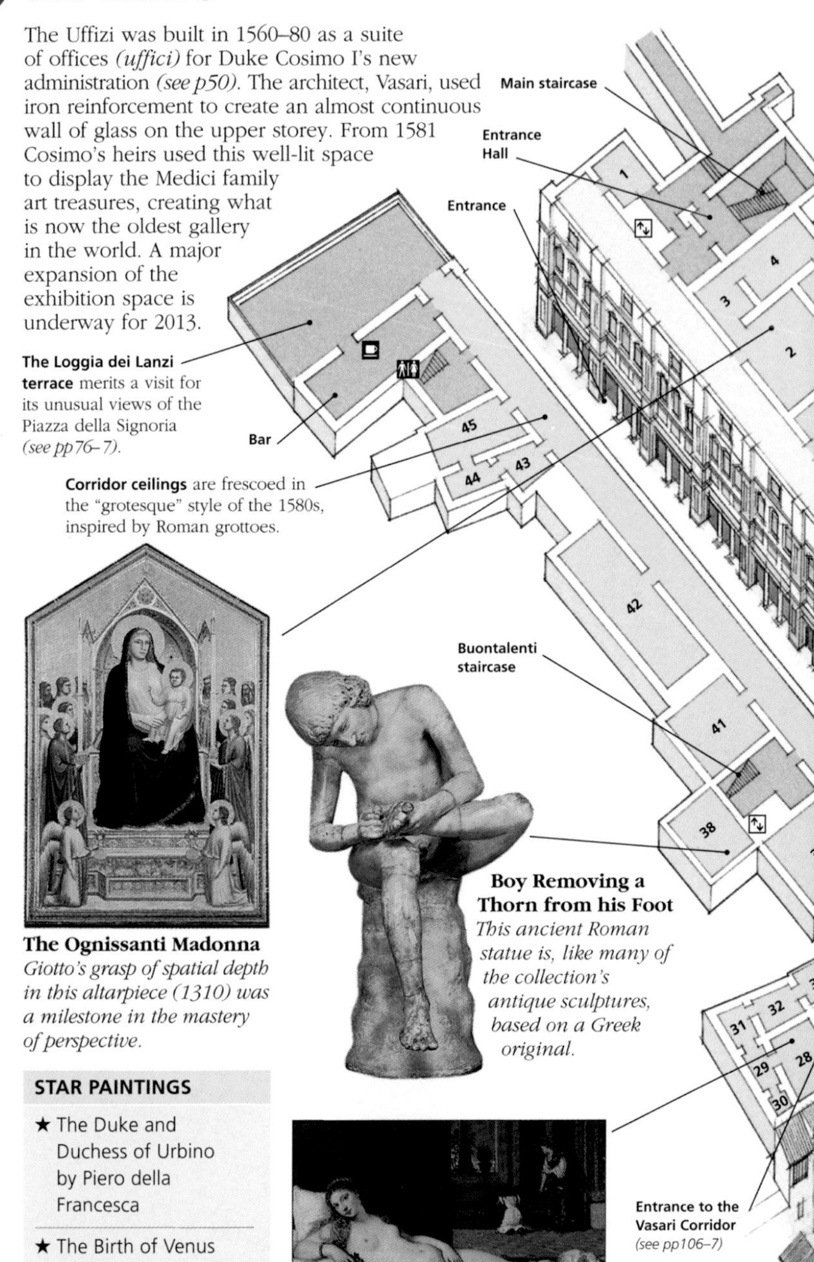

The Loggia dei Lanzi terrace merits a visit for its unusual views of the Piazza della Signoria *(see pp76–7).*

Corridor ceilings are frescoed in the "grotesque" style of the 1580s, inspired by Roman grottoes.

The Ognissanti Madonna
Giotto's grasp of spatial depth in this altarpiece (1310) was a milestone in the mastery of perspective.

Boy Removing a Thorn from his Foot
This ancient Roman statue is, like many of the collection's antique sculptures, based on a Greek original.

★ The Venus of Urbino *(1538)*
Titian's sensuous nude was condemned for portraying the goddess in such an immodest pose.

STAR PAINTINGS

- ★ The Duke and Duchess of Urbino by Piero della Francesca
- ★ The Birth of Venus by Botticelli
- ★ The Holy Family by Michelangelo
- ★ The Venus of Urbino by Titian

★ The Duke and Duchess of Urbino *(1460)*
Piero della Francesca's panels are among the first true Renaissance portraits. He even recorded the Duke's hooked nose – broken by a sword blow.

VISITORS' CHECKLIST

Loggiato degli Uffizi 6. **Map** 4 D1 (6 D4). ***Tel*** *055 238 86 51 (info); 055 29 48 83 (reservations). Line open: 8:30am–6:30pm Mon–Sat (to 12:30pm Sat).* *B, 23.* *8:15am–6:50pm Tue–Sun (occasional extended hours in summer; last adm: 45 mins before closing).* *1 Jan, 1 May, 25 Dec.* **www**.uffizi.firenze.it

The Tribune, decorated in red and gold, contains the works that the Medici valued most.

★ The Birth of Venus *(1485)*
Botticelli's captivating image shows the Roman goddess of love, born in a storm in the Aegean sea. Blown ashore by the winds, she is greeted by nymphs, ready to wrap her in a cloak.

GALLERY GUIDE

Ancient Greek and Roman sculptures are in the corridor around the inner side of the horseshoe-shaped building. The paintings are hung in a series of rooms off the main corridor, in chronological order, to show the development of Florentine art from Gothic to Renaissance and beyond. Many well-known paintings are in rooms 7–18. Five new rooms opened on the ground floor in 2004 and a major expansion of the gallery, due to be completed in 2013, is underway. Pick up a gallery guide for advice on layout changes during building works. To avoid queues, book your ticket and visiting time in advance using Firenzemusei (see p299).

Vasari's Classical Arno façade

★ The Holy Family *(1506)*
Michelangelo's painting, the first to break with the convention of showing Christ on the Virgin's lap, inspired Mannerist artists through its expressive handling of colour and posture (see p27).

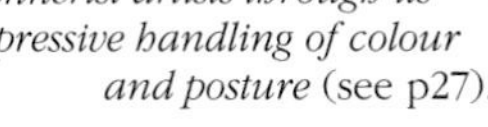

KEY

- East Corridor
- West Corridor
- Arno Corridor
- Gallery Rooms 1–45
- Non-exhibition space

Exploring the Uffizi's Collection

The Uffizi offers an unrivalled opportunity to see some of the greatest works of the Renaissance. The collection was born from the immense wealth of the Medici family *(see pp50–51)*, who commissioned work from many great Florentine masters. Francesco I housed the family collection at the Uffizi in 1581. His descendants added to it until 1737, when Anna Maria Lodovica, last of the Medici, bequeathed it to the people of Florence.

GOTHIC ART

Following the collection of antiquities in room 1, the gallery's next six rooms are devoted to Tuscan Gothic art from the 12th to 14th centuries.

Giotto (1266–1337) introduced a degree of naturalism that was new in Tuscan art. The angels and saints in his *Ognissanti Madonna* (1310), in room 2, express a range of human emotions, from awe and reverence to puzzlement. The throne in this painting, and the temple in Lorenzetti's *Presentation in the Temple* (1342) in room 3, show a concern for three-dimensional depth quite at odds with the flatness of much Gothic art.

Giotto's naturalism extends throughout the works in room 4, devoted to the 14th-century Florentine School. One of the most obvious examples is the *Pietà* (1360–65), attributed to Giottino. Look at the difference between the characters' expressions, their medieval, rather than Biblical, style of dress and the blood, still fresh on the cross.

EARLY RENAISSANCE

A better understanding of geometry and perspective allowed Renaissance artists to create an illusion of space and depth in their works. Paolo Uccello (1397–1475) was obsessed with perspective; witness his nightmarish *The Battle of San Romano* (1456) *(see p48)* in room 7.

Also in this room are two panels by Piero della Francesca (1410–92), depicting the Duke and Duchess of Urbino on one side and representations of their virtues on the other. Painted between 1465 and 1470, these are two of the first Renaissance portraits.

If these works seem coldly experimental, Fra Filippo Lippi's *Madonna and Child with Angels* (1455–66), in room 8, is a masterpiece of warmth and humanity. Like so many Renaissance artists, Lippi uses a religious subject to celebrate earthly delights, such as feminine beauty and the Tuscan landscape.

***Madonna and Child with Angels* (1455–66) by Fra Filippo Lippi**

BOTTICELLI

The Botticelli paintings in rooms 10–14 are the highlight of the Uffizi's collection. The brilliant colours and crisp draughtsmanship of, for instance, *The Birth of Venus* (about 1485) *(see p81)*, are a reminder that Renaissance artists often experimented with

***Primavera* (1480) by Botticelli**

new pigments to achieve striking colour effects. The subject of this painting, the Roman goddess Venus, is also significant. By painting Venus instead of the Christian Virgin, Botticelli expressed the fascination with Classical mythology common to many Renaissance artists.

The same is true of his other famous work, *Primavera* (about 1480). It breaks with the tradition of Christian religious painting by illustrating a pagan rite of spring. Other works to see here include the *Adoration of the Magi* (about 1475), a thinly disguised Medici family portrait *(see p51)*.

LEONARDO DA VINCI

Detail from *The Annunciation* (1472–5) by Leonardo da Vinci

Room 15 contains works attributed to the young Leonardo. Still under the influence of his teachers, he was already developing his own masterly style, as in *The Annunciation* (1472–5) and the unfinished *Adoration of the Magi* (1481).

THE TRIBUNE

The octagonal tribune, with its mother-of-pearl ceiling, was designed in 1584 by Buontalenti so that Francesco I could display all his favourite works from the Medici collection in one room.

Notable paintings include Bronzino's portrait (1545) of Eleonora di Toledo with her son, Giovanni *(see p51)*, and the same artist's portrait of Bia, Cosimo I's illegitimate daughter. It was painted just before her

Portrait of *Bia* (1542) by Bronzino

early death in 1542. *The Medici Venus*, probably dating to the 1st century BC, is a Roman copy of the Greek original by Praxiteles. A small room off the Tribune contains a copy of the Hellenistic sculpture, *The Hermaphrodite*.

NON-FLORENTINE ART

The works in rooms 19 to 23 show how rapidly the artistic ideas and techniques of the Renaissance spread beyond Florence. Umbrian artists like Perugino (1446–1523) and Northern European painters such as Dürer (1471–1528) are well represented.

THE ARNO CORRIDOR

The corridor overlooking the Arno, which links the east and west wings of the Uffizi, offers fine views of the hills to the south of Florence.

The ancient Roman statues displayed here were mainly collected by the Medici during the 15th century. Their anatomical precision and faithful portraiture were much admired and copied by Renaissance artists, who saw themselves as giving rebirth to Classical perfection in art.

The Roman statues were equally popular during the 17th and 18th centuries with visitors on their way to Rome on the Grand Tour *(see p55)*. The Renaissance works, which attract visitors today, were largely ignored until John Ruskin, the art historian, wrote about them in the 1840s.

HIGH RENAISSANCE AND MANNERISM

Michelangelo's *The Holy Family* (1506–8), in room 25, is striking for its vibrant colours and the unusually twisted pose of the Virgin *(see p81)*. This painting proved to be enormously influential with the next generation of Tuscan artists, notably Bronzino (1503–72), Pontormo (1494–1556) and Parmigianino (1503–40). The latter's *Madonna of the Long Neck* (about 1534) in room 29, with its contorted anatomy and bright, unnatural colours, is a remarkable example of what came to be known as the Mannerist style.

Two other masterpieces of the High Renaissance are located nearby. Raphael's tender *Madonna of the Goldfinch* (1506), in room 26, still shows signs of earthquake damage dating to 1547. Titian's *The Venus of Urbino* (1538), said to be one of the most beautiful nudes ever painted, is in room 28.

***Madonna of the Goldfinch* (1506) by Raphael**

LATER PAINTINGS

Works by Rubens (1577–1640) and Van Dyck (1599–1641) are in rooms 41 and 42 (sometimes closed), while Rembrandt (1606–69) can be found in room 44. New rooms on the ground floor hold paintings by Caravaggio (1573–1610) and his school, as well as by Guido Reni (1577–1642).

CITY CENTRE NORTH

This area of Florence is stamped with the character of Cosimo il Vecchio. The man who founded the great Medici dynasty maintained his position of power by astute management of the city's financial affairs, as opposed to resorting to threats and violence. Cosimo was a highly educated and sophisticated man with a passion for building, and he wanted the churches, palazzi and libraries that he built to last a thousand years, like the buildings of ancient Rome. To this end, he commissioned some of the greatest architects and artists of the time to build the churches of San Lorenzo and San Marco as well as the Medici's first home, the Palazzo Medici Riccardi. He is regarded as one of the great innovators of the Renaissance in Florence. Even after the Medici family had moved across the river Arno to the Palazzo Pitti in 1550, the Grand Dukes made their final journey back to the north of the city to be buried in the extravagant Cappelle Medicee in San Lorenzo. For the tombs in the New Sacristy, Michelangelo contributed his magnificent allegorical sculptures, *Day and Night*, and *Dawn and Dusk*.

Roundel on Spedale degli Innocenti

SIGHTS AT A GLANCE

Churches and Synagogues
San Lorenzo pp90–91 ❷
San Marco pp96–7 ❼
Santa Maria Maddalena dei Pazzi ⓰
Santissima Annunziata ⓮
Tempio Israelitico ⓱

Historic Buildings
Palazzo Medici Riccardi ❺
Palazzo Pucci ❹
Spedale degli Innocenti ⓬

Museums and Galleries
Cenacolo di Sant'Apollonia ❻
Conservatorio ❿
Galleria dell'Accademia ❾
Museo Archeologico ⓯
Opificio delle Pietre Dure ⓫

Gardens
Giardino dei Semplici ❽

Streets, Piazzas and Markets
Mercato Centrale ❶
Piazza della Santissima Annunziata ⓭
Piazza di San Lorenzo ❸

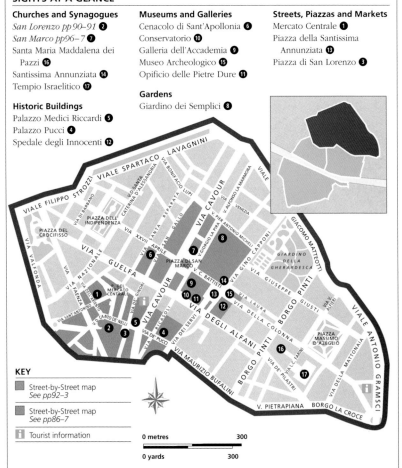

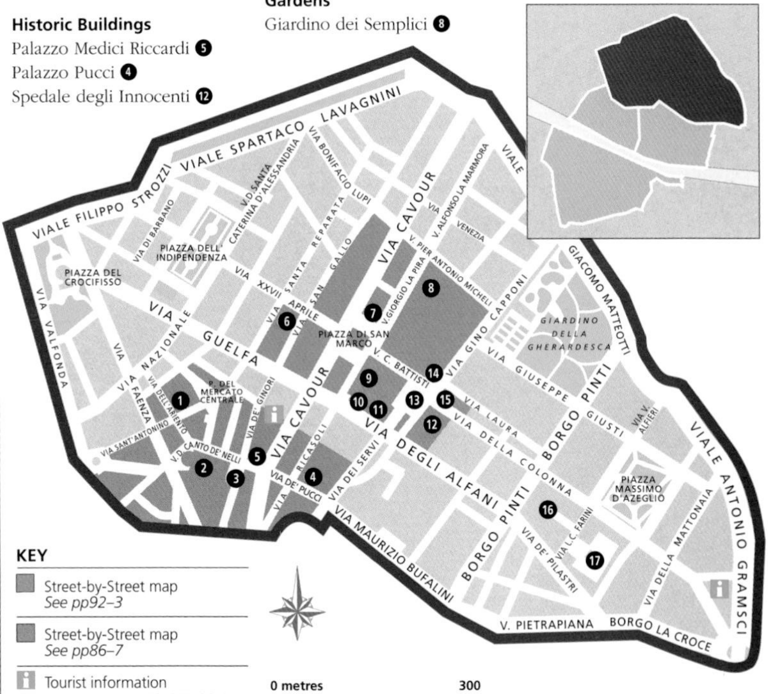

KEY

Street-by-Street map *See pp92–3*

Street-by-Street map *See pp86–7*

Tourist information

0 metres 300

0 yards 300

◁ ***Virgin and Child*** **by Fra Angelico (c.1440) in San Marco**

Street-by-Street: Around San Lorenzo

Bust, Palazzo Medici Riccardi

This area is stamped with the character of Cosimo il Vecchio, founder of the Medici dynasty, who commissioned San Lorenzo and the Palazzo Medici Riccardi. Around San Lorenzo, a huge general market fills the streets, its colourful awnings almost obscuring the various monuments. The market is a reminder that Florence has always been a city of merchants. Many of the products on sale – leather goods and silk, wool and cashmere garments – are very good value especially if, like the Florentines, you are prepared to bargain.

Cheap cafés and cooked meat stalls abound in the vicinity of the market. They sell traditional Italian take-away foods, such as tripe and roast suckling pig, chicken and rabbit.

Mercato Centrale
Built in 1874, the central market is packed with fish, meat and cheese stalls downstairs, while fruit and vegetables are sold upstairs beneath the glass and cast-iron roof ❶

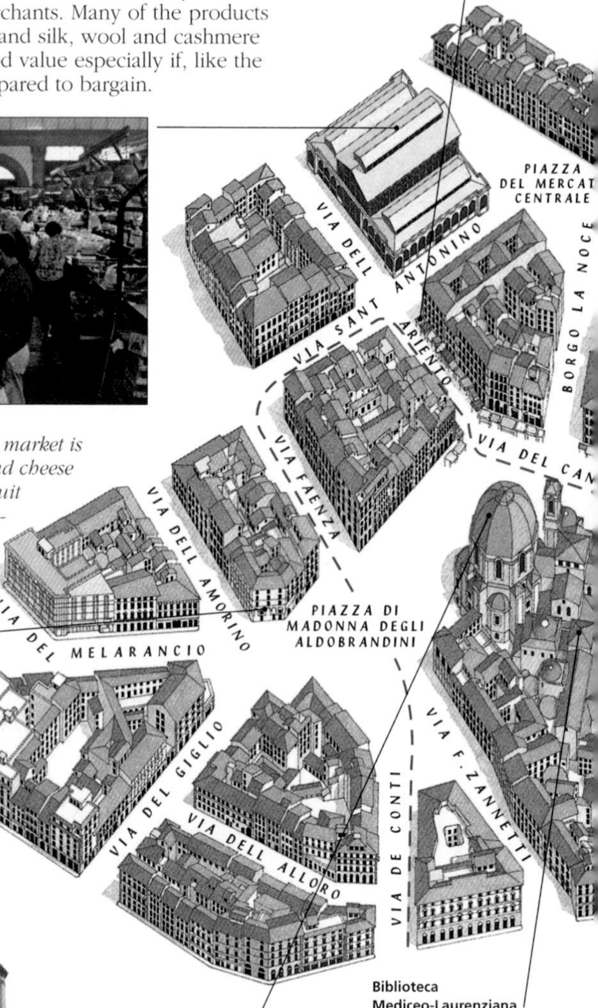

Palazzo Riccardi-Manelli, begun in 1557, stands on the site of the house where Giotto was born in 1266.

Biblioteca Mediceo-Laurenziana

The Cappelle Medicee are situated in San Lorenzo, but are reached from a separate entrance in Piazza di Madonna degli Aldobrandini. Michelangelo designed the New Sacristy and two Medici tombs. Some of his pencil sketches survive on the walls inside.

STAR SIGHTS

★ San Lorenzo

★ Palazzo Medici Riccardi

For hotels and restaurants in this area see pp251–52 and p271

The Biblioteca Riccardiana, founded in the 16th century, was opened to the public in 1715. It comprises a series of frescoed reading rooms which house a collection of precious manuscripts, including Dante's *Divine Comedy*.

CITY CENTRE NORTH
CITY CENTRE WEST
CITY CENTRE EAST
Arno

LOCATOR MAP

See Florence Street Finder maps 5, 6

Via de' Ginori is lined with fine 16th-century palazzi.

San Giovannino degli Scolopi church was begun by Ammannati in 1579.

★ Palazzo Medici Riccardi
The palazzo, built between 1444–64, served as the Medici family home and the headquarters of their banking empire ❺

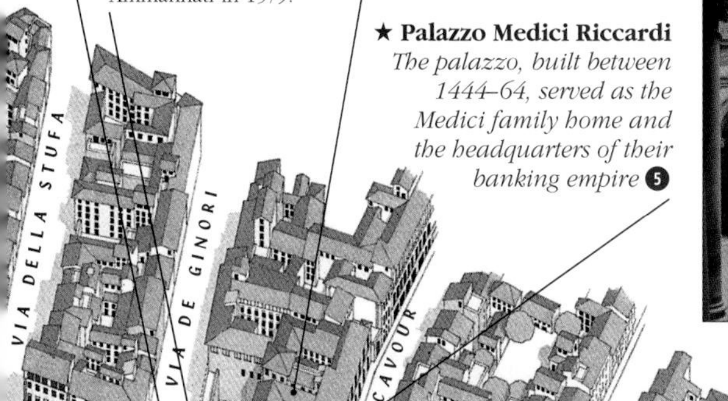

Palazzo Pucci
This is the ancestral home of the late designer Emilio Pucci ❹

VIA DELLA STUFA
VIA DE GINORI
VIA CAVOUR
DE NELLI
VIA DE GORI
VIA DE PUCCI
VIA RICASOLI
PIAZZA DI SAN LORENZO
BORGO SAN LORENZO
VIA DE MARTELLI
VIA DE BIFFI

★ San Lorenzo
The unfinished façade belies the noble interior, which was designed for the Medici by Brunelleschi in 1425–46 ❷

Giovanni delle Bande Nere, Grand Duke Cosimo I's father *(see p51)*, is depicted in battle dress in this statue by Baccio Bandinelli (1540).

KEY

– – – Suggested route

0 metres 100

0 yards 100

Mercato Centrale

Mercato Centrale ❶

Via dell'Ariento 10–14. **Map** 1 C4 (5 C1). ◯ *7am–2pm Mon–Sat.* **Underground car park** ◯ *24 hours a day, seven days a week.*

Right in the heart of the San Lorenzo street market is Florence's busiest food market, the bustling Mercato Centrale. It is housed in a vast two-storey building made of cast-iron and glass, which was built in 1874 by Giuseppe Mengoni. During restoration in 1980, a mezzanine floor was constructed and a car park was added in the basement. For reduced rate parking, have a market vendor stamp your receipt. On the ground floor there are dozens of stalls selling meat, fish, cheese and typical Tuscan takeaway foods, such as *porchetta* (roast suckling pig). Fruit, vegetables and flowers are sold on the top floor.

San Lorenzo ❷

See pp90–91.

Piazza di San Lorenzo ❸

Map 1 C5 (6 D1). *9am–7:30pm Tue–Sat.*

At the western end of the piazza, near the entrance to San Lorenzo church, there is a statue of Giovanni delle Bande Nere, mercenary and father of Cosimo I, first Medici Grand Duke *(see p49)*. It was carved by Baccio Bandinelli in 1540, and is almost hidden from view among the market stalls stretching all the way up the side of San Lorenzo church and into the streets leading off the piazza. The stalls closest to the church cater mostly for tourists, selling leather goods, T-shirts and souvenirs. In the streets around the market, everything from lentils to bargain-priced clothes is sold. The neighbouring shops have become an integral part of the market, selling cheeses, hams, home-baked bread, pastries, fabrics and table linen.

San Lorenzo street market

Statue of Giovanni delle Bande Nere in Piazza di San Lorenzo

Palazzo Pucci ❹

Via de' Pucci 6. **Map** 2 D5 (6 E1). ***Tel*** *055 28 30 61.* ● *to the public.*

The Palazzo Pucci is the ancestral home of clothes designer Emilio Pucci, Marchese di Barsento. The Pucci family, traditionally friends and allies of the Medici, feature prominently in Florence's history, and this large palace was built in the 16th century to designs by Bartolomeo Ammannati.

Emilio Pucci's boutique can be found at Via de' Tornabuoni 22r. In the past, *haute couture* clients were fitted out in palatial rooms above the showroom. Pucci is most famous for smart but casual clothes, and designed the stylish blue uniforms worn by Florentine traffic police, the *vigili urbani (see p301).*

Palazzo Medici Riccardi ❺

Via Cavour 1. **Map** 2 D5 (6 D1). ***Tel*** *055 276 03 40.* **Cappella dei Magi** *9am–7pm Thu–Tue.* *1 May, 25 Dec.* *Booking is advisable in busy periods.*

Home of the Medici for 100 years from 1444, the palazzo was later acquired by the Riccardi family and now houses government offices. It was built to an austere design by Michelozzo for Cosimo il Vecchio, who rejected Brunelleschi's original plans as being too flamboyant – Cosimo did not want to flaunt his wealth. The windows on either side of the entrance were added in 1517 and designed by Michelangelo.

Through the main door, the courtyard walls are covered in ancient Roman masonry fragments. The roundels above the arcade show scenes copied from antique intaglios now on display in the Museo degli Argenti *(see p123)*. Donatello's statue of David (now in the Bargello, *see pp68–9*) used to be here, but today the place of honour is given to Bandinelli's marble statue of *Orpheus*.

Only a few rooms in the palazzo are open to the public. In the Cappella dei Magi is a colourful fresco of *The Procession of the Magi* painted in 1459–60 by Benozzo Gozzoli. It depicts several members of the Medici dynasty *(see pp48–9)*. The Sala di Luca Giordano is named after the Neapolitan artist who painted its walls with *The Apotheosis of the Medici in* High Baroque style in 1683. A selection of marble sculptures from the Medici Riccardi collection is on display in a recently renovated wing. The palazzo often plays host to temporary art exhibitions, for which there is an additional admission charge.

Statuary in the garden of the Palazzo Medici Riccardi

The Last Supper **(1445–50) by Andrea del Castagno in Sant'Apollonia**

Cenacolo di Sant'Apollonia ❻

Via XXVII Aprile 1. **Map** 2 D4. ***Tel*** *055 238 86 07.* *8:15am–1:50pm daily.* *1st, 3rd & 5th Sun, 2nd & 4th Mon of the month.*

The cloister and refectory of what was originally a convent for the Camaldolite order of nuns are now used by the students of Florence University. On the main wall of the refectory is a fresco of *The Last Supper* painted in 1445–50, one of the few surviving works by Andrea del Castagno, pupil of Masaccio and among the first Renaissance artists to begin to experiment with perspective. Here Judas sits isolated in the foreground of the picture, disrupting its balance and breaking up the long white strip of tablecloth. He is shown in profile with the face of a satyr: a mythological creature, half-man, half-goat, often used in Renaissance paintings to represent evil.

San Marco ❼

See pp96–7.

Giardino dei Semplici ❽

Via Micheli 3. **Map** 2 E4. ***Tel*** *055 275 74 02.* *9am–1pm Sun–Fri.* *1 Jan, 6 Jan, 25 Apr, Easter Sun & Mon, 1 May, 13–17 Aug, 1 Nov, 24–26 Dec, 31 Dec.*

Giardino dei Semplici

The word "Semplici" refers to the raw ingredients, "simples", used by medieval apothecaries in preparing medicine – thus the Giardino dei Semplici was where medicinal herbs were grown and studied. It was set up in 1545 by Niccolò Tribolo for Cosimo I in the area between Via Micheli, Via Giorgio la Pira and Via Gino Capponi. The garden retains its original layout but now the collection includes tropical plants as well as flora native to Tuscany.

Around the garden are small specialist museums: a geology collection includes fossils; the mineralogy section shows the geological structure of Elba, whose ores attracted bronze traders in the 10th century BC. The botanical museum has specimens of rare plants.

San Lorenzo ❷

San Lorenzo was the parish church of the Medici family, and they lavished their wealth on its adornment. Brunelleschi rebuilt the church in Renaissance Classical style in 1419, although the façade was never completed. In 1520 Michelangelo began work on the Medici tombs and designed the Biblioteca Mediceo-Laurenziana in 1524 to house the manuscripts collected by the Medici. In both the New Sacristy and the Cappella dei Principi, extensive scaffolding has been erected (for an indefinite period) to protect visitors from falling marble.

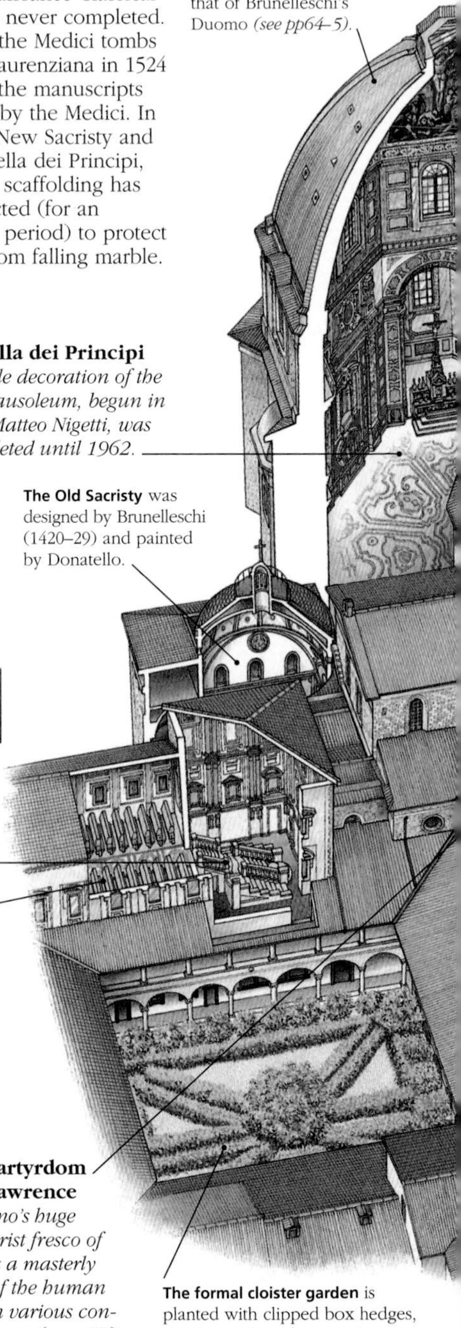

The huge dome by Buontalenti echoes that of Brunelleschi's Duomo *(see pp64–5).*

★ Cappella dei Principi
The marble decoration of the Medici mausoleum, begun in 1604 by Matteo Nigetti, was not completed until 1962.

The Old Sacristy was designed by Brunelleschi (1420–29) and painted by Donatello.

★ Michelangelo's Staircase
The Mannerist pietra serena *sandstone staircase to the Biblioteca is one of Michelangelo's most innovative designs. It was built by Ammannati in 1559.*

Michelangelo designed the desks and ceiling of the Biblioteca, which is entered from Manetti's graceful, tiered cloister, built in 1462.

The Martyrdom of St Lawrence
Bronzino's huge Mannerist fresco of 1569 is a masterly study of the human form in various contorted poses (see p27).

The formal cloister garden is planted with clipped box hedges, pomegranate and orange trees.

★ Medici Tombs
Michelangelo's monumental funerary figures, symbolizing Night, Day, Dawn and Dusk, are among his greatest works.

VISITORS' CHECKLIST

Piazza di San Lorenzo (Basilica and Biblioteca), Piazza di Madonna degli Aldobrandini (Cappelle Medicee). **Map** 1 C5 (6 D1). *many routes.* **Basilica *Tel*** *055 21 66 34.* *10am–5:30pm Mon–Sat (Mar–Oct also 1:30–5:30pm Sun).* *8am, 9:30am, 6pm Mon–Sat, 9:30am, 11am, 6pm Sun & religious hols.* **Biblioteca *Tel*** *055 21 07 60.* *Apr–Jun & during exhibitions (call for opening times).* *public hols.* **Cappelle Medicee *Tel*** *055 238 86 02 (055 29 48 83 to book).* *8:15am–2pm daily; (to 1:50pm Sun & holidays).* *1st, 3rd & 5th Mon, 2nd & 4th Sun of the month.*

Six Grand Dukes are buried in the Cappella dei Principi.

The campanile was built in 1740.

Donatello's Pulpits
Donatello was 74 when he began work on the bronze pulpits in the nave in 1460; they depict Christ's Passion and Resurrection.

A simple stone slab marks the unostentatious grave of Cosimo il Vecchio (1389–1464), founder of the Medici dynasty.

St Joseph and Christ in the Workshop
Pietro Annigoni (1910–88) is one of the few modern artists whose work is seen in Florence.

Michelangelo submitted several designs for the façade of San Lorenzo, but it remains unfinished.

Entrance to church

STAR FEATURES

- ★ Michelangelo's Staircase
- ★ Cappella dei Principi
- ★ Medici Tombs by Michelangelo

Street-by-Street: Around San Marco

The buildings in this part of Florence once stood on the fringes of the city, serving as stables and barracks. The Medici menagerie, including lions, elephants and giraffes, was housed here. Today it is the student quarter, and in term-time Piazza di San Marco is filled with young people waiting for lectures at the university or at the Accademia di Belle Arti. This is the world's oldest art school, set up in 1563, with Michelangelo as a founder *(see p94)*.

The Palazzo Pandolfini was designed by Raphael in 1516.

Michelangelo taught himself to draw from the statues in the Medici gardens.

★ San Marco
This Dominican convent is now a museum housing Savonarola's cell and the spiritual paintings of Fra Angelico (1395–1455) ❼

Piazza di San Marco is a lively meeting-place for students.

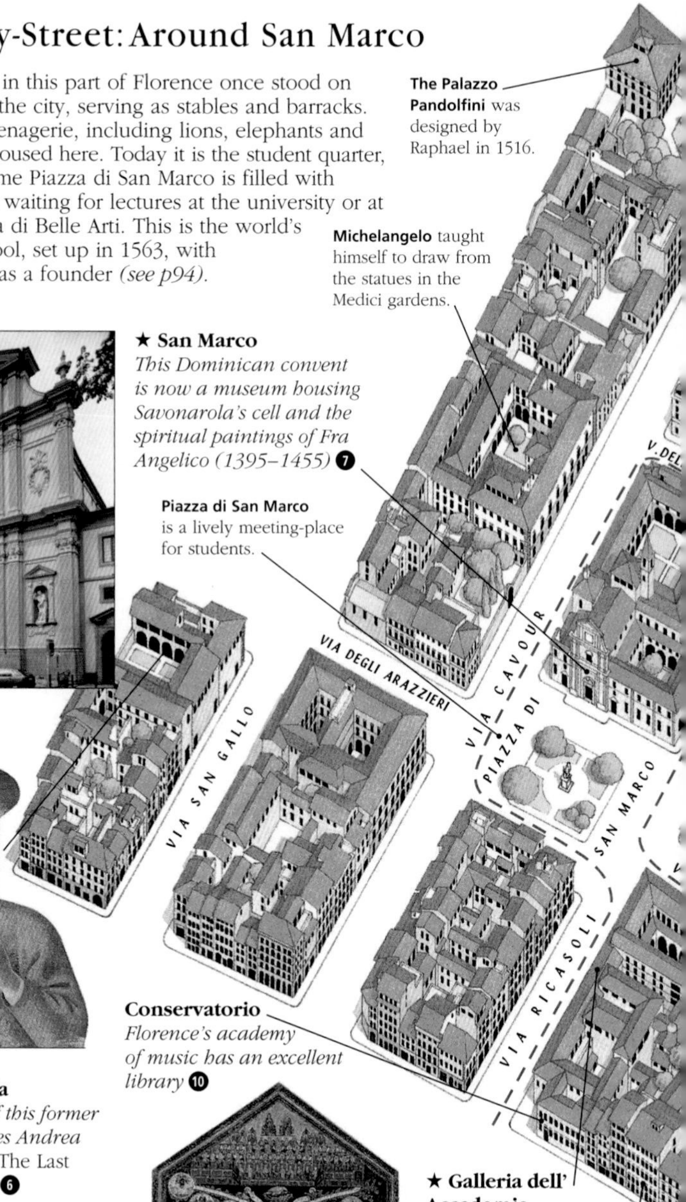

Cenacolo di Sant'Apollonia
The refectory of this former convent features Andrea del Castagno's The Last Supper *(1450)* ❻

Conservatorio
Florence's academy of music has an excellent library ❿

★ Galleria dell' Accademia
This gallery, famous for Michelangelo's David, *also contains Bonaguida's* Tree of the Cross *(1330)* ❾

Opificio delle Pietre Dure
Precious mosaics are restored here ⓫

STAR SIGHTS

- ★ Galleria dell'Accademia
- ★ San Marco
- ★ Spedale degli Innocenti

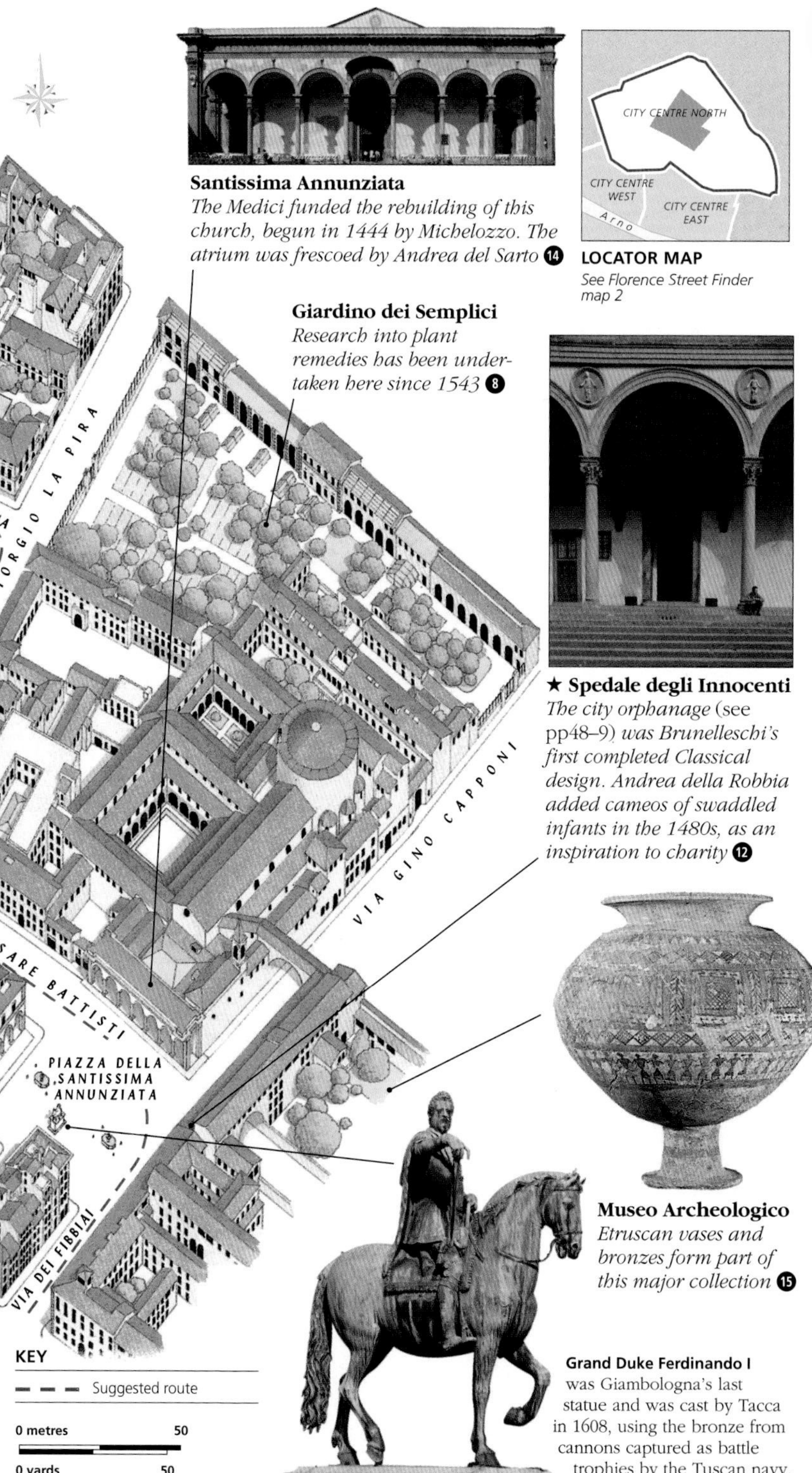

Santissima Annunziata
The Medici funded the rebuilding of this church, begun in 1444 by Michelozzo. The atrium was frescoed by Andrea del Sarto ⓮

LOCATOR MAP
See Florence Street Finder map 2

Giardino dei Semplici
Research into plant remedies has been undertaken here since 1543 ❽

★ Spedale degli Innocenti
The city orphanage (see pp48–9) was Brunelleschi's first completed Classical design. Andrea della Robbia added cameos of swaddled infants in the 1480s, as an inspiration to charity ⓬

Museo Archeologico
Etruscan vases and bronzes form part of this major collection ⓯

Grand Duke Ferdinando I was Giambologna's last statue and was cast by Tacca in 1608, using the bronze from cannons captured as battle trophies by the Tuscan navy.

KEY

— — — Suggested route

0 metres 50

0 yards 50

The central section of the 15th-century *Cassone Adimari* by Scheggia

Galleria dell'Accademia ❾

Via Ricasoli 60. **Map** 2 D4 (6 E1). ***Tel*** *055 238 86 09 (information); 055 29 48 83 (reservations). 8:15am–6:50pm Tue–Sun (occasional extended hours in summer). 1 Jan, 1 May, 25 Dec.*

The Academy of Fine Arts in Florence was founded in 1563 and was the first school in Europe set up to teach the techniques of drawing, painting and sculpture. The art collection displayed in the gallery was formed in 1784 with the aim of providing the students of the academy with material to study and copy.

Since 1873, many of Michelangelo's most important works have been in the Accademia. Perhaps the most famous of all dominates the collection: Michelangelo's *David* (1504). This colossal Classical statue (5.2 m/17 ft) depicts the biblical hero who killed the giant Goliath. It was commissioned by the city of Florence and positioned in front of the Palazzo Vecchio. This established Michelangelo, then aged 29, as the foremost sculptor of his time. In 1873 it was moved to the Accademia, to protect it from the weather and pollution. One copy of *David* is now to be found in its original position in Piazza della Signoria *(see pp76–7)* and a second stands in the middle of Piazzale Michelangelo *(see p131)*.

***Madonna del Mare* (c.1470) by Sandro Botticelli**

Michelangelo's other masterpieces include a statue of St Matthew finished in 1508, and the *Quattro Prigionieri* (the four prisoners) which were sculpted between 1521 and 1523 and intended to adorn the tomb of Pope Julius II. Presented to the Medici in 1564 by Michelangelo's cousin, the muscular figures struggling to free themselves from the stone are among the most dramatic of his works. The statues were moved to the Grotta Grande in the Boboli Gardens in 1585, where casts of the originals can now be seen *(see pp124–5)*.

***David* by Michelangelo**

The gallery contains an important collection of paintings by 15th- and 16th-century local artists: contemporaries of Michelangelo such as Fra Bartolomeo, Filippino Lippi, Bronzino and Ridolfo del Ghirlandaio. There are many major works including the *Madonna del Mare* (Madonna of the Sea), attributed to Botticelli (1445–1510), and *Venus and Cupid* by Jacopo Pontormo (1494–1556), based upon a preparatory drawing by Michelangelo. Also on display is an elaborately painted wooden chest, the *Cassone Adimari*, by Scheggia, Masaccio's step-brother. Dating from around 1440, it was originally used as part of a bride's trousseau, and is covered with details of Florentine daily life, clothing and architecture. The bridal party are pictured standing in front of the Baptistry.

Pacino di Bonaguida's *Tree of Life* (1310) is a prominent painting among the collections of Byzantine and late 13th- and 14th-century religious art, much of which is stylized and heavily embossed with gold.

The Salone della Toscana (Tuscany Room) is full of 19th-century sculpture and paintings by members of the Accademia, and a series of original plaster models by the sculptor Lorenzo Bartolini. Born in 1777, he became professor at the Accademia in 1839, a post he held until his death in 1850. His work includes busts of major figures such as the poet Lord Byron and the composer Franz Liszt.

Detail from 14th-century *Madonna and Saints* in the Accademia

Conservatorio Musicale Luigi Cherubini ❿

Piazza delle Belle Arti 2. **Map** 2 D4 (6 E1). ***Tel*** *055 29 21 80.*
Library ● *to the public.*

Some of Italy's finest musicians trained at this musical academy, named after the Florentine composer Luigi Cherubini (1760–1842). The conservatory owns a range of ancient musical instruments, now on display in the Palazzo Vecchio *(see pp78–9)*. The collection was acquired by Ferdinando, the last of the Medici Grand Dukes, and includes violins, violas and cellos made by Stradivari, Amati and Ruggeri. There is also a harpsichord by Bartolomeo Cristofori, who invented the piano in the early 18th century. He was responsible for many of the most important acquisitions. The conservatory has one of the best music libraries in Italy, holding many original manuscripts by composers like Monteverdi and Rossini.

***Pietre dure* table (1849) by Zocchi**

Opificio delle Pietre Dure ⓫

Via degli Alfani 78. **Map** 2 D4 (6 F1). ***Tel*** *055 24 98 83.* *8:15am–2pm Mon–Sat (to 7pm Thu).*
● *public hols.*

Situated in the former monastery of San Niccolò, the *opificio* (factory) is a national institute specializing in teaching the Florentine craft of producing inlaid pictures using marble and semi-precious stones. This tradition has flourished since the end of the 16th century, when it was funded through the patronage of the Medici Grand Dukes, who decorated their mausoleum with *pietre dure*.

There is a museum in the same building displaying 19th-century workbenches, tools, vases and portraits showing *pietre dure* work. Several table tops decorated with *pietre dure* are on display: one inlaid with a harp and garlands by Zocchi, made in 1849, another with flowers and birds, designed by Niccolò Betti in 1855. A stockpile of exquisite marbles and other semi-precious stones dates back to Medici times.

Spedale degli Innocenti ⓬

Piazza della Santissima Annunziata 12. **Map** 2 D4 (6 F1). ***Tel*** *055 249 17 08.* *8:30am–7pm Mon–Sat, 8:30am–2pm Sun; last adm 30 mins before closing.* ● *1 Jan, Easter, 25 Dec.*

This "hospital" is named after Herod's biblical Massacre of the Innocents following the birth of Jesus. It opened in 1444 as the first orphanage in Europe, and part of the building is still used for this purpose. UNICEF, the United Nations Children's Fund, also has offices here. Brunelleschi's arcaded loggia *(see pp48–9)* is decorated with glazed terracotta roundels, added by Andrea della Robbia around 1487, showing babies wrapped in swaddling bands. At the left-hand end of the portico is the *rota*, a rotating stone cylinder on which mothers could place their unwanted children anonymously and ring the orphanage bell. The stone was then turned around and the child was taken in.

Within the building there are two elegant cloisters built to Brunelleschi's designs. The larger Chiostro degli Uomini (Men's Cloister), built between 1422 and 1445, is decorated with *sgraffito* designs of cherubs and roosters scratched into the wet plaster. The smaller Women's Cloister (1438) leads to a gallery which has several paintings donated by children from the orphanage who became successful in later life. Among these is the *Adoration of the Magi* (1488) painted by Domenico del Ghirlandaio, showing the massacre in the background.

Andrea della Robbia's roundels (c.1487) on the Spedale degli Innocenti

San Marco ❼

Dominican friar in grey habit

The convent of San Marco was founded in the 13th century and enlarged in 1437 when Dominican monks from nearby Fiesole moved here at the invitation of Cosimo il Vecchio. He paid a considerable sum to have the convent rebuilt by his favourite architect, Michelozzo, whose simple cloisters and cells are the setting for a remarkable series of devotional frescoes (c.1438–45) by Fra Angelico.

Cells 38 and 39 were reserved for Cosimo il Vecchio when he retreated to the convent to find spiritual sustenance and peace.

The Mocking of Christ
Fra Angelico's beautiful allegorical fresco (c.1440) shows Jesus blindfolded and being struck by a Roman guard.

Cells 12 to 15 contain relics of the religious fanatic Savonarola, made prior of San Marco in 1491 *(see pp52–3).*

An ancient cedar stands in Michelozzo's Sant'Antonino cloister.

Entrance to the church (Chiesa di San Marco)

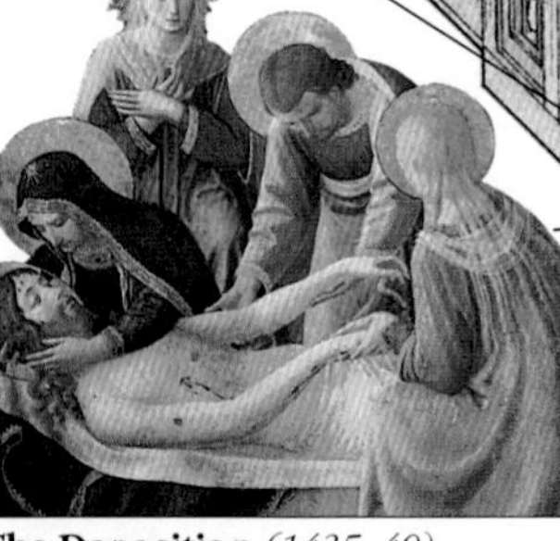

Entrance to Museo di San Marco

The Deposition *(1435–40)*
This poignant scene of the dead Christ, and other works by Fra Angelico and his School, are displayed in the former Pilgrims' Hospice.

KEY TO FLOORPLAN

- Ground floor
- First floor
- Non-exhibition space

Sant'Antonino cloister

The dormitory cells contain scenes from *The Life of Christ*, intended to inspire prayer and contemplation.

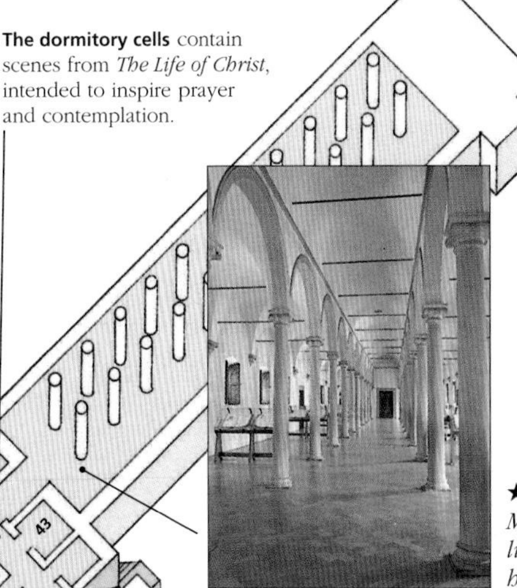

★ Library
Michelozzo designed Europe's first public library, in a light and airy colonnaded hall, for Cosimo il Vecchio in 1441.

★ The Annunciation *(c.1440)*
Fra Angelico shows his mastery of perspective by placing Gabriel and the Virgin in an elaborate loggia, inspired by Michelozzo.

The Entombment
Fra Angelico's tender fresco (c.1442) in Cell 2 shows Mary Magdalene and St. John mourning Christ.

Staircase to first floor

★ The Crucifixion *(1441–42)*
Fra Angelico was moved to tears as he painted this image of the Crucifixion of Christ in the Chapter House.

VISITORS' CHECKLIST

Piazza di San Marco. **Map** 2 D4. *many routes.* **Church** ***Tel*** *055 28 76 28. 7am–noon, 4–8pm. 7:30am, 6:30pm Mon–Sat; 10:30am, 11:30am, 12:30pm, 6:30pm Sun & relig hols.* **Museum** ***Tel*** *055 238 86 08 (reservations: 055 29 48 83). 8:15am–1:50pm daily (to 5pm Sat, to 7pm Sun; last adm: 30 mins before closing). 2nd & 4th Mon & 1st, 3rd & 5th Sun of month; 1 Jan, 1 May, 25 Dec.*

STAR FEATURES

★ The Annunciation by Fra Angelico

★ The Crucifixion by Fra Angelico

★ Library by Michelozzo

Mannerist fountain by Pietro Tacca in Piazza della Santissima Annunziata

Piazza della Santissima Annunziata ⓭

Map 2 D4.

The delicate nine-bay arcade on the eastern side of this elegant square was designed by Brunelleschi in 1419 and forms the façade to the Spedale degli Innocenti *(see p48)*. Brunelleschi's round arches gave rise to the Classical style widely copied by Renaissance architects. In the centre of the square is an equestrian statue of Duke Ferdinando I, started by Giambologna towards the end of his career. It was finished in 1608 by his assistant, Pietro Tacca, who also designed the two stylized Mannerist bronze fountains in the square.

A fair is held annually in the piazza on the feast of the Annunciation, 25 March, when homemade sweet biscuits called *brigidini* are sold from the stalls.

Santissima Annunziata ⓮

Piazza della Santissima Annunziata. **Map** 2 E4. ***Tel*** *055 26 61 81.* *7:30am–12:30pm, 4–6:30pm daily.*

The Church of the Holy Annunciation was founded by the Servite order in 1250 and later rebuilt by Michelozzo between 1444 and 1481. There is a series of early 16th-century frescoes in the atrium by Mannerist artists Rosso Fiorentino, Andrea del Sarto and Jacopo Pontormo, but many of these frescoes have suffered from damp and are fading. The most celebrated are *The Journey of the Magi* (1511) and *The Birth of the Virgin* (1514) by del Sarto.

The interior is dark and heavily decorated, with a frescoed ceiling completed by Pietro Giambelli in 1669.

The church also boasts one of the most revered shrines in Florence, a painting of the Virgin Mary begun in 1252 by a monk. Devout Florentines believe it was finished by an angel, and many newly wed couples traditionally come here after their wedding ceremony to present a bouquet of flowers to the Virgin and pray for a long and fruitful marriage. Nine chapels radiate from the sanctuary. The central one was reconstructed by Giambologna to use as his tomb, and contains bronze reliefs and a crucifix sculpted by him.

Through the door in the north transept of the church is the Chiostro dei Morti (Cloister of the Dead), so called because it was originally used as a burial ground and is packed with memorial stones. The fresco above the entrance porch is by Andrea del Sarto. Painted in 1525, it shows the Holy Family resting on their flight to Egypt and is usually known as *La Madonna del Sacco*, since Joseph is depicted leaning on a sack.

The Cappella di San Luca off the cloister has been owned by the Accademia delle Arte del Disegno since 1565 and a special service dedicated to artists is held here every year on St Luke's day (which falls on 18 October). Benvenuto Cellini is among the artists buried in the vault below.

The Birth of the Virgin **(1514) by Andrea del Sarto**

The François Vase, covered in figures from Greek mythology

Museo Archeologico ⓯

Via della Colonna 36. **Map** 2 E4. ***Tel*** *055 23 57 50.* *2–7pm Mon; 8:30am–7pm Tue, Thu; 8:30am–2pm Wed & Fri–Sun.* *1 Jan, 1 May, 25 Dec.*

The Archaeological Museum is in a palazzo built by Giulio Parigi for the Princess Maria Maddalena de' Medici in 1620. It now exhibits outstanding collections of Etruscan, Greek, Roman and ancient Egyptian artifacts.

A section on the second floor is dedicated to Greek vases, with a room given over to the François Vase, found in an Etruscan tomb at Fonte Rotella near Chiusi *(see p228).* Painted and signed in 570 BC, it is decorated with six rows of black and red figures depicting scenes from Greek mythology. The Etruscan collection was very badly damaged by the 1966 floods in Florence *(see p57)* and restoration of some pieces is still ongoing.

In addition to the splendid series of bronze Etruscan statues, on the first floor of the museum there are two famous bronzes. The *Chimera (see p42)*, sculpted in the 4th century BC, is a mythical lion with a goat's head imposed on its body and a serpent for a tail, shown here cowering in terror. It was ploughed up in a field near Arezzo in 1553 and presented to Cosimo I de' Medici by Giorgio Vasari, the artist, author and critic. The *Arringatore* (Orator) was found c.1566 near Lake Trasimeno in central Italy and is inscribed with the name of an Etruscan aristocrat, Aulus Metullus. The sculpture dates from the 1st century BC, and the figure, splendidly dressed in a Roman toga, appears to be addressing his audience.

Part of the Egyptian collection was acquired during a joint French and Tuscan expedition in 1829. It is especially rich in wooden, cloth and bone artifacts, which were well preserved in the dry atmosphere of the desert tombs in which they were found. They include a near-complete chariot of bone and wood found in a tomb near Thebes (dating to c.15th century BC), along with textiles, hats, ropes, furniture, purses and baskets.

Bronze Etruscan warrior

Santa Maria Maddalena dei Pazzi ⓰

Borgo Pinti 58. **Map** 2 E5. ***Tel*** *055 247 84 20.* **Church and chapter house** *9am–noon, 3–7pm daily.* *for mass 5:30–6pm.*

This former convent has been restored following the floods of 1966. Originally run by the Cistercian order, it was taken over by Carmelites in 1628, and Augustinian monks have lived here since 1926. The chapterhouse, which is entered from the crypt, contains the famous *Crucifixion and Saints fresco* painted in 1493–6 by Perugino (his real name was Pietro Vannucci), who was one of the founders of the Umbrian School of artists. This beautiful and well-preserved fresco is regarded as a masterpiece, bearing all Perugino's trademarks, most notably the background, which is a detailed landscape of wooded hills and winding streams painted in soft blues and greens. The main chapel, decorated with coloured marble by Ciro Ferri (1675), is one of the best examples of the High Baroque style in a Florentine church. In 1492 Giuliano da Sangallo designed the church's unusual and striking portico, with its square-topped, Ionic-style arcades.

Tempio Israelitico ⓱

Via Farini 4. **Map** 2 F5. ***Tel*** *055 24 52 52.* **Synagogue and Museum** *Oct–Mar: 10am–1pm, 2–4pm Sun–Thu, 10am–1pm Fri; Apr–Oct: 10am–1pm, 2–5pm Sun–Thu, 10am–1pm Fri.* *Jewish hols.*

Interior of the Tempio Israelitico

The green copper-covered dome of Florence's main synagogue stands out on the horizon as you look down on the city from the surrounding hills. As elsewhere in Europe, Jews in Florence were alternately welcomed and persecuted over the years. In the early 17th century they flocked to Livorno and then to Florence when it was freed from its strong political ties with Spain by Grand Duke Ferdinando I (1549–1609).

In the Inquisition, Grand Duke Cosimo III (1642–1723) passed laws forbidding Christians to work for Jewish families and businesses. In the 1860s the Jewish ghetto was cleared to make way for the Piazza della Repubblica *(see p112).* The synagogue was built by Marco Treves in 1874–82 in Spanish-Moorish style. It has a museum of ritual objects dating to the 17th century.

CITY CENTRE WEST

At one end of this part of Florence is the main railway station – a rare example of modern architecture in the city centre. At the other end, a magnet for visitors and Florentines alike, is the Ponte Vecchio, the city's oldest bridge. It is lined with jewellers' shops, here since 1593, and presents a scene little changed since.

Between these two focal points there is something to interest most people, from the frescoes of Santa Maria Novella and Santa Trinità to the luxurious 14th-century interiors of the Palazzo Davanzati and the awe-inspiring scale of Palazzo Strozzi.

Detail from Strozzi Chapel in Santa Maria Novella

Nearby is Piazza della Repubblica, originally laid out as part of the grandiose plans to remodel Florence when it was briefly the nation's capital. Most locals may consider it an eyesore, but the cafés here have always been very popular. This is also the part of Florence in which to shop, from the leather goods, silks and woollens of the Mercato Nuovo to the elegant showrooms of the top couturiers in Via della Vigna Nuova and Via de' Tornabuoni. In the smaller streets off these, local artisans continue Florence's proud tradition of craftsmanship, from stonecutting to restoration work.

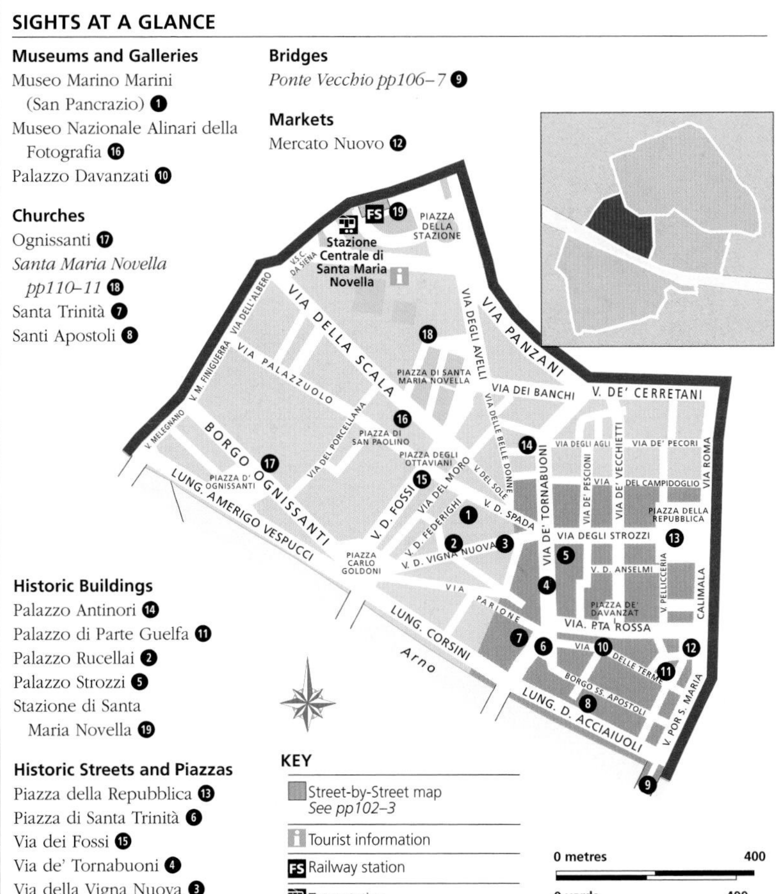

SIGHTS AT A GLANCE

Museums and Galleries
Museo Marino Marini (San Pancrazio) ❶
Museo Nazionale Alinari della Fotografia ⓰
Palazzo Davanzati ❿

Churches
Ognissanti ⓱
Santa Maria Novella pp110–11 ⓲
Santa Trinità ❼
Santi Apostoli ❽

Historic Buildings
Palazzo Antinori ⓮
Palazzo di Parte Guelfa ⓫
Palazzo Rucellai ❷
Palazzo Strozzi ❺
Stazione di Santa Maria Novella ⓳

Historic Streets and Piazzas
Piazza della Repubblica ⓭
Piazza di Santa Trinità ❻
Via dei Fossi ⓯
Via de' Tornabuoni ❹
Via della Vigna Nuova ❸

Bridges
Ponte Vecchio pp106–7 ❾

Markets
Mercato Nuovo ⓬

KEY
Street-by-Street map *See pp102–3*
Tourist information
FS Railway station
Tram station

0 metres 400
0 yards 400

◁ **View from Ponte Santa Trinità towards Piazza di Santa Trinità**

Street-by-Street: Around Piazza della Repubblica

Underlying the street plan of modern Florence is the far older pattern of the ancient Roman city founded on the banks of the Arno. Nowhere is this more evident than in the rectilinear grid of narrow streets in the western half of the city centre. Here the streets lead north from the river Arno to the Piazza della Repubblica, once the site of the forum, the main square of the ancient Roman city. It later became the city's main food market *(see p54)* until the city authorities decided to tidy it up in the 1860s, building the triumphal arch that now stands in today's café-filled square.

Palazzo Strozzi
This monumental palazzo dominates the square ❺

Piazza di Santa Trinità
The square is marked by an ancient Roman column ❻

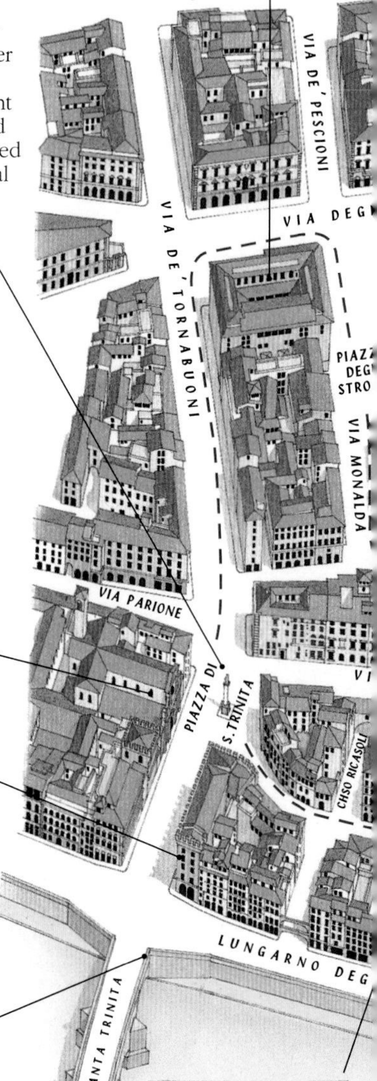

★ Santa Trinità
Ghirlandaio's frescoes, The Life of St Francis *(1483), depict scenes that took place in this area. Here, a child is restored to life, after falling from the Palazzo Spini-Ferroni* ❼

Palazzo Spini-Ferroni, a medieval palazzo featured in Ghirlandaio's frescoes in Santa Trinità, now houses the fashion boutique of Salvatore Ferragamo *(see p108)*.

The statues of the Four Seasons decorating the approaches to Ponte Santa Trinità were erected in 1608 to celebrate the wedding of Cosimo I.

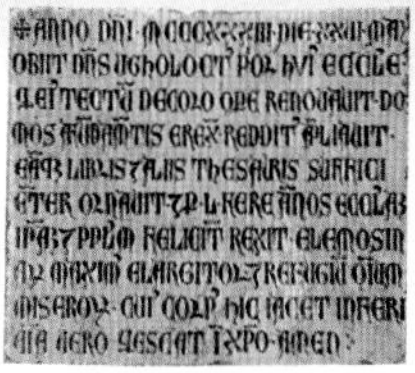

Santi Apostoli
A plaque claims Charlemagne as founder ❽

KEY

— — — Suggested route

0 metres 200

0 yards 200

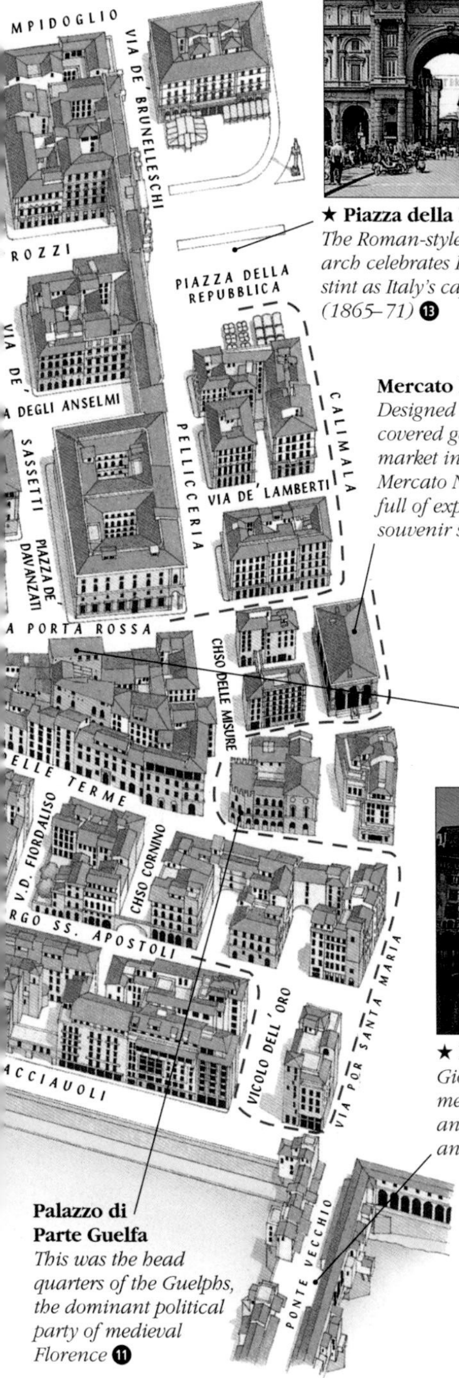

★ Piazza della Repubblica
The Roman-style triumphal arch celebrates Florence's stint as Italy's capital (1865–71) ⓭

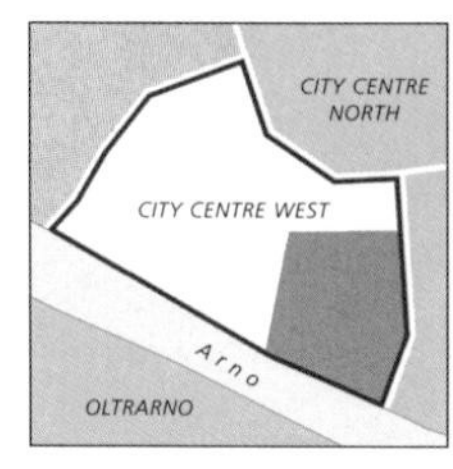

LOCATOR MAP
See Florence Street Finder maps 5, 6

Mercato Nuovo
Designed as a covered general market in 1547, Mercato Nuovo is full of expensive souvenir stalls ⓬

Palazzo Davanzati
Frescoes with exotic birds decorate the Sala dei Papagalli, which was once the dining room of this 14th-century palazzo ❿

★ Ponte Vecchio
Giotto's pupil, Taddeo Gaddi, designed this medieval bridge in 1345. It is the oldest – and most popular – of Florence's bridges and retains many of its original features ❾

Palazzo di Parte Guelfa
This was the head quarters of the Guelphs, the dominant political party of medieval Florence ⓫

STAR SIGHTS

★ Piazza d. Repubblica

★ Ponte Vecchio

★ Santa Trinità

Museo Marino Marini (San Pancrazio) ❶

Piazza San Pancrazio. **Map** 1 B5 (5 B2). ***Tel*** *055 21 94 32.*
10am–5pm Mon, Wed–Sat.
public hols.
www.museomarinomarini.it

The former church of San Pancrazio has been turned into a museum devoted to the work of Italy's best known abstract artist, Marino Marini (1901–80). Marini was born in Pistoia, where more of his work can be seen in the Palazzo del Comune and in the Centro Marino Marini *(see p186)*. Marini studied art in Florence before moving on to teaching in Monza and at the prestigious Brera Academy in Milan. He sought to reinterpret Etruscan and medieval art forms and is noted for rugged and elemental bronzes. Many of these are on the theme of horse and rider, expressing a range of moods and experiences, from sombre weariness to joyous eroticism.

San Pancrazio itself is one of the oldest churches in Florence. It was founded in the 9th century, though its most attractive features are from the Renaissance period, including a graceful Classical façade and porch (1461–7) by Leon Battista Alberti.

San Pancrazio was the parish church of the wealthy merchant Giovanni Rucellai. Inside, in the Cappella di San Sepolcro, built by Alberti in 1467, is Rucellai's tomb, which is modelled on the Holy Sepulchre in Jerusalem (the tomb of Christ).

Bronze statue, *Cavaliere* (1949), by Marini in the Museo Marino Marini

Palazzo Rucellai ❷

Via della Vigna Nuova 16. **Map** 1 C5 (5 B2). **www**.palazzorucellai.com

Built in 1446–51, this is one of the most ornate Renaissance palaces in the city. It was commissioned by Giovanni Rucellai, whose wealth derived from the family business, the import of a rare and costly red dye made from a lichen found only on Majorca. The dye was called *oricello*, from which the name Rucellai is derived.

Giovanni commissioned several buildings from the architect Leon Battista Alberti, who went on to write an influential architectural treatise called *De Re Aedificatoria* (Concerning Architecture) in 1452. Alberti designed the Palazzo Rucellai almost as a textbook illustration of the major Classical orders. In ascending order of complexity, the pilaster strips on the ground floor are Doric, those above are Ionic and those on the top floor are Corinthian. The construction of the palace combined eight medieval houses into one structure.

Two symbols are carved into the entablature: the Rucellai's billowing sails of Fortune and the ring symbol of the Medici family. The ring is a reminder that Bernardo Rucellai formed an alliance with the Medici in the 1460s by marrying Lorenzo de' Medici's sister, Lucrezia. The Loggia del Rucellai, opposite the palace, was most likely built to commemorate the marriage. The Loggia is now a shop, but it is still possible to see the architrave.

Today the Palazzo remains the property of the Rucellai family. It is located on a prominent shopping street and is within easy walking distance of several main sights and the Stazione di Santa Maria Novella. Part of the building is used as an educational center, the Institute at Palazzo Rucellai, which provides a liberal arts, study abroad programme for students of North American colleges. On site are fully-equipped classrooms, a library and a Fine art studio for classes and student exhibitions.

19th-century view of Lungarno degli Acciaiuoli, from Palazzo Rucellai

For hotels and restaurants in this area see pp252–54 and p271

Via della Vigna Nuova ❸

Map 3 B1 (5 B3).

Reflecting its associations with wealthy Renaissance Florentines, such as the Rucellai, Via della Vigna Nuova has a number of fashionable clothes shops. Nearly all the major Italian designers can be found here, as well as several smaller shops selling quality silks, cashmeres and lingerie.

Fashion houses doing business along Via della Vigna Nuova are La Perla (No. 17), Mariella Burani (No. 32r) and Beltrami (No. 70r) for leather goods.

Pucci window display, Via de' Tornabuoni

Via de' Tornabuoni ❹

Map 1 C5 (5 C2). **Ferragamo Museum** ***Tel*** *055 336 04 56.* *10am–6pm Wed–Mon.* *for groups of 10 or more.*

This is the most elegant shopping street in Florence, lined with boutiques such as Salvatore Ferragamo (No. 14r), Pucci (No. 20r), Roberto Cavalli (No. 83r), Gucci (No. 73r), Prada for men (No. 67r), Prada for women (No. 53r), Armani (No. 48/50r), Bulgari (No. 61r) and Cartier (No. 40r). The Ferragamo Museum (No. 2) focuses on the firm's efforts in shoe-making. The medieval tower at the end of the street, now a hotel, used to be a private club for local aristocrats.

THE BIGGEST PALAZZO IN FLORENCE

The Strozzi family were exiled from Florence in 1434 for their opposition to the Medici, but in 1466 the banker Filippo Strozzi, having built up a fortune in Naples, returned to the city, determined to outdo his great rivals. He became a man obsessed. For years he bought up and demolished other palaces around his home. At last, he acquired enough land to achieve his ambition: to build the biggest palace ever seen in Florence. Having spent so much money to get this far, nothing was left to chance. Astrologers were brought in to choose the most favourable day on which to lay the foundation stone, and the walls of the monumental palace began to rise in 1489. Two years later Filippo Strozzi was dead, and, though his heirs struggled on with the building, the cost of pursuing Filippo's grandiose vision finally left them penniless and bankrupt.

Filippo Strozzi (1428–91)

Palazzo Strozzi ❺

Piazza degli Strozzi. **Map** 3 C1 (5 C3). ***Tel*** *055 264 51 55.* *for exhibitions.*

The Strozzi Palace is awesome because of its sheer size: 15 buildings were demolished to make way for it, and although it is only three storeys high, each floor is as tall as a normal palazzo. The palace was commissioned by the wealthy banker Filippo Strozzi, but he died in 1491, only two years after the foundation stone was laid.

The building was not completed until 1536, and three major architects had a hand in its design – Giuliano da Sangallo, Benedetto da Maiano and Simone del Pollaiuolo (also known as Cronaca). The exterior, built of huge rusticated masonry blocks, remains unspoiled. Look out for the original Renaissance torch-holders, lamps and rings for tethering horses, which adorn the corners and façades.

The elegance of the courtyard itself has been destroyed by a huge iron fire escape, constructed when the building was converted to a major exhibition venue. In recent years, it has hosted world-class exhibitions of art and antiquities. During major exhibitions, visitors can also access "La Strozzina" free of charge. This is a vaulted gallery space at basement level with changing displays. When there are no exhibitions, visitors may access only the central courtyard.

The palace also houses various learned institutes and an excellent library, the Gabinetto Vieusseux, named after the 19th-century Swiss scholar Gian Pietro Vieusseux. He founded a scientific and literary association in 1818, which was attended by, among others, the French author Stendhal.

Exterior of Palazzo Strozzi, with masonry block rustication

Ponte Vecchio ⑨

The Ponte Vecchio, or Old Bridge – indeed, the oldest bridge in Florence – was built in 1345. It was the only bridge in the city to escape being blown up during World War II. There have always been workshops on the bridge, but the butchers, tanners and blacksmiths who were here originally (and who used the river as a convenient rubbish tip) were evicted by Duke Ferdinando I in 1593 because of the noise and stench they created. The workshops were rebuilt and let to the more decorous goldsmiths, and the shops lining and overhanging the bridge continue to specialize in new and antique jewellery to this day.

Private Corridor
The aerial corridor built by Vasari along the eastern side of the bridge is hung with the self-portraits of many great artists, including Rembrandt, Rubens and Hogarth.

Medieval Workshops
Some of the oldest workshops have rear extensions overhanging the river, supported by timber brackets called sporti.

The three-arched medieval bridge rests on two stout piers with boat-shaped cutwaters.

VASARI'S CORRIDOR

The Corridoio Vasariano was built in 1565 by Giorgio Vasari and links the Palazzo Vecchio to the Palazzo Pitti, via the Uffizi. This private elevated walkway, also known as *Percorso del Principe* ("Prince's Route"), allowed members of the Medici family to move between their residences without having to step into the street below and mix with the crowds. The Corridor is occasionally open by guided tour only; tickets must be booked in advance.

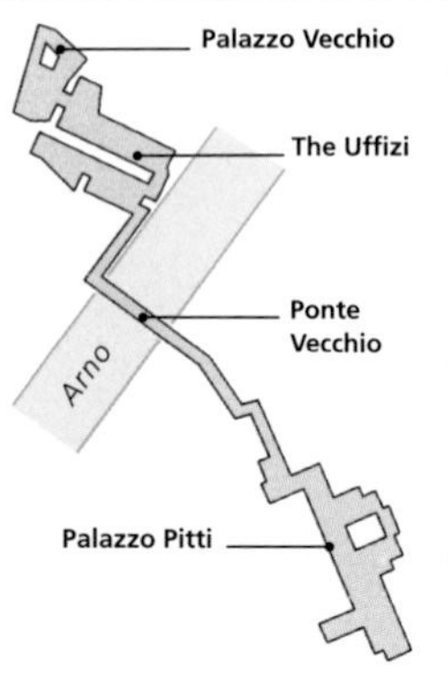

Bust of Cellini
A bust of Benvenuto Cellini (1500–71), the most famous of all Florentine goldsmiths, was placed in the middle of the bridge in 1900.

For hotels and restaurants in this area see pp252–54 and p271

★ Bridge at Sunset
The Ponte Vecchio is especially attractive when viewed in the setting sun from Ponte Santa Trinità, or from one of the river embankments.

★ Jewellers' Shops
The shops sell everything from affordable modern earrings to precious antique rings.

VISITORS' CHECKLIST

Map 3 C1 (5 C4). *B, D.* **Vasari Corridor** ***Tel*** *055 29 48 83.*

Mannelli Tower
This medieval tower was built to defend the bridge. The Mannelli family stubbornly refused to demolish it to make way for the Vasari Corridor.

The Vasari Corridor, supported on brackets, circumvents the Mannelli tower.

Circular windows called *oculi* (eyes) light the corridor.

Viewpoint
There are few better places for enjoying the river views; buskers, portrait painters and street traders congregate on the bridge, adding to the colour and bustle.

STAR FEATURES

★ Jewellers' Shops

★ Bridge at Sunset

Piazza di Santa Trinità

Piazza di Santa Trinità ❻

Map 3C1 (5C3).

Noble Palazzi line this busy square. To the south is the Palazzo Spini-Ferroni, originally built in 1290 but much rebuilt in the 19th century; today the ground floor houses the famous boutique of Salvatore Ferragamo *(see p284)*, specializing in shoes and leather goods. To the north, on the corner with Via delle Terme, is the Palazzo Bartolini-Salimbeni. Built during 1520–29, it is one of the city's best examples of High Renaissance architecture. In between the two palazzi is a column of oriental granite originally from the Baths of Caracalla in Rome and given to Cosimo I by Pope Pius IV in 1560. The figure of Justice on top was made in 1581.

Just south of the square is the Ponte Santa Trinità, considered the most beautiful bridge in Florence. It affords fine views of the surrounding hills and especially of the Ponte Vecchio *(see pp106–7)*. It was originally built in wood in 1252, and then rebuilt by Ammannati in 1567 as a monument to Cosimo I's defeat of Siena. Michelangelo is credited with the elegant design, based on an intriguing elliptical curve echoing those on the famous Medici tombs *(see p91)*. The statues of the Four Seasons at each end were added in 1608 for Cosimo II's marriage to Maria of Austria. The bridge was restored after it was blown up by the Germans in 1944, and the statues were dredged up from the river bed.

Look west from here to the golden-yellow Palazzo Corsini (1648–56), with statues on the roof balustrade. It is one of the best examples of Baroque architecture in Florence.

Ponte Santa Trinità

Santa Trinità ❼

Piazza di Santa Trinità. **Map** 3 C1 (5 C3). ***Tel*** *055 21 69 12.*
7am–noon, 4–7pm daily.

The nave of Santa Trinità

The original church, built in the second half of the 11th century by the Vallombrosan monastic order, was very plain – a reflection of the austerity of the order, which was founded in Florence in 1092 to restore the simplicity of monastic rule. Gradually, the building became more ornate, with a Baroque façade added in 1593. Inside, the east wall shows traces of its Romanesque predecessor.

Ghirlandaio's frescoes in the Sassetti Chapel (right of the High Altar) show what the church looked like in 1483–6. In one scene St Francis of Assisi performs a miracle in the Piazza di Santa Trinità, with the church and the Palazzo Spini-Ferroni in the background. The donors of the chapel, Francesco Sassetti and his wife Nera Corsi, are portrayed on either side of the altar. In another scene, St Francis is receiving the Rule of the Franciscan order from Pope

Honorius III in the Piazza della Signoria. Sassetti, who was general manager of the Medici bank, is shown with his son, Teodoro, and with Lorenzo de' Medici to his right, along with Antonio Pucci. Lorenzo's sons are climbing up steps with their tutors, led by the Humanist scholar Agnolo Poliziano, or Politian. The altar painting, *The Adoration of the Shepherds* (1485), is also by Ghirlandaio; he is the first, dark-haired shepherd. The black sarcophagi of Sassetti and his wife are by Giuliano da Sangallo.

Santi Apostoli ❽

Piazza del Limbo. **Map** 3 C1 (5 C4). ***Tel*** *055 29 06 42. 10am–noon, 4–7pm daily.*

The little church of the Holy Apostles is, along with the Baptistry, among the oldest surviving churches in Florence. Florentines like to think that the church was founded in 800 AD by the first Holy Roman Emperor, Charlemagne, but it more likely dates to 1059–1100. The church has a simple Romanesque façade and the basilican plan typical of early Christian churches, but with 16th-century side aisles.

Santi Apostoli fronts Piazza del Limbo, so called because there was a cemetery here for infants who died before they were baptized. Hence, according to medieval theology, their souls dwelt in limbo – halfway between heaven and hell.

Della Robbia glazed terracotta tabernacle in Santi Apostoli

Ponte Vecchio ❾

See pp106–7.

Fresco in a bedroom in the Palazzo Davanzati

Palazzo Davanzati ❿

Via Porta Rossa 13. **Map** 3 C1 (5 C3). ***Tel*** *055 238 86 10. 8:15am–1:50pm daily; second and third floors closed. 1st, 3rd & 5th Mon and 2nd & 4th Sun of the month; 1 Jan, 1 May, 25 Dec.*

Also known as the Museo dell'Antica Casa Fiorentina, the Palazzo Davanzati is preserved as a typical house of wealthy Florentines of the 14th century. The entrance courtyard was designed to trap unwanted visitors; holes in the vaulted ceiling were used for dropping missiles. In the more peaceful inner courtyard, a staircase links all the floors. In one corner is a well and a pulley system so buckets of water could be raised to each floor – this ingenious mechanism was quite a luxury since most households had to fetch all their water from a public fountain.

The main living room on the first floor looks plain, but hooks beneath the ceiling show that the walls would have been hung with tapestries. Many rooms have bathrooms attached, and are decorated with frescoes of scenes from a French romance. The restored Salone Madornale, where large gatherings would have been held, and the Sala dei Pappagalli (Parrots Room), with its frescoes and rich tapestries, are impressive. Restoration in two rooms dedicated to lace is ongoing.

Palazzo di Parte Guelfa ⓫

Piazza di Parte Guelfa. **Map** 3 C1 (6 D3). *to the public.*

This characterful building served as the headquarters of the Guelph party and the residence of its captains from around 1266, after the Guelphs began to emerge as the stronger of the two medieval factions struggling for control over Florence. In the complex politics of the period, the Guelphs supported the Pope and the Ghibellines took the side of the Holy Roman Emperor in the dispute over who should rule northern Italy *(see p46)*.

Emblem of the Guelphs

The lower part of the building dates to the 13th century, but the upper part was added by Brunelleschi in 1431. There are *stemmae* (coats-of-arms) under the crenellations. The elegant open staircase, added in 1589, is by Vasari.

Santa Maria Novella ⓲

The Gothic church of Santa Maria Novella contains some of the most important works of art in Florence. The church was built by the Dominicans from 1279 to 1357. Beside the church is a cemetery walled in with *avelli* (grave niches), which continue along the façade and the wall beyond. The cloisters form a museum. Here, the frescoes in the Spanish Chapel show the Dominicans as whippets – *domini canes* or hounds of God – rounding up the "stray sheep".

Green Cloister
The name comes from the green tinge to Uccello's Noah and the Flood *frescoes, unfortunately damaged by the 1966 floods.*

Monastic buildings

★ Spanish Chapel
The chapel used by the Spanish courtiers of Eleonora of Toledo, the wife of Cosimo I (see p51), *has dramatic frescoes on the theme of salvation and damnation.*

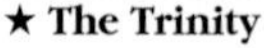

★ The Trinity
Masaccio's pioneering work is a masterpiece of perspective and portraiture (see p26).

Entrance to museum

Main door

The billowing sail emblem of the Rucellai *(see p104)* appears on the façade because they paid for its completion in 1470.

Alberti added the volutes in 1458–70 to hide the roofs over the side chapels.

Entrance (via courtyard)

Strozzi Chapel
The 14th-century frescoes by Nardo di Cione and his brother, Andrea Orcagna, were inspired by Dante's epic poem, The Divine Comedy. *Dante himself is portrayed in the* Paradise *fresco on the left, along with members of the Strozzi family.*

VISITORS' CHECKLIST

Piazza di Santa Maria Novella.
Map 1 B5 (5 B1).
A, 6, 11, 36, 37.
Church ***Tel*** *055 28 21 87.*
9am–5pm Mon–Thu & Sat; 1–5pm Fri & Sun.
7:30am, 6pm Mon–Sat; 8:30am, 10:30am, noon, 6pm Sun & religious hols.
Museum ***Tel*** *055 28 21 87.*
9am–5pm Mon–Thu & Sat; 9am–2pm Sun.
8 Dec, 25 Dec.

The arcade arches are emphasized by grey and white banding.

★ Tornabuoni Chapel
Ghirlandaio's famous fresco cycle, The Life of John the Baptist *(1485), portrays Florentine aristocrats and contemporary costumes and furnishings. Opposite is his other masterpiece,* The Life of the Virgin.

★ Filippo Strozzi Chapel
Filippino Lippi's dramatic frescoes show St John raising Drusiana from the dead and St Philip slaying a dragon. Boccaccio set the beginning of The Decameron *in this chapel.*

The walls of the old cemetery are decorated with the emblems and badges of wealthy Florentines.

Interior
The nave piers are spaced closer at the east end to create the illusion of an exceptionally long church.

STAR FEATURES

★ The Trinity by Masaccio

★ Filippo Strozzi Chapel

★ Tornabuoni Chapel

★ Spanish Chapel

Mercato Nuovo ⓬

Map 3 C1 (6 D3). *Apr–Oct: 9am–7pm daily; Nov–Mar: 9am–7pm Tue–Sat.*

The Mercato Nuovo (New Market) is sometimes called the "Straw Market" because goods woven out of straw, such as hats and baskets, were sold here from the end of the 19th century until the 1960s. In fact, it was originally built in 1547–51 as a central market for silk and other luxury goods. Today's stallholders sell leather goods and souvenirs, and on summer evenings buskers gather to entertain visitors.

To the south of the market is a little fountain called Il Porcellino. This is a 17th-century copy in bronze of the Roman marble statue of a wild boar that can be seen in the Uffizi. Its snout gleams like gold, thanks to the superstition that any visitor who rubs it will return to Florence some day. Coins dropped in the water basin below are collected and distributed to the city's charities.

Bronze boar in Mercato Nuovo

Piazza della Repubblica ⓭

Map 1 C5 (6 D3).

Until 1890, when the present square was laid out, this had been the site of the Mercato Vecchio (Old Market) and before that of the ancient Roman forum. A single column from the old market still stands on the square, topped by an 18th-century statue of Abundance. Dominating the western side of the square is a triumphal arch built in 1895 to celebrate

One of the many pavement cafés in Piazza della Repubblica

the fact that Florence was then the capital of Italy. The demolition of the Old Market was intended as the first step in a wholesale remodelling of Florence, but leading members of the English community led an international campaign opposing this grand scheme, which would have led to the destruction of almost every historic building in the city centre. Fortunately, the campaign was successful and the demolition halted.

The square, popular with both tourists and locals, is lined with pavement cafés, such as the very smart Gilli (No. 39r) or the Giubbe Rosse (No. 13–14r), so called because of the red jackets of the waiters. In the early part of this century, the Giubbe Rosse was the haunt of writers and artists, including those of Italy's avant-garde Futurist movement. Rinascente, one of Florence's department stores *(see p287)*, is on the eastern side of the square.

Palazzo Antinori ⓮

Piazza Antinori 3. **Map** 1 C5 (5 C2). *to the public.* **Cantinetta Antinori** ***Tel*** *055 29 22 34. 12:30–2:30pm, 7–10:30pm Mon–Fri (also open 12 Saturdays a year at the manager's discretion).*

The Palazzo Antinori, originally the Palazzo Boni e Martelli, was built in 1461–6 and with its elegant courtyard is considered one of the finest small Renaissance *palazzi* of Florence. It was acquired by the Antinori family in 1506 and has remained with them since.

The family owns large and productive estates all over Tuscany and in the neighbouring region of Umbria, producing a range of well-regarded wines, olive oils and liqueurs. You can sample these in the frescoed wine bar to the right of the courtyard, the Cantinetta Antinori.

The wine bar also specializes in typical Tuscan cuisine, with dishes such as *crostini alla toscana,* together with traditional cheeses and a range of other produce from the Antinori estates.

Via dei Fossi ⓯

Map 1 B5 (5 B3).

Shop in Via dei Fossi selling reproduction statuary

Via dei Fossi and the nearby streets contain some of the most absorbing shops in Florence, many of them specializing in antiques and works of art and statuary, and in classic Florentine products. Bottega Artigiana del Libro (Lungarno Corsini 40r) stocks handmade marbled papers, albums, notebooks and carnival masks. Fallani Best (Borgo Ognissanti 15r) has Art Nouveau and Art Deco furnishings and sculpture, and Antonio Frilli (Via dei Fossi 26r) specializes in marble sculpture – original Art Nouveau works and copies of famous Renaissance pieces. Neri (Via dei Fossi 57r) also sells top-quality antiques and G Lisio (Via dei Fossi 41r), makes handwoven tapestries and rich Renaissance-style fabrics. Attached to the convent of the same name, the frescoed Farmacia di Santa Maria Novella (Via della Scala 16r) dates to the 16th century and sells toiletries and liqueurs made by Dominican monks.

Museo Nazionale Alinari della Fotografia ⓰

Piazza Santa Maria Novella 14a. **Map** 1 B5 (5 B2). ***Tel*** *055 21 63 10.* *10am–7pm Thu–Tue.*

The Alinari brothers began taking pictures of Florence in the 1840s, soon after the invention of photography. The firm they set up in 1852 specialized in supplying top-quality prints, postcards and art books to foreigners who flocked to the city during the 1800s. Today, this archive provides a fascinating insight into the social history of Florence over the last 150 years. The museum also houses a collection of cameras, documents and objects that illustrate the history of photography. There are around six temporary exhibitions a year held here.

Ognissanti ⓱

Borgo Ognissanti 42. **Map** 1 B5 (5 A2). ***Tel*** *055 239 87 00.* *7:45am–noon & 4:45–6:30pm Mon–Sat.* *Fri morning and first and last Mon of month.*
Cenacolo del Ghirlandaio
9am–noon Mon, Tue & Sat (call 055 239 68 02 to book appointments for other times).

The church of All Saints, or Ognissanti, was the parish church of the merchant family of the Vespucci, one of whose members, the 15th-century navigator Amerigo, gave his name to the New World. Amerigo is depicted in Ghirlandaio's fresco of the *Madonna della Misericordia* (1472) in the second chapel on the right. Amerigo Vespucci was the first to realize that the land discovered by Columbus was a new continent, not the eastern shore of the Indies. He made two voyages following Columbus's route and, because his letters enabled cartographers to draw the first maps *(see p75)* of the new land, it was given his name.

Ognissanti is also the burial place of Sandro Botticelli. His fresco of *St Augustine* (1480) can be seen on the south wall. It is complemented by Ghirlandaio's *St Jerome* (1480) on the opposite wall.

Alongside the church is a cloister and refectory, containing Ghirlandaio's fresco The *Last Supper* (1480), with its background of birds and trees.

The cloister of Ognissanti with 17th-century frescoes

Santa Maria Novella ⓲

See pp110–11.

Stazione di Santa Maria Novella ⓳

Map 1 B4 (5 B1). *1:30–4:15am daily.* **Train information** *7am–9pm daily.* **Ticket office** *5:45am–11pm daily.* **Bag deposit** *6am–midnight daily.* **Assistance** *7am–9pm daily.* ***Tel*** *055 235 61 20.* **Disabled passengers assistance** *7am–9pm daily.* ***Tel*** *055 235 22 75.* *8:30am–5:30pm Mon–Sat.* **Chemist** *24 hrs.*

A fine example of modern architecture in Italy, the central railway station was designed in 1935 by a group of Tuscan "Functionalist" artists, including Piero Berardi and Giovanni Michelucci. They believed that a building's form should reflect its purpose. The exterior was designed to compliment the Gothic architecture of the city centre, while the interior uses metal and glass to create a feeling of space and light.

Ghirlandaio's *Madonna della Misericordia* (1472) in Ognissanti, with the boy Amerigo Vespucci

OLTRARNO

Oltrarno means "across the Arno", and living on the south bank of the river was once considered inferior. Here lived people who did not have sufficient wealth to build a palazzo within the city centre. That stigma did not change until the household of the Medici Grand Dukes moved to Oltrarno in 1550.

Statue, Museo Bardini

MEDICI POWER BASE

The Palazzo Pitti became the base from which Tuscany was ruled for the next 300 years. Eleonora di Toledo, the Spanish wife of Cosimo I, purchased the Palazzo Pitti in 1549. Suffering from a wasting disease, perhaps malaria or tuberculosis, Eleonora persuaded Cosimo that her health might well improve if they lived in the relatively rural setting of Oltrarno. Over the years the Palazzo Pitti increased almost threefold in size in comparison with the original plans, and the Boboli Gardens were laid out on the land around it. A few Florentine aristocrats followed the Medici lead and moved across the river to make their homes here. In the late 16th and 17th centuries, many palazzi were built in the area surrounding Via Maggio and Piazza di Santo Spirito. Today, this is primarily a quiet area full of artisan workshops and antique shops, contrasting with the elegant palazzi and the unfinished austere façade of Santo Spirito. The local merchants' association organizes guided tours, events and fairs to expose visitors to the artisan treasures on the south bank. It is a fascinating area to wander around and discover the true character of Florence.

SIGHTS AT A GLANCE

Churches

Brancacci Chapel pp126–7 ❿
Santa Felicità ❺
San Frediano in Cestello ⓫
Santo Spirito ❶

Museums and Galleries

Cenacolo di Santo Spirito ❷
Museo Bardini ❽
Museo "La Specola" ❾
Palazzo Pitti pp120–21 ❻

Gardens

Boboli Gardens pp124–5 ❼

Streets and Piazzas

Piazza di Santo Spirito ❸
Via Maggio ❹

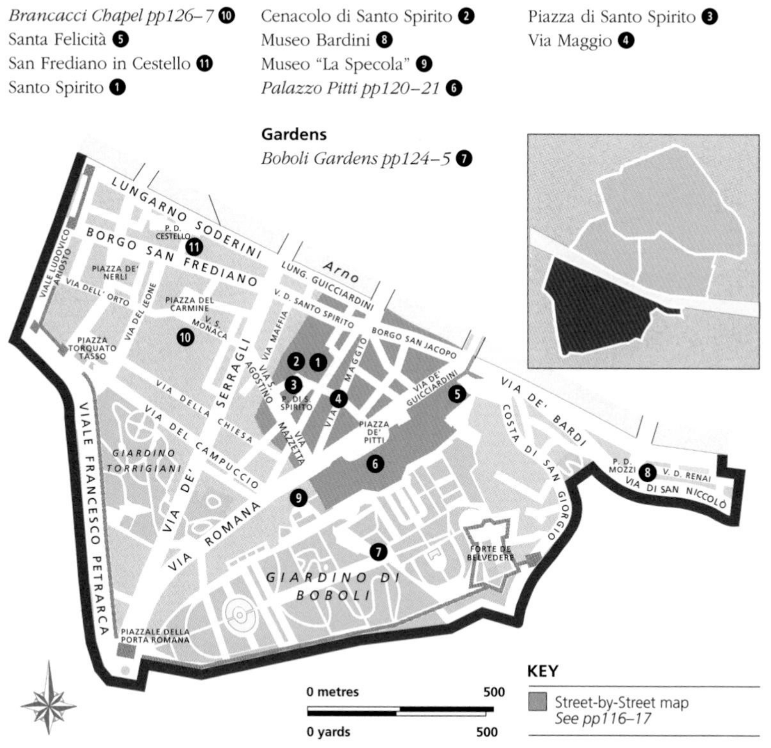

◁ **Rooftops of the Oltrarno and the spire and dome of Santo Spirito**

Street-by-Street: Oltrarno

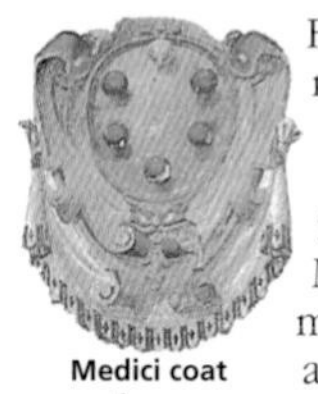

Medici coat of arms

For the most part, the Oltrarno area consists of relatively small houses and shops selling antiques, bric-à-brac and foodstuffs. The Via Maggio breaks this pattern, with its numerous imposing 16th-century palazzi close to the Medici's Palazzo Pitti. As it is one of the main routes into the city, the road is busy and there is constant traffic noise. Step into the side streets, however, and you escape the noise and bustle to discover traditional Florence; restaurants are authentic and reasonably priced, and the area is full of workshops restoring antique furniture.

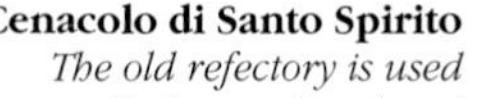

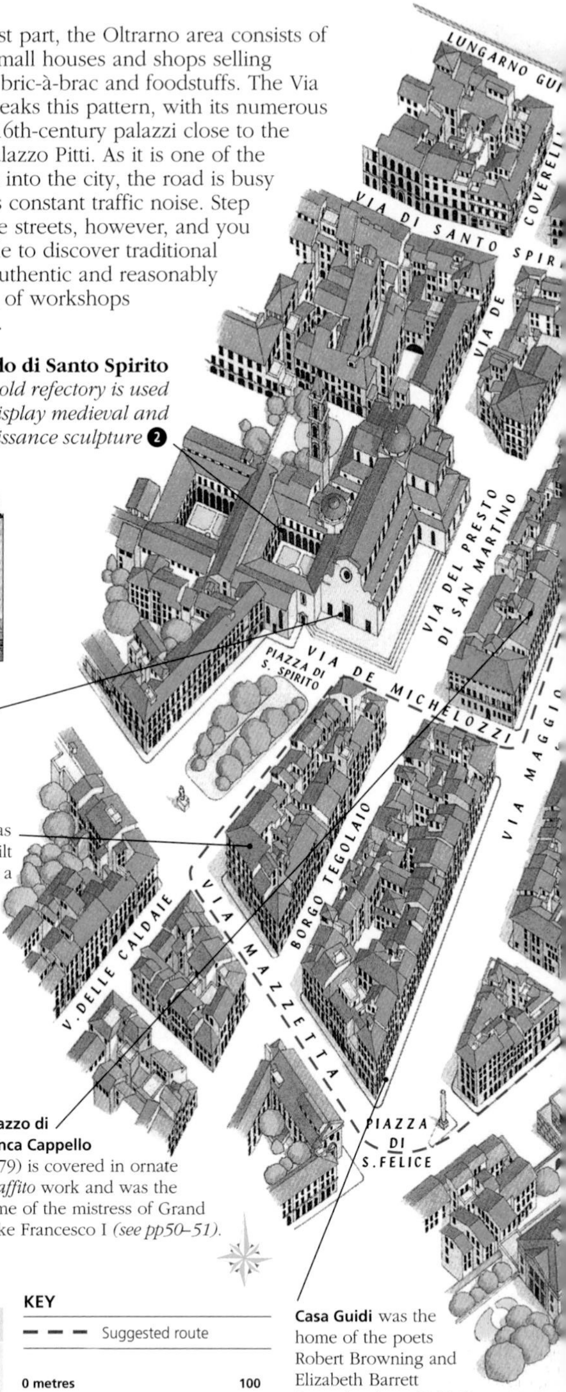

Cenacolo di Santo Spirito
The old refectory is used to display medieval and Renaissance sculpture ❷

Santo Spirito
Simplicity is the keynote of Brunelleschi's last church. It was completed after his death in 1446 ❶

Palazzo Guadagni (1500) was the first in the city to be built with a rooftop loggia, setting a trend among the aristocracy.

Palazzo di Bianca Cappello (1579) is covered in ornate *sgraffito* work and was the home of the mistress of Grand Duke Francesco I *(see pp50–51)*.

Casa Guidi was the home of the poets Robert Browning and Elizabeth Barrett Browning from 1846–61, after their secret wedding.

LUNGARNO GUI
VIA DI SANTO SPIRITO
COVERELLI
VIA DE
VIA DEL PRESTO DI SAN MARTINO
PIAZZA DI S. SPIRITO
VIA DE MICHELOZZI
VIA MAGGIO
BORGO TEGOLAIO
VIA MAZZETTA
V. DELLE CALDAIE
PIAZZA DI S.FELICE

STAR SIGHTS

★ Palazzo Pitti

★ Boboli Gardens

KEY

– – – Suggested route

0 metres 100

0 yards 100

For hotels and restaurants in this area see p255 and pp272–73

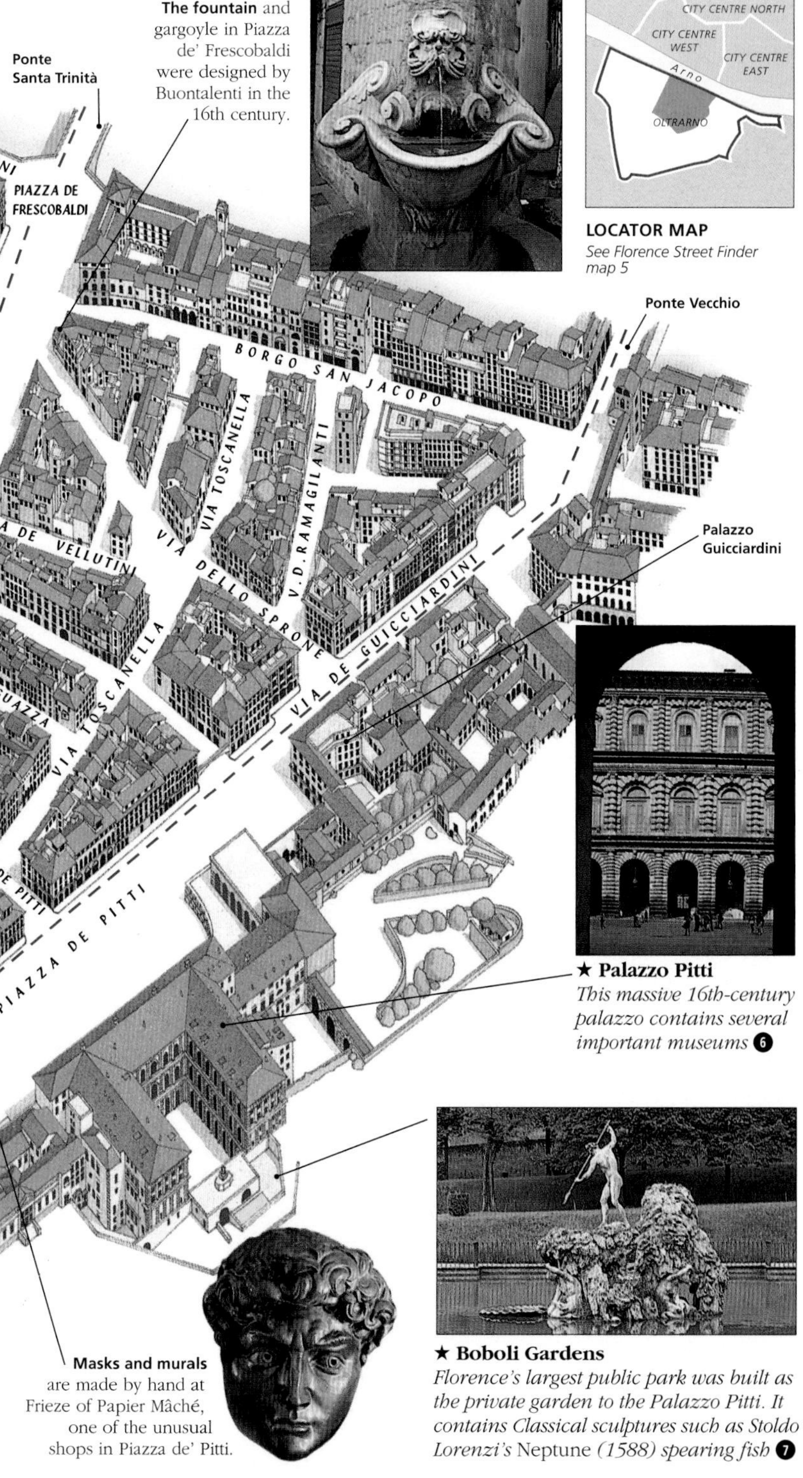

The fountain and gargoyle in Piazza de' Frescobaldi were designed by Buontalenti in the 16th century.

LOCATOR MAP
See Florence Street Finder map 5

★ Palazzo Pitti
This massive 16th-century palazzo contains several important museums ❻

Masks and murals are made by hand at Frieze of Papier Mâché, one of the unusual shops in Piazza de' Pitti.

★ Boboli Gardens
Florence's largest public park was built as the private garden to the Palazzo Pitti. It contains Classical sculptures such as Stoldo Lorenzi's Neptune *(1588) spearing fish* ❼

Santo Spirito ❶

Piazza di Santo Spirito. **Map** 3 B2 (5 B4). *D.* ***Tel*** *055 21 00 30.*
9:30am–12:30pm, 3–5:30pm Thu–Sat & Mon–Tue, 3–5:30pm Sun.
Wed.

The Augustinian foundation of this church dates from 1250. The present building has an unfinished 18th-century façade, which dominates the northern end of Piazza di Santo Spirito. Brunelleschi designed the church in 1435, but it was not completed until the late 1400s, well after his death.

Inside, the harmony of the proportions has been somewhat spoiled by the elaborate Baroque baldacchino and the High Altar, which was finished in 1607 by Giovanni Caccini. The church has 38 side altars, decorated with 15th- and 16th-century Renaissance paintings and sculpture, among them works by Cosimo Rosselli, Domenico Ghirlandaio and Filippino Lippi. The latter painted a *Madonna and Child* (1466) for the Nerli Chapel in the south transept.

In the north aisle, a door beneath the organ leads to a vestibule with an ornate coffered ceiling. It was designed by Simone del Pollaiuolo, more commonly known as Cronaca, in 1491. The sacristy adjoining the vestibule was designed by Giuliano da Sangallo in 1489.

Cenacolo di Santo Spirito ❷

Piazza di Santo Spirito 29. **Map** 3 B1 (5 B4). ***Tel*** *055 28 70 43.*
Apr–Nov: 9am–2pm Tue–Sun; Dec–Mar: 10:30am–1:30pm Sat.
1 Jan, Easter Sun, 1 May, 15 Aug, 25 Dec.

All that survives of the monastery that stood next to Santo Spirito is the refectory *(cenacolo)*, now a small museum. Inside is a fresco, *The Crucifixion* (1360–65), attributed to the followers of Andrea Orcagna and his brother Nardo di Cione. In a city that has a wealth of Renaissance art, this is a rare and beautiful example of High Gothic religious work.

The Fondazione Salvatore Romano, a collection of 11th-century Romanesque sculpture, is displayed in the refectory.

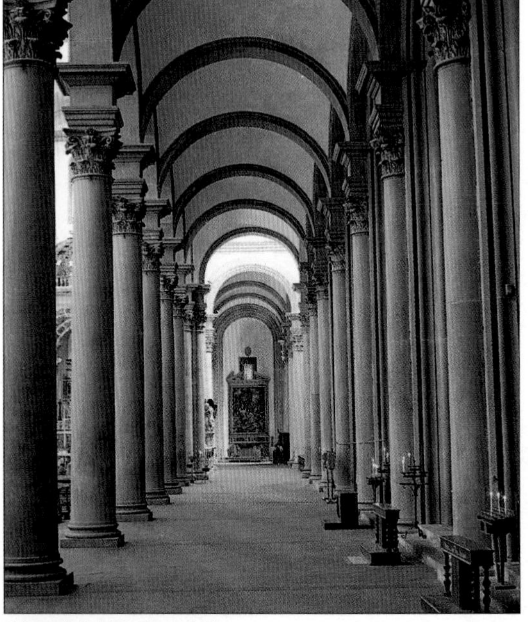

Colonnaded aisle in Santo Spirito

The façade of Palazzo Guadagni

Piazza di Santo Spirito ❸

Map 3 B2 (5 B5). *D.*
2nd (Antiques) & 3rd (Organic) Sun of month.

This part of Florence is best appreciated by wandering around the square and its market, looking at the many furniture restorers' workshops and medieval palazzi. The biggest house in the square is the Palazzo Guadagni at No. 10, on the corner with Via Mazzetta. It was built around 1505, probably to the designs of Cronaca. The windows have distinctive stone surrounds with tear-drop shaped keystones. The top floor forms an open loggia, the first of its kind to be built in the city. The loggia set a fashion among 16th-century Florentine aristocrats, who incorporated the design into their own palazzi.

Via Maggio ❹

Map 3 B2 (5 B5).

Opened in the mid-13th century, this road became a fashionable residential area after the Medici Grand Dukes moved to the Palazzo Pitti in 1550 *(see pp120–21)*. It is lined with 15th- and 16th-century palazzi, such as the Palazzo Ricasoli at No. 7, and antique shops. Via Maggio runs into Piazza di San Felice, where a plaque marks the Casa Guidi. The English poets Elizabeth and Robert Browning rented an apartment here after eloping in 1847. Inspired by Tuscan art and landscape, this is where they wrote much of their best poetry.

For hotels and restaurants in this area see p255 and pp272–73

The Virgin from *The Annunciation* (1528) by Pontormo

Santa Felicità ❺

Piazza di Santa Felicità. **Map** 3 C2 (5 C5). ***Tel*** *055 21 30 18.* *9am–noon, 3:30–6:30pm Mon–Sat.*

A church has stood on this site since the 4th century AD, but the current building dates from the 11th century. It was extensively remodelled by Ferdinando Ruggieri in 1736–9, but some original Gothic features and the porch added by Vasari in 1564 were retained.

The Capponi family chapel to the right of the entrance houses two works by Mannerist artist Jacopo da Pontormo: a panel depicting *The Deposition* and an *Annunciation* fresco. Painted in 1525–8, they make use of vivid colours such as salmon pink, light green, apricot and gold. The roundels at the base of the ceiling vault depict the Four Evangelists, also painted by Pontormo, with help from his pupil Agnolo Bronzino.

Palazzo Pitti ❻

See pp120–23.

Boboli Gardens ❼

See pp124–5.

Museo Bardini ❽

Piazza de' Mozzi 1. **Map** 4 D2 (6 E5). ***Tel*** *055 234 24 27.* *for restoration until further notice. Call for more information.*

Stefano Bardini was a 19th-century antiquarian and avid collector of architectural materials – mostly salvaged from the churches and palazzi demolished when the Piazza della Repubblica was built in the 1860s *(see p112).* In 1883 he built his palazzo in Piazza de' Mozzi almost entirely from recycled medieval and Renaissance masonry, including carved doorways, chimney pieces and staircases as well as painted and coffered ceilings. The rooms are full of sculpture, statues, paintings, armour, musical instruments, ceramics and antique furnishings. In 1922 this collection of antiquities was bequeathed to the people of Florence.

Museo Bardini, Piazza de' Mozzi

Museo "La Specola" ❾

Via Romana 17. **Map** 3 B2 (5 B5). ***Tel*** *055 22 88 251.* *9:30am–4:30pm Tue–Sun.* *public hols.* *in English, on request.*

This unusual museum is in the Palazzo Rottigiani, built in 1775 and now used by the natural science faculty of Florence University. The name "la Specola" refers to the observatory built on the roof of the building by Grand Duke Pietro Leopoldo in the late 18th century. It now contains the museum, which has a zoological section exhibiting vast numbers of preserved animals, insects and fish, and an anatomical section with some extremely realistic 18th-century wax models showing various grotesque aspects of human physiology and disease. Not for the faint-hearted!

Brancacci Chapel ❿

See pp126–7.

San Frediano in Cestello ⓫

Piazza di Cestello. **Map** 3 B1 (5 A3). *D, 6.* ***Tel*** *055 21 58 16.* *10–11:30am, 4:30–6pm Mon–Sat; 5–6:30pm Sun.*

The San Frediano area, with its small, low houses, has long been associated with the wool and leather industries. The parish church of San Frediano in Cestello stands beside the Arno looking across the river. It has a bare stone exterior with a large dome that is a local landmark. It was rebuilt on the site of an older church in 1680–89 by Antonio Maria Ferri: the fresco and stuccowork inside are typical of the late 17th and early 18th centuries. Nearby is a well-preserved stretch of the 14th-century city walls. The Porta San Frediano, built in 1324, has a tower overlooking the road to Pisa. Its wooden doors have retained their original 14th-century locks and detailed ironwork.

The dome and plain façade of San Frediano in Cestello

Palazzo Pitti ❻

The Palazzo Pitti, begun in 1457, was originally built for the banker Luca Pitti. Its huge scale was developed into its actual shape by the Medici, who one century later bought the palazzo when building costs bankrupted Pitti's heirs. In 1550 it became the main Medici residence and subsequently all Florentine rulers lived here. Today the richly decorated rooms exhibit treasures from the Medici collections *(see pp122–3)* and the Habsburg-Lorraine court.

Inner Courtyard
Ammannati designed the courtyard in 1560–70. The Artichoke Fountain by Francesco Susini (1641) was topped by a bronze artichoke, since lost.

The Boboli Gardens were laid out where stone had been quarried to build the Palazzo Pitti *(see pp124–5).*

★ Palatine Gallery
The gallery contains many masterpieces, among which is the highest concentration of Raphael's paintings.

The side wings were added in 1828 by the Dukes of Lorraine, who ruled the city after the Medici.

Frescoes by Pietro da Cortona (1641–5) cover the ceilings in the Palatine Gallery.

Brunelleschi is thought to have designed the façade of the palazzo, which was later extended to three times its original length.

★ Museo degli Argenti
As well as silverware, the museum displays gold, stone and glassware. This view of Piazza della Signoria (see pp76–7) *is made of precious stones.*

STAR FEATURES

- ★ Palatine Gallery
- ★ Museo degli Argenti

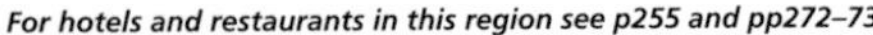

Galleria d'Arte Moderna
The gallery, on the second floor of the palazzo, spans the years from 1784 to 1924. The Tuscan Maremma *(c.1850), by Giovanni Fattori, is a highlight of the collection.*

The Carriage Museum offers another glimpse of the sumptuous, opulent life of the dukes.

Galleria del Costume
The clothes reflect changing fashion at the court of the Grand Dukes during the 18th and 19th centuries.

VISITORS' CHECKLIST

Piazza Pitti. **Map** 3 C2 (5 B5). *D, 11, 36, 37.* ***Tel*** *055 29 48 83 (booking & information).* **Palatine Gallery & Royal Apartments, Galleria d'Arte Moderna, Galleria del Costume** *8:15am–6:50pm Tue–Sun.* *1 Jan, 1 May, 25 Dec.* **Museo degli Argenti** *&* **Museo delle Porcellane** (enter via Boboli Gardens, *see p125*). *Mar: 8:15am–5:30pm daily; Apr–May & Sep–Oct: 8:15am–6:30pm; Jun–Aug: 8:15am–7:30pm.* *2nd & 4th Sun and 1st & 5th Mon of the month & public hols.* ***Ticket offices close 45 mins before the museums.*** *for each museum.* **Palatine Gallery** *ticket admits to* **Royal Apartments. Galleria d'Arte Moderna** *ticket admits to* **Galleria del Costume**. *Occasional temporary exhibitions – call for details.* **www**.polomuseale.firenze.it

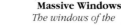

Entrance to museums and galleries

Massive Windows
The windows of the Palazzo Pitti were built to be larger than the main door of the Palazzo Medici Riccardi.

Royal Apartments
The south wing was used for ceremonial occasions and receiving ambassadors.

Exploring the Palazzo Pitti

The Palatine gallery was realized by the Medici family and the Habsburg-Lorraine duchies in the 1600s and 1700s. The frescoed halls were hung with works from their private collection and the gallery was opened to the public in 1833. Other attractions include the royal apartments, the Medici collection of jewellery and treasures, the gallery of modern art and an exhibition of Italian clothing from the 18th, 19th and 20th centuries.

THE PALATINE GALLERY

The gallery contains a superb collection of works dating from the Renaissance and Baroque. They are hung as the 17th- and 18th-century Grand Dukes wished, placed purely for their effect, regardless of subject or chronology. The decoration of the rooms in the gallery reflects the tastes and preoccupations of the time. Rooms 4 to 8 are painted with Baroque ceiling frescoes begun by Pietro da Cortona between 1641–7, and finished by his pupil Ciro Ferri in 1666. They allegorize the education of a prince by the gods. In Room 1, the prince is torn from the love of Venus by Minerva (knowledge) and in the following rooms he is taught science from Apollo, war from Mars and leadership from Jupiter. Finally Saturn welcomes him to Mount Olympus, home of the gods in Roman mythology.

The other rooms in the gallery were private apartments and range from the opulence of the formal drawing rooms to the severity of Napoleon's bathroom (Room 27) *(see p55)*, in a suite of rooms designed by Giuseppe Cacialli for the emperor in 1813 following his conquest of northern Italy.

Mary Magdalene **by Titian (c.1535)**

Although some of the Medici collection has been transferred to the Uffizi over the years, the Palatine Gallery is still packed with masterpieces by artists such as Botticelli, Perugino, Titian, Andrea del Sarto, Pontormo, Tintoretto, Veronese, Caravaggio, Rubens and Van Dyck, among others. There are approximately 1,000 paintings here, providing a vast survey of 16th- and 17th-century European painting.

The Sala di Venere (Venus) is dominated by the statue of *Venus Italica* by Antonio Canova, commissioned by Napoleon in 1810 as a replacement for *The Medici Venus* in the Uffizi Gallery, which was to be taken to Paris. Napoleon was not normally so generous, as his agents were renowned for stealing a large number of fine works of art from Italy during the Napoleonic Wars.

Several of Titian's works in the following rooms were commissioned by the Duke of Urbino. *La Bella* (1536) is a portrait of a lovely but unknown woman, whom he also used as a model in other paintings. His portrait, *Mary Magdalene*, in the Sala di Apollo, was painted between 1530–35 in an overtly sensual manner, bathed in soft light.

Some of Raphael's best High Renaissance work is in the Palatine, including *Portrait of a Woman* (c.1516) and

THE PALATINE GALLERY

The gallery is on the first floor of the Palazzo Pitti.

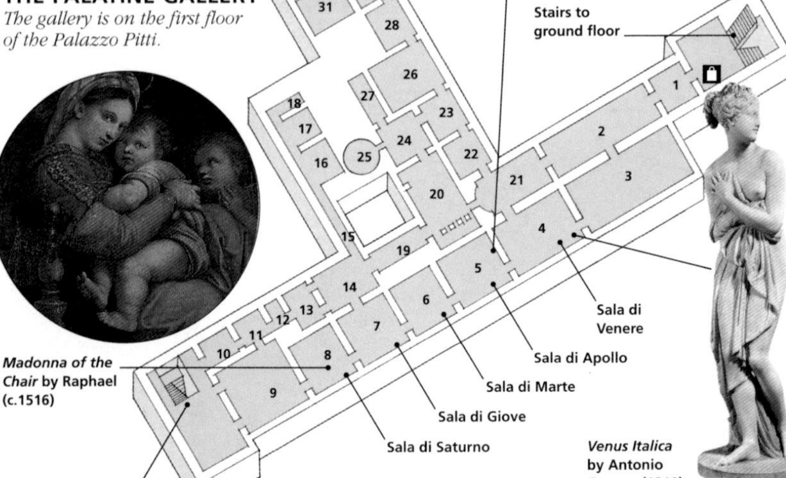

Madonna of the Chair (c.1510) in the *tondo* (roundel) form which became very popular during the Renaissance.

The Consequences of War by Peter Paul Rubens (1638) is an allegorical painting of the Thirty Years War (1618–48), showing Venus preventing Mars from unleashing his fury on the cowering, beleaguered figure of Europe, completely robed in black mourning.

ROYAL APARTMENTS

The Throne Room

The Royal Apartments on the first floor of the south wing of the palazzo were built in the 17th century. They are decorated with frescoes by various Florentine artists and a series of portraits of the Medici by the Flemish painter Justus Sustermans, who worked at the court between 1619–81. In the late 18th and early 19th centuries, the apartments were completely revamped in Neo-Classical style by the Dukes of Lorraine when they succeeded the Medici dynasty as the rulers of Florence *(see pp54–5)*.

The apartments are lavishly appointed with ornate gold and white stuccowork ceilings and rich decoration, as on the walls of the Parrot Room, which are covered with an opulent crimson fabric detailed with a bird design. The apartments' varied ownership is revealed in their design, which embraces three distinct artistic periods.

MUSEO DEGLI ARGENTI

This museum is on the ground and mezzanine floors, below the Palatine Gallery, in the rooms used by the Medici as their summer apartments. It displays the massive private wealth of the Medici dynasty: the collection encompasses rare and beautiful examples of ancient Roman glassware, ivory, carpets, crystal and amber and fine works by Florentine and German goldsmiths. The pride of the collection are 16 *pietre dure* vases displayed in the Sala Buia. These belonged to Lorenzo the Magnificent and are from the ancient Roman and Byzantine periods.

14th-century gold and jasper vase

The family's lavish tastes are reflected in the museum's polished ebony furniture inlaid with semi-precious marbles and stones. Portraits of the Medici hang throughout the rooms, including a series of the Grand Duchesses, and Cosimo I and his family carved in an onyx cameo.

GALLERIA D'ARTE MODERNA

Here the paintings span the period from 1784 to 1924; many of them were collected by the Dukes of Lorraine to decorate the Palazzo Pitti. The present museum has combined this collection with pictures donated by the state and various private collectors. The museum contains Neo-Classical, Romantic and religious works, but probably the most important collection is of the group of late 19th-century artists known as the *Macchiaioli* (spot-makers), similar to French Impressionists. The *Macchiaioli* used bright splashes of colour to represent the sun-dappled Tuscan landscape. This collection was given to the city of Florence in 1897 by the art critic Diego Martelli, and includes paintings by Giovanni Fattori *(see p121)* and Giovanni Boldini. Two works by Camille Pissarro hang in the same room.

GALLERIA DEL COSTUME

Opened in 1983, the gallery is on the ground floor of the Palazzo Meridiana. This was designed in 1776 by Gaspare Maria Paoletti for the Royal Family; they lived until the abolition of the monarchy *(see p52)*. The exhibits reflect the changing tastes in the courtly fashion of the late 18th century up to the 1920s. Some rooms have been restored to correspond to a 1911 inventory, while the rest of the gallery has been renovated.

The Italian Camp after the Battle of Magenta (c.1855) by Giovanni Fattori

Boboli Gardens ❼

The Boboli Gardens were laid out for the Medici in 1550, one year after they bought the Palazzo Pitti. A perfect example of stylized Renaissance gardening, they were opened to the public in 1766. The more formal parts of the garden, nearest the palazzo, consist of box hedges clipped into symmetrical geometric patterns. These lead to wild groves of ilex and cypress trees, planted to create a contrast between artifice and nature. Statues of varying styles and periods are dotted around, and the vistas were planned to give views over Florence.

★ Amphitheatre
Stone for the Palazzo Pitti was quarried here and the hollow was turned into a stage for the first-ever opera performances.

Kaffeehaus
The Rococo-style pavilion, built in 1774, now houses a coffee house. It is open during the summer and offers beautiful views over the city.

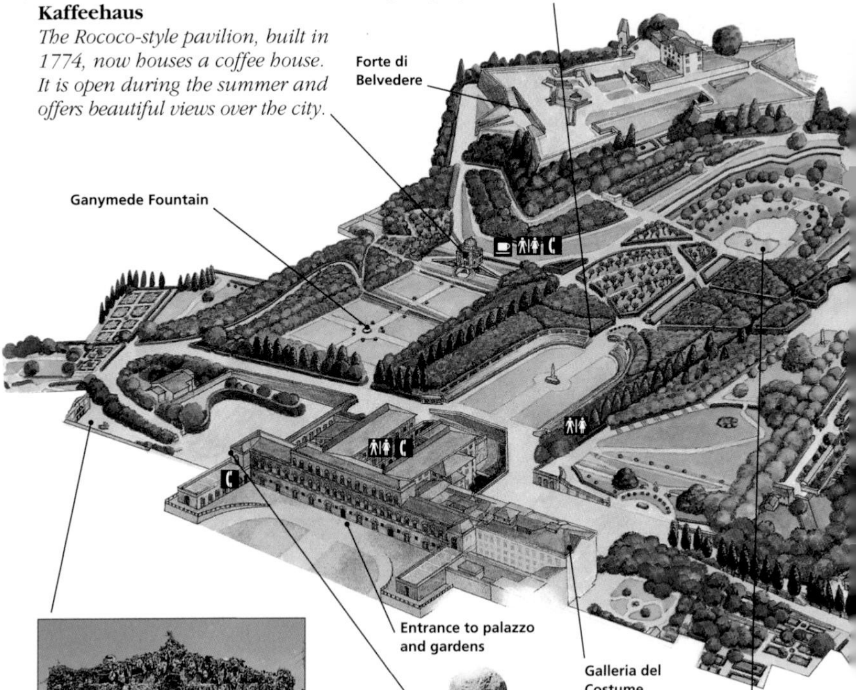

Forte di Belvedere

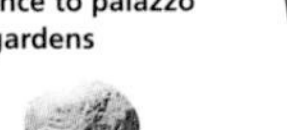

Galleria del Costume

The Neptune Fountain was built between 1565–8 by Stoldo Lorenzi.

★ La Grotta Grande
The casts of Michelangelo's Quattro Prigioni (see p94) *are built into the walls of this Mannerist folly (1583–93), which also houses Vincenzo de' Rossi's* Paris with Helen of Troy *(1560) and* Venus Bathing *(1565) by Giambologna.*

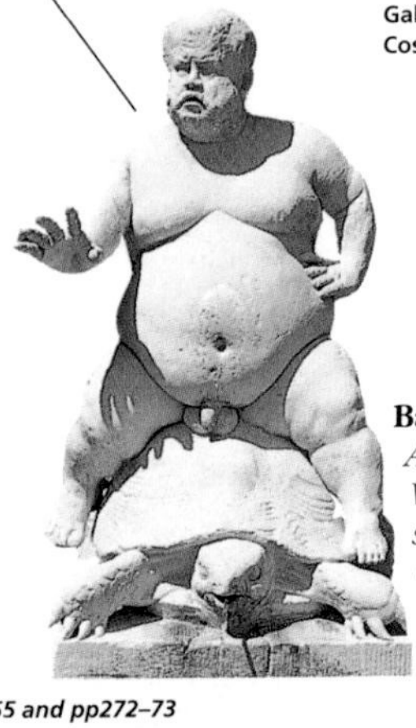

Bacchus Fountain *(1560)*
A copy of the original by Valerio Cioli, the statue shows Pietro Barbino, Cosimo I's court dwarf, as Bacchus, the Roman god of wine, astride a turtle.

For hotels and restaurants in this area see p255 and pp272–73

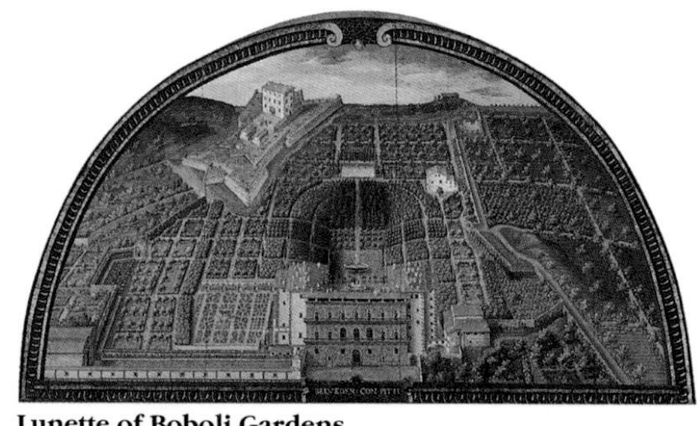

Lunette of Boboli Gardens
The Flemish artist Giusto Utens painted this picture of the Palazzo Pitti and Boboli Gardens in 1599.

VISITORS' CHECKLIST

Piazza de' Pitti. **Map** 3 B2 (5 B5). **Boboli Gardens** ***Tel*** *055 29 48 83.* *D, 11, 36, 37.* *Jun–Aug: 8:15am–7:30pm daily; Apr, May, Sep & Oct: 8:15am–6:30pm daily; Nov–Feb: 8:15am–4:30pm daily; Mar: 8:15am–5:30pm daily.* *1st & 4th Mon of month; 1 Jan, 1 May, 25 Dec.* **Museo degli Argenti** & **Museo delle Porcellane** ***Tel*** *see p121.* *as for Boboli Gardens, above.*

The Porcelain Museum is accessed via the Rose Garden.

Viottolone
The avenue of cypress trees, planted in 1612, is lined with Classical statues.

★ L'Isolotto (Little Island)
The centrepiece of the moated garden is Giambologna's Oceanus Fountain *(1576). The original statue of Oceanus has been moved to the Bargello* (see pp68–9).

Hemicycle (semicircular lawn)

Entrance

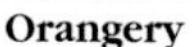

Orangery
Zanobi del Rosso's Orangery (1777–8) was built to protect rare, tender plants from frost.

STAR FEATURES

★ La Grotta Grande

★ Amphitheatre

★ L'Isolotto (Little Island)

Brancacci Chapel ⑩

The church of Santa Maria del Carmine is famous for *The Life of St Peter* frescoes in the Brancacci Chapel, commissioned by the Florentine merchant Felice Brancacci around 1424. Masolino began the work in 1425 but many of the scenes are by his pupil, Masaccio, who died before completing the cycle. Filippino Lippi finished the work 50 years later, in 1480. Masaccio's use of perspective in *The Tribute Money* and the tragic realism of his figures in *The Expulsion of Adam and Eve* placed him at the vanguard of Renaissance painting. Many great artists, including Michelangelo, later visited the chapel to study his pioneering work.

St Peter Heals the Sick
Masaccio's realistic portrayal of cripples and beggars was revolutionary in his time.

In every scene, St Peter is distinguished from the crowds as the figure in the orange cloak.

The grouping of stylized figures in Masaccio's frescoes reflects his interest in the sculpture of his contemporary Donatello *(see p69)*.

Masaccio's simple style allows us to focus on the figures central to the frescoes without distracting detail.

Expulsion of Adam and Eve
Masaccio's ability to express emotion is well illustrated by his harrowing portrait of Adam and Eve being driven out of the Garden of Eden, their faces wracked by misery, shame and the burden of self-knowledge.

KEY TO THE FRESCOES: ARTISTS AND SUBJECTS

- Masolino
- Masaccio
- Lippi

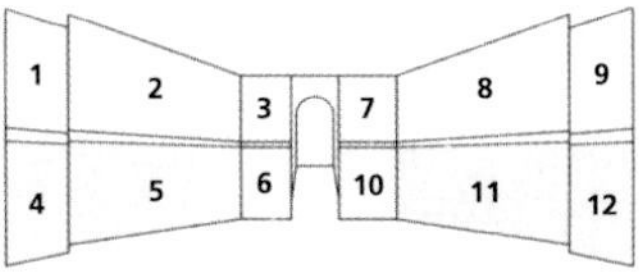

1 Expulsion of Adam and Eve
2 The Tribute Money
3 St Peter Preaching
4 St Peter Visited by St Paul
5 Raising the Emperor's Son; St Peter Enthroned
6 St Peter Healing the Sick
7 St Peter Baptizing the Converts
8 St Peter Healing the Cripple; Raising Tabitha
9 Temptation of Adam and Eve
10 St Peter and St John Giving Alms
11 Crucifixion; Before the Proconsul
12 The Release of St Peter

VISITORS' CHECKLIST

Piazza del Carmine. **Map** 3 A1 (5 A4). ***Tel*** *055 238 21 95.* *D.* *10am–5pm Mon, Wed–Sat; 1–5pm Sun (reservation required – call 055 276 85 58).* *Tue, public hols.*

Masolino's *Temptation of Adam and Eve* is gentle and decorous, in contrast with the emotional force of Masaccio's painting on the opposite wall.

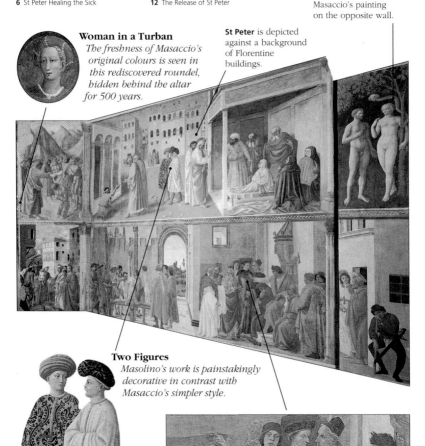

Woman in a Turban
The freshness of Masaccio's original colours is seen in this rediscovered roundel, hidden behind the altar for 500 years.

St Peter is depicted against a background of Florentine buildings.

Two Figures
Masolino's work is painstakingly decorative in contrast with Masaccio's simpler style.

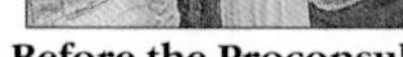

Before the Proconsul
Filippino Lippi was called in to complete the unfinished cycle of frescoes in 1480. He added this emotional scene showing the Proconsul sentencing St Peter to death.

FOUR GUIDED WALKS

In Florence the countryside is never very far away, and you can be walking down quiet, rural lanes within just a few minutes of leaving the Ponte Vecchio *(see pp106–7)*, in the bustling heart of the city. The first walk is popular with the Florentines, who like to stroll on a Sunday beneath the city walls and take in the panoramic views that can be enjoyed from San Miniato al Monte and the Piazzale Michelangelo. Fiesole, the setting for the second walk, is 8 km (5 miles) north of Florence. It was once a powerful Etruscan city, but was later eclipsed by the rise of Florence, so that it is now merely a village. There are archaeological remains to provide a hint of its previous glory. The third walk shows Renaissance Florence at its best, taking in Brunnelleschi's cupola and many of the grand palazzi. The last walk ends in the serene Piazza Santo Spirito after exploring the Florentine backstreets.

Bust, Museo Faesulanum

Roman ruins in Fiesole
(see Fiesole walk pp132–3)

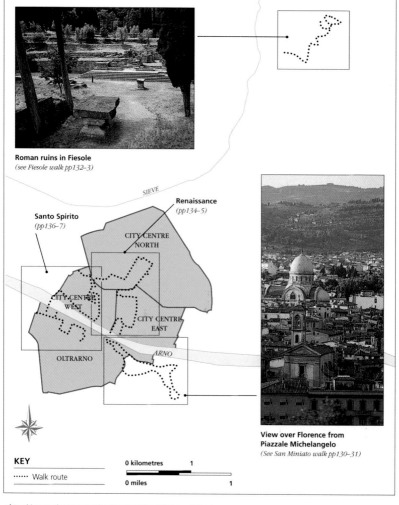

SIEVE

Renaissance
(pp134–5)

Santo Spirito
(pp136–7)

CITY CENTRE NORTH

CITY CENTRE WEST

CITY CENTRE EAST

ARNO

OLTRARNO

View over Florence from Piazzale Michelangelo
(See San Miniato walk pp130–31)

KEY

······ Walk route

0 kilometres 1

0 miles 1

◁ **Looking up the steps to the church of San Miniato al Monte**

A Two-Hour Walk to San Miniato al Monte

This walk takes you from the centre of Florence to the exquisitely decorated church of San Miniato al Monte high on a hill in the south of the city. The route follows quiet lanes along the city walls, and then takes in the bustling Piazzale Michelangelo, packed with souvenir stalls, before returning to the town centre.

No. 19 Costa di San Giorgio ③

From the Ponte Vecchio ① walk south down Via de' Guicciardini and take the second turning left into the square fronting Santa Felicità ②. On the left of the church, take the steep road to the right, Costa di San Giorgio. No. 19 ③ was once the home of Galileo. The Porta San Giorgio (St George's Gate) ④ is straight ahead at the end of the lane.

Built in 1260, this is the oldest city gate to survive in Florence. The weathered fresco within the arch is *The Virgin with St George and St Leonard* by Bicci di Lorenzo (1460). On the outer face of the arch is a carving of St George fighting the dragon, a copy of the original 1284 work, which has been removed and is currently being restored.

The Forte di Belvedere ⑤ is to the right through the gate, and was designed by Bernardo Buontalenti in 1590. Originally the fortress was built to guard the city against attack from its political rivals, but it soon became a private refuge for the Medici Grand Dukes. From here there are extensive views over the Boboli Gardens ⑥ below, and across to the olive groves and cypress trees in the countryside south of the city. Head downhill along Via di Belvedere, which runs along a stretch of city walls (to the left) dating from 1258. Porta San Miniato ⑦, a small arch in the wall, is situated at the bottom of the hill.

San Miniato al Monte

Turn right into Via del Monte alle Croci and walk uphill for 500 m (550 yds) to the Viale Galileo Galilei. Bear right and cross the road to the vast stone steps leading to the terrace in front of San Miniato al Monte ⑧. Catch your breath and admire the view of the Forte di Belvedere.

San Miniato al Monte is one of the most unspoiled of all the Romanesque churches in Tuscany. It was built in 1018 over the shrine of the early Christian martyr, San Miniato (St Minias). He was a rich Armenian merchant beheaded for his beliefs by Emperor Decius in the 3rd century. The façade was begun around 1090 and has geometric patterning in green-grey and white marble, typical of the Romanesque style. The statue on the gable shows an eagle carrying a bale of cloth, the symbol of the powerful Arte di Calimala (guild of wool

The façade of San Miniato al Monte ⑧

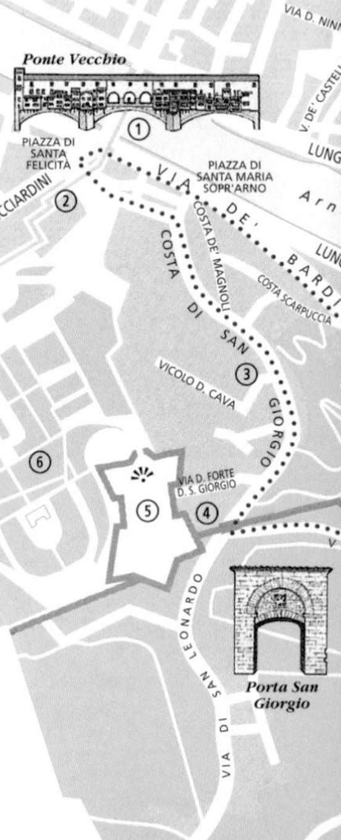

View across to San Miniato al Monte from Forte di Belvedere ⑤

importers) who financed the church in the Middle Ages. The restored 13th-century mosaic below the gable shows Christ, the Virgin and St Minias. Inside the church, the High Altar is raised above the nave and there is a Byzantine-style mosaic in the apse, again of St Minias with Christ and the Virgin. Below this is the crypt, built using columns salvaged from ancient Roman buildings. The floor of the nave is covered with seven marble mosaic panels of lions, doves and the signs of the Zodiac (1207); similar intarsia work panels can be seen on the raised marble choir and pulpit. In the north wall is the funeral chapel of the 25-year-old Cardinal of Portugal, Iacopo di Lusitania, who died in Florence in 1439. Antonio Rossellino carved the figure of the cardinal guarded by angels on the elaborate marble tomb (1466). The terracotta roundels on the ceiling, showing the Holy Spirit and Virtues, were sculpted by Luca della Robbia (1461). Outside, the massive belltower was begun in 1523 by Baccio d'Agnolo, but was never finished. Cannons were installed here to shoot at the Medici troops during the Siege of Florence *(see pp52–3)*. The cemetery ⑨ surrounding the church opened in 1854 and this contains tombs the size of miniature houses, built to show off family wealth.

13th-century mosaic on San Miniato façade

Leave San Miniato by an arch in the buildings to the west and follow the path that threads down to the church of San Salvatore al Monte ⑩. Here steps lead down to the Viale Galileo Galilei; take a right turn to reach Piazzale Michelangelo ⑪. The piazzale was laid out in the 1860s by Giuseppe Poggi, and is dotted with copies of Michelangelo's famous statues. It is lined with souvenir stalls and has far-reaching views over the rooftops of central Florence.

San Salvatore al Monte ⑩

Either take the No. 13 bus back to the city centre, or the stone steps on the west side of the piazza down to Porta San Niccolò ⑫, a 14th-century gateway in the city wall. Go left along Via di San Niccolò and Via de' Bardi, lined with medieval buildings. This includes the 13th-century Palazzo de' Mozzi ⑬ on Via de' Bardi; the Museo Bardini ⑭ *(see p119)* is opposite. From here you can return along the Arno to the Ponte Vecchio ①.

David **in Piazzale Michelangelo ⑪**

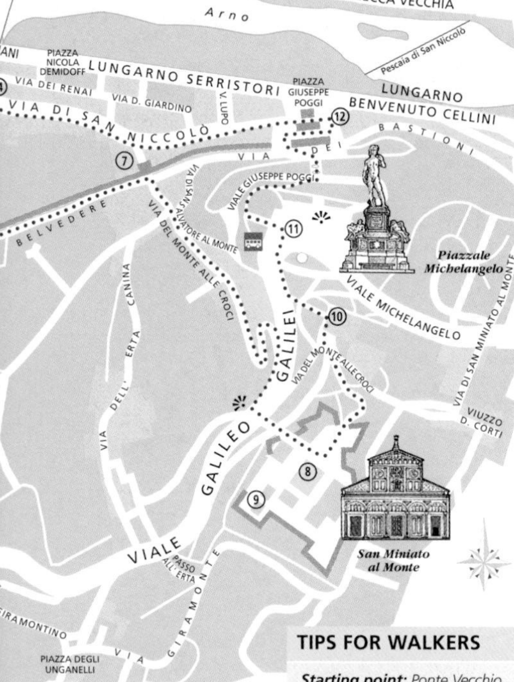

KEY

······ Walk route

Viewing point

0 metres **500**

0 yards **500**

TIPS FOR WALKERS

Starting point: *Ponte Vecchio.*
Length: *3 km (2 miles).*
San Miniato al Monte: *Open Apr–Oct: 8am–7:30pm daily; Nov–Mar: 8am–1pm, 2:30–6pm daily.*
Stopping-off points: *There are several cafés along the route.*

A Two-Hour Walk through Fiesole

The village of Fiesole stands in the foothills of the Mugello region, 8 km (5 miles) north of Florence, and has substantial Roman and Etruscan remains. The area has been a popular summer retreat since the 15th century, thanks to its fresh breezes and hilltop position.

The belltower of the Duomo ②

Piazza Mino da Fiesole

The No. 7 bus arrives at its last stop, in Fiesole's main square ①, after a 30-minute journey from Florence through countryside dotted with villas. Settled in the 7th century BC, Fiesole was a powerful force in central Italy by the 5th century BC. It began to decline after the Romans founded Florence in the 1st century BC, but kept its independence until 1125, when Florentine troops razed most of the city. The Duomo of San Romolo ② in the piazza was begun in 1028 and has a massive belltower. The bare Romanesque interior has columns which are topped with reused Roman capitals.

From here, walk up the square to the front of the 14th-century Palazzo Comunale ③. Here there is a bronze statue of King Vittorio Emanuele II and Garibaldi, called *Incontro di Teano* (Meeting at Teano) ④. Returning to the church, take the first turning right, down Via Dupre, to the Roman theatre ⑤ and into the archaeological park.

The bronze statue *Incontro di Teano* ④

After its defeat by Florence in 1125, Fiesole went into a decline, and many Etruscan and Roman remains went undisturbed until excavation in the 1870s. The Teatro, built in the 1st century BC, is used for the annual Estate Fiesolana festival *(see pp38–9)*. Its tiers of stone seats can hold 3,000 spectators. Next to the theatre is the Museo Faesulanum ⑥, built in 1912–14. Inside are finds from the Bronze Age onwards: coins, jewellery and ceramics, bronzes and marble sculpture. The building is a copy of the 1st-century Roman temple whose remains are in the northern part of the complex. It is built on Etruscan foundations, and part of the Roman frieze dating from the 1st century BC is still intact. There are some partly restored Roman baths close by ⑦, and, at

Roman theatre complex ⑤

TIPS FOR WALKERS

Starting point: *Piazza Mino da Fiesole.*
Length: *1.5 km (1 mile). Allow 2–3 hours for the walk to include time to visit the various museums. Note that Via di San Francesco is steep.*
Badia Fiesolana: *Open Sunday morning for services.*
Getting there: *No. 7 bus from Piazza di San Marco in Florence.*
Stopping-off points: *There are several cafés around Piazza Mino da Fiesole. The tiny ice-cream parlour Il Tucano (Via Gramsci 8) is also worth a stop.*

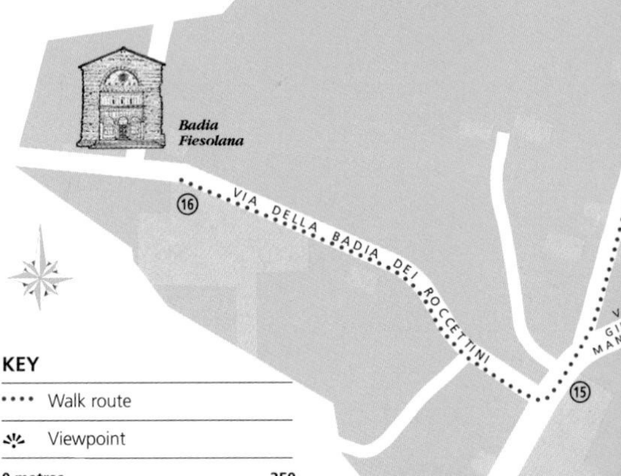

the northern edge of the park, 4th-century BC Etruscan walls ⑧. From the theatre turn into Via Dupre to Museo Bandini ⑨ to the right, with a collection of medieval religious paintings built up by local aristocrat Angelo Bandini in the 19th century.

Back in Piazza Mino da Fiesole, turn right down Via di San Francesco to the left of the Palazzo Vescovile ⑩. There are views over Florence and back to Fiesole ⑪ on the road up to Sant'Alessandro church ⑫, which has a Neo-Classical façade combined with a 9th-century

Fiesole from Via di San Francesco

Romanesque interior. Original Roman columns used in the nave are made out of *cipollino* (onion ring) marble. From here carry on up to San Francesco ⑬, a Franciscan friary founded in 1399 and restored in 1907. It has a pretty cloister and a museum of artifacts collected by the monks.

From Fiesole to San Domenico

Retrace your steps or walk through the park back to the town centre. Continue down Via Vecchia Fiesolana. On the left is the Villa Medici ⑭, built in 1461 by Michelozzo for Cosimo de' Medici. Walk down Via Bandini and Via Vecchia Fiesolana to San Domenico. In this little hamlet is the 15th-century church of San Domenico ⑮, with two good works by Fra Angelico, Dominican prior of the monastery here until 1437. The *Madonna with Angels* and *The Crucifixion* are in the chapter house and were both painted around 1430.

Opposite, Via della Badia dei Roccettini leads to the Badia Fiesolana ⑯, a pretty church with a Romanesque façade of inlaid marble. The interior is decorated with local grey sandstone, *pietra serena*. The No. 7 bus back to Florence can be caught from the village square in San Domenico.

Façade of Badia Fiesolana ⑯

The 15th-century church of San Francesco ⑬

A 90-Minute Walk Around Renaissance Florence

This walk takes in the Renaissance heart of the city and passes some of its greatest landmarks. Ideally, it should be done early on in your visit to get a real feel for the place, and if you incorporate a climb up Giotto's Campanile, you will get a bird's eye view of the narrow streets, the characteristic red-tiled rooftops and the many towers that are not so easy to see from ground level.

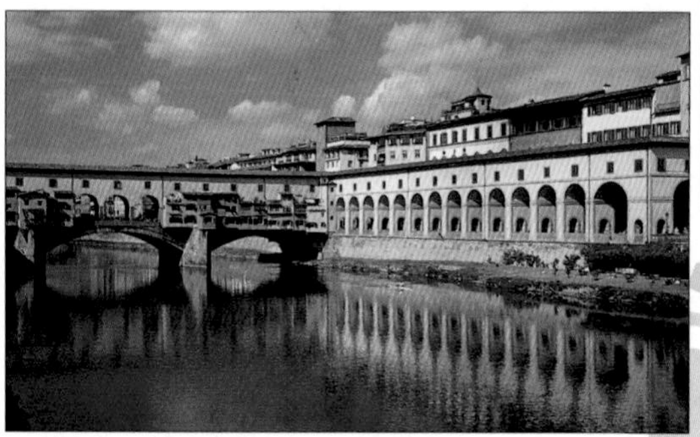

View of Ponte Vecchio and Vasari corridor ①

Ponte Vecchio to Piazza di San Firenze

The walk begins in the centre of the Ponte Vecchio ① *(see pp106–7)*, where butcher's and grocery shops were first built in the 13th century, then replaced by goldsmiths at the end of the 16th century. The bust here is of Benvenuto Cellini, the most famous goldsmith of them all. Note the Vasari Corridor with its round windows running over the shops on the eastern side of the bridge. Walk north up Via Por Santa Maria. A short way along on the right is Vicolo Santo Stefano and the ancient, deconsecrated church of Santo Stefano al Ponte ②, which was badly damaged in 1993 when a car bomb exploded in nearby Via Lambertesca. Further up Por Santa Maria is the Mercato Nuovo ③ *(see p112)*, a site on which there has been a market for centuries. The famous bronze "*porcellino*" (wild boar) is on the southern side; he is a copy of a copy of a sculpture by Tacca. It is said that if you rub his snout you will return to Florence one day. Turn right into Piazza della Signoria, past the open air sculpture gallery of the Loggia dei Lanzi ④ and turn right to walk the length of the Uffizi gallery portico *(see pp80–81)* and back along the opposite side. Turn right and take Via della Ninna out of the square; turn left at the end into Piazza di San Firenze ⑤. On the corner of Via dei Gondi stands Sangallo's late 15th-century Palazzo Gondi, which has a very graceful courtyard. The huge Baroque building opposite (1772–5) houses the law courts; to its left is the 17th-century church of San Filippo Neri, which has a painted ceiling.

Via del Proconsolo to Via dei Servi

At the north end of the square on the left, its tall, slim tower rising above the surrounding rooftops, is the Badia Fiorentina ⑥, one of the city's oldest churches. Across the street is the forbidding ex-prison building that now houses the Bargello museum ⑦ *(see pp68–9)* and its superb collection of sculpture. Continue north up Via Proconsolo. At no. 10 stands Palazzo Pazzi-Quaratesi, once the home of the Pazzi family of bankers, protagonists in the famous Pazzi conspiracy against the Medici of 1478. At no. 12 is Buontalenti's Palazzo Nonfinito *(see p70)* begun in 1593 and "unfinished", which today houses the Anthropological Museum and its wonderfully old-fashioned collection of curios. Via Proconsolo emerges at the east end of the Duomo ⑧ *(see pp64–5)*. Skirt around the south side of this massive building, past the stone plaque known as "*Il Sasso di Dante*" ⑨, where the poet would sit and contemplate the construction of the cathedral; it's on the left just before Via dello Studio.

Neptune Fountain in Piazza della Signoria ④

Enter Piazza di San Giovanni with its extraordinary religious buildings, crowds of visitors, and postcard sellers. Just south of the Baptistery at the top of Via de' Calzaiuoli is

PIAZZA DELLA STAZIONE
VIA SANT'ANTONINO
VIA FAENZA
PIAZZA DELL'UNITÀ ITALIANA
VIA DEL MELARANCIO
VIA DEGLI AVELLI
⑰
VIA PANZANI
VIA DEL GIGLIO
PIAZZA DI SANTA MARIA NOVELLA
VIA DELLA SCALA
VIA DEI BANCHI
VIA D. RONDINELLI
VIA DELLE BELLE DONNE
VIA DEL SOLE
V. D. TORNABUONI
VIA DEGLI AGLI
V. D. STRO
V. PO ROS
VIA DELL
B. SANTI A
LUNGA D. ACCIAI

the 14th-century Loggia del Bigallo ⑩. Piazza di San Giovanni is the heart of religious Florence and if you have the time and energy to climb the 400-odd steps of the Giotto's Campanile, you will be rewarded by a close-up of the great dome by Brunelleschi *(see pp64–5)*, and a view of the city below. Afterwards, walk round the north side of the Duomo and turn left up Via dei Servi. At no. 10 is Palazzo Niccolini with its typical mid-16th century façade ⑪. If the main door is open, you can see into the courtyard and small garden beyond with its double loggia. A little further up, take a right turn into Via degli Alfani where Brunelleschi's octagonal Rotonda di Santa Maria degli Angeli ⑫ is on the right.

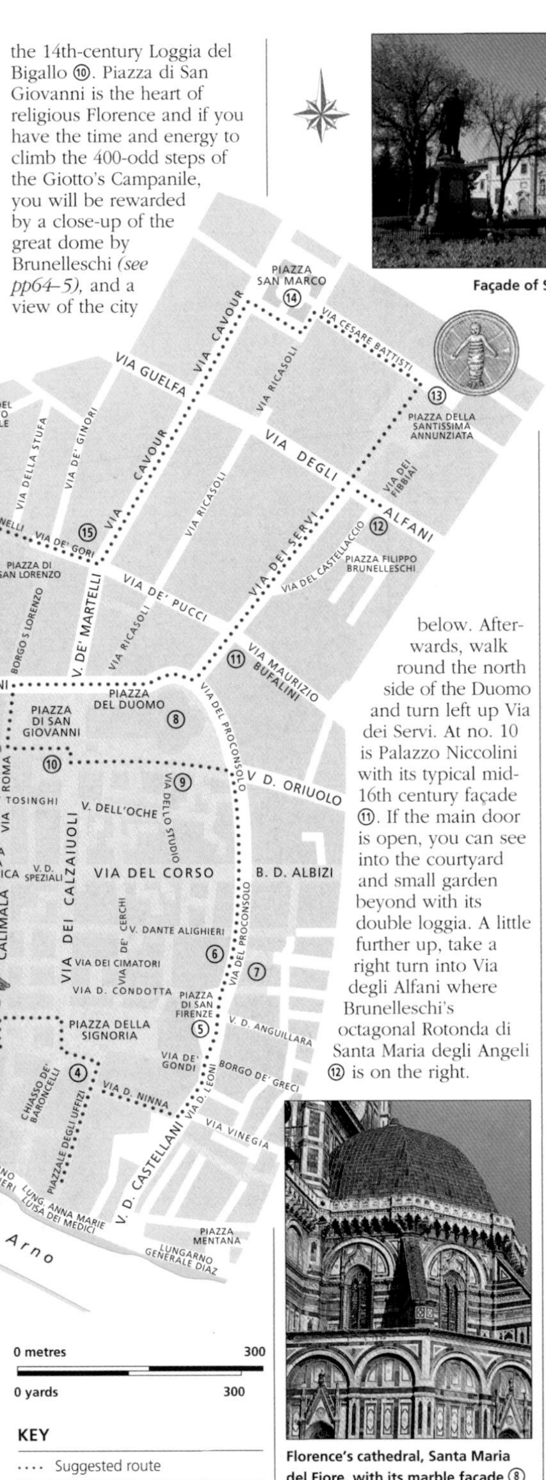

Façade of San Marco from Piazza San Marco ⑭

Florence's cathedral, Santa Maria del Fiore, with its marble façade ⑧

Piazza Santissima Annunziata to Santa Maria Novella

Go back to Via dei Servi and right to Piazza Santissima Annunziata ⑬ *(see p98)*, flanked on the right side by Brunelleschi's loggia and the *Spedale degli Innocenti (see p95)*. Turn left out of the square on Via Cesare Battisti and enter the Piazza San Marco ⑭. The portico immediately left dates from 1384 and was once part of a hospital. Today, it is home to the Accademia di Belle Arti, an art school founded in 1784. Also in the piazza is the convent of San Marco *(see pp96–7)* where Fra Angelico's sublime frescoes are housed. Walk south down Via Cavour to Palazzo Medici-Riccardi ⑮ *(see p89)*, where the Cappella dei Magi is painted with Benozzo Gozzoli's delightfully vivid fresco. Turn right along Via de' Gori to the church of San Lorenzo and the Medici Chapels ⑯ *(see pp90–91)*.

Walk past the chapels and bear right down Via del Melarancio. Cross Piazza dell'Unita Italiana and Via Panzani to make your way into Piazza di Santa Maria Novella where the walk finishes at the Santa Maria Novella church, under Alberti's glorious symmetrical façade ⑰ *(see pp110–11)*. To return to the Duomo, catch the no. 1 bus from the Piazza.

TIPS FOR WALKERS

Starting point: *The Ponte Vecchio*
Length: *3 km (2 miles)*
Getting there: *The bridge is an easy walk from the city centre.*
Stopping-off points: *There are plenty of bars and cafés along the way.*

A 90-Minute Walk to Piazza Santo Spirito

This walk begins under the clock at the Santa Maria Novella train station, which is one of the city's few significant modern buildings. It takes you to one of Florence's greatest churches, leads along one of the city's most fashionable shopping streets, and visits Piazza Santa Trinità, with its elegant medieval palaces. You cross the Arno river into the western limits of the Oltrarno area with its fascinating artisan workshops, taking in Piazza del Carmine and finishing in the heart of the Bohemian district at Piazza Santo Spirito.

View across the Piazza Santa Maria Novella to the parish church ③

Stazione di Santa Maria Novella

Begin under the digital clock on the south side of Florence's main train station ① *(see p113)*. Designed in 1935, this is one of the few important "modern" buildings in a city dominated by Medieval and Renaissance architecture. The Italians invented the digital clock and the one here is an early version. Cross over Piazza della Stazione and bear left towards the back of the great parish church of Santa Maria Novella *(see pp110–11)* ②. Follow the arched recesses along one side of the church, which were once the family vaults of Florentine nobles, and you will emerge in the Piazza Santa Maria Novella ③, a once scruffy square that has undergone renovation. At the southern end is the Loggia di San Paolo, a copy of Brunelleschi's famous Loggia degli Innocenti dating from 1489. In the 17th century the piazza was used for carriage races and the two obelisks sitting on turtles marked the turning points. Exit the square on the south side along Via dei Fossi and turn left into Via della Spada, a busy local shopping street. On the right is the former church of San Pancrazio ④, one of the oldest in Florence and, today, home to the Museo Marino Marini *(see p104)*. Turning left into Via delle Belle Donne, right into Via del Trebbio and right again will bring you out in Via de' Tornabuoni with its impressive mansions and designer shops *(see p105)*. On the corner is Palazzo Antinori ⑤ *(see p112)*, built by Giuliano da Maiano from 1461–69; you can walk into the splendid courtyard. Note the 17th-century church of San Gaetano across the road with its a fine Baroque façade.

A designer shop in chic Via de' Tornabuoni

Piazza Santa Trinità

Walk past Palazzo Strozzi *(see p105)* and down to Piazza Santa Trinità ⑥ *(see p108)*, which marks the meeting of three ancient Roman roads and is lined with noble palaces. Walk towards the river and turn right along Lungarno Corsini. At no. 2 is Palazzo Masetti ⑦, today occupied by the British Consulate but once the home of Bonnie Prince Charlie's widow, the Countess of Albany, who later married the dramatist Vittorio Alfieri.

The huge building a little further down on the right is Palazzo Corsini ⑧; it houses the Corsini family's private art collection (entrance on Via del Parione), which includes works by artists such as Botticelli.

At Piazza Carlo Goldoni (named after the playwright whose statue is on the far side), continue west along Borgo Ognissanti which opens onto the Arno at Piazza Ognissanti ⑨. Palazzo Lenzi, on the right, was built in the mid-15th century and has a

0 metres 300

0 yards 300

KEY

····· Suggested route

Train station

façade decorated with sgraffiti; today it is home to the French Consulate. Overlooking the square is the church of Ognissanti *(see p113)*, which contains Botticelli's tomb and frescoes by Ghirlandaio. The latter's famous *The Last Supper*, is housed in the convent refectory next door, reached through a frescoed cloister.

One of the artisan workshops in the Oltrano area

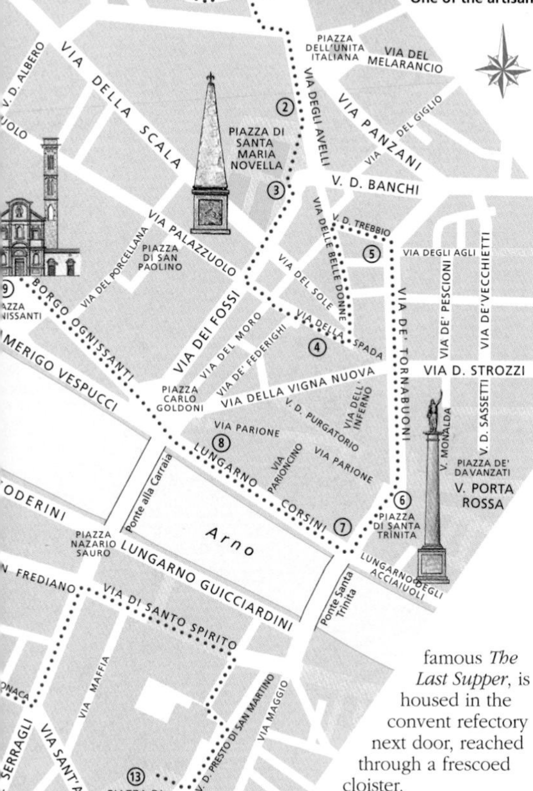

Across the River Arno

Cross the Ponte Amerigo Vespucci and walk on to Borgo San Frediano, a delightful area that's filled with artisan workshops and characteristic houses set on narrow streets. To the right is Porta San Frediano ⑩, built in 1324, whose massive wooden doors are still intact. The adjoining stretch of city wall is particularly well preserved.

Double back along Borgo San Frediano and turn left down Via Cestello into Piazza del Cestello ⑪, where the entrance to the church of San Frediano in Cestello *(see p119)* faces the river. Return to Borgo San Frediano turning right into Piazza del Carmine ⑫. The church of Santa Maria del Carmine is famous for its Brancacci Chapel *(see pp126–7)*, which is decorated with frescoes begun by Masolino and Masaccio, and finished by Filippino Lippi.

Leave the square at the southernmost corner along Via Santa Monaca and turn left into Via dei Serragli where there is a pretty tabernacle. Walk towards the river and turn right into Via di Santo Spirito. Note the Medici Crest at no. 58r, the 13th–14th-century Torre de' Lanfredini stands at no. 40r and Palazzo Frescobaldi (home of the wine-growing Frescobaldi family) is at nos. 5-13. Turn into Via de' Coverelli and walk to Piazza Santo Spirito ⑬, the heart of this Bohemian district and the walk's end. To return to the city centre, catch bus no. 11 to the Duomo.

A pavement café in the Piazza di Santo Spirito ⑬

TIPS FOR WALKERS

Starting point: *Santa Maria Novella Train Station.*
Length: *3.5 km (2 miles)*
Getting there: *You can walk to the station from the city centre.*
Stopping-off points: *There are plenty of bars and cafés along the way.*

FLORENCE STREET FINDER

Map references given for sights, restaurants, hotels and shops in Florence refer to the maps in the *Florence Street Finder* only *(see* How the Map References Work *opposite)*.

Where two map references are provided, the second (in brackets) relates to the large-scale maps, 5 and 6.

A complete index of street names is on pages 146–7. The key map below shows the area of Florence covered by each of the six maps in the *Florence Street Finder*. The maps encompass the four city-centre areas (colour-coded pink), which include all the sights. *(See also* Florence City Centre, *pp16–17.)*

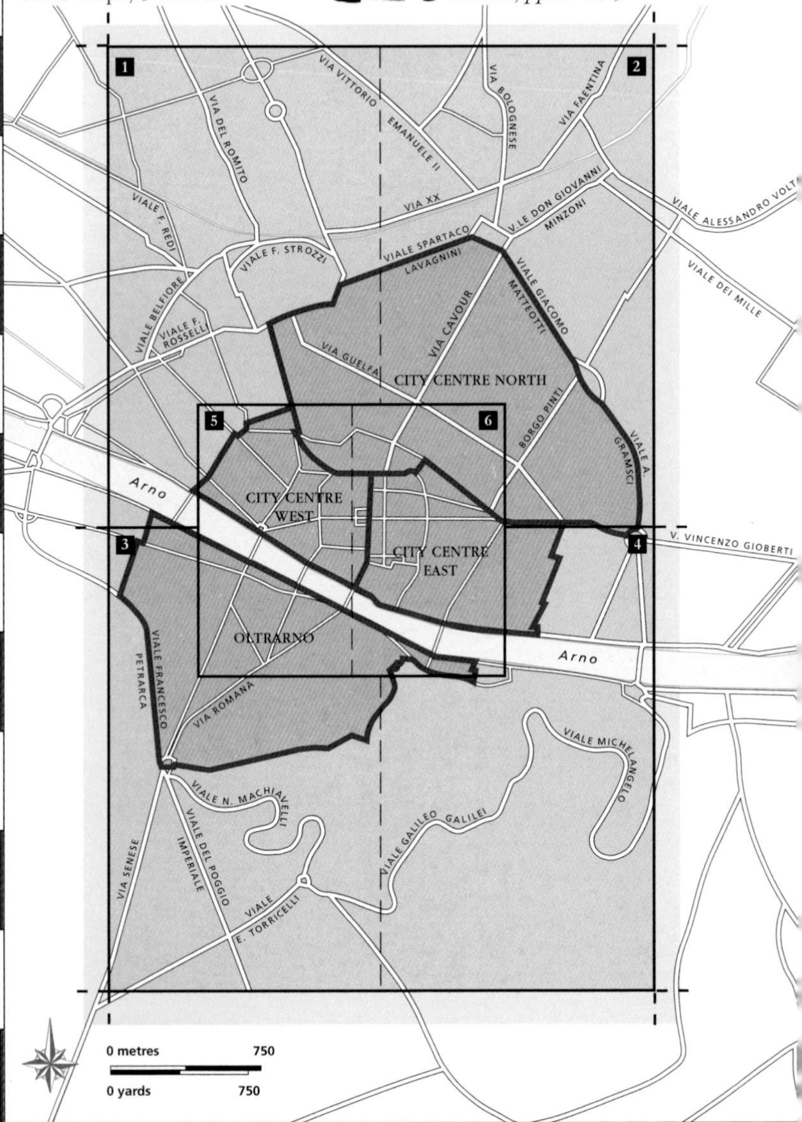

1
2
3
4
5
6
VIA VITTORIO EMANUELE II
VIA BOLOGNESE
VIA FAENTINA
VIA DEL ROMITO
VIA XX
V.LE DON GIOVANNI MINZONI
VIALE ALESSANDRO VOLTA
VIALE F. REDI
VIALE F. STROZZI
VIALE SPARTACO LAVAGNINI
VIALE DEI MILLE
VIALE BELFIORE
VIALE F. ROSSELLI
VIA CAVOUR
VIALE GIACOMO MATTEOTTI
VIA GUELFA
CITY CENTRE NORTH
BORGO PINTI
VIALE A. GRAMSCI
Arno
CITY CENTRE WEST
CITY CENTRE EAST
V. VINCENZO GIOBERTI
OLTRARNO
Arno
VIALE FRANCESCO PETRARCA
VIA ROMANA
VIALE MICHELANGELO
VIALE N. MACHIAVELLI
VIALE GALILEO GALILEI
VIA SENESE
VIALE DEL POGGIO IMPERIALE
VIALE E. TORRICELLI
0 metres 750
0 yards 750

HOW THE MAP REFERENCES WORK

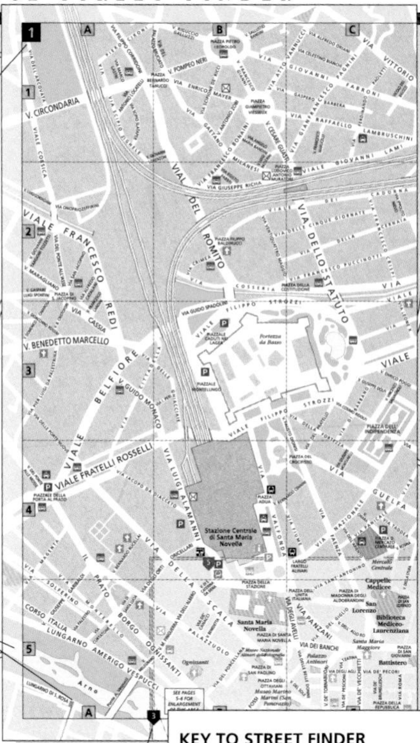

The first figure tells you which Street Finder map to turn to.

Ognissanti 17

Borgo Ognissanti 42. **Map** 1 B5 (5 A2) ***Tel*** *055 239 87 00.* ***Open*** *8am–noon, 4–7pm.*

The letter and number are a grid reference. You will find the letters at the top and bottom of the map and the numbers at the sides.

The second reference refers to the large-scale maps of Florence (5 & 6). It is read in exactly the same way as the first.

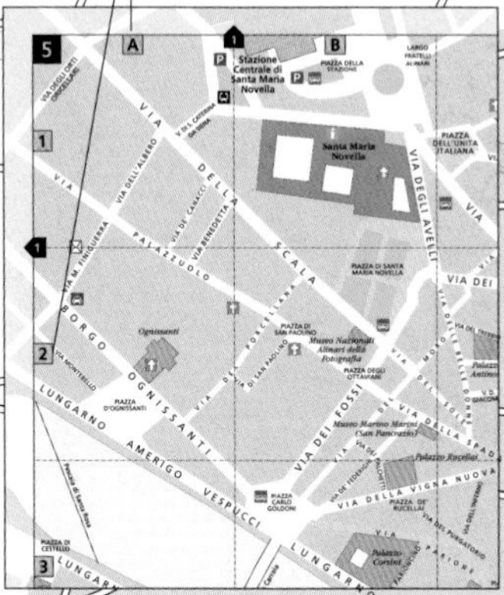

The map continues on map 3 of the Street Finder.

The key to the abbreviations used in the Street Finder is on page 146.

KEY TO STREET FINDER

- Major sight
- Places of interest
- Railway station
- Bus terminus
- Tram station
- Coach terminus
- Parking
- Tourist information office
- Hospital with casualty unit
- Police station
- Church
- Synagogue
- Post office
- Railway line
- Pedestrianized street
- City wall

SCALE OF MAPS 1–2 & 3–4

0 metres 200

0 yards 200

1:11,000

SCALE OF MAPS 5–6

0 metres 125

0 yards 125

1:6,000

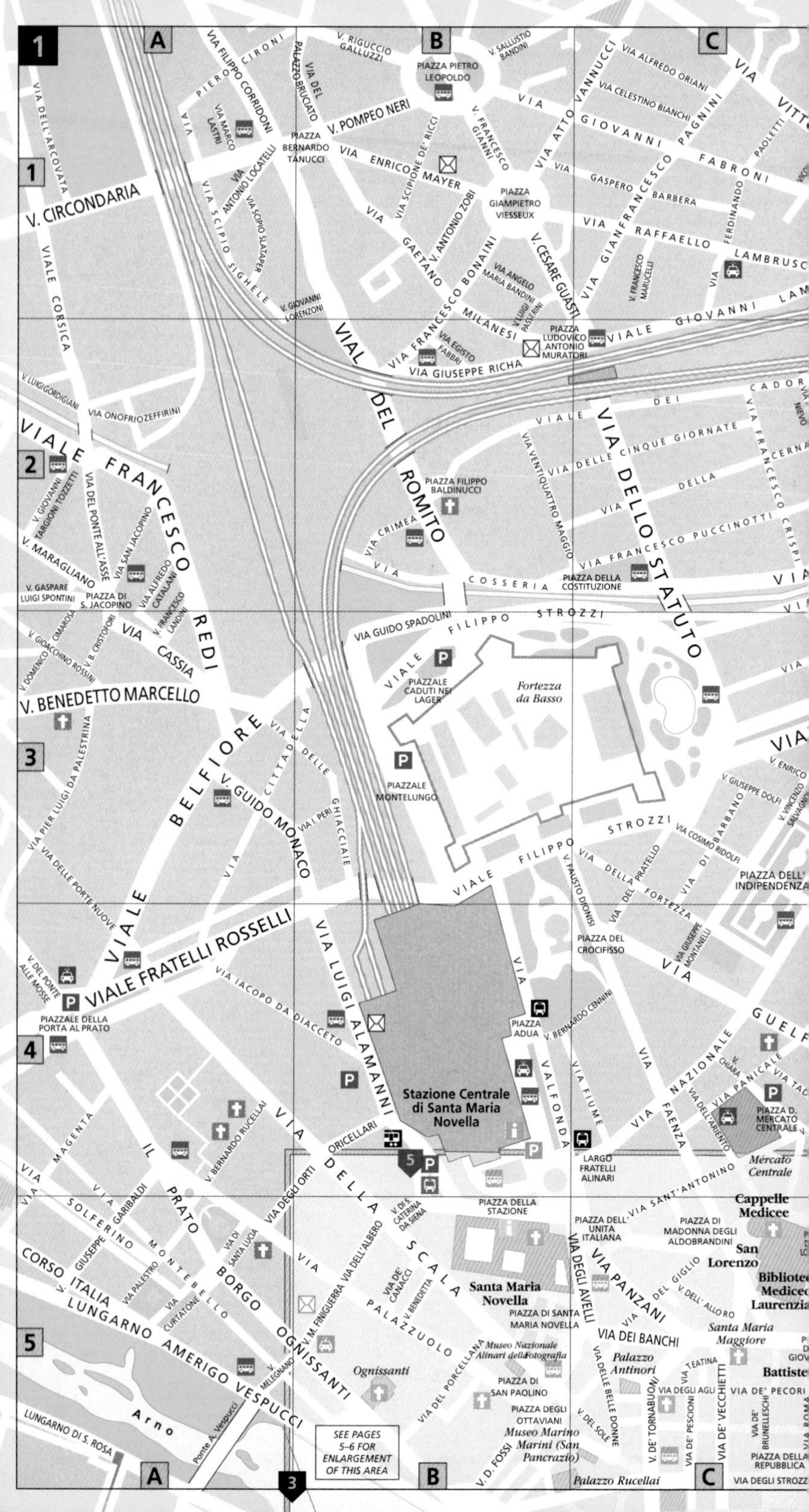
1
A
B
C
VIA DELL'ARCOVATA
VIA FILIPPO CORRIDONI
VIA PIERO CIRONI
VIA DEL PALAZZO BRUCIATO
V. RIGUCCIO GALLUZZI
PIAZZA PIETRO LEOPOLDO
V. SALLUSTIO BANDINI
VIA ATTO VANNUCCI
VIA ALFREDO ORIANI
VIA CELESTINO BIANCHI
VIA VITT
VIA MARCO LASTRI
V. POMPEO NERI
PIAZZA BERNARDO TANUCCI
VIA SCIPIONE DE' RICCI
V. FRANCESCO GIANNI
VIA GIOVANNI PAGNINI
VIA ENRICO MAYER
PIAZZA GIAMPIETRO VIESSEUX
VIA GASPERO BARBERA
VIA FABRONI
PAOLETTI
V. CIRCONDARIA
VIA ANTONIO LOCATELLI
VIA SCIPIO SLATAPER
VIA SCIPIO SIGHELE
V. ANTONIO ZOBI
VIA GAETANO MILANESI
VIA FRANCESCO BONAINI
VIA ANGELO MARIA BANDINI
V. CESARE GUASTI
VIA GIANFRANCESCO
VIA RAFFAELLO LAMBRUSCHINI
VIA FERDINANDO
V. FRANCESCO MARUCELLI
VIALE CORSICA
V. GIOVANNI LORENZONI
V. LUIGI PASSERINI
PIAZZA LUDOVICO ANTONIO MURATORI
VIALE GIOVANNI LAMI
VIAL DEL ROMITO
VIA FRANCESCO FABBRI
VIA EGISTO FABBRI
VIA GIUSEPPE RICHA
V. LUIGI GORDIGIANI
VIA ONOFRIO ZEFFIRINI
VIALE DEI CADORINI
VIA NIEVO
VIALE FRANCESCO REDI
2
V. GIOVANNI TARGIONI TOZZETTI
VIA DEL PONTE ALL'ASSE
VIA SAN JACOPINO
VIA DELLO STATUTO
VIA VENTIQUATTRO MAGGIO
VIA DELLE CINQUE GIORNATE
VIA FRANCESCO CRISPI
VIA DELLA CERNAIA
PIAZZA FILIPPO BALDINUCCI
VIA FRANCESCO PUCCINOTTI
VIA CRIMEA
V. MARAGLIANO
VIA ALFREDO CATALANI
V. GASPARE LUIGI SPONTINI
PIAZZA DI S. JACOPINO
VIA COSSERIA
PIAZZA DELLA COSTITUZIONE
VIA GUIDO SPADOLINI
VIALE FILIPPO STROZZI
V. FRANCESCO LANDINI
V. CIMAROSA
V. B. CRISTOFORI
VIA CASSIA
V. DOMENICO
V. GIOACCHINO ROSSINI
PIAZZALE CADUTI NEI LAGER
Fortezza da Basso
V. BENEDETTO MARCELLO
VIALE BELFIORE
VIA DELLE CITTADELLA
3
VIA PIER LUIGI DA PALESTRINA
V. GUIDO MONACO
PIAZZALE MONTELUNGO
V. ENRICO
V. GIUSEPPE DOLFI
V. VINCENZO SALVAGNOLI
VIA I. PERI
VIA DEI GHIACCIAIE
VIA DI BARBANO
VIA COSIMO RIDOLFI
VIA DELLE PORTE NUOVE
V. FAUSTO DIONISI
VIA DEL PRATELLO
VIA DELLA FORTEZZA
PIAZZA DELL' INDIPENDENZA
VIALE FRATELLI ROSSELLI
VIA LUIGI ALAMANNI
PIAZZA DEL CROCIFISSO
VIA GIUSEPPE MONTANELLI
V. DEL PONTE ALLE MOSSE
VIA IACOPO DA DIACCETO
PIAZZALE DELLA PORTA AL PRATO
4
PIAZZA ADUA
V. BERNARDO CENNINI
VIA GUELFA
VIA NAZIONALE
V. CHIARA
VIA PANICALE
VIA TADDEA
VIA VALFONDA
VIA FIUME
Stazione Centrale di Santa Maria Novella
VIA FAENZA
VIA DELL'ARIENTO
PIAZZA D. MERCATO CENTRALE
VIA MAGENTA
V. BERNARDO RUCELLAI
VIA DELLA SCALA
ORICELLARI
LARGO FRATELLI ALINARI
Mercato Centrale
VIA SOLFERINO
VIA GIUSEPPE GARIBALDI
IL PRATO
VIA DEGLI ORTI
V. DI S. CATERINA DA SIENA
PIAZZA DELLA STAZIONE
VIA SANT'ANTONINO
Cappelle Medicee
CORSO ITALIA
VIA PALESTRO
VIA MONTEBELLO
VIA DI SANTA LUCIA
BORGO OGNISSANTI
VIA DELL'ALBERO
PIAZZA DELL' UNITA ITALIANA
PIAZZA DI MADONNA DEGLI ALDOBRANDINI
San Lorenzo
V. LUNGARNO AMERIGO VESPUCCI
VIA CURTATONE
VIA DE' CANACCI
VIA PALAZZUOLO
V. BENEDETTA
Santa Maria Novella
VIA DEGLI AVELLI
VIA PANZANI
VIA DEL GIGLIO
V. DELL' ALLORO
Biblioteca Medicea Laurenziana
PIAZZA DI SANTA MARIA NOVELLA
5
V.M. FINIGUERRA
V. MELEGNANO
Museo Nazionale Alinari della Fotografia
VIA DEI BANCHI
Santa Maria Maggiore
Ognissanti
VIA DEL PORCELLANA
PIAZZA DI SAN PAOLINO
Palazzo Antinori
VIA DELLE BELLE DONNE
VIA TEATINA
VIA DEGLI AGLI
VIA DE' PECORI
Battistero
Arno
LUNGARNO DI S. ROSA
Ponte A. Vespucci
SEE PAGES 5–6 FOR ENLARGEMENT OF THIS AREA
PIAZZA DEGLI OTTAVIANI
Museo Marino Marini (San Pancrazio)
V. DEL SOLE
V. DE' TORNABUONI
VIA DE' PESCIONI
VIA DE' VECCHIETTI
VIA DE' BRUNELLESCHI
PIAZZA DELLA REPUBBLICA
V. D. FOSSI
Palazzo Rucellai
VIA DEGLI STROZZI
3

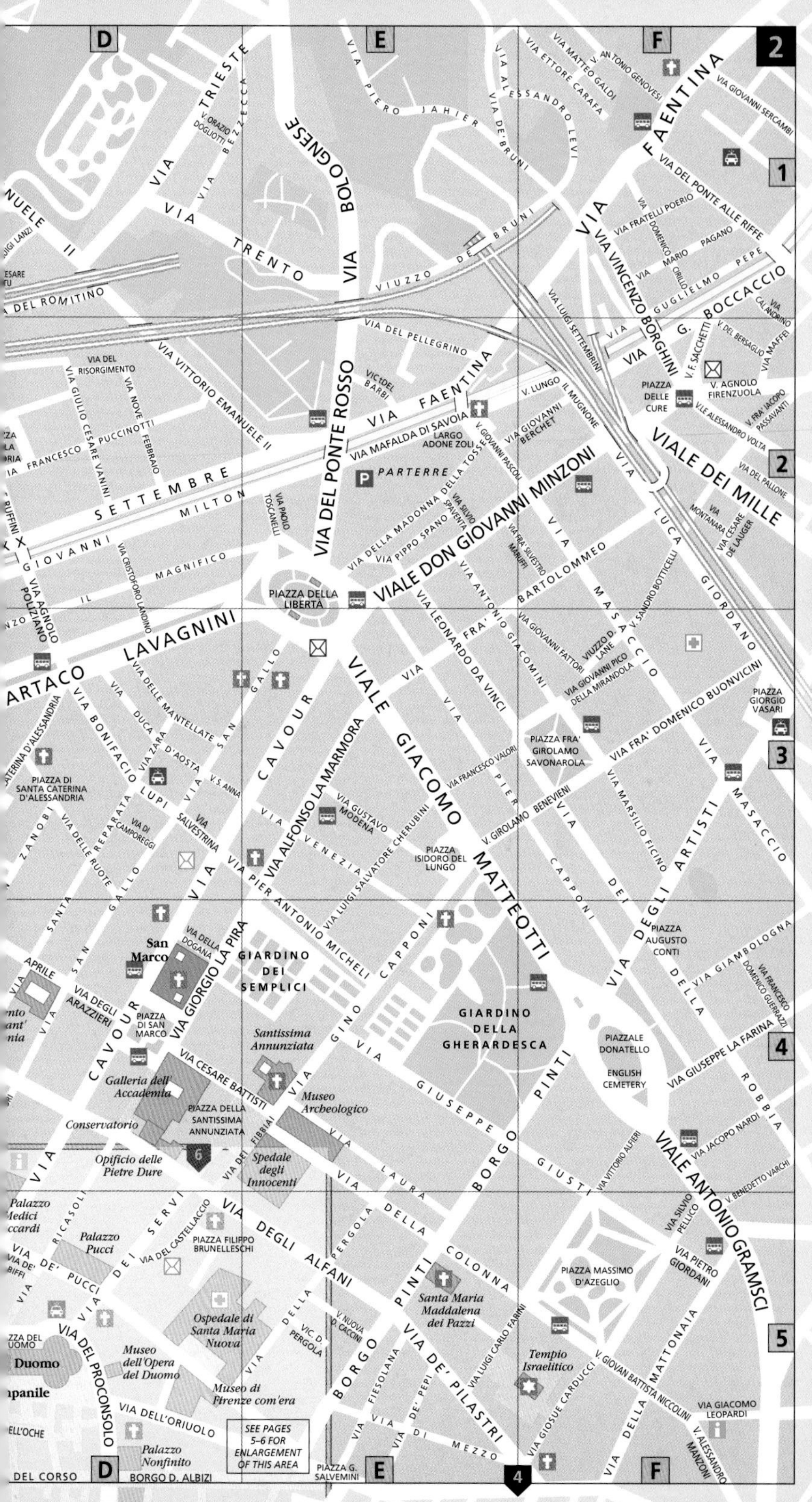
D
E
F
2
1
2
3
4
5
VIA FAENTINA
VIA BOLOGNESE
VIA TRENTO
VIA TRIESTE
VIA DEL PONTE ROSSO
VIA VITTORIO EMANUELE II
SETTEMBRE
VIA GIOVANNI MILTON
VIALE DON GIOVANNI MINZONI
PIAZZA DELLA LIBERTÀ
PARTERRE
VIALE DEI MILLE
PIAZZA DELLE CURE
VIA VINCENZO BORGHINI
VIA G. BOCCACCIO
LAVAGNINI
VIA CAVOUR
VIALE GIACOMO MATTEOTTI
VIA ALFONSO LA MARMORA
VIA LEONARDO DA VINCI
VIA FRA' BARTOLOMMEO
VIA MASACCIO
VIA LUCA GIORDANO
PIAZZA FRA' GIROLAMO SAVONAROLA
VIA FRA' DOMENICO BUONVICINI
PIAZZA GIORGIO VASARI
VIA DEGLI ARTISTI
PIAZZA DI SANTA CATERINA D'ALESSANDRIA
PIAZZA ISIDORO DEL LUNGO
VIA PIER ANTONIO MICHELI
VIA GIORGIO LA PIRA
San Marco
GIARDINO DEI SEMPLICI
PIAZZA DI SAN MARCO
GIARDINO DELLA GHERARDESCA
PIAZZA AUGUSTO CONTI
PIAZZALE DONATELLO
ENGLISH CEMETERY
Santissima Annunziata
Galleria dell' Accademia
PIAZZA DELLA SANTISSIMA ANNUNZIATA
Museo Archeologico
Conservatorio
Opificio delle Pietre Dure
Spedale degli Innocenti
VIA GIUSEPPE GIUSTI
BORGO PINTI
VIALE ANTONIO GRAMSCI
VIA DEGLI ALFANI
VIA DELLA COLONNA
Palazzo Medici Riccardi
Palazzo Pucci
PIAZZA FILIPPO BRUNELLESCHI
Ospedale di Santa Maria Nuova
Santa Maria Maddalena dei Pazzi
PIAZZA MASSIMO D'AZEGLIO
Tempio Israelitico
Duomo
Museo dell'Opera del Duomo
Museo di Firenze com'era
VIA DEL PROCONSOLO
VIA DELL'ORIUOLO
VIA DE' PILASTRI
VIA DELLA MATTONAIA
Palazzo Nonfinito
BORGO D. ALBIZI
PIAZZA G. SALVEMINI
VIA GIACOMO LEOPARDI
SEE PAGES 5–6 FOR ENLARGEMENT OF THIS AREA
6
4

3
SEE PAGES 5–6 FOR ENLARGEMENT OF THIS AREA
LUNGARNO SODERINI
BORGO SAN FREDIANO
LUNGARNO CORSINI
LUNGARNO GUICCIARDINI
LUNGARNO D. ACCIAIUOLI
BORGO SAN JACOPO
VIA DI SANTO SPIRITO
Cappella Brancacci (Santa Maria del Carmine)
San Frediano in Cestello
Palazzo Corsini
Palazzo Strozzi
Santa Trinita
Palazzo Spini-Feroni
Palazzo Bartolini-Salimbeni
Palazzo Davanzati
Palazzo di Parte Guelfa
Santi Apostoli
Orsanmichele
Mercato Nuovo
Santo Spirito
Cenacolo di Santo Spirito
Santa Felicita
Palazzo Pitti
Museo La Specola
GIARDINO TORRIGIANI
GIARDINO DI BOBOLI
Forte di Belvedere
PIAZZA DELLA CALZA
PIAZZALE DELLA PORTA ROMANA
VIALE FRANCESCO PETRARCA
VIALE NICCOLÒ MACHIAVELLI
VIA SENESE
VIALE DEL POGGIO IMPERIALE
V.LE EVANGELISTICA TORRICELLI
PIAZZALE GALILEO
VIA DI SAN LEONARDO
VIA ROMANA
VIA DE' SERRAGLI
VIA MAGGIO
VIA DEL GELSOMINO
VIA DANTE DA CASTIGLIONE

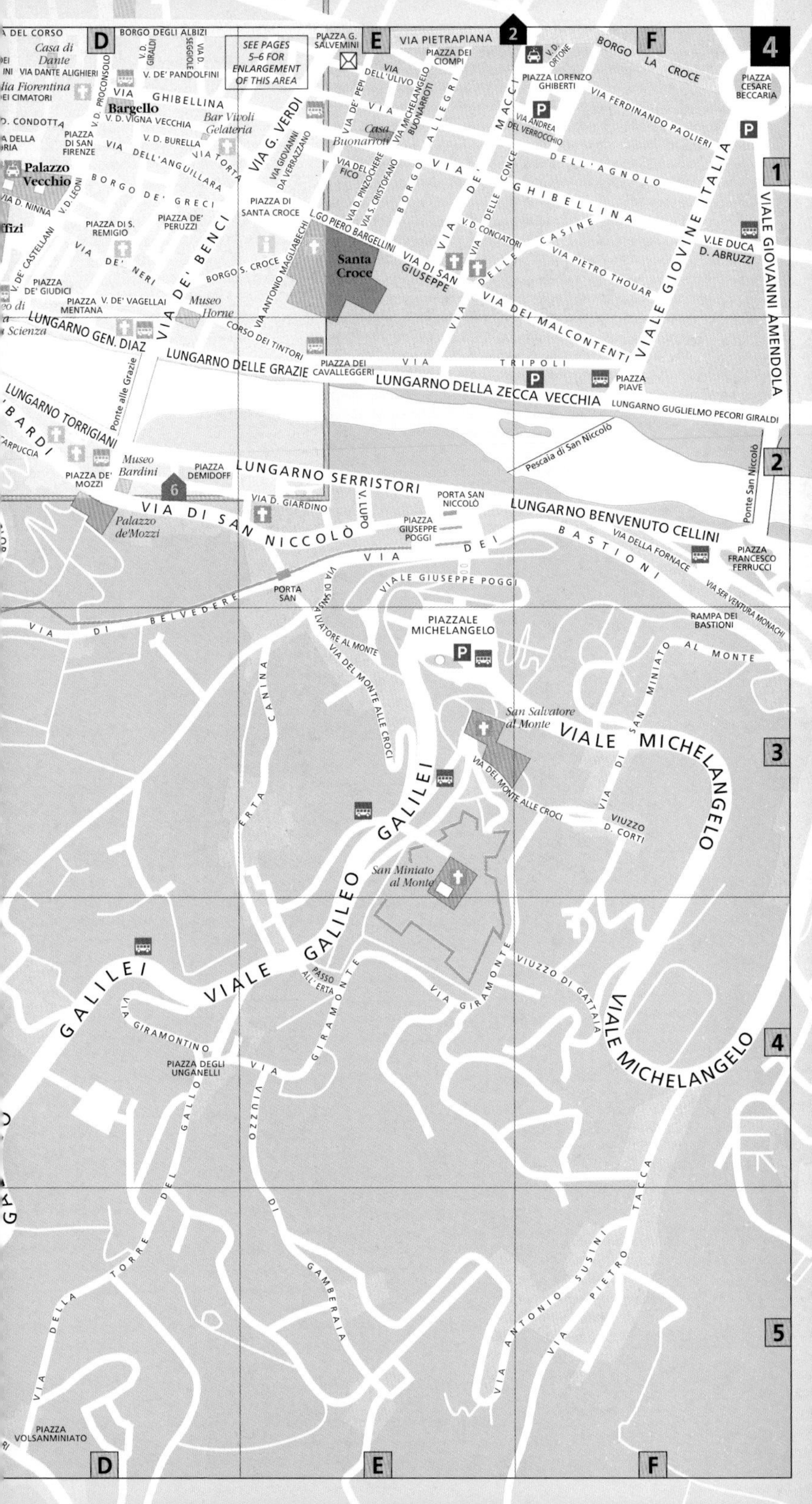

D
E
F
4
2
1
2
3
4
5
6
SEE PAGES 5–6 FOR ENLARGEMENT OF THIS AREA
BORGO DEGLI ALBIZI
PIAZZA G. SALVEMINI
VIA PIETRAPIANA
BORGO LA CROCE
PIAZZA CESARE BECCARIA
Casa di Dante
VIA DANTE ALIGHIERI
V. DE' PANDOLFINI
VIA GHIBELLINA
Bargello
V. D. VIGNA VECCHIA
Bar Vivoli Gelateria
VIA G. VERDI
PIAZZA DEI CIOMPI
PIAZZA LORENZO GHIBERTI
VIA FERDINANDO PAOLIERI
VIA ANDREA DEL VERROCCHIO
Casa Buonarroti
VIA MICHELANGELO BUONARROTI
VIA DELL'ULIVO
VIA DE' PEPI
VIA ALLEGRI
VIA DE' MACCI
VIA DELL'AGNOLO
PIAZZA DI SAN FIRENZE
V. D. BURELLA
VIA DELL'ANGUILLARA
VIA TORTA
VIA GIOVANNI DA VERRAZZANO
VIA DEL FICO
Palazzo Vecchio
BORGO DE' GRECI
PIAZZA DI SANTA CROCE
VIA D. PINZOCHERE
VIA S. CRISTOFANO
BORGO S. CROCE
VIA DELLE CONCE
VIA GHIBELLINA
VIALE GIOVINE ITALIA
VIALE GIOVANNI AMENDOLA
PIAZZA DI S. REMIGIO
PIAZZA DE' PERUZZI
L.GO PIERO BARGELLINI
Santa Croce
VIA DI SAN GIUSEPPE
V. D. CONCIATORI
VIA DELLE CASINE
VIA PIETRO THOUAR
V.LE DUCA D. ABRUZZI
VIA DE' NERI
VIA DE' BENCI
BORGO S. CROCE
VIA ANTONIO MAGLIABECHI
PIAZZA DE' GIUDICI
PIAZZA MENTANA
V. DE' VAGELLAI
Museo Horne
VIA DEI MALCONTENTI
LUNGARNO GEN. DIAZ
CORSO DEI TINTORI
LUNGARNO DELLE GRAZIE
PIAZZA DEI CAVALLEGGERI
VIA TRIPOLI
PIAZZA PIAVE
LUNGARNO DELLA ZECCA VECCHIA
LUNGARNO GUGLIELMO PECORI GIRALDI
Ponte alle Grazie
LUNGARNO TORRIGIANI
Pescaia di San Niccolò
Museo Bardini
PIAZZA DEMIDOFF
PIAZZA DE' MOZZI
LUNGARNO SERRISTORI
Ponte San Niccolò
PORTA SAN NICCOLÒ
V. LUPO
VIA D. GIARDINO
LUNGARNO BENVENUTO CELLINI
Palazzo de'Mozzi
VIA DI SAN NICCOLÒ
PIAZZA GIUSEPPE POGGI
VIA DEI BASTIONI
VIA DELLA FORNACE
PIAZZA FRANCESCO FERRUCCI
VIALE GIUSEPPE POGGI
VIA SER VENTURA MONACHI
PORTA SAN
VIA DI BELVEDERE
VIA DI SAN SALVATORE AL MONTE
PIAZZALE MICHELANGELO
RAMPA DEI BASTIONI
VIA DEL MONTE ALLE CROCI
VIA DI SAN MINIATO AL MONTE
San Salvatore al Monte
VIALE MICHELANGELO
ERTA CANINA
VIA DEL MONTE ALLE CROCI
VIUZZO D. CORTI
VIALE GALILEO GALILEI
San Miniato al Monte
VIUZZO DI GATTAIA
PASSO ALL'ERTA
VIA GIRAMONTE
VIA GIRAMONTINO
PIAZZA DEGLI UNGANELLI
VIUZZO DI GAMBERAIA
VIA DEL GALLO
VIA TORRE DEL GALLO
VIA DELLA TORRE
VIA PIETRO TACCA
VIA ANTONIO SUSINI
PIAZZA VOLSANMINIATO

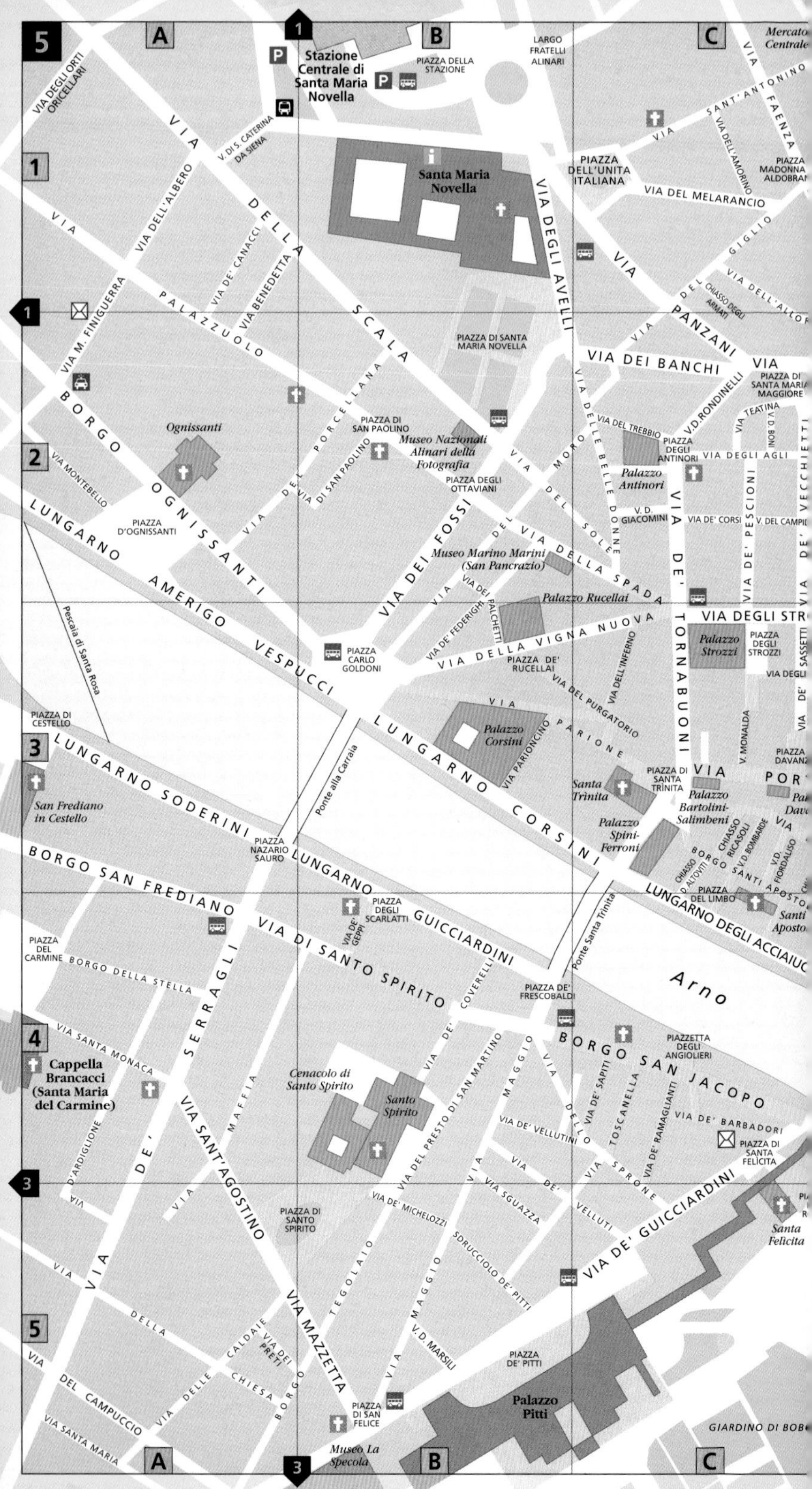
5
A
B
C
1
2
3
4
5
Stazione Centrale di Santa Maria Novella
Piazza della Stazione
Largo Fratelli Alinari
Mercato Centrale
Santa Maria Novella
Piazza di Santa Maria Novella
Piazza dell'Unita Italiana
Via degli Orti Oricellari
Via della Scala
Via dell'Albero
V. di S. Caterina da Siena
Via degli Avelli
Via Sant'Antonino
Via Faenza
Via dell'Amorino
Piazza Madonna Aldobrandini
Via del Melarancio
Via del Giglio
Via dell'Alloro
Via Panzani
Chiasso degli Armati
Via dei Banchi
Via M. Finiguerra
Via de' Canacci
Via Benedetta
Via Palazzuolo
Via della Porcellana
Borgo Ognissanti
Ognissanti
Via Montebello
Piazza d'Ognissanti
Piazza di San Paolino
Via di San Paolino
Museo Nazionali Alinari della Fotografia
Piazza degli Ottaviani
Via del Moro
Via delle Belle Donne
Via del Trebbio
V.D. Rondinelli
Via Teatina
Piazza di Santa Maria Maggiore
Piazza degli Antinori
Via degli Agli
Palazzo Antinori
V. D. Giacomini
Via de' Corsi
V. del Campidoglio
Via de' Pescioni
Via de' Vecchietti
V.D. Boni
Via del Sole
Via della Spada
Via dei Fossi
Museo Marino Marini (San Pancrazio)
Via dei Palchetti
Via de' Federighi
Palazzo Rucellai
Via della Vigna Nuova
Via de' Tornabuoni
Via degli Strozzi
Palazzo Strozzi
Piazza degli Strozzi
Via de' Sassetti
Lungarno Amerigo Vespucci
Pescaia di Santa Rosa
Piazza Carlo Goldoni
Piazza de' Rucellai
Via dell'Inferno
Via del Purgatorio
Via Parione
Palazzo Corsini
Via Parioncino
Piazza di Cestello
Lungarno Soderini
San Frediano in Cestello
Ponte alla Carraia
Lungarno Corsini
Piazza di Santa Trinita
Santa Trinita
Palazzo Spini-Feroni
Palazzo Bartolini-Salimbeni
V. Monalda
Piazza Davanzati
Via Porta Rossa
Palazzo Davanzati
Chiasso Ricasoli
V.D. Bombarde
V.D. Fiordaliso
Chiasso D. Altoviti
Borgo Santi Apostoli
Piazza del Limbo
Santi Apostoli
Lungarno degli Acciaiuoli
Piazza Nazario Sauro
Lungarno Guicciardini
Borgo San Frediano
Piazza degli Scarlatti
Via de' Geppi
Via di Santo Spirito
Ponte Santa Trinita
Arno
Piazza del Carmine
Borgo della Stella
Via de' Serragli
Via de' Coverelli
Piazza de' Frescobaldi
Borgo San Jacopo
Piazzetta degli Angiolieri
Via Santa Monaca
Cappella Brancacci (Santa Maria del Carmine)
Via Maffia
Cenacolo di Santo Spirito
Santo Spirito
Via del Presto di San Martino
Via Maggio
Via dello Sprone
Via de' Sapiti
Toscanella
Via de' Ramaglianti
Via de' Barbadori
Piazza di Santa Felicita
Via de' Vellutini
Via d'Ardiglione
Via Sant'Agostino
Via de' Velluti
Via Sguazza
Via de' Michelozzi
Piazza di Santo Spirito
Via de' Guicciardini
Santa Felicita
Sdrucciolo de' Pitti
Via della Chiesa
Via delle Caldaie
Via dei Preti
Via Mazzetta
Via Tegolaio
V.D. Marsili
Piazza de' Pitti
Via del Campuccio
Via delle ...
Borgo ...
Piazza di San Felice
Palazzo Pitti
Via Santa Maria
Museo La Specola
Giardino di Bob...

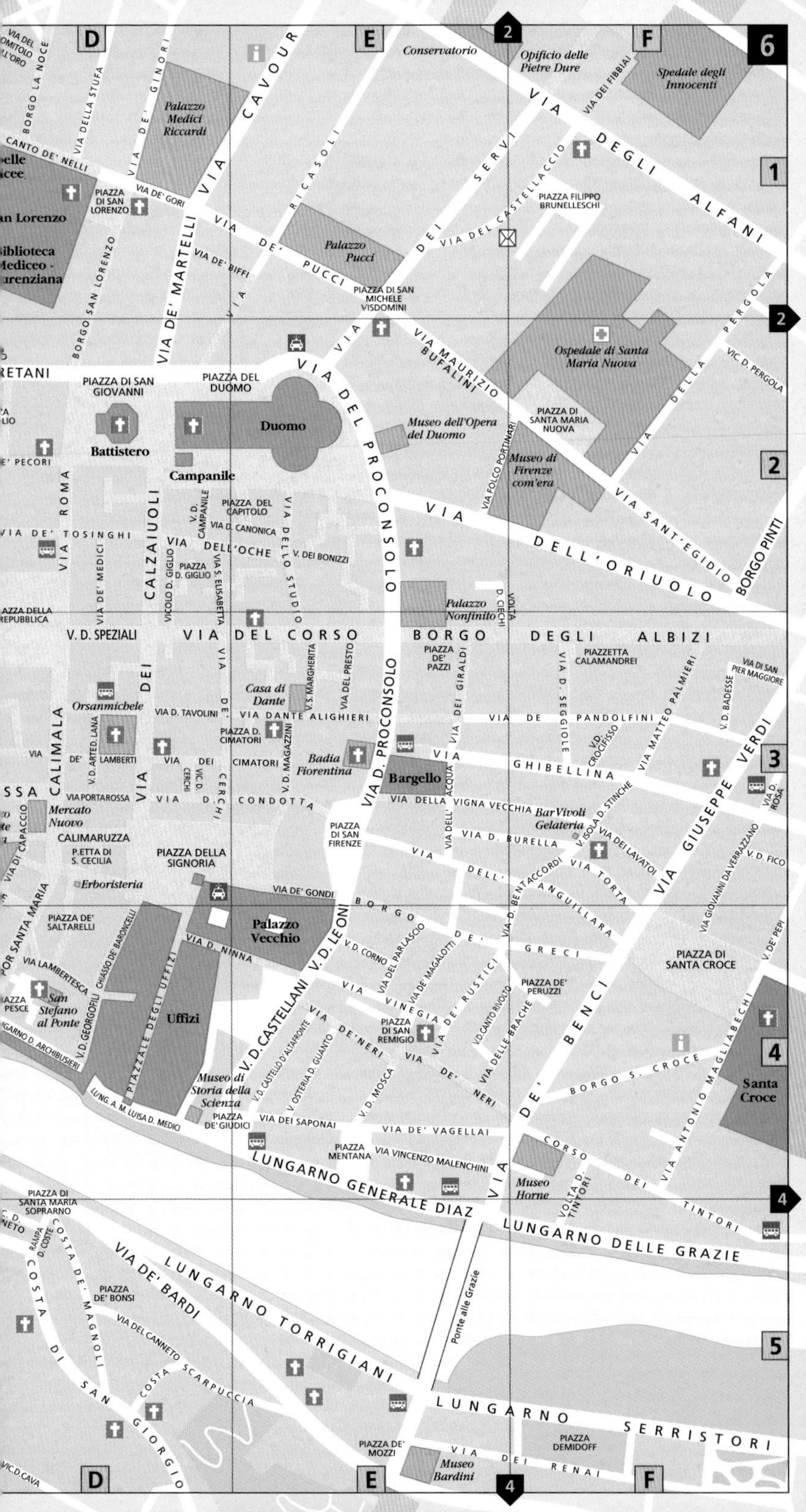

6
D
E
F
1
2
3
4
5
Palazzo Medici Riccardi
Conservatorio
Opificio delle Pietre Dure
Spedale degli Innocenti
San Lorenzo
Biblioteca Mediceo-Laurenziana
Palazzo Pucci
Ospedale di Santa Maria Nuova
Battistero
Campanile
Duomo
Museo dell'Opera del Duomo
Museo di Firenze com'era
Palazzo Nonfinito
Casa di Dante
Orsanmichele
Badia Fiorentina
Bargello
Mercato Nuovo
Bar Vivoli Gelateria
Erboristeria
Palazzo Vecchio
Uffizi
San Stefano al Ponte
Museo di Storia della Scienza
Santa Croce
Museo Horne
Museo Bardini
Ponte alle Grazie
VIA CAVOUR
VIA DEGLI ALFANI
VIA DEI SERVI
VIA RICASOLI
VIA DE' MARTELLI
VIA DE' PUCCI
VIA DEL PROCONSOLO
VIA MAURIZIO BUFALINI
VIA DELL'ORIUOLO
VIA DEL CORSO
BORGO DEGLI ALBIZI
VIA CALZAIUOLI
VIA ROMA
VIA DANTE ALIGHIERI
VIA GHIBELLINA
VIA GIUSEPPE VERDI
VIA DE' BENCI
BORGO DE' GRECI
LUNGARNO GENERALE DIAZ
LUNGARNO DELLE GRAZIE
LUNGARNO TORRIGIANI
LUNGARNO SERRISTORI
VIA DE' BARDI
COSTA DI SAN GIORGIO
PIAZZA DI SAN GIOVANNI
PIAZZA DEL DUOMO
PIAZZA DI SAN LORENZO
PIAZZA FILIPPO BRUNELLESCHI
PIAZZA DI SANTA MARIA NUOVA
PIAZZA DELLA SIGNORIA
PIAZZA DI SAN FIRENZE
PIAZZA DI SANTA CROCE
PIAZZA DE' GIUDICI
PIAZZA MENTANA
PIAZZA DE' MOZZI
PIAZZA DEMIDOFF
PIAZZA DE' BONSI
PIAZZA DI SANTA MARIA SOPRARNO

Street Finder Index

KEY TO ABBREVIATIONS USED IN THE STREET FINDER

d.	di, del, dell', dello, della, dei, de', delle, degli	**Lung.**	Lungarno	**P.te**	Ponte	**V.**	Via
		P.	Piazza	**S.**	San, Sant', Santa, Santo	**Vic.**	Vicolo
		P.ta	Porta	**SS.**	Santi, Santissima	**V.le**	Viale

Map references in parentheses refer to the larger scale map.

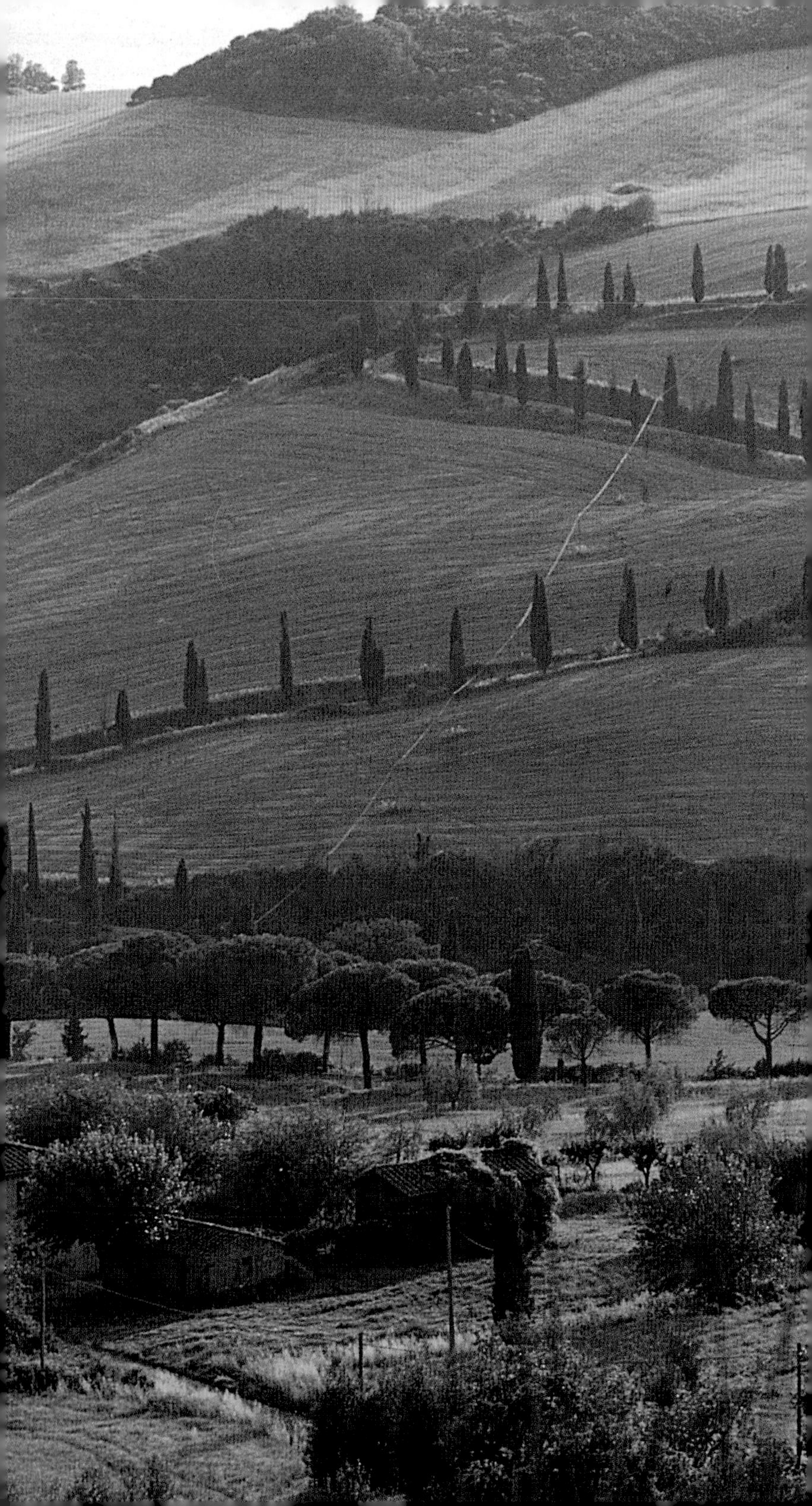

TUSCANY AREA BY AREA

Tuscany at a Glance

Tuscany is rich in culture and landscape. Out of Florence, most visitors' first port of call is Pisa, in Western Tuscany, with its Leaning Tower. Northern Tuscany has mountains and beaches, and Eastern Tuscany the lush forests of the Mugello. Siena and San Gimignano in Central Tuscany draw their own visitors, while Southern Tuscany with its sparse vegetation and unspoiled beaches is more off the beaten track.

Sights in Tuscany are grouped within their own sections in this book, corresponding with the colour-coded map below.

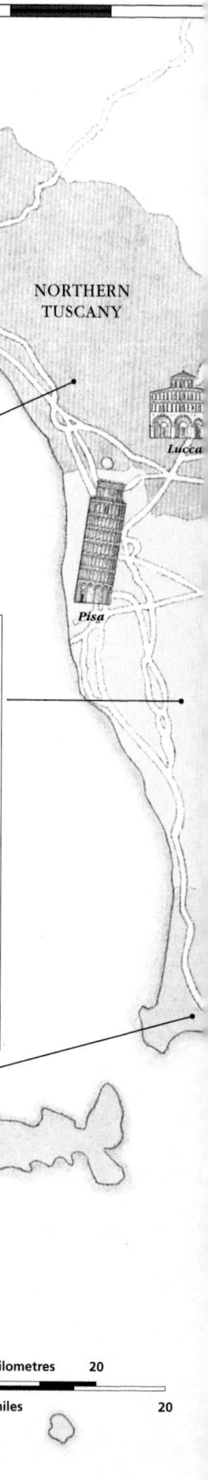

NORTHERN TUSCANY

Lucca

Pisa

NORTHERN TUSCANY
Pages 168–189

WESTERN TUSCANY
Pages 152–167

SOUTHERN TUSCANY
Pages 230–241

0 kilometres 20

0 miles 20

◁ **View of the beautiful Tuscan countryside**

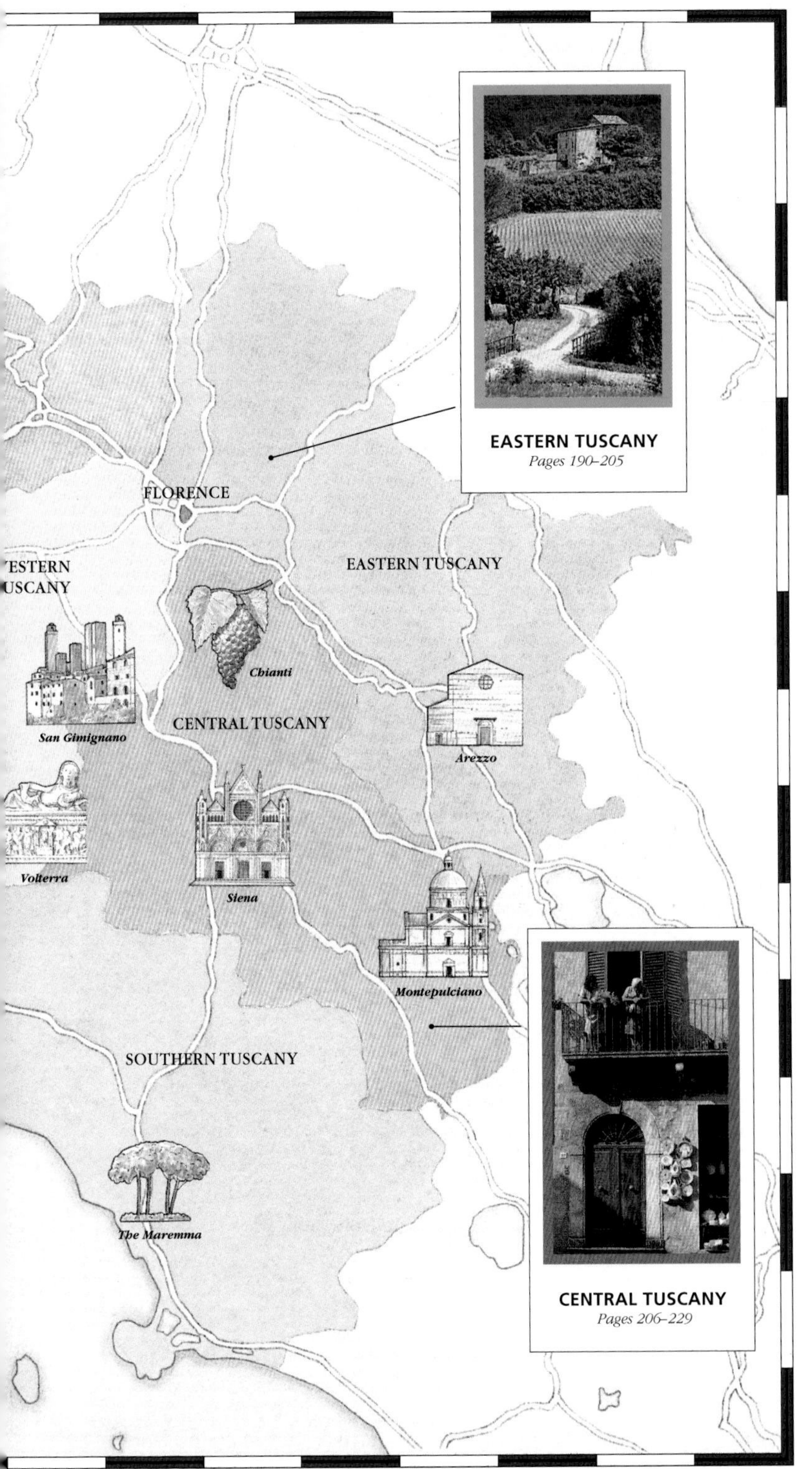
EASTERN TUSCANY
Pages 190–205
FLORENCE
'ESTERN
USCANY
EASTERN TUSCANY
Chianti
San Gimignano
CENTRAL TUSCANY
Arezzo
Volterra
Siena
Montepulciano
SOUTHERN TUSCANY
The Maremma
CENTRAL TUSCANY
Pages 206–229

WESTERN TUSCANY

Tuscany's hard-working economic engine, this area is characterized by its factories and ports, particularly Livorno. There are also some extraordinary sights, most famously the Leaning Tower of Pisa. To the south, the windswept ancient Etruscan town of Volterra, standing high on a barren plateau, has some of the finest museums and medieval architecture in Italy.

From the 11th to the 13th centuries, when at the height of its powers, Pisa dominated the Western Mediterranean. Its strong navy opened up extensive trading links with North Africa, and brought to Italy the benefits of Arabic scientific and artistic achievement.

These new ideas had a profound effect on 12th- and 13th-century architects working in western Tuscany. Many of the era's splendid buildings, for instance Pisa's Duomo, Baptistry and Campanile, are decorated with complex geometric patterns made from beautiful inlaid marble, alternating with bizarre arabesques.

During the 16th century the Arno estuary began to silt up, ending Pisan supremacy. In 1571, work began to establish Livorno as the region's main port. This proved so successful that it remains Italy's second busiest port. Pisa, meanwhile, is the gateway to Tuscany following the extensive development of Galileo Galilei airport. The Arno valley is mainly an industrial area, with huge factories producing glass, furniture, motorcycles, leather and textiles. Even so, there are some rewarding sights lurking within the urban sprawl, like the Romanesque church of San Piero a Grado or the entertaining museum in Vinci, which contains models of many of Leonardo da Vinci's brilliant inventions.

South of the Arno valley, the landscape is pleasant but unremarkable, consisting of rolling hills and expanses of agricultural land. But the imposing ancient town of Volterra, with its unmatched collection of Etruscan artifacts, demands a visit.

Landscape of rolling hills near Volterra

◁ The Leaning Tower, rising above the terracotta roofs of Pisa

Exploring Western Tuscany

Pisa, with its world-famous leaning tower, and Volterra, with a wealth of ancient Etruscan remains, are the highlights of the region. There is, however, much more to see, especially in the gentle hilly countryside that rises on either side of the Arno valley. It was here that Renaissance architects pioneered new styles of villa building; their work can be admired at Poggio a Caiano and Artimino. San Miniato is gloriously sited on a hilltop commanding extensive views; the museum in Vinci, on the other side of the valley, celebrates the inventive genius of Leonardo da Vinci.

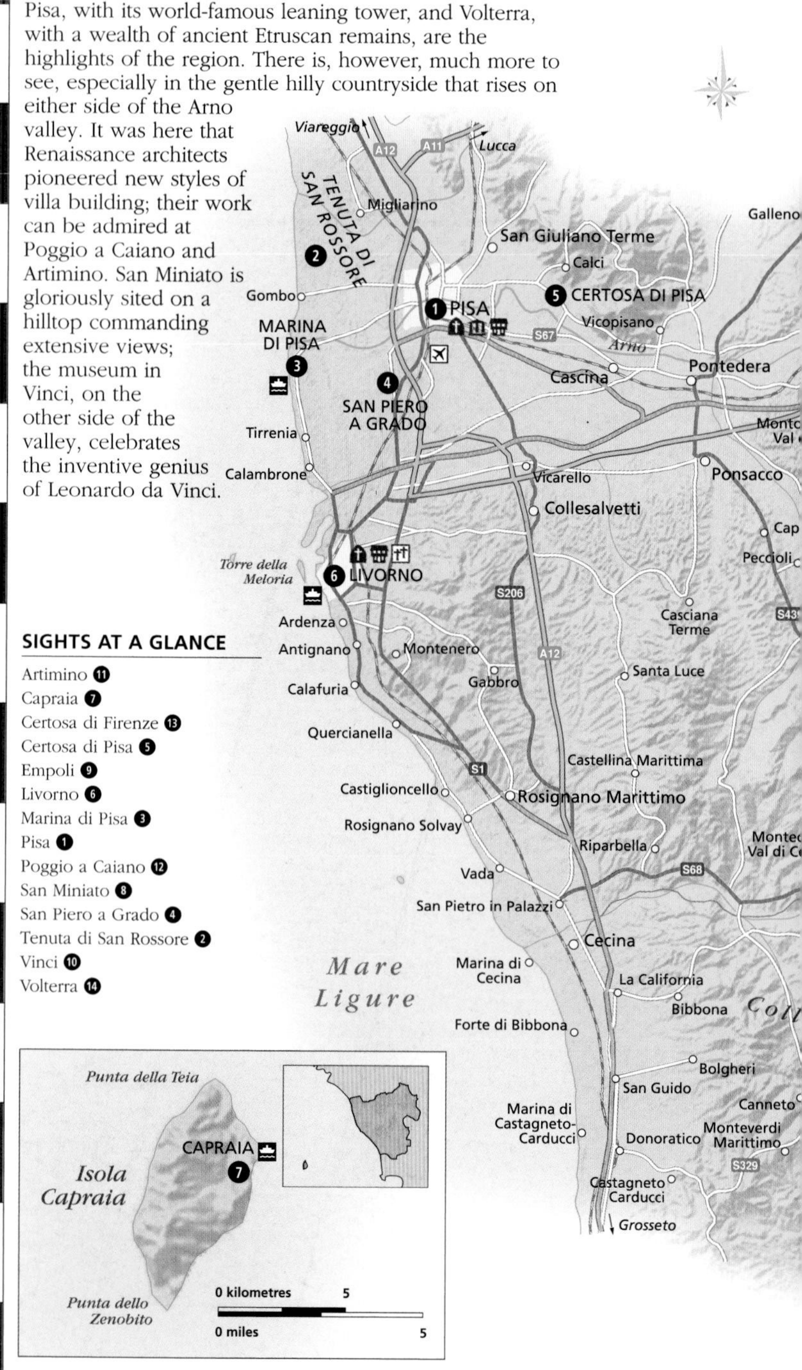

SIGHTS AT A GLANCE

- Artimino 11
- Capraia 7
- Certosa di Firenze 13
- Certosa di Pisa 5
- Empoli 9
- Livorno 6
- Marina di Pisa 3
- Pisa 1
- Poggio a Caiano 12
- San Miniato 8
- San Piero a Grado 4
- Tenuta di San Rossore 2
- Vinci 10
- Volterra 14

For additional map symbols *see back flap*

Venezia Nuova in Livorno, with its canals and waterways

GETTING AROUND

Western Tuscany has a number of busy roads. An express route, the Fi–Pi–Li motorway, links Pisa with Florence, but travellers may find the old S67 more convenient for reaching the sights lining the Arno valley. The S1 coastal road skirts Livorno on its way to Rome.

The region is well served by buses and trains. A regular rail service runs between Florence and Pisa, stopping at the major Arno valley towns.

It can be difficult to reach Volterra, as there is no train service, but several buses depart each day from Florence, Pisa and Livorno.

KEY

- Motorway
- Major road
- Secondary road
- Minor road
- Main railway
- Minor railway
- Summit

0 kilometres 10

0 miles 10

The S68 highway to Volterra

Pisa ❶

Inlaid marble, Duomo façade

From the 11th to the 13th centuries, Pisa's powerful navy ensured the city's dominance in the Western Mediterranean. Trading links with Spain and North Africa led to a cultural revolution *(see p46)* reflected in the splendid buildings of the era: the Duomo, Baptistry and Campanile. Pisa's decline was assured when the Arno began to silt up. Salt marsh, partly a nature reserve, now divides the city from the sea.

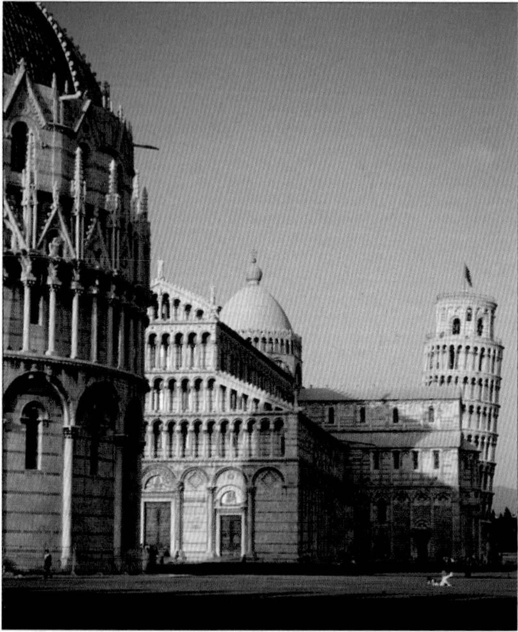
Campo dei Miracoli

Campo dei Miracoli

See pp158–9.

Museo delle Sinopie

Piazza del Duomo. ***Tel*** *050 387 22 10.* *10am–5pm daily.*

This fascinating museum displays sketches from the fresco cycle that once covered the walls of Campo Santo cemetery *(see pp158–9)*. The frescoes disintegrated when the cemetery was bombed in 1944, but the underlying sketches survived. They were removed from the walls for conservation before being rehoused in the museum. There are also displays showing how fresco artists went about their work.

Museo dell'Opera del Duomo

Piazza Duomo. ***Tel*** *050 387 22 10.* *Apr–Sep: 8am–8pm daily; Mar & Oct: 9am–6pm daily; Nov–Feb: 10am–5pm daily.*

Housed in the cathedral's 13th-century former Chapter House, the museum was opened in 1986. All the exhibits were formerly in the Duomo and Baptistry. Modern display methods ensure that they are excellently presented. Exhibits such as the intricately inlaid marble arabesque panels and fine Corinthian capitals reveal the twin influences of Rome and Islam on Pisan architects in the 12th and 13th centuries. Be sure to see the imposing 10th-century hippogriff (half horse, half gryphon); this statue, cast in bronze by Islamic craftsmen, was looted by Pisan adventurers during the wars against the Saracens.

The museum also contains 13th-century statues and sculptures by Nicola and Giovanni Pisano, including Giovanni's ivory *Virgin and Child* (1300) carved for the Duomo's High Altar. There are paintings from the 15th to 18th centuries, a fine Roman and Etruscan archaeological collection, and ecclesiastical treasures and vestments dating from the 12th century.

The museum cloister offers a wonderful view of the Leaning Tower *(see p160)*.

Piazza dei Cavalieri

The Piazza dei Cavalieri stands at the heart of Pisa's student quarter. The huge building on the north side of the square, covered in exuberant black and white *sgraffito* decoration (designs scratched into wet plaster), is the Palazzo dei Cavalieri and houses one of Pisa University's most prestigious colleges: the Scuola Normale Superiore. The site was originally occupied by Pisa's medieval town hall, but Cosimo I ordered its destruction when the city fell under Florentine rule. The council chamber, however, was spared and is now a lecture hall. The present flamboyant building was designed in 1562 by Vasari, as the headquarters of the Cavalieri di San Stefano, an order of knights created by Cosimo in 1561. An equestrian statue of Cosimo by Pietro Francavilla (1596) stands outside. Santo Stefano dei Cavalieri

10th-century bronze hippogriff

***Virgin and Child* polyptych (1321) by Simone Martini**

(1565–9), the knights' church, stands next to the Palazzo dei Cavalieri. Also designed by Vasari, it has a splendid gilded and coffered ceiling. The walls are hung with figureheads and battle standards. There is also a splendid organ (look out for notices of recitals).

On the other side of the Palazzo dei Cavalieri is the Palazzo dell'Orologio, incorporating the medieval town jail. The building, which is now housing a library, was the scene of a most shameful and gruesome historical episode. In 1288 Count Ugolino, mayor of Pisa, was accused of treachery and walled up with his sons and grandsons. The entire male side of the Ugolino family was wiped out.

Museo Nazionale di San Matteo

Piazzetta San Matteo in Soarta. ***Tel*** *050 54 18 65. 8:30am–7pm Tue–Sun (to 1pm Sun). 1 Jan, 1 May, 15 Aug, 25 Dec.*

The medieval convent of San Matteo, with its elegant Gothic façade, is located alongside the River Arno. Many exhibits in the museum inside are poorly labelled and the rooms leading off the cloister are unnumbered. Nevertheless, the museum presents a unique opportunity to examine the complete sweep of Pisan and Florentine art from the 12th to the 17th centuries.

Most of the earliest works portray the Virgin and Child. These include Simone Martini's fine polyptych (1321) and a 14th-century statue, the *Madonna del Latte*, attributed to Nino Pisano, another member of the talented family of sculptors. The half-length statue, in gilded marble, shows Christ feeding at his mother's breast. A number of early Renaissance pieces deserve to be sought out, particularly Masaccio's *St Paul* (1426), Gentile da Fabriano's radiant 15th-century *Madonna and Child*, and Donatello's reliquary bust of *San Rossore* (1424–7).

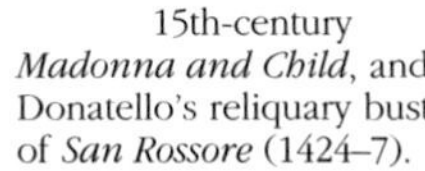

Grand Duke Cosimo I

VISITORS' CHECKLIST

Road map B2. *98,929. Galileo Galilei. Centrale, Viale Gramsci. Piazza Duomo (050 56 04 64). Piazza Vittorio Emanuele 16 (050 422 91). Airport (050 50 37 00). Wed, Sat.* **Shops** *Mon am. Gioco del Ponte* (see p38). **www**.pisaonline.it

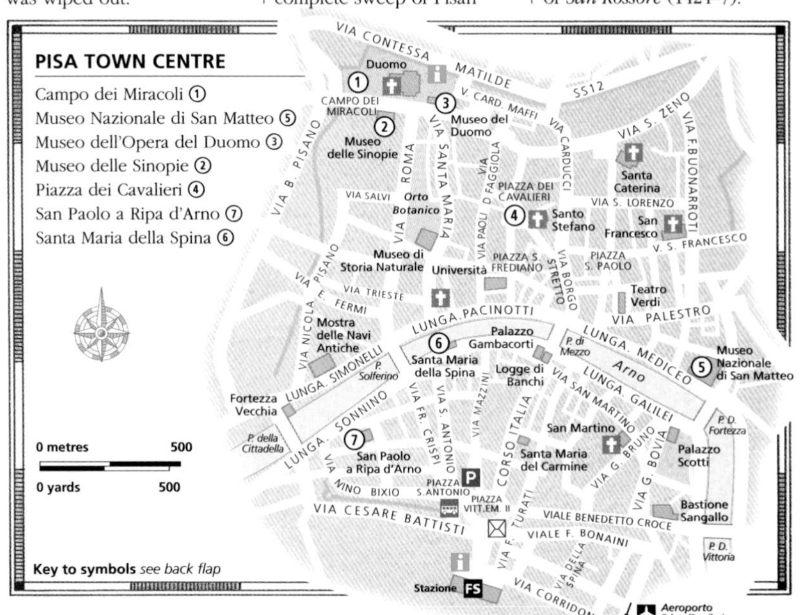

Campo dei Miracoli

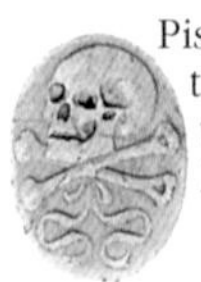

Cemetery memorial

Pisa's world famous Leaning Tower is just one of the splendid religious buildings that rise from the emerald-green lawns of the "Field of Miracles". Lying to the northwest of the city centre, it is partnered by the Duomo, begun in 1063, the Baptistry of 1152–1284 and the Campo Santo cemetery begun in 1278. These buildings combine definite Moorish elements, such as inlaid marble in geometric patterns (arabesques), with delicate Romanesque colonnading and spiky Gothic niches and pinnacles.

Campo Santo
The cemetery contains earth from the Holy Land and carved Roman sarcophagi.

The Triumph of Death
These late 14th-century frescoes depict various allegorical scenes such as this of a knight and lady overwhelmed by the stench of an open grave.

The domed Cappella del Pozzo was added in 1

★ **Baptistry Pulpit**
Nicola Pisano's great marble pulpit, completed in 1260, is carved with lively scenes from The Life of Christ.

Upper gallery

VISITORS' CHECKLIST

Piazza dei Miracoli. ***Tel** 050 387 22 10.* 🚌 *3, 11.* **Duomo** ◯ *daily. Jan & Dec: 10am–12:45pm, 2–5pm; Feb & Nov: 10am–12:45pm; Mar: 10am–6pm; Apr–Sep: 10am–8pm; Oct: 10am–7pm.* ✝ *8am, 9:30am daily; also 11am, 12:10pm, 6pm Sun (5pm in winter).* 🚫 📷 **Baptistry & Campo Santo** ◯ *daily. Nov–Mar: 10am–5:30pm; Apr–Sep: 8:30am–8pm (till 11pm Jun–Aug); Oct: 9am–7pm.* 🚫 📷 **Tower** ◯ *daily (30 people admitted every half hour).* **www**.opapisa.it

★ Portale di San Ranieri
Bonanno Pisano's bronze panels for the south transept doors depict The Life of Christ. *Palm trees and Moorish buildings show Arabic influence.*

Frescoes were added to the dome's interior after a fire in 1595.

The Leaning Tower *(see p160)* was completed in 1350, when its seven bells were hung.

Fragments of the 11th-century marble floor survive beneath the dome.

A frieze shows that work began in 1173.

Gleaming white Carrara marble decorates the walls.

Cathedral Pulpit
The carved supports for Giovanni Pisano's pulpit (1302–11) symbolize the Arts and Virtues.

This 12th-century wall tomb is for Buscheto, the Duomo's original architect.

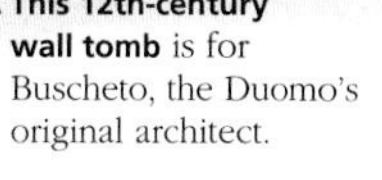

★ Duomo Façade
Coloured sandstone, glass and majolica plates decorate the lombard-style 12th-century façade. Its patterned surface includes knots, flowers and animals in inlaid marble.

STAR FEATURES

- ★ Baptistry Pulpit by Nicola Pisano
- ★ Portale di San Ranieri
- ★ Duomo Façade

The Leaning Tower of Pisa

All the buildings of the Campo dei Miracoli lean because of their shallow foundations and sandy silt subsoil, but none tilts so famously as the Torre Pendente – the Leaning Tower. Begun in 1173, the tower began to tip sideways before the third storey was completed. Even so, construction continued until its completion in 1350. Over ten years of engineering interventions to 2008 have succeeded in stabilizing the tower and should keep it stable for at least 200 years.

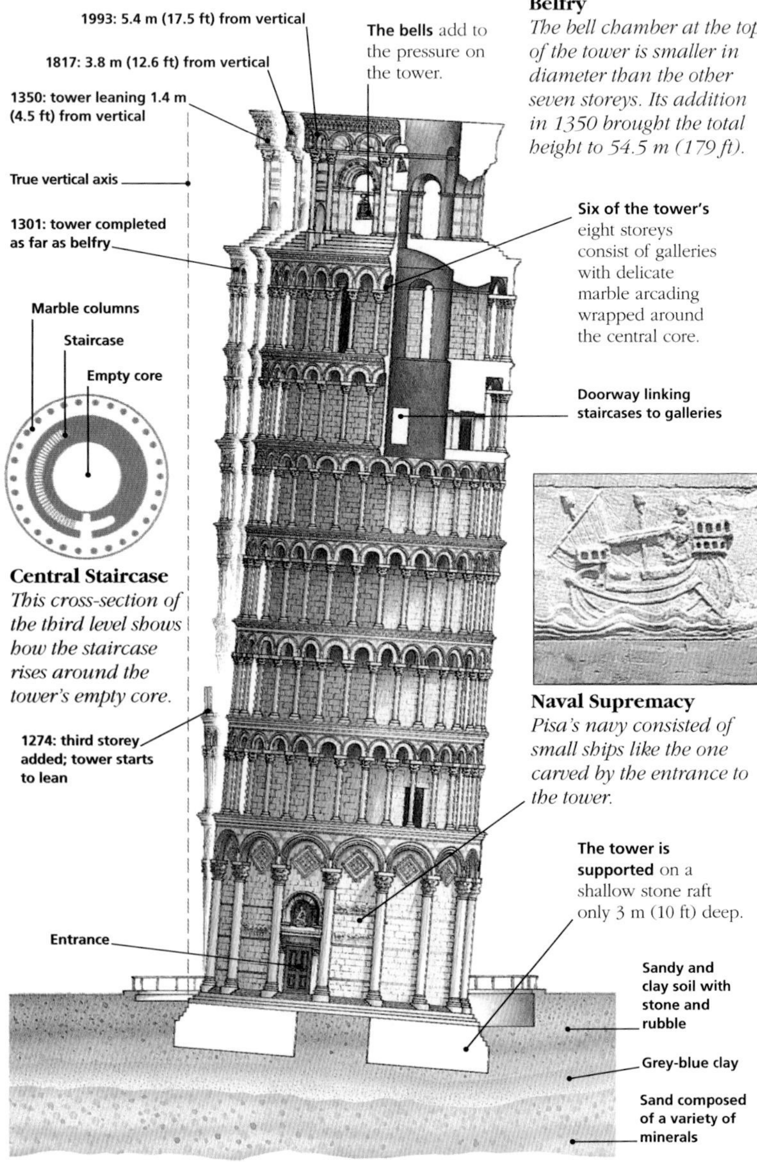

Belfry
The bell chamber at the top of the tower is smaller in diameter than the other seven storeys. Its addition in 1350 brought the total height to 54.5 m (179 ft).

Central Staircase
This cross-section of the third level shows how the staircase rises around the tower's empty core.

Naval Supremacy
Pisa's navy consisted of small ships like the one carved by the entrance to the tower.

Santa Maria della Spina by the river Arno in Pisa

Santa Maria della Spina

Lungarno Gambacorti. ***Tel*** *055 321 54 46.* *Mar–Oct: 10am–1:30pm, 2:30–6pm Tue–Fri, 10am–7pm Sat & Sun; Nov–Feb: 10am–2pm Tue–Fri, 10am–1:30pm, 2:30–6pm Sat & Sun.*

The roofline of Santa Maria della Spina bristles with spiky Gothic pinnacles, miniature spires and niches sheltering statues of apostles and saints. The church was built to house an unusual relic: a thorn from the Crown of Thorns forced on to Christ's head during the cruel mock coronation that preceded His crucifixion.

San Paolo a Ripa d'Arno

Piazza San Paolo a Ripa d'Arno. ***Tel*** *050 415 15.* *by appt.*

Worth visiting for its impressive 12th-century façade, this church was built in the same Pisan-Romanesque style as the Duomo *(see pp158–9).*

The Romanesque chapel *(see p44)* at the east end is dedicated to St Agatha. It is built entirely from brick, with a cone-shaped roof; Islamic influence is said to account for its unusual octagonal shape.

Tenuta di San Rossore ❷

Road map B2. *Pisa.* ***Tel*** *050 52 55 00 (050 53 01 01 or 53 37 55 for tours).* *8am–5:30pm Sat, Sun & pub hols (Apr–Sep: to 7:30).* *8am–2pm Mon–Fri (in English by appt).*

North of the Arno, this area is part of the Parco Naturale di San Rossore, a nature reserve stretching to the north of Tuscany. Wild boar and deer roam among the pine forests and salt marsh. Gombo, to the west, is where the drowned body of the poet Shelley was found in 1822.

Marina di Pisa ❸

Road map B2. *3,000.* *Sun in summer, Tue in winter.*

Moorings at Marina di Pisa, at the mouth of the river Arno

Much of the salt marsh to the west of Pisa has now been drained and reclaimed, and a large US Air Force base (Camp Darby) now occupies the area south of the Arno. There are extensive sandy beaches on the Arno estuary, and here lies Marina di Pisa, a seaside resort with some pretty Art Nouveau houses, backed by pine woods.

On the drive there you may catch sight of grazing camels – these are the descendants of a large herd established under Duke Ferdinand II in the mid-17th century. The village of Tirrenia, with its sandy beaches, lies 5 km (3 miles) south of Marina di Pisa.

San Piero a Grado ❹

Road map B2. ***Tel*** *050 96 00 65.* *8am–7pm daily.*

San Piero is a handsome 11th-century church built on the spot where St Peter is believed to have first set foot on Italian soil in AD 42. According to the New Testament Book of Acts, he arrived at a set of landing steps by the Arno. Archaeologists have discovered the foundations of Roman port buildings underneath the present church, which stands at the point where the Arno once flowed into the sea. Silt deposits mean that the church now stands some 6 km (3.5 miles) from the shore.

An unusual feature of the church is the lack of any façade. Instead, it has semi-circular apses at both the east and west ends. The exterior is decorated with blind arcading and with Moorish-style ceramic plates set into the masonry around the eaves – an unusual feature that it shares with the Duomo in San Miniato *(see p163).*

The present church was built during the reign of Pope John XVIII (1004–9) and the varied capitals of the nave come from ancient Roman buildings. High up on the nave walls there are frescoes by Deodato Orlandi, painted around 1300, on *The Life of St Peter.* These are interspersed with portraits of all the popes from St Peter to John XVII.

Interior of San Piero a Grado, with frescoes by Deodati Orlandi

The 18th-century Certosa di Pisa

Certosa di Pisa ❺

Road map C2 (località Calci). *from Pisa.* ***Tel*** *050 93 84 30.* *8:30am–6:30pm Tue–Sat; 8:30am–12:30pm Sun (adm half past the hour; last adm: 1 hour before closing).*

This Carthusian monastery was founded in 1366 and rebuilt during the 18th century. The splendid church is lavishly decorated, and some buildings form the University of Pisa's **Museo di Storia Naturale**. Exhibits include 16th-century anatomical wax models.

Nearby is the **Pieve di Calci**, a fine 11th-century Romanesque church. The unfinished campanile is alongside.

Museo di Storia Naturale
Certosa di Pisa. ***Tel*** *050 221 29 70.* *mid-Sep–mid-Jun: 9am–6pm Tue–Sat, 10am–7pm Sun; mid-Jun–mid-Sep: 10am–7pm Tue–Sat, 10am–8pm Sun.* *public hols.* *partial.*

Pieve di Calci
Piazza della Propositura, Calci. *daily.*

Livorno ❻

Road map B3. *168,370.* *Piazza Cavour 6. (0586 20 46 11).*

The fact that Livorno is now a bustling city, Italy's second busiest container port, is . thanks to Cosimo I. In 1571 he chose Livorno, then a tiny fishing village, as the site for Tuscany's new port after Pisa's harbour silted up. From 1607–21 the English marine engineer Sir Robert Dudley built the great sea wall that protects the harbour.

In 1608 Livorno was declared a free port, open to all traders, regardless of religion or race. People fleeing wars or religious persecution, including Jews, Protestants and Greeks, settled here and contributed greatly to the city's success.

Piazza Grande

When the architect Buontalenti planned the new city of Livorno in 1576, he envisaged the huge Piazza Grande at the heart of a network of wide avenues.

The square's original appearance has, however, been lost. This is partly due to controversial post-war rebuilding, which cut the square into two halves: the present Piazza Grande, to the south, and the Largo Municipio, to the north.

Duomo

Piazza Grande. *daily.*

A prominent victim of Livorno's wartime bombing was the late 16th-century cathedral by Pieroni and Cantagallina. It was rebuilt in 1959, retaining the original entrance portico, with its Doric arcades.

The original building was designed by Inigo Jones, who served his apprenticeship under the architect Buontalenti. Jones later used an almost identical design for the arcades of his Covent Garden piazza in London.

Piazza Micheli

The piazza, with its views of the 16th-century Fortezza Vecchia, contains Livorno's best-known monument: the *Monumento dei Quattro Mori*.

Bandini's bronze figure of Duke Ferdinand I dates to 1595; but Pietro Tacca's four Moorish slaves, also cast in bronze, were not added until 1626. Naked and manacled, the dejected slaves are a stark reminder that Livorno once had a thriving slave market.

Venezia Nuova canals

Venezia Nuova

Originally laid out in the middle of the 17th century, this area, which includes the 18th-century octagonal church of Santa Caterina, is spread between a handful of canals, reminiscent of Venetian waterways. Although it only covers a few blocks, Venezia Nuova is one of the city's most scenic areas.

Monumento dei Quattro Mori by Bandini and Tacca in Piazza Micheli

Fortezza Vecchia, Livorno harbour

The Fortezza Nuova, surrounded by a moat, dates to 1590. Its interior has been converted to a public park.

Piazza XX Settembre

Lying south of the Fortezza Nuova, the piazza is renowned for its bustling "American Market". The market's name derives from the large amounts of American army surplus sold here after World War II.

A US army base, Camp Darby, still operates to the north of Livorno.

English Cemetery

Via Giuseppe Verdi 63. ***Tel** 0586 83 97 72. by appt.*

The 19th-century memorials to British and American emigrés, long untended, are considerably overgrown. Among them is the grave of Tobias Smollett (1721–71), the misanthropic Scottish novelist. He claimed to live in Italy for health reasons, and, predictably, constantly complained about the place.

Museo Civico

Via San Jacopo Acquaviva. ***Tel** 0586 80 80 01. 10am–1pm, 4–7pm Tue–Sun. Easter, 1 May.*

The Museo Civico houses temporary exhibitions and several paintings by Giovanni Fattori (1825–1908), an artist of the *Macchiaioli* School *(see p123)*, whose work was similar to that of the French Impressionists.

Capraia 7

from Livorno. 300. Pro Loco, The Port (0586 90 51 38).

This tiny mountainous island appeals mainly to keen bird watchers and divers who go to explore the rocky coastline.

Nearby Gorgona, a penal colony, can also be visited by booking in advance. Contact the tourist information office in Livorno.

San Miniato 8

Road map C2. *3,852. Piazza del Popolo 1 (0571 427 45). Tue, 1st & 2nd Sun of each month.*

San Miniato suffers from its proximity to the vast industrial conurbation of the Arno valley. Straddling the crest of one of the region's highest hills, it manages, however, to remain somewhat aloof. There are a number of fine historic buildings, including the 13th-century Rocca (castle) built for Frederick II (1194–1250), the German Holy Roman Emperor.

The town played a major part in Frederick's Italian military campaigns. He dreamed of rebuilding the ancient Roman empire that lay divided between papal and Imperial authority. To this end he conquered large areas of Italy. His battles fuelled fierce local struggles between the imperial Ghibellines and the papal Guelphs *(see p46)*.

Local people still refer to the town as San Miniato *al Tedesco* (of the German).

Façade of Duomo in San Miniato

Duomo

Piazza del Duomo. *daily.*

Only the red-brick façade survives from the original 12th-century building. The majolica plates set within it show evidence of trade with Spain or North Africa. They seem to represent the North Star and the constellations of Ursus Major and Minor: key reference points for early navigators.

The campanile, the Torre di Matilda, is named in honour of the great Countess Matilda *(see p45)*, who was born in Livorno in 1046.

Piazza della Repubblica

The Piazza della Repubblica (also known as the Piazza del Seminario) occupies a long, narrow space dominated by the decorated façade of the 17th-century seminary. The frescoes and *sgraffito* (scenes scratched out of plaster) on the façade show allegories of the Virtues painted below quotations from key religious texts, for instance the writings of Pope Gregory (540–604).

To the right of the seminary are several well-restored 15th-century shops. Buildings like these can be seen in many medieval frescoes, such as Lorenzetti's 14th-century *Good Government (see p46).*

Façade of the seminary in Piazza della Repubblica

Museo Diocesano d'Arte Sacra

Piazza Duomo. ***Tel*** *0571 41 82 71.* *10am–1pm, 3–7pm Tue–Sun (Nov–Mar: to 6pm).*

Located next to the Duomo, the Museo Diocesano d'Arte Sacra contains a number of important 15th-century works gathered from local churches. These include a *Crucifixion* by Filippo Lippi and a terracotta bust of Christ attributed to Verrocchio.

Rocca

10am–7pm Tue–Sun.

A staircase behind the Museo Diocesano leads towards Frederick II's ruined 13th-century Rocca (castle). While the remains are run down, the site offers extraordinary views along the entire Arno valley, from Fiesole to Pisa.

Piazza Farinata degli Uberti in Empoli

Empoli 9

Road map C2. *43,500.* FS *Via Giuseppe del Papa 98 0571 76 115).* *Thu.*

An industrial town, specializing in textiles and glass manufacturing, Empoli is worth visiting for the excellent Museo della Collegiata.

Piazza Farinata degli Uberti

Empoli's arcaded main square is surrounded by a number of 12th-century buildings, notably the church of Sant'Andrea, with its black and white marble façade. The large fountain dating to 1827, with water nymphs and lions, is by Luigi Pampaloni.

Museo della Collegiata di Sant'Andrea

Piazza della Propositura 3. ***Tel*** *0571 762 84.* *9am–noon, 4–7pm Tue–Sun.* *public & relig hols.*

The museum contains a collection of Renaissance paintings and sculpture. Of particular interest are Masolino's *Pietà* fresco (1425) and a marble font by Rossellino, dating to 1447.

Santo Stefano

Via dei Neri. *for concerts & exhibitions.*

Visitors to Santo Stefano can see fresco fragments by Masolino, dating to 1424, and two 15th-century Annunciation statues by Rossellino. Bicci di Lorenzo's painting, *St Nicholas of Tolentino* (1445), in the second chapel on the north side, shows Empoli as it was in the mid-15th century.

Vinci 10

Road map C2. *2,000.* *Wed.*

This hilltop town is the birthplace of Leonardo da Vinci (1452–1519). To celebrate his extraordinary genius, the 13th-century castle in the centre of the town was restored in 1952 to create the **Museo Leonardiano**. Among the displays are wooden models of Leonardo's machines and inventions, based on the drawings from his notebooks, copies of which are shown alongside. These range from his conception of a car, to an armoured tank and even a machine-gun. A pair of skis, designed for walking on water, show that he could occasionally miss the mark. The museum is best avoided on Sundays, when it can be extremely crowded.

Pietà **by Masolino in Museo della Collegiata**

Close to the museum is Santo Stefano church and the font in which Leonardo was baptized. His actual birthplace, the **Casa di Leonardo**, is 2 km (1.25 miles) from the town centre at Anchiano. This simple farmhouse is worth visiting if you feel like a pleasant, undemanding walk through superb poppy fields; but don't expect

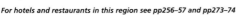

For hotels and restaurants in this region see pp256–57 and pp273–74

to be overawed by the exhibits, which mostly consist of a few reproduction drawings.

Museo Leonardiano
Castello dei Conti Guidi.
Tel *0571 560 55.* *Mar–Oct: 9:30am–7pm daily; Nov–Feb: 9:30am–6pm daily.*

Casa di Leonardo
Anchiano. ***Tel*** *0571 560 55.*
Mar–Oct: 9:30am–7pm daily; Nov–Feb: 9:30am–6pm daily.

Model bicycle based on drawings by Leonardo, Museo Leonardiano

Artimino ⓫

Road map C2.

Artimino is a fine example of a *borgo*, a small fortified hamlet, and is remarkable for the unspoiled Romanesque church of San Leonardo. Outside the walls, higher up the hill, lies the **Villa di Artimino**, designed by Buontalenti in 1594 for Grand Duke Ferdinando I. It is often referred to as the "Villa of a Hundred Chimneys", because of the numerous and highly ornate chimney pots crowding the roofline. The building is now used as a conference centre, but the Museo Archeologico Etrusco in the basement, which exhibits Etruscan and Roman artifacts, is open to the public.

The church of **San Michele** in Carmignano, only 5 km (3 miles) north of Artimino, contains Pontormo's (1494–1557) great masterpiece, *The Visitation* (1530).

Villa di Artimino
Via Papa Giovanni XXIII. ***Tel*** *055 875 14 27.* *Tue am (by appointment).* *compulsory.* *partial.*

San Michele
Pza. SS Francesco e Michele, Carmignano.
Tel *055 871 20 46.* *daily.*

Poggio a Caiano ⓬

Road map C2. ***Tel*** *055 87 70 12.*
daily (except 2nd and 3rd Mon of each month).

The Villa di Poggio a Caiano, built by Giuliano da Sangallo for Lorenzo de' Medici *(see p50)* in 1480, was the first Italian villa to be designed in the Renaissance style. Its original severity is now softened by the graceful, curved staircase (added in 1802–7) leading up to the terrace, with its views of the park beyond.

The villa's barrel-vaulted *salone* contains 16th-century frescoes by Andrea del Sarto and Franciabigio. They were commissioned by the future Leo X, the Medici pope, to portray his family as great statesmen in the manner of ancient Roman figures.

Villa di Artimino

The *salone* also contains Pontormo's colourful *Conette* fresco (1521). It portrays the Roman garden deities, Vertumnus and Pomona – a perfect evocation of a Tuscan summer afternoon.

Certosa di Firenze ⓭

Road map D2. Via Buca di Certosa 2. ***Tel*** *055 204 92 26.*
daily. *compulsory.*

The Charterhouse of Florence lies in the suburb of Galluzzo, where the Ema and Greve rivers meet. The high, fortress-like walls have sheltered a small community of monks since 1341, when the monastery was founded here.

The cloister and Palazzo degli Studi within contain several artworks, including a damaged but still beautiful series of 16th-century frescoes by Pontormo depicting scenes from the Passion of Christ.

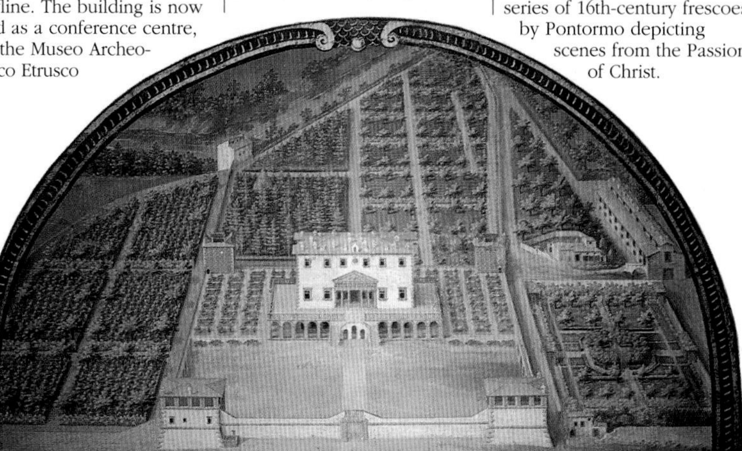

Villa di Poggio a Caiano **from the set of lunettes by Giusto Utens** ***(see p71)***

Volterra ⓮

Stucco figure in the Duomo

Situated, like many Etruscan cities, on a high plateau, Volterra offers uninterrupted views over the surrounding hills. In many places the ancient Etruscan walls still stand. Volterra's famous Museo Guarnacci contains one of the best collections of Etruscan artifacts in Italy. Many of the exhibits were gathered from the numerous local tombs. After its museums and medieval buildings, the city is famous for its craftsmen who carve beautiful white statues from locally mined alabaster.

Museo Etrusco Guarnacci

Via Don Minzoni 15. ***Tel*** *0588 863 47.* *9am–7pm daily (2 Nov–15 Mar: 9am–1:30pm).* *1 Jan, 25 Dec.* *(also allows entry at the Pinacoteca e Museo Civico and the Museo d'Arte Sacra).*

The pride of the Guarnacci Museum is its collection of 600 Etruscan funerary urns. Adorned with detailed carving, they offer a unique insight into Etruscan customs and beliefs *(see pp42–3).*

The museum's two main exhibits are on the first floor. Room 20 contains the terracotta "Married Couple" urn. The elderly couple on the lid are portrayed realistically, with haggard, careworn faces. Room 22 contains the elongated bronze known as the *Ombra della Sera* (Shadow of the Evening). This name was bestowed by the poet Gabriele d'Annunzio, who said that the bronze reminded him of the shadow thrown by a human figure in the dying light of the evening sun. It is probably a votive figure dating to the 3rd century BC, but it is difficult to speak of it with any certainty; unusually, it was cast with no clothes or jewellery to indicate rank, status or date. It is only by chance that this remarkable figure survived. Ploughed up by a farmer in 1879, it was used as a fire poker until someone recognized it as a masterpiece of Etruscan art.

Ombra della Sera

Detail from The Deposition (1521) by Rosso Fiorentino

Pinacoteca e Museo Civico

Via dei Sarti 1. ***Tel*** *0588 875 80.* *mid-Mar–Nov: 9am–7pm daily; Dec–mid-Mar: 9am–1:30pm daily.* *1 Jan, 25 Dec.* *(also allows entry at the Museo Etrusco Guarnacci and the Museo d'Arte Sacra).*

Volterra's excellent art gallery is situated in the 15th-century Palazzo Minucci-Solaini. The best works are by Florentine artists. In Ghirlandaio's *Christ in Majesty* (1492), Christ hovers above an idealized Tuscan landscape. It was meant for the San Giusto monastery, which was abandoned after a landslip like the one shown in the middle distance and beyond. Luca Signorelli's *Madonna and Child with Saints* (1491) shows his debt to Roman art through the reliefs on the base of the Virgin's throne. His *Annunciation* (1491) is another beautiful composition.

The museum's main exhibit is Rosso Fiorentino's Mannerist work *(see p27), The Deposition* (1521). Attention is focused on the grief-stricken figures in the foreground and the pallid, empty shell of Christ's body, its dead weight symbolizing that His spirit is elsewhere.

Duomo

Piazza San Giovanni. *daily.*

Work on Volterra's cathedral began in the 1200s and continued intermittently over the next two centuries.

To the right of the High Altar stands a Romanesque wood-carving of *The Deposition* (1228). The Altar itself is flanked by graceful marble angels carved by Mino da Fiesole in 1471; they face the same artist's elegant tabernacle, carved with figures of Faith, Hope and Charity.

The nave, remodelled in 1581, has an unusual coffered ceiling with stucco figures of bishops and saints painted in rich blue and gold. The pulpit, in the middle of the nave, dates to 1584, but was created using sculptural reliefs from the late 12th and early 13th centuries. The *Last Supper* panel, facing into the nave and thought to be the work of the

View from Volterra over the surrounding landscape

Detail from one of the panels decorating the Duomo pulpit

Pisan artist Guglielmo Pisano, has a number of humorous details including a monster snapping at the heels of Judas. Nearby, in the north aisle, Fra Bartolomeo's *The Annunciation* (1497) hangs above one of the side chapel altars.

More sculptures are housed in the oratory off the north aisle, near the main entrance. The best is a tableau of the Epiphany, preserved behind glass. The remarkably humane painted terracotta figures of the Virgin and Child in the foreground are believed to be by Zaccaria da Volterra (1473–1544), a local sculptor.

Museo d'Arte Sacra

Via Roma 13. ***Tel*** *0588 862 90.* *9am–1pm, 3–6pm daily (Nov–mid-Mar: 9am–1pm only).* *1 Jan, 1 May, 25 Dec.* *(also allows entry at the Museo Etrusco Guarnacci and the Pinacoteca e Museo Civico).*

This museum, in the Palazzo Arcivescovile, contains sculpture and architectural fragments from the Duomo and a few local churches. The main exhibit is a 15th-century della Robbia terracotta of St Linus, Volterra's patron saint.

The collection also has a range of church bells, from the 11th to 15th centuries, some church silver and several illuminated manuscripts.

Teatro Romano

Viale Ferrucci. *mid-Mar–Oct: 10:30am–5:30pm daily; Nov–mid-Mar: 10am–2pm Sat, Sun (not when raining).* *1 Jan, 25 Dec.*

Just outside the city walls, the ancient Roman theatre, dating to the first century BC, is one of the best-preserved in Italy. Enough of the original structure has survived to enable an almost complete reconstruction.

VISITORS' CHECKLIST

Road map C3. *12,200.* *Via G Turazza 2 (0588 861 50).* *Sat.* *Astiludio (1st Sun in Sep).* **www**.volterratur.it

Piazza dei Priori

This fine square is dominated by the Palazzo dei Priori, dating to 1208. A sober building, it is said to have been the model for the Palazzo Vecchio in Florence *(see pp78–9)*.

The 13th-century Porcellino tower, on the other side of the square, is named after the small pig, now almost worn away, carved at its base.

Plaque outside the Palazzo dei Priori

Arco Etrusco

One of Volterra's more unusual sights, the Etruscan arch is in fact part Roman. Only the columns and the severely weathered basalt heads, representing Etruscan gods, date to the 6th-century BC original. The features of each head are now barely visible.

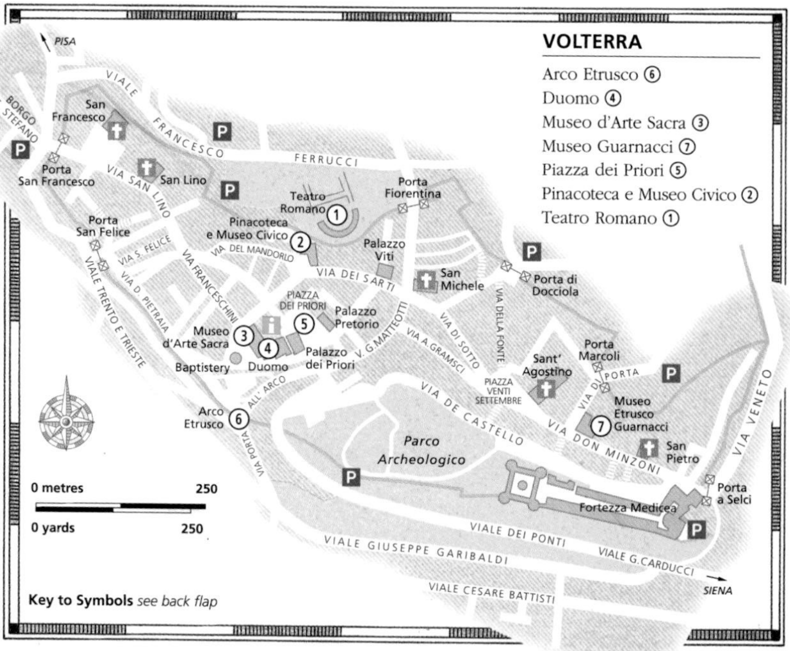

VOLTERRA

Arco Etrusco ⑥
Duomo ④
Museo d'Arte Sacra ③
Museo Guarnacci ⑦
Piazza dei Priori ⑤
Pinacoteca e Museo Civico ②
Teatro Romano ①

0 metres 250
0 yards 250

Key to Symbols *see back flap*

NORTHERN TUSCANY

Of all the regions of Tuscany, this one offers something for everyone. The historic towns are rich in art, architecture and music festivals, while many sporting activities can be enjoyed along the coast or in the mountains. The landscape, too, is marked by a vast range of features, from marble quarries to market gardens, and from mountain ranges and nature reserves to beaches.

The heavily populated Lucchese plain between Florence and Lucca is dominated by industry: the textile factories of Prato produce three out of every four woollen garments exported from Italy. But in spite of their large suburbs, cities such as Prato, Pistoia and, above all, Lucca have rewarding churches, museums and galleries within their historic city centres.

The land between the cities is fertile and is therefore intensively cultivated. Asparagus and cut flowers are two of the most important crops, and the wholesale flower market at Pescia is one of the biggest in Italy. East of Lucca towards Pescia are garden centres and nurseries where huge quantities of young trees and shrubs are grown in long, neat rows.

North of the Lucchese plain the scenery is very different again. A series of foothills is covered in olive groves which produce some of the finest oil in Italy. Then, the land rises to the wild and mountainous areas of the Garfagnana, the Alpi Apuane (Apuan Alps) and the Lunigiana, with its fortified towns and castles built by the Dukes of Malaspina. Here you will find some of Tuscany's highest peaks, rising to 2,000 m (6,550 ft) or more. Vast areas of the mountains are designated as nature parks and the wild scenery attracts ramblers, trekkers and riders as well as hang-gliding enthusiasts.

Finally, the coastal area, known as the Versilia, includes some of Italy's most elegant and popular beach resorts. It stretches from the famous marble-quarrying town of Carrara in the north down to the area's main town, Viareggio, and to Torre del Lago Puccini, the lakeside home of Giacomo Puccini, where he wrote nearly all his operas.

Lucca's Piazza del Mercato, echoing the shape of the original Roman amphitheatre

◁ **The village of Vagli di Sotto on Lago di Vagli in the Parco Naturale delle Alpi Apuane**

Exploring Northern Tuscany

The beautiful town of Lucca is a favourite base for exploring. Northwards, industrial suburbs give way to the olive groves, chestnut woods and bare mountains of the Alpi Apuane and the Garfagnana region, a popular area for outdoor sports, from trekking and canoeing to skiing. Castles dot the rugged Lunigiana, while beaches line the Versilia. Due east are large towns with historic centres: Pistoia and Prato.

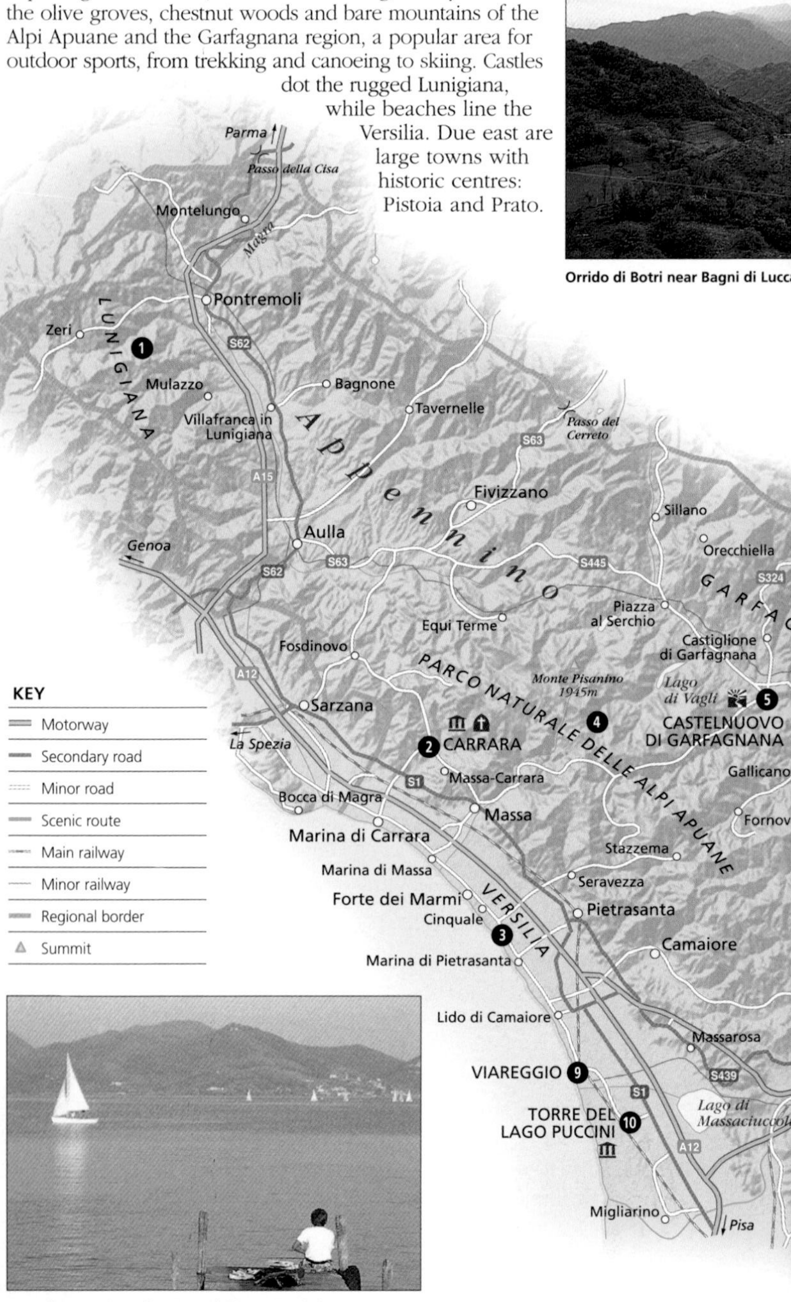

Orrido di Botri near Bagni di Lucca

Lago di Massaciuccoli at Torre del Lago Puccini

GETTING AROUND

Lucca, Montecatini Terme, Prato and Pistoia are all on the A11 autostrada and are easy to reach by car from Pisa, Florence and other major cities outside Tuscany, such as Bologna. There are several trains a day between Pisa and Florence via Lucca, Montecatini Terme, Prato and Pistoia, and along the coast between Pisa and Carrara. From Lucca you can also travel by train up the Serchio valley to Castelnuovo di Garfagnana. But, since this is a mountainous region, much of it is only accessible by car.

SIGHTS AT A GLANCE

Bagni di Lucca 8
Barga 6
Carrara 2
Castelnuovo di Garfagnana 5
Collodi 12
The Garfagnana 7
Lucca 11
The Lunigiana 1
Montecatini Terme 14
Parco Naturale delle Alpi Apuane 4
Pescia 13
Pistoia 15
Prato 16
Torre del Lago Puccini 10
The Versilia 3
Viareggio 9

The hamlet of Montefegatesi in the Alpi Apuane

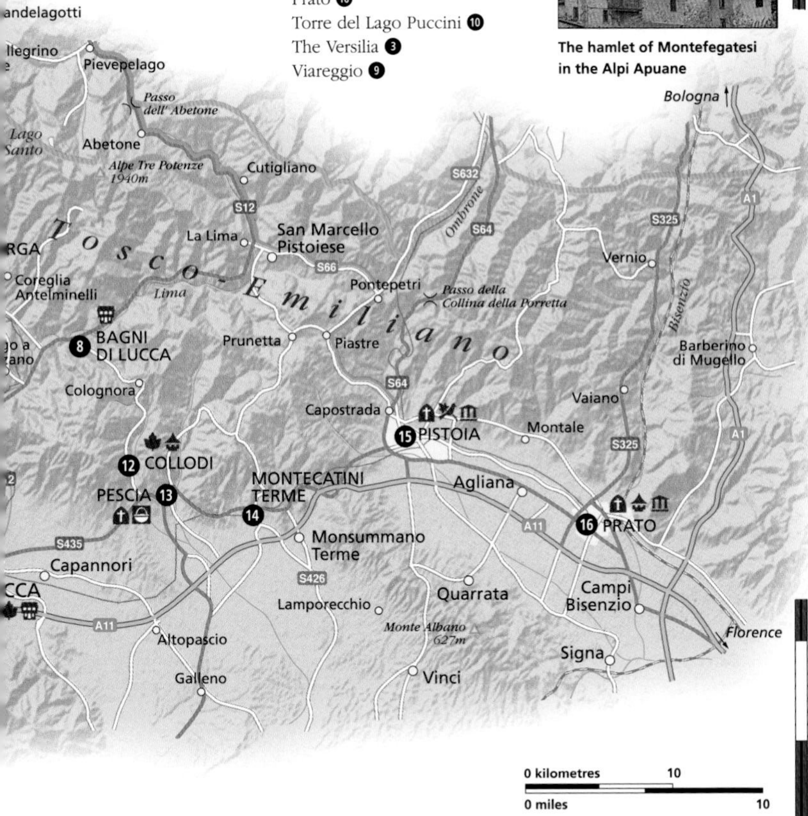

Sun, sand and sea – essential components of a holiday at a beach resort of the Versilia

The Lunigiana ❶

Road map A1. FS *Aulla.* *Via Salucci 5, Aulla (0187 42 14 39).*

The Lunigiana (Land of the Moon) area is named after the port of Luni – so called because of the moon-like luminescence of the marble shipped from here in Roman times. From the 16th century onwards, the Dukes of Malaspina fortified villages against banditry and built castles at Massa, Fosdinovo, Aulla, Fivizzano and Verrucola.

At Pontremoli, the 14th-century Castello del Piagnaro houses the **Museo delle Statue-Stele Lunigianesi**, which shows prehistoric carved stone figures from the region.

Museo delle Statue-Stele Lunigianesi
Castello del Piagnaro, Pontremoli. ***Tel*** *0187 83 14 39.* *Apr–Sep: 9am–1pm, 2:30–6:30pm Tue–Sun; Oct–Mar: 9:30am–12:30pm, 2:30–5:30pm Tue–Sun.*

Carrara ❷

Road map B1. *70,000.* FS *Piazza Cesare Battisti 1 (0585 64 14 22).* *Mon.*

Carrara is world famous for its white marble. The 300 or so quarries near the town date to Roman times, making this the oldest industrial site in continuous use in the world. In Carrara itself there are numerous showrooms and workshops where the marble is sawn into sheets or sculpted into statues and ornaments. Many of the workshops welcome visitors. You can also discover more about the techniques of crafting marble at the **Museo Civico del Marmo**.

Carrara's **Duomo** uses the local marble to good effect in its Pisan-Romanesque façade featuring a rose window. In the same square is the house where Michelangelo used to stay on his visits to buy marble for his sculptures. The façade is marked by a plaque and by carvings of the sculptor's tools.

Tour buses from Carrara regularly visit the quarries at Colonnata and at Fantiscritti, where a museum displays various marble quarrying techniques. You can also drive there, following the numerous signs that say "Cave di Marmo".

Museo Civico del Marmo
Viale XX Settembre. ***Tel*** *0585 84 57 46.* *Oct–Apr: 9am–5pm Mon–Sat; May–Sep: 10am–6pm Mon–Sat (Jul & Aug: to 8pm).*

Duomo
Piazza del Duomo. *daily.*

The Versilia ❸

Road map B2. FS *Viareggio.* *Viale Carducci 10, Viareggio (0584 96 22 33).* **www**.aptversilia.it

The Versilia, sometimes called the Tuscan Riviera because of the many beach resorts that line this 30-km (18-mile) strip, stretches from Marina di Carrara in the north down to Marina di

A quarry in the marble-bearing hills around Carrara

Torre del Lago Puccini. In the 1820s, towns such as Massa, Pietra Santa and Camaiore developed marinas and lidos along the part of the coast they controlled. These inland towns are linked by roads to their coastal twins. Here villas and hotels with fine walled gardens line the streets, with the mountains of the Alpi Apuane as a backdrop.

The beaches are divided into numerous bathing establishments run by hotels or private operators, who charge for use of the beach and its facilities. Forte dei Marmi is perhaps the most beautiful of these resorts, much favoured by wealthy Florentines and Milanese.

Poster for the Versilia

Parco Naturale delle Alpi Apuane ❹

Road map B1. FS 🚌 *Castelnuovo di Garfagnana.* ℹ *Piazza Delle Erbe 1, Castelnuovo di Garfagnana (0583 64 42 42).*

The Parco Naturale delle Alpi Apuane, northwest of Castelnuovo di Garfagnana, was designated a nature reserve in 1985. Monte Pisanino is the highest peak in the area at 1,945 m (6,320 ft). It towers above Lago di Vagli, an artificial lake covering the drowned village of Fabbrica. Nearby are Vagli di Sotto *(see p168)* and Vagli di Sopra, ancient villages with rugged stone houses.

To the south, in the valley of the Turrite Secca, a spectacular mountain road leads to Seravezza, passing through a white-walled tunnel called the Galleria del Cipollaio. Northwest, at Arni, are the Marmitte dei Giganti (Giants' Cooking Pots), great hollows left by the glaciers of the Ice Age.

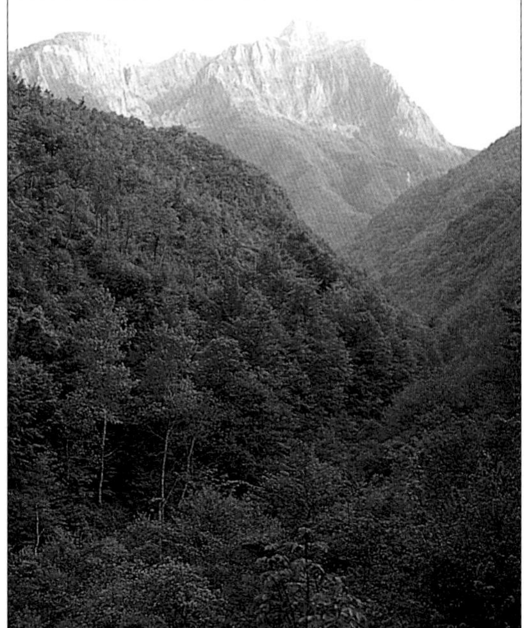
The Turrite Secca valley in the Parco Naturale delle Alpi Apuane

Southeast at Calomini is a 12th-century rock-cut hermitage, home to a Capuchin monk; at Fornovolasco is the Grotta del Vento (Cave of the Wind). To the east, past Barga, at Coreglia Antelminelli, is the **Museo della Figurina di Gesso**, devoted to the history of locally made plaster figurines, once sold all over Europe.

The 13th-century Rocca at Castelnuovo di Garfagnana

Museo della Figurina di Gesso
Via del Mangano 17, Coreglia Antelminelli. ***Tel*** *0583 780 82.* *9am–1pm Mon–Fri, 10am–1pm Sat & Sun.*

Castelnuovo di Garfagnana ❺

Road map B1. *6,300.* FS 🚌 ℹ *Via Cavalieri di Vittorio Veneto (0583 64 10 07).* *Thu.*

Visitors to the Garfagnana use the town as a base for sporting activities. For details, head to the information office or the **Cooperativa Garfagnana Vacanze**. The 13th-century Rocca (castle) houses the town hall. Ludovico Ariosto, author of the epic poem *Orlando Furioso* (1516), was town governor in 1522–25.

Cooperativa Garfagnana Vacanze
Piazza delle Erbe 1. ***Tel*** *0583 651 69.* *Jun–Sep: 9am–1pm, 3–7pm daily; Oct–May: 9am–1pm, 3:30–5:30pm daily.*

Barga ❻

Road map C1. 11,000. FS Sat.

Barga is the most attractive of the towns that line the Serchio valley leading northwards from Lucca, and it makes an excellent base for touring the Garfagnana area. The little walled town with its steep streets paved with stone is the setting for a highly regarded opera festival held in July and August in the 18th-century Teatro dell'Accademia dei Differenti. The festival is always well attended.

View over Barga rooftops

Duomo

Propositura. daily.

Barga's Duomo stands on a grassy terrace at the highest point in the town. There are glorious views from here of the gleaming white marble and limestone peaks of the Alpi Apuane.

The 11th-century Duomo is dedicated to San Cristoforo (St Christopher). The exterior is decorated with interesting Romanesque carvings of interlaced knots, wild beasts and knights in armour. Over the north portal, a frieze thought to be a scene from a folk tale depicts a banquet.

Inside, a huge wooden statue of St Christopher dates to the 12th century, and there is a gilded tabernacle guarded by two charming terracotta angels by Luca della Robbia.

Most impressive of all is the massive marble pulpit, standing fully 5 m (16.5 ft) tall, supported by pillars which in turn rest on the back of man-eating lions. The pulpit is the work of Guido Bigarelli of Como and dates to the early 13th century. The lively sculptures on the upper part depict the Evangelists, the Three Magi, the Annunciation, the Nativity and the Baptism of Christ.

The Garfagnana ❼

Road map C1. FS *Castelnuovo di Garfagnana.* *Via Cavalieri di Vittorio Veneto, Castelnuovo di Garfagnana (0583 64 10 07).*

This mountainous region can be explored from Barga, Seravezza, or Castelnuovo di Garfagnana *(see p173)*. Here too is the Parco Naturale delle Alpi Apuane *(see p173)*. From Castelnuovo a scenic drive takes you to the Alpe Tre Potenze. You can return via San Pellegrino in Alpe with its **Museo Etnografico**, and also visit the nature park **Parco dell' Orecchiella** and the **Orto Botanico Pánia di Corfino** with its collection of local Alpine plants.

Romanesque sculpture in Pieve di Brancoli

Museo Etnografico

Via del Voltone 15, San Pellegrino in Alpe. ***Tel*** *0583 64 90 72.* *Sep–Jun: Tue–Sun; Jul & Aug: daily.*

Parco dell'Orecchiella

Centro Visitatori, Orecchiella. ***Tel*** *058 3 61 90 02.* *Jun & Sep: Sat & Sun; Jul–15 Sep: daily; Apr–Nov: Sun.*

Orto Botanico Pánia di Corfino

Parco dell'Orecchiella. *Jul–Aug daily; May–Jun & Sep: Sun.*

Bagni di Lucca ❽

Road map C2. 7,402. *Via del Casino (0583 80 57 45).* *Wed & Sat.*

Visitors come to Bagni di Lucca for its lime sulphate springs. In the 19th century it was one of Europe's most fashionable spa towns *(see p185)*: the Casino, built in 1837, was the first to be licensed in Europe. Also from that time are the Neo-Gothic **English Church**, the elegant **Palazzo del Circolo dei Forestieri** restaurant and the **Cimitero Anglicano** (Protestant Cemetery). Bagni di Lucca makes a good base for exploring the surrounding hills cloaked in chestnut woods. You can walk to Montefegatesi, a hamlet surrounded by the peaks of the Alpi Apuane, and then continue to Orrido di Botri, a dramatic gorge.

To the south of Bagni is San Giorgio or **Pieve di Brancoli**, one of many Romanesque churches in the area founded during the reign of Countess Matilda (1046–1115) *(see p45)*.

The Ponte della Maddalena is a hump-backed bridge across the River Serchio just north of the village of Borgo a Mozzano. It is called Ponte del Diavolo (Devil's Bridge) because, according to local legend, the Devil offered to build the bridge in return for possession of the first soul to

Ponte della Maddalena or "Devil's Bridge" near Bagni di Lucca

A seaside café in the popular beach resort of Viareggio

cross it; the canny villagers agreed and, when it was finished, sent a dog across.

English Church
Via Crawford. ***Tel*** *0583 80 84 62.* *by appt.*

Palazzo del Circolo dei Forestieri
Piazza Varraud 10. ***Tel*** *0583 860 38.* *Fri–Sun.*

Cimitero Anglicano
Via Letizia. ***Tel*** *0583 80 84 62.* *by appt.*

Pieve di Brancoli
Vinchiana. ***Tel*** *0583 96 52 81.* *by appt.*

Viareggio 9

Road map B2. *60,000.* *Viale Carducci 10 (0584 96 22 33).* *Thu.*

Viareggio is famous for its elegant "Liberty" style (Art Nouveau) villas and hotels, built in the 1920s after the original boardwalk and timber chalets of the resort went up in flames in 1917. One example is the Gran Caffè Margherita, designed by Galileo Chini *(see p194)*. The harbour has an interesting mix of boatyards, luxury yachts and fishing boats, and offers fine views of the Versilia coastline. Viareggio's carnival, held on Sundays from February to Lent and on Shrove Tuesday, is famous throughout Italy *(see p38)*.

Torre del Lago Puccini 10

Road map B2. *11,500.* *Viale Kennedy 2 (0584 35 98 93).* *Fri (Jul & Aug: also Sun).* **Teatro Opera Puccini** ***Tel*** *0584 35 93 22.*

The composer Giacomo Puccini (1858–1924) *(see p179)* lived here, beside Lago di Massaciuccoli, to indulge his passion for shooting waterfowl. He and his wife are buried in the **Museo Villa Puccini,** in the mausoleum between the piano room and the gun room where he kept his rifle ("my second favourite instrument"). The operas are performed in the open-air theatre in summer *(see p35)*. The reed-fringed lake is now a nature reserve.

Museo Villa Puccini
Piazzale Belvedere Puccini 266. ***Tel*** *0584 34 14 45.* *Tue–Sun. Apr–Oct: 10am–12:30pm, 3–6pm (to 6:30pm Jun–Oct); Dec–Mar: 10am–12:30pm, 2:30–5:30pm.* *Nov, 25 Dec.*
www.giacomopuccini.it

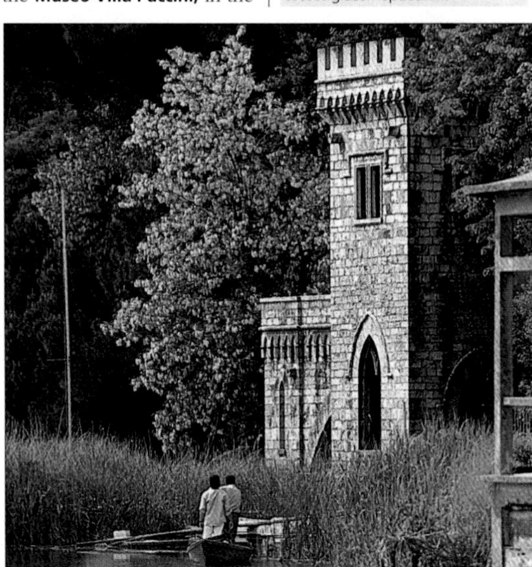

Near Puccini's lakeside home at Torre del Lago Puccini

Street-by-Street: Lucca ⓫

Lucca became a colony of ancient Rome in 180 BC, and the town's Roman legacy is still evident in the regular grid pattern of its streets. The remarkable elliptical shape of the Piazza del Mercato *(see p169)* is a survival of the amphitheatre. The name of the church of San Michele in Foro indicates that it stands beside the Roman forum, laid out as the city's main square in ancient times and still serving that function to this day. San Michele is just one of Lucca's many churches built in the 12th and 13th centuries in the elaborate Pisan-Romanesque style.

Most of the Renaissance palazzi of Piazza San Michele are now offices.

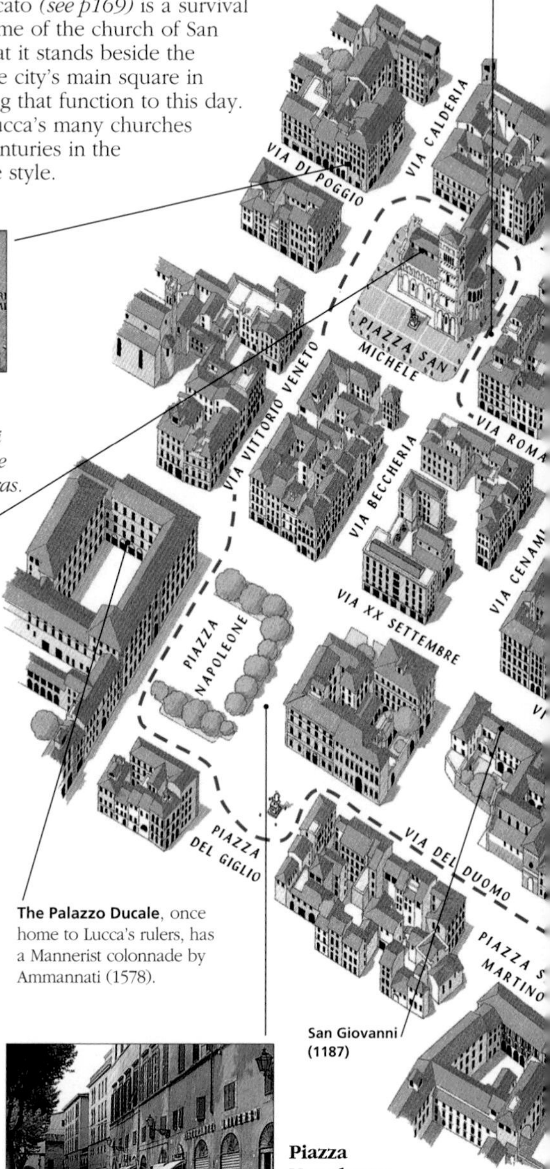

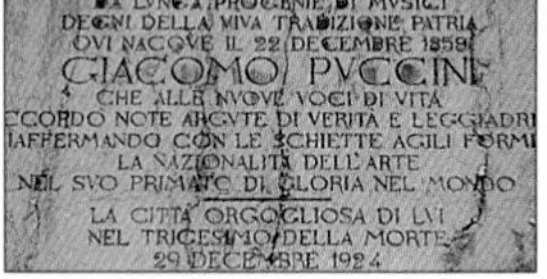

Casa di Puccini
This plaque marks the birthplace of Giacomo Puccini (1858–1924), composer of some of the world's most popular operas.

★ San Michele in Foro
The Madonna on the south-west corner of the church is a copy of the original inside, carved by Matteo Civitali (1436–1501).

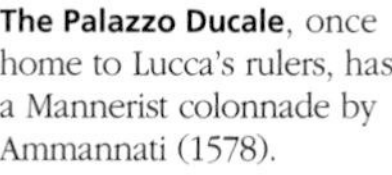
The Palazzo Ducale, once home to Lucca's rulers, has a Mannerist colonnade by Ammannati (1578).

San Giovanni (1187)

Piazza Napoleone
The square is named after Napoleon, whose sister, Elisa Baciocchi, was ruler of Lucca (1805–15). The statue is of her successor, Marie Louise de Bourbon.

STAR SIGHTS

- ★ San Martino
- ★ San Michele in Foro

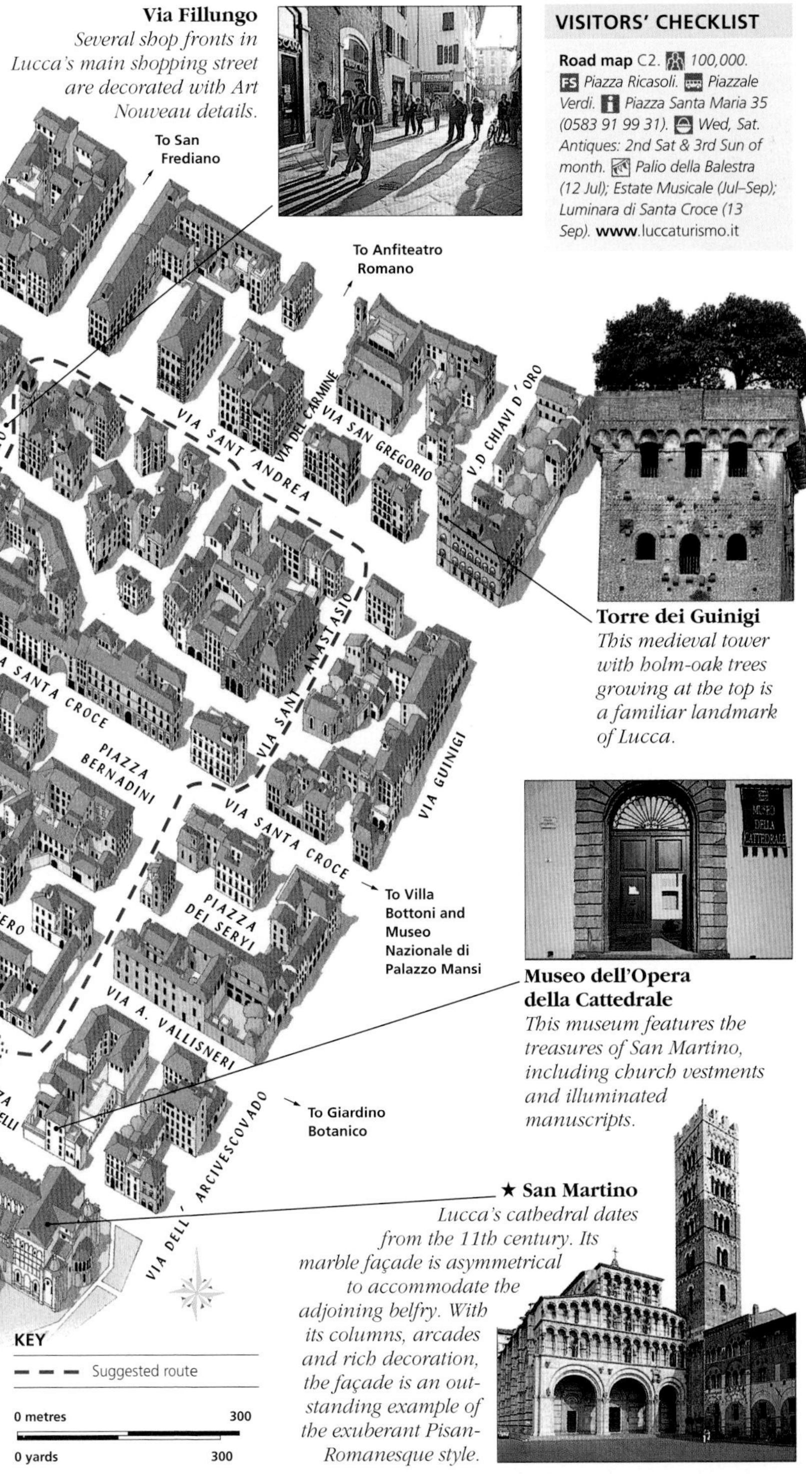

Via Fillungo
Several shop fronts in Lucca's main shopping street are decorated with Art Nouveau details.

VISITORS' CHECKLIST

Road map C2. *100,000.* FS *Piazza Ricasoli.* *Piazzale Verdi.* *Piazza Santa Maria 35 (0583 91 99 31).* *Wed, Sat. Antiques: 2nd Sat & 3rd Sun of month.* *Palio della Balestra (12 Jul); Estate Musicale (Jul–Sep); Luminara di Santa Croce (13 Sep).* **www**.luccaturismo.it

Torre dei Guinigi
This medieval tower with holm-oak trees growing at the top is a familiar landmark of Lucca.

Museo dell'Opera della Cattedrale
This museum features the treasures of San Martino, including church vestments and illuminated manuscripts.

★ San Martino
Lucca's cathedral dates from the 11th century. Its marble façade is asymmetrical to accommodate the adjoining belfry. With its columns, arcades and rich decoration, the façade is an outstanding example of the exuberant Pisan-Romanesque style.

Exploring Lucca

Mosaic in San Frediano

Lucca is enclosed by massive red brick walls which help to give the city its special character by shutting out traffic and the modern world. Built in 1504–1645, the walls are among the best-preserved Renaissance defences in Europe. Within these walls, Lucca is a peaceful city of narrow lanes, preserving intact its original ancient Roman street plan. Unlike several of Tuscany's hilltop cities, Lucca is flat: many locals use bicycles, which lends the city added charm.

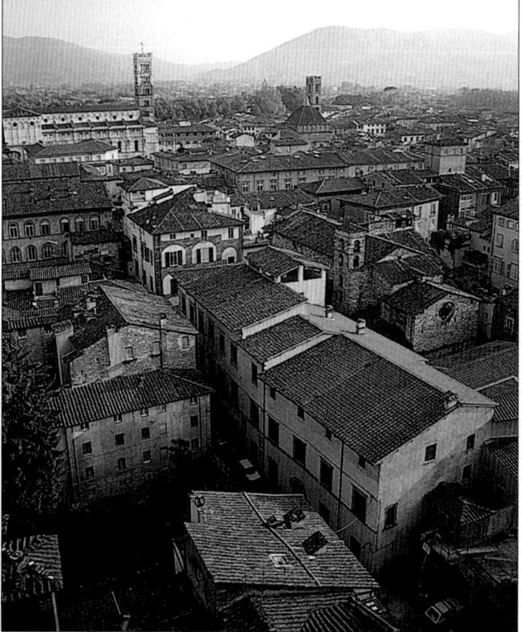

Lucca viewed from the top of the Guinigi Tower

San Martino

See pp180–81.

Anfiteatro Romano

Piazza del Mercato.

Almost none of the ancient Roman amphitheatre survives: the stone was gradually stolen for use elsewhere, leaving the atmospheric arena-shaped Piazza del Mercato of today *(see p169)*. The piazza is enclosed by medieval houses that were built up against the walls of the amphitheatre. Its shape, perfectly preserved, is a striking reminder that Lucca was founded by the Romans around 180 BC. Low archways at north, south, east and west mark the gates through which beasts and gladiators would once have entered the arena.

Palazzo dei Guinigi

Via Sant'Andrea 41. ***Tel*** *0583 31 68 46.* **Tower** *daily. Apr–May: 9am–6:30pm; Jun–Sep: 9:30am–7:30pm; Oct: 9:30am –5:30pm; Nov–Feb: 9:30am–4:30pm. 25 Dec.*

This house was once owned by the powerful Guinigi family, rulers of the city in the 15th century. They kept Florence at bay, so Lucca was never conquered by the Medici, remaining independent until the late 1700s. The red brick palazzo, built in the late 14th century, has late-Gothic windows. The striking 41-m (133-ft) defensive tower alongside, the Torre del Guinigi, has a small roof garden, hence the ilex (holm-oak) trees sprouting incongruously at the top.

Giardino Botanico

Via dell'Orto Botanico 14. ***Tel*** *0583 44 21 60. 10am–5pm daily (to 6pm May & Jun; to 7pm Jul–Sep). Sun (Nov–Mar).*

Lucca's delightful botanical garden, tucked into an angle of the city walls, was laid out in 1820. It displays a wide range of Tuscan plants.

Museo della Cattedrale

Piazza Antelminelli 5. ***Tel*** *0583 49 05 30. Nov–Mar: 10am–3pm daily (to 5pm Sat, Sun); Apr–Oct: 10am–6pm daily. 1 Jan, Easter, 25 Dec.*

Housed in the 14th-century former Archbishop's Palace, the museum displays the treasures of the Duomo, San Martino. These include the 11th-century carved stone head of a king from the original façade. There is also a rare 12th-century Limoges enamel casket, which possibly held a relic of St Thomas à Becket. The Croce di Pisani made by Vincenzo di Michele in 1411 is a masterpiece showing Christ hanging from the Tree of Redemption, surrounded by angels, the Virgin, St John and the other Evangelists.

Museo Nazionale Villa Guinigi

Via della Quarquonia. ***Tel*** *0583 49 60 33. 8:30am–7pm Tue–Sat (to 1pm Sun). 1 Jan, 1 May, 25 Dec. (a cumulative ticket also allows entry at the Museo Nazionale di Palazzo Mansi).*

This Renaissance villa was built for Paolo Guinigi, who ruled Lucca from 1400 until 1430. The ground floor holds sculpture from Lucca and surrounds, including fine Romanesque reliefs from Lucca's churches. The gallery on the floor above displays paintings and choir

Romanesque lion at Museo Nazionale Guinigi

The beautiful galleried staircase at Palazzo Pfanner

stalls from Lucca's cathedral, inlaid with marquetry views of the city in 1529.

Palazzo Pfanner

Via degli Asili 33. ***Tel*** *058 395 40 29.*
Mar–Oct: 10am–6pm daily, Nov–Feb: by appt.

The imposing Palazzo Pfanner, built in 1667, has a delightful formal garden to the rear, which can also be viewed from the ramparts. Laid out in the 18th century, the garden's central avenue is lined with Baroque statues of ancient Roman gods and goddesses, alternating with lemon trees in huge terracotta pots.

The house itself contains an interesting collection of furniture, antiques and medical instruments.

Piazza Napoleone and Piazza del Giglio

Piazza Napoleone was laid out in 1806 when Lucca was under the imposed rule of Elisa Baciocchi, Napoleon's sister. The statue in the square is of her successor, Marie Louise de Bourbon. She faces the massive Palazzo Ducale, with its elegant colonnade built by Ammannati in 1578. Behind her is the Piazza del Giglio, with the Teatro del Giglio (1817) on the south side of the square. The theatre is famous for its productions of operas by Puccini, who was born in Lucca.

Casa di Puccini

Corte San Lorenzo 8 (Via di Poggio). ***Tel*** *0583 35 91 54.*
for restoration.

The 15th-century house in which Giacomo Puccini (1858–1924) was born contains many interesting artifacts, including portraits of the great composer, costume designs for his operas and the piano he used when composing his last opera, *Turandot*. Left unfinished at his death, the composition was completed by Franco Alfano and first performed two years later at La Scala, Milan.

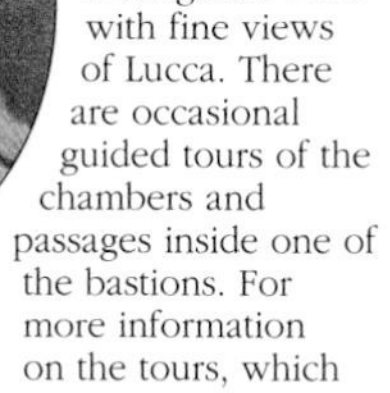
The composer Giacomo Puccini

Museo Nazionale di Palazzo Mansi

Via Galli Tassi 43. ***Tel*** *0583 555 70.*
8:30am–7pm Tue–Sat (to 1pm Sun). (a cumulative ticket also allows entry at the Museo Nazionale Guinigi).

Lucca's picture gallery is in the impressive 17th-century Palazzo Mansi, with paintings and furnishings of the same period, typical of the time when Mannerism was being superseded by Baroque and Rococo art. There are also works by Bronzino, Pontormo, Sodoma, Andrea del Sarto, Tintoretto and Salvatore Rosa.

Ramparts

Complete circuit: 4.2 km (2.5 miles).

A promenade runs along the top of the city walls, built in 1504–1645. Marie Louise de Bourbon made the ramparts into a public park in the early 19th century, with a double avenue of trees. It makes a delightful walk with fine views of Lucca. There are occasional guided tours of the chambers and passages inside one of the bastions. For more information on the tours, which should be booked in advance, contact Compagnia Balestrieri Lucca on 338 237 1277.

The Porta San Donato along the tree-lined ramparts walk

San Martino

Lucca's extraordinary cathedral, with its façade abutting incongruously on to the campanile, is dedicated to St Martin. He is the Roman soldier depicted on the façade dividing his cloak with a sword to share with a needy beggar. This and other scenes from the life of the saint form part of the complex decorations covering the 13th-century façade. There are also reliefs depicting *The Labours of the Months* and intricate panels of inlaid pink, green and white marble showing hunting scenes, peacocks and flowers.

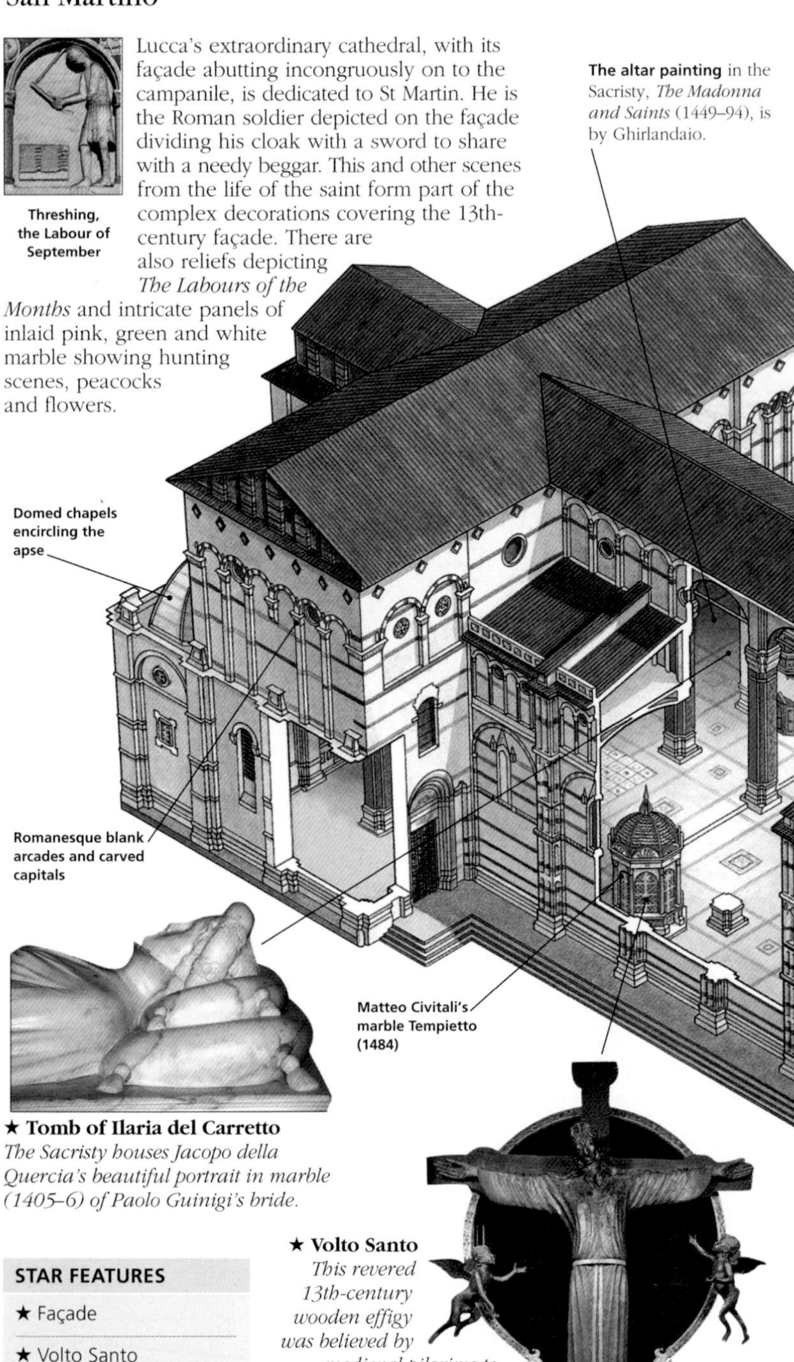

Threshing, the Labour of September

The altar painting in the Sacristy, *The Madonna and Saints* (1449–94), is by Ghirlandaio.

Domed chapels encircling the apse

Romanesque blank arcades and carved capitals

Matteo Civitali's marble Tempietto (1484)

★ Tomb of Ilaria del Carretto

The Sacristy houses Jacopo della Quercia's beautiful portrait in marble (1405–6) of Paolo Guinigi's bride.

★ Volto Santo

This revered 13th-century wooden effigy was believed by medieval pilgrims to have been carved by Christ's follower, Nicodemus, at the time of the Crucifixion.

STAR FEATURES

- ★ Façade
- ★ Volto Santo
- ★ Tomb of Ilaria del Carretto

★ Façade
The gabled façade has three tiers of ornate colonnading (1204). Every one of the carved columns is different, and there are lively hunting scenes above them.

The campanile was built in 1060 as a defensive tower. The upper two tiers were added in 1261 when the tower was joined to the cathedral.

VISITORS' CHECKLIST

***Tel** 0583 95 70 68.* *7am–7pm daily (to 5pm Oct–Mar).* *8am, 10:30am, noon Sun & relig hols, 9am, 6pm Mon–Sat.*
Sacristy & Museum *daily; hours vary.*

St Martin
This sculpture of the saint dividing his cloak to share it is a copy. The 13th-century original is now just inside the cathedral entrance.

Circular clerestory windows, in the nave and above the aisle roof, light the unusually tall nave of the cross-shaped church.

Inlaid Marble
Scenes from daily life, myths and poems cover the façade. Look out for the maze pattern on the right pier of the porch.

Nicola Pisano (1200–78) carved *The Journey of the Magi* and *The Deposition* round the left doorway.

Doorway Sculptures
This 13th-century relief depicts the beheading of St Regulus. The Labours of the Months *round the central door show the tasks appropriate to each season.*

Apostles from the mosaic on the façade of San Frediano in Lucca

San Frediano

Piazza San Frediano. *daily.*

The striking façade of Lucca's San Frediano church features a colourful 13th-century mosaic, *The Ascension,* by the School of Berlinghieri. Inside, to the right, is a splendid Romanesque font which could easily be mistaken for a fountain, because it is so big and impressive. The sides are carved with scenes from *The Life of Christ* and the story of Moses. One dramatic scene shows Moses and his followers dressed in 12th-century armour, looking like Crusaders, as they pass through the divided Red Sea with an entourage of camels.

Amico Aspertini's frescoes (1508–9) in the second chapel in the north aisle tell the story of Lucca's precious relic, the Volto Santo *(see p180)*, and give a good idea of what the city looked like in the early 16th century.

Also in the church is a coloured wooden statue of the Virgin, carved by Matteo Civitali, and an altarpiece carved from a single block of marble by Jacopo della Quercia in the Cappella Trenta. It is carved in the shape of a polyptych with five Gothic-spired niches.

San Michele in Foro

Piazza San Michele. *daily.*

As its name suggests, this church stands on the site of the ancient Roman forum. It has a wonderfully rich Pisan-Romanesque façade that competes in splendour with that of San Martino *(see pp180–81)*. John Ruskin, the English artist and art historian whose work did so much to revive interest in Italian art during the 19th century *(see p55)*, spent many hours sketching the rich mixture of twisted marble columns and Cosmati work (inlaid marble). The façade is almost barbaric in its exuberance, and the inlaid marble scenes depict wild beasts and huntsmen on horseback rather than Christian subjects. Only the huge winged figure of St Michael, standing on the pediment and flanked by two angels, marks this out as a church. The splendour of the façade, built over a long period from the 11th to the 14th centuries, is matched by the arcading of the belltower.

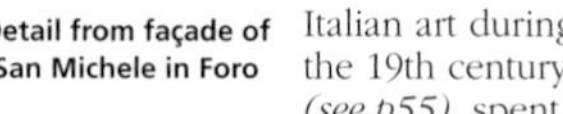
Detail from façade of San Michele in Foro

The interior has little of interest except for Filippino Lippi's restored *Saints Helena, Jerome, Sebastian and Roch*, among the most beautiful of his paintings.

The square outside is circled by 15th- and 16th-century palazzi, which are now mostly occupied by banks, while the portico of the Palazzo Pretorio to the south shelters a 19th-century statue of Lucca's greatest artist and architect, Matteo Civitali (1436–1501).

Via Fillungo

Lucca's principal shopping street winds its way through the heart of the city towards the Anfiteatro Romano *(see p178)*. It is a good place to stroll in the cool of the early evening. The upper end, towards San Frediano church, has several shops with Art Nouveau ironwork, while San Cristoforo, the 13th-century church halfway down the street, holds exhibitions of work by local artists.

Villa Bottini

Via Elisa. ***Tel*** *0583 49 14 49.*

Garden *9am–6pm daily.*

The pretty walled garden of this late 16th-century building is open to the public. It is also used occasionally in summer for outdoor concerts.

Villa Bottini and garden

A Day Out around Lucca

This motoring tour takes you by a scenic route to the best of the villas around Lucca. After leaving Lucca the first stop is the Romanesque church of San Giorgio at Pieve di Brancoli; then comes the ancient hump-backed Ponte della Maddalena, also known as Devil's Bridge *(see p174)*. In the spa town of Bagni di Lucca the pretty suspension bridge across the Lima dates from 1840. On reaching Collodi, explore the village on foot, as the streets are too steep and narrow for cars. The Villa Garzoni, with its splendid gardens, lies below the town, and the Pinocchio Park is on the other side of the road. Continue to the Villa Torrigiani, which is set in a fine park and contains 13th–18th- century porcelain and furnishings. The tour ends at the 17th-century Villa Mansi, with its Baroque façade and a garden enlivened by statues of Diana and other pagan deities.

Bagni di Lucca ③
Drive on along the S12 for 5 km (3 miles) to the spa-town. Then continue along the same road through the town.

Villa Garzoni ④
Turn left at the T-junction on the S12 for Abetone, then right for Collodi and the Villa Garzoni with its terraced gardens.

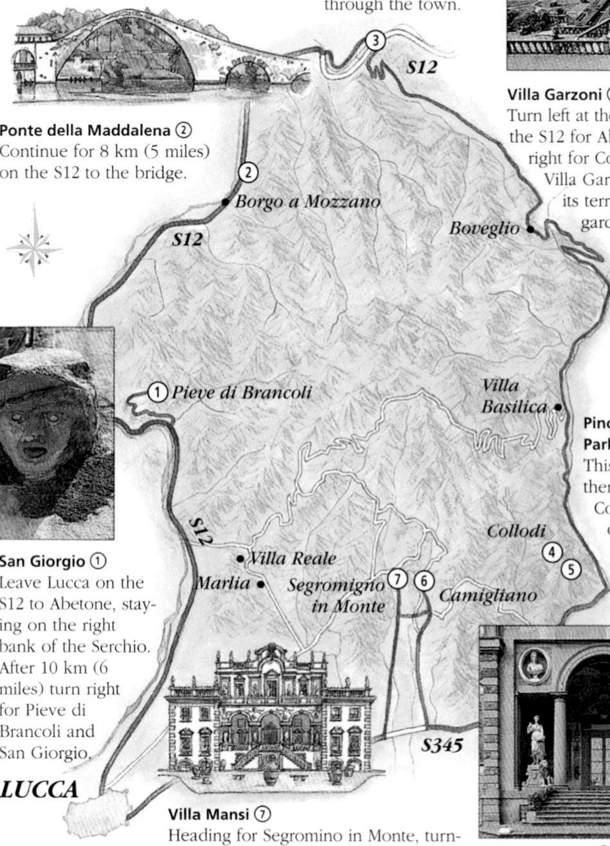

Ponte della Maddalena ②
Continue for 8 km (5 miles) on the S12 to the bridge.

Pinocchio Park ⑤
This children's theme park in Collodi is based on the famous puppet's adventures.

San Giorgio ①
Leave Lucca on the S12 to Abetone, staying on the right bank of the Serchio. After 10 km (6 miles) turn right for Pieve di Brancoli and San Giorgio.

Villa Mansi ⑦
Heading for Segromino in Monte, turn right at the first junction into Via Piaggiori; then follow signs to Villa Mansi.

Villa Torrigiani ⑥
South of Collodi turn right on the S435 for Lucca. After Borgonuovo, turn right for Camigliano Santa Gemma and left after 1.5 km (1 mile) for the villa.

KEY

Tour route

Other roads

0 kilometres 5

0 miles 2

Terme Tettuccio, Montecatini's oldest and most famous spa, rebuilt in 1925–8

Collodi ⓬

Road map C2. 3,000. *Piazza Collodi (0572 42 96 60).*

There are two main sights in this town: the **Villa Garzoni** with its theatrical terraced gardens tumbling down the hillside and, for children, the **Pinocchio Park** *(see p183)*.

The author of *The Adventures of Pinocchio* (1881), Carlo Lorenzini, was born in Florence but his uncle was custodian of the Villa Garzoni and Lorenzini frequently stayed here as a child. Fond memories led him to use Collodi as his pen name and in 1956 the town decided to repay the compliment by setting up the theme park.

The park consists of gardens featuring mosaics and sculptural tableaux based on the adventures of the puppet, plus a maze, playground, exhibition centre and children's restaurant.

Villa Garzoni
Tel *0572 42 95 90.*
Villa *for restoration.*
Garden *9am–5pm daily.*

Pinocchio Park
Tel *0572 42 93 42.*
8:30am–sunset daily.
partial. **www**.pinocchio.it

Pescia ⓭

Road map C2. *18,000.* *Via Fratelli Rosselli 2 (0572 49 09 19).* *Sat.*

Pescia's wholesale flower market is one of Italy's biggest, and there are some interesting sights to visit.

In the church of **San Francesco** are frescoes on *The Life of St Francis* (1235) by Bonaventura Berlinghieri (1215–74). The artist knew St Francis *(see p47)* and it is claimed that the frescoes are an accurate portrait of the saint. The **Duomo**, remodelled in Baroque style by Antonio Ferri in 1693, has a massive campanile that was originally built as a tower within the city walls. It was given its onion-dome "cap" in 1771.

There is a small collection of religious paintings and illuminated manuscripts in the **Museo Civico**, and the **Museo Archeologico della Valdinievole** displays material excavated from nearby Valdinievole, the pretty "Vale of Mist".

San Francesco
Piazza San Francesco. *daily.*

Duomo
Piazza del Duomo. *daily.*

Museo Civico
Palazzo Galeotti, Piazza Santo Stefano 1. ***Tel*** *0572 47 79 44.*
for restoration.

Museo Archeologico della Valdinievole
Piazza Leonardo da Vinci 1.
Tel *0572 47 75 33.* *8:30am–1pm Mon–Fri, 3–5:30pm Tue & Thu.*

Montecatini Terme ⓮

Road map C2. *22,500.* *Viale Verdi 66 (0572 77 22 44).* *Thu.*

Of all Tuscany's many spa towns, Montecatini Terme is the most interesting. It has beautiful formal gardens and the architecture of its spas is particularly distinguished.

Terme Leopoldine (1926), built in the style of a Classical temple, is named after Grand Duke Leopoldo I, who first

The Pescia river, running through a fertile, cultivated landscape

Theatre building in Montecatini Alto's main square

encouraged the development of Montecatini Terme in the 18th century.

The most splendid is the Neo-Classical Terme Tettuccio (1925–8) with its circular, marble-lined pools, fountains and Art Nouveau tiles depicting languorous nymphs.

Terme Torretta, named after its mock medieval tower, is noted for its tea-time concerts, while Terme Tamerici has beautifully tended gardens.

Visitors can obtain day tickets to the spas to drink the waters and relax in the reading, writing and music rooms. More information is available from the Direzione delle Terme at Viale Verdi 41.

A popular excursion from Montecatini Terme is to take the funicular railway up to the ancient fortified village of Montecatini Alto. In the quiet main piazza, there are antique shops and well-regarded restaurants with outdoor tables. From the Rocca (castle) you can take in sweeping views over the mountainous countryside.

Nearby at Ponte Buggianese, in **San Michele** church, you can see modern frescoes by the Florentine artist Pietro Annigoni (1910–88) on the theme of Christ's Passion.

At Monsummano Terme, another of Tuscany's well known spa towns, the **Grotta Giusti** spa prescribes the inhalation of vapours from hot sulphurous springs found in the nearby caves.

Above Monsummano Terme is the fortified hilltop village of Monsummano Alto, with its ruined castle. Today, few people live in the sleepy village, with its pretty 12th-century church and crumbling houses, but there are some fine views from here.

San Michele
Ponte Buggianese.
by appointment.

Grotta Giusti
Monsummano Terme.
Tel *0572 907 71.*
9am–7pm daily.
www.grottagiustispa.com

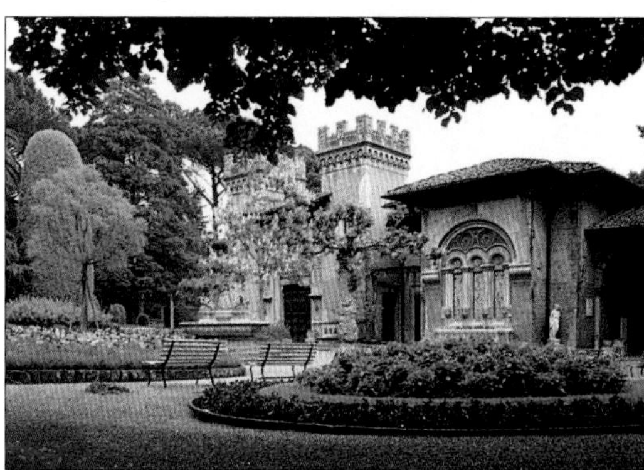

The Terme Tamerici, built in Neo-Gothic style in the early 20th century

TAKING THE WATERS IN TUSCANY

The therapeutic value of bathing was first recognized by the ancient Romans. They were also the first to exploit the hot springs of volcanic origin that they found all over Tuscany. Here they built bath complexes where the army veterans who settled in towns such as Florence and Siena could relax. Some of these spas, as at Saturnia *(see p238)*, are still called by their original Roman names.

Other spas came into prominence during the Middle Ages and Renaissance: St Catherine of Siena (1347–80) *(see p219)*, who suffered from scrofula, a form of tuberculosis, and Lorenzo de' Medici (1449–92), who was arthritic, both bathed in the sulphurous hot springs at Bagno Vignoni *(see p226)* to relieve their ailments. Tuscan spas really came into their own in the early 19th century when Bagni di Lucca was one of the most fashionable spa centres in Europe, frequented by emperors, kings and aristocrats *(see p174)*. However, spa culture in the 19th century had more to do with social life: flirtation and gambling took precedence over health cures.

1920s spa poster

Today treatments such as inhaling sulphur-laden steam, drinking the mineral-rich waters, hydro massage, bathing and application of mud packs are prescribed for disorders ranging from liver complaints to skin conditions and asthma. Many visitors still continue the tradition of coming to fashionable spas such as Montecatini Terme or Monsummano Terme, not just for the benefits of therapeutic treatment but also for relaxation and in search of companionship.

Pistoia ⓯

The Cappella del Tau symbol

The citizens of Pistoia acquired a reputation for viciousness and intrigue in the 13th century and the taint has never quite disappeared. The cause was a feud between two of the city's rival factions, the Neri and Bianchi (Blacks and Whites), that spread to involve other cities. Assassination in Pistoia's narrow alleyways was commonplace. The favoured weapon was a tiny but deadly dagger called the *pistole* made by the city's ironworkers, who also specialized in surgical instruments. The city still thrives on metalworking: everything from buses to mattress springs is made here. Its historic centre has several fine buildings.

Baptistry opposite the Cattedrale

Cattedrale di San Zeno

Piazza del Duomo. ***Tel*** *0573 250 95.* *8am–12:30pm, 3:30–7pm daily.* *side entrance.*
Cappella di San Jacobo *daily.*

Piazza del Duomo, the city's main square, is dominated by the Cattedrale di San Zeno and its bulky campanile, which was originally built in the 12th century as a defensive watchtower in the city walls.

The interior is rich in funerary monuments, including the tomb of poet Cino da Pistoia, in the south aisle. He is depicted in a relief (1337) lecturing to a class of young boys.

Nearby is the Cappella di San Jacobo, with its extraordinary silver altar decorated with over 600 statues and reliefs. The earliest of these date from 1287 and the altar was not completed until 1456. During that time, nearly every silversmith of note in Tuscany contributed to the extraordinarily rich design. Among them was Brunelleschi, who began his career working in metal before switching to architecture. Also in Piazza del Duomo, facing the Cattedrale, is the octagonal Baptistry, which was finished in 1359.

Museo di San Zeno

Palazzo dei Vescovi, Piazza del Duomo. ***Tel*** *0573 36 92 72.* *10am–1pm, 3–5pm Tue, Thu & Fri.* *partial.*

In the beautifully restored Palazzo dei Vescovi (Bishop's Palace) is the Museo della Cattedrale. In the basement, you can see the excavated remains of Roman buildings, and upstairs there are some fine reliquaries, crucifixes and chalices made by local goldsmiths in the 13th–15th centuries.

Museo Civico

Palazzo del Comune, Piazza del Duomo. ***Tel*** *0573 37 12 96.* *10am–5pm Tue, Fri, Sat (to 6pm in summer), 3–6pm Wed (4–7pm in summer), 11am–5pm Sun (to 6pm in summer).* *Mon.*

On the opposite side of the square is the Palazzo del Comune (Town Hall), which has the Museo Civico upstairs. Exhibits here range from medieval altar paintings to the work of 20th-century Pistoian artists, architects and sculptors.

Centro Marino Marini

Palazzo del Tau, Corso Silvano Fedi 30. ***Tel*** *0573 302 85.* *10am–5pm Mon–Fri, 9:30am–12:30pm Sat.*

The work of Marino Marini (1901–80), Pistoia's most famous 20th-century artist, is housed in a museum in the Palazzo del Tau. On display are drawings and casts, which trace the development of his style. Marini specialized in sculpting primitive forms in bronze or clay. His subjects included a horse and rider *(see p104)*, and Pomona, the ancient Roman goddess of fertility.

Pomona **by Marino Marini**

Cappella del Tau

Corso Silvano Fedi 70. ***Tel*** *0573 322 04.* *9am–1pm Mon–Sat.*

This chapel owes its name to the letter T (*tau* in Greek) which appeared on the cloaks of the monks who built it and which symbolized a crutch.

Inside the chapel there are frescoes on *The Creation* and the life of St Anthony Abbot, who founded the order, which is dedicated to tending the sick and crippled.

The Fall**, in the Cappella del Tau**

San Giovanni Fuorcivitas

Via Cavour. *daily.*

Just north of the Cappella del Tau is the 12th-century church of San Giovanni Fuorcivitas ("St John outside the city", since the church once stood beyond the city walls). Its north flank is strikingly clad in banded marble and there is a Romanesque relief of *The Last Supper* over the portal. Inside is Giovanni Pisano's holy water basin, carved in marble with figures of the Virtues, and an equally masterly pulpit by Guglielmo

Detail of frieze (1514–25) by Giovanni della Robbia, Ospedale del Ceppo

da Pisa, carved in 1270 with New Testament scenes. Both works are among the finest of this period, when artists were reviving the art of carving.

Sant'Andrea

Via Sant'Andrea 21. ***Tel*** *0573 219 12.* *8am–12:30pm, 3–6:30pm daily.*

This church is reached by walking through Piazza della Sala, the site of Pistoia's lively open-air market. There is a good Romanesque relief of *The Journey of the Magi* over the portal, and inside is Giovanni Pisano's pulpit (completed in 1301). This is considered by some to be his masterpiece, even more accomplished than the pulpit he later made for Pisa cathedral *(see p159)*. It is decorated with reliefs depicting scenes from the life of Christ.

San Bartolomeo in Pantano

Piazza San Bartolomeo 6. *daily.*

The beautiful Romanesque church of San Bartolomeo in Pantano, dating from 760, houses another celebrated pulpit, carved in 1250 by Guido da Como.

Ospedale del Ceppo

Piazza Giovanni XXIII.

This hospital and orphanage, founded in 1277, was named after the ceppo, or hollowed-out tree trunk, that was used in medieval times to collect donations for its work. The striking façade of the main building features coloured terracotta panels (1514–25) by Giovanni della Robbia illustrating the Seven Works of Corporeal Mercy. The portico is by Michelozzo.

VISITORS' CHECKLIST

Road map C2.
93,000.
FS *Piazza Dante Alighieri.*
Piazza San Francesco.
Palazzo dei Vescovi, Piazza del Duomo 4 (0573 216 22).
Wed & Sat.
Giostra dell'Orso (25 Jul).

Zoo

Via Pieve a Celle 160a. ***Tel*** *0573 91 12 19.* *9am–5pm daily (to 7pm in summer).* **www**.zoodipistoia.it

There is a small, well-kept zoo just 4 km (2.5 miles) northwest of Pistoia at La Verginina.

Façade of San Bartolomeo

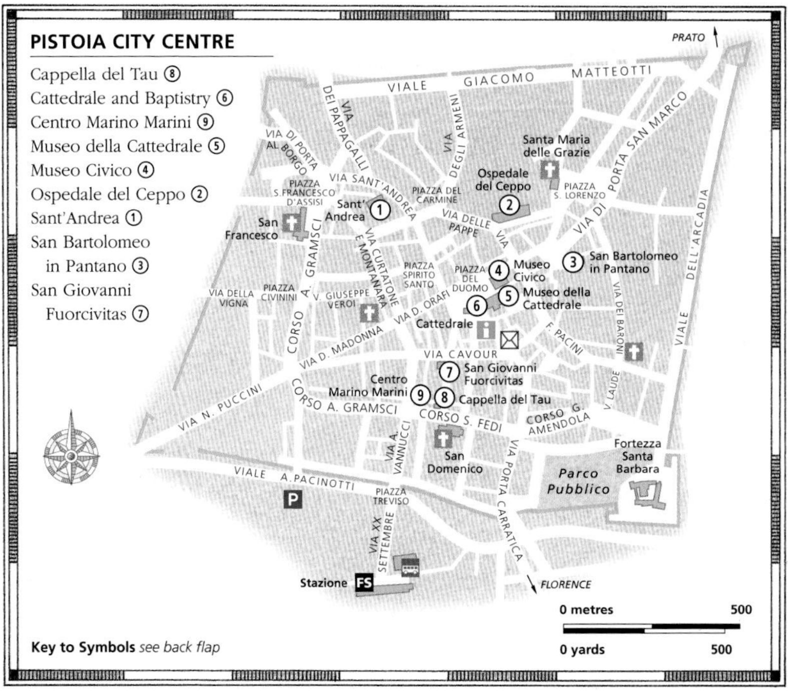

PISTOIA CITY CENTRE

Cappella del Tau ⑧
Cattedrale and Baptistry ⑥
Centro Marino Marini ⑨
Museo della Cattedrale ⑤
Museo Civico ④
Ospedale del Ceppo ②
Sant'Andrea ①
San Bartolomeo in Pantano ③
San Giovanni Fuorcivitas ⑦

Key to Symbols *see back flap*

0 metres 500
0 yards 500

Prato ⑯

Prato has been one of Italy's most important textile-manufacturing cities since the 13th century. One of its most famous citizens was the immensely wealthy Francesco di Marco Datini (1330–1410), who has been immortalized by Iris Origo in *The Merchant of Prato* (1957). Datini left all his money to charity, and the city contains several reminders of him, particularly in his own Palazzo Datini. Prato also attracts pilgrims from all over Italy who come to see the Virgin's Girdle, a prized relic kept in the Duomo and on view five times a year.

Madonna del Ceppo by Fra Filippo Lippi in the Museo Civico

Duomo façade and pulpit

Duomo

Piazza del Duomo. ***Tel*** *0574 26 234.* *7am–noon, 3:30–7pm Mon–Sat; 7am–1pm, 3:30–8pm Sun.*

The Duomo stands on the main square, with the Pulpit of the Holy Girdle to the right of its façade, its frieze of dancing cherubs designed by Donatello (1438). Inside, the first chapel on the left holds the Virgin's Girdle, which is displayed from the pulpit on religious holidays. Frescoes by Agnolo Gaddi (1392–5) relate how the girdle reached Prato. In 1141 a local merchant married a Palestinian woman who brought it with her after inheriting it from the Apostle Thomas, who had been given it by the Virgin herself. Also in the Duomo is Fra Filippo Lippi's masterpiece, *The Life of John the Baptist* (1452–66).

Museo dell'Opera del Duomo

Piazza del Duomo 49. ***Tel*** *0574 293 39.* *10am–1pm, 3–6:30pm Mon–Sat.* *(a cumulative ticket allows entry at the Museo Civico and the Castello dell'Imperatore,* see p189*).* *partial.*

Donatello's original panels for the Holy Girdle pulpit are on display here. The museum also houses the reliquary (1446) made for the Girdle by Maso di Bartolomeo, and *St Lucy* by Filippino Lippi, the son of Fra Filippo Lippi.

Piazza del Comune

The streets around the Duomo contain several important buildings. The city's main street, Via Mazzoni, leads west to the Piazza del Comune with its Bacchus fountain. The original, made in 1659, is in the nearby Palazzo Comunale.

Museo Civico

Palazzo Pretorio, Piazza del Comune 19. ***Tel*** *0574 183 6302.* *for restoration.* *(see Museo dell'Opera del Duomo).* *partial.*

The Museo Civico houses the altar painting *The Story of the Holy Girdle* by Bernardo Daddi (1312–48) and Fra Filippo Lippi's *Madonna del Ceppo*, featuring a portrait of Francesco Datini, a patron of the Ceppo charity *(see p187)*. During restoration work, many paintings are on display at the Museo di Pittura Murale (Piazza S Domenico 8, 0574 440 501).

Palazzo Datini

Via Ser Lapo Mazzei 43. ***Tel*** *0574 213 91.* *9am–12pm, 4–7:30pm Mon–Sat.*

This house where Francesco Datini lived is now a museum. Its archive contains 140,000 business letters and Datini's account books, on which Iris Origo based her biography.

The Story of the Holy Girdle **by Bernardo Daddi in the Museo Civico**

Santa Maria delle Carceri

Piazza delle Carceri. *7am–noon, 4–7pm daily.*

Prato's most important church stands on the site of a prison *(carceri)* on whose wall an image of the Virgin miraculously appeared in 1484. With its harmoniously proportioned interior, the domed church (1485–1506) is a fine work by Renaissance architect Giuliano da Sangallo. Andrea della Robbia created the blue and white glazed terracotta roundels of the Evangelists (1490).

Castello dell'Imperatore

Piazza delle Carceri. *Wed–Sat, Sun morning & Mon. (see Museo dell'Opera del Duomo).*

This castle (1237) was built by the German Holy Roman Emperor Frederick II during his campaign to conquer Italy.

Museo del Tessuto

Via Santa Chiara 24. ***Tel*** *0574 61 15 03. 10am–7pm daily.*

www.museodeltessuto.it

The history of Prato's textile industry, the basis of its wealth, is charted in this textile museum. Located on the city's southern outskirts, it houses historic looms and examples of various types of cloth, such as lush Renaissance embroidery, velvets, lace and damask.

VISITORS' CHECKLIST

Road map D2. *170,000.* *Prato Centrale and Porta al Serraglio.* *Piazzas Ciardi, San Francesco & Stazione.* *Piazza delle Carceri 15 (0574 241 12). 9am–6:30pm Mon–Sat (daily in the summer).* *Mon.*

The imposing Castello dell'Imperatore (1237), built by Frederick II

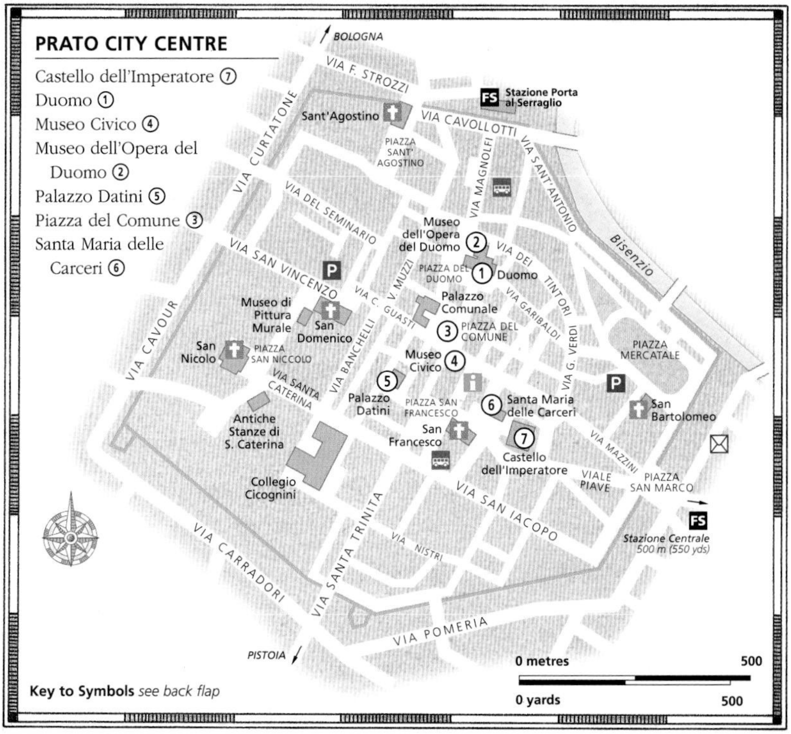

Centro per l'Arte Contemporanea Luigi Pecci

Viale della Repubblica 277.
Tel *0574 53 17. 10am–7pm Wed–Mon.*

www.centropecci.it

Near the Prato Est Autostrada exit, the Luigi Pecci cultural centre is used for changing displays of contemporary art, concerts and films. The centre is also worth a visit for the interesting modern building in which it is housed.

PRATO CITY CENTRE

Castello dell'Imperatore ⑦
Duomo ①
Museo Civico ④
Museo dell'Opera del Duomo ②
Palazzo Datini ⑤
Piazza del Comune ③
Santa Maria delle Carceri ⑥

BOLOGNA
Via F. Strozzi
Stazione Porta al Serraglio
Sant'Agostino
Via Cavollotti
Piazza Sant' Agostino
Via Curtatone
Via Magnolfi
Via Sant'Antonio
Via del Seminario
Bisenzio
Museo dell'Opera del Duomo ②
Via dei Tintori
Via San Vincenzo
Piazza del Duomo
① Duomo
Via C. Guasti
V. Muzzi
Palazzo Comunale
Via Garibaldi
Museo di Pittura Murale
San Domenico
③ Piazza del Comune
Via G. Verdi
Via Cavour
San Nicolo
Piazza San Niccolo
Via Banchelli
Museo Civico ④
Piazza Mercatale
Via Santa Caterina
⑤ Palazzo Datini
Piazza San Francesco
⑥ Santa Maria delle Carceri
San Bartolomeo
Antiche Stanze di S. Caterina
San Francesco
⑦ Castello dell'Imperatore
Via Mazzini
Viale Piave
Piazza San Marco
Collegio Cicognini
Via San Iacopo
Via Santa Trinita
Via Nistri
Stazione Centrale 500 m (550 yds)
Via Carradori
Via Pomeria
PISTOIA

0 metres 500
0 yards 500

Key to Symbols *see back flap*

EASTERN TUSCANY

From the forests of the Mugello and the Casentino to the heights of La Verna, this is an area of outstanding natural beauty. Hermits and mystics have long favoured its more remote reaches, where ancient monastic orders continue to flourish. Only this part of Tuscany could have produced an enigmatic artist like Piero della Francesca, whose celebrated frescoes decorate San Francesco in Arezzo.

Eastern Tuscany's main transport route, the A1 Autostrada, channels speeding traffic southwards along the Arno valley towards Arezzo and Rome. Away from this busy artery, Eastern Tuscany is a little-visited region of steep hills cloaked in beech, oak and sweet chestnut trees. It is particularly attractive in autumn, when the huge forests of the Mugello and the Casentino take on fiery shades of red and gold. This is also the season when mushrooms and truffles abound. Driving through the region at this time of year, you'll see them for sale at roadside stalls.

The tiny mountain pastures to the east of the region are grazed both by sheep, whose milk is made into cheese, and by beautiful white cattle, which were once highly prized by the Romans as sacrificial beasts.

This is also a land of saints, hermits and monasteries. The mountain-top sanctuary of La Verna is reputed to be the place where St Francis received the stigmata – marks resembling Christ's wounds. The 11th-century hermitage at Camaldoli was intended as the site for a Benedictine order who wished to live in complete isolation, but proved so popular with religious day-trippers that a visitors' centre soon had to be built nearby. The monastery at Vallombrosa has such glorious woodlands that John Milton was moved to describe them in his epic poem, *Paradise Lost* (1667).

For art-lovers, eastern Tuscany is the region of Piero della Francesca. His frescoes in Arezzo, largely ignored until the late 19th century, form one of the world's greatest fresco cycles.

Pieve di Santi Ippolito e Donato in Pratovecchio, between Poppi and Stia

◁ **Fertile countryside surrounding Monterchi**

Exploring Eastern Tuscany

The ancient city of Arezzo and the hilltop town of Cortona, with its steep streets, narrow, ladder-like alleys and ancient houses, will amply satisfy visitors in search of culture, art and architecture. The region will also appeal to those who love nature. The woodlands, meadows and streams are ideal for exploring on foot. There are plenty of well-marked paths and picnic areas to encourage you, especially within the beautiful ancient forests surrounding the monasteries at Vallombrosa and Camaldoli.

KEY

- Motorway
- Major road
- Secondary road
- Minor road
- Main railway
- Regional border
- △ Summit
-)(Pass

0 kilometres 10

0 miles 10

Cortona, with its steep streets and medieval towers

GETTING AROUND

The region's main highways, the A1 Autostrada and the S71, linking Bibbiena, Poppi and the Casentino, offer swift access to most of the region. The remaining roads are delightfully rural, particularly the S70, with its fine views near Vallombrosa, but be prepared for steep gradients and hairpin bends. Some roads in the Casentino are very narrow. There are passing places, but a speed limit of 40 km/h (25 mph) means you should leave plenty of time for your journey.

Bus and rail transport is very limited. An intercity train service links Florence to Arezzo, from where there are irregular bus services to other major towns in the region.

For additional map symbols *see back flap*

SIGHTS AT A GLANCE

Anghiari 12
Arezzo 14
Bibbiena 7
Borgo San Lorenzo 2
Camaldoli 5
Caprese Michelangelo 10
The Casentino 9
Cortona 17
La Verna 8
Lucignano 16
Monte San Savino 15
Monterchi 13
The Mugello 1
Poppi 6
Sansepolcro 11
Stia 4
Vallombrosa 3

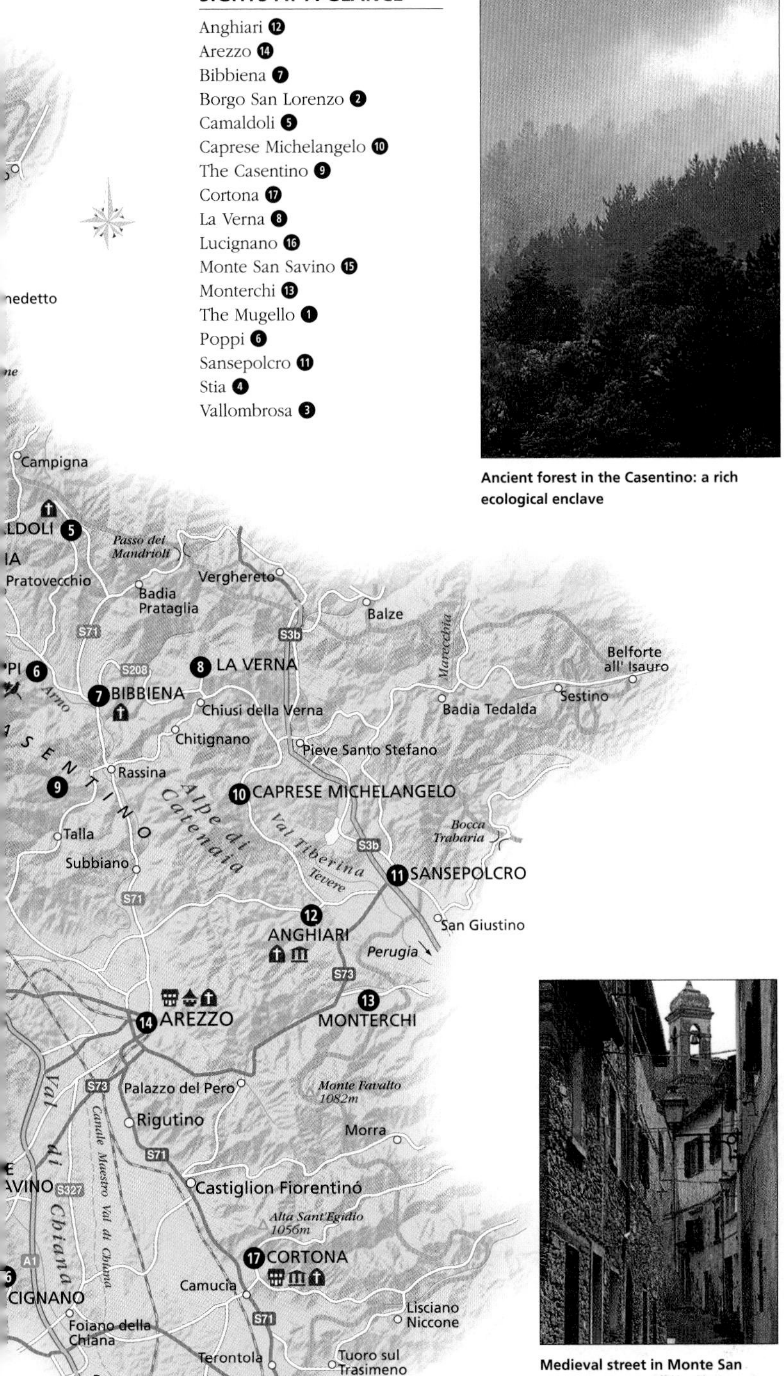

Ancient forest in the Casentino: a rich ecological enclave

Medieval street in Monte San Savino

The Mugello ❶

Road map D2.
FS *Borgo San Lorenzo.*
Largo La Vacchini (055 845 62 30).

The Mugello is the area to the north and east of Florence.

The scenic S65 passes the **Parco Demidoff** at Pratolino, to the south of the region. Here you can see a giant statue of the mountain god, Appennino, carved by Giambologna in 1580. Just to the north, the **Convento di Montesenario** offers excellent views. Further east lies the wine town of Rufina, with its **Museo della Vita e del Vino della Val di Sieve**.

Parco Demidoff
Via Fiorentina 6, Pratolino.
***Tel** 055 40 94 27.* *Apr–Sep: Thu–Sun; Mar & Oct: Sun (call for times).*

Convento di Montesenario
Via Montesenario 1, Bivigliano.
***Tel** 055 40 64 41.* **Church** *daily.* **Convent** *by request.*

Museo della Vita e del Vino della val di Sieve
Villa di Poggio Reale, Rufina.
***Tel** 055 839 79 32.*

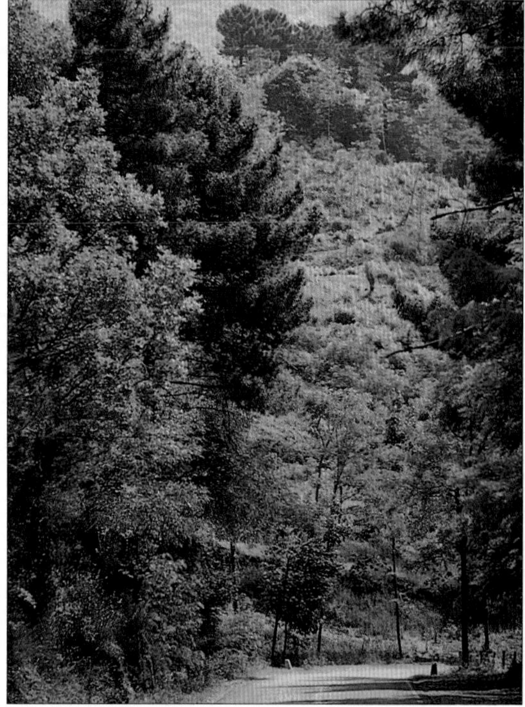

Woodland landscape at Vallombrosa

Borgo San Lorenzo ❷

Road map D2. *15,500.* FS
Largo La Vacchini (055 845 62 30). *Tue.*

Substantially rebuilt after an earthquake in 1919, this is the largest town of the Mugello. The parish church, the **Pieve di San Lorenzo**, has an odd Romanesque campanile, circular in its lower stages and hexagonal above. In the apse, the wall paintings (1906) are by the Art Nouveau artist Galileo Chini. He also worked on the Tabernacle of St Francis (1926), a shrine outside the church, and the Santuario del Santissimo Crocifisso, a church on the edge of town.

To the west are the **Castello del Trebbio**, with its gardens, and the **Villa di Cafaggiolo**, with its bulging clock tower. Among the first Medici villas, both were built for Cosimo il Vecchio by Michelozzo di Bartolommeo (1396–1472).

Tabernacle of St Francis in Borgo San Lorenzo

Pieve di San Lorenzo
Via Cocchi 4. *Mon–Sat, Sun pm.*

Castello del Trebbio
San Piero a Sieve. ***Tel** 055 845 87 93 (Mon, Wed, pm Fri).* *Nov–Easter: Tue–Fri by appt.*

Villa di Cafaggiolo
Cafaggiolo, Barberino di Mugello.
***Tel** 055 849 81 03 (Mon, Wed, Fri am).* *for restoration until late 2011.*

Vallombrosa ❸

Road map D2. *from Florence.* ***Tel** 055 86 20 03.* **Church** *from 3:30pm daily.* **Abbey** *by appt.*

Like the monasteries of the Casentino *(see p196)*, the abbey buildings at Vallombrosa are surrounded by woodland. The routes to this sight are all very scenic.

The Vallombrosan order was founded by Saint Giovanni Gualberto Visdomini in 1038. He aimed to persuade like-minded aristocrats to join him in relinquishing their wealth and adopting a life of great austerity. Contrary to these worthy ideals, the order grew wealthy and powerful during the 16th and 17th centuries. It was then that today's fortress-like abbey was built. Today, the order comprises some 20 monks.

In 1638 the English poet John Milton (1608–74) visited the abbey. The beautiful scenery of this area inspired a passage in his epic poem, *Paradise Lost*.

Façade of Santa Maria Assunta in Stia

Stia ❹

Road map D2. 3,017. *Piazza Tanucci 65 (0575 50 41 06) (summer only). Tue.*

Stia is a bustling, attractive village on the Arno. In the main piazza is the Romanesque church of **Santa Maria Assunta**, with a rather plain façade. Inside is a 16th-century terracotta *Madonna and Child* by Andrea della Robbia.

There are two medieval Guidi family castles close by: **Castello di Palagio**, with an attractive garden, and the **Castello di Porciano**, which houses an agricultural museum.

Santa Maria Assunta
Piazza Tanucci. *daily.*

Castello di Palagio
Via Vittorio Veneto.
Tel *0575 58 33 88.*
Jul–Sep: Sat–Sun, Tue.

Castello di Porciano
Porciano. ***Tel*** *3290 20 92 58.*
by appointment only.

Camaldoli ❺

Road map E2. *from Bibbiena.* ***Tel*** *0575 55 60 12.* **Monastery** *9am–1pm, 2:30–7pm daily (to 7:30pm in summer).* **Hermitage** ***Tel*** *0575 55 60 21. 8:30–11:15am, 3–6pm daily.* **Museo Ornitologico Forestale** ***Tel*** *0575 55 61 30.*

The monastery was founded in 1046 and today houses 40 Carthusian monks. Visitors to Camaldoli will want to see not only the monastery but the original *eremo* (hermitage), 2.5 km (1.5 miles) away. A narrow, winding road leads up from the monastic complex to the hermitage through thick forest. This ancient woodland, which is some of the most ecologically rich in Europe, was declared a National Park in 1991.

The hermitage dates back to 1012 when San Romualdo (St Rumbold) came here with a small group of followers, to cut themselves off completely from the outside world.

Today's monks lead a more gregarious life, running a small café in the monastery below. As you descend to the monastery complex you will also pass numerous picnic spots and some of the many local footpaths.

The monks still tend the magnificent beech and chestnut woodland that surrounds the ancient monastery, as their predecessors have for nearly 1,000 years. A pharmacy, dating to 1543, now sells soaps, toiletries and liqueurs made by the monks.

There is a small, privately owned ornithological museum across the road from the monastery, opposite the car park, which illustrates the area's rich bird life.

Poppi ❻

Road map E2. *6,700.* *Via Cesare Battisti 23 (0575 52 96 82). Tue.*

The older part of Poppi is located high above the town's bus and train termini. Its splendid castle, the imposing **Castello di Poppi**, can be seen from as far away as Bibbiena *(see p196)*. Just to the south of the town is the **Zoo Fauna Europa**, which specializes in the conservation of endangered European species like the Apennine wolf and the lynx.

Visible from Poppi, a short drive to the northwest up the Arno valley, is the 11th-century **Castello di Romena** where Dante stayed as a guest of the local rulers in the early 14th century. Romena's *pieve*, dating to 1152, is a typical example of a Romanesque village church.

Castello di Poppi
Tel *0575 52 99 64.*
Apr–Oct: daily; Nov–Mar: Thu–Sun.
partial.

Zoo Fauna Europa
Poppi. ***Tel*** *0575 52 90 79. 9am–sunset daily.*

Castello di Romena
Pratovecchio.
Tel *Call Tourist Office for info. for restoration.*

Castello di Poppi, which towers over Poppi and overlooks the entire Casentino

Casentino landscape

Bibbiena 7

Road map E2. *11,000.* *Bibbiena train station (0575 59 30 98).* *Thu.*

One of the oldest towns in the region, Bibbiena was the subject of intense territorial feuding between Arezzo and Florence in medieval times. It is now the commercial centre of the Casentino region, surrounded by sprawling factories and industrial buildings.

The town's main attraction is the **Pieve di Santi Ippolito e Donato**. Dating from the 12th century, this church contains some fine Siena School paintings and an altarpiece by Bicci di Lorenzo (1373–1452).

Bibbiena's main square, the Piazza Tarlati, offers excellent views of Poppi *(see p195)*.

Pieve di Santi Ippolito e Donato
Piazza Tarlati. *8am–noon, 3–6pm daily.*

La Verna 8

Road map E2. *from Bibbiena.* ***Tel*** *0575 53 41.* *7am–7pm daily.* *partial.*

The rocky outcrop on which La Verna monastery stands, called La Senna, was split, according to legend, by an earthquake when Christ died on the Cross. The site was given to St Francis by the local ruler, Count Orlando Cattani, in 1213, and it was here, in 1224, that the saint was miraculously marked with the stigmata – the wounds of Christ.

Today, the monastery is both a popular tourist sight and a charismatic religious centre. Its modern buildings are not particularly attractive, but they contain numerous sculptures by the della Robbia workshops. There are several waymarked paths through the surrounding woodland, leading to some excellent viewpoints.

The Casentino 9

Road map E2. *from Bibbiena.* *Bibbiena.*

The vast Casentino region, an area of tiny villages dotted among hills covered with ancient woodland, lies to the north of Arezzo. The river Arno has its source here, on the slopes of Monte Falterona. Countless streams run down the region's valleys to join it, creating stunning waterfalls.

A favourite destination for walkers, the area is renowned for its abundant autumn mushroom crop *(see p202)*.

The monastery at La Verna, founded by St Francis in 1213

Caprese Michelangelo 10

Road map E2. *1,671.* *from Arezzo.* *Via Capoluogo 1 (0575 79 37 76).*

Michelangelo Buonarroti was born in Caprese on 6 March 1475, while his father served as the town's *podestà* – a combination of magistrate, mayor and chief of police. His birthplace is now a museum, the **Comune Casa Natale Michelangelo**, housing photos and copies of the artist's work. The town walls feature modern sculptures and have fine views over the alpine landscape. Michelangelo attributed his keen mind to the mountain air he breathed here as a child.

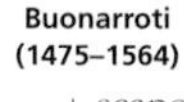
Michelangelo Buonarroti (1475–1564)

Comune Casa Natale Michelangelo
Casa del Podestà, Via Capoluogo 1. ***Tel*** *0575 79 37 76.* *daily; call ahead for up-to-date details of opening hours.* *Tue (Oct–May).*

Sansepolcro 11

Road map E3. *15,700.* *Via Matteotti 8 (0575 74 05 36).* *Tue, Sat.*

Sansepolcro is a busy industrial town, famous as the birthplace of the artist Piero della Francesca (1410–92). The **Museo Civico**, housed in the 14th-century Palazzo Comunale, contains a collection of his work. The most famous exhibit is Piero's fresco *The Resurrection* (1463), in which a curiously impassive Christ strides out of his tomb. The sleeping soldiers at his feet, in their Renaissance armour, seem trapped in time, while the Son of God takes possession of a primitive, eternal landscape. Other works by Piero are displayed in the same room, notably the *Madonna della Misericordia* (1462).

Sansepolcro is home to a number of other major works. Chief among these are Luca Signorelli's 15th-century *Crucifixion* (also in the Museo Civico) and Rosso Fiorentino's Mannerist *Deposition* in **San Lorenzo** church.

Museo Civico
Via Aggiunti 65. ***Tel*** *0575 73 22 18.* *Oct–May: 9:30am–1pm, 2:30–6pm daily; Jun–Sep: 9am–1:30pm, 2:30–7:30pm daily.* *1 Jan, 25 Dec.* *(partial).*

San Lorenzo
Via Santa Croce. ***Tel*** *0575 74 05 36.* *10am–1pm, 3–6pm daily.*

Anghiari ⓬

Road map E3. *5,874.* *Via Matteotti 103 (0575 74 92 79).* *Wed.*

The Battle of Anghiari, between Florence and Milan in 1440, was to have been the subject of a fresco by Leonardo in Florence's Palazzo Vecchio. It was never painted – one of the greatest "lost" works of the Renaissance. Today, this historic little town sits peacefully amid fields of tobacco, a traditional crop of the upper valley of the river Tevere (Tiber), which rises nearby on the slopes of Monte Fumaiolo.

Anghiari, a typical medieval walled town

Museo dell'Alta Valle del Tevere
Piazza Mameli 16. ***Tel*** *0575 78 80 01.* *8:30am–7pm Tue–Sat, 9am–1pm Sun.* *1 Jan, 1 May, 25 Dec.*
Several major works, such as Jacopo della Quercia's fine wooden *Madonna* (1420), can be seen here. There are also displays of locally made furniture and toys.

Santa Maria delle Grazie
Propositura. *daily.*
The town's main church, dating to the 18th century, contains a High Altar and tabernacle from the della Robbia workshops. There is also a 15th-century *Madonna and Child* painted by Matteo di Giovanni.

Museo della Misericordia
Via Francesco Nenci 13. ***Tel*** *0575 78 95 77.* *by appointment.*
The Misericordia, a charitable organization, was founded in the 13th century to look after ailing pilgrims on their way to Rome. Today it operates Tuscany's efficient ambulance service *(see p301)*. This small museum records their work.

The Resurrection **(1463) by Piero della Francesca in Sansepolcro**

Monterchi ⓭

Road map E3. *1,910.* *Arezzo.* *Sun.*

The cemetery chapel at Monterchi was the site chosen in 1460 by Piero della Francesca for his *Madonna del Parto* (Pregnant Madonna) *(see p28)*, possibly because his mother may be buried here. The recently restored fresco is now in the **Museo Madonna del Parto**. A work of haunting ambiguity, it simultaneously captures the Virgin's pride in the impending birth, the weariness of pregnancy and the sorrow borne of knowing that her child will be no ordinary man.

Museo Madonna del Parto
Via Reglia 1. ***Tel*** *0575 707 13.* *9am–1pm, 2–7pm daily (to 5pm Nov–Mar).* *25 Dec.* *(partial).*

Arezzo ⓮

One of the wealthiest cities in Tuscany, Arezzo produces gold jewellery for shops all over Europe. It is famous for Piero della Francesca's frescoes and for its antiques market. Following World War II, there was much rebuilding – broad avenues have replaced many of the medieval alleys. The Chimera fountain near the station is a reminder of the city's past. It is a copy of an Etruscan bronze *(see p42)* cast here in 380 BC.

Duomo façade, completed as recently as 1914

Chimera fountain

San Francesco

See pp200–201.

Pieve di Santa Maria

Corso Italia 7. ***Tel*** *0575 226 29.* *8:30am–12:30pm, 3–6:30pm daily.* **www**.pievesantamaria.it

Arezzo's main shopping street, Corso Italia, leads uphill to the Pieve di Santa Maria, which has a beautifully ornate Romanesque façade. Sadly, the complex filigree of interlaced arches has weathered badly.

The splendid campanile, the "tower of a hundred holes", dates to 1330. Its name derives from the many arches running through it.

Piazza Grande

The square is famous for its antiques market *(see p286)*. On the west side, the façade of the Palazzo della Fraternità dei Laici is decorated with a relief of the Virgin (1434) by Bernardo Rossellino. The lower half of the building dates from 1377. The belfry and clock tower date from 1552.

The north side of the square features a handsome arcade designed by Vasari in 1573.

Fortezza Medicea e Parco il Prato

Tel *0575 37 76 78.* *summer: 7am–8pm; winter: 7:30am–6:30pm.*

Antonio da Sangallo the Younger's imposing fortress was built for Cosimo I during the 16th century. It was partly demolished in the 18th century, leaving only the ramparts intact. With its excellent views across the Arno valley, it remains an excellent spot for a picnic.

The same can be said of the city's large public park, the Parco il Prato, with its extensive lawns. It contains a huge statue (1928) of the great poet Petrarch. The house where he was born stands at the entrance to the park.

Duomo

Piazza del Duomo. *daily.*

Begun in 1278, the Duomo remained incomplete until 1510; its façade dates to 1914. A huge building, its Gothic interior is lit through windows containing beautiful 16th-century stained glass by Guillaume de Marcillat, a French artist who settled in Arezzo.

High on the wall to the left of the 15th-century High Altar can be seen the tomb of Guido Tarlati, bishop and ruler of Arezzo from 1312 until his death in 1327. Carved reliefs depict scenes from his unconventional life. Next to the tomb is a small fresco of Mary Magdalene by Piero della Francesca (1410–92).

The Lady Chapel, fronted by an intricate wrought-iron screen (1796), contains a terracotta *Assumption* by Andrea della Robbia (1435–1525).

Museo del Duomo

Piazzetta behind the Duomo 13. ***Tel*** *0575 239 91.* *10am–noon Thu–Sat. Ask the sacristan to let you in.*

Among the artifacts removed from the cathedral are three wooden crucifixes, dating from the 12th and 13th centuries. The oldest of these was painted by Margaritone di Arezzo in 1264.

Also of interest are Bernardo Rossellino's terracotta bas-relief of *The Annunciation* (1434), a number of frescoes by Vasari (1512–74) and an *Annunciation* by Spinello Aretino (1373–1410).

Apse of Pieve di Santa Maria and Palazzo della Fraternità dei Laici in Piazza Grande

For hotels and restaurants in this region see pp258–59 and pp276–78

Casa del Vasari

Via XX Settembre 55. ***Tel*** *0575 40 90 40.* *8:30am–7pm Mon, Wed–Sat (to 1pm Tue, Sun & pub hols).*

Vasari (1512–74) built this house for himself in 1540 and decorated the ceilings and walls with portraits of fellow artists, friends and mentors. He also painted himself looking out of one of the windows. A prolific painter and architect, Vasari is most famous for his book, *Lives of the Most Excellent Painters, Sculptors and Architects* (1550). An account of many great Renaissance artists, it has, in spite of an often cavalier attitude to the truth, led to Vasari being described as the first art historian.

Detail of fresco from Casa del Vasari

Museo Statale d'Arte Medioevale e Moderna

Via di San Lorentino 8. ***Tel*** *0575 40 90 50.* *9am–7pm daily.* *1 Jan, 1 May, 25 Dec.*

The museum is housed in the graceful 15th-century Palazzo Bruni. Its courtyard contains architectural fragments and sculptures dating from the 10th to the 17th centuries.

The collection includes one of the best displays of majolica pottery in Italy. There are also several terracottas by Andrea della Robbia and his followers; frescoes by Vasari and Signorelli; and paintings by 19th-and 20th-century artists, including members of the Italian *Macchiaioli* School *(see p123)*.

Anfiteatro Romano e Museo Archeologico

Via Margaritone 10. ***Tel*** *0575 222 59.* **Amphitheatre** *8:30am–6pm daily (to 8pm in summer).* **Museum** *8:30am–7:30pm daily.* *1 Jan, 1 May, 25 Dec.* *for the museum.*

A ruined Roman amphitheatre stands near the Museo Archeologico. Famous for its extensive collection of Roman Aretine ware, the museum has a display showing how this high-quality red-glazed pottery was produced and exported throughout the Roman Empire during the 1st century BC.

1st-century BC Aretine ware

VISITORS' CHECKLIST

Road map E3. *92,000.* **FS** *Piazza della Repubblica.* *P. della Repubblica 28 (0575 37 76 78).* *Sat.* *Giostra del Saracino (3rd Sun in Jun and 1st Sun in Sep).* ***Early closing*** *Sat (Mon am in winter).* **www**.apt.arezzo.it

Santa Maria delle Grazie

Via di Santa Maria. *8am–7pm daily.*

Completed in 1449 and set in its own walled garden, this church, fronted by Benedetto da Maiano's pretty loggia (1482), stands on the south-eastern outskirts of the town. The High Altar, by Andrea della Robbia (1435–1525), encloses Parri di Spinello's fresco of the Virgin (1430). A damaged fresco by Lorentino d'Arezzo (1430–1505) is on the right of the altar.

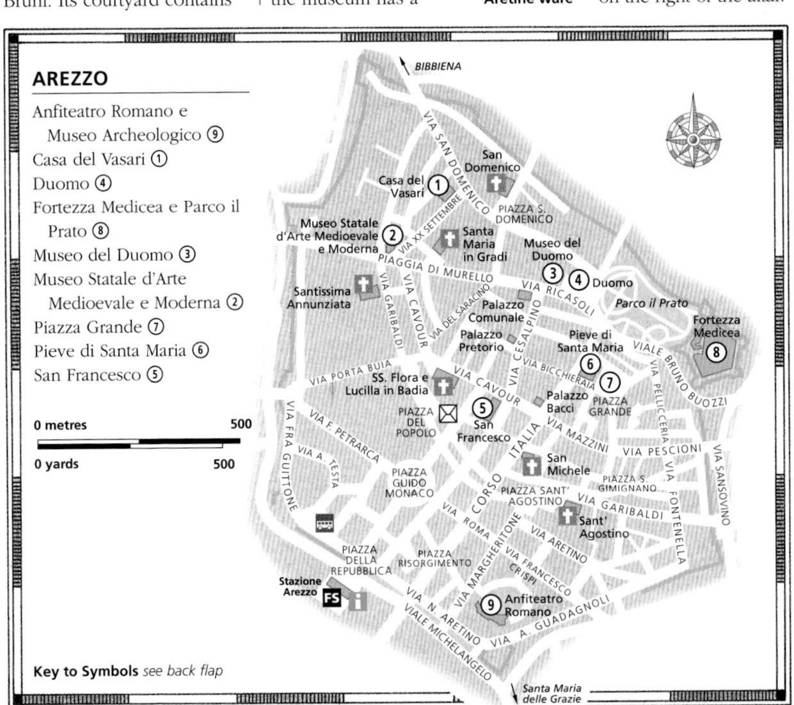

San Francesco

The 13th-century church of San Francesco contains Piero della Francesca's *Legend of the True Cross* (1452–66), one of Italy's greatest fresco cycles. The frescoes, now visible again after a long restoration, show how the Cross was found near Jerusalem by the Empress Helena. Her son, the Emperor Constantine, adopted it as his battle emblem. In reality, Constantine granted the Christian faith official recognition through the Edict of Milan, signed in 313. He is said to have bequeathed the Empire to the Church in 337, although this was still hotly disputed when Piero painted the frescoes. Visitors have a limited time in the chapel and advance booking is mandatory.

Exaggerated Hats
Piero often depicted historical figures in Renaissance garb.

Judas reveals where the Cross is hidden.

The Cross returns to Jerusalem.

Painted Crucifix
The 13th-century Crucifix forms the focal point of the fresco cycle. The figure at the foot of the Cross represents St Francis.

The Empress Helena watches the Cross being dug up. The town shown in the background, symbolizing Jerusalem, is an accurate representation of 15th-century Arezzo.

The Annunciation, with its stately figures and aura of serenity, is typical of Piero's enigmatic style.

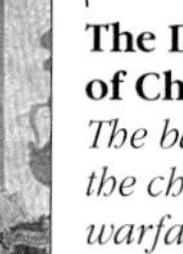

The Defeat of Chosroes
The battle scene shows the chaos of Renaissance warfare. Piero was influenced by ancient Roman carving, especially the battle scenes that often decorated sarcophagi.

The Death of Adam
This vivid portrayal of Adam and Eve in old age illustrates Piero's masterly treatment of anatomy. He was one of the first Renaissance artists to paint nude figures.

VISITORS' CHECKLIST

Piazza San Francesco. ***Tel*** *0575 206 30.* *9am–6pm Mon–Sat (to 5:30 Sat); 1–5:30pm Sun. Book ahead (0575 35 27 27).* **www**.pierodellafrancesca.it

The prophets appear to play no part in the narrative cycle; their presence may be for purely decorative reasons.

The buildings in the fresco reflect the newly fashionable Renaissance style in architecture *(see p25).*

The wood of the Cross is buried in a pit.

Constantine dreams of the Cross on the eve of battle.

Constantine adopts the Cross as his battle emblem.

The Queen of Sheba recognizes the wood of the Cross.

Solomon's Handshake
The Queen's handshake with Solomon, King of Israel, symbolizes 15th-century hopes for a union between the Orthodox and Western churches.

Mushrooms in Tuscany

Champignon
(Marasmius oreades)

The people of Tuscany consider mushrooms a great delicacy. Collecting fungi can be dangerous, unless you are an expert, but you can sample the best varieties in the region's restaurants. The smaller edible varieties are sometimes chopped and combined with mashed garlic to make a pasta sauce. As starters, many menus include *funghi trifolati* (sautéed mushrooms with garlic and parsley), or the region's most popular mushrooms, porcini, served *in gratella* (grilled). The prized truffle is often simply grated over home-made pasta; it has a pronounced flavour and should be used sparingly.

Gathering chanterelles *(right)* and saddle fungus *(left)*

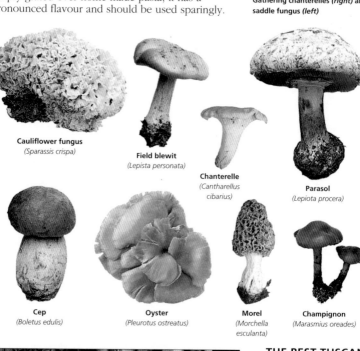

Cauliflower fungus
(Sparassis crispa)

Field blewit
(Lepista personata)

Chanterelle
(Cantharellus cibarius)

Parasol
(Lepiota procera)

Cep
(Boletus edulis)

Oyster
(Pleurotus ostreatus)

Morel
(Morchella esculanta)

Champignon
(Marasmius oreades)

THE BEST TUSCAN MUSHROOMS

Prized species have a rich flavour and a firm texture. They are sold from mid-September to late November at shops and markets throughout the region.

Porcini
This popular mushroom, known in England as the cep, is one of the few wild species available all year, either fresh or dried.

Monte San Savino 15

Road map E3. 7,794. FS
Piazza Gamurrini 3 (0575 817 71). *Wed.*

The town stands on the western edge of the Valdichiana, once a marshy and malaria-ridden plain that was drained by Cosimo I in the 16th century. It is now an area of rich farmland used to rear cattle whose meat is used for *Bistecca alla Fiorentina*, the famous beefsteaks served in Florentine restaurants *(p267)*.

Agriculture has made the town prosperous, and its streets are lined with handsome buildings and churches. Some of these are by the High Renaissance sculptor and architect Andrea Contucci, known as Sansovino (1460–1529), who was born in the town; a number are by Antonio da Sangallo the Elder (1455–1537), his contemporary.

The town's main street, Corso Sangallo, starts at the Porta Fiorentina town gate, built in 1550 to Giorgio Vasari's design. The street leads past the 14th-century Cassero, or Citadel, whose exterior walls are now almost entirely hidden by 17th-century houses. There are good views from the interior, which contains the tourist office and the small

Corso Sangallo in Monte San Savino

Lucignano, with its circular street plan

Museo del Cassero with its extensive collection of local work. Further up the street is the handsome Classical Loggia dei Mercanti (1518–20), designed by Sansovino, and the Palazzo Comunale, originally built as the Palazzo di Monte by Sangallo for Cardinal Antonio di Monte in 1515. Sansovino's house can be seen in the Piazza di Monte. He laid out the square, built the fine double loggia with Ionic columns that fronts **Sant'Agostino** church and went on to design the cloister standing alongside it. Inside the church is a series of 15th-century frescoes illustrating scenes from *The Life of Christ*, and Vasari's *Assumption* altarpiece (1539). Sansovino's worn tomb slab lies beneath the pulpit.

Locally made vase, Museo di Ceramica

Museo del Cassero
Piazza Gamurrini. ***Tel*** *0575 817 71.*
by appt.

Sant'Agostino
Piazza di Monte. *daily.*

Lucignano 16

Road map E3. 3,349.
Piazza del Tribunale 22 (0575 838 01). Thu.

An attractive medieval town, Lucignano contains many well-preserved 14th-century houses. The street plan is extremely unusual, consisting of a series of four concentric rings encircling the hill upon which the town sits, sheltered by its ancient walls. There are four small piazzas at the centre.

The **Collegiata** is fronted by some attractive steps whose circular shape reflects the town's street plan. Completed by Orazio Porta in 1594, the church contains some fine gilded wooden angels added in 1706.

The 14th-century Palazzo Comunale houses the **Museo Comunale**. Its highlight is a massive gold reliquary, 2.5 m (8 ft) high, to which numerous artists contributed over the period 1350–1471. Because of its shape, it is known as the *Tree of Lucignano*.

Also of note are two 14th-century paintings by Luca Signorelli: a lunette showing St Francis of Assisi miraculously receiving the wounds of Christ to his hands and feet, and a *Madonna and Child*. There are several fine 13th- to 15th-century Siena School paintings and a small painting of the Madonna by Lippo Vanni (1341–75).

The vaulted ceiling of the main chamber, the Sala del Tribunale, has frescoes of famous biblical figures and characters from Classical mythology painted from 1438–65 by various Siena School artists.

Collegiata
Costa San Michele.
Tel *0575 83 61 22.*

Museo Comunale
Piazza del Tribunale 22. ***Tel*** *0575 83 80 01. 10am–1pm, 3–6pm Tue, Thu–Sun; by appt Wed (winter: open only Sat & Sun).*

Cortona ⓱

Cortona is one of the oldest cities in Tuscany. It was founded by the Etruscans *(see p42)*, whose work can still be seen in the foundations of the town's massive stone walls. The city was a major seat of power during the medieval period, able to hold its own against larger towns like Siena and Arezzo; its decline followed defeat by Naples in 1409, after which it was sold to Florence and lost its autonomy. The main street, Via Nazionale, is remarkably flat in comparison with the rest of Cortona. The numerous ladder-like alleys leading off it, for instance the Vicolo del Precipizio (Precipice Alley), are far more typical.

Medieval houses in Via Janelli

Palazzo Comunale

Palazzo Comunale

● *to the public.*

Dating from the 13th century, the building was enlarged at the beginning of the 16th century, to incorporate the distinctive tower. Its ancient steps are the ideal place to linger in the early evening.

Museo dell'Accademia Etrusca

Palazzo Casali, Piazza Signorelli 9. ***Tel*** *0575 63 72 35.* ◯ *Apr–Oct: 10am–7pm daily; Nov–Mar: 10am–5pm Tue–Sun.* ● *1 Jan, 25 Dec.* *partial.*

This is one of the region's most rewarding museums. It contains a number of major Etruscan artifacts, including a unique bronze chandelier *(see p43)* dating from the 4th century BC. There are also a number of Egyptian objects. These include a wooden model funerary boat dating to the second millennium BC.

On the west wall of the main hall is a beautiful fresco of Polymnia, the muse of song. It was once believed to be Roman and date from the 1st- or 2nd-century AD, but it is now known to be a brilliant 18th-century fake.

Duomo

Piazza del Duomo. ◯ *daily.*

The present Duomo was designed by Giuliano da Sangallo in the 16th century. Remains of an earlier Romanesque building were incorporated into the west façade. The entrance is through an attractive doorway (1550) by Cristofanello.

Museo Diocesano

Piazza del Duomo 1. ***Tel*** *0575 628 30.* ◯ *Apr–Oct: 10am–7pm daily; Nov–Mar: 10am–5pm Tue–Sun.*

Housed in the 16th-century church of Gesù, the museum contains several masterpieces. Chief among these are Fra Angelico's *Annunciation* (1428–30), a *Crucifixion* by Pietro Lorenzetti (c.1280–1348) and a *Deposition* by Luca Signorelli (1441–1523). There is also a Roman sarcophagus, featuring Lapiths and Centaurs, which was much admired by Donatello and Brunelleschi.

Via Janelli

The medieval houses in this short street are some of the oldest to survive in Italy. A striking feature is their overhanging upper floors, built out on massive timbers.

San Francesco

Via Maffei. ● *to the public.*

The church was built in 1245 by Brother Elias, a native of Cortona, who succeeded St Francis as leader of the Franciscan order. He and the Painter Luca Signorelli (1441–1523), also born locally, are buried here.

The Annunciation **(1428–30) by Fra Angelico in the Museo Diocesano**

Piazza Garibaldi

Located on the eastern edge of town, this square is a favourite haunt of American students who come to Cortona each summer. It offers superb views of the handsome Renaissance church of Santa Maria delle Grazie al Calcinaio.

Via Crucis and Santa Margherita

The Via Crucis, a long uphill lane with gardens on either side, leading to the 19th-century church of Santa Margherita, was laid out as a war memorial in 1947. It is decorated with Futurist mosaics depicting episodes in Christ's Passion by Gino Severini (1883–1966).

The church, rebuilt from 1856–97 in the Romanesque-Gothic style, has excellent views over the surrounding country-side. Inside, to the right of the altar, lie a number of Turkish battle standards and lanterns captured during 18th-century naval battles. A single rose window remains from the original church.

Santa Maria delle Grazie

Santa Maria delle Grazie

Calcinaio. daily.

A 15-minute stroll from the centre of town, this remarkable Renaissance church (1485) is one of the few surviving works by Francesco di Giorgio Martini (1439–1502). The building is opened on request – ask at the caretaker's house, beyond a garden to the right of the main entrance.

The attractive High Altar (1519), built by Bernardino Covatti, contains a 15th-century image of the Madonna del Calcinaio. The stained glass is by Guillaume de Marcillat *(see p198)*.

VISITORS' CHECKLIST

Road map E3. *22,620.* *Camucia, 5 km (3 miles) SE.* *Piazza Garibaldi.* *Via Nazionale 42 (0575 63 03 52).* *Sat.* *Sagra della Bistecca (14–15 Aug).* ***Shops*** *Mon am.*

Tanella di Pitagora

Maestà del Sasso, on the road to Sodo. ***Tel*** *0575 63 04 15. daily. Book one day in advance at the Museo dell'Accademia Etrusca (see p204).*

"Pythagoras's tomb" draws its name from a mix-up between Cortona and Pythagoras's birthplace, Crotone. Two Etruscan tombs nearby are called "melons" because of the grassy mounds around them.

Tanella di Pitagora, a Hellenic-style tomb on the plain below Cortona

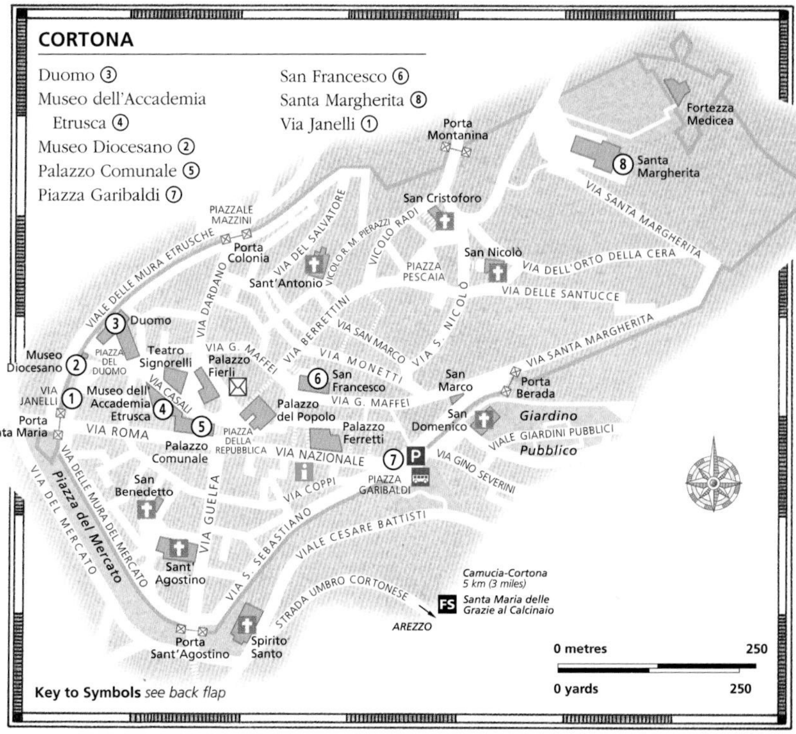

CORTONA

Duomo ③
Museo dell'Accademia Etrusca ④
Museo Diocesano ②
Palazzo Comunale ⑤
Piazza Garibaldi ⑦
San Francesco ⑥
Santa Margherita ⑧
Via Janelli ①

0 metres 250
0 yards 250

Key to Symbols *see back flap*

37

CENTRAL TUSCANY

With Siena at its heart, this is an agricultural area of great scenic beauty, noted for its historic walled towns such as San Gimignano and Pienza. To the north of Siena is the Chianti Classico region, where some of Italy's best wines are produced; to the south is the Crete, with landscapes characterized by round clay hillocks, eroded of topsoil by heavy rain over the centuries.

The vine-clad hills to the north of Siena are dotted with farmhouses, villas and baronial castles. Many are now turned into luxury hotels or rental apartments, offering various leisure facilities such as tennis courts, swimming pools and riding stables: this is now one of the most popular areas for family holidays in the Tuscan countryside.

To the south of Siena, in the Crete, shepherds tend sheep whose milk is used to produce the *pecorino* cheese popular throughout Tuscany. Cypress trees, planted to provide windbreaks along roads and around isolated farms, are an important sculptural feature in this empty and primeval landscape.

Linking the two regions is the S2 highway, an ancient road along which pilgrims made their way in the Middle Ages, followed by travellers on the Grand Tour *(see p55)* in the 18th and 19th centuries. Romanesque churches line the roads, and the valleys and passes are defended by castles and garrison towns, most of which have hardly changed over the years.

CONSTANT CONFLICT

The history of the region is of a long feud between the two city states of Florence and Siena. Siena's finest hour was its victory in the Battle of Montaperti in 1260, but when Siena finally succumbed to the Black Death, and subsequently to a crushing defeat by Florence in the siege of 1554–5, the city went into decline.

As several other Central Tuscan cities experienced the same fate, this lovely region became a forgotten backwater, frozen in time. But after centuries of neglect, the graceful late-medieval buildings in many of the towns are now being well restored, making this the most architecturally rewarding part of Tuscany to explore.

The beautifully preserved fortified town of Monteriggioni

◁ **A house in San Quirico d'Orcia, bathed in the morning light**

Exploring Central Tuscany

The beautiful city of Siena, with its narrow streets and medieval buildings of rose-coloured brick, is the natural starting place for exploring the heart of Tuscany. From here it is only a short drive to the castle-dotted landscapes of Chianti to the north, or to historic towns such as San Gimignano and Montepulciano. Although these towns are full of visitors during the day, at night they revert to their timeless Tuscan character and many have first-class restaurants serving local fare. The landscape is of cypresses, olive groves, vineyards, simple churches and stone farmhouses.

Wicker-covered *damigiane* (demijohns) transporting local Chianti wine

GETTING AROUND

The S2 is the main road south through Siena. The S222 links Florence with Siena and is known as the *Chiantigiana* (Chianti Way) as it passes through the Chianti wine-growing area. Both routes are well served by bus services, and tour operators in both cities offer tours of the main sites. Train services are limited to one line between Florence and Siena. A car is a great advantage, especially for visiting the Chianti wine estates.

KEY

- Motorway
- Major road
- Secondary road
- Minor road
- Scenic route
- Main railway
- Minor railway
- Regional border
- △ Summit

0 kilometres 10

0 miles 10

View over Siena from the surrounding hills

For additional map symbols *see back flap*

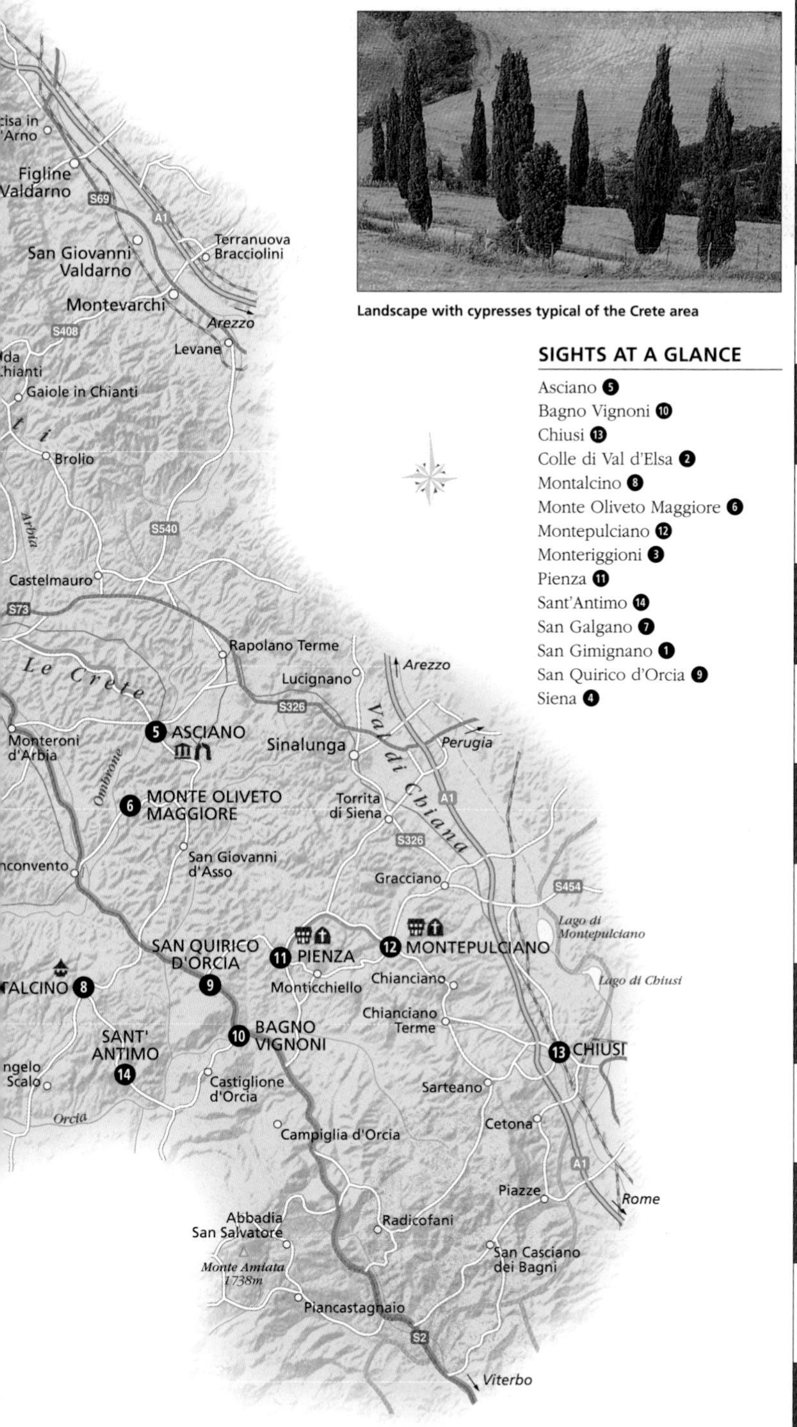

Landscape with cypresses typical of the Crete area

SIGHTS AT A GLANCE

Asciano 5
Bagno Vignoni 10
Chiusi 13
Colle di Val d'Elsa 2
Montalcino 8
Monte Oliveto Maggiore 6
Montepulciano 12
Monteriggioni 3
Pienza 11
Sant'Antimo 14
San Galgano 7
San Gimignano 1
San Quirico d'Orcia 9
Siena 4

Palazzo Campana, the gateway to Colle Alta

San Gimignano ❶

See pp212–15

Colle di Val d'Elsa ❷

Road map C3. *17,200.* *Via Campana 43 (0577 92 27 91).* *Fri.*

Colle di val d'Elsa has a lower and an upper town. Colle Alta, the upper town, is of great medieval architectural interest. Arnolfo di Cambio, who built the Palazzo Vecchio in Florence *(see pp78–9)*, was born here in 1232. In the modern lower town shops sell locally made crystal glass.

Palazzo Campana

to the public.

This Mannerist palazzo was built on a viaduct in 1539 by Baccio d'Agnolo, forming a gateway to Colle Alta.

Duomo

Piazza del Duomo. *4–5pm Mon–Fri, Sun morning (for Mass only).*

The Duomo has a marble Renaissance pulpit carved with bas-reliefs of the Madonna (1465), attributed to Giuliano da Maiano. The façade was rebuilt in 1603.

Museo Archeologico

Palazzo Pretorio, Piazza del Duomo. ***Tel*** *0577 92 04 90.* *Oct–Apr: 3:30–5:30pm Tue–Fri, 10am–noon, 3–6pm Sat & Sun; May–Sep: 10am–noon, 5–7pm Tue–Sun (from 4pm Sat & Sun).*

The museum houses many Etruscan funerary urns. The building was once a jail: Communist slogans written on the walls survive from the 1920s.

Museo d'Arte Sacra

Via del Castello 31. ***Tel*** *0577 92 38 88.* *see Museo Civico.*

Part of the Museo Civico, this museum features 14th-century frescoes of hunting scenes by Bartolo di Fredi, Sienese paintings and a collection of Etruscan pottery.

Sgraffito cherub, Museo Civico

Museo Civico

Via del Castello 31. ***Tel*** *0577 92 38 88.* *Apr–Oct: 10am–noon, 4–7pm Tue–Sun; Nov–Mar: 10:30am–12:30pm, 3:30–5:30pm Tue–Sun.*

The museum is housed in the ancient Palazzo dei Priori, whose façade is decorated with *sgraffito* work scratched in the plaster, incorporating cherubs and Medici coats of arms. There is a small collection of Siena School paintings and some fine examples of Etruscan pottery. The chapel next to the main room has a portico decorated with frescoes by Simone Ferri in 1581.

Santa Maria in Canonica

Via del Castello. *sporadically.*

The Romanesque church has a simple belltower and a stone façade decorated with brickwork. The interior was altered in the 17th century, and now contains a tabernacle by Pier Francesco Fiorentino, showing scenes from the lives of the Madonna and Child.

Porta Nova

Via Gracco del Secco. *daily.*

This large Renaissance fortress was designed by Giuliano da Sangallo in the 15th century to guard against attack from the Volterra road. Two heavily fortified cylindrical towers are on the outside of the building.

Monteriggioni ❸

Road map D3. *720.* *Piazza Roma 23 (0577 30 48 10).*

Monteriggioni is a gem of a medieval hilltop town. It was built in 1203 and ten years later became a garrison town. It is totally encircled by high walls with 14 heavily fortified towers, built to guard the northern borders of Siena's territory against invasion by Florentine armies.

Dante used the town as a simile for the abyss at the

Craft shop in the main piazza of Monteriggioni

heart of his *Inferno*, which compares Monteriggioni's "ring-shaped citadel … crowned with towers" to giants standing in a moat.

The walls, which are still perfectly preserved, are best viewed from the direction of the Colle di Val d'Elsa road. Within the walls, the sleepy village consists of a large piazza, a pretty Romanesque church, a few houses, a couple of craft shops, restaurants, and shops selling many of the excellent local Castello di Monteriggioni wines.

Siena ❹

See pp216–23.

Asciano ❺

Road map D3. *6,250.* FS *Corso Matteotti 78 (0577 71 88 11).* *Sat.*

The road from Siena to Asciano passes through the strange Crete landscape of clay hillocks, almost bare of vegetation and looking like massive anthills. Asciano itself is medieval, and retains much of its fortified wall, built in 1351. The main street, Corso Matteotti, is lined with smart shops and Classical *palazzi*. At the top of the street, in Piazza della Basilica, there is a large fountain built in 1472. Facing it is the late 13th-century Romanesque **Basilica di Sant'Agata**.

The Romanesque Basilica di Sant'Agata in Asciano

***Temptation of St Benedict* (1508) by Sodoma in Monte Oliveto Maggiore**

The **Museo Civico Archeologico e d'Arte Sacra** in the Palazzo Corboli unites two previously separate museums under one roof. Included in the collection are late Siena School masterpieces – Duccio's *Madonna and Child* and Ambrogio Lorenzetti's unusual *St Michael the Archangel*. Also on display are local Etruscan finds from the **Necropoli di Poggio Pinci**, 5 km (3 miles) east of the village. The artifacts come from tombs built between the 7th and 4th centuries BC. On Via Mameli, the **Museo Amos Cassioli** has a display of portraits by Cassioli, who lived here from 1832–91, and other modern works by local artists.

Basilica di Sant'Agata
Piazza della Basilica. *daily.*

Museo Civico Archeologico e d'Arte Sacra
Palazzo Corboli, Corso Matteotti 118. ***Tel*** *0577 71 95 24.* *Apr–Oct: 10:30am–1pm, 3–6:30pm Wed–Sun; Nov–Mar: 10:30am–1pm, 3–5:30pm Thu–Sun.*

Necropoli di Poggio Pinci
Poggio Pinci. *call tourist office for opening times.*

Museo Amos Cassioli
Via Mameli. ***Tel*** *0577 71 72 33.* *Tue, Thu, Fri & Sat.*

Monte Oliveto Maggiore ❻

Road map D3. ***Tel*** *0577 70 70 18.* *9:15am–noon, 3:15–5:45pm daily (to 6pm in the summer).*

The approach to this abbey is through thick cypresses, with stunning views of eroded cliffs and sheer drops to the valley floor. It was founded in 1313 by the Olivetan order, who were dedicated to restoring the simplicity of Benedictine monastic rule. The 15th-century rose-pink abbey church is a Baroque building with outstanding choir stalls of inlaid wood.

Alongside is the Great Cloister (1427–74), whose walls are covered by a cycle of frescoes on the life of St Benedict, begun by Luca Signorelli, a pupil of Piero della Francesca, in 1495. He completed nine panels; the remaining 27 were finished by Sodoma in 1508. The cycle, which begins on the east wall with Benedict's early life, is considered a masterpiece of fresco painting for its combination of architectural and naturalistic detail.

Street-by-Street: San Gimignano ❶

The distinctive skyline of San Gimignano must have been a welcome sight to the faithful in medieval times, for the town lay on the main pilgrim route from northern Europe to Rome. This gave rise to its great prosperity at that time, when its population was twice what it is today. The plague of 1348, and later the diversion of the pilgrim route, led to its economic decline. Following World War II there was a rapid recovery thanks to tourism and local wine production. For a small town, San Gimignano is rich in works of art, and good shops and restaurants.

Sant'Agostino
Here Bartolo di Fredi painted Christ, Man of Sorrows.

To Sant'Agostino

La Buca, Via San Giovanni, selling local wine and wild boar ham

Via San Matteo, in contrast with the more commercial Via San Giovanni, caters mainly for the local residents, selling food and wine, clothes and other typical Tuscan products.

Rocca (1353)

★ Collegiata
This 11th-century church is covered in delightful frescoes, including The Creation *(1367) by Bartolo di Fredi.*

Museo Ornitologico

Museo d'Arte Sacra
The museum contains religious paintings, sculpture and liturgical objects from the Collegiata.

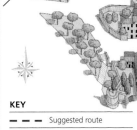

STAR SIGHTS

- ★ Collegiata
- ★ Piazza del Duomo
- ★ Palazzo del Popolo

KEY

— — — Suggested route

0 metres 250

0 yards 250

★ Piazza del Duomo
Among the historic buildings located here is the Palazzo Vecchio del Podestà (1239), whose tower is probably the town's oldest.

VISITORS' CHECKLIST

Road map C3. 7,041. Porta San Giovanni. Piazza del Duomo 1 (0577 94 00 08). Thu. ***Shops*** Mon am (summer); souvenir shops stay open. Patron Saints' Festivals: 31 Jan, 12 Mar; Ferie delle Messi: 3rd weekend of June; Fiera di Santa Fina: 1st wk of Aug; Fiera di Sant' Agostino: 29 Aug; Festa della Madonna di Pancole: 8 Sep.
www.comune.sangimignano.si.it

There are spectacular views from the top of the Torre Grossa.

★ Palazzo del Popolo
The impressive town hall (1288–1323) has a huge Maestà *by Lippo Memmi in the council chamber.*

Piazza della Cisterna is named after the well at its centre.

Via San Giovanni is lined with shops selling local goods.

Museo Civico
This gallery, found on the upper floors of the Palazzo del Popolo, houses The Madonna with Saints Gregory and Benedict *(1511), which was one of the last works to be painted by Pinturicchio.*

Exploring San Gimignano

Fresco in Sant'Agostino

The "city of beautiful towers" is one of the best-preserved medieval towns in Tuscany. Its stunning skyline bristles with tall towers dating from the 13th century: 14 of the original 76 have survived. These windowless towers were built to serve both as private fortresses and symbols of their owners' wealth. In the Piazza della Cisterna, ringed by a jumble of unspoilt 13th- and 14th-century *palazzi*, is a wellhead built in 1237. Shops, galleries and jewellers line the two main streets, Via San Matteo and Via San Giovanni, which still retain their medieval feel.

San Gimignano's skyline, almost unchanged since the Middle Ages

Palazzo Vecchio del Podestà

Piazza del Duomo. *to the public.*

The Palazzo Vecchio del Podestà (the old mayor's palace) is in a group of public buildings clustered around the central Piazza del Duomo. It has a vaulted loggia and the 51-m (166-ft) Torre della Rognosa, one of the oldest towers in San Gimignano. A law was passed in 1255 forbidding any citizen to build a higher tower, but the rule was often broken by rival families.

Museo Civico

Palazzo del Popolo, Piazza del Duomo. ***Tel*** *0577 99 03 12.*

Museum & Tower *Mar–Oct: 9:30am–7pm daily; Nov–Feb: 10am–5:30pm daily.* *31 Jan.*

The Museo is on the south side of the Piazza del Duomo, in the Palazzo del Popolo (town hall). Its tower, finished in 1311, is the tallest in the city, at 54 m (175 ft). This is open to the public and the views from the top are quite stunning. Worn frescoes in the courtyard feature the coats of arms of city mayors and magistrates, as well as a 14th-century *Virgin and Child* by Taddeo di Bartolo. The first public room is the Sala di Dante, where an inscription records the poet's plea to the city council in 1300 to support the Guelph (pro-pope) alliance led by Florence. The walls are covered with hunting scenes and a huge *Virgin Enthroned* by Lippo Memmi (1317).

The floor above has a small art collection, which includes Pinturicchio's *Madonna with Saints Gregory and Benedict* (1511) painted against a landscape of blues and greens. The painting of *San Gimignano and his Miracles* by Taddeo di Bartolo shows the saint holding the town – recognizably the same city we see today. The *Wedding Scene* frescoes by Memmo di Filippucci (early 14th-century) show a couple sharing a bath and going to bed – an unusual record of life in a wealthy household in 14th-century Tuscany.

12th-century well and medieval *palazzi* in the triangular Piazza della Cisterna

Museo d'Arte Sacra

Piazza Pecori. ***Tel*** *0577 94 03 16.* *Apr–Oct: 9:30am–7:10pm Mon–Fri (to 5:10pm Sat), 12:30–5:10pm Sun; Nov–Mar: 9:30am–4:40pm daily (from 12:30pm Sun).* *4 weeks in winter.*

The museum is entered from Piazza Pecori, where buskers play in summer. A chapel on the ground floor contains elaborate tomb slabs. The first floor houses paintings, sculpture and liturgical objects from the Collegiata. A marble bust (1493), by Benedetto da Maiano, commemorates the scholar Onofrio di Pietro.

Collegiata

Piazza del Duomo. ***Tel*** *0577 94 03 16.* *as Museo d'Arte Sacra, above.* *21 Jan–28 Feb.*

The plain façade of this 12th-century Romanesque church belies its exotic interior; it is one of the most frescoed churches in Italy. The arches bordering the central aisle are painted in striking blue and white stripes, and the deep blue paint of the vaulted roof is speckled with gold stars. The aisle walls are extensively covered with dramatic fresco cycles of scenes from the Bible. In the north aisle the frescoes are on three levels and comprise 26 episodes from the Old Testament, including *The Creation*

The ceiling of the Collegiata, painted with gold stars

of Adam and Eve, Noah and his Ark, Moses Crossing the Red Sea and The Afflictions of Job, finished by Bartolo di Fredi in 1367. On the opposite walls are scenes from the life of Christ, dated 1333–41, now attributed to Lippo Memmi, a pupil of Simone Martini. At the back of the church, on the nave walls, are scenes from *The Last Judgment*, painted by Taddeo di Bartolo (1393–6). They depict the souls of the damned being tortured in hell by devils relishing their task.

The tiny Santa Fina chapel, off the south aisle, is covered with a cycle of frescoes by Ghirlandaio (1475) telling the life story of St Fina; legend has it that she spent most of her short life in prayer. The towers of San Gimignano feature in the background of the funeral scene.

Under an arch to the left of the Collegiata is a courtyard containing the loggia to the Baptistry, frescoed with an *Annunciation* painted in 1482 by Ghirlandaio.

Rocca

Piazza Propositura. *daily.*

The Rocca, or fortress, was built in 1353. It now has only one surviving tower following its dismantling by Cosimo I de' Medici in the 16th century. It encloses a public garden filled with fig and olive trees, and commands superb views over the vineyards where wine has been produced for hundreds of years.

Sant'Agostino

Piazza Sant'Agostino. ***Tel*** *0577 90 70 12.* *7am–noon, 3–7pm Tue–Sun (from 10am Dec–Mar).*

This church was consecrated in 1298 and has a simple façade, contrasting markedly with the heavily decorated Rococo interior (c.1740) by Vanvitelli, architect to the kings of Naples. Above the main altar is the *Coronation of the Virgin* by Piero del Pollaiuolo, dated 1483, and the choir is entirely covered in a cycle of frescoes of *The Life of St Augustine* (1465), by the Florentine artist Benozzo Gozzoli and his assistants.

In the Cappella di San Bartolo, on the right of the main entrance, is an elaborate marble altar completed by Benedetto da Maiano in 1495. The bas-relief carvings show the miracles performed by St Bartholomew, all topped by flying angels and a roundel of the Madonna and Child.

Detail from *The Life of St Augustine*

Museo Ornitologico

Via Quercecchio. ***Tel*** *0577 94 13 88.* *Apr–Sep: 11am–5:30pm daily.*

The museum is in an elaborate 18th-century Baroque church. This is in total contrast to the sturdy cases of stuffed birds that form the collection, put together by a local dignitary.

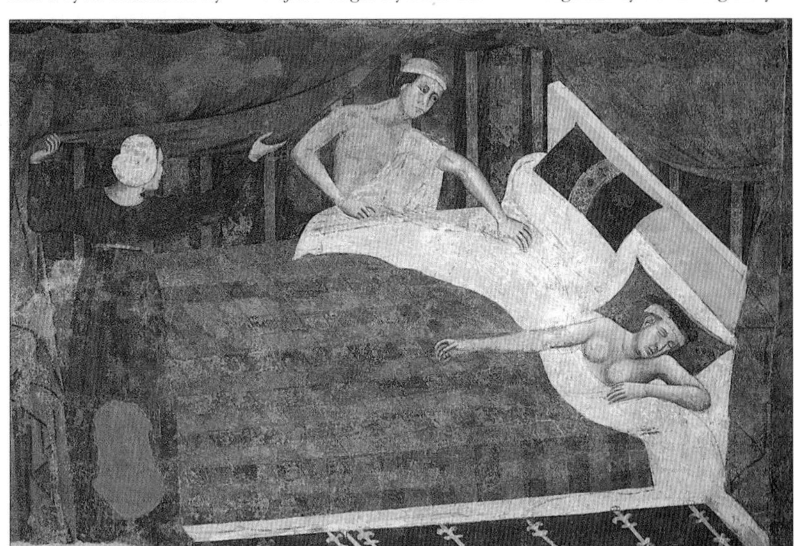

Fresco from the early 14th-century *Wedding Scene* cycle by Memmo di Filippucci in the Museo Civico

Street-by-Street: Siena ❹

Unicorn *contrada* symbol

The principal sights of Siena are found in the network of narrow streets and alleys around the fan-shaped Piazza del Campo. Scarcely any street is level, as Siena, like Rome, is built on seven hills. This adds to the pleasure of exploring: one minute the city is laid out to view before you and the next you are in a warren of medieval houses. Packed into Siena are the 17 *contrade* (parishes) whose animal symbols are everywhere on carvings, plaques and car stickers.

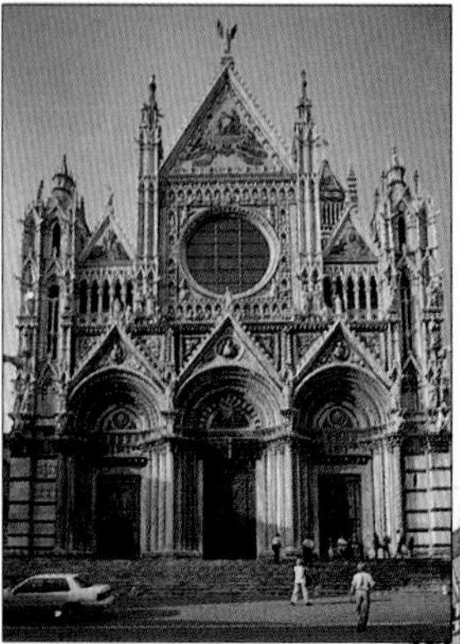

★ Duomo
Statues of prophets carved by Giovanni Pisano in the 1290s fill the Gothic niches of the marble façade (see pp220–21).

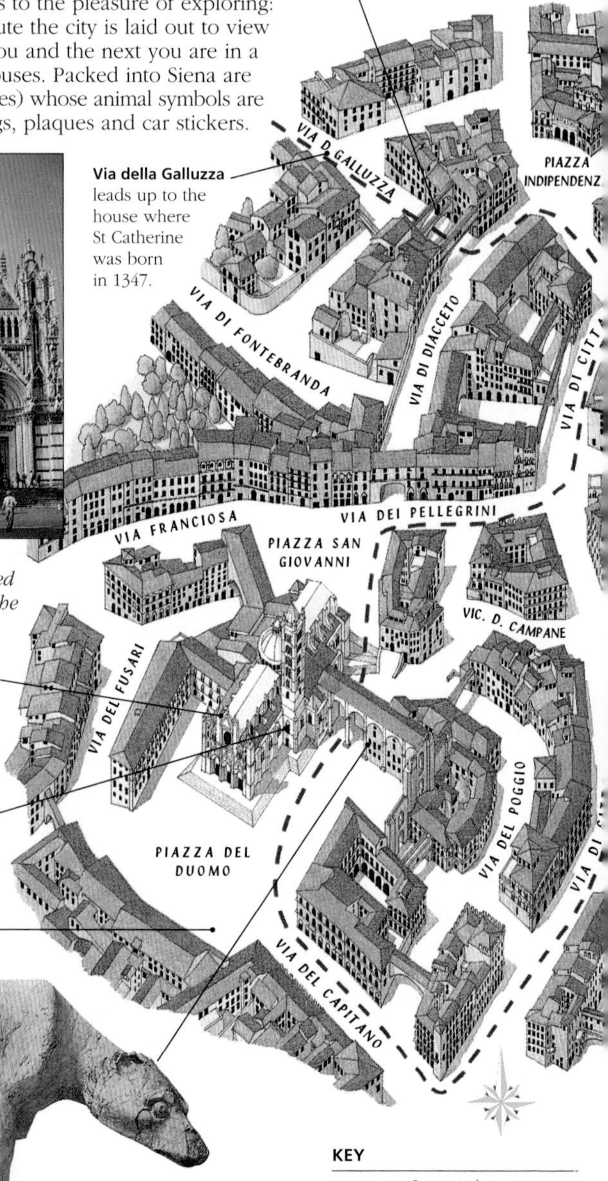

Aerial bridges and corridors linking buildings on opposite sides of the street are characteristic of Siena.

Via della Galluzza leads up to the house where St Catherine was born in 1347.

Each tier of the Duomo's belltower has one window fewer than the floor above.

Antique shops line the streets near the Duomo square.

Museo dell'Opera Metropolitana
Statue of Remus. Legend tells that his son Senius founded Siena.

KEY

— — — Suggested route

0 metres 300

0 yards 300

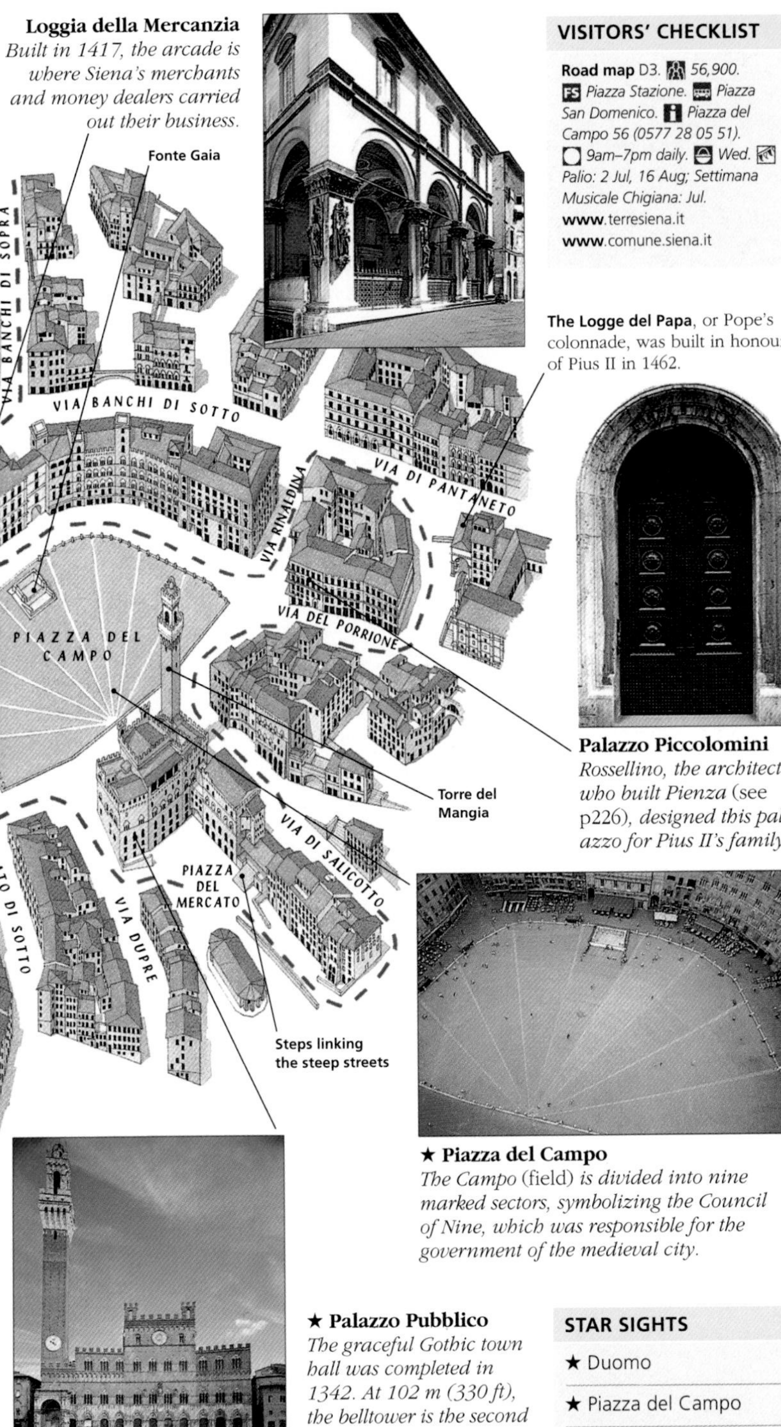

Loggia della Mercanzia
Built in 1417, the arcade is where Siena's merchants and money dealers carried out their business.

VISITORS' CHECKLIST

Road map D3. 56,900. *Piazza Stazione.* *Piazza San Domenico.* *Piazza del Campo 56 (0577 28 05 51).* *9am–7pm daily.* *Wed.* *Palio: 2 Jul, 16 Aug; Settimana Musicale Chigiana: Jul.*
www.terresiena.it
www.comune.siena.it

The Logge del Papa, or Pope's colonnade, was built in honour of Pius II in 1462.

Palazzo Piccolomini
Rossellino, the architect who built Pienza (see p226), *designed this palazzo for Pius II's family.*

★ Piazza del Campo
The Campo (field) *is divided into nine marked sectors, symbolizing the Council of Nine, which was responsible for the government of the medieval city.*

★ Palazzo Pubblico
The graceful Gothic town hall was completed in 1342. At 102 m (330 ft), the belltower is the second highest medieval tower to be built in Italy.

STAR SIGHTS

★ Duomo

★ Piazza del Campo

★ Palazzo Pubblico

Exploring Siena

Siena is a city of steep medieval alleys surrounding the Piazza del Campo. The buildings around the square symbolize the golden age of the city between 1260 and 1348, when wealthy citizens contributed to a major programme of civic building. Siena's decline began in 1348 when the Black Death hit the city, killing a third of the population; 200 years later many more died in an 18-month siege ending in defeat by the Florentines. The victors repressed all further development and building in Siena, which remained frozen in time, crammed with many renovated medieval buildings.

Aerial view of Siena's Piazza del Campo and surrounding palazzi

Piazza del Campo

The shell-shaped 12th-century Piazza del Campo is bordered by elegant *palazzi*. It has an elaborate fountain as its focal point, the Fonte Gaia, a rectangular marble basin decorated by statues. The fountain now seen in the square is a 19th-century copy of the original, which was carved by Jacopo della Quercia in 1409–19. This was removed to preserve it from the ravages of the weather.

The reliefs on the fountain depict Adam and Eve, the Madonna and Child, and the Virtues. Water is fed into it by a 25-km (15-mile) aqueduct, which has brought fresh water into the city from the hills since the 14th century.

Torre del Mangia

Piazza del Campo. ***Tel*** *055 29 26 14.* *10am–4pm (mid-Mar–Oct: to 7pm).* *25 Dec.*

The belltower to the left of the Palazzo Pubblico is the second-highest in Italy, at 102 m (330 ft). Built by the brothers Muccio and Francesco di Rinaldo between 1338–48, it is named after the first bell ringer, who was nicknamed *Mangiaguadagni* (literally "eat the profits") because of his great idleness. (It was the bell ringer's responsibility to warn the citizens of impending danger.) There are 505 steps to the top of the tower, which has views across Tuscany.

Palazzo Pubblico

Piazza del Campo 1. ***Tel*** *055 29 26 14.* **Museo Civico** *Daily. Mar: 10am–6pm; Apr–Oct: 10am–7pm; Nov–Feb: 10am–5:30pm.* *2 Jul, 16 Aug, 25 Dec.*

The Palazzo Pubblico serves as the town hall, but the state rooms are open to the public. The main council chamber is called the Sala del Mappamondo, after a map of the world painted by Ambrogio Lorenzetti in the early 1300s. One wall is covered by Simone Martini's *Maestà* (Virgin in Majesty). Painted in 1315, it depicts the Virgin Mary as the Queen of Heaven, attended by the Apostles, saints and angels. Opposite is Martini's fresco of the mercenary Guidoriccio da Fogliano (1330).

The walls of the adjacent chapel are covered with frescoes of the *Life of the Virgin* (1407) by Taddeo di Bartolo, and the choir stalls (1428) feature wooden panels inlaid with biblical scenes.

The Sala della Pace contains the famous *Allegory of Good and Bad Government*, a pair of frescoes by Ambrogio Lorenzetti, finished in 1338. In *The Good Government* *(see pp46–7)* civic life flourishes, while *The Bad Government* reveals ruins and rubbish-strewn streets. The Sala del Risorgimento is

Fonte Gaia in Piazza del Campo

***Guidoriccio da Fogliano* by Simone Martini (1330) in the Palazzo Pubblico**

covered with late 19th-century frescoes illustrating events leading up to the unification of Italy under King Vittorio Emanuele II *(see pp54–5)*.

Palazzo Piccolomini

Via Banchi di Sotto 52. ***Tel** 0577 24 71 45. entrances at 9:30am, 10:30am & 11:30am Mon–Sat by appt only. 1st two weeks in Aug & public hols.*

This imposing private palazzo was built in the 1460s by Rossellino for the very wealthy Piccolomini family. It houses the *Tavolette di Biccherna*, municipal ledgers from the 13th century, with covers by Sano di Pietro, Ambrogio Lorenzetti, Domenico Beccafumi and others.

Pinacoteca Nazionale

Via San Pietro 29. ***Tel** 0577 28 11 61. 8:15am–7:15pm Tue–Fri (to 1pm Sun & Mon). 1 Jan, 1 May, 25 Dec.*

Housed in the 14th-century Palazzo Buonsignori, this gallery contains important works by the Siena School. Lorenzetti's *Two Views*, painted in the 14th century, are early examples of landscape painting, and Pietro da Domenico's *Adoration of the Shepherds* (1510) shows how the art of the Siena School remained stylized long after Renaissance naturalism had influenced the rest of Europe. There is also a striking *Deposition* (1502) by Sodoma.

Duomo

See pp220–21.

Museo dell'Opera Metropolitana

Piazza del Duomo 8. ***Tel** 0577 28 30 48. mid-Mar–Oct: 9:30am–7pm daily (to 8pm Jun–Aug); Nov–mid-Mar: 10am–5pm daily. 1 Jan, 25 Dec.*

This museum is built into the unfinished side aisle of the Duomo *(see pp220–21)*. Part of it houses the sculpture from the exterior of the Duomo, which had become eroded outside. Duccio's double-sided *Maestà*, one of the best Siena School works, has a room to itself. Painted between 1308–11, it depicts the Madonna and Child on one side and scenes from *The Life of Christ* on the other. A loggia on the top floor offers views of the town and countryside.

Pisano's *Simone* (c.1300) in the Museo dell'Opera del Duomo

Santa Maria della Scala

Piazza del Duomo. ***Tel** 0577 53 45 70. 10:30am–6:30pm daily.*

This former hospital is now a museum housing a collection of paintings and sculpture. In the Sala del Pellegrino, frescoes by Domenico di Bartolo depict hospital scenes from the 1440s, including monks attending to the sick.

Cloister of Casa di Santa Caterina

Santuario e Casa di Santa Caterina

Costa di Sant'Antonio. ***Tel** 0577 247 393. 9am–12:30pm, 2:30–6pm daily (3:30–6pm in winter).*

Siena's patron saint, Catherine Benincasa (1347–80), was the daughter of a tradesman. She took the veil aged eight, and experienced many visions of God, from whom she also received the stigmata. Her eloquence persuaded Gregory XI to return the seat of the papacy to Rome in 1376, after 67 years of exile in Avignon. She died in Rome and was canonized in 1461. Today, her house is surrounded by chapels and cloisters. It is decorated with paintings of events from her life by artists such as Pietro Sorri and Francesco Vanni, both her contemporaries.

Siena Duomo

Siena's Duomo (1136–1382) is one of the most spectacular in Italy, and one of the few to have been built south of the Alps in full Gothic style. Many ordinary citizens helped to cart the black and white stone used in its construction from quarries on the outskirts of the city. In 1339, the Sienese decided to build a new nave to the south with the aim of making it the biggest church in Christendom. This plan came to nothing when plague hit the city soon afterwards, killing off much of the population. The uncompleted nave now contains a museum of Gothic sculpture.

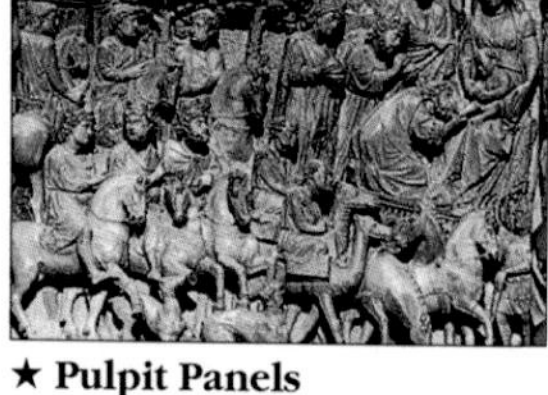

★ Pulpit Panels
Carved by Nicola Pisano in 1265–8, the panels on the octagonal pulpit depict scenes from The Life of Christ.

★ Inlaid Marble Floor
The Massacre of the Innocents *is one of a series of scenes in the inlaid marble floor. The marble is usually uncovered each year, in September and October.*

Nave
Black and white marble pillars support the vault.

Chapel of St John the Baptist

STAR FEATURES

- ★ Inlaid Marble Floor
- ★ Piccolomini Library
- ★ Pulpit Panels by Pisano

★ Piccolomini Library
Pinturicchio's frescoes (1509) portray the life of Pope Pius II (see p226). *Here he presides at the betrothal of Frederick III to Eleonora of Portugal.*

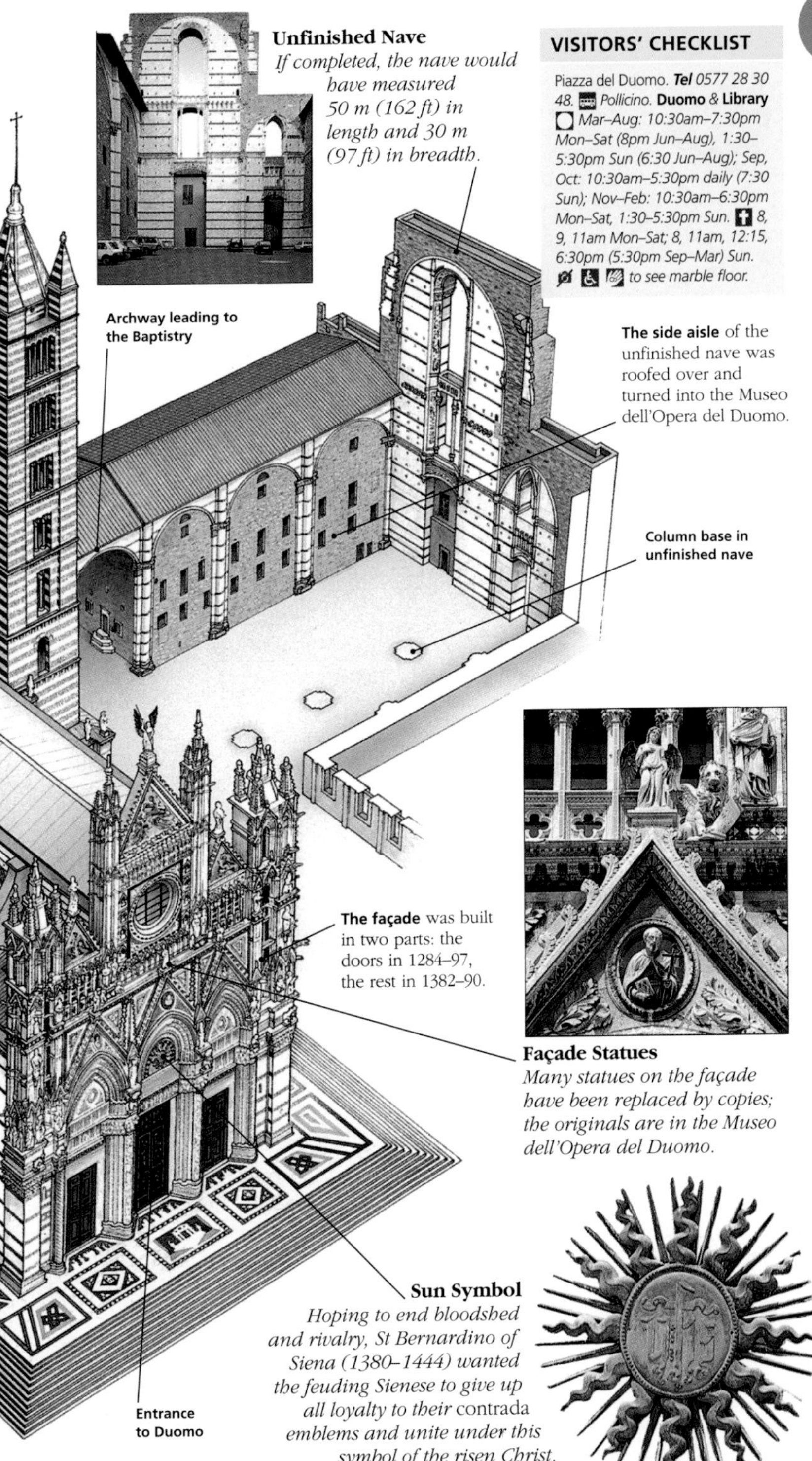
Archway leading to the Baptistry
The side aisle of the unfinished nave was roofed over and turned into the Museo dell'Opera del Duomo.
Column base in unfinished nave
The façade was built in two parts: the doors in 1284–97, the rest in 1382–90.
Entrance to Duomo

Unfinished Nave
If completed, the nave would have measured 50 m (162 ft) in length and 30 m (97 ft) in breadth.

Façade Statues
Many statues on the façade have been replaced by copies; the originals are in the Museo dell'Opera del Duomo.

Sun Symbol
Hoping to end bloodshed and rivalry, St Bernardino of Siena (1380–1444) wanted the feuding Sienese to give up all loyalty to their contrada *emblems and unite under this symbol of the risen Christ.*

VISITORS' CHECKLIST

Piazza del Duomo. ***Tel*** *0577 28 30 48.* *Pollicino.* **Duomo** & **Library** *Mar–Aug: 10:30am–7:30pm Mon–Sat (8pm Jun–Aug), 1:30–5:30pm Sun (6:30 Jun–Aug); Sep, Oct: 10:30am–5:30pm daily (7:30 Sun); Nov–Feb: 10:30am–6:30pm Mon–Sat, 1:30–5:30pm Sun.* *8, 9, 11am Mon–Sat; 8, 11am, 12:15, 6:30pm (5:30pm Sep–Mar) Sun.* *to see marble floor.*

The Sienese Palio

One of the contrada symbols

The Palio is Tuscany's most celebrated festival and takes place on 2 July and 16 August each year in the Campo *(see p218)*. It is a bareback horse race and was first recorded in 1283, but may have had its origins in Roman military training. The jockeys represent the 17*contrade* or districts; the horses are chosen by the drawing of straws and are then blessed at the local *contrada* churches. The races are preceded by heavy betting and pageantry, but only last about 90 seconds each. The winner is awarded a *palio* (banner).

Ringside View
Huge sums are paid for a view of the races.

Flag-Throwing
The Sienese display their flag-throwing skills in the procession and pageantry before the race.

Medieval Knight
The traditional outfits worn in the processions are all hand-made.

Racing Crowds
Thousands of people cram into the piazza to watch the race, and rivalry is intense between competitors.

Galloping towards the finish

Traditional drummer taking part in pre-race pageant

View across the Campo during a race

The façade of San Domenico

San Domenico

Piazza San Domenico. ◯ *daily.*

This barn-like Gothic church was begun in 1226 and its belltower was added in 1340. Inside is an exquisite chapel dedicated to St Catherine *(see p219)*. It was built in 1460 to store her preserved head, which is now kept in a gilded marble tabernacle on the altar. This is surrounded by frescoes showing Catherine in a state of religious fervour, painted by Sodoma in 1526. The marble pavement is attributed to Giovanni di Stefano.

Catherine experienced many of her visions and received her stigmata in the Cappella delle Volte at the west end of the church. Here there is an authenticated portrait of her by contemporary Andrea Vanni, dated around 1380.

Fortezza Medicea

Viale Maccari. **Fortezza** ◯ *daily.* **Theatre** ◯ *Nov–Apr: performances only.* ● *May–Oct.*

This huge red-brick fortress was built for Cosimo I by Baldassarre Lanci in 1560, following Siena's defeat by the Florentines in the 1554–5 war. The fortress now houses an open-air theatre, and from the entrance bastions there are fine views of the countryside.

Accademia Musicale Chigiana

Palazzo Chigi Saracini, Via di Città 89. ***Tel*** *0577 220 91.* ◯ *for concerts and exhibitions – call or check website for details.* **www**.chigiana.it

Founded by Count Guido Chigi Saracini in 1932, the Accademia holds master classes for the principal musical instruments. Housed in one of the finest buildings in Siena, there is also a fine art collection, a museum of musical instruments and a library containing original manuscripts. Concerts and occasional exhibitions are also held here.

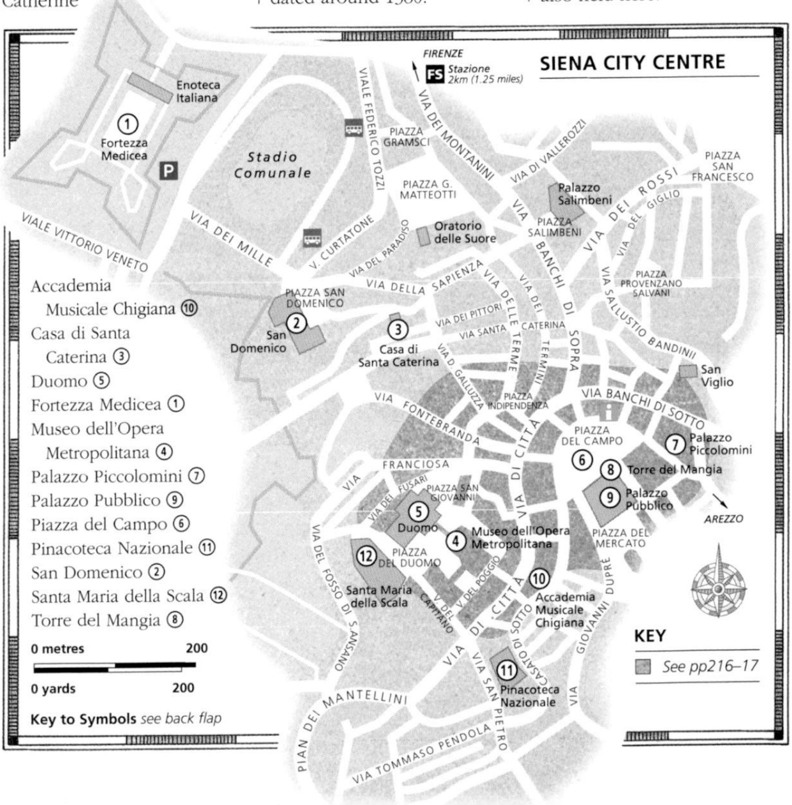

SIENA CITY CENTRE

Accademia Musicale Chigiana ⑩
Casa di Santa Caterina ③
Duomo ⑤
Fortezza Medicea ①
Museo dell'Opera Metropolitana ④
Palazzo Piccolomini ⑦
Palazzo Pubblico ⑨
Piazza del Campo ⑥
Pinacoteca Nazionale ⑪
San Domenico ②
Santa Maria della Scala ⑫
Torre del Mangia ⑧

0 metres 200
0 yards 200

Key to Symbols *see back flap*

KEY

See pp216–17

The ruined abbey at San Galgano, surrounded by dense woodland

San Galgano 7

Road map D4 (località Chiusdino). *from Siena.*
Abbey and oratory *daily.*

The ruined Cistercian abbey is surrounded by woodland and in a superb setting. It is very remote but well worth the effort of getting there for the beauty of the surroundings and the majesty of the roofless building. Begun in 1218, the abbey is Gothic in style; unusual in Tuscany, this reflects the French origins of the Cistercian monks who designed and built it.

The monks avoided contact with civilization and divided their lives between prayer and labour, clearing the hills of vegetation to graze their sheep. Despite the Cistercian emphasis on poverty, the monks became wealthy from the sale of wool; by the middle of the 14th century, the abbey was corruptly administered and gradually fell into decline.

In the late 14th century, the English mercenary Sir John Hawkwood sacked the abbey and by 1397 the abbot was the sole occupant. Numbers recovered for a time but the abbey was eventually dissolved in 1652. Empty for many years, the cloister and other monastic buildings alongside the church are now being restored for the Olivetan order of nuns.

On a hill above the abbey is the beehive-shaped chapel of Montesiepi, built on the site of St Galgano's hermitage around 1185, a few years after his death in 1181.

St Galgano's sword stands embedded in a stone just inside the door of the circular oratory. The 14th-century stone walls of the side chapel are covered with frescoes showing scenes from Galgano's life by Ambrogio Lorenzetti (1344); some are now in a poor state of repair.

The shop alongside the chapel sells locally-made herbs, wines, olive oils and toiletries along with books on the history of the region.

Montalcino 8

Road map D4. *5,100.* *Costa del Municipio 8 (0577 84 93 31).* *Mon.* *Fri.*

Montalcino's foremost activity is wine-producing, as is evident from the number of shops where you can both sample and buy the excellent local Brunello wines *(see p268)*.

The town, situated on the top of a hill, is of timeless character and the streets are narrow, winding and steep. The highest point is the 14th-century **Fortezza** and its impressive ramparts, built by Cosimo I in 1571.

THE LEGEND OF ST GALGANO

Galgano was born in 1148, the son of noble parents, and grew into a brave but dissolute young knight. He saw his life as futile and turned to God, renouncing the material world. When he tried to break his sword against a rock as a symbol of his rejection of war, it was swallowed by the stone. This he interpreted as a sign of God's approval. He built a hut on the site of today's chapel at Montesiepi, and died a hermit in 1181. In 1185 Pope Urban III declared him a saint and an example to all Christian knights.

Montalcino's 14th-century Fortezza

Spectacular views over the surrounding countryside are available from the walkway on the ramparts.

There is an Enoteca (wine shop) in the grounds of the Fortezza, where the Brunello red wines are on sale.

Inside the fortress there is an ancient Sienese battle standard, a reminder that the town gave refuge to a band of rebels after Florence conquered Siena in 1555. In remembrance of this, flag-bearers from the village of Montalcino are given the honour of leading the parade before the Palio in Siena every year *(see p222)*.

As you walk down into the town from the Fortezza, the monastery of Sant'Agostino and its 14th-century church, with an attractive rose window, are on the right. Just beyond is the **Palazzo Vescovile**, formerly the bishop's palace. The **Palazzo Comunale** stands on the Piazza del Popolo. Constructed in the 13th and 14th centuries, its tall, slim tower rises above the town.

The Duomo, San Salvatore, was designed in 1818–32 by Agostino Fantastici, and replaced the original Romanesque church building.

Fortezza
Piazzale della Fortezza. ***Tel*** *0577 84 92 11.* **Enoteca** *Nov–Mar: 9am–6pm daily; Apr–Oct: 9am–8pm daily.* *for ramparts.*

Palazzo Vescovile
Via Spagni 4. ***Tel*** *0577 84 81 68.* *to the public.*

Palazzo Comunale
Costa del Municipio 1. ***Tel*** *0577 84 93 31.* *to the public.*

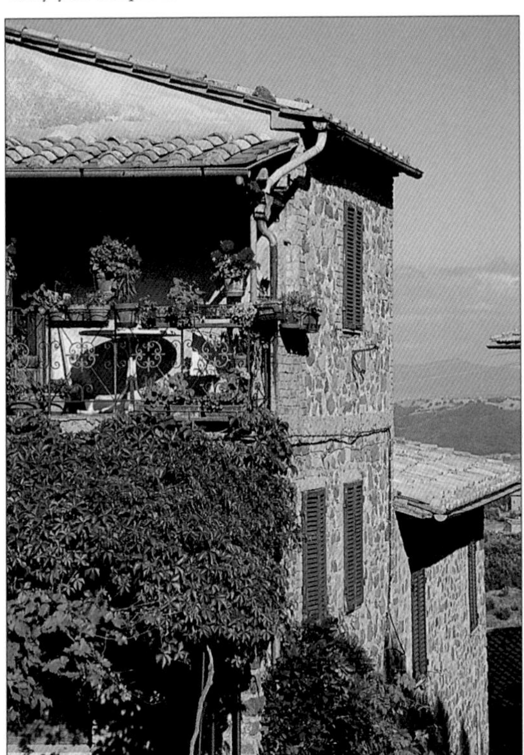

Flower-covered house in the pretty town of Montalcino

San Quirico d'Orcia 9

Road map E4. *2,390.* *Piazza Chigi 2 (0577 89 97 24).* *2nd & 4th Tue of month.*

Collegiata in San Quirico

Standing just inside the city walls, San Quirico d'Orcia's pride is the **Collegiata**, featuring three ornately carved Romanesque portals built onto an 8th-century structure. Begun in 1080, the capitals and lintels of the portals are carved with details of dragons, mermaids and other mythical beasts.

The church commemorates the 3rd-century martyr St Quiricus, who was killed at the age of five by the Romans for the simple act of declaring himself a Christian. Quiricus is depicted in the elaborate altar piece by Sano di Pietro, along with the Virgin and Child and other saints.

Next to the church is the 17th-century **Palazzo Chigi**, whose frescoed interior has recently been restored. The **Horti Leonini** nearby is a 16th-century garden of box hedges nestling within the town walls. It was intended as a refuge for pilgrims, and is now used as a public sculpture garden during the summer months.

Collegiata
Via Dante Alighieri. ***Tel*** *0577 89 72 36.* *8am–5pm daily.*

Palazzo Chigi
Piazza Chigi. *10am–1pm, 4–7pm (Oct–Mar: 3:30–6:30pm) Tue–Sun.*

Horti Leonini
Piazza Libertà. ***Tel*** *0577 89 72 11.* *sunrise–sunset daily.* *partial.*

The Terme di Bagno Vignoni

Bagno Vignoni ⑩

Road map D4. *32. from Siena.* *0577 88 73 65.*

This is a tiny medieval spa village which consists of a handful of houses built round a huge piazza containing an arcaded, stone-lined pool. Constructed by the Medici, it is full of hot sulphurous water which bubbles up to the surface from the volcanic rocks deep underground. The healing quality of the water has been known since Roman times and, according to legend, famous people who have sought a cure in Bagno Vignoni include St Catherine of Siena *(see p219)* and Lorenzo the Magnificent (to relieve his arthritis). The pool is no longer open for bathing but is still well worth a visit to admire the architecture. Sulphur pools in the grounds of the Posta Marcucci hotel are open for swimming.

Pienza ⑪

Road map E4. *1,300.* *Corso il Rossellino 59 (0578 74 90 71).* *Fri.*

The centre of Pienza was completely redesigned in Renaissance times by Pope Pius II *(see p49)*. Born here in 1405, when it was called Corsignano, Aeneas Sylvius Piccolomini became known as a leading Humanist scholar and philosopher. He was elected pope in 1458 and in the following year decided to commission a new centre in Corsignano and rename it Pienza in his own honour. He planned to transform his birthplace into a model Renaissance town, but the grand scheme never progressed beyond the handful of buildings around the Piazza Pio II. The architect Bernardo Rossellino was commissioned to build a Duomo, papal palace and town hall, which were finished in three years. Subsequently Rossellino was caught embezzling papal funds, but Pius II forgave him because he was so delighted with his new buildings.

The isolated monastery of Sant'Anna in Camprena with its wondeful frescoes painted by Sodoma is nearby. The original monastery dates from the 13th century, however the present building is 16th century.

Duomo

Piazza Pio II. *daily.*

The Duomo was built by the architect Rossellino in 1459, and is now suffering from subsidence at its eastern end. There are cracks in the walls and floor of the nave, but this does not detract at all from the splendid Classical proportions of this Renaissance church. It is flooded with light from the vast stained-glass windows requested by Pius II; he wanted a *domus vitrea* (literally "a house of glass") which would symbolize the spirit of intellectual enlightenment of the Humanist age.

Coat of arms of Pope Pius II

Palazzo Piccolomini

Piazza Pio II. ***Tel*** *0578 74 85 03.* *10am–1pm, 2–6:30pm Tue–Sun (guided tours only).* *mid-Nov–early Dec & mid-Feb–early Mar.*

The palazzo is next door to the Duomo and was home to Pius II's descendants until 1968. Rossellino's design for the building was influenced by Leon Battista Alberti's Palazzo Rucellai in Florence *(see p104)*. The apartments open to the public include Pius II's bedroom and library, which are full of his belongings. At the rear of the palazzo there is an arcaded courtyard and a triple-tiered loggia. The spectacular view looks across the garden and takes in the wooded slopes of Monte Amiata.

Courtyard in Palazzo Piccolomini

Pieve di Corsignano

Via delle Fonti. ***Tel*** *0578 74 82 03.* *by appt or through tourist office.*

Pope Pius II was baptized in this 11th-century Romanesque parish church on the outskirts of Pienza. It has an unusual round tower and a doorway decorated with flower motifs.

Pienza's piazza and the town hall, viewed from the steps of the Duomo

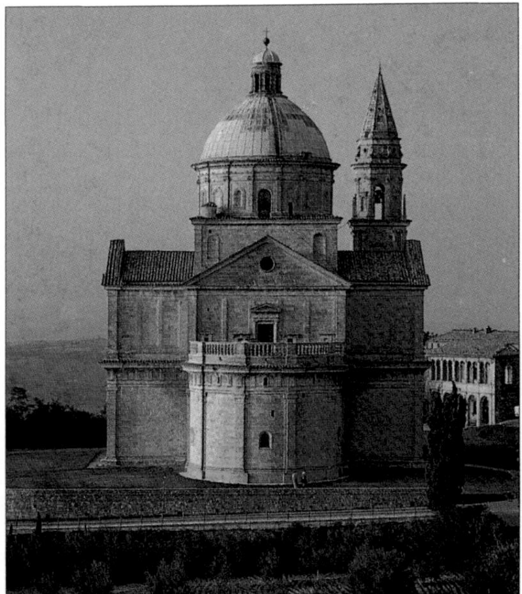

The church of Madonna di San Biagio on the outskirts of Montepulciano

Montepulciano ⓬

Road map E4. *14,000.*
Piazza Don Minzoni 1 (0578 75 73 41). *Thu.*

Montepulciano is built along a narrow limestone ridge and, at 605 m (1,950 ft) above sea level, is one of the highest of Tuscany's hilltop towns. The town is encircled by walls and fortifications designed by Antonio da Sangallo the Elder in 1511 for Cosimo I. Inside the walls the streets are crammed with Renaissance-style palazzi and churches, but the town is chiefly known for its good local Vino Nobile wines *(see p268)*. A long winding street called the Corso climbs up into the main square, which crowns the summit of the hill.

On the Corso is the Art Deco Caffè Poliziano, which has an art gallery in the basement. In July the café hosts a jazz festival and the town fills with musicians who perform at the Cantiere Internazionale d'Arte *(see p35)*, an arts festival directed by the German composer Hans Werner Henze.

In August there are two festivals: the Bruscello takes place on the 14th, 15th and 16th, when scenes from the town's turbulent history are re-enacted. For the Bravio delle Botti, on the last Sunday in August, there is a parade through the streets followed by a barrel race and a banquet.

Madonna di San Biagio

Via di San Biagio 14.
8:30am–7pm daily.

This beautiful church with a restored façade on the outskirts of Montepulciano is perched on a platform below the city walls. Built of honey- and cream-coloured travertine, it is Sangallo's masterpiece, a Renaissance gem begun in 1518. The project occupied him until his death in 1534.

Palazzo Bucelli

Via di Gracciano del Corso 73.
to the public.

The lower façade of the palazzo (1648) is studded with ancient Etruscan reliefs and funerary urns collected by its 18th-century antiquarian owner, Pietro Bucelli.

Sant'Agostino

Piazza Michelozzo. *daily.*

Michelozzo built the church in 1427, with an elaborate carved portal featuring the Virgin and Child flanked by St John and St Augustine.

Palazzo Comunale

Piazza Grande 1. ***Tel*** *0578 71 73 00.*
Tower *Apr–Oct: 10am–6pm daily.* **Museum** *10am–1pm, 3–6pm Tue–Sun (Aug: to 7pm).*

In the 15th century, Michelozzo added a tower and façade on to the original Gothic town hall. The building is now a smaller version of the Palazzo Vecchio *(see pp78–9)*.

Palazzo Tarugi

Piazza Grande. *to the public.*

This imposing 16th-century palazzo is located next to the town hall.

Duomo

Piazza Grande. *8:30am–1pm, 3–7pm daily.*

The Duomo was designed between 1592 and 1630 by Ippolito Scalza. The façade is unfinished and plain, but the interior is Classical in proportions. It is the setting for an earlier masterpiece from the Siena School, the Assumption of the Virgin triptych painted by Taddeo di Bartolo in 1401. Placed over the High Altar, it is rich in bright, jewel-like colours and heavily embossed with gold leaf.

Taddeo di Bartolo's triptych (1401)

Santa Maria dei Servi

Via del Poliziano. *by appt.*

The Corso continues from the Piazza up to the Gothic church of Santa Maria dei Servi. The wine bar alongside sells Vino Nobile from medieval storage cellars cut out of the limestone cliffs below the town.

Etruscan frieze in the Museo Nazionale Etrusco in Chiusi

Chiusi ⓭

Road map E4. 10,000. FS
Piazza Duomo 1 (0578 22 76 67). Mon, Tue.

Chiusi was one of the most powerful cities in the Etruscan league, reaching the height of its influence in the 7th and 6th centuries BC *(see pp42–3)*. There is a large number of Etruscan tombs in the surrounding countryside.

Museo Archeologico Nazionale

Via Porsenna 93. ***Tel*** *0578 201 77.*
9am–8pm daily.
The museum, founded in 1871, is packed with cremation urns, vases decorated with black figures and Bucchero ware, burnished to resemble bronze. Most of these were excavated from local tombs, which can be visited by arrangement with the museum.

Duomo

Piazza del Duomo. *daily.*
The Romanesque cathedral is built from recycled Roman pillars and capitals. The decorations on the nave walls seem to be mosaics, but in fact were painted by Arturo Viligiardi in 1887. There is a Roman mosaic under the High Altar.

Museo della Cattedrale

Piazza del Duomo. ***Tel*** *0578 22 64 90.*
Jun–mid-Oct: 9:30am–12:45pm, 4–7pm daily; mid-Oct–May 9:30am–12:45pm Mon–Sat, 3:30–6:30pm Sun (Jan–Mar: open only Tue, Thu, Sat). *partial.*
The museum has a display of Roman, Lombardic and medieval sculpture. Visits can be arranged here to the underground galleries beneath the city, dug by the Etruscans and used as Christian catacombs in the 3rd–5th centuries.

Sant'Antimo ⓮

Road map D4. ***Custodian*** *0577 83 56 59.* *10:30am–12:30pm, 3–6:30pm Mon–Sat, 9:15–10:45am, 3–6pm Sun.*

This beautiful abbey church *(see pp44–5)* has inspired many poets and painters and enchants everyone who comes here. The creamy travertine church is set against a background of tree-clad hills in the Starcia valley. The very earliest surviving church on the site dates back to the 9th century, but locals prefer to think the church was founded by the Holy Roman Emperor Charlemagne in 781. The main part of the church was built in 1118 in the French Romanesque style, and the exterior is decorated with interlaced blank arcades carved with the symbols of the Four Evangelists.

The soft, honey-coloured alabaster interior has an odd luminous quality which is seen to change according to time of day and season. The capitals in the nave are carved with geometric designs, leaf motifs and biblical scenes. Recorded plainsong echoes around the walls, adding to the eerie atmosphere.

The Augustinian monks who tend the church sing Gregorian chant at mass every Sunday and there are organ concerts in the church during July and August.

The beautiful abbey church of Sant'Antimo

A Day Out in Chianti

This tour takes in the main villages of the Chianti Classico wine region. Castles and wine estates line the route, and vineyards offer tastings and sell direct to the public. Look for signs along the way saying "vendita diretta".

The first stop on leaving Siena is the Castello di Brolio, which has been owned by the Ricasoli family since 1167. From Brolio, drive to Gaiole, diverting to see the 13th-century castle at Meleto. Gaiole is a very quiet agricultural town with a stream running down the main street; wine can be sampled here at the local cooperative. In Badia a Coltibuono there is a restaurant *(see p292)* and a Romanesque church, and Radda in Chianti offers extensive views over the Parco Naturale della Viriglia. At Castellina in Chianti, there is a 15th-century underground passage built for defence purposes, and the Enoteca Vini Gallo Nero (Via della Rocca 13), which is a showcase for the region's wines *(see pp268–9)*.

Badia a Coltibuono ④
At the crossroads in Gaiole, follow the signs to Montevarchi and divert to the left off the main road before heading right towards the village of Badia.

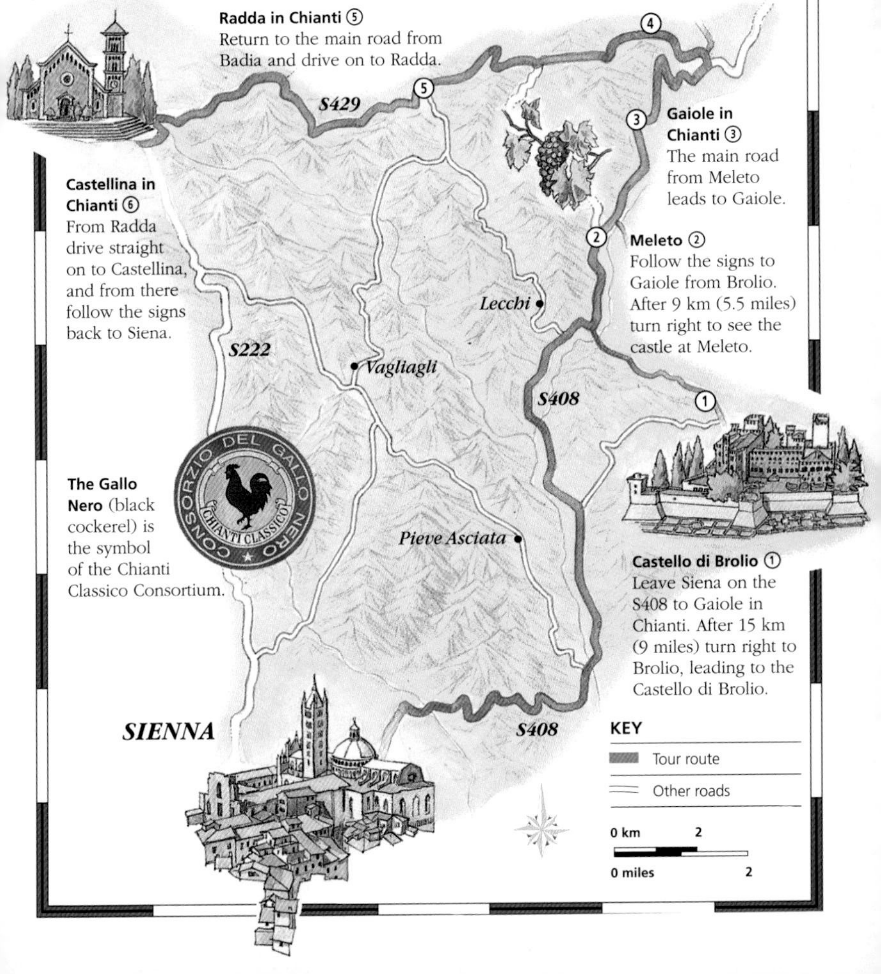

Radda in Chianti ⑤
Return to the main road from Badia and drive on to Radda.

Gaiole in Chianti ③
The main road from Meleto leads to Gaiole.

Castellina in Chianti ⑥
From Radda drive straight on to Castellina, and from there follow the signs back to Siena.

Meleto ②
Follow the signs to Gaiole from Brolio. After 9 km (5.5 miles) turn right to see the castle at Meleto.

The Gallo Nero (black cockerel) is the symbol of the Chianti Classico Consortium.

Castello di Brolio ①
Leave Siena on the S408 to Gaiole in Chianti. After 15 km (9 miles) turn right to Brolio, leading to the Castello di Brolio.

S429
S222
S408
Lecchi
Vagliagli
Pieve Asciata
CONSORZIO DEL GALLO NERO
CHIANTI CLASSICO
SIENNA

KEY

Tour route

Other roads

0 km 2

0 miles 2

SOUTHERN TUSCANY

The southernmost part of Tuscany and the island of Elba have a very different feel to any other Tuscan region. Thanks to the hotter, drier and sunnier climate, the hills are cloaked in aromatic Mediterranean scrub, known as macchia. *Palm trees grow in towns and also edge the sandy beaches, and strands of prickly pear cactus are traditionally used to mark field boundaries in the countryside.*

The coastline, lined with fishing villages and beaches, is very popular in the summer, with numerous holiday villages and caravan sites. Resorts such as Monte Argentario have a much more exclusive image, and are favoured by the wealthy, yacht-owning Italians from Rome and Milan. Inland, the region's wild and unspoiled hills are popular with sportsmen, who come to hunt for wild boar and deer.

The transformation of the marshy coastal strip, known as the Maremma, into a holiday playground is a recent development. The ancient Etruscans, followed by the Romans *(see p42)*, drained its swamps to create richly fertile farming land. After the collapse of the Roman Empire, the drainage channels became choked, turning the Maremma into an inhospitable wilderness of marshland and stagnant pools plagued by malaria-carrying mosquitoes. Re-draining of the land began again in the late 18th century and, with the help of insecticides, the malaria-mosquito was finally eliminated in the 1950s.

LITTLE DEVELOPMENT

The region slumbered from Roman times and for long periods was virtually uninhabited except for farmers and fishermen. Consequently there are few cities or major architectural and artistic monuments. On the other hand, archaeological remains have survived because there were few people here to salvage the stone for new buildings. The relative lack of intensive farming means the region is still rich in wildlife, from butterflies and orchids to tortoises and porcupines.

Detail of Romanesque *tympanum* on the Duomo at Massa Marittima

◁ **Looking across the old harbour of Portoferraio on the island of Elba**

Exploring Southern Tuscany

Away from the coastal resorts, this region remains relatively undiscovered; quiet roads and a lack of tourists only add to the pleasure of exploring rock-cut tombs in Sovana, bathing in hot sulphurous springs at Saturnia or wandering through the Maremma spotting the wildlife. For a busier atmosphere, visit the resorts of Orbetello and Monte Argentario, which have plenty of choice for shopping, restaurants and nightlife.

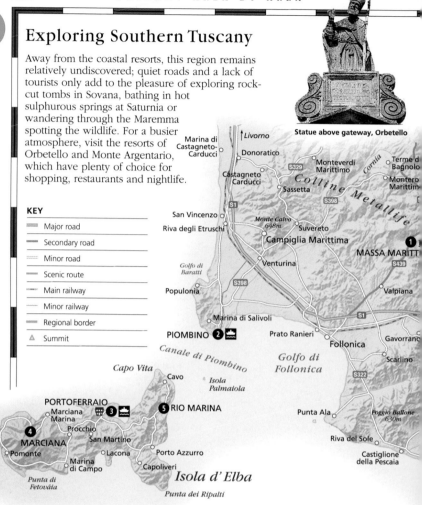

Statue above gateway, Orbetello

KEY

- Major road
- Secondary road
- Minor road
- Scenic route
- Main railway
- Minor railway
- Regional border
- △ Summit

Livorno
Marina di Castagneto-Carducci
Donoratico
Monteverdi Marittimo
Terme di Bagnolo
Cornia
S329
Castagneto Carducci
Colline Metallifere
Sassetta
Montero Marittimo
S398
S1
San Vincenzo
Monte Calvo 648m
Riva degli Etruschi
Suvereto
Campiglia Marittima
1 MASSA MARITTIMA
Venturina
S439
Golfo di Baratti
S398
Populonia
Valpiana
S1
Marina di Salivoli
PIOMBINO 2
Prato Ranieri
Gavorrano
Follonica
Canale di Piombino
Golfo di Follonica
Scarlino
Capo Vita
Cavo
Isola Palmaiola
S322
PORTOFERRAIO 3
5 RIO MARINA
Punta Ala
Poggio Ballone 630m
Marciana Marina
Procchio
4 MARCIANA
San Martino
Riva del Sole
Pomonte
Lacona
Porto Azzurro
Castiglione della Pescaia
Marina di Campo
Capoliveri
Isola d'Elba
Punta di Fetováia
Punta dei Ripalti

GETTING AROUND

The S1 coastal route cannot cope with the traffic in summer and is best avoided. A busy railway line runs alongside; most trains stop at Grosseto and Orbetello, and buses from Grosseto serve most towns in the area. Vehicle and passenger ferries depart from Piombino to Elba every 30 minutes during the day in summer. Bus services from Portoferraio cover all parts of the island.

View across the rooftops of Massa Marittima to the hills beyond

For additional map symbols *see back flap*

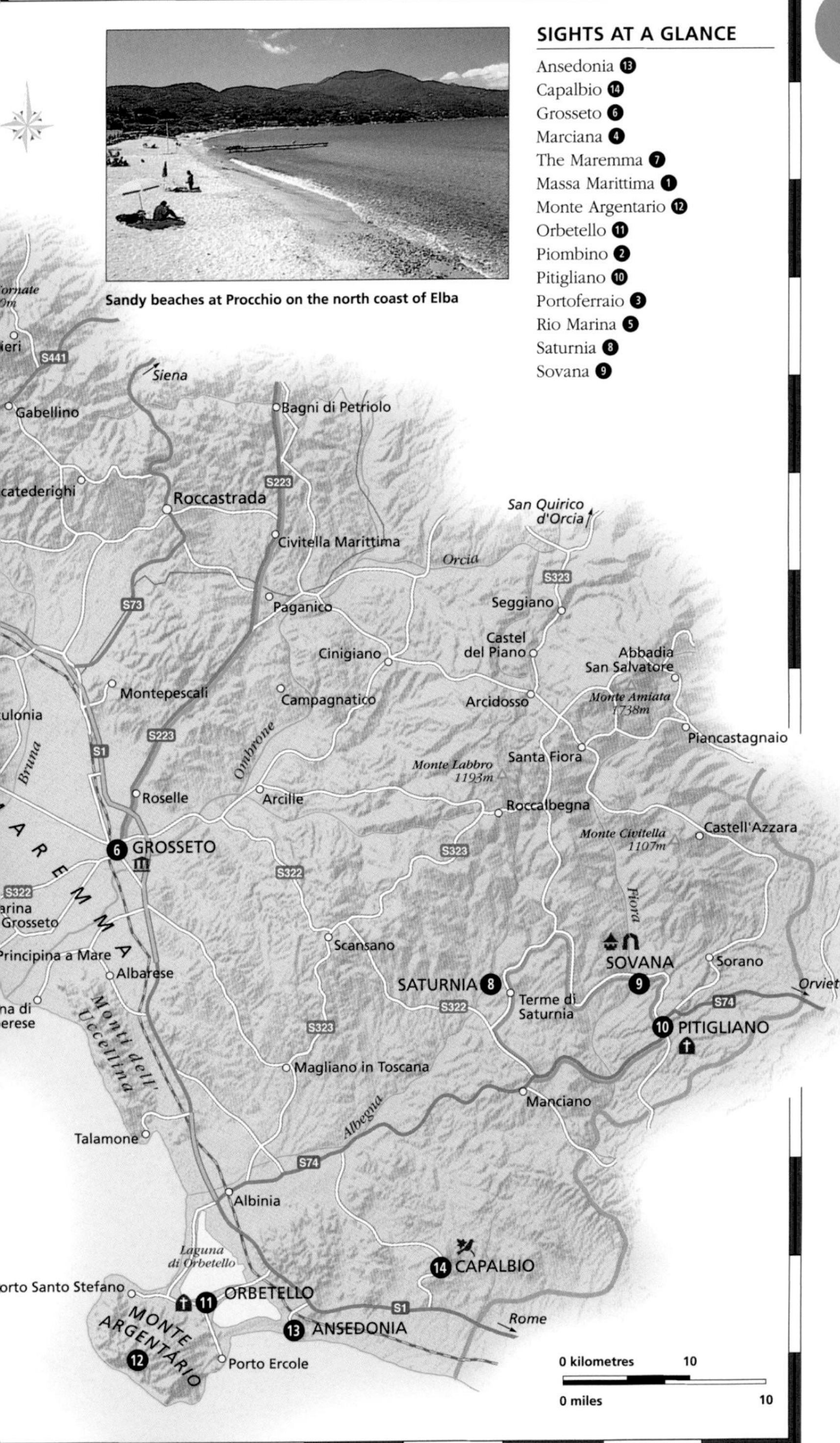

Sandy beaches at Procchio on the north coast of Elba

SIGHTS AT A GLANCE

Ansedonia 13
Capalbio 14
Grosseto 6
Marciana 4
The Maremma 7
Massa Marittima 1
Monte Argentario 12
Orbetello 11
Piombino 2
Pitigliano 10
Portoferraio 3
Rio Marina 5
Saturnia 8
Sovana 9

Massa Marittima ❶

Road map C4. 9,469.
Amatur, Via Todini 3–5 (0566 90 27 56). *Wed.*

Set in the Colline Metallifere (metal-bearing hills), from which lead, copper and silver ores were mined, Massa Marittima is far from being a grimy industrial town. Its history is closely associated with mining and there are some excellent examples of Romanesque architecture.

Duomo

The Romanesque cathedral is dedicated to St Cerbone, a 6th-century saint whose story is told in stone above the door.

The skyline of Massa Marittima

Museo Archeologico

Palazzo del Podestà, Piazza Garibaldi. ***Tel*** *0566 90 22 89.* *Tue–Sun.*

An archaeological museum with material from Paleolithic to Roman times.

Museo d'Arte Sacra

Convento di San Pietro all'Orto, Corso Diaz 36. ***Tel*** *0566 90 22 89.* *daily.*

Art from local churches and basilicas can be admired here.

Museo della Miniera

Via Corridoni. ***Tel*** *0566 90 22 89.* *Tue–Sun.* *compulsory.*

Parts of this museum of mining are located within a worked-out mine shaft.

Piombino ❷

Road map C4. 36,774. FS
Via Ferruccio 1 (0565 22 56 39). *Wed.*

Piombino is a busy town dominated by iron and steel works. It is at the end of the Massoncello peninsula and

A Day Out on Elba

Elba's most famous resident was Napoleon, who spent nine months here after the fall of Paris in 1814. Today the island is mainly populated by holidaymakers, who come by ferry from Piombino, 10 km (6 miles) away on the mainland. The main town is Portoferraio, with an old port and a modern seafront with smart hotels. The landscape of the island is varied: on the west coast there are sandy beaches, suitable for all water sports; inland, olive groves and vineyards line hillsides, and vegetation covers the mountains. The east coast is more rugged, with high cliffs and stony beaches.

Marciana Marina ③
Return to the main road and follow the coast round, past Procchio with its long sandy bays. From here it is 7.5 km (4.5 miles) to the marina.

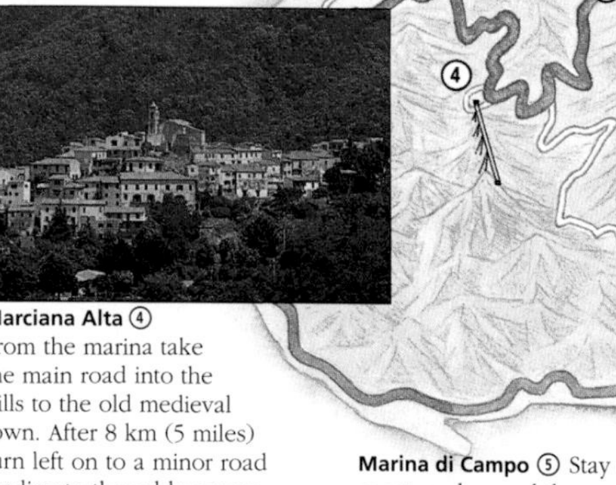

Marciana Alta ④
From the marina take the main road into the hills to the old medieval town. After 8 km (5 miles) turn left on to a minor road leading to the cable car up to the top of Monte Capanne.

Marina di Campo ⑤ Stay on the coast road, round the west end of the island, until Marina di Campo.

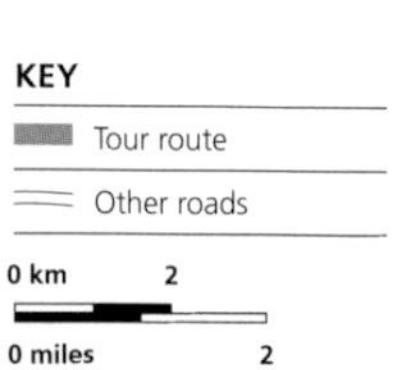

For hotels and restaurants in this region see pp262–63 and pp280–81

was originally an island. It is the main port for ferries to Elba, which run every half hour in summer and at frequent intervals in winter. Nearby are the extensive ruins of Etruscan Populonia and the **Museo Etrusco Gasparri**, which contains a collection of bronze and terracotta works found in the surrounding necropolises.

Museo Etrusco Gasparri
Populonia. ***Tel*** *0565 296 66* *9am–12:30pm, 2–7pm daily.*

Portoferraio ❸

Road map B4. *11,500.* *Calata Italia 43 (0565 29 46 71).* *Fri.*

The ferry from mainland Piombino arrives here. The town has a pretty harbour but the main sights are Napoleon's two houses. In the centre of Portoferraio is the **Palazzina Napoleonica** (also known as the Villetta dei Mulini), a modest house built around two windmills. **Villa San Martino**, his country residence, had a Classical façade imposed on it by the Russian emigré, Prince Demidoff, in 1851. Egyptian-style frescoes in the house, painted in 1814, are a reminder of Napoleon's Nile campaigns of 1798–9.

Palazzina Napoleonica
Villa Napoleonica dei Mulini. ***Tel*** *0565 91 58 46.* *9am–7pm Wed–Mon in summer, 9am–4pm in winter (to 1pm Sun & public hols).*

Villa San Martino
San Martino. ***Tel*** *0565 91 46 88.* *9am–7pm Tue–Sun (to 1pm Sun), 9am–4pm in winter.*

Marciana ❹

Road map B4. *3,000.* *Municipio, Marciana Alta (0565 90 12 15).*

On Elba's Northwest coast is Marciana Marina, and further inland the well-preserved medieval town of Marciana Alta. The **Museo Civico Archeologico** houses exhibits from Etruscan ships wrecked off Elba. From here, take the cable car up Monte Capanne, Elba's highest peak at 1,018 m (3,300 ft).

Shady beaches and inlets at Marciana Marina on Elba

Museo Civico Archeologico
Via del Pretorio, Marciana Alta. ***Tel*** *0565 90 12 15.* *Apr–Sep: daily.*

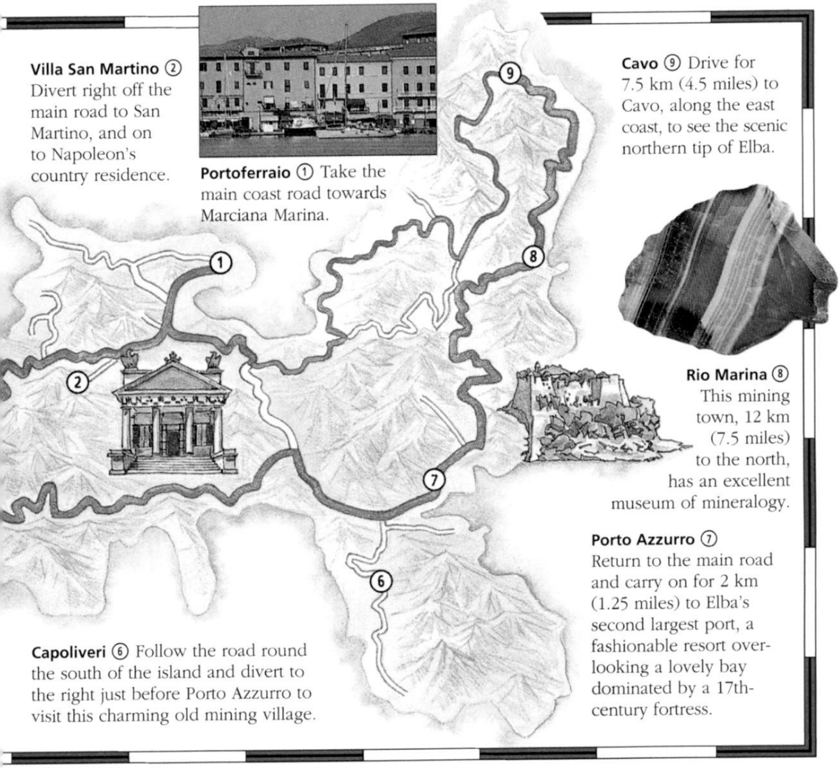

Portoferraio ① Take the main coast road towards Marciana Marina.

Villa San Martino ② Divert right off the main road to San Martino, and on to Napoleon's country residence.

Capoliveri ⑥ Follow the road round the south of the island and divert to the right just before Porto Azzurro to visit this charming old mining village.

Porto Azzurro ⑦ Return to the main road and carry on for 2 km (1.25 miles) to Elba's second largest port, a fashionable resort overlooking a lovely bay dominated by a 17th-century fortress.

Rio Marina ⑧ This mining town, 12 km (7.5 miles) to the north, has an excellent museum of mineralogy.

Cavo ⑨ Drive for 7.5 km (4.5 miles) to Cavo, along the east coast, to see the scenic northern tip of Elba.

The Maremma ❼

Maremma butterfly

The ancient Romans were the first to cultivate the marshes of the Maremma, but after the collapse of their empire the area went virtually uninhabited until the 18th century. The land has since been reclaimed, the irrigation canals unblocked and farming developed on the fertile soil. The Parco Naturale dell'Uccellina was set up in 1975 to protect the abundant local flora and fauna and prevent more development taking place.

Wildlife
The undergrowth and marshes are home to wild boar and other wildlife.

Entry permits are sold at Alberese.

This salt marsh, cut by irrigation canals, is home to herons, storks and other wading birds.

Canoes can be hired to explore the irrigation canals.

There are picnic tables on the beach in the shade of pine trees.

Sea lilies and hollies grow along the sandy shoreline, backed by groves of parasol pines, mastic trees and juniper.

Beaches
The shoreline south of Marina di Alberese has wide, sandy beaches sheltered by steep cliffs.

Torre di Castelmarino
The cliffs are crowned by 16th-century watchtowers, part of a defence system built by the Medici to protect the coastal region from attack.

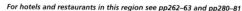

For hotels and restaurants in this region see pp262–63 and pp280–81

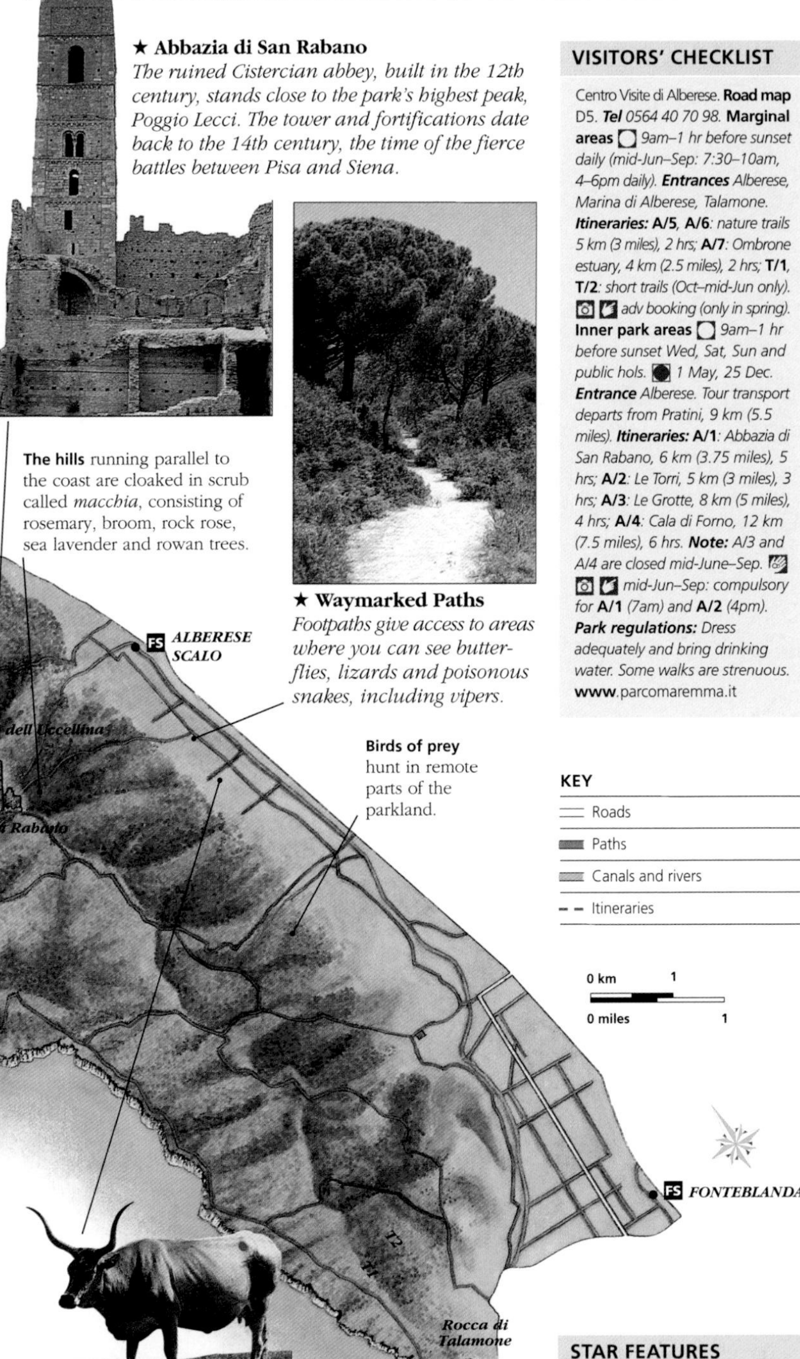

★ Abbazia di San Rabano
The ruined Cistercian abbey, built in the 12th century, stands close to the park's highest peak, Poggio Lecci. The tower and fortifications date back to the 14th century, the time of the fierce battles between Pisa and Siena.

The hills running parallel to the coast are cloaked in scrub called *macchia*, consisting of rosemary, broom, rock rose, sea lavender and rowan trees.

★ Waymarked Paths
Footpaths give access to areas where you can see butterflies, lizards and poisonous snakes, including vipers.

Birds of prey hunt in remote parts of the parkland.

Long-horned Cattle
The docile white Maremma cattle are raised by cowboys (butteri) *who also stage rodeos.*

Talamone is a fishing village.

VISITORS' CHECKLIST

Centro Visite di Alberese. **Road map** D5. ***Tel*** *0564 40 70 98.* **Marginal areas** *9am–1 hr before sunset daily (mid-Jun–Sep: 7:30–10am, 4–6pm daily).* ***Entrances*** *Alberese, Marina di Alberese, Talamone.* ***Itineraries:*** **A/5**, **A/6**: *nature trails 5 km (3 miles), 2 hrs;* **A/7**: *Ombrone estuary, 4 km (2.5 miles), 2 hrs;* **T/1**, **T/2**: *short trails (Oct–mid-Jun only).* *adv booking (only in spring).* **Inner park areas** *9am–1 hr before sunset Wed, Sat, Sun and public hols.* *1 May, 25 Dec.* ***Entrance*** *Alberese. Tour transport departs from Pratini, 9 km (5.5 miles).* ***Itineraries:*** **A/1**: *Abbazia di San Rabano, 6 km (3.75 miles), 5 hrs;* **A/2**: *Le Torri, 5 km (3 miles), 3 hrs;* **A/3**: *Le Grotte, 8 km (5 miles), 4 hrs;* **A/4**: *Cala di Forno, 12 km (7.5 miles), 6 hrs.* **Note:** *A/3 and A/4 are closed mid-June–Sep.* *mid-Jun–Sep: compulsory for* **A/1** *(7am) and* **A/2** *(4pm).* ***Park regulations:*** *Dress adequately and bring drinking water. Some walks are strenuous.* **www**.parcomaremma.it

KEY

- Roads
- Paths
- Canals and rivers
- Itineraries

STAR FEATURES

- ★ Waymarked Paths
- ★ Abbazia di San Rabano

Rio Marina ❺

Road map B4. 2,038. *Lungomare G Marconi 2, Gli Spiazzi (0565 96 20 04). Mon.*

Around Rio Marina there are still open-cast mines which extract the ores that attracted the Etruscans to Elba. The **Museo dei Minerali** explains the geology of the island. Shops in the town centre sell jewellery made of local semi-precious stones.

Museo dei Minerali
Palazzo Comunale. ***Tel*** *0565 96 20 88. Apr–mid-Oct: daily; mid-Oct–Mar: by appt.*

Grosseto ❻

Road map D4. *71,472.* FS *Via Monterosa 206 (0564 46 26 11). Thu.*

Grosseto is the largest town in southern Tuscany. World War II destroyed many buildings, but the 16th-century walls still stand and several of the bastions are now parks.

Museo Civico Archeologico e d'Arte della Maremma
Piazza Baccarini 3. ***Tel*** *0564 48 87 53. Nov–Feb: 9am–1pm Tue–Sun (also 4:30–7pm Sat); Mar–Apr: 9:30am–1pm, 4:30–7pm Tue–Sun; May–Oct: 10am–1pm, 5–8pm Tue–Sun. 1 Jan, 1 May, 25 Dec.*
The museum has Etruscan and Roman artifacts from Roselle and Vetulonia. There is also a collection of coins, intaglios (carved stones) and pottery.

Grosseto, a busy town full of narrow streets and shops

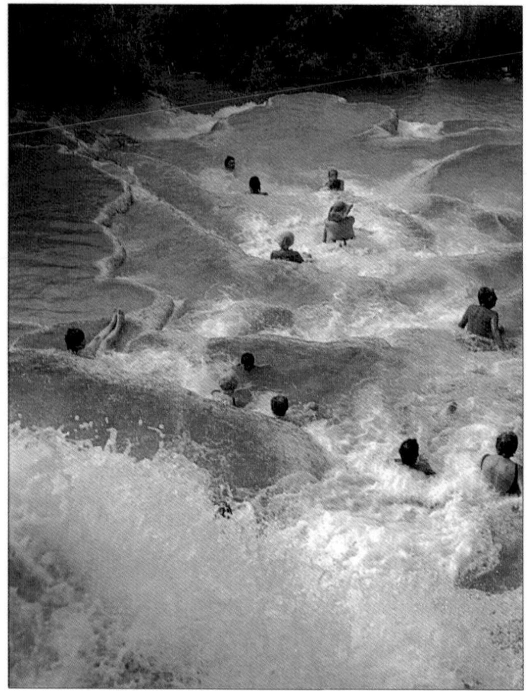

Cascate del Gorello, free for all to enjoy in Saturnia

The Maremma ❼

See pp236–7.

Saturnia ❽

Road map D5. *550. Via Mazzini 4 (0564 60 12 80).*

Holidaymakers come to Saturnia to enjoy the good Maremma food or seek a health cure in the modern spa of Terme di Saturnia. Others prefer to bathe for free in the hot sulphurated waters of the waterfall at Cascate del Gorello on the Montemerano road. This is a pretty spot, with its pools and rocks stained coppery green.

Sovana ❾

Road map E5. *100.*

Sovana sits on a ridge high above the Lente valley. Its main street is lined with cafés, restaurants and shops. The 13th-century Romanesque **Rocca Aldobrandesca**, named after the Teutonic family that ruled in the area until 1608, is now in ruins.

The frescoes of the late 15th-century Siena School in the medieval church of **Santa Maria** were discovered under the whitewashed walls. The main altar is sheltered by a 9th-century canopy that was originally in the Romanesque **Duomo**. This 12th-century building incorporates sculpture from earlier churches built on the same site.

The Etruscans dug tombs nearby in the soft limestone cliffs bordering the river Lente. The most complete set of **Necropoli Etrusca** can be found in a valley just to the west of Sovana.

Rocca Aldobrandesca
Via del Pretorio. *to the public.*

Santa Maria
Piazza del Pretorio. *daily.*

Duomo
Piazza del Pretorio. *daily in summer; Sat, Sun only in winter.*

Necropoli Etrusca
Poggio di Sopra Ripa. ***Tel*** *0564 61 40 74. Mar–Nov: 9am–7pm daily; Dec–Feb: 9am–5pm Sat & Sun.*

Cafés and shops in Sovana's medieval piazza

Pitigliano ⑩

Road map E5. 4,361. Piazza Garibaldi 51 (0564 61 71 11). Wed.

Pitigliano looks spectacular perched on a plateau, high above cliffs carved out by the river Lente. The houses seem to grow out of the cliffs, which are riddled with caves cut out of soft limestone. The caves have been used for many years to store wines and olive oils.

A maze of tiny medieval streets passes through the Jewish ghetto, formed when Jews fleeing from Catholic persecution took refuge here in the 17th century. The Palazzo Orsini in the town centre has its water supply brought in by an aqueduct, built in 1545, that overhangs Via Cavour. The **Museo Palazzo Orsini** in the palazzo has a small exhibition of work by the artist Francesco Zuccarelli (1702–88). He also painted two of the altarpieces in the medieval **Duomo**, whose huge belltower supports a bell which weighs 3 tonnes.

The **Museo Etrusco** contains finds from ancient local settlements.

Museo Palazzo Orsini
Piazza della Fortezza Orsini. ***Tel*** *0564 61 60 74.* *10am–1pm, 3–7pm (to 5pm in winter) Tue–Fri.*

Duomo
Piazza San Gregorio.
daily.

Museo Etrusco
Piazza della Fortezza Orsini 59.
Tel *0564 61 40 67.*
summer: 10am–1pm, 3–7pm Thu–Tue; call to check times in winter.

Orbetello ⑪

Road map D5. 15,455. FS Piazza della Repubblica 1 (0564 86 04 47). Sat.

Orbetello is a crowded resort bordered by two tidal lagoons. Part of the northernmost lagoon is managed by the Worldwide Fund for Nature as a wildlife park.

The town was the capital of a tiny Spanish state, called the Presidio, from 1557 until 1808, when it was absorbed into the Grand Duchy of Tuscany. The Porta del Soccorso bears the coat of arms of the king of Spain. Inside the gates is the **Polveriera Guzman**, which was originally used as an arsenal. The Duomo, **Santa Maria Assunta**, also has Spanish-style decoration, but the altar in the Cappella di San Biagio is typically Romanesque in design.

Coat of arms on the Porta del Soccorso

The Fontone di Talamone, in Piazza della Repubblica, is a terracotta plinth from the Roman-Etruscan era.

Polveriera Guzman
Viale Mura di Levante. *Call Tourist Information for details.*

Santa Maria Assunta
Piazza del Duomo. *daily.*

View over Pitigliano showing soft limestone cliffs and caves bordering the river Lente

Porto Ercole, near Monte Argentario

Monte Argentario ⓬

Road map D5. *14,000.*
Piazzale Sant'Andrea, Porto Santo Stéfano (0564 81 42 08). *Tue.*

Monte Argentario was an island until the early 18th century, when the shallow waters separating it from the mainland began to silt up, creating two sandy spits of land, known as *tomboli*, that enclose the Orbetello lagoon. Orbetello itself was linked to the island in 1842, when a dyke was constructed linking the mainland to Terrarossa.

The two harbour towns of Porto Ercole and Porto Santo Stéfano are both favoured by wealthy yacht owners. There are good fish restaurants in both towns *(see p263)*, and from the Strada Panoramica there are views over rocky coves, cliffs and bays. Ferries from Porto Santo Stéfano go to the island of Giglio, popular with Italian tourists for its sandy beaches and rich wildlife.

In the summer the Porto Santo Stéfano ferry also calls at Giannutri, a privately owned island where visitors are not allowed to stay overnight.

Ansedonia ⓭

Road map D5. *300.*

Ansedonia is a prosperous village of luxurious villas and gardens, high on a hill above the coast. The ruins of the city of Cosa, founded by the Romans in 173 BC, are on the summit of the hill looking over Ansedonia. The **Museo di Cosa**, containing relics from the ancient settlement, is close by. East of Ansedonia is a long stretch of sandy beach and the remains of the Etruscan Canal. The date and purpose of the canal

An Etruscan Tour

The Etruscans gained much of their wealth from Tuscany's vast mineral resources, and their monied classes were cultured and worldly. Both their elaborate burial sites and the artifacts found in their tombs give us an insight into their lives *(see pp42–3)*. Etruscan burial sites were carved into soft rock or built of huge stone slabs with rock-cut roads leading down to the tombs.

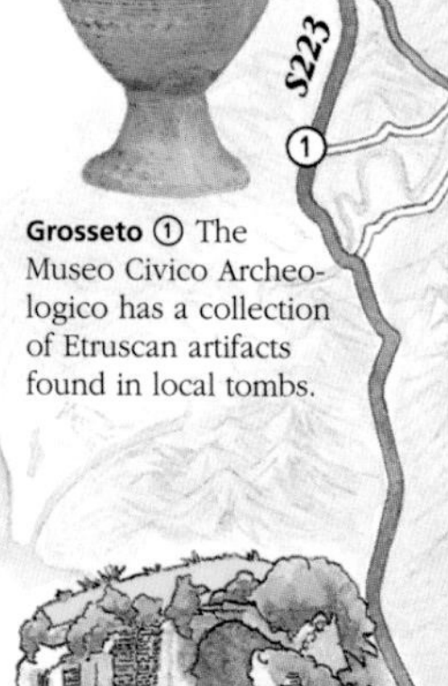

Grosseto ① The Museo Civico Archeologico has a collection of Etruscan artifacts found in local tombs.

Talamone ⑦ Follow the S74 to the S1. Turn right and after 8 km (5 miles) fork off to the left, into the Maremma, for the Etruscan temple, Roman villa and baths.

ALSO WORTH SEEING

Museo Archeologico, Florence *(see p99)*.

Museo Etrusco, Volterra *(see p166)*.

Vulci and **Tarquinia** These excavated sites, just over the Tuscany border in Lazio, have impressive Etruscan ruins, painted tombs and art collections.

This Etruscan bone brooch, called a *fibula*, was found near Grosseto and is now in the Museo Archeologico in Florence.

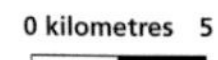

The Etruscan Canal at Ansedonia

are debatable, but it may have been dug in Roman times to keep the harbour free of silt. Alternatively, it may have been part of a canal leading to the Lago di Burano, 5 km (3 miles) down the coast. This lagoon is 4 km (2.5 miles) long and has been turned into a wildlife refuge *(rifugio faunistico)* by the Worldwide Fund for Nature. It is a very important habitat for wading birds.

Museo di Cosa
Via delle Ginestre 35, Ansedonia. ***Tel*** *0564 88 14 21. 9am–7pm daily. 1 Jan, 25 Dec.*

Capalbio ⓮

Road map D5. *4,049. Wed.*

Capalbio is another village which is popular with wealthy Italians. The hilltop town has several restaurants and hotels and is busy all year round. Summer tourists come for the beaches, and winter visitors flock to hunt deer and wild boar in the surrounding woodland, which is now managed as a game reserve. A game festival is held in September each year.

Giardino dei Tarocchi
Garavicchio, Pescia Fiorentina. ***Tel*** *0564 89 51 22. Apr–mid-Oct: 2:30–7:30pm daily; mid-Oct–Mar: group reservations only.*

At Pescia Fiorentina, southeast of Capalbio, is a modern sculpture garden created by the late French artist Niki de Saint-Phalle in 1982. It was inspired by the figures of the Tarot and was over ten years in the making. The bigger pieces each represent one card from the Tarot pack. Among the sculptures is *The Tower*, a glittering three-storey edifice made out of broken mirrors.

View across the rooftops of Capalbio

Roselle ② Head north on the S223 to the most important excavated Etruscan and Roman remains in Tuscany.

Saturnia ③ Continue east for 54 km (34 miles) for the rock-cut tombs below this tiny village of Etruscan origin.

Sovana ④ From Saturnia, drive towards Sovana to the famous Ildebranda Tomb in a valley to the west.

Scansano

S322

Manciano

S74

Pitigliano ⑤ The town, on the junction with the S74, is built on tufa cliffs riddled with Etruscan tombs and tunnels, now used for storing produce.

Marsiliana ⑥ Head west on the S74 through Manciano to the vast necropolises on the outskirts of Marsiliana.

KEY

Tour route

Other roads

TRAVELLERS' NEEDS

WHERE TO STAY

Of all Italy's regions, Tuscany has some of the most charming places to stay. Inland these range from ancient villas to elegant town houses. Smaller, family-run establishments excel in their cuisine and are sometimes filled with antiques. The major cities also offer B&B accommodation. Hotels on the riviera tend to be less distinctive, but the popularity of coastal resorts in summer means that standards are high. Many visitors opt for self-catering holidays. Often the accommodation is a small flat or house on a farm, and the prices can prove very reasonable. Other options include hostels and dormitories and, for walking enthusiasts, there are mountain huts throughout the region. For more information on hotels in Florence and Tuscany see the listings on pages 250–63.

Sign showing hotel rating

Terrace at Hotel Continentale, Florence *(see p251)*

WHERE TO LOOK

Florence has a wide range of hotels, but prices can be high. The most attractive locations are along the north bank of the Arno, the historic centre and in nearby Fiesole. Parking is a problem in the city centre, so if you have a car it is best to choose a hotel which has parking facilities.

Accommodation in central Pisa is generally sub-standard but there are some lovely Tuscan villa hotels a short drive from the centre.

Though large, Arezzo has relatively few hotels and those in the centre are mostly geared for business people. If you can, stay outside the town and travel in to visit the centre.

The hill towns of central Tuscany offer a number of quality villa hotels, manor houses and even former palaces. The Chianti region is rich in converted villa hotels, with excellent regional restaurants, particularly around Radda and Gaiole. Siena's more attractive options are outside the city, such as the tiny hamlet of Strove.

Street sign showing the direction and location of hotels

HOTEL PRICES

During the low season (November to March) prices are cheaper and often negotiable. Florence is less busy than other parts of Tuscany in July and August, but this is the peak holiday season on the coast. Avoid the city during certain weeks of January and July when fashion shows fill the top hotels, raising low-season prices.

Single room rates are higher than individual rates for two people sharing a double room. Prices include tax and service. Bear in mind that accommodation in Florence and Siena is more expensive than elsewhere in the region.

HIDDEN EXTRAS

Before making a reservation, establish whether breakfast is included in the price. Garage parking, laundry and snacks in the hotel or from the minibar may be pricey and telephone charges from your hotel room can be phenomenal. Check the rates first if you are concerned. Some hotels may expect you to take full- or half-board during the high season.

HOTEL GRADINGS AND FACILITIES

Hotels in Italy are classified by a star-rating system, from one to five stars. However, each province sets its own levels for grading; consequently, standards for each category may vary from one area to another. Some hotels may not have a restaurant but those that do will usually welcome non-residents to stop by and eat.

Some of the converted castles and ancient villas are not air-conditioned, but as the stone walls are thick the

◁ Houses in Cortona, one of the oldest cities in Tuscany

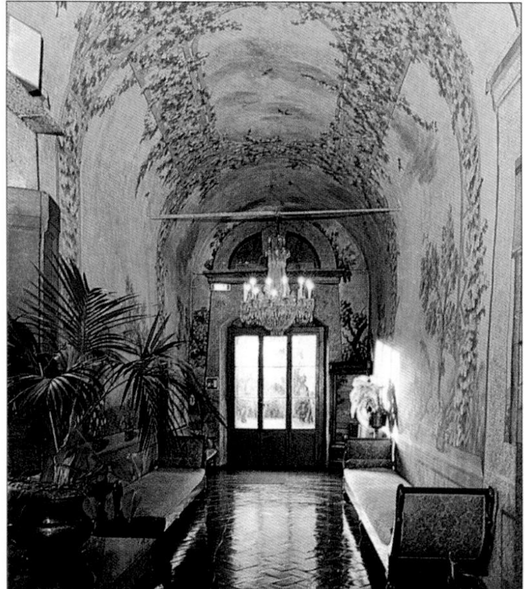

The gallery entrance of Hotel Villa Villoresi, just outside Florence *(see p256)*

midsummer heat barely penetrates the buildings.

Children are welcome but the smaller hotels generally have limited facilities. Often, more up-market hotels will arrange a baby-sitting service.

WHAT TO EXPECT

In Florence, street numbers can be confusing *(see p305)*, so refer to the map references in the listings.

Hotel proprietors are obliged by law to register you with the police, so they will ask for your passport when you arrive. Make sure you take it back, as you will need some form of identification to change money or travellers' cheques.

Even a humble *pensione* should have a reasonably smart bathroom. Rooms without a bathroom will usually have wash basins and towels.

As far as hotel decoration goes, you may sometimes have to sacrifice smart decor for the charm of an old establishment.

The Italian breakfast is light – a cappuccino and a pastry *(brioche)*. Most hotels serve a continental breakfast of coffee, tea or hot chocolate, bread rolls and jam. However, it may be cheaper to go to a local bar or a *pasticceria*.

Florence can be very noisy. Top-class hotels usually have some form of soundproofing, but ask for a room facing away from the street if you are easily disturbed by noise.

Check-out time is usually noon in four- and five-star hotels and between 10am and noon in other establishments. If you stay longer you will be asked to pay for an extra day. However, many hotels will store your baggage if you plan on leaving the city several hours after check-out time. Most hotels offer Internet access and accept credit cards but be sure to check when booking, if you require these or any other facilities.

BOOKING AND PAYING

Book at least two months in advance if you want to stay in a particular hotel in high season or at Easter. The local tourist office will have listings of all the hotels in the area and will be able to advise you on the best hotels for each category. Most hotels take credit cards, but check which ones when booking. You can usually pay the deposit by credit card, or send an international money order. Confirm your reservation by fax or e-mail including the dates of your stay and your credit card details.

Under Italian law, a booking is valid as soon as the deposit is paid and confirmation is received. As in restaurants, you are required by law to keep your hotel receipt until you leave Italy.

DISABLED TRAVELLERS

Facilities for the disabled are usually limited. The hotel listings on pages 250–63 indicate which hotels have these facilities.

HOTELS IN HISTORIC BUILDINGS

The Tuscany regional tourist board publishes a leaflet which lists hotels in historic buildings and those of artistic interest. Some of the best are included in the listings here. The booklet is also available from national Italian tourist offices worldwide. **Relais & Châteaux** produces a guide that includes a number of fine Tuscan hotels and hotel restaurants of historic interest, all of high quality.

Villa San Michele, a former monastery, in Fiesole *(see p256)*

Terrace at the Gallery Hotel Art in Florence *(see p250)*

AGRITURISMOS

Farm and villa holiday accommodation abounds in Tuscany. Tourist offices can help visitors arrange a rural stay with an *agriturismo*. These vary from B&Bs to working farms, and give the visitor an opportunity to experience traditional rural life, and sample locally sourced food.

SELF-CATERING

There are many international agencies offering self-catering holidays around Florence such **Your Way to Florence**. Other agents include **Cuendet** in Monteriggioni and **Prima Italia** in Grosseto. **Tastes of Italy** is based in the UK, and **Interhome** has offices in the UK, the US and Australia.

Prices for self-catering vary enormously depending on the season and location. Generally, a four-person villa within a complex in the low season will cost around €450 per week, while an individual villa in its own grounds can cost as much as €1,750 per week during the peak season.

STAYING IN PRIVATE HOMES

Rooms in private homes can usually be rented through one of the recreational associations such as **AB&BA** (Associazione Bed & Breakfast Affittacamere) in Florence. Meals are not provided but can sometimes be arranged on request.

RESIDENTIAL HOTELS

Throughout Tuscany there are former palaces or villas that have been converted into

DIRECTORY

HISTORIC HOTELS

Relais & Châteaux
5 Dovedale Studios,
465 Battersea Park Road,
London SW11 4LR.
Tel *00800 2000 0002.*
Fax *020 7228 5483.*
www.relaischateaux.com

SELF-CATERING AGENCIES

Your Way to Florence
www.yourwaytoflorence.com

Cuendet
Strada di Strove 17,
53035 Monteriggioni.
Tel *0577 57 63 30.*
www.cuendet.com

Interhome
Tel *UK: 020 8780 6633.*
Tel *US: 800 882 6864.*
www.interhome.com

Prima Italia
Viale Tirreno 19, 58046
Principina a Mare
(Grosseto). **Tel** *0564 300 09.* **www**.primaita.it

Tastes of Italy
9 Lydden Road,
London SE18 4LT.
Tel *UK: 020 8874 3490.*
www.tastesofitaly.co.uk

PRIVATE HOMES

AB&BA
Via Pietro Mastri 26,
50135 Florence.
Tel *055 654 08 60.*
www.abba-firenze.it

RESIDENTIAL HOTELS

Mini Residence
Via Giulio Caccini 20,
50141 Florence.
Tel *055 41 08 76.*

Palazzo Ricasoli
Via delle Mantellate 2,
50129 Florence. **Map** 2 D3. **Tel** *055 35 21 51.*
www.ricasoli.com

Residence San Niccolò
Piazza Piave 1a, 50122
Florence. **Map** 4 F2.
Tel *055 234 52 87.*

La Valle
Via Sanminiatese,
Loc. La Valle, 50050
Montaione (Florence).
Tel *0571 69 80 59.*
www.agricolalavalle.it

HOTEL COOPERATIVES

Chianti Slow Travel
Tel *055 854 62 99.*
www.chiantislowtravel.it

Family Hotels
Viale Don Minzoni 11R,
50129 Florence.
Map 2 E2.
Tel *055 33 40 41.*
www.familyhotels.com

Florence Promhotels
Viale Alessandro Volta 72,
50131 Florence.
Map 2 F2.
Tel *055 55 39 41.*
www.promhotels.it

BUDGET ACCOMMODATION

Associazione Italiana Alberghi per la Gioventù
Viale Augusto
Righi 2–4, 50137
Florence.
Tel *055 60 03 15.*
www.ostellionline.org

Europa Villa Camerata
Viale Augusto
Righi 2–4, 50137
Florence.
Tel *055 60 14 51.*

MOUNTAIN REFUGES AND CAMP SITES

Club Alpino Italiano
Via E Petrella 19,
20124 Milan.
Tel *02 205 72 31.*
www.cai.it

Touring Club Italiano
Corso Italia 10,
20122 Milan.
Tel *02 852 61.*
www.touringclub.it

complexes of small apartments, often with swimming pools or bars. The minimum period of stay is usually a week, but there is more flexibility in low season.

Residential hotels in Florence include **Residence San Niccolò** and **Palazzo Ricasoli**. The local tourist offices can help.

Poster (about 1918) for a Pisan hotel

HOTEL COOPERATIVES

These are not chains but consortiums of different hotel types. **Family Hotel** specializes in small, intimate family hotels and B&Bs, while **Florence Promhotels** provides a wider range of accommodation. **Chianti Slow Travel** books rooms in villas, castles and farmhouses in the Chianti region.

BUDGET ACCOMMODATION

For one- and two-star budget hotels, visitors should expect to pay from €30 to €50 per person per night. They are generally small, family-run establishments that were originally known as *pensioni*. The term is no longer in use; however, many places retain the name and personal character that has made them so popular. Most offer breakfast and some have rooms with private bathrooms, but do not expect particularly high standards of service.

Hostel and dormitory accommodation can often be found in convents and religious institutions. Dormitory accommodation can be arranged through the local tourist office. The **Associazione Italiana Alberghi per la Gioventù** (Italian Youth Hostel Association) in Rome has lists of youth hostels in Italy. The main youth hostel in Florence is **Europa Villa Camerata**.

Full lists and booking facilities for youth hostels are available through the Italian tourist board (ENIT) worldwide or from the local tourist offices. Go to www.enit.it; alternatively, log on to www.ostellionline.org.

ALBERGHI

Albergo is Italian for hotel but the term tends to refer to the upper categories. Room sizes vary considerably: in city centres even expensive hotels can have far smaller rooms than their counterparts in other countries, whereas outside the city your room may be more like a small suite. In general, *alberghi* will have private showers in all rooms and the more luxurious have baths. In city centres you may come across the sign *albergo diurno*. This is a day hotel without accommodation but with bathroom, showers, hairdressing, drying and other cleaning facilities you may need when travelling. Day hotels are usually situated at or near the main railway station.

MOUNTAIN REFUGES AND CAMP SITES

If you are likely to be trekking, backpacking or walking, there are mountain refuges and huts dotted throughout Tuscany. The Garfagnana in the north west of Tuscany is worthy of note for these outdoor activities. This area caters for tourists well and is renowned for its outstanding natural beauty. There are also camp sites on the fringes of most towns. A list of camp sites and mountain refuges is available from www.enit.it or local tourist offices. **Club Alpino Italiano** in Milan owns most of the huts in the mountain districts of Italy, including Tuscany. The **Touring Club Italiano** publishes a list of camp sites in *Campeggi e Villaggi Turistici in* Italy.

Vaulted entrance hall of Hotel Porta Rossa ***(see p253)***

Florence's Best Hotels

In a city renowned for its splendid architecture, it is hardly surprising that many of Florence's hotels are favoured by visitors for their charm and individual character. Former palazzi, monasteries such as Villa San Michele, and town villas offer a range of accommodation, though usually at a high price. Original features are sometimes preserved at the expense of modern comforts: among the older establishments listed on pages 250–56 we try to include those that combine both. The hotels shown here are a selection of the best.

Hotel Beacci Tornabuoni
This family-run former palace is particularly welcoming and furnished with fine antiques. (See p253.)

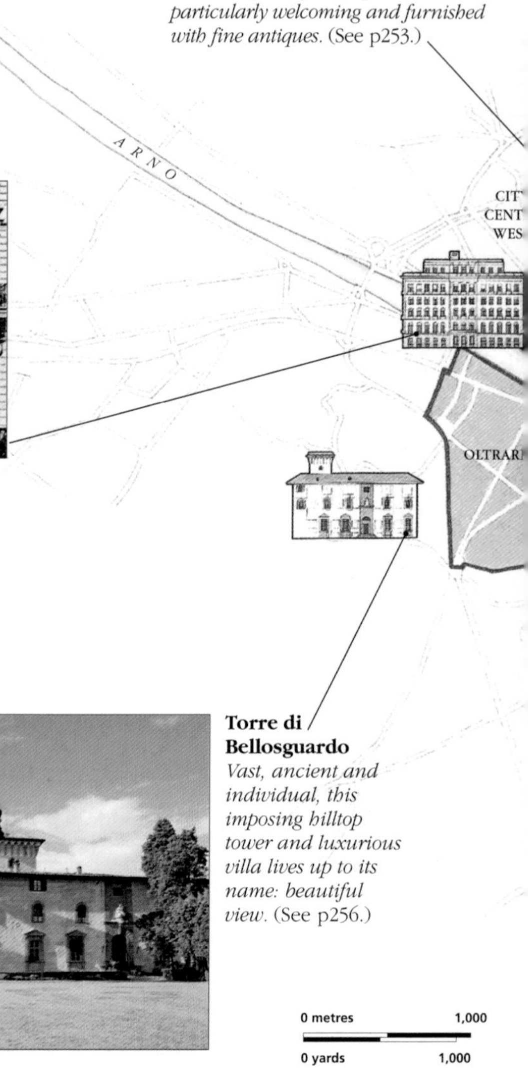

ARNO

CIT
CENT
WES

Hotel Excelsior
On a 13th-century square near the river Arno, this beautiful hotel epitomizes luxury, with well-appointed bedrooms and 19th-century fittings. (See p253.)

OLTRARI

Torre di Bellosguardo
Vast, ancient and individual, this imposing hilltop tower and luxurious villa lives up to its name: beautiful view. (See p256.)

0 metres 1,000

0 yards 1,000

Villa San Michele
This peaceful monastery in Fiesole is said to have been designed by Michelangelo. (See p256.)

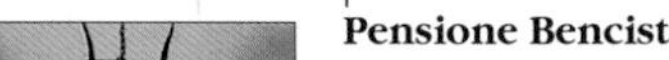

Pensione Bencistà
A haven in the hills behind the city, this lovingly kept pensione *has luxurious period furniture.* (See p255.)

CITY CENTRE NORTH

CITY CENTRE EAST

Four Seasons
This fresco-filled sanctuary in the city has its own ancient parkland as well as sumptuous accommodation and attentive service. (See p250.)

Palazzo Vecchietti
Exquisite interior decoration and butler service are the hallmarks of this town house with every home comfort. (See p254.)

Choosing a Hotel

Many hotels in Florence and Tuscany, even budget ones, offer very charming decor and environs. The best among them are reviewed on the following pages. For more information on other types of accommodation, see pages 244–9. Map references are either to the Street Finder on pages 140–47, or the road map on the inside back cover.

PRICE CATEGORIES
For a double room per night, including breakfast, tax and service:

€ under €100
€€ €100–€150
€€€ €150–€200
€€€€ €200–€250
€€€€€ over €250

FLORENCE

CITY CENTRE EAST Hotel Locanda Orchidea €

Borgo degli Albizi 11, 50122 ***Tel/Fax*** *055 248 03 46* ***Rooms*** *10* ***Map*** *6 F3*

Value-for-money accommodation at its best, the Locanda is a ten-minute walk from the heart of the city. Situated inside a 12th-century building, the hotel prides itself on its old-fashioned simplicity. Fans instead of air conditioning, and no en suite bathrooms. All rooms are refreshingly unique. **www.hotelorchideaflorence.it**

CITY CENTRE EAST Soggiorno Battistero €

Piazza San Giovanni 1, 50129 ***Tel*** *055 29 51 43* ***Fax*** *055 26 81 89* ***Rooms*** *6* ***Map*** *6 D2*

On the third floor of a 14th-century palazzo, this modest *pensione* is reasonably priced and excellently located. Most of the rooms have a splendid view of the Duomo and the Baptistery. The Museo del Bigallo is located on the ground floor. The decor is unremarkable but pleasant. Wi-fi in rooms. **www.soggiornobattistero.it**

CITY CENTRE EAST Dei Mori B&B €€

Via Dante Alighieri 12, 50122 ***Tel*** *055 21 14 38* ***Fax*** *055 238 22 16* ***Rooms*** *5* ***Map*** *6 3E*

This clean and cosy establishment is a very popular haunt, so book early. Don't be fooled by the dimly-lit stairway since it leads into a spacious lounge, and tastefully decorated rooms. The hosts are charming and helpful. All rooms in this gay-friendly inn overlook the tranquil courtyard. **www.deimori.com**

CITY CENTRE EAST Martin Dago B&B €€

Via de Macci 84, 50122 ***Tel*** *055 234 14 15* ***Fax*** *055 234 14 15* ***Rooms*** *6* ***Map*** *4 E1*

This charming little place near Santa Croce is close to the lively Sant'Ambrogio market and Cibreo restaurant *(see p271)*. There are frescoes, canopied beds and en-suite bathrooms in the six bedrooms, and a terrace at the top of the house. The gay-friendly owner gives tips on local artisans and shopping. **www.bbmartindago.com**

CITY CENTRE EAST Hotel Balestri €€€

Piazza Mentana 7, 50122 ***Tel*** *055 21 47 43* ***Fax*** *055 239 80 42* ***Rooms*** *46* ***Map*** *6 E4*

Open for business since 1888, this hotel is located in a little piazza on the riverfront halfway between the Ponte Vecchio and Santa Croce. Extensively renovated, the rooms are clean, pretty and have all amenities. Thirty rooms face the Arno, while the rest overlook a quiet courtyard. **www.hotel-balestri.it**

CITY CENTRE EAST Bernini Palace €€€€€

Piazza San Firenze 29, 50122 ***Tel*** *055 28 86 21* ***Fax*** *055 26 82 72* ***Rooms*** *74* ***Map*** *6 E3*

An ideal choice if easy access to the main sights is a priority. This hotel is on the road leading from Piazza del Duomo to the river, and is equidistant from Piazza della Signoria and Santa Croce. The double-glazed windows mute the street noise. The decor veers towards a shabby chic. Rooms are spacious. **www.baglionihotels.com**

CITY CENTRE EAST Four Seasons Florence €€€€€

Borgo Pinti 99, 50121 ***Tel*** *055 262 61* ***Fax*** *055 262 65 00* ***Rooms*** *116* ***Map*** *2 F4*

A lengthy renovation turned two Renaissance palaces into this sumptuous hotel. Frescoes, bas-reliefs and original decorations give it a museum-like gravitas, yet the attentive service makes it feel like home. There's also a large and delightful walled garden, an exclusive spa and excellent restaurant, Il Palagio. **www.fourseasons.com/florence**

CITY CENTRE EAST Gallery Hotel Art €€€€€

Vicolo dell'Oro 5, 50123 ***Tel*** *055 272 63* ***Fax*** *055 26 85 57* ***Rooms*** *74* ***Map*** *6 D4*

The lobby and library of this eight-storey boutique hotel also double as a contemporary art gallery. Fax and modem lines along with cutting-edge sound and video systems in every room. The penthouse suites feature linen sheets and cashmere blankets. The sushi bar offers a fusion of Italian, French and Japanese cuisine. **www.lungarnohotels.com**

CITY CENTRE EAST Hotel Calzaiuoli €€€€€

Via Calzaiuoli 6, 50123 ***Tel*** *055 21 24 56* ***Fax*** *055 26 83 10* ***Rooms*** *45* ***Map*** *6 D3*

Halfway down the pedestrianised street that links the Duomo and the Piazza della Signoria, this small hotel is located close to all the action. All the rooms are on the upper floors, and are large and comfortable. Some have views of Brunelleschi's dome. The buffet breakfast is excellent. Advance booking is essential. **www.calzaiuoli.it**

Key to Symbols *see back cover flap*

CITY CENTRE EAST Hotel Continentale €€€€€

Vicolo dell'Oro 6r, 50123 **Tel** *055 272 62* **Fax** *055 28 31 39* **Rooms** *43* **Map** *6 D4*

This trendy, contemporary hotel is designed to impress. The entrance lobby features installations by the leading Italian artist, Fabrizio Corneli. The rooms are chic and have good views – in most cases of the Ponte Vecchio. The fitness and wellness centre is housed in the medieval tower. **www.lungarnohotels.com**

CITY CENTRE EAST J and J €€€€€

Via di Mezzo 20, 50121 **Tel** *055 263 12* **Fax** *055 24 02 82* **Rooms** *19* **Map** *2 E5*

A 16th-century convent is now this superb hotel. The large rooms, some of which are on two levels, are all decorated differently. All boast antique furniture and handwoven fabrics. Rooms either overlook the red-tiled rooftops or the cloister garden, where breakfast and drinks can be enjoyed in the summer. **www.jandj.hotelinfirenze.com**

CITY CENTRE EAST Plaza Hotel Lucchesi €€€€€

Lungarno della Zecca Vecchia 38, 50122 **Tel** *055 262 36* **Fax** *055 248 09 21* **Rooms** *97* **Map** *4 E2*

A private home built in 1860, the building was converted into a hotel in the 1940s. Furnished in a warm and cosy style, the rooms have outstanding views of the city. Some have sprawling terraces with views of the Arno or Santa Croce. The restaurant, La Serra, specializes in Tuscan cuisine. **www.plazalucchesi.it**

CITY CENTRE EAST Relais Santa Croce €€€€€

Via Ghibellina 87, 50122 **Tel** *055 234 22 30* **Fax** *055 234 11 95* **Rooms** *24* **Map** *4 F1*

This wonderful hotel, in an 18th-century palazzo, is just a short stroll from Michelangelo's house. Most of its luxurious rooms overlook the street. The music room and smoking room retain the splendour of their grand past. The restaurant serves Tuscan delicacies. **www.relaissantacroce.it**

CITY CENTRE NORTH Casa di Barbano €

Via di Barbano 1, 50129 **Tel** *055 47 50 16* **Fax** *055 47 50 16* **Rooms** *3* **Map** *1 C3*

The simple and elegant ground-floor rooms are furnished with a practised eye at this family-run guesthouse, which is reasonably priced while maintaining high standards. All rooms are en-suite. Breakfast is served in your room. The charming owner gives dining tips, books museum tickets and even lends out umbrellas. **www.casadibarbano.it**

CITY CENTRE NORTH Casa Rovai €

Via Fiesolana 1, 50122 **Tel** *055 20 01 647* **Fax** *055 200 16 47* **Rooms** *6* **Map** *2 E5*

A renovated family home has been converted into a lovely and comfortable guesthouse. All the spacious rooms are en-suite, and some have nice frescoes. The friendly staff and owner make a real difference, as do their restaurant tips. There is a terrace which gives a good view over the centre of town. **www.casarovai.it**

CITY CENTRE NORTH Residenza Johanna II €

Via Cinque Giornate 2, 50129 **Tel** *055 47 33 77* **Fax** *055 47 33 77* **Rooms** *10* **Map** *1 C2*

This Liberty-style villa is very clean, comfortable and pleasantly furnished. You get your own keys to the front door as the staff go home at 7pm. Rooms are simple, with high ceilings and pale, pastel floral prints. Breakfast is basic and served in your room. There is free parking in the courtyard behind. No credit cards. **www.johanna.it**

CITY CENTRE NORTH Antica Dimora Firenze €€

Via San Gallo 72, 50129 **Tel** *055 462 72 96* **Fax** *055 463 44 50* **Rooms** *6* **Map** *2 D3*

Of the Johanna & Johlea group of guesthouses, Antica Dimora is the most sumptuous, with splendid four-poster beds in the individually decorated bedrooms. There is a DVD library for the use of guests. The afternoon tea, which is served in the homely lounge, is a real treat. **www.anticadimorafirenze.it**

CITY CENTRE NORTH Palazzo Benci €€

Piazza Madonna Aldobrandini 3, 50123 **Tel** *055 21 38 48* **Fax** *055 28 83 08* **Rooms** *35* **Map** *1 C5*

Once belonging to the famous Benci family, this 16th-century palazzo has a breathtakingly beautiful courtyard-garden. Contemporary furnishings set off the original features of the carefully restored building. All rooms have double-glazed windows, and those at the back overlook the Medici Chapels. **www.palazzobenci.com**

CITY CENTRE NORTH Hotel Botticelli €€€

Via Taddea 8, 50123 **Tel** *055 29 09 05* **Fax** *055 29 43 22* **Rooms** *34* **Map** *2 E5*

A few steps from the market of San Lorenzo is this hotel, located in a 16th-century palazzo that has undergone restoration. The Renaissance architecture and vaulted, frescoed ceilings give it a thoroughly Florentine feel. Views of San Lorenzo and the cathedral's dome can be enjoyed from the covered terrace. **www.hotelbotticelli.it**

CITY CENTRE NORTH Hotel Liana €€€

Via Vittorio Alfieri 18, 50121 **Tel** *055 24 53 03* **Fax** *055 234 45 96* **Rooms** *24* **Map** *2 F4*

This wonderful hotel is just across the *viale* (boulevard) that marks the edge of the historic centre, but only a five-minute walk from Santa Croce. It was the British embassy for a few years in the 19th-century. The rooms are large and gorgeous with their frescoed ceilings and original floors. There is a delightful garden to relax in. **www.hotelliana.com**

CITY CENTRE NORTH Orto de' Medici €€€

Via San Gallo 30, 50129 **Tel** *055 48 34 27* **Fax** *055 46 12 76* **Rooms** *31* **Map** *2 D4*

Ten minutes on foot from the Duomo, and five from the Accademia, this mid-19th century building has large frescoes in its lounges and breakfast room. A delightful flower-filled terrace overlooks San Marco. The banqueting suites make the hotel popular with the locals for festive occasions. All rooms non-smoking. **www.ortodeimedici.it**

CITY CENTRE NORTH Hotel Unicorno €€€

Via dei Fossi 27, 50123 ***Tel*** *055 28 73 13* ***Fax*** *055 26 83 32* ***Rooms*** *27* ***Map*** *1 B5*

This centrally located hotel, in the heart of the antique shop district and within walking distance of all the sights, is situated in a renovated 15th-century building with cosy Tuscan furnishings. Staff are friendly and helpful, rooms are spacious and there is a good breakfast buffet. **www.hotelunicorno.it**

CITY CENTRE NORTH Monna Lisa €€€

Borgo Pinti 27, 50121 ***Tel*** *055 247 97 51* ***Fax*** *055 247 97 55* ***Rooms*** *45* ***Map*** *2 E5*

Close to Santa Croce, the hotel is in a 14th-century palazzo with terracotta floors, white stucco walls and *pietra serena* (a type of Italian sandstone) detailing. Some rooms are enormous, with old furniture and high ceilings. There are two more recent buildings in the courtyard but these, though quieter, have less character. **www.monnalisa.it**

CITY CENTRE NORTH Residenza Johlea €€€

Via San Gallo 80, 50129 ***Tel*** *055 463 32 92* ***Fax*** *055 463 45 52* ***Rooms*** *6* ***Map*** *2 D3*

A cosy town house with marble bathrooms and bedrooms furnished with antiques. Breakfast is available in the breakfast room, and guests may also take trays back to their room. Room 4 (Johlea Classic) is opposite the bar/breakfast room and can be noisy. There is a sitting room on the top floor and a nice roof terrace. **www.johanna.it**

CITY CENTRE NORTH Il Guelfo Bianco €€€€

Via Cavour 29, 50129 ***Tel*** *055 28 83 30* ***Fax*** *055 29 52 03* ***Rooms*** *40* ***Map*** *6 E1*

A short walk from the Duomo, this impressive hotel comprises two adjacent 17th-century buildings. The rooms are very spacious, many resplendent with frescoed ceilings and period furniture. The view is always pleasant, regardless of whether you overlook the garden, rooftops or street. Free Internet access. **www.ilguelfobianco.it**

CITY CENTRE NORTH Loggiato dei Serviti €€€€

Piazza SS. Annunziata 3, 50122 ***Tel*** *055 28 95 92* ***Fax*** *055 28 95 95* ***Rooms*** *39* ***Map*** *2 D4*

Built in the 16th-century by the Serviti order to house travelling priests, this hotel is the mirror-image of the Spedale degli Innocenti across the square. The opulent decor belies its monastic origins. Rooms either overlook the piazza or the Accademia di Belle Arti garden. Book well in advance. **www.loggiatodeiservitihotel.it**

CITY CENTRE NORTH Morandi alla Crocetta €€€€

Via Laura 50, 50121 ***Tel*** *055 234 47 47* ***Fax*** *055 248 09 54* ***Rooms*** *10* ***Map*** *2 E4*

Once a convent, this small hotel has many admirers. Rooms are furnished in different styles, but all are equally delightful. Two have terraces and room 29 has a frescoed wall. Most of the rooms overlook the street, but the quaint interiors are the real attraction. It is essential to book in advance. **www.hotelmorandi.it**

CITY CENTRE NORTH Lorenzo il Magnifico €€€€€

Via Lorenzo il Magnifico 25, 50129 ***Tel/Fax*** *055 463 08 78* ***Rooms*** *31* ***Map*** *2 E2*

Lying between the station and Piazza Libertà, this recently converted villa offers exquisite bed and bath linens, as well as a Jacuzzi bath or shower in every room. One suite faces the luxuriant garden. Most major sights are walking distance but parking is available as is a convenient bus service. **www.lorenzoilmagnifico.net**

CITY CENTRE NORTH Palazzo Niccolini al Duomo €€€€€

Via dei Servi 2, 50122 ***Tel*** *055 28 24 12* ***Fax*** *055 29 09 79* ***Rooms*** *10* ***Map*** *2 D5*

In a prime location facing the Duomo, this 16th-century palazzo is run by descendants of the original owners. Public rooms feature period paintings, antiques and chandeliers. Some rooms have frescoed walls or ceilings. Bathrooms are marbled. The suite upstairs offers a unique view of Brunelleschi's dome. **www.niccolinidomepalace.com**

CITY CENTRE WEST Hotel Cestelli €

Borgo Santi Apostoli 25, 50123 ***Tel/Fax*** *055 21 42 13* ***Rooms*** *8* ***Map*** *5 C3*

Proprieter Alessio Lotti and his Japanese wife Asumi add to the charm of this affordable eight-room hotel housed in a 12th-century palazzo. Only three rooms have private baths. Despite much refurbishing, the hotel retains its original 16th-century floors. All rooms non-smoking. No breakfast served. **www.hotelcestelli.com**

CITY CENTRE WEST Casa Howard €€

Via della Scala 18, 50129 ***Tel*** *06 69 92 45 55* ***Fax*** *06 67 94 644* ***Rooms*** *13* ***Map*** *5 B1*

The individual, characterful rooms combine original features with modern furnishings. One room has a large, private terrace for pet owners; another has a playroom for children. Communal sitting room and terrace, with an honesty bar. Guests in the Garden Room have exclusive use of the Turkish bath. Breakfast is extra. **www.casahoward.com**

CITY CENTRE WEST Floroom 2 €€

Via del Sole, 50123 ***Tel/Fax*** *055 21 66 74* ***Rooms*** *4* ***Map*** *5 C2*

With just four rooms, all with their own bathroom, this hotel is defiantly modern. Decorated in wood, glass and steel – a masterful combination of old and new – and complete with Wi-Fi and high-tech facilities, it's like having a design hotel all to yourself. Floroom 1 offers more of the same on the other side of the river. **www.floroom.com**

CITY CENTRE WEST Hotel Alessandra €€

Borgo Santi Apostoli 17, 50123 ***Tel*** *055 28 34 38* ***Fax*** *055 21 06 19* ***Rooms*** *27* ***Map*** *5 C3*

Located on the second and third floors of a 16th-century building, this central hotel, with its vaulted ceilings, retains an aura of grandeur. Rooms overlooking the Arno are larger and more expensive. The Piazzetta del Limbo and the church of Santi Apostoli can be glimpsed from other rooms. **www.hotelalessandra.com**

Key to Price Guide *see p250* **Key to Symbols** *see back cover flap*

CITY CENTRE WEST Hotel Torre Guelfa €€

Borgo Santi Apostoli 8, 50123 **Tel** *055 239 63 38* **Fax** *055 239 85 77* **Rooms** *29* **Map** *5 C3*

On the third floor of a medieval palazzo, this hotel incorporates the tallest privately-owned tower in the city. This tower's terrace is a residents-only bar in summer. The hotel has a rustic, robust appeal. Book early to get the top-floor suite with its own terrace. The six newer rooms on the second floor are cheaper. **www.hoteltorreguelfa.com**

CITY CENTRE WEST Pensione Scoti €€

Via Tornabuoni 7, 50123 **Tel/Fax** *055 29 21 28* **Rooms** *11* **Map** *5 C3*

An upmarket address with very good prices – perfect if shopping is your priority. The rooms are all en-suite, simply decorated, clean and comfortable. There are wonderful, faded floor-to-ceiling frescoes in the sitting room. Reception is open 24 hours and the staff very helpful. There is a bar and restaurant. Breakfast €5 extra. **www.hotelscoti.com**

CITY CENTRE WEST Davanzati Hotel €€€

Via Porta Rossa 5, 50123 **Tel** *055 28 66 66* **Fax** *055 265 82 52* **Rooms** *21* **Map** *6 D3*

This imposing 14th-century building was renovated in 2004, and combines the old and the new magnificently. The service in this family-run outfit is impeccable, and good English is spoken. Competitively-priced for a central location, there is free Internet access in all rooms and a complimentary *aperitivo* every evening. **www.hoteldavanzati.it**

CITY CENTRE WEST Della Signoria €€€

Via delle Terme 1, 50123 **Tel** *055 21 45 30* **Fax** *055 21 61 01* **Rooms** *27* **Map** *6 D3*

Run by the same family for over 50 years, the hotel is located on the corner of Por Santa Maria, a great central location, if a little bit noisy. Ask for a room on the side street Via delle Terme, or one overlooking the rear of the building. **www.hoteldellasignoria.com**

CITY CENTRE WEST Hotel Martelli €€€

Via Panzani 8, 50129 **Tel** *055 21 71 51* **Fax** *055 26 85 04* **Rooms** *52* **Map** *1 C5*

Located on the busy main street leading from the station to the Duomo, the Martelli is fairly quiet and comfortable. Four of the rooms are furnished in Florentine style and are the most in demand. The others have a more contemporary look. The building was originally a palazzo belonging to the Medici. **www.hotelmartelli.com**

CITY CENTRE WEST Porta Rossa €€€

Via Porta Rossa 19, 50123 **Tel** *055 28 75 51* **Fax** *055 28 21 79* **Rooms** *78* **Map** *6 D3*

While the current building dates from 1500, documents confirm that a hotel stood here as early as 1386, making this one of Italy's oldest hotels. The vaulted entrance hall is decorated in the unique Italian Art Nouveau tradition (Liberty style) with beautiful stained glass. Rooms are large and furnished with antiques. **www.hotelportarossa.com**

CITY CENTRE WEST Beacci Tornabuoni €€€€

Via de' Tornabuoni 3, 50123 **Tel** *055 21 26 45* **Fax** *055 28 35 94* **Rooms** *40* **Map** *5 C3*

With a rich history of hospitality, this hotel takes up the top three floors of a 15th-century palazzo. Once a classic *pensione*, the hotel has been refitted so guests can now choose between junior suites, deluxe and standard rooms – all with antique furniture and tapestries. The rooftop terrace is lovely. **www.tornabuonihotels.com**

CITY CENTRE WEST Hotel de la Ville €€€€

Piazza Antinori 1, 50123 **Tel** *055 238 18 06* **Fax** *055 238 18 09* **Rooms** *71* **Map** *5 C2*

This palazzo is located at the end of Via Tornabuoni and is ideal for those who want to shop till they drop, before settling into the lap of luxury. The rooms are spacious, elegant and soundproofed. The breakfast is exceptional. The bar is open until midnight and light meals are available throughout the day. **www.hoteldelaville.it**

CITY CENTRE WEST Hotel Goldoni €€€€

Borgo Ognissanti 8, 50123 **Tel** *055 28 40 80* **Fax** *055 28 25 76* **Rooms** *20* **Map** *1 B5*

Mozart was a guest in this hotel in 1770, and the Goldoni still retains the aura of an era gone by. Located on the second floor of an old palace, all but three rooms overlook a quiet private garden. The rooms are spacious and the decor elegant. Closed 2 weeks Dec. **www.hotelgoldoni.com**

CITY CENTRE WEST Baglioni €€€€€

Piazza Unità Italiana 6, 50123 **Tel** *055 235 80* **Fax** *055 235 888 95* **Rooms** *193* **Map** *1 C5*

Ever since it opened its doors in 1903, this hotel has been charming guests with its plush interiors and lush gardens. Rooms are well-appointed, many with leaded glass windows. The beauty of the rooftop garden restaurant adds to the eating experience. Its full range of conference facilities are ideal for business travellers. **www.hotelbaglioni.it**

CITY CENTRE WEST Berchielli €€€€€

Lungarno Acciaiuoli 14, 50123 **Tel** *055 26 40 61* **Fax** *055 21 86 36* **Rooms** *76* **Map** *5 C4*

This Art Nouveau gem was once a 15th-century palazzo. The rooms have an understated, traditional elegance and are wonderful to relax in. About 25 of them overlook the river, while the rest either face Piazza del Limbo or the narrow side alleys. The service is excellent. **www.berchielli.it**

CITY CENTRE WEST Excelsior €€€€€

Piazza Ognissanti 3, 50123 **Tel** *055 271 51* **Fax** *055 21 02 78* **Rooms** *171* **Map** *5 A2*

The Excelsior excels with its marble floors and columns, grand staircases, stained-glass windows, statues and period paintings. The rooms are equally opulent, while the staff add warmth to it all. On the downside, breakfast is not included in the price. Its restaurant, Il Cestello, is celebrated for its cuisine. **www.starwoodhotels.com/westin**

CITY CENTRE WEST Grand Hotel €€€€€

Piazza Ognissanti 1, 50123 ***Tel*** *055 28 87 81* ***Fax*** *055 21 74 00* ***Rooms*** *107* ***Map*** *5 A2*

Crowned heads and other VIPs favour this classic hotel that lives up to its name. The rooms, furnished in Renaissance or Empire style, afford views either of the Arno or of a delightful courtyard filled with potted orange trees. This hotel is also home to a good restaurant. Sister to the Excelsior across the piazza. **www.starwood.com/grandflorence**

CITY CENTRE WEST Grand Hotel Minerva €€€€€

Piazza Santa Maria Novella 16, 50123 ***Tel*** *055 272 30* ***Fax*** *055 26 82 81* ***Rooms*** *102* ***Map*** *1 B5*

With its rooftop swimming pool, the Grand Minerva does full justice to the romance of Florence. Watching the sunset from here or from the adjacent bar is a memorable experience. Recently refurbished, this hotel has welcomed many famous guests, including Henry James. Family suites have two bathrooms. **www.grandhotelminerva.com**

CITY CENTRE WEST Grand Hotel Villa Medici €€€€€

Via Il Prato 42, 50123 ***Tel*** *055 238 13 31* ***Fax*** *055 238 13 36* ***Rooms*** *100* ***Map*** *1 A4*

This 18th-century villa conversion is the only hotel within the city limits to have an open-air pool in its own gardens. Located by Porta al Prato, it is within walking distance of the centre of town. The plush rooms are furnished with antiques. The fitness centre features a sauna and Turkish bath. **www.villamedicihotel.com**

CITY CENTRE WEST Helvetia & Bristol €€€€€

Via dei Pescioni 2, 50123 ***Tel*** *055 266 51* ***Fax*** *055 28 83 53* ***Rooms*** *67* ***Map*** *5 C2*

With five-star traditions but a more boutique feel, this hotel is full of pieces from the owner's art collection – you might find a 17th- or 18th-century painting above your bed. The rooms are ornate and decently sized and the location is great. Everyone from Stravinsky to Gorbachev has stayed here, and for good reason. **www.royaldemeure.com**

CITY CENTRE WEST Hotel Aprile €€€€€

Via della Scala 6, 50123 ***Tel*** *055 21 62 37* ***Fax*** *055 28 09 47* ***Rooms*** *28* ***Map*** *1 B5*

Once owned by the Medici, this palazzo features frescoed ceilings, period paintings and spacious rooms. Traces of *The Triumph of David* can be seen on the interesting façade. Ask for a room overlooking the courtyard since the streets can be quite noisy. Breakfast is served in the colourful courtyard garden in summer. **www.hotelaprile.it**

CITY CENTRE WEST Hotel Golden Tower €€€€€

Piazza Strozzi 11r, 50123 ***Tel*** *055 28 78 60* ***Fax*** *055 265 80 44* ***Rooms*** *27* ***Map*** *5 C3*

An elegant boutique hotel occupying the medieval tower where Filippo Strozzi *(see p105)* lived while his palace was being built next door. Rooms are thoughtfully furnished, with en-suite marble bathrooms. Two rooms have Jacuzzis. The tower rooms are the most atmospheric and have original features. **www.goldentowerhotel.it**

CITY CENTRE WEST Hotel Roma €€€€€

Piazza Santa Maria Novella 8, 50123 ***Tel*** *055 21 03 66* ***Fax*** *055 21 53 06* ***Rooms*** *57* ***Map*** *1 B5*

This large hotel flaunts many elegant touches such as marble floors, wood panelling and intriguing stained-glass works by Galileo and Tito Chini. Rooms facing the piazza are larger although they can be noisy. For a quieter stay, ask to be accommodated in a different part of the hotel. **www.hotelromaflorence.com**

CITY CENTRE WEST Hotel Savoy €€€€€

Piazza della Repubblica 7, 50123 ***Tel*** *055 273 51* ***Fax*** *055 273 58 88* ***Rooms*** *102* ***Map*** *6 D3*

Architecturally magnificent with lavish interiors, the stylishly appointed rooms here are sleek and spacious. The sixth-floor gym affords spectacular views of the Duomo and Giotto's Campanile. L'Incontro bar on the piazza is a favourite rendezvous point for Florentines. Breakfast is not included in the price. **www.hotelsavoy.it**

CITY CENTRE WEST JK Place €€€€€

Piazza Santa Maria Novella 7, 50123 ***Tel*** *055 264 51 81* ***Fax*** *055 265 83 87* ***Rooms*** *20* ***Map*** *5 B2*

A hip town house hotel with contemporary lines and a high design ethos. There is a stunning rooftop terrace – its Lounge is Florence's coolest bar. The bedrooms feature muted colours and top quality furnishings. The atmosphere is unstuffy but attentive, with check-in done over drinks around an 18th-century walnut table. **www.jkplace.com**

CITY CENTRE WEST Montebello Splendid €€€€€

Via Garibaldi 14, 50123 ***Tel*** *055 274 71* ***Fax*** *055 274 77 00* ***Rooms*** *60* ***Map*** *1 A5*

This 19th-century villa with its own *giardino all'Italiana* (Italian-style garden) was totally refurbished in 2004. Rooms are airy and bathrooms have marble fittings. There is no charge for children under six sharing a room with their parents. **www.montebellosplendid.com**

CITY CENTRE WEST Palazzo Vecchietti €€€€€

Via degli Strozzi 4, 50123 ***Tel*** *055 230 28 02* ***Rooms*** *14* ***Map*** *5 C3*

This 15th-century palace is a chic home-from-home. All suites feature full kitchens, marble bathrooms, walk-in wardrobes and butler service. The breakfast room is the only public room. The contemporary decor is finished to a high quality, with classic elegant furnishings and period details. **www.palazzovecchietti.com**

CITY CENTRE WEST Santa Maria Novella €€€€€

Piazza Santa Maria Novella 1, 50124 ***Tel*** *055 27 18 40* ***Fax*** *055 27 18 41 99* ***Rooms*** *38* ***Map*** *5 B2*

Furnished in Empire style, this superb hotel couples grandeur with tranquility. Standard doubles overlook Via delle Belle Donne, while the superiors face Santa Maria Novella and the Piazza. One junior suite has a roof terrace. The service is of a consistently high quality. The bar serves snacks and light meals. **www.hotelsantamarianovella.it**

Key to Price Guide *see p250* **Key to Symbols** *see back cover flap*

OLTRARNO Istituto Gould €

Via dei Serragli 49, 50100 **Tel** *055 21 25 76* **Fax** *055 28 02 74* **Rooms** *41* **Map** *3 B2*

The combination of unbelievably low rates with their contribution to a good cause (disadvantaged children), makes it easier to fully appreciate this sparsely furnished hostel-like outfit. The rooms are spotless, and the gardens make for a very attractive view. Ideal for those who want safety and basic comfort on a tight budget. **www.istitutogould.it**

OLTRARNO Hotel Annalena €€

Via Romana 34, 50125 **Tel** *055 22 24 02* **Fax** *055 22 24 03* **Rooms** *20* **Map** *3 B2*

Opposite the Boboli Gardens, and on the second floor of a 15th-century palazzo (once a convent), this *pensione* has a fascinating history. The single and double rooms come with their own little terrace. Rooms are decorated with antique pieces. The atmospheric hotel prides itself on its Florentine authenticity. **www.hotelannalena.it**

OLTRARNO Pitti Palace €€

Borgo San Jacopo 3, 50125 **Tel** *055 239 87 11* **Fax** *055 239 88 67* **Rooms** *72* **Map** *3 C1*

As close to the Ponte Vecchio as you can get, this hotel is in a modernised 13th-century tower, with two terraces on the sixth floor. You can soak in the splendid vista of the city and the Boboli Gardens as you enjoy breakfast. Small and functional, but well-priced for such a good location. Try to book the top-floor suite. **www.vivahotels.com**

OLTRARNO Sorelle Bandini €€

Piazza Santo Spirito 9, 50125 **Tel** *055 21 53 08* **Rooms** *13* **Map** *5 B5*

This historic building might be considered shabby, but its unbeatable location makes it a popular choice. There are 13 rooms but only five come with a private bathroom. The romantic *loggia* overlooks all the action in the square below. Zeffirelli's *Tea with Mussolini* (1999) was shot here, a testament to the beauty of the place.

OLTRARNO Villa Betania €€

Viale del Poggio Imperiale 23, 50125 **Tel** *055 22 22 43* **Fax** *055 22 05 32* **Rooms** *20* **Map** *3 A4*

This family-run hotel has been warmly welcoming guests since 1945. Set in its own lush grounds, the southern city gate of Porta Romana is only a 10-minute walk downhill. The rooms are quiet, elegant and offer excellent value. Private parking and a regular bus service make it a convenient base. Superior breakfast. **www.villabetania.it**

OLTRARNO Hotel Silla €€

Via de'Renai 5, 50100 **Tel** *055 234 28 88* **Fax** *055 234 14 37* **Rooms** *35* **Map** *6 F5*

Located in a beautiful 16th-century building, this family-run hotel on the Oltrarno side of the river is reached through an elegant courtyard. A grand staircase leads to the first floor. The rooms and decor are a delight, and the staff are friendly. Guests can enjoy the terrace which overlooks the river. **www.hotelsilla.it**

OLTRARNO Marignolle Relais & Charme €€€

Via di San Quirichino a Marignolle16, 50124 **Tel** *055 228 69 10* **Fax** *055 204 73 96* **Rooms** *6*

Located just off the Via Senese, this is an ideal location for those who want to explore the Chianti countryside, and perhaps play a little golf, while still being able to spend time in Florence. The large rooms are decorated impeccably, and the terrace offers breathtaking views of the city. The pool is set in a delightful garden. **www.marignolle.com**

OLTRARNO Lungarno €€€€€

Borgo San Jacopo 14, 50125 **Tel** *055 272 61* **Fax** *055 26 84 37* **Rooms** *73* **Map** *5 C4*

This boutique hotel sports a crisp and cool look that is refreshing to the eye. Many of the rooms have their own terraces jutting out over the river, offering great views of the Ponte Vecchio. Some rooms are in an adjacent medieval tower, while the Lungarno Suites across the river are available for longer stays. **www.lungarnohotels.com**

OLTRARNO Palazzo Magnani Feroni €€€€€

Borgo San Frediano 5, 50124 **Tel** *055 239 95 44* **Fax** *055 260 89 08* **Rooms** *13* **Map** *5 A3*

On the Oltrarno side of the river, this 16th-century palazzo features massive halls and a sweeping staircase. Large bedrooms and sitting rooms fitted with chandeliers and Renaissance-style furniture. The billiard room and rooftop terrace add to its appeal. Two apartments are available for rent by the week. **www.palazzomagnaniferoni.com**

FURTHER AFIELD Pensione Bencistà €€€

Via Benedetto da Maiano 4, 50014 **Tel/Fax** *055 591 63* **Rooms** *40*

Choose between full board, half board or just breakfast in this 1500s villa-turned-hotel. However, the place is so welcoming, and the views so lovely that people are usually happy to stick around all day. Watch the sun set over the Florentine countryside from the stone balcony. Advance booking is advisable. **www.bencista.com**

FURTHER AFIELD Una Hotel Vittoria €€€

Via Pisana 59, 50143 **Tel** *055 227 71* **Fax** *055 227 72* **Rooms** *85*

With bright colours and crazy designs, this is an antidote to the antiques or tasteful contemporary interiors which characterize most Florence hotels. Rare materials such as mosaics, leather and printed lamé are used in all rooms, and all have Internet connection and plasma screen TVs. Parking and half-board available. **www.unahotels.it**

FURTHER AFIELD Riva Lofts €€€€

Via Baccio Bandinelli 98, 50142 **Tel** *055 713 02 72* **Fax** *055 71 11 03* **Rooms** *8*

This collection of self-contained suites overlooks the river on one side and the Cascine park on the other. The light, airy rooms feature clean, modern lines with a monochrome theme, and most have a kitchenette. The modern lounge/ breakfast room has an honesty bar with lots to read, and the garden has a pool. Fantastic staff. **www.rivalofts.com**

FURTHER AFIELD Villa le Rondini €€€€

Via Bolognese Vecchia 224, 50139 ***Tel*** *055 40 00 81* ***Fax*** *055 26 82 12* ***Rooms*** *42*

Set in a sprawling garden amid olive groves, this villa affords stunning views of the Arno valley. Book early to ensure a room in the main house that boasts quaint, traditional furnishings and beamed ceilings. Rooms with terraces are very popular and with good reason. The outdoor pool is available from June to September. **www.villalerondini.com**

FURTHER AFIELD Hotel Villa Villoresi €€€€€

Via Ciampi 2, 50019 ***Tel*** *055 44 32 12* ***Fax*** *055 44 20 63* ***Rooms*** *28*

Halfway between the city and the countryside, this is an ideal hideaway. Built as a military stronghold in the 12th-century and then converted to a villa in the 1400s, it is now a national monument. Frescoes, murals and antique furniture perfect the atmosphere. Not all rooms are air conditioned. Garden with lemon trees. **www.villavilloresi.it**

FURTHER AFIELD Il Salviatino €€€€€

Via del Salviatino 21, Fiesole, 50137 ***Tel*** *055 904 11 11* ***Fax*** ***Rooms*** *45*

A palatial 15th-century villa has been converted into a superb hotel offering a 21st-century perspective on its aristocratic past. Frescoes and handcrafted leather sit alongside modern technologies, while the large garden overlooks Florence from the heights of Fiesole. The innovative restaurant serves dinner in the grounds. **www.salviatino.com**

FURTHER AFIELD Torre di Bellosguardo €€€€€

Via Roti Michelozzi 2, 50124 ***Tel*** *055 229 81 45* ***Fax*** *055 22 90 08* ***Rooms*** *16*

Far from the crowds, but with the city at its feet, the views from the 16th-century tower of this 14th-century villa are unparalleled. It is equally breathtaking indoors, with vast public areas and huge rooms decorated with antique furniture and Persian carpets. Two landscaped pools and a beautiful garden. **www.torrebellosguardo.com**

FURTHER AFIELD Villa San Michele €€€€€

Via Doccia 4, 50014 ***Tel*** *055 567 82 00* ***Fax*** *055 567 82 50* ***Rooms*** *45*

Once a monastery, the design of this hotel's façade is attributed to Michelangelo. Standing in sprawling 37-acre grounds, the views are spectacular, the best being from the loggia, where dinner is served in summer. Ask for a room overlooking the city. Closed end-Nov–mid-Mar. **www.villasanmichele.orient-express.com**

WESTERN TUSCANY

ARTIMINO Hotel Paggeria Medicea €€

Viale Papa Giovanni XXIII 1, 59015 ***Tel*** *0558 751 41* ***Fax*** *0558 75 14 70* ***Rooms*** *37* ***Road map*** *C2*

In the converted servant quarters of Artimino's famous Medici villa, La Ferdinanda, this hotel is complete with original furniture, terracotta floors and decorative frescoes. Adding to the experience are riding stables, the restaurant (Biagio Pignatta) and a farm shop that also sells local wines. There are 44 apartments for weekly rental. **www.artimino.com**

CRESPINA Poggio al Casone €€€€

Via Volpaia 16, 56042 ***Tel*** *050 64 22 59* ***Fax*** *050 64 46 11* ***Rooms*** *10* ***Road map*** *C3*

These 10 self-catering apartments are on a working organic wine estate run by a charming family. All are furnished in Tuscan country style, with tiled floors, beamed ceilings and some canopied beds. Two are detached, so good for families. Guests can join in activities in the vineyards or go on organized trips. **www.poggioalcasone.com**

PISA Hotel Roseto €

Via Mascagni 24, 56127 ***Tel*** *050 425 96* ***Fax*** *050 420 87* ***Rooms*** *24* ***Road map*** *B2*

This small two-star hotel is handy for visitors on a tight budget. The Roseto makes a quiet and comfortable base in central Pisa very near the railway station and within walking distance of the Leaning Tower. Rooms are airy with large windows and high ceilings. **www.hotelroseto.it**

PISA Hotel Francesco €€

Via Santa Maria 129, 56126 ***Tel*** *050 55 54 53* ***Fax*** *050 55 61 45* ***Rooms*** *13* ***Road map*** *B2*

Within walking distance of the Leaning Tower of Pisa, the terrace of this small, welcoming hotel offers some beautiful views over the city. The rooms are clean, bright and minimally furnished. Non-smoking rooms available on request. Bike and moped hire organized by the hotel. **www.hotelfrancesco.com**

PISA Hotel Villa Kinzica €€

Piazza Arcivescovado 2, 56126 ***Tel*** *050 56 04 19* ***Fax*** *050 55 12 04* ***Rooms*** *30* ***Road map*** *B2*

In an imposing 18th-century villa, the Kinzica offers comfortable rooms with modern furnishings. The price is very reasonable given its central location. The best rooms retain many of the building's original features, including stone fireplaces and frescoed ceilings. Some have views over the Piazza dei Miracoli. **www.hotelvillakinzica.it**

PISA Royal Victoria Hotel €€

Lungarno Pacinotti 12, 56126 ***Tel*** *050 94 01 11* ***Fax*** *050 94 01 80* ***Rooms*** *48* ***Road map*** *B2*

One of Pisa's most historic buildings, the hotel occupies a 10th-century tower built for the Winemakers' Guild. It became Pisa's first hotel in 1837, combining several medieval tower houses in the process. Run by the welcoming Piegaja family, the rooms are charming in their size and decor. Bike rental and private garage. **www.royalvictoria.it**

Key to Price Guide *see p250* **Key to Symbols** *see back cover flap*

PISA Grand Hotel Duomo €€€

Via Santa Maria 94, 56126 **Tel** *050 56 18 94* **Fax** *050 56 04 18* **Rooms** *93* **Road map** *B2*

Though it may not be the most exciting place to stay, this modern hotel is very well located. Within walking distance of the Leaning Tower of Pisa, it is a good base for exploring the Piazza dei Miracoli and its associated attractions. The restaurant's specialties offer an accessible insight into local cuisine. **www.grandhotelduomo.it**

PISA Hotel Relais dell'Orologio €€€€€

Via della Faggiola 12/14, 56126 **Tel** *050 83 03 61* **Fax** *050 55 18 69* **Rooms** *25* **Road map** *B2*

This five-star hotel is in a renovated manor house built near the remains of a 14th-century tower. Rooms are thoughtfully decorated with tartan rugs and curtains, antique furnishings and original fireplaces. Some have Jacuzzis. Breakfast is served in the manor garden, and the restaurant is very good. **www.hotelrelaisorologio.com**

RIGIOLI Relais dell' Ussero €€

Via Statale 12, 56010 **Tel** *050 81 81 93* **Fax** *050 81 88 97* **Rooms** *12* **Road map** *B2*

The former country residence of Italian nobility, this spectacular hotel is in a 16th-century Baroque building. It has been a hotel since 1980, and rooms are luxurious with frescoed ceilings and antique furnishings. You will also find a 1700s café and old church in the grounds. A large park surrounds this establishment. **www.corliano.it**

VOLTERRA Hotel La Locanda €€

Via Guarnacci 24/28, 56048 **Tel** *0588 815 47* **Fax** *0588 815 41* **Rooms** *19* **Road map** *C3*

A converted convent close to Volterra's Roman amphitheatre, this is a relatively new four-star hotel. Its former owner, Anton Filippo Giacchi, a historian, added excavated Etruscan relics to the building's façade. Rooms are elegant with antique furniture and private bathrooms. The restaurant enjoys a good reputation. **www.hotel-lalocanda.com**

VOLTERRA Hotel San Lino €€

Via S. Lino 26, 56048 **Tel** *0588 852 50* **Fax** *0588 806 20* **Rooms** *43* **Road map** *C3*

Within the medieval walls of Volterra, this 1400s convent was converted into a hotel in 1982. The rooms are modernly furnished, but in keeping with the building's illustrious past. Windows look out over the town's cobbled streets or into the hotel's garden. The small restaurant, La Monache, is very popular. **www.hotelsanlino.com**

VOLTERRA Albergo Villa Nencini €€€

Borgo Santo Stefano 55, 56048 **Tel** *0588 863 86* **Fax** *0588 806 01* **Rooms** *35* **Road map** *C3*

This family-run country house hotel in a magnificent location just outside of town has views as far as the Tuscany Archipelago. Rooms are airy with light furnishings. The hotel *enoteca* in the converted stables serves a range of local wines. You can swim in the pool next to a garden of luxuriant oak trees. **www.villanencini.it**

VOLTERRA Hotel le Fonti €€€

Via di Fontecorrenti 8, 56048 **Tel** *0588 852 19* **Fax** *0588 927 28* **Rooms** *66* **Road map** *C3*

Ten minutes' walk from the centre of Volterra, Hotel Le Fonti was renovated in 2002 to its current modern design. If you want to splash out, ask for the main suite, La Torre, with its lavish antiques and sumptuous fabrics. Large panoramic terrace. There are two pools and a lush, green park surrounds the hotel. **www.parkhotellefonti.com**

NORTHERN TUSCANY

BALBANO Villa Casanova €

Via di Casanova 1004, 55050 **Tel** *0583 54 84 29* **Fax** *0583 36 89 55* **Rooms** *48* **Road map** *B2*

A charming hotel in a converted 1600s farmhouse, Villa Casanova retains part of the walls of an older Lucchese military fortress. Just 12km (7 miles) from Lucca, the Villa is very suitable for hiking and cycling excursions. The restaurant serves traditional dishes using locally farmed ingredients. Tennis courts. **www.villacasanova.net**

LUCCA Locanda Vigna Ilaria €

Via Per Pieve S.Stefano 967/C **Tel** *0583 33 20 91* **Fax** *0583 33 19 08* **Rooms** *4* **Road map** *C2*

This small inn just outside of Lucca has modern and artfully decorated rooms with bright carpets, pastel walls and ceilings with wooden beams. Located on Lucca's Strada del Vino (wine road), the popular Tuscan restaurant has a list of over 300 wines. Booking recommended. **www.locandavignailaria.it**

LUCCA Piccolo Hotel Puccini €

Via di Poggio 9, 55100 **Tel** *0583 554 21* **Fax** *0583 534 87* **Rooms** *14* **Road map** *C2*

This friendly little hotel is in an attractive stone building, located just over the road from the house in which Giacomo Puccini was born (now a museum). It is also very close to the busy central square of San Michele. The rooms are small but reasonably priced considering the location. Courtesy car to airport and train station. **www.hotelpuccini.com**

LUCCA Albergo San Martino €€

Via della Dogana 9, 55100 **Tel** *0583 46 91 81* **Fax** *0583 99 19 40* **Rooms** *9* **Road map** *C2*

With a great location in Lucca's historical centre, just a brief stroll from the cathedral, this small three-star hotel offers large rooms at a reasonable price. The hotel prides itself on its personal touch and the service is exemplary. The breakfast is also a veritible feast. There is a car park, and bicycles can be rented. **www.albergosanmartino.it**

LUCCA Hotel Universo  €€

Piazza del Giglio 1, 55100 **Tel** *0583 49 36 78* **Fax** *0583 95 48 54* **Rooms** *60* **Road map** *C2*

Located in the centre of town near the Palazzo Ducale, this 19th-century building houses 60 comfortable rooms, some with views over Lucca's cathedral. The recently restored restaurant serves delicious Tuscan fare in an elegant and tranquil setting. Parking is available. The hotel is open all year. **www.universolucca.com**

LUCCA Grand Hotel Guinigi €€€€

Via Romana 1247, 55100 **Tel** *0583 49 91* **Fax** *0583 49 98 00* **Rooms** *168* **Road map** *C2*

This large four-star hotel is popular with both leisure and business travellers for its luxury rooms and conference facilities. Ideally placed in Lucca's ramparts, the many accoutrements include a gym and sauna. The cocktail bar and gourmet restaurant are advantages. Event and entertainment booking facilities available. **www.grandhotelguinigi.it**

LUCCA Locanda L'Elisa €€€€€

Via Nuova per Pisa 1952, 55050 **Tel** *0583 37 97 37* **Fax** *0583 37 90 19* **Rooms** *10* **Road map** *C2*

Five-star accommodation in a stately 18th-century home, this Relais & Chateaux chain hotel stands at the foot of a range of softly rolling hills. The luxury rooms are spacious with lounge areas full of antique furnishings, paintings and draperies. Understandably, it is a popular choice for couples on a romantic trip. **www.locandalelisa.it**

LUCCA Villa la Principessa €€€€€

Via Nuova per Pisa 1616, 55050 **Tel** *0583 37 00 37* **Fax** *0583 37 91 36* **Rooms** *40* **Road map** *C2*

The former home and court of Castruccio Castracani, Lord and Duke of Lucca at the turn of the 13th-century, Villa la Principessa stands at the base of the hills surrounding Lucca. The rooms are charmingly rustic, and the shared lounge has a fireplace and 13th-century furniture. The garden is tranquil and soothing. **www.hotelprincipessalucca.it**

PIETRASANTA Palazzo Guiscardo €€€€€

Via Provinciale 16, 55045 **Tel** *0584 73 52 98* **Fax** *0584 73 52 98* **Rooms** *9* **Road map** *B2*

A small *palazzo* houses this quietly elegant hotel offering friendly service. Each bathroom is made from a different kind of local marble. Bedrooms come with canopied beds, flatscreen televisions and antique furniture. The breakfast is splendid and you can expect a warm welcome. **www.palazzoguiscardo.it**

PISTOIA Hotel Piccolo Ritz €

Via A. Vannucci 67, 51100 **Tel** *0573 267 75* **Fax** *0573 277 98* **Rooms** *21* **Road map** *C2*

This popular budget three-star hotel is near the city walls, and close to the train station. The rooms are small but luxurious. The coffee bar has a stunning frescoed ceiling. Even though it is close to a busy and sometimes noisy road, this hotel is still an economical option given its proximity to the city's major sightseeing attractions.

PISTOIA Il Convento €€

Via San Quirino 33, 51030 **Tel** *0573 45 26 51* **Fax** *0573 45 35 78* **Rooms** *32* **Road map** *C2*

Once a 19th-century Franciscan monastery, this ambient hotel has simple but appealing rooms overlooking a picturesque courtyard and cloister. The rooms are in the monks' former cells, and the restaurant in the refectory. The garden, surrounded by woodlands, has views as far as Florence cathedral. **www.ilconventohotel.com**

PRATO Hotel Hermitage €

Via Ginepraia 112, 59016 **Tel** *0558 772 44* **Fax** *0558 79 70 57* **Rooms** *59* **Road map** *C2*

Located in a quiet residential area near the 15th-century Medicean Villa Ambra, this three-star hotel sits on top of a hill in a lush parkland. A great spot for touring the nearby vineyards. Rooms are unfussy and comfortable, and some come with stunning views. The restaurant serves Tuscan specialties. **www.hotelhermitageprato.it**

VIAREGGIO Hotel President €€€€

Viale Carducci 5, 55049 **Tel** *0584 96 27 12* **Fax** *0584 96 36 58* **Rooms** *39* **Road map** *B2*

This Liberty-style beachfront hotel, built in 1949, is typical of Viareggio's architecture. Its good reputation is justified by the comfortable, modern rooms with a real seaside feel. Restaurant Gaudì serves a generous buffet breakfast, and boasts an evening menu of Tuscan and international cuisine. Bicycle rental and playground. **www.hotelpresident.it**

VIAREGGIO Hotel Astor €€€€€

Lungomare Carducci 54, 55049 **Tel** *0584 503 01* **Fax** *0584 551 81* **Rooms** *68* **Road map** *B2*

A luxury hotel alongside the white sand beaches of Viareggio, the Astor has a panoramic sundeck overlooking the town's Liberty-style promenade with its elegant shops and colourful attractions. The popular seafood restaurant, La Conchiglia, serves up a real treat with alfresco dining in the summer months. **www.astorviareggio.com**

EASTERN TUSCANY

AREZZO B&B Casa Bellavista €€

Località Creti, 52044 **Tel** *0575 61 03 11* **Fax** *0575 61 07 49* **Rooms** *3* **Road map** *E3*

This family house on the hills outside Arezzo has only three guestrooms. The charming garden overlooks cypress-lined hills. You can be sure to get excellent, personalised service at this welcoming B&B. Breakfasts consist of delicacies made using great-grandmother Teresa's recipes. Cooking courses on request. **www.casabellavista.it**

Key to Price Guide *see p250* **Key to Symbols** *see back cover flap*

AREZZO Castello di Gargonza €€

Località Monte San Savino, 52048 **Tel** *0575 84 70 21* **Fax** *0575 84 70 54* **Rooms** *30* **Road map** *E3*

This atmospheric castle-residence in the hills between Arezzo and Siena offers rooms by the night, and self-catering apartments by the week. Restaurant La Torre di Gargonza is just outside the main walls. Hiking and nature trails in the 600 acres of surrounding parkland. The frescoed chapel in the grounds is an added attraction. **www.gargonza.it**

AREZZO Hotel Il Patio €€€

Via Cavour 23, 52100 **Tel** *0575 40 19 62* **Fax** *0575 274 18* **Rooms** *10* **Road map** *E3*

Just a few metres from the Church of San Francesco, this charismatic hotel is in an 18th-century palazzo on the antique shop-lined Via Cavour. Each room is decorated to reflect the travels of author Bruce Chatwin (China, India, Morocco and so on). The effect, coupled with wood-beamed ceilings, is enchanting. **www.hotelpatio.it**

AREZZO Relais la Commenda €€€€

Località Commenda 6, 52031 **Tel** *0575 72 33 56* **Fax** *0575 72 39 21* **Rooms** *7* **Road map** *E3*

This 11th-century monastery has been converted into apartments and suites by the Barboni family. The three buildings are surrounded by a glorious, ancient parkland. Rooms are striking with terracotta floors, exposed stone walls and Tuscan crafted furniture. Suites booked by night and apartments by week. **www.relaislacommenda.com**

BARBERINO DI MUGELLO Villa le Maschere €€€€€

Via Nazionale 75, 50031 **Tel** *055 84 74 32* **Fax** *055 847 17 44* **Rooms** *65* **Road map** *D2*

This stunning Renaissance villa features modern Italian design and furniture made exclusively for the hotel. Rooms are bright and luxurious, with original columns, frescoes and even statues, but there's no clutter. The public rooms are grand with a contemporary aesthetic. Spa, swimming pools, and a glass lift with views! **www.villalemaschere.it**

CASTIGLION FIORENTINO Relais San Pietro €€€€€

Loc. Polvano 3, 52043 **Tel** *0575 65 01 00* **Fax** *0575 65 02 55* **Rooms** *10* **Road map** *E3*

This delightful 17th century farmhouse enjoys an idyllic location overlooking a valley in the hilltop town of Castiglion Fiorentino. Accommodation is either in a converted priest's house or in the main building, and the decor is typically Tuscan – wood beams, tiled ceilings and wrought iron bed heads. Dinner is served on the terrace in summer. **www.polvano.com**

CORTONA Hotel Italia €

Via Ghibellina 5–7, 52044 **Tel** *0575 63 02 54* **Fax** *0575 60 57 63* **Rooms** *26* **Road map** *E3*

Just off the main square of medieval Cortona, this hotel is located in an ancient palace dating back to the 1600s. Though no longer a family-run establishment, the service is exceedingly personalised and friendly. The large roof terrace has panoramic views over the Chiana valley and the Trasimeno lake. **www.planhotel.com**

CORTONA Hotel San Michele €€€

Via Guelfa 15, 52044 **Tel** *0575 60 43 48* **Fax** *0575 63 01 47* **Rooms** *43* **Road map** *E3*

A beautifully restored Renaissance palazzo in the heart of Cortona, this hotel has fabulous bedrooms featuring exposed brickwork and wood-beamed ceilings. The rooms offer scenic views over the city and the hotel's interior courtyard. The hotel organizes excursions around town and into the countryside. **www.hotelsanmichele.net**

CORTONA Relais Villa Baldelli €€€€€

San Pietro a Cegliolo 420, 52044 **Tel** *0575 61 24 06* **Fax** *0575 61 24 07* **Rooms** *15* **Road map** *E3*

Located in a restored 17th-century villa, Relais Villa Baldelli is surrounded by a tranquil parkland. The peaceful rooms are decorated with pastoral frescoes and vintage paintings. The shared lounge features an antique stone fireplace. Segments of 17th-century altars embellish the ground floor. **www.villabaldelli.com**

REGELLO I Bonsi €€€€€

Via i Bonsi 47, 50066 **Tel** *055 28 46 15* **Fax** *055 28 95 95* **Rooms** *6* **Road map** *D2*

A tree-lined avenue leads to a turreted villa, built in 1400 and set in parkland overlooking the Arno valley. The villa has been converted into six luxury apartments, tastefully decorated in typical Tuscan style. The farm produces its own honey, wine and olive oil (available for purchase) and dinner can be arranged on request. **www.agriturismoibonsi.it**

CENTRAL TUSCANY

CASTELLINA IN CHIANTI Colle Etrusco Salivolpi €€

Via Fiorentina 89, 53011 **Tel** *0577 74 04 84* **Fax** *0577 74 09 98* **Rooms** *19* **Road map** *D3*

An elegant country house surrounded by vineyards, olive groves and cypress trees, this hotel is within walking distance of Castellina in Chianti. The rooms are warmly decorated with authentic rustic Tuscan furniture including wrought-iron beds, terracotta floors and wooden beams. Large lounge room and garden. **www.hotelsalivolpi.com**

CASTELLINA IN CHIANTI Tenuta di Ricavo €€€€€

Località Scotoni, 53011 **Tel** *0577 74 02 21* **Fax** *0577 74 10 14* **Rooms** *22* **Road map** *D3*

This charming resort in a lovingly restored medieval hamlet rests in the middle of a natural park, offering a unique combination of history and nature. Bedrooms contain parts of the original furnishings, including terracotta tiles and wooden beams. The gourmet restaurant, Percora Nera, dishes out delicious meals. **www.ricavo.com**

CHIUSI Villa il Patriarca €€€€€

Strada Statale 146, Località Querce al Pino, 53043 **Tel** *0578 274407* **Fax** *0578 274407* **Rooms** *23* **Road map** *E4*

Romantic and sumptuous with an acclaimed, innovative restaurant, this villa has a swimming pool and fantastic grounds. There is a casual restaurant as well as the more formal Il Salotti. Look for the Etruscan remains under the villa, which have been incorporated into the hotel's first-floor reception. **www.ilpatriarca.it**

GAIOLE IN CHIANTI Residence San Sano €€

Località San Sano 21, 53100 **Tel** *0577 74 61 30* **Fax** *0577 74 61 56* **Rooms** *14* **Road map** *D3*

The appealing rooms in this renovated 13th-century watchhouse show off whitewashed walls and wood-beamed ceilings. A three-course menu of Tuscan specialties is served under the well-known restaurant's stone arches. Meals can be enjoyed in the garden terrace during the summer months. **www.sansanohotel.it**

GAIOLE IN CHIANTI Castello di Spaltenna €€€€€

Località Spaltenna, 53013 **Tel** *0577 74 94 83* **Fax** *0577 74 92 69* **Rooms** *38* **Road map** *D3*

In an ancient feudal hamlet with a splendid medieval church and belltower, this beautiful converted monastery has fabulous views over the valley and its abundant vineyards. Rooms are luxurious with four-poster beds, large lounge areas and Jacuzzis. Gourmet restaurant. Horse riding by arrangement. **www.spaltenna.it**

GREVE Fattoria de Rignana €€€€€

Via di Rignana 15, 50022 **Tel** *055 85 20 65* **Fax** *055 856 08 21* **Rooms** *11* **Road map** *D3*

A splendid converted farmhouse with wonderful grounds, great views, an infinity swimming pool and exceptional rooms. Some come with frescoes, while a public sitting room is frescoed from floor to ceiling. Rooms can be arranged into self-catering apartments. Try the delicious wines from the farm. **www.rignana.it**

PANZANO IN CHIANTI Villa le Barone €€€€€

Via San Leolino 19, 50020 **Tel** *055 85 26 21* **Fax** *055 85 22 77* **Rooms** *28* **Road map** *D3*

The home of the Della Robbia family since the 16th century, Villa le Barone has been renovated into a cheerful, welcoming hotel crammed full of antique furnishings, old prints and bright fabrics. The restaurant in the old winery serves typical Tuscan food and Chianti wines. The hotel also organizes sightseeing excursions. **www.villalebarone.it**

RADDA IN CHIANTI Relais Fattoria Vignale €€€

Via Panigiani 9, 53017 **Tel** *0577 73 83 00* **Fax** *0577 73 85 92* **Rooms** *40* **Road map** *D3*

Right in the middle of the Chianti Classico heartland, this hotel is the perfect stop for wine-loving tourists. The former manor house of a large wine estate, the hotel still has a busy wine shop, tavern and popular restaurant. Bedrooms are furnished with antiques. There is a wisteria and jasmine-covered breakfast terrace. **www.vignale.it**

RADDA IN CHIANTI La Locanda €€€€

Località Montanino, 53017 **Tel** *0577 73 88 32* **Fax** *0577 73 92 63* **Rooms** *7* **Road map** *D3*

This family-run hotel, in a converted 16th-century farmhouse, offers breathtaking views over the Chianti countryside. A nearby stone building houses a cosy drawing room with a bar and dining area. A large panoramic terrace beside the pool, along with a big garden are incentives to sit outdoors. Minimum stay of two nights. **www.lalocanda.it**

SAN CASCIANO VP Villa Mangiacane €€€€€

San Casiano VP, 50026 **Tel** *055 829 01 23* **Fax** *055 829 03 58* **Rooms** *26* **Road map** *D2*

A richly furnished 15th-century villa, a short drive south of Florence, that once belonged to the Machiavelli family. It has sumptuously decorated bedrooms filled with antiques. Olive groves and vineyards fill the grounds – try some of their award-winning wines. Enjoy the spa or the sculpture garden, or take a dip in the pools. **www.mangiacane.it**

SAN GIMIGNANO Albergo Leon Bianco €€

Piazza della Cisterna 13, 53037 **Tel** *0577 94 12 94* **Fax** *0577 94 21 23* **Rooms** *25* **Road map** *C3*

Overlooking the historical Piazza della Cisterna in the heart of San Gimignano, Hotel Leon Bianco boasts one of the best locations in town. It is also housed in an extremely interesting building – an 11th-century palazzo with exposed brickwork and wood-beamed ceilings in the bedrooms. **www.leonbianco.com**

SAN GIMIGNANO Casa de' Potenti €€

Piazza della Erbe 10, 53037 **Tel/Fax** *0577 94 31 90* **Rooms** *6* **Road map** *C3*

This unfussy place, in a private town house in the historic centre of the city, serves as one of the most economical options in the region. Located on the second floor of a 14th-century stone house, the rooms are small and simple, with views over the nearby Piazza della Cisterna. There is a cafè on the ground floor. **www.casadeipotenti.com**

SAN GIMIGNANO Hotel Villa Belvedere €€

Via Dante 14, 53037 **Tel** *0577 94 05 39* **Fax** *0577 94 03 27* **Rooms** *15* **Road map** *C3*

With a cypress-filled garden and comfortably refurbished rooms, this isolated medieval villa just outside San Gimignano is good value for money. The rooms are simple but intimate, with shared lounge areas and a breakfast terrace by the pool. Turn to the staff for helpful sightseeing advice on the area. **www.hotelvillabelvedere.net**

SAN GIMIGNANO La Cisterna €€

Piazza della Cisterna 23, 53037 **Tel** *0577 94 03 28* **Fax** *0577 94 20 80* **Rooms** *50* **Road map** *C3*

In a 14th-century palazzo in the centre of town, its rooms are furnished in traditional Florentine style and have great views over both the main square and the surrounding countryside. The restaurant, Le Terrazze (open since 1918) is split into two parts – one of which, Loggia Rustica, has gloriously high wooden ceilings. **www.hotelcisterna.it**

Key to Price Guide *see p250* **Key to Symbols** *see back cover flap*

SAN GIMIGNANO Albergo Relais Santa Chiara €€€€€

Via Matteotti 15, 53037 ***Tel*** *0577 94 07 01* ***Fax*** *0577 94 20 96* ***Rooms*** *41* ***Road map*** *C3*

An eclectic mix of historic and modern decor, this four-star hotel is situated on a hill just outside San Gimignano. The rooms are somewhat small, but clean and cheerful – try to book one with a balcony. A swimming-pool with Jacuzzi, garden and private parking add to its appeal. Wine-tasting and horse riding by arrangement. **www.rsc.it**

SAN GIMIGNANO La Collegiata €€€€€

Località Strada 27, 53037 ***Tel*** *0577 94 32 01* ***Fax*** *0577 94 05 66* ***Rooms*** *20* ***Road map*** *C3*

This outstanding Relais & Chateaux hotel in a converted Franciscan convent, offers stunning views of the towers of San Gimignano. The 16th-century *pietra serena* building is surrounded by ancient cypresses and Italian-style gardens. Indulge yourself in the restaurant and wine bar, or lounge in the spa and wellbeing centre. **www.lacollegiata.it**

SAN GIMIGNANO Villa San Paolo €€€€€

Strada per Certaldo, 53037 ***Tel*** *0577 95 51 00* ***Fax*** *0577 95 51 13* ***Rooms*** *18* ***Road map*** *C3*

Bounded by a rambling park, the isolated 18th-century country villa is now an exceptionally delightful four-star hotel just outside San Gimignano. It has recently been restored with plush double rooms that complement the architecture. Tennis courts and mountain bikes for hire. Three-night minimum stay. **www.hotelvillasanpaolo.com**

SAN GUSME Relais San Arceno €€€€€

Località Castelnuovo Berardenga, 53100 ***Tel*** *0577 35 92 92* ***Fax*** *0577 35 92 76* ***Rooms*** *40* ***Road map*** *D3*

This stately 17th-century villa hotel features large bedrooms with high vaulted ceilings and luxury reproduction antique furnishings. Rooms have views of the surrounding park and lake. Many activities are on offer such as wine tasting and cookery courses. Excursions to Siena on foot, by bike and on horseback.

SIENA Antica Torre €€

Via di Fieravecchia 7, 53100 ***Tel/Fax*** *0577 22 22 55* ***Rooms*** *8* ***Road map*** *D3*

Along Siena's southeast walls, this small hotel is in a stunning 16th-century tower. The rooms are quiet and romantic, while the old travertine stone staircase, stone arches, wooden beams and original brick vaults add lots of character. The breakfast room occupies a medieval potter's shop. Close to all the main sights. **www.anticatorresiena.it**

SIENA Hotel Chiusarelli €€

Viale Curtatone 15, 53100 ***Tel*** *0577 28 05 62* ***Fax*** *0577 27 11 77* ***Rooms*** *49* ***Road map*** *D3*

Within walking distance of Piazza del Campo, this tranquil villa is one of the oldest hotels in town. Built in 1870 by the Chiusarelli family, the rooms are furnished in Neo-Classical style with views over the church of San Domenico. Ask for a room with a balcony. Generous buffet breakfast served on the veranda. **www.chiusarelli.com**

SIENA Palazzo Bruchi di Masignani €€

Via Pantaneto 105, 53100 ***Tel/Fax*** *0577 28 73 42* ***Rooms*** *9* ***Road map*** *D3*

In an 18th-century palazzo in the heart of Siena, this friendly B&B is within easy walking distance of Piazza del Campo. Lovely view of the palazzo garden and the ancient city walls. Luxury rooms come with frescoed ceilings and old-fashioned furnishings. Standard rooms are traditionally furnished with wall tapestries. **www.palazzobruchi.it**

SIENA Villa Piccola Siena €€

Via Petriccio Belriguardo 7, 53100 ***Tel*** *0577 58 80 44* ***Fax*** *0577 58 95 10* ***Rooms*** *13* ***Road map*** *D3*

Close to Siena's historic centre, this three-star hotel provides traditionally decorated rooms, small terrace garden, a gourmet restaurant, cookery courses, guided tours, bicycle rentals and horse riding by arrangement. The staff is friendly and baby-sitting can be arranged. **www.villapiccolasiena.com**

SIENA Hotel Athena €€€

Via P Mascagni 55, 53100 ***Tel*** *0577 28 63 13* ***Fax*** *0577 481 53* ***Rooms*** *100* ***Road map*** *D3*

Situated in a quiet residential area, this modern four-star hotel is just a short way from the Siena Duomo. Rooms are fairly large and comfortable though the decor is not very distinctive. The rooftop terrace has fantastic views over Siena and beyond. The fine restaurant serves authentic local cuisine. Private parking. **www.hotelathena.com**

SIENA Pensione Palazzo Ravizza €€€

Pian dei Mantellini 34, 53100 ***Tel*** *0577 28 04 62* ***Fax*** *0577 22 15 97* ***Rooms*** *30* ***Road map*** *D3*

This well-located, quiet *pensione* is in a renovated Renaissance palace. Rooms come with original terracotta floors, frescoed ceilings, carved doorways and antique furnishings. Suites have their own lounge areas. The gourmet restaurant and splendid terrace garden add to the Ravizza's considerable charm. **www.palazzoravizza.it**

SIENA Residence Bosco della Spina €€€

Lupompesi, Murlo, 53016 ***Tel*** *0577 81 46 05* ***Fax*** *0577 81 46 06* ***Rooms*** *14* ***Road map*** *D3*

Fourteen apartments managed as a hotel, this residence-restaurant occupies the renovated barns, granaries, haylofts and stables of a medieval farmhouse outside Siena. Rooms have been renovated in antique style by using terracotta, stone, solid wood and wrought iron. The superb restaurant has a panoramic terrace. **www.boscodellaspina.com**

SIENA Sangallo Park Hotel €€€

Strada di Vico Alto 2, 53100 ***Tel*** *0577 33 41 49* ***Fax*** *0577 33 33 06* ***Rooms*** *50* ***Road map*** *D3*

Two kilometres (one mile) from Siena's historical centre, the Sangallo offers the perfect base for exploring the Chianti and Val d'Orcia countryside by car, bike or foot. The rooms are large with modern decor. The generous breakfast is served on the panoramic terrace, and there is also a pretty garden to relax in. **www.sangalloparkhotel.it**

SIENA Piccolo Hotel Oliveta €€€€

Via E.S.Piccolomini 35, 53100 **Tel** *0577 28 39 30* **Fax** *0577 27 00 09* **Rooms** *15* **Road map** *D3*

In a converted 18th-century farmhouse, this welcoming three-star hotel is within walking distance of Siena's major monuments and tourist attractions. Rooms have preserved all the original architectural features, including beamed ceilings, terracotta tiles and the original brickwork. The wine bar offers light snacks as well. **www.oliveta.com**

SIENA Villa Scacciapensieri €€€€

Strada Scacciapensieri 10, 53100 **Tel** *0577 414 41* **Fax** *0577 27 08 54* **Rooms** *32* **Road map** *D3*

Located in a hilly parkland outside of Siena, this converted 19th-century villa overlooks the city walls and has a wonderful old-world charm. The lovely rooms have whitewashed walls and wood-beamed ceilings. Meals are served outside on one of the many atmospheric terraces with views over the Chianti hills. **www.villascacciapensieri.it**

SIENA Grand Hotel Continental €€€€€

Via Banchi di Sopra 85, 53100 **Tel** *0577 560 11* **Fax** *0577 560 15 55* **Rooms** *51* **Road map** *D3*

Just off the Piazza del Campo, the Continental has quickly built up an impressive reputation since opening in 2002. In a majestic 1600s palazzo, the rooms are filled with priceless antiques, stunning fabrics and frescoed ceilings. A shuttle service links to the sister hotel (Park Hotel) with its golf, tennis and swimming facilities. **www.ghcs.it**

SIENA Hotel Certosa di Maggiano €€€€€

Strada di Certosa 82, 53100 **Tel** *0577 28 81 80* **Fax** *0577 28 81 89* **Rooms** *17* **Road map** *D3*

Part of the Relais & Chateaux chain of luxury hotels, this converted monastery lies in the countryside just outside Siena. Built in 1314, the hotel is internationally renowned for its antique paintings and fine silk furnishings. The vast grounds include olive groves, vineyards and a helipad. **www.certosadimaggiano.it**

SIENA Palace Hotel Due Ponti €€€€€

Viale Europa 12, 53100 **Tel** *0577 460 55* **Fax** *0577 24 79 07* **Rooms** *44* **Road map** *D3*

On the outskirts of Siena, the Palace Hotel Due Ponti is popular with business travellers since it is equipped with all mod-cons including a solarium, private parking and conference facilities. Rooms are clean and simply furnished. A large restaurant serves Tuscan fare and there is a very pleasant garden. **www.palacehoteldueponti.com**

SIENA Villa Patrizia €€€€€

Via Fiorentina 58, 53100 **Tel** *0577 504 31* **Fax** *0577 504 42* **Rooms** *38* **Road map** *D3*

A short walk from Siena's northernmost city walls, this converted villa offers a haven of tranquility in its garden and oak-filled park. Rooms are simply furnished and comfortable. The restaurant (open Apr–Oct) offers an authentic mix of local dishes including *pici* (hand-rolled pasta) with porcini mushrooms. **www.villapatrizia.it**

SINALUNGA Locanda dell'Amorosa €€€€€

Loc. L'Amorosa, 53048 **Tel** *0577 67 72 11* **Fax** *0577 63 20 01* **Rooms** *20* **Road map** *E3*

This idyllic 14th-century villa graces the rolling Sienese hills. Rooms are splendid with antique Tuscan furniture, prints and paintings. Visitors can enjoy the elegant restaurant which now occupies the ancient stables. The surrounding park, farm and vineyards capture the essence of the countryside and are ideal for long walks. **www.amorosa.it**

STROVE Albergo Casalta €

Loc. Monteriggioni, 53035 **Tel/Fax** *0577 30 10 02* **Rooms** *10* **Road map** *D3*

A small hamlet in the centre of Strove is home to this welcoming, family-run hotel. The 1,000-year old stone building houses rooms that are beautifully furnished in a rustic style with simple antiques, exposed stone fireplaces and wood-beamed ceilings. An elegant restaurant serves traditional regional dishes. **www.chiantiturismo.it**

STROVE San Luigi Residence €€€

Via della Cerreta 38, 53035 **Tel** *0577 30 10 55* **Fax** *0577 30 11 67* **Rooms** *73* **Road map** *D3*

Set in a vast park, the emphasis at San Luigi is on sport and relaxation. Accommodation is in a range of farm buildings (including 10 apartments) that are tastefully restored in rustic Tuscan style. The restaurant serves traditional local cuisine. Tennis, volleyball and basketball courts, as well as a cookery school. **www.borgosanluigi.it**

SOUTHERN TUSCANY

CASTIGLIONE DELLA PESCAIA L'Andana €€€€€

Tenuta La Badiola, Località Badiola, 58043 **Tel** *0564 94 48 00* **Fax** *0564 944577* **Rooms** *41* **Road map** *C4*

This property has friendly staff, a world-class spa, fragrant gardens and inspired rooms in French country house style, some with contemporary touches. There is a golf course and two swimming pools. The acclaimed restaurant, Trattoria Toscana, housed in a converted barn, has a Michelin star. Cookery courses are available. **www.andana.it**

CINIGIANO Castello di Vicarello €€€€€

Poggi del Sasso, 58044 **Tel** *0564 990718* **Fax** *0564 99 07 18* **Rooms** *7* **Road map** *D4*

A unique and charming hotel, this remote 11th-century castle has seven suites with eclectic decor. There is fine food and wine from the grounds, as well as two swimming pools, a spa and gardens with stunning views over the wild Maremma countryside. The charming hosts are extremely welcoming. Great for a tranquil break. **www.vicarello.it**

Key to Price Guide *see p250* **Key to Symbols** *see back cover flap*

ELBA Hotel Ilio €

Via Sant'Andrea 5, 57030 ***Tel*** *0565 90 80 18* ***Fax*** *0565 90 80 87* ***Rooms*** *19* ***Road map*** *B4*

This fabulous "all nature" boutique hotel is located on the edge of a natural park. The rooms are named after the plants around them – you can stay in the Lemon, Oleander or Geranium room among others. The beach is close and the owners organize nature walks. The restaurant serves typically Elban dishes. Open Apr–Oct. **www.ilio.it**

ELBA Hotel Antares €€

Lido di Capoliveri, 57031 ***Tel*** *0565 94 01 31* ***Fax*** *0565 94 00 84* ***Rooms*** *49* ***Road map*** *B4*

With the beach on one side, and a garden on the other, this hotel has a bright, cheerful look. Rooms are spacious and contemporary. The private beach has surfboards, sailing boards and motorboats for hire. Motorboat tours take visitors to the small, quiet coves that are inaccessible by land. Open Apr–Oct. **www.elbahotelantares.it**

ELBA Hotel Montecristo €€

Lungomare Nomellini 11, 57034 ***Tel*** *0565 97 68 61* ***Fax*** *0565 97 65 97* ***Rooms*** *43* ***Road map*** *B4*

This four-star hotel is simply furnished with a stunning poolside terrace and restaurant, with views across the bay of Marina di Campo. Steps from the hotel lead down to the sandy beach and to the adjacent pine forest. There is a spa and wellbeing centre. Diving by arrangement. Open Apr–Oct. **www.hotelmontecristo.it**

ELBA Albergo Locanda del Volterraio €€€€

Località Bagnaia, 57039 ***Tel*** *0565 96 12 19* ***Fax*** *0565 96 12 89* ***Rooms*** *18* ***Road map*** *B4*

Part of a complex beside the seaside village of Bagnaia, this exclusive four-star hotel shares 400 acres of private parkland with the apartments of Residenza Sant'Anna. The health conscious can enjoy the tennis courts and spa, and later relax at the beach bar. Baby-sitting facilities and the children's pool are also advantages. Open Apr–Oct. **www.volterraio.it**

ELBA Hotel Hermitage €€€€€

Località La Biodola, 57037 ***Tel*** *0565 97 40* ***Fax*** *0565 96 99 84* ***Rooms*** *130* ***Road map*** *B4*

The most luxurious hotel in Elba's most exclusive bay, the Hermitage has its own private beach, three pools, three restaurants, a piano bar, a six-hole golf course and nine tennis courts. Accommodation is split between the main building and smaller cottages in the grounds. Three-day minimum stay. Open Apr–Oct. **www.hotelhermitage.it**

GIGLIO CAMPESE Hotel Campese €€€

Località Giglio Campese, 58012 ***Tel*** *0564 80 40 03* ***Fax*** *0564 80 40 93* ***Rooms*** *39* ***Road map*** *C5*

In the charming bay of Campese, northwest of the island of Giglio, Hotel Campese is simple but welcoming, with a private beach and an excellent restaurant that serves great seafood. The mountainous backdrop evokes a feeling of wild isolation. Terrace garden with glorious views over the quiet fishing bay at sunset. **www.hotelcampese.com**

GIGLIO PORTO Castello Monticello €€

Via Provinciale, 58013 ***Tel*** *0564 80 92 52* ***Fax*** *0564 80 94 73* ***Rooms*** *29* ***Road map*** *C5*

Beautifully situated in the midst of Giglio's lush Mediterranean vegetation, this hotel was originally built as a private mansion. Rooms are tastefully decorated with superb views of the sea. A panoramic terrace, tennis court, and children's playground add to its appeal. Courtesy shuttle to the beach and ferry. **www.hotelcastellomonticello.com**

PITIGLIANO/SORANO Hotel della Fortezza €€

Piazza Cairoli 5, 58010 ***Tel*** *0564 63 20 10* ***Fax*** *0564 63 32 09* ***Rooms*** *16* ***Road map*** *E5*

A short drive from Pitigliano, this elegant three-star hotel is located within the walls of Sorano's most important medieval structure, the historical Fortezza Orsini. Room furnishings date from the 19th-century, but the ancient beams, tiled ceilings and winding pathways are much older. Closed in February. **www.fortezzahotel.it**

PORTO ERCOLE Hotel Don Pedro €€

Via Panoramica 7, 58018 ***Tel*** *0564 83 39 14* ***Fax*** *0564 83 31 29* ***Rooms*** *44* ***Road map*** *D5*

The only hotel in town, the simply furnished rooms of the Don Pedro offer breathtaking views over Porto Ercole's yacht-filled port and Fortezza Spagnola. The hotel has its own private beach in the pebble-filled bay, with a bar and breakfast terrace. The restaurant serves a seasonal range of locally caught fish. **www.hoteldonpedro.it**

PORTO ERCOLE Il Pellicano €€€€€

Località Sbarcatello, 58018 ***Tel*** *0564 85 81 11* ***Fax*** *0564 83 34 18* ***Rooms*** *50* ***Road map*** *D5*

Touted as one of the best hotels in Italy, this is pure luxury overlooking the beach. There is an air of understated elegance, with vistas over the sea, and bright, modern rooms, many with their own terrace. Privacy is highly valued, and service is attentive and discreet. The restaurant has a Michelin star. **www.pellicanohotel.com**

PUNTA ALA Baglioni Residence Alleluja €€€€€

Via del Porto, 58040 ***Tel*** *0564 92 20 50* ***Fax*** *0564 92 07 34* ***Rooms*** *38* ***Road map*** *C4*

This luxury four-star seaside hotel is in the middle of the Punta Ala nature park, and boasts a private beach of fine white sand. Rooms are decorated in characteristic Tuscan-farmhouse style. Some double rooms have their own sitting rooms. Tennis courts on site and nearby golf club. Baby-sitting services on request. **www.baglionihotels.com**

TALAMONE Hotel Torre dell'Osa €€€

SS Aurelia KM156, 58010 ***Tel*** *0564 88 49 53* ***Fax*** *0564 88 49 54* ***Rooms*** *14* ***Road map*** *D5*

South of the Parco della Maremma, this friendly hotel is on the Talamone promontory. The fabulous rural location is offset by classically furnished rooms with wood-beamed ceilings. Five minutes to the beach and golf course. An ideal choice for an isolated romantic break. Motorboat tours along the coast can be arranged. **www.torredellosa.it**

RESTAURANTS, CAFES AND BARS

Food is one of the great Italian passions, and eating out on a balmy summer's evening can be a memorable experience. Few restaurants in Tuscany serve anything but Italian food, and most concentrate on the robust fare that typifies the region's cuisine. Most Tuscans take their lunch *(pranzo)* around 1pm, and have dinner *(cena)* from 8pm. Restaurants may shut for several weeks during the winter and also during the holiday season in summer. If in doubt, phone first to check that the restaurant is open. Finding the restaurants in Florence can be confusing due to the dual numbering of the streets *(see p305)*, so use the map references. The restaurants listed on pages 270–281 have been selected from the best the city and region can offer across all price ranges.

Italian waiter at your service

TYPES OF RESTAURANTS AND BARS

Italian restaurants have a bewildering variety of names, but in practice there's little difference between a *trattoria, osteria* or *ristorante* in terms of price, cooking or ambience. Both a *birreria* and *spaghetteria* are more down-market establishments, and sell beer, pasta dishes and snacks. A *pizzeria* is a cheap, informal restaurant with pasta, meat and fish on the menu as well as pizzas. It is usually open only in the evening, especially if it has wood-fired ovens.

At lunchtime you could visit a *tavola calda,* which will offer a range of hot and cold pasta dishes, vegetables and meats. A *rosticceria* offers spit-roast chicken to take away, often with other fast foods. Most bars sell filled rolls *(panini)* and sandwiches *(tramezzini)* and small pizza bars sell slices of pizza *(pizza taglia)* to eat on the street.

Old-fashioned wine bars *(vinaii* or *fiaschetterie)* are a dying breed, but they are atmospheric places to grab a snack or a glass of wine. Ice cream parlours *(gelaterie)*, by contrast, are thriving, and Florence has some of the best in Italy.

VEGETARIAN FOOD

Most Italians find it hard to understand vegetarianism, and Florence boasts only a couple of vegetarian restaurants. However, in the wake of mad-cow disease, restaurants are offering a wider vegetarian selection and you should have no trouble assembling a meat-free meal, particularly if you eat fish and seafood. Starters *(antipasti)* will usually include some suitable dishes. There are also vegetable-based soups and pasta sauces, although you will need to check that they have been cooked with vegetable stock *(brodo vegetariano)*.

I Latini, Florence *(see p272)*

HOW MUCH TO PAY

Prices are often higher in Florence than elsewhere. In the cheaper eating establishments and pizzerias you can have a two-course or a fixed-price *(menù turistico)* meal with half a litre of wine for around €15–€20. Average prices for a three-course meal are €20–€30, and in up-market restaurants you could easily pay as much as €40–€50.

Nearly all restaurants have a cover charge *(pane e coperto)*, usually no more than €3. Many also add a 10 per cent service charge *(servizio)* to the bill *(il conto)*, so always establish whether or not this is the case. Where leaving a tip is a matter of your own discretion, 12–15 per cent is acceptable.

Restaurants are obliged by law to give you a receipt *(una ricevuta)*. Scraps of paper with an illegible scrawl are illegal, and you are perfectly within your rights to ask for a proper bill.

A convivial atmosphere at Teatro del Sale in Florence *(see p271)*

The 13th-century Il Pozzo in Monteriggioni *(see p279)*

Cash is the preferred form of payment in most cafés and bars, but many restaurants, particularly the more expensive, will accept major credit cards. Check which cards are accepted when booking.

Chic, modern decor at Osteria Tornabuoni, Florence *(see p272)*

MAKING RESERVATIONS

Florence's best restaurants in all price ranges are well patronized. It is therefore advisable to try and reserve a table, even in the more down-market places. Where restaurants do not accept bookings, try to arrive early to avoid queuing.

SMOKING

Legislation requires restaurants and bars throughout Italy to provide separate no-smoking areas or they will be fined. At cafés and restaurants that do not provide sealed-off areas, smoking is limited to outside tables.

CHOICE OF WINE

House wines will usually be Chiantis or some close cousin. The cheaper establishments usually have only house wine, or a small choice of other Tuscan wines. Those in the €40–€50 price range will have a fuller selection of regional wines, as well as wines from other parts of Italy. At the top of the scale, there should be a wide range of Italian and local wines, and, as at the Enoteca Pinchiorri *(see p271)*, a selection of French and other foreign vintages. *(See also pp268–9.)*

CHILDREN

Children are generally welcome in restaurants, but less so in the evening and in more up-market places. Special facilities such as high chairs are not commonly provided. Check the menu for the option of a small portion *(una porzione piccola)*: most restaurants will prepare a half portion *(mezza porzione)* if requested.

WHEELCHAIR ACCESS

Few restaurants make special provision for wheelchairs, though a word when you are booking should ensure a conveniently situated table and assistance on arrival.

DRESS CODE

Italians are relaxed about eating out, but nevertheless like to dress up to dine. If in doubt, check if formal dress is required when booking.

READING THE MENU

A meal in a restaurant will usually start with *antipasti,* or hors d'œuvres (hams, olives, salamis, crostini), followed by *primi* (soups, pasta or rice). Main courses – *secondi* – will be meat or fish, either served alone or accompanied by vegetables *(contorni)* or a salad *(insalata)*.

To finish, there will probably be a choice of fruit *(frutta)*, cheese *(formaggio)*, puddings *(dolci)*, or a combination of all three. Coffee – always espresso, never cappuccino – is ordered at the end of a meal, often with a *digestivo (see p269)*. In cheaper restaurants, the menu *(il menù* or *la lista)* may be written on a blackboard and in many establishments the waiter *(cameriere)* will recite the chef's daily specials at your table.

The dark wood interior of Osteria le Logge in Siena *(see p280)*

The Flavours of Florence and Tuscany

Tuscany is the orchard and vegetable garden of Italy, a vision of rolling, vine-clad hills and silvery grey olive groves, while the Ligurian sea yields a fabulous bounty of fish and seafood. The cuisine is rustic and simple, but always using the finest ingredients. It is said that Tuscany is where Italian cooking was born, thanks to Catherine de'Medici, an accomplished gourmet. Tuscans are known as *mangiafagioli* (bean eaters), because pulses are used so much in soups and robust stews. Juicy steaks from prized Valdichiana cattle, pork and game all feature strongly. Fungi are highly prized; even more so are truffles – "black gold".

Black truffles

Freshly harvested Tuscan olives, for pressing into olive oil

FIRST AND FOREMOST

Tuscan olive oil is simply outstanding in quality. This "liquid gold" has countless uses and is an integral part of *crostini*, slices of toasted bread smeared with olive oil on which are spread different toppings, such as *crostini alla Toscana*, topped sautéed with chickens livers. *Salumi* producers are an important feature of the region and *prosciutto di cinghiale* (wild boar ham) is a rich, gamey delicacy. Soups and minestrones are also very popular, often made with beans, especially the white kidney beans known as *cannellini*. The most typical pasta is papardelle, broad noodles that are often served with a rich hare sauce, called *papardelle alla lepre*.

EARTH AND WATER

The shining star of meat dishes is tender, succulent beef steak, *bistecca alla fiorentina*. The best is from cattle raised in Valdichiana, south of Arezzo, delicious marinated with extra virgin olive oil and herbs, grilled over an open fire and usually served very rare. Tuscans are passionate hunters and

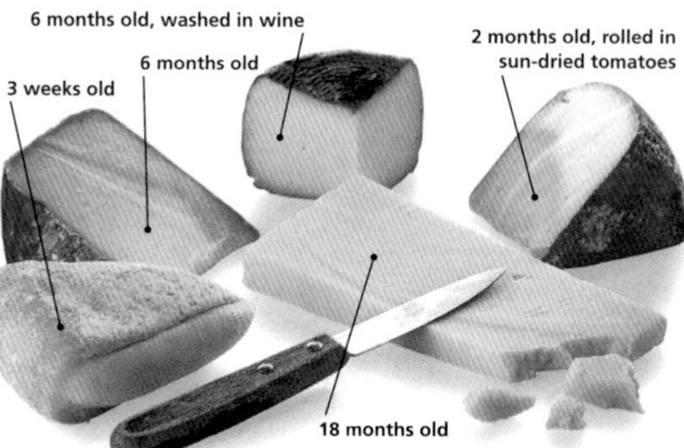

Some of the varieties of ewe's milk Pecorino cheese found in Tuscany

REGIONAL DISHES AND SPECIALITIES

The olive is the staple ingredient – even the branches of the tree are used for grilling. Soups vary from those enriched with beans such as *ribollita* ("boiled again"), a rich soup of beans, herbs and vegetables whose second boiling makes it thicker and intensifies the flavour, to the simple, thin vegetable *acquacotta* (literally meaning "cooked water") to which an egg is added before serving. The vast array of salamis and cold cuts includes *finocchiona*, salami flavoured with wild fennel. Robust stews include *lepre in dolce e forte*. This hare stew is cooked with citrus fruits, cocoa, garlic, rosemary, vegetables and red wine. For the sweet-toothed, Tuscany offers *ricciarelli* (diamond-shaped almond cakes), *cantucci* (above) and *torta di riso* – a golden, rich rice cake that is mouthwateringly delicious.

Cantucci

Minestrone alla fiorentina
This thick vegetable and bean soup may also contain chicken and pork giblets.

A colourful assortment of local produce

everything from the smallest songbird to the largest wild boar features on menus. Hare is a special favourite.

Seafood and fish includes especially good red mullet *(triglie)* from Livorno and *cacciucco* soup, claimed as the ancestor of *bouillabaisse*.

FUNGI FORAYS

From late August to early October Tuscans are seized by fungi fever. Armies of people with baskets make an annual pilgrimage to the Garfagna, Mugello and Maremma for prize pickings. The most sought-after are *porcini* (boletus or cep). Picking tends to be limited by licence and is certainly only advisable to those who know their edible fungi. Out of season, dried wild mushrooms accompany many dishes. But the star and most highly prized fungi hide underground, waiting to be sniffed out by hunters with their keen-scented dogs – the truffle *(tartufo)*. The location of truffle troves is a closely-guarded secret as they are, literally, worth their weight in gold. San Miniato produces about a quarter of Italy's truffle crop, including the prized white truffle.

An array of beans on display in a Tuscan market square

SWEET DELIGHTS

Chestnuts are plentiful and have many uses. They, with almonds and honey, are the main ingredients in some favourite and famous recipes. Castelnuovo della Garfagnana produces a superb chestnut cake, called *torta garfagnana*. Panforte, the Christmas cake originating from Siena, is a rich mix of fruits, nuts and spices. For something a little less rich, almond *cantucci* biscuits are sublime dipped into sweet *vin santo* wine.

TUSCAN TREATS

Cacciucco di Livorno Rich tomatoey fish soup served over toasted garlic bread.

Cantucci Sweet, very hard almond biscuits.

Cheeses Ricotta, Mucchino, (cow's milk made near Lucca), Pecorino, and Cacciotte (made with ewe, cow and goat milk).

Chestnuts Made into flour, pancakes, soup and sweet cakes like *castagnaccio*, flavoured with rosemary.

Chianti The fine Tuscan red wine, used in many recipes.

Crostini Toasted bread which is smeared with olive oil and rubbed with garlic.

Pappardelle alla Lepre *Thick noodles are served with a sauce of hare cooked with herbs and red wine.*

Arista alla Fiorentina *Pork loin is roasted with rosemary in a recipe dating from the 15th century.*

Zuccotto *In this Tuscan speciality, sponge cake is filled with almonds, hazelnuts, chocolate and cream.*

What to Drink in Florence and Tuscany

Medieval engraving of a grape crusher

Tuscany is a major wine-producing region whose wines make ideal partners for the robust local food. Both reds and whites are made here, ranging from light, house wine *(vino della casa)* to the very best Europe can produce. The most famous reds, notably Brunello di Montalcino, Vino Nobile di Montepulciano and Chianti, are made from the Sangiovese grape and are produced inland, on the hills of Tuscany. A number of estates, particularly in Chianti Classico, also experiment with non-Italian grape varieties with considerable success. Throughout Tuscany, bars and cafés are open all day serving drinks from wine to beer and coffee. See also *A Day Out in Chianti* on page 229.

Il Poggione is an excellent producer of Brunello di Montalcino.

Carmignano, a good dry red, is made north of Florence.

RED WINE

Chianti is made in seven defined zones, but the best wines generally come from the hilly areas of Classico and Rufina. Brunello, from further south, needs ageing and can be expensive but Rosso di Montalcino, made for younger drinking, often offers better value. Tuscan table wine can be cheap or expensive – the top-priced wines may not fit the traditional Chianti regulations, but are likely to be extremely good. Sassicaia, made from the French Cabernet Sauvignon grape, is an example. Other fine reds include Fontalloro, Cepparello and Solaia.

Solaia

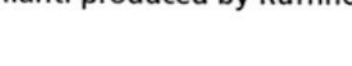

Chianti produced by Ruffino

Sassicaia is made from Cabernet Sauvignon grapes.

Galestro

WHITE WINE

Tuscany's white wines are less interesting than the reds, although some producers are experimenting with a handful of quality whites from grapes such as Chardonnay and Sauvignon. Most Tuscan white wine is made from the Trebbiano grape, at its lightest in the spritzy style called Galestro, but usually sold as plain dry Bianco della Toscana. Vernaccia di San Gimignano, from the Vernaccia grape, is sometimes good and Montecarlo, from near Lucca, a blend of grapes, offers more interesting drinking. Most Tuscan whites need to be drunk young.

Vin Santo

VIN SANTO

Vin Santo, or "Holy Wine", is a traditional wine once made on farms throughout the region and now seeing a revival of interest from modern producers. The best versions are sweet, though it can be found as a dry wine. It is often offered with *cantucci*, small almond biscuits, in Tuscan restaurants and homes. Vin Santo is made from Trebbiano and Malvasia grapes which are semi-dried, made into wine and then aged in small barrels for a number of years before bottling. The best are very concentrated in flavour. Quality varies, but superb versions are made by Avignonesi and Isole e Olena.

HOW CHIANTI IS MADE

Chianti is made as soon as possible after the October harvest. The quality of the wine can be very high, as wineries have combined the best of traditional and modern techniques.

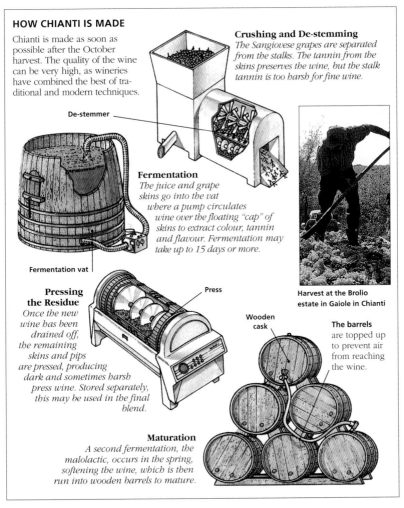

Crushing and De-stemming
The Sangiovese grapes are separated from the stalks. The tannin from the skins preserves the wine, but the stalk tannin is too harsh for fine wine.

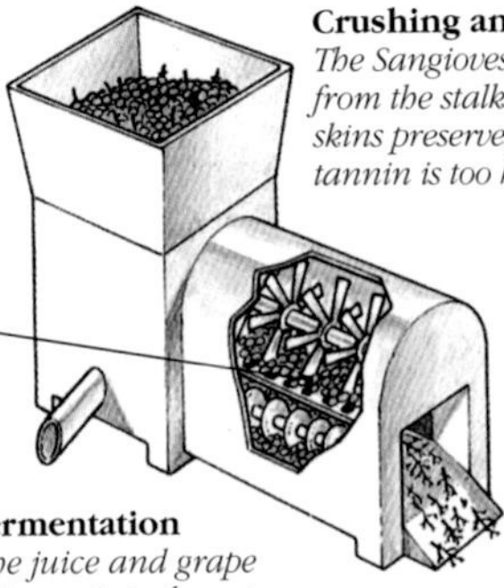

De-stemmer

Fermentation
The juice and grape skins go into the vat where a pump circulates wine over the floating "cap" of skins to extract colour, tannin and flavour. Fermentation may take up to 15 days or more.

Fermentation vat

Harvest at the Brolio estate in Gaiole in Chianti

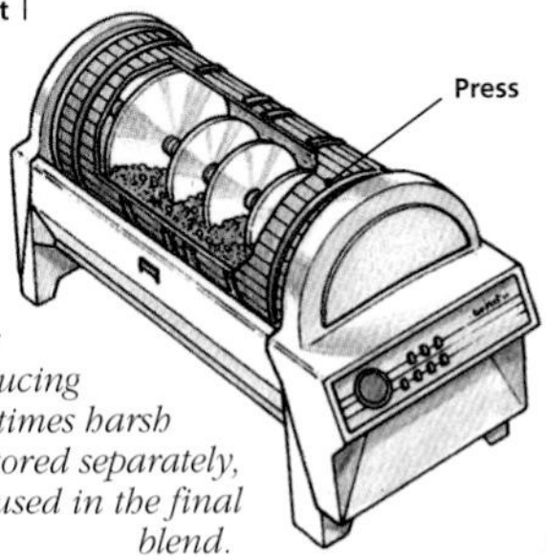

Pressing the Residue
Once the new wine has been drained off, the remaining skins and pips are pressed, producing dark and sometimes harsh press wine. Stored separately, this may be used in the final blend.

Press

Wooden cask

The barrels are topped up to prevent air from reaching the wine.

Maturation
A second fermentation, the malolactic, occurs in the spring, softening the wine, which is then run into wooden barrels to mature.

Cinzano, a popular early evening *aperitivo*

APERITIFS AND DIGESTIFS

Pre- and post-meal tipples include Campari, Cinzano and the artichoke-based Cynar, as well as Crodino, the best-known of several non-alcoholic drinks. The herb-flavoured *amaro* or a *grappa* commonly round off a meal; otherwise try a *limoncello*, a sweet, lemon-based liqueur, the aniseed-scented Sambuca or almond-flavoured Amaretto.

BEER

Beer can be a great thirst-quencher, especially in the summer heat. Draught beer *(birra alla spina)* is less expensive than bottled beer, and is sold by the measure. Good Italian lager-style beers include Peroni and Moretti.

OTHER DRINKS

Fruit juices are sold in small bottles *(succo di frutta)* or freshly squeezed *(spremuta)*. In summer, iced tea or coffee can be refreshing. Italian coffee is drunk with frothy milk for breakfast *(cappuccino)* or black after meals *(espresso)*. An *espresso* with a spot of milk is called a *macchiato*.

Espresso Cappuccino

Choosing a Restaurant

These restaurants have been selected across a wide price range for their exceptional food, good value and location. They are listed by area and within these by price, for Florence and Tuscany, and the areas surrounding them. Map references refer either to the Street Finder, pages 138–147, or the road map on the inside back cover.

PRICE CATEGORIES
For a three-course meal for one, including a half-bottle of house wine, cover charge, tax and service.

€ under €20
€€ €20–€30
€€€ €30–€40
€€€€ €40–€50
€€€€€ over €50

FLORENCE

CITY CENTRE EAST Cantinetta del Verrazzano €
Via del Tavolini 18-20, 50122 ***Tel*** *055 26 85 90* **Map** *6 D3*

Perfect for lunch in the city or an after-shopping snack, this popular place is part-bakery and part wine bar. It belongs to the Verrazzano wine estate, and sells their wines exclusively. Sample a glass with some fine local cheeses. They serve a wonderful lunch of mixed Tuscan toasts or sandwiches, and also light cooked dishes. Open till 9pm.

CITY CENTRE EAST Semolina €
Piazza Ghiberti 87, 50122 ***Tel*** *055 234 75 84* **Map** *4 F1*

Try excellent thin crust pizzas at this lively pizzeria on the other side of Sant'Ambrogio market. Regular pasta dishes and Florentine specialities such as *bistecca Fiorentina* are also available. It has a bright decor with tribal African touches. Service is cheeky and the atmosphere is fun and noisy.

CITY CENTRE EAST L'Antico Noe €€
Volta di San Pietro 6, off Bargo degli Albizi, 50122 ***Tel*** *055 234 08 38* **Map** *6 F3*

L'Antico Noe is a rustic little eatery hidden under an arched alleyway. It is typically Tuscan, with cured hams and copperware hanging on the walls, exuberant service and excellent food made from seasonal ingredients. The grilled meats and the traditional Florentine T-bone steak are very good, and there is a range of fresh pasta dishes.

CITY CENTRE EAST Baldovino €€
Via San Giuseppe 22r, 50122 ***Tel*** *055 24 17 73* **Map** *4 E1*

Big, noisy and lively, Baldovino is one of those places where you can eat anything, from a salad or a plate of cheese to a full meal. In between there are excellent pizzas, good pasta dishes, a choice of fish or meat main courses and a number of vegetarian options. Puddings are particularly good and there's a long wine list.

CITY CENTRE EAST Boccadama €€
Piazza Santa Croce 25–26r, 50122 ***Tel*** *055 24 36 40* **Map** *6 F4*

This wine bar/restaurant enjoys a superb position on Piazza Santa Croce with a handful of outside tables; shelves of wine line the walls of the cosy interior. Wine can be ordered by the glass or the bottle from a long list. You can either nibble on a selection of cheese or cold meats or go for a full meal; the food is good and quite imaginative.

CITY CENTRE EAST Coquinaros €€
Via delle Oche 15r, 50122 ***Tel*** *055 230 21 53* **Map** *6 E2*

A convenient, cosy little place, just behind the Duomo, where you can eat at almost any time of the day or evening. There are some delicious pasta dishes (try the ravioli with pecorino and pears). You can also order a salad, a plate of cheese or cured meats or a toasted open sandwich. There are good wines by the glass and bottle too.

CITY CENTRE EAST Antico Fattore €€€
Via Lambertesca 1/3r, 50123 ***Tel*** *055 28 89 75* **Map** *6 D4*

This trattoria, a favoured haunt of the Florentine literati, was founded in 1908. Though it has lost some of its old charm, having been badly damaged by the 1993 Uffizi bomb, the food and service are still of a refreshingly old-fashioned kind. Try the pasta with wild boar and the *involtini* (meat wraps) with artichoke hearts.

CITY CENTRE EAST Buca dell'Orafo €€€
Via de Girolami 28, 50122 ***Tel*** *055 21 36 19* **Map** *6 D4*

This Florentine "cellar" restaurant is down steep stairs in an alley by the Ponte Vecchio. The fantastic Tuscan fare is prepared from fresh local ingredients – try *spaghettini* with fresh peas or an omelette of fried artichokes in season, before the must-have *bistecca Fiorentina*, which is always perfectly cooked and served with a slick of oil.

CITY CENTRE EAST Frescobaldi Wine Bar €€€
Via dei Magazzini 2/4r, 50122 ***Tel*** *055 28 47 24* **Map** *6 E3*

This wine bar and restaurant is owned by one of Tuscany's foremost wine producers. Lunch is a casual affair while dinner is a little more formal, with white cloths and gleaming crystal. Creative, elegant food is accompanied by some fine, in-house wines; if you just want a snack and a glass, pop into Frescobaldino next door.

Key to Symbols *see back cover flap*

CITY CENTRE EAST Teatro del Sale €€€

Via de' Macci 111, 50122 ***Tel*** *055 200 14 92* ***Map*** *4 E1*

An inventive mix of private members' club, canteen and theatre, this is another venture from Fabio Picchi of Cibreo fame. Typically Tuscan dishes, such as tripe and risotto, are offered buffet style – with unlimited refills. A €5 membership fee gives access to the buffet lunch for €15, including wine and coffee.

CITY CENTRE EAST Osteria del Caffè Italiano €€€€

V Isola delle Stinche 11/13r, 50122 ***Tel*** *055 28 93 68* ***Map*** *6 F3*

You can eat at any time of the day in this beautifully appointed restaurant; at mealtimes there is a full menu of mainly Tuscan dishes, but in between times, you can snack on excellent cheeses or cured meats and choose from a selection of Tuscan wines. The next door pizzeria is under the same ownership.

CITY CENTRE EAST Cibreo €€€€€

V Andrea del Verrocchio 8r, 50122 ***Tel*** *055 234 11 00* ***Map*** *4 F1*

This restaurant offers superbly prepared traditional Tuscan dishes. There is no pasta, but an array of sublime soups and thoroughly Florentine dishes such as tripe, cockscomb or kidneys. Safer options include lamb with artichokes or stuffed pigeon. Desserts are fabulous. Next door is the cheaper Cibreo Trattoria, serving food from the same kitchen.

CITY CENTRE EAST Enoteca Pinchiorri €€€€€

Via Ghibellina 87, 50122 ***Tel*** *055 24 27 57* ***Map*** *4 E1*

Michelin-starred Pinchiorri is frequently described as Italy's finest restaurant and it has one of Europe's best stocked cellars with over 80,000 bottles. On the ground floor of a 15th-century palazzo, the ambience is very special too, but the food (ultra-refined Tuscan/French) and the fussy service will not please all.

CITY CENTRE NORTH Da Rocco €

Sant'Ambrogio market, 50122 No phone ***Map*** *4 F1*

Only lunch is served at this busy market eatery which offers Florentine food such as hearty bread soup (*ribollita*) and *pappa al pomodoro* made from fresh tomatoes and bread. Creamy lasagne and succulent roast beef are also available. It's speedy, very cheap and good, and always packed with locals so be prepared to wait and share a table.

CITY CENTRE NORTH Trattoria Mario €

Via Rosina 2r, 50123 ***Tel*** *055 21 85 50* ***Map*** *1 C4*

This lively trattoria is always packed with a mix of stall owners, business people and tourists who all come for the good, traditional, homely food at very reasonable prices. The daily handwritten menu is posted on the wall near the kitchen and features hearty soups, simple pastas and a number of meat and side dishes.

CITY CENTRE NORTH Il Vegetariano €

Via delle Ruote 30r, 50129 ***Tel*** *055 47 50 30* ***Map*** *2 D3*

One of Florence's few vegetarian restaurants, this place has been around for a long time, but continues to be popular. The decor is rustic and the food wholesome and cheap; choose from the menu written on a blackboard, pay at the desk and take your receipt to the counter to collect your food. There's a great salad bar.

CITY CENTRE NORTH Da Sergio €€

Piazza San Lorenzo 8r, 50129 ***Tel*** *055 28 19 41* ***Map*** *1 C5*

A popular, family-run eatery in the San Lorenzo area, Sergio's trattoria is hidden behind the market stalls. Big tables (you may end up sharing) are laid with white cloths in two airy rooms. The food is quintessentially Tuscan *casalinga* (traditional) cooking and very good; there's always tripe on Mondays and Thursdays and fresh fish on Fridays.

CITY CENTRE NORTH Trattoria Za Za €€

Piazza del Mercato 26r, 50129 ***Tel*** *055 21 54 11* ***Map*** *1 C4*

Though a bit touristy, with wooden stools and tressle tables, this old-style trattoria is great value. Soups, such as *ribollita, pappa al pomodoro* (thick soup of bread and tomato) and *pasta e fagioli* (bean soup with pasta), are a speciality. The *arista*, roast pork spiked with garlic or rosemary, is reliable. Finish with apple tart *alla zaza*.

CITY CENTRE NORTH Il Grande Nuti €€€

Via Borgo San Lorenzo 22/24, 50123 ***Tel*** *055 21 01 45* ***Map*** *6 D1*

This well located restaurant in San Lorenzo is an established classic. It has a wood-burning oven for classic pizzas, as well as serving traditional Tuscan dishes. Start with Tuscan *crostini*, little toasts with toppings such as chopped chicken liver and fresh tomatoes, and then follow with Florentine steak served rare and bloody, as it should be.

CITY CENTRE NORTH Don Chisciotte €€€€

Via C. Rodolfi 4–6, 50129 ***Tel*** *055 47 54 30* ***Map*** *1 C3*

This small restaurant near Fortezza Basso serves inventive Italian food, with an emphasis on fish and vegetable dishes. Try squid filled with ricotta and Sardinian cheese, or tagliatelle with asparagus and prawns. The lighting is soft and the surroundings are elegant, with intimate corners for the romantically inclined.

CITY CENTRE NORTH La Taverna del Bronzino €€€€€

Via delle Ruote 25–27r, 50129 ***Tel*** *055 49 52 20* ***Map*** *2 D3*

The 15th-century palazzo housing this restaurant was designed by the Florentine painter Bronzino, hence the name. Businessmen on expense account lunches and well-heeled tourists make up the clientele. The atmosphere in the airy, vaulted room is reserved and the food (elegant Tuscan) is of the highest quality.

CITY CENTRE WEST Cantinetta Antinori €€

Piazza Antinori 3, 50123 ***Tel*** *055 292 234* **Map** 5 C2

More than just a wine bar, yet not a full-blown restaurant, this room on the ground floor of one of Florence's finest Renaissance palaces makes a lovely place to eat. There are traditional Florentine dishes such as tripe and pasta with duck sauce, and a fine selection of Antinori wines.

CITY CENTRE WEST Obika €€

Via de Tornabuoni 16, 50123 ***Tel*** *055 277 35 26* **Map** 5 C2

This mozzarella bar, part of a small chain, serves fantastic fresh buffalo mozzarella and great salads, and has a stunning setting in the inner courtyard of the Palazzo Tornabuoni in the heart of town. You can taste three different hand-made mozzarellas, or there are light meals such as aubergine parmigiana, and aubergine and smoked rice tart.

CITY CENTRE WEST Colle Bereto €€€

Piazza Strozzi 4–6, 50123 ***Tel*** *055 28 31 56* **Map** 5 C3

Florence's most fashionable bar is also a popular lunch spot with a great terrace, right opposite Palazzo Strozzi. Light meals are the order of the day, with gourmet hamburgers, pastas and grilled succulent cuts of beef. Dinners are more elaborate. Good wine list and a buzzing atmosphere in a lounge setting.

CITY CENTRE WEST I Latini €€€

Via dei Palchetti 6r, 50123 ***Tel*** *055 21 09 16* **Map** 5 B3

There is always a crowd of both foreigners and locals clamouring for a table outside I Latini's large, noisy trattoria, where huge hams hang from the ceiling. The food is traditional and portions are enormous. Bypass the pasta and try the succulent grilled and roasted meats; *bistecca alla fiorentina* (broiled T-bone steak) is an experience.

CITY CENTRE WEST Garga €€€€

Via del Moro 48r, 50123 ***Tel*** *055 239 88 98* **Map** 5 B2

A Florentine classic presided over by Giuliano, one of the city's great characters, Garga is fun and often full. The walls are daubed in garish frescoes and you eat in one of a series of cosy rooms. Some dishes are better than others but *taglierini del Magnifico* (pasta with a creamy orange-and-mint flavoured sauce) is superb.

CITY CENTRE WEST Osteria Tornabuoni €€€€

Via de Corsi 5, 50123 ***Tel*** *055 27 73 51* **Map** 5 C2

This chic *osteria* is frequented by Florence's VIP crowd and features modern Tuscan food cooked with flair, an extensive wine list and a chic, modern decor comprising clean lines and row upon row of wine bottles. The Chianina beef melts in the mouth and the *peposa*, a slow-cooked stew, is divine. Book ahead.

CITY CENTRE WEST Oliviero €€€€€

Via delle Terme 51r, 50123 ***Tel*** *055 21 24 21* **Map** 5 C3

A vaguely retro atmosphere prevails at this elegant restaurant in the centre of town, but the food is up-to-the-minute creative Tuscan and delicious too. Choose between interesting fish and meat dishes – try galantine of rabbit or seared tuna steak with ginger and white beans. Service is professional and there's an excellent wine list.

OLTRARNO Antica Porta €

Via Senese 23, 50124 **Map** 3 A5

Possibly the best pizzeria in the city, Antica Porta is always crowded, so be prepared to queue. The pizzas are thin and absolutely perfect, with dollops of melting mozzarella, cooked in a huge wood oven. There are some shared tables at the front. Try to get a table at the back to avoid the crowds.

OLTRARNO Al Tramvai €€

Piazza T Tasso 14r, 50124 ***Tel*** *055 22 51 97* **Map** 3 A1

A typically Florentine place, styled as the interior of the old trams, with long bench seats. There is also a cosy back room. The traditional Tuscan food is always excellently cooked – the fried artichokes and zucchini are crisp, never greasy or heavy. The rabbit is extremely good, and this is the place to try fried brain – it's light, fluffy and delicious.

OLTRARNO Fuori Porta €€

Via Monte alle Croci 10r, 50125 ***Tel*** *055 234 24 83* **Map** 4 E3

One of Florence's classic *enoteche*, this is a popular place where you can go for a glass of wine or settle down to something more substantial. Choose wine from a list featuring over 600 labels. The *crostini* (toasted open sandwiches) make a particularly good accompaniment, but there are also excellent pastas and salads.

OLTRARNO La Casalinga €€

Via del Michelozzo 9r, 50125 ***Tel*** *055 21 86 24* **Map** 5 B5

In spite of the high numbers of tourists that flock to this no-frills trattoria, it is still very much a family-run eatery where the food is wholesome and plentiful. Go for the local dishes – *ribollita* (bread and vegetable soup), *arista* (roast pork) or *bollito misto* (mixed, boiled meats), served with a tangy *salsa verde*. Try the home-made *tiramisù*.

OLTRARNO Da Ruggero €€€

Via Senese 89, 50124 ***Tel*** *055 22 05 42* **Map** 3 A5

A very popular family trattoria beloved by locals south of the river. There are always queues to get in, so do book ahead. The fantastic hearty cooking is straight from mamma's kitchen, with Florentine favourites such as bread soup *(ribollita)* and large ravioli with butter and sage. It's an unfussy place, full of people who have been coming for years.

Key to Price Guide *see p270* **Key to Symbols** *see back cover flap*

OLTRARNO 4 Leoni €€€
Via dei Vellutini 1r, 50125 **Tel** *055 21 85 62* **Map** *5 B4*

This restaurant is conveniently situated five minutes from the city centre, near the Ponte Vecchio. In warm weather, tables at this revamped trattoria are set out on the pretty Piazza della Passera, but the ambience is pleasant inside too. Though no longer the simple, traditional place it once was, the service is always friendly and the setting charming.

OLTRARNO Ristorante Ricchi €€€€
Piazza Santo Spirito 8r, 50125 **Tel** *055 21 58 64* **Map** *3 B2*

With elegant, modern decor and a lovely terrace, this small fish restaurant is situated on one of Florence's most beautiful squares. Oriental influences are evident in dishes such as pasta with shrimps and mint, sword fish with sichuan pepper and salt cod in a spice crust. There's a limited choice for carnivores too.

OLTRARNO San Jacopo €€€€
Borgo San Jacopo 62r, 50125 **Tel** *055 28 16 61* **Map** *5 C4*

The San Jacopo enjoys a fabulous setting on the south bank of the Arno. Ask for one of the coveted tables on the tiny terrace. The chic and breezy atmosphere suits the unpretentious but beautifully served food very well. Fish fans should try *brodetto* (fish soup), an Adriatic speciality.

OLTRARNO Nove €€€€€
Piazza degli Scarlatti 1r, 50125 **Tel** *055 29 00 76* **Map** *5 B4*

Trendy and bustling, Nove has a sleek, modern look that wouldn't be out of place in London or New York. The imaginative food, however, is firmly rooted in Italian traditions and is generally very good. The menu, featuring both fish and meat, changes regularly and there is an interesting wine list.

OLTRARNO Onice €€€€€
Viale Michelangelo 78, 50125 **Tel** *055 68 16 31* **Map** *4 F3*

This restaurant, with a Michelin star, is part of the smart Villa La Vedetta hotel that overlooks the city from near Piazzale Michelangelo. The ambience is elegant and contemporary, while the food is superb and prepared with minimum fuss. Menu changes with the season.

FURTHER AFIELD Da Burde €€
Via Pistoiese 6r, 50145 **Tel** *055 31 72 06*

It's worth trekking 6 km (4 miles) from the city centre to this family-run trattoria, to soak up an air of a time gone by. All the classics of traditional Florentine cooking are to be found on the menu – *fettunta* (Tuscan garlic bread), *ribollita* (Tuscan bread soup), *trippa alla fiorentina* (tripe) and *spezzatino* (meat stew).

FURTHER AFIELD Targa €€€€
Lungarno C Colombo 7, 50136 **Tel** *055 67 73 77*

Background jazz and a warm wood-and-glass interior, softened by lots of greenery, make for a relaxed setting in this bistro, set 2 km (1 mile) from the city centre on the Arno. The food is understated and based on seasonal local traditions; crêpes with artichokes and *taleggio* (cheese), rack of lamb with asparagus and broad beans. Fantastic wine list.

FURTHER AFIELD Fuor d'Acqua €€€€€
Via Pisana 37r, 50143 **Tel** *055 22 22 99*

Many locals say that this is the best fish restaurant in Florence – and one of the most expensive. The fish is very fresh indeed, coming straight off the boats in Versilia and cooked with the minimum of fuss. Some crustaceans are served raw. Try the black *tagliolini* (pasta) with calamari and sage.

WESTERN TUSCANY

ARTIMINO da Delfina €€€€
Via della Chiesa 1, 59015 **Tel** *055 871 80 74* **Road map** *C2*

Surrounded by vineyards and some interesting historic villas, this delightful restaurant is located in a walled medieval village just 22 km (14 miles) from Florence. Owner Carlo Cioni renews the culinary traditions of his mother, Delfina. The rabbit galantine and *maccheroni* (pasta) with duck sauce are simply exquisite.

CASCIANA TERME Il Merlo €€€€
Piazza Minati 5, 56034 **Tel** *0587 64 40 40* **Road map** *C3*

Bean soup, mushrooms, chestnuts and wild boar are the main ingredients for winter dishes in this friendly little eatery. In the summer, fish comes to the fore: anchovies, seafood salad, linguine with squid ink and fish soup. There is a good selection of local cheeses, and a discerning wine list, with a few contributions from smaller producers.

CASTAGNETO CARDUCCI Nettare degli Dei €€€
Salita San Lorenzo, 57022 **Tel** *0565 76 51 18* **Road map** *C3*

This small eatery on two levels offers dishes based on fish from the morning's catch. A classic that usually features is *crudités di mare* (raw seafood dressed with lemon, excellent local oil, herbs and pepper). Try the gnocchetti with scorpionfish sauce. Interesting wine list and desserts.

FUCECCHIO Le Vedute €€€€

Via Romana Lucchese 121, 50054 ***Tel*** *0571 297 498* **Road map** *C2*

This elegant restaurant is located in a scenic wooded area easily accessible by car. The menu is seasonal but always features a selection of fish dishes and home-made desserts. There is an outside terrace and two interior rooms, one with a fireplace. White truffle and porcini mushrooms feature on the menu when in season. Closed Mon, first week in Jan, Aug.

LIVORNO Cantina Nardi €

Via Leonardo Cambini 6/8, 57100 ***Tel*** *0586 80 80 06* **Road map** *B3*

Friendly, family-run tavern open only for lunch. The day's menu, written on a blackboard, offers tasty local dishes such as fish soup, octopus and potatoes, spelt with vegetables, salt cod with mushrooms. The desserts include excellent fruit tarts. This is also a good place for a glass of wine and a snack.

LIVORNO La Barcarola €€

Viale Carducci 39, 57122 ***Tel*** *0586 40 23 67* **Road map** *B3*

Though Livorno may not be Tuscany's prettiest city, it is not without gastronomic charm. Fish-based dishes abound, including the hearty *cacciucco* (fish stew), for which this friendly restaurant is renowned. Much of your future meal can be seen swimming in ample tanks. Pleasantly comprehensive wine list.

LIVORNO Da Galileo €€€

Via della Campana 20, 57122 ***Tel*** *0586 88 90 09* **Road map** *B3*

For two generations the Piagneri family has been delighting diners with authentic local cuisine in this reassuringly simple restaurant. Over the years, Da Galileo's passion for gastronomy has not waned. Fish prevails, including various soups, seafood fettuccine and salt cod cooked with onions, Livorno-style.

MONTOPOLI VAL D'ARNO Trattoria dell'Orcio Interrato €€€

Piazza San Michele 2, 56020 ***Tel*** *0571 46 68 78* **Road map** *C2*

Those with a taste for history will find a palatable welcome at this trattoria, in the converted wine cellars of what is now the Albergo Quattro Gigli. The restaurant specializes in medieval and Renaissance recipes, interpreted with inventive flair: cockerel cooked with pomegranate or tripe with egg and saffron.

PISA Osteria I Santi €

Via S Maria 71-73, Pisa, 56126 ***Tel*** *050 280 81* **Road map** *B2*

A good, reasonably priced restaurant close to the Leaning Tower. Service is friendly and the decor is bright and cheerful with wonderfully kitsch art. Try *baccalà*, salted cod, or the hearty *zuppa Toscana*. There is a very decent tourist menu for €10. Expect a lively atmosphere and be prepared to chat with the locals at the rows of long tables.

PISA Osteria dei Cavalieri €€€

Via San Frediano 16, 56126 ***Tel*** *050 58 08 58* **Road map** *B2*

This friendly tavern occupies the ground floor of a medieval tower-house halfway between Pisa's two most prestigious centres of further education. It's common to find a scholarly-looking crowd enjoying the special all-in-one lunch dishes. The menu expands in the evening. Try the beef with beans and mushrooms.

PISA Ristorante V Beni €€€€

Piazza Gambacorti Chiara 22, 56125 ***Tel*** *050 250 67* **Road map** *B2*

The speciality of this small restaurant is fresh fish, expertly prepared. The place is so popular, it is wise to book in advance, even at lunchtime. In the summer months, you can enjoy your meal alfresco, with a view on to one of Pisa's lively squares, only a 15-minute walk from the Leaning Tower. Closed Sun, 3 wks in Aug.

SAN MINIATO Collebrunacchi €€€

Via Collebrunacchi 6a, 59028 ***Tel*** *0571 40 95 93* **Road map** *C2*

A hospitable family-run restaurant a short drive outside of San Miniato, in a setting with glorious panoramic views of the surrounding countryside and a cool breeze that is a welcome change from the torrid Tuscan summer heat. In November, try the *tartufo bianco* (white truffle), a regional speciality. Closed Mon, 10 days in Jan.

SAN MINIATO Il Convio €€€

Via San Maiano 2, 56028 ***Tel*** *0571 40 81 14* **Road map** *C2*

Just outside town, a fine, old 19th-century farmhouse has been converted into a restaurant serving classic local cuisine. Many of the dishes are made with home-grown ingredients, including the olive oil. Since San Miniato is renowned for its truffles, in November this "food of the gods" also features prominently on the menu.

VOLTERRA Il Sacco Fiorentino €€

Piazza XX Settembre 18, 56048 ***Tel*** *0588 885 37* **Road map** *C3*

Located in a nicely restored 17th-century palazzo, this restaurant focuses on seasonal fare such as the delectable savoury flan with courgettes, lard and porcini mushrooms, or the fettuccine pasta with spelt, beans and pecorino. There's a good selection of cheeses as well as an enticing wine list.

VOLTERRA Del Duca €€€€

Via del Castello 2, 56048 ***Tel*** *0588 815 10* **Road map** *C3*

A charming 16th-century palazzo houses this small restaurant with its ancient wine cellar and secret garden. Try the fried pumpkin flowers stuffed with ricotta and tomato. The pigeon breast cooked with locally grown saffron and olives is another speciality. There's a good cheese platter.

Key to Price Guide *see p270* **Key to Symbols** *see back cover flap*

NORTHERN TUSCANY

CASTELNUOVO DI GARFAGNANA Vecchio Mulino €

Via Vittorio Emanuele 12, 55032 **Tel** *0583 621 92* **Road map** *B1*

This traditional wine bar has changed little in aspect since the early 1900s. Run by Andrea Bertucci and his family, it now offers a fine choice of wines, plus some of Italy's best (and rarest) salamis, cold cuts and cheeses. The home-made quiches and steaming pots of polenta are a further delight. Only one table outside.

LUCCA Da Giulio in Pelleria €

Via delle Conce 47, 55100 **Tel** *0583 559 48* **Road map** *C2*

You must book ahead and enter into the spirit of this bright, boisterous and extremely busy neighbourhood restaurant. This is the reign of hearty local dishes such as *zuppa di farro* (Tuscan white bean and spelt soup) and polenta, so expect no gastronomic surprises. The prices are remarkably reasonable.

LUCCA Locanda Buatino €

Via Borgo Giannotti 508, 55100 **Tel** *0583 34 32 07* **Road map** *C2*

The eatery attached to this traditional inn also caters to locals who appreciate good food at extremely reasonable prices. So don't be alarmed at the lack of a menu with prices. Choose from the great soups, various pasta dishes, and *secondi* such as salt cod, pig's liver, sausages and beans. Good house wine and home-made desserts.

LUCCA Vecchia Trattoria Buralli €€

Piazza Sant'Agostino 10, 55100 **Tel** *0583 95 06 11* **Road map** *C2*

Exceptionally vegetarian-friendly, this trattoria provides a complete vegetarian menu on Friday evenings. Try the vegetable-based *zuppa alla frantoiana*. For dessert, go for *buccellato di Lucca*, a warm pudding of fried bread, anise and raisins soaked in Vin Santo. The wine list features Luccan recipes and wines.

LUCCA Buca di Sant'Antonio €€€

Via della Cervia 3, 55100 **Tel** *0583 558 81* **Road map** *C2*

This duly restored 19th-century tavern, with an excellent location, serves classic local fare with the occasional innovative touch. The stuffed rabbit *en croute* with mushrooms is excellent. In winter, several dishes feature locally-grown chestnuts. Try *buccellato*, the tasty local pudding. Interesting wines.

LUCCA Giglio €€€

Piazza del Giglio 2, Lucca, 55100 **Tel** *0583 49 40 58* **Road map** *C2*

Occupying an 18th-century palace decorated with grand frescoes and chandeliers, Giglio's restaurant serves traditional cuisine made from the freshest local ingredients. Try fresh spelt pasta with rabbit sauce or the excellent spaghetti with crab pulp. The dining room is elegant, and there is an atmospheric terrace overlooking the Teatro Giglio.

LUCCA La Mora €€€

Via Ludovica 1748, Località Ponte Moriano, 55029 **Tel** *0583 40 64 02* **Road map** *C2*

Situated 9 km (5.5 miles) from Lucca, this nicely appointed restaurant focuses on local cuisine, using prime produce, much of it home-grown. Start with the exquisite ravioli with a hint of marjoram, best followed by the pigeon casserole. The desserts usually comprise *cialda garfagnanina*, a sort of creamy pancake.

LUCCA Vipore €€€

Pieve Santo Stefano 44–69, 55100 **Tel** *0583 39 40 65* **Road map** *C2*

Located 8 km (5 miles) from Lucca in the surrounding hills, this 18th-century farmstead offers amazing views and an excellent opportunity to explore the Tuscan landscape. Seasonal produce is used to create dishes such as *tagliata di manzo alla erbe aromatiche* (strips of beef with aromatic herbs). Wide range of Tuscan wines.

MONTECATINI Ristorante Montaccolle €€€

Via Marlianese 27, 51016 **Tel** *0572 724 80* **Road map** *C2*

Just outside Montecatini, this restaurant has an ideal location, overlooking both the town and the valley below, a relaxed atmosphere and exceptional hospitality. The excellent cuisine is typically Tuscan – try the *Spaghetti al Chianti* – and the interior is rustic. For the best views choose a table outside.

MONTECATINI TERME Enoteca Giovanni €€€€€

Via Garibaldi 25–27, 51016 **Tel** *0572 716 95* **Road map** *C2*

Chef Giovanni Rotti's approach to local cuisine is both innovative and winningly in keeping with the fine collection of wines in his cellar. This memorable dining experience is further enhanced by superb service. Try his pigeon with grapes and pine nuts, and seek his assistance in choosing what to drink with it.

PESCIA Cecco €€€

Via Francesco Forti 96/98, 51017 **Tel** *0572 47 79 55* **Road map** *C2*

This quiet, easy-going restaurant is the best place to sample Pescia's famous *asparagi* (asparagus). Other examples of traditional fare include *pollo al mattone* (chicken cooked under a brick) and *fagioli al fiasco* (beans cooked in a flask). On cold days, try the pudding – *cioncia* – a delicious house speciality.

PIETRASANTA Enoteca Marcucci €€€€

Via Garibaldi 40, Pietrasanta, 55045 **Tel** *0584 79 19 62* **Road map** *B2*

This wine bar is well stocked with local and international labels, and is known for its excellent restaurant. There is a lively buzz and the food is incredibly tasty and well presented, while the service is sweetly informal. Be sure to admire the range of local art exhibited on the walls. Book ahead.

PISTOIA La Bottegaia €€

Via del Lastrone 17, 51100 **Tel** *0573 36 56 02* **Road map** *C2*

Looking onto the old market square to one side and the cathedral to the other, this cheerful, unpretentious wine bar boasts 300 of Italy's best wines. The food menu features cheeses, cold cuts and other toothsome delicacies, such as fish carpaccio, to go with the wines. Superb desserts. Service is friendly.

PRATO La Vecchia Cucina di Soldano €

Via Pomeria 23, Prato, 59100 **Tel** *0574 346 65* **Road map** *D2*

You'll find red-checked tablecloths at this unpretentious trattoria run by the Mattei family. The cooking is old-fashioned and hearty, with pasta and beans and filling *ribollita* soup on offer. The house speciality is *francesina*, an aromatic beef and onion stew. The wild boar, roe deer and meat cooked with celery are also excellent dishes.

PRATO Osteria Cibbè €€

Piazza Mercatale 49, 59100 **Tel** *0574 60 75 09* **Road map** *D2*

Housed in a medieval building in the city centre, this cosy little family-run eatery serves good local cold cuts and crostini for antipasto, followed by classic Tuscan fare such as pappardelle with game sauce. The desserts are home-made too: try the apple and spelt tart. Interesting wine list.

PRATO Enoteca Barni €€€

Via Ferrucci 22, 59100 **Tel** *0574 60 78 45* **Road map** *D2*

This minimalist eatery, related to the family-run deli next door, offers quick, informal lunches at very reasonable prices. The dinner menu, much more elaborate, features a range of choices such as pheasant tortelli with pig's cheek, onions and rosemary; spelt timbale with kale and shellfish; lamb in almond crust with *foie gras* sauce.

VIAREGGIO La Darsena €€€

Via Virgilio 150, 55049 **Tel** *0584 39 27 85* **Road map** *B2*

Located in the lively docks area, this friendly trattoria offers excellent fish dishes at reasonable prices. The antipasti comprise little samples of all sorts of things based on the morning's catch. For a dish of pasta, try the tagliolini with fresh anchovies. Good desserts and some fine Italian white wines.

VIAREGGIO Cabreo €€€€

Via Firenze 14, 55049 **Tel** *0584 546 43* **Road map** *B2*

The main focus of this pleasant restaurant, located in a little side street, is seafood simply cooked and served in the way that best enhances its natural aromas. Specialities include spaghetti with clams, gnocchi with lobster sauce, and baked fish. It is advisable to leave enough room for the delicious home-made desserts.

VIAREGGIO Romano €€€€€

Via Mazzini 122, 55049 **Tel** *0584 313 82* **Road map** *B2*

Although Romano is expensive, few other places give such value for money. Wines are fairly priced and the fixed-price menu has ten full courses. The owner, Romano, at the front of house is unfailingly courteous, and his wife, Franca, prepares dishes that are simple, immaculately presented and often inventive.

EASTERN TUSCANY

ANGHIARI Da Alighiero €€€

Via Garibaldi 8, 52031 **Tel** *0575 78 80 40* **Road map** *E3*

Anghiari is a gastronomic crossroads between Tuscany and Umbria. Suitably surrounded by thick stone walls of a 15th-century origin, this restaurant pays homage to that mixed, historic tradition. Try fresh pasta with porcini mushrooms, followed by roast breast of duck, and enjoy the discerning wine list.

AREZZO Antica Osteria l'Agania €€

Via Mazzini 10, 52100 **Tel** *0575 29 53 81* **Road map** *E3*

This typical family-run tavern serves local dishes among plenty of noisy chatter and laughter. Home-made pasta, *ribollita* soup, tripe, roast meats are on offer. No-frills service but good value for money. This is not the place for an intimate *diner à deux*, but ideal for a quick, lively lunch with friends.

AREZZO La Torre di Gnicche €€

Piaggia S. Martino 8, 52100 **Tel** *0575 35 20 35* **Road map** *E3*

Looking out over the beautiful Piazza Vasari, this is first and foremost a place for wine-lovers, with its great list of Tuscan wines, and some from other regions. The freshly-cooked food is as good, and uses ingredients depending on the season. There's no menu, so just be adventurous and try anything.

Key to Price Guide *see p270* **Key to Symbols** *see back cover flap*

AREZZO Buca di San Francesco €€€

Via San Francesco 1, 52100 ***Tel*** *0575 232 71* ***Road map*** *E3*

Set alongside the church of San Francesco in the historic centre, the Buca is ideal for those who have been sight-seeing in the frescoed church. The restaurant is found in the basement of a 14th-century building. Here, you can sample the famous Tuscan *ribollita* (cabbage and bread soup), or try the Chianti beef stew.

AREZZO Logge Vasari €€€

Via Vasari 19, 52100 ***Tel*** *0575 29 58 94* ***Road map*** *E3*

In the frescoed rooms of a 16th-century building, Logge Vasari serves dishes based on local recipes revisited with creative flair. Try *tortelli del casentino* with partridge sauce, or fillet of Chianina beef cooked in Brunello. All the bread is home-made. There's an enticing choice of desserts and a good selection of wines.

AREZZO Ristorante I Tre Bicchieri €€€€€

Piazzetta Sopra i Ponti 3, 52100 ***Tel*** *0575 265 57* ***Road map*** *E3*

Brothers Sefano and Lionello put great care and inventive spirit into this refined but unpretentious restaurant. Superb ingredients are handled with flair. Try the ravioli – two black and two white – stuffed with lobster and served in an exquisite flame-coloured tomato reduction. There's a fantastic wine list.

BORGO SAN LORENZO Ristorante degli Artisti €€€€

Piazza A. Romagnoli 1, 50032 ***Tel*** *055 845 77 07* ***Road map*** *D2*

This pleasant restaurant is located in a charming, old building in the historic centre. The menu boasts Tuscan cuisine interpreted with flair. Try the pheasant terrine with black truffles and larded croutons, or *strappati* pasta with duck sauce. Good cheeses too. The wine list offers plenty of choice.

CAMALDOLI Il Cedro €€

Via di Camaldoli 20, Località Moggiona, 52010 ***Tel*** *0575 55 60 80* ***Road map*** *E2*

One of the most popular restaurants in the region, Camadoli is known for its finely-cooked specialities such as venison and boar, no doubt hunted in the thickly forested Casentino Mountains that provide breathtaking views. In spring and summer, delicate fried vegetables are also a treat. Booking advised.

CASTELNUOVO BERARDENGA Bengodi €€

Via della Società Operaia 11, 53019 ***Tel*** *0577 35 51 16* ***Road map*** *D3*

This small, intimate *enoteca* (wine bar) is situated in the bustling main square. The walls are lined with hundreds of different wines that you can choose to sample with your meal. The home-made desserts are a real treat. Afternoon and early evening *aperitivi* are served in the hours between lunch and dinner. Closed Mon.

CASTELNUOVO BERARDENGA La Bottega del 30 €€€€€

Via Santa Caterina 2, Località Villa a Sesta, 53019 ***Tel*** *0577 35 92 26* ***Road map*** *D3*

This is a serious, award-winning restaurant run by Franco Camelia and his French wife Hélène. The menu inlcudes a renowned *petto di anatra con il finocchio selvatico* (breast of dusk with wild fennel). Pasta dishes are cooked with a difference. There's also superb home-made spaghetti with nettle, wild mint and porcini. Fine wine list.

CORTONA Osteria del Teatro €€

Via Maffei 2, 52044 ***Tel*** *0575 63 05 56* ***Road map*** *E3*

This classic trattoria serves well prepared traditional dishes. Apart from the excellent soups, try the risotto with porcini and saffron, or *caramelle al radicchio rosso* (pasta stuffed with red chicory and ricotta). The guinea fowl with mushrooms is also good. There are some nice wines to wash it all down.

CORTONA Preludio €€

Via Guelfa 11, 52044 ***Tel*** *0575 63 01 04* ***Road map*** *E3*

Cheese soufflé with pears and truffles: this creative combination of flavours is typical of a restaurant that uses unusual combinations of local ingredients to gratify the taste buds. Succulent meat dishes are based on Chianina beef, the renowned local breed. The menu also offers children-friendly dishes.

LUCIGNANO La Rocca €€

Via Matteotti 15–17, 52046 ***Tel*** *0575 83 67 75* ***Road map*** *E3*

While this easy-going restaurant serves all the classics of local cuisine, it also boasts something a bit different to the usual fare. One of the specialities is the delicious *zuppa dei tarlati* (chicken soup made with wild fennel and served with croutons). For a taste of the sublime, try the fried eggs topped with truffle shavings.

LUCIGNANO Il Goccino €€€

Via Matteotti 88/90, 52046 ***Tel*** *0575 83 67 07* ***Road map*** *E3*

The tasting menu greets you with a sparkling *aperitivo* and then leads you through four excellent courses. There's also an option to choose from an inventive menu: in spring, there may be maltagliati pasta with asparagus, pears and pecorino. Good wine list, with many bottles that can be tasted by the glass.

POPPI Antica Cantina €€

Via Lapucci 2, 52014 ***Tel*** *0575 52 98 44* ***Road map*** *E2*

A stone's throw from the imposing Castello dei Conti Guidi, this restaurant is located in a cellar dating back to the 12th century. Chestnut ravioli and *tagliata di manzo con porcini* (beef strips with porcini mushrooms) are among the temptations on the menu. A good wine list with bottles from various Italian regions. The menu changes every four months.

SANSEPOLCRO Il Convivio €€

Via Traversari 1, 52037 ***Tel*** *0575 73 65 43* ***Road map*** *E3*

Located in the historic Palazzo Bourbon del Monte, this restaurant provides a pleasant showcase for the local culinary tradition. Mushrooms and truffles prevail, and meats range from succulent steaks to game. The antipasti include a tasty game terrine. Good soups as well as pasta dishes can also be found on the menu.

SANSEPOLCRO Fiorentino €€€

Via Luca Pacioli, 60, 52037 ***Tel*** *0575 74 20 33* ***Road map*** *E3*

Run by the same family for over 50 years, the Fiorentino occupies a Renaissance dining room with a magnificent ceiling and fireplace. The menu includes Tuscan *hors d'oeuvres*, home-made pasta dishes, succulent Chianina beef, and traditional recipes based on Renaissance cooking. There's also a good range of Tuscan wines.

SANSEPOLCRO Ristorante da Ventura €€€

Via Aggiunti 30, 52037 ***Tel*** *0575 74 25 60* ***Road map*** *E3*

This charming family-run restaurant serves delectable *agnolotti al tartufo* (stuffed pasta with truffles). Another of their classic dishes is the veal cooked slowly in Chianti. Mushrooms often feature too. Even the cantucci biscuits for dipping in Vin Santo are home-made.

TERRANUOVA BRACCIOLINI Il Canto del Maggio €€

Località Penna 30/D, 52028 ***Tel*** *055 970 51 47* ***Road map*** *D3*

In a tiny hamlet between Terranuova and Loro Ciuffenna you'll find this gem of a restaurant restored and run by Mauro Quirini and his family. Surrounded by blossoms and aromatic herbs, enjoy the rare, peppery beef dish known as *peposo alla fornacina*, along with a wine from the excellent cellar.

CENTRAL TUSCANY

BAGNO VIGNONI Hotel Terme €€€

Piazza delle Sorgenti 13, 53027 ***Tel*** *0577 88 71 57* ***Road map*** *D4*

A fantastic location and an injection of youthful energy have turned an average hotel restaurant into a cool eatery offering good food well matched with fine wines. You don't have to eat the whole three-course lunch, and the opening times are less rigid than most restaurants. A must-try is the delicious *carabaccia* (sweet onion soup).

BARBERINO VAL D'ELSA I Paese dei Campanelli €€€

Loc. Petrognano Semifonte, Barberino Val d'Elsa, 50021 ***Tel*** *055 807 53 18* ***Road map*** *D3*

Stone walls, linen tablecloths and candles lend a wonderful atmosphere to this well regarded restaurant close to Florence. It is popular with chic Florentines who come here to enjoy the traditional Tuscan dishes which are given an imaginative twist. Fillet of beef with breadcrumbs and pesto is popular, as is anything seasonal.

CHIANCIANO Patry €€€

Viale G. di Vittorio 80, 53042 ***Tel*** *0578 630 14* ***Road map*** *E4*

Unprepossessing though Chianciano may be, it is worth a visit for its Archeological Museum and for Patry, an impressive fish restaurant. The menu depends on the day's catch, so let yourself be guided by Danilo, the affable restaurateur. The cooking style is simple, and the flavours speak for themselves.

CHIUSI Il Salotti €€€€

Il Patriarca Hotel, Strada Statale 146, Località Querce al Pino, Chiusi, 53043 ***Tel*** *0578 27 44 07* ***Road map*** *E4*

A Michelin star distinguishes this gourmet jewel in the Il Patriarca hotel, a testament to the chef's efforts to produce traditional yet innovative dishes made from seasonal ingredients. All wines on the extensive wine list can be sampled by the glass, courtesy of the "wine cart". There are only 15 tables, so booking is advisable.

COLLE VAL D'ELSA Arnolfo €€€€€

Via XX Settembre 50/52A, 53034 ***Tel*** *0577 92 05 49* ***Road map*** *D3*

French-trained chefs have earned this intimate three-roomed restaurant one of Tuscany's few Michelin stars. The wines, food and service are all impeccable, though the reverential hush feels a bit odd for Italy. Typical dishes include a sublime *ribollita* (Tuscan bread soup), and pigeon cooked with wine, prunes and pine nuts.

COLLE VAL D'ELSA L'Antica Trattoria €€€€€

Piazza Arnolfo 23, 53034 ***Tel*** *0577 92 37 47* ***Road map*** *D3*

This well-run family restaurant features classic Tuscan fish and meat dishes as well as some more inventive fare. For instance, the saddle of venison is cooked in grape must and juniper. There are also some inviting desserts such as orange *semifreddo*. The cheese board is extensive and the wine list decent.

GAIOLE IN CHIANTI Castello di Spaltenna €€€€

Località Pieve di Spaltenna, 53013 ***Tel*** *0577 74 94 83* ***Road map*** *D3*

This lovely stone-walled, flower-filled restaurant forms part of a peaceful hotel in a castle just outside Gaiole in Chianti. Popular with expatriates, it offers refined versions of Tuscan classics such as pigeon cooked in Chianti, fresh porcini mushrooms, chickpea soup and, occasionally, more offbeat innovations.

Key to Price Guide *see p270* **Key to Symbols** *see back cover flap*

GREVE La Cantinetta di Rignana €€€

Loc. Rignana, Greve in Chianti, 50022 **Tel** *055 85 26 01* **Road map** *D3*

With incredible views from its large terrace, this country restaurant serves breathtaking yet simple Tuscan food. The pasta with chestnuts is rich and creamy – and you won't taste a fresher salad. Roast pigeon is tender, and the rabbit delectable. Upstairs is rowdier than the cosier room downstairs, but the large terrace is best of all.

MONTALCINO Il Boccon Divino €€€€

Località Colombaio, 53024 **Tel** *0577 84 82 33* **Road map** *D4*

Perfect for summer dining alfresco, this restaurant offers some interesting dishes and a magnificent view. The *carabaccia* (onion soup) is a must, and the *scottiglia di cinghiale* (wild boar stew) is excellent. Not exclusively local, the cheese board is also interesting. Excellent wine list, as befits the town.

MONTEFOLLONICO La Chiusa €€€€

Via della Madonnina, 88, Montefollonico, 53040 **Tel** *0577 66 96 68* **Road map** *E4*

Brick arches, antiques and wild flowers furnish what is reputedly the best restaurant in southern Tuscany. Staying true to its farming roots, the restaurant's cuisine is in the peasant tradition, and includes bread soup and pulse soup, as well as excellent courgette flowers and vegetable flans. Local truffles and porcini mushrooms are used in season.

MONTEPULCIANO La Grotta €€€

Località San Biagio, 53045 **Tel** *0578 75 76 07* **Road map** *E4*

A restaurant for discerning diners, La Grotta is located right opposite one of the foremost expressions of Renaissance architecture in Tuscany: Sangallo the Elder's Church of San Biagio. Specialities include the excellent *pici* (local pasta strips) with duck and saffron sauce. Also good is the fillet of Chianina beef with asparagus and truffles.

MONTERIGGIONI Il Pozzo €€€

Piazza Roma 20, 53035 **Tel** *0577 30 41 27* **Road map** *D3*

Occupying 13th-century stables, Il Pozzo is an ideal place for lunch. The food is rigorously Tuscan, essentially simple, but never banal. Try the truffle-fragrant *tortelli al cartoccio* (tortelli cooked in tinfoil), which comes wrapped up like a packet to conserve the aromas. Equally delicious is the stuffed pigeon.

PANZANO IN CHIANTI Solociccia €€

5 Via Chiantigiana, Panzano in Chianti, 50022 **Tel** *055 85 27 27* **Road map** *D3*

Butcher Dario Cecchini's quest to promote all cuts of meat is the impetus behind this innovative restaurant serving a set six-course meal. Modern design and communal tables provide the backdrop for the dishes, which include every cut but the *bistecca*. Cecchini also has another restaurant nearby. Book ahead. Open Thu–Sat pm and Sun lunch only.

PIENZA La Pergola €€€

Via dell'Acero 2, 53026 **Tel** *0578 74 80 51* **Road map** *E4*

Unpretentious but inventive, La Pergola is the best restaurant in the area. Chef Emanuele injects a little of his Abruzzo origins into Tuscan fare, conjuring up dishes that have real flair. Try the *sformato di verdura con crema di porri e patata*, a vegetable flan with a leek and potato sauce. Excellent wine list.

POGGIBONSI La Galleria €€

Galleria Cavalieri V. Veneto 20, Poggibonsi, 53036 **Tel** *0577 98 23 56* **Road map** *D3*

The setting – in a shopping arcade in industrial Poggibonsi – is unpromising but loyal locals swear the chef here is one of the best in Tuscany. You'll get traditional Tuscan food with more than a dash of flair, including good fish and seafood. Probably the best reason to stop in Poggibonsi.

SAN CASCIANO Nello €€

Via 4 Novembre 66, San Casciano in Val di Pesa, 50026 **Tel** *055 82 01 63* **Road map** *D2*

Nello's serves simple but excellent food and is just a short drive from Florence. The restaurant is large and the decor unfussy, while the food includes tasty bean dishes as well as *pappardelle* with wild boar, and ravioli in the house sauce. On Fridays fish appears on the menu, including excellent *spaghetti al vongole*.

SAN GIMIGNANO Osteria delle Catene €€

Via Mainardi 18, 53037 **Tel** *0577 94 19 66* **Road map** *C3*

This small restaurant specializes in regional cooking enhanced with its own special touch. You could start off with cold cuts made from wild boar, then continue with a saffron soup made according to a medieval recipe. The hare cooked in local wine is also good, and the home-made desserts are worth leaving room for.

SAN GIMIGNANO Dorandò €€€€

Vicolo dell'Oro 2, 53037 **Tel** *0577 94 18 62* **Road map** *C3*

This restaurant is small and very select, so booking is advised. Impressive wine list, and dishes to go with it. The pasta with pigeon sauce on a bed of creamed mushrooms is delicious. There are various fish specialities, including angler fish in a nutty crust served with leeks. Take your time to enjoy it all.

SANT'ANGELO IN COLLE SCALO Il Marrucheto €€

Località Sant'Angelo in Colle Scalo, 53020 **Tel** *0577 80 80 00* **Road map** *D4*

Il Marrucheto is known for its simplicity, warmth and good value: a combination that's becoming increasingly rare in Tuscany. The focus is fish, or pizza, though there are meat dishes too. Try the seafood spaghetti, which is very filling. The *zuppa di cozze*, or clam soup, is also good. Finish up with a simple salad.

SARTEANO Santa Chiara €€€

Via Costa S. Chiara 30, 53047 ***Tel*** *0578 26 54 12* **Road map** *E4*

A small hotel with a good restaurant, Santa Chiara is located in an old convent with lovely views across the valley. Home-made pasta, including exquisite ravioli stuffed with dandelion and borage leaves, is a speciality. Mushrooms also feature on the menu when they're in season. The rabbit with wild fennel makes a perfect *secondo*.

SEGGIANO Silene €€€

Località Pescina, 58038 ***Tel*** *0564 95 08 05* **Road map** *D4*

A little distance up the road from Seggiano, just past Daniel Spoerri's sculpture garden, you will come to this mountain hamlet with an inn serving excellent food, prepared and presented to perfection. The pigeon ravioli and small gnocchi with truffles are exquisite. Great wines and memorable desserts.

SIENA Enoteca I Terzi €€

Via dei Termini 7, 53100 ***Tel*** *0577 443 29* **Road map** *D3*

This restaurant has a nice vaulted space and a friendly atmosphere in which to enjoy a good bottle of wine accompanied by a wide range of premium cold cuts, *carpaccio*, smoked meats, steak tartare, and cheeses from all over Italy. In addition, each day there are three cooked dishes which change with the seasons.

SIENA La Taverna del Capitano €€

Via del Capitano 6/8, 53100 ***Tel*** *0577 28 80 94* **Road map** *D3*

Located up near the Duomo, this restaurant with vaulted ceilings and dark wood furnishings is quintessentially Sienese. The *ribollita* soup; *pici* with pecorino and pepper, stewed rabbit and tasty beef tagliata, all speak for unbroken tradition. What's more, the house wine is good too.

SIENA La Compagnia dei Vinattieri €€€

Via delle Terme 79, 53100 ***Tel*** *0577 23 65 68* **Road map** *D3*

An impressive underground, vaulted space with a magnificent wine cellar and some interesting food to go with it. You can sip by the glass, with a platter of cheese and salami, or enjoy a bottle with a hot meal such as salt cod soup. Good desserts and unusual sweet wines. Only one table outside.

SIENA La Sosta di Violante €€€

Via di Pantaneto 115, 53100 ***Tel*** *0577 437 74* **Road map** *D3*

Close to Piazza del Campo, La Sosta di Violante provides two small rooms in which you can relish local seasonal ingredients cooked with imagination: aubergine rolls containing Scamorza cheese and pine nuts, for instance, or *pici* (pasta) with duck sauce. Great care is taken in matching the meat dishes with suitable wines.

SIENA Osteria Le Logge €€€€

Via del Porrione 33, 53100 ***Tel*** *0577 480 13* **Road map** *D3*

Siena's prettiest, and often full, restaurant has a dark wood and marble interior. The tables are laid with crisp linen cloths and decorated with plants. Home-produced oils and Montalcino wines accompany dishes that wander slightly from mainstream Tuscan cooking. The stuffed guinea fowl is delicious.

SOUTHERN TUSCANY

CAPALBIO Da Maria €€€

Via Nuovo 3, 58011 ***Tel*** *0564 89 60 14* **Road map** *D5*

Capalbio's holiday population of Roman politicians and media types sit down with locals in this pleasant eatery to enjoy genuine Maremma cuisine. Dishes include stuffed pasta with truffles, spelt soup, *cinghiale alla cacciatora* (rich, spicy wild boar) and an enticing warm apple and pear tart.

CASTIGLIONE DELLA PESCAIA Pierbacco €€€

Piazza Repubblica 24, 58043 ***Tel*** *0564 93 35 22* **Road map** *C4*

Located in a building dating back to the 1500s, this restaurant largely serves seafood: the little potato gnocchi with lobster sauce is just one example. The mixed seafood platter varies in content daily but is alway excellent. To further enhance your enjoyment, there is an impressive wine list.

CECINA Il Doretto €€€€

Via Pisana Livornese 32, San Pietro in Palazzi, Cecina, 57023 ***Tel*** *0586 66 83 63* **Road map** *C3*

There are rustic interiors with elegant touches in this restaurant, which gives equal emphasis to both meat and fish. *Fritto misto*, assorted fried fish, is very good – crispy but not dry. In season, the wild boar is also excellent. The feel of the place is cosy, although the tables can be a tad too close. Closed Wed.

ELBA Rendez-Vous da Marcello €€

Piazza della Vittoria 1, Marciana Marina, 57033 ***Tel*** *0565 992 51* **Road map** *B4*

Outdoor tables on the harbour front at this noted fish restaurant make a pleasant retreat from the summer crowds of Marciana Marina. Clearly, the dishes reflect the morning's catch. Most dishes are pleasantly simple, but on occasions the menu also embraces the fashionable culinary fads of the moment.

Key to Price Guide *see p270* **Key to Symbols** *see back cover flap*

ELBA Publius €€€

Piazza del Castagneto, Località Poggio Marciana, 57030 ***Tel*** *0565 992 08* ***Road map*** *B4*

Food with a view. Not only does this historic trattoria have perhaps the best cellar on the island, but it also provides an alternative to the seafood that prevails elsewhere. In addition to fish, you can eat poultry, game, lamb roasted in herbs and a choice of pecorino and other cheeses.

MAGLIANO IN TOSCANA Da Sandra €€€

Via Garibaldi 20, 58051 ***Tel*** *0564 59 21 96* ***Road map*** *D5*

This quietly classy establishment showcases some of the best wines, now made in this promising area. The menu reflects the changing seasons. Pasta with truffles or mushrooms, wild asparagus (growing abundantly in the spring sun), game, including beautifully cooked wild boar. Good desserts.

MAGLIANO IN TOSCANA Antica Trattoria Aurora €€€€

Via Chiasso Lavagnini 12/14, 58051 ***Tel*** *0564 59 27 74* ***Road map*** *D5*

With its lovely hanging gardens for summer eating, this attractive restaurant serves dishes that add flair to local traditions. The tortelli with duck cooked in Morellino wine is excellent. Likewise, the delectable breast of goose is perfectly offset by a slightly tart bilberry sauce. Wine is also served by the glass.

MARINA DI BIBBONA La Pineta €€€€

27 Via dei Cavalleggeri Nord, Marina di Bibbona, 57020 ***Tel*** *0586 60 00 16* ***Road map*** *C3*

La Pineta is not much more than a shack on the beach, but foodies swear this is the best place for seafood in southern Tuscany. Owner-chef Zazzeri is a former fisherman who still gets the daily catch from the family's boats. There is a cookbook, so you can take the magic home. Great service and wine list.

MASSA MARITTIMA Da Tronca €€

Vicolo Porte 5, 58024 ***Tel*** *0566 90 19 91* ***Road map*** *C4*

Da Tronca has a rustic ambience befitting the well-cooked, simple fare. The *zuppa dell'osteria* (kale and cannellini beans on garlic-rubbed bread drizzled with oil) is delicious. There's also a good chickpea soup, served hot. Otherwise try the tripe, or the rabbit baked with potatoes. Good local wine list.

MASSA MARITTIMA Taverna Vecchio Borgo €€

Via Norma Parenti 12, 58024 ***Tel*** *0566 90 39 50* ***Road map*** *C4*

Ancient barrel-vaulted rooms with an enticingly well-stocked wine cellar. The menu usually features pasta stuffed with ricotta and dressed with a sauce of nuts and herbs as well as *acquacotta* bread soup. The wild boar cooked with olives and the pheasant breast done in Vin Santo are also recommended.

MASSA MARITTIMA Bracali €€€€€

Via di Perolla 2, Località Ghirlanda, 58020 ***Tel*** *0566 90 23 18* ***Road map*** *C4*

If you drive a small distance north out of Massa Marittima, you will come across this attractive family-run restaurant, where local culinary traditions are revisited with flair. The aubergine flan, served with a potato and anchovy sauce, is a case in point; likewise the hare cooked with fennel and juniper.

ORBETELLO I Pescatori €

Via Leopardi 9, Orbetello, 58015 ***Tel*** *0564 86 06 11* ***Road map*** *D5*

This simple place run by the local fishermen's cooperative serves only fish caught in the lagoon on which it is located. Order and pay at entry, take a seat and await the fresh fish and seafood which can be washed down with local wines. Specialities include smoked eel and fillet of grey mullet.

ORBETELLO Osteria del Lupacante €€€

Corso Italia 103, 58015 ***Tel*** *0564 86 76 18* ***Road map*** *D5*

This pleasant osteria sticks to old ways in a place increasingly overrun by affluent out-of-towners. Based on seafood, the cooking is light in touch and quite adventurous. The *zuppa di pesce* (fish soup) is excellent. The risotto with prawns and pine nuts and the sole with almonds and onions are also good.

PITIGLIANO Il Tufo Allegro €€€€

Vicolo della Costituzione 5, 58017 ***Tel*** *0564 61 61 92* ***Road map*** *E5*

This little restaurant features local Maremma cuisine with a subtle difference. There are *pappardelle* with a lamb ragout, and lasagne with artichokes, mature cheese and rabbit ragout. The saddle of rabbit with wild fennel is excellent, as is the courgette and goat's cheese flan.

PORTO SANTO STEFANO I Due Pini €€€€

Località la Soda, Porto Santo Stefano, Monte Argentario, 58019 ***Tel*** *0564 81 40 12* ***Road map*** *D5*

Try this restaurant for its beautiful beachside setting and some of the best seafood on the coast. Have a simple meal of fish fresh from the boats, grilled to perfection, or try the *spaghetti al nero di seppia* (black squid ink pasta) followed by *spezzatino di pesce spada* (swordfish stew). There's live music at night, with the sunset as backdrop.

SATURNIA Bacco e Cerere €€€

Via Mazzini 4, 58050 ***Tel*** *0564 60 12 35* ***Road map*** *D5*

The wide range of antipasti at this small, friendly place is a great introduction to the traditional Maremma cuisine. The *zuppa di ricotta* makes a delectable change from the traditional *acquacotta* (vegetable soup served over toast). The *enoteca* of the same name offers an interesting range of wines. Occasional live music in summer. Closed Wed.

Light Meals and Snacks in Florence

The traditional pavement café is not as much a part of local life in Florence as in other Italian cities. However, small, hole-in-the-wall bars can be found on most of the city's streets. Here, you can have alcoholic and soft drinks, as well as a range of tempting breakfast and lunch-time snacks. Old-fashioned wine bars provide alternative eating and drinking venues, and the city has plenty of take-away establishments, especially near Santa Maria Novella station, if you want to eat on the move.

Sitting down at a bar or café can be expensive, as there is a charge for taking a table. If you only want a quick snack, it may be cheaper to eat at the stand-up counter. It is also worth noting that some cafés and bars may close during August.

BARS

Locals generally use bars as stop-offs for a coffee, quick snack, an early morning apéritif, to make a phone call or to use the toilet *(il bagno)*. Some bars may stay open late, particularly during the summer, but most are busiest during the day. Most of them have a stand-up counter rather than tables.

Some bars also double as a pastry shop *(pasticceria)* and virtually all serve filled rolls *(panini)* or sandwiches *(tramezzini)* for lunch.

Breakfast is usually *un caffè* (a short espresso) or *un cappuccino* (milky coffee) with a plain jam or custard-filled croissant *(una brioche or un cornetto)*.

The cheapest way to buy beer at a bar is from the keg *(una birra alla spina)* either as a *piccola, media* or *grande* measure. Italian bottled beers such as Peroni are also reasonably priced but foreign beers are expensive. Other drinks available are freshly squeezed fruit juice *(una spremuta)*, grappa and wine by the glass *(un bicchiere di vino)*.

Once you have chosen what to eat or drink, you must first pay at the cash desk *(la cassa)*, and then take your receipt *(lo scontrino)* to the bar, where you will be served. A small tip on the counter will usually ensure quicker service.

There are numerous bars dotted around Florence, and many are convenient for the sights. For example, **Il Caffè** is opposite the Palazzo Pitti.

WINE CELLARS

Though wine cellars of the rustic style *(vinaii* or *fiaschetterie)* are a dying breed, they are quickly being replaced by modern, upscale versions, where you can sample from a wide range of Tuscan and Italian wines, accompanied by *antipasti*, often featuring local salamis, cheeses, and a variety of *crostini* and other light snacks.

CAFES

Four of Florence's handful of old-world cafés stand around the dour perimeter of Piazza della Repubblica. **Gilli**, renowned for its cocktails, dates back to 1733. It has two rear panelled rooms still redolent of an earlier age. **Giubbe Rosse**, once the haunt of the city's turn-of-the century literati, also evokes its former glory with dazzling chandeliers. However, like the neighbouring cafés, it is overpriced and likely to be filled with wealthy foreigners rather than elegant Florentines. Instead, locals head for the **Rivoire**, also expensive, but with more genuine class and a beautiful marble interior. Bars which offer Manaresi, a locally roasted coffee, are usually worth a stop. This coffee is considered by many to be the best in Italy.

The young and fashionable hang out at **Noir**, an elegant bar/bistro along the river, or at **Procacci**, justly renowned for its delicious truffle rolls *(tartufati)*.

TAKE-AWAY FOOD

Traditional street food includes tripe and *lampredotto* (pig's intestines) sandwiches, sold from the stalls at the Mercato Centrale *(see p88)*, around the Mercato Nuovo *(see p112)*, as well as in the Piazza dei Cimatori. The Mercato Centrale is a great place to buy picnic provisions if you are planning a day's excursion out of the city.

In the same areas there are often vans selling *porchetta*, crispy slices of suckling pig in bread rolls. Small shops selling pizza by weight or slice *(al taglio)* are found all over the city, especially around Santa Maria Novella station.

As well as bread, bakeries sell *schiacciata*, a focaccia sold plain, with oil and salt, or with herbs and spices. Bars offer other take-away options including *panini, tramezzini* and ice cream. Some *vinaii*, notably in Via dei Cimatori and Piazza dell'Olio, serve *crostini* and sandwiches to eat out on the pavement.

Snack bars, such as **Gastronomia Vera**, selling burgers, chips and flavoured milk shakes, are becoming increasingly popular.

ICE-CREAM PARLOURS

Florentines often round off a meal or the evening *passeggiata* (walk) with an ice cream *(gelato)*. No day in the city is complete without one visit to an ice-cream parlour *(gelateria)*. You can choose between a cone *(un cono)* and a cup *(una coppa)* and pay by size, usually starting at €1 and working up in 50-cent stages to enormous multi-scoop offerings at €5.

It's best to avoid bars where the selection is limited and the ice cream is made off the premises. Make instead for **Bar Vivoli Gelateria** *(see p71)*, thought by many to make the best ice cream in Italy, or to **Badiani**, famed for its egg-rich *Buontalenti*. **Carabè** is well known for its Sicilian ice granitas, made with coffee or fruit.

DIRECTORY

CITY CENTRE EAST

Bars and Cafés

Caffè Caruso
Via Lambertesca 14–16r.
Map 6 D4.

Chiaroscuro
Via del Corso 36r.
Map 4 D1.

Dolci Dolcezze
Piazza Cesare Beccaria 8r.
Map 4 F1.

Galleria degli Uffizi
Piazzale degli Uffizi 6.
Map 6 D4.

Red Garter
Via de' Benci 33.
Map 4 D1 (6 F4).

Rivoire
Piazza della Signoria 5.
Map 4 D1 (6 D3).

Robiglio
Via de' Tosinghi 11.
Map 6 D2.

Scudieri
Piazza di San Giovanni 19.
Map 1 C5 (6 D2).

Trattoria Santa Croce
Borgo Santa Croce 31r.
Map 4 D1 (6 F4).

Wine Cellars

Boccadama
Piazza Santa Croce 25–26r.
Map 4 E1 (6 F4).

Bottiglieria Torrini
Piazza dell'Olio, 15r.
Map 6 D2

Cantinetta del Verrazzano
Via dei Tavolini 18–20r.
Map 4 D1 (6 D3).

Enoteca Baldovino
Via San Giuseppe, 18r.
Map 4 E1.

Enoteca De' Giraldi
Via De' Giraldi 4r.
Map 4 D1 (6 E3).

Fiaschetteria Balducci
Via de' Neri 2r.
Map 4 D1 (6 E4).

Giovacchino
Via de' Tosinghi 34r.
Map 6 D2.

Vini del Chianti
Via dei Cimatori.
Map 4 D1 (6 D3).

Vini e Panini
Via dei Cimatori 38r.
Map 4 D1 (6 D3).

Take-Away Food

La Ghiotta
Via Pietrapiana 7r.
Map 4 E1.

Ice-Cream Parlours

Bar Vivoli Gelateria
Via Isola delle Stinche 7r.
Map 6 F3.

Gelateria de' Ciompi
Via dell'Agnolo 121r.
Map 4 E1.

Gelateria Veneta
Piazza Cesare Beccaria.
Map 4 F1.

Perchè No!
Via dei Tavolini 19r.
Map 4 D1 (6 D3).

CITY CENTRE NORTH

Bars and Cafés

Da Nerbone
Mercato Centrale.
Map 1 C4 (5C1).

Rex Café
Via Fiesolana 23–25r.
Map 2 E5.

Wine Cellars

Casa del Vino
Via del Ariento.
Map 1 C4.

Take-Away Food

Forno Pugi
Piazza San Marco 10.
Map 2 D4.

Lì Per Lì
Via XXVII Aprile 42r.
Map 2 D4.

Ice-Cream Parlours

Badiani
Via dei Mille 20.
Map 2 F2.

Carabè
Via Ricasoli 60r.
Map 2 D5.

Vestri
Borgo Albizi 11r.
Map 2 D5.

CITY CENTRE WEST

Bars and Cafés

Alimentari
Via Parione 12r.
Map 3 B1 (5 B3).

Caffè Amerini
Via della Vigna Nuova 61–63.
Map 3 B1 (5 B3).

Caffè Strozzi
Piazza degli Strozzi 16r.
Map 3 C1 (5 C3).

Caffè Voltaire
Via della Scala 9r.
Map 1 A4 (5 A1).

Donnini
Piazza della Repubblica 15r.
Map 1 C5 (6 D3).

Gilli
Piazza della Repubblica 39r.
Map 1 C5 (6 D3).

Giubbe Rosse
Piazza della Repubblica 13–14r.
Map 1 C5 (6 D3).

Il Barretto Piano Bar
Via Parione 50r.
Map 3 B1 (5 B3).

La Vigna
Via della Vigna Nuova 88.
Map 3 B1 (5 B3).

Noir
Lungarno Corsini 12r.
Map 3 B1 (5 B3).

Paszkowski
Piazza della Repubblica 6r.
Map 1 C5 (6 D3).

Procacci
Via de' Tornabuoni 64r.
Map 1 C5 (5 C2).

Rose's Bar
Via Parione 26r.
Map 3 B1 (5 B3).

Ice-Cream Parlours

Banchi
Via dei Banchi 14r.
Map 1 C5 (5 C2).

OLTRARNO

Bars and Cafés

Café Ricchi
Piazza di Santo Spirito 9r.
Map 3 B2 (5 A5).

Caffè La Torre
Lungarno Cellini 65r.
Map 4 F2.

Caffè Santa Trìnita
Via Maggio 2r.
Map 3 B2 (5 B5).

Caffeteria Henry
Via dei Renai 27a.
Map 4 D2 (6 E5).

Cennini
Borgo San Jacopo 51r.
Map 3 C1 (5 C4).

Dolce Vita
Piazza del Carmine.
Map 3 A1 (5 A4).

Gastronomia Vera
Piazza de' Frescobaldi 3r.
Map 3 B1 (5 B4).

Il Caffè
Piazza de' Pitti 11–12r.
Map 3 B2 (5 B5).

Il Rifrullo
Via di San Niccolò 55r.
Map 4 D2.

La Loggia
Piazzale Michelangelo 1.
Map 4 E3.

Marino
Piazza Nazario Sauro 19r.
Map 3 B1 (5 A3).

Pasticceria Maioli
Via de' Guicciardini 43r.
Map 3 C2 (5 C5).

Tiratoio
Piazza de' Nerli.
Map 3 A1.

Wine Cellars

Enoteca Fuoriporta
Via Monte alle Croci 10r.
Map 4 E3.

Le Volpi e l'Uva
Piazza de' Rossi 1r.
Map 5 C5.

Take-Away Food

Gastronomia Vera
Piazza de' Frescobaldi 3r.
Map 3 B1 (5 B4).

Ice-Cream Parlours

Fa Chi Sa
Via San Miniato 5r.
Map 4 E2.

Il Innocenti
Piazza Sauro 25r.
Map 3 B1 (5 A3).

SHOPS AND MARKETS

Shopping in Florence can be a unique experience as you wander through its ancient and medieval streets, exploring the city's renowned tradition of crafts and family-run businesses. Few cities of comparable size can boast such a profusion and variety of high-quality goods. Walking around the city you will find shops selling Italian fashion, antiques and jewellery as well as typical Florentine crafts. Tuscany is dwarfed by Florence when it comes to shopping possibilities. However, the rich traditions of many outlying towns and villages boast a variety of local crafts and specialities. These range from ceramics, hand-woven materials to the region's many gastronomic delicacies. *(See also pp30–31.)*

Protective bag with designer label

A colourful shop display of elegant handbags

WHEN TO SHOP

Generally, shops open around 9am and close at 1pm. In the afternoon they re-open from 3:30pm to 7:30pm, though food shops tend to open earlier in the morning and remain closed from 1pm to 5pm. Most shops are shut on Monday morning but food stores are closed on Wednesday afternoon.

Almost all shops close on Saturday afternoon in summer, and shops and markets tend to close for two or three weeks around 15 August, the national holiday *(ferragosto)*.

HOW TO PAY

Major credit cards are usually accepted in larger shops, but smaller ones prefer cash. Travellers' cheques are now rarely accepted for goods and services.

Shopkeepers and market stallholders should by law give you a receipt *(ricevuta fiscale)*. If a purchased item is defective, most shops will change the article or give you a credit note, as long as you show the till receipt. Cash refunds are uncommon.

VAT EXEMPTION

Visitors from non-EU countries can reclaim the 20 per cent sales tax (IVA) on purchases from the same shop exceeding €160. Ask for an invoice *(la fattura)* when you buy the goods and inform the shop of your intention to reclaim the tax. You will need to show your passport and the shop will fill out and stamp a form which can be taken to the relevant office at the airport.

SHOPPING IN FLORENCE

The centre of Florence is packed with shops selling everything from designer clothes to second-hand books. It is compact and easy to get around, as many streets are pedestrianized. It is also worth exploring the streets away from the centre around Piazza di Santa Croce, Piazza dei Ciompi and Piazza di Santo Spirito for furniture and gift shops where craftsmen are busy at work. The best time for bargains is during the January and July sales *(saldi)*.

Window shopping in the Via de' Tornabuoni, Florence

DEPARTMENT STORES

The city's main chain store is **Coin**, a popular independent department store with branches in Montecatini Terme and Livorno. This store stocks mid-range casual clothing, shoes, toiletries, children's clothing and toys, and a huge range of fashion accessories, including hosiery, sunglasses, bags and scarves. It also has an extensive home collection.

Rinascente in Piazza della Repubblica has designer clothing, lingerie, household items and a rooftop bar with direct views of the Duomo. **Principe** has classic menswear and women's and children's clothes as well as upmarket home accessories.

CLOTHING

In Florence the big names in Italian fashion – **Gucci**, **Armani**, **Ferragamo**, **Versace**, **Prada** and **Roberto Cavalli** – are mostly found in Via de' Tornabuoni *(see p105)*. This elegant street is also home to the French designer **Yves Saint Laurent** and, at the top of the street in Piazza Antinori, is **Hermès**. Opposite the imposing Palazzo Strozzi is **Louis Vuitton**, with its impressive collections of footwear, clothing and luggage; **Dolce & Gabbana** is in Via degli Strozzi nearby and **Valentino** is in Via dei Tosinghi.

On Via della Vigna Nuova *(see p105)*, you willl find affordable fashions at **Mariella**

Burani and designer underwear at **La Perla**, while younger styles can be found at **Gioel** and **Intimissimi**.

Luisa Via Roma and **Raspini** stock top-designer clothing and shoes, while **Eredi Chiarini** and **Matucci** have more casual styles. **Emilio Pucci** *(see p88)*, famous for his extravagant 1960s print clothes is in Via de' Tornabuoni.

There are opulent hand-woven fabrics, fine silks and vintage fabrics at **Casa dei Tessuti**, and embroidered linen can be found at **Taf**. Those looking for discounts on Italian designer clothing and shoes should venture out to **The Mall** or **Barberino Designer Outlet**. Both these outlets are located approximately 30 minutes away from Florence so require a special trip.

Classic leather goods at Beltrami

SHOES

Italy is renowned worldwide for its shoes and, with the local Tuscan tanneries, there is nowhere better than Florence to find footwear for all tastes. Some shops design and make classic shoes by hand in-store, while others stock huge collections of new styles for each season.

At the top end, the refined finishing and elegance of **Ferragamo's** shoes are sought-after by Hollywood stars, and **Gucci** and **Prada** are both meccas for admirers of designer Italian shoes. If you prefer more classic styles then head across the Arno to **Francesco**, a tiny shop that sells simple handmade shoes and sandals, or **Quercioli** for high quality hand-stitched leather shoes for both men and women. The mid-priced range is well represented by **Romano**, which stocks collections of shoes and boots in good-quality leather. For more casual and sporty styles, try the reasonably-priced **Peluso**. Alternatively stroll down Via de' Cerretani, which houses many affordable shoe shops including the popular **Divarese**.

Trendy sandals at Ferragamo

LEATHER GOODS

Piazza di Santa Croce *(see pp72–3)* and the adjoining streets are filled with leather shops and workshops. Inside the cloisters of the church itself is the **Scuola del Cuoio**, where leather craftsmen work in front of the customers. Classic leather bags and gifts are sold at **Bojola**, **Il Bisonte** and **Beltrami**, and more contemporary styles can be found at **Coccinelle** and **Furla**. **Peruzzi** stocks leather clothing and accessories for men and women. The best place to buy gloves is **Madova**. For good value bags, belts and leather jackets try the **Mercato di San Lorenzo** or the market stalls in Via Pellicceria *(see p287)*.

TOILETRIES

For toiletries and beauty products head to a *profumeria* (perfumery), such as **Aline**, **Profumeria Inglese** or **Le Vanita'**, which also has a beauty centre and solarium. *Erboristerie* (herbalists) sell a range of natural products. Try the **Erboristeria di Palazzo Vecchio** *(see p75)* for unique handmade perfumes. The **Erboristeria Inglese** on Via de' Tornabuoni dispenses natural remedies and tisanes, and stocks natural beauty products, perfumes and gifts. Also worth a visit is the **Farmacia di Santa Maria Novella**, a frescoed apothecary, selling products from the elixirs of the Camaldoli monks to perfumes, herbal remedies and sweets.

JEWELLERY

Florence has always been noted for its gold and sliver-smiths. Go to **Torrini**, whose family has produced jewellery for six centuries, and to **Pommellato's** stunning shop on Via de' Tornabuoni, for its famous chunky white gold rings with huge semi-precious gems. **Bulgari** is on the same street, and so is **Parenti**, which has beautiful Baccarat rings and unique antique jewels. Try **Aprosio & Co**. for decorative jewellery made from precious metals and tiny glass stones.

The tiny wooden shops on the Ponte Vecchio *(see pp106-7)* are all jewellery shops, some with beautiful antiques from Italy and abroad, others with high-quality new Italian gold pieces.

A vibrant array of fabrics in Casa dei Tessuti, Florence

Typical antiques shop in Florence

ART AND ANTIQUES

Florence has always been a centre of artistic excellence. This heritage has translated into a wealth of antiques and fine art shops. The antiques shops are mostly clustered around Via dei Fossi *(see pp112-3)*, Via Maggio *(see p118)* and Via dei Serragli.

For top-quality antiques go to **Neri** or the nearby **Cei**. **Romanelli** has bronze statuary and works encrusted in semi-precious stones, while **Ducci** has an exquisite selection of handmade boxes, prints and sculpture in marble and wood. For lovers of modern art, there is **Galleria Tornabuoni**, while modern art objects and gifts can be found at **Armando Poggi**. **Ugo Poggi** has a selection of household objects, including elegant porcelain.

Ugolini and **Mosaico di Pitti** create tables and framed pictures using the age-old technique of marble inlay. **Arredamenti Castorina** has a wonderful selection of picture frames, mouldings, brassware and intricate intarsias. More contemporary styles are at **Mirabili**, which showcases furniture and interior designers.

GIFTS

Florence is a treasure trove for unusual gifts and souvenirs. Via de' Guicciardini and the area between Piazza di Santa Croce and Piazza della Signoria are good places to look for gifts.

Housed in a converted wine cellar, **Signum** has postcards, posters and prints, and items such as miniature shop models and tiny packs of cards. **Mandragora** in Piazza del Duomo has a wide choice of gifts based on famous artworks in the city, while the renowned **Pineider** has upmarket stationery and office gifts in leather, linen and paper.

For locally made terracotta and decorative glazed ceramics visit **Sbigoli Terracotte**. **La Bottega dei Cristalli** has Murano glass kitchenware, chandeliers and decorative objects. **Passamaneria Valmar** sells decorative key and curtain tassels, tapestries and soft furnishings in silks and wools, while **Lisa Corti Home Textile Emporium** has hand-printed cotton throws, bedcovers and cushions as well as a range of children's clothes and pottery.

BOOKS AND PAPER

The main bookshops in Florence are **Feltrinelli International**, which sells publications in various languages, and **Edison**, which stocks magazines, maps, books in English as well as coffee-table photography books, and also houses a café. **Paperback Exchange** has an extremely wide selection of new and second-hand books in English.

Typical Florentine crafts include bookbinding and handmade marbled paper, which is used to decorate a variety of gift objects. These are easily available at **Giulio Giannini**, **Il Papiro** and **Il Torchio**; it's worth going to the latter just to see bookbinding in action, as you can wach it being done on the balcony workshop.

Feltrinelli International bookshop

FOOD AND WINE

Those shopping for food should go to **Pegna**, a mini-supermarket in the heart of Florence that stocks fresh, as well as vast selection of gourmet, foods. The **Bottega dell'Olio** has shelves of extra virgin Tuscan olive oils, spice-flavoured oils and gifts. For typically British items such as teas and speciality foods go to **Old England Stores**.

Dolceforte sells chocolate souvenirs in the shape of the Duomo and the statue of David. A huge selection of biscuits and chocolates fills the front half of **Alessi**, while at the back and in the cellar are fine wines, spirits and liqueurs. Another good place to buy wine is **Zanobini**,

Fresh vegetables at a Florentine market stall

where you can mix with the locals and sample the wines. At **Procacci** in Via de' Tornabuoni, shoppers can stop for a glass of wine and a canapé while choosing between pots of black or white truffles and other delicacies to take away.

FLORENCE'S MARKETS

Florence's central street market is the **Mercato di San Lorenzo**, which caters mostly for tourists *(see p88)*. Nearby, in Via dell'Ariento, is the covered **Mercato Centrale**, the city's main food market *(see p88)*. The **Mercato di Sant'Ambrogio** also has fresh fruit and vegetable stalls, as well as clothing and household goods. Beneath the 16th-century Loggia del Porcellino, is the **Mercato Nuovo**, or Straw Market, which sells leather goods and souvenirs *(see p112)*. On Tuesday mornings, there is an enormous market at the **Parco delle Cascine** with cheap clothing, shoes and food. The **Mercato delle Pulci** is a flea market, selling antiques and bric-à-brac. Garden enthusiasts might want to check out the **Mercato delle Piante** held on Thursday mornings under the porticoes of Via Pellicceria, selling flowers, houseplants and herbs.

Occasional markets spring up in Piazza Santa Croce and Piazza Santa Maria Novella, notably the German gift market in the weeks before Christmas and the monthly antiques market in **Piazza Santo Spirito**.

DIRECTORY

DEPARTMENT STORES

Coin
Via dei Calzaiuoli 56r.
Map 6 D3.
Tel *055 28 05 31.*

Principe
Via delle Belle Donne 1/9r–15r.
Map 1 C5 (5 C2).
Tel *055 29 27 64.*

Rinascente
Piazza della Repubblica 1.
Map 1 C5 (6 D3).
Tel *055 21 91 13.*

CLOTHING

Armani
Via de' Tornabuoni 48/50r.
Map 1 C5 (5 C2).
Tel *055 21 90 41.*

Barberino Designer Outlet
A1 Firenze–Bologna, exit Barberino di Mugello.
Map 2D.
Tel *055 58 42 16.*

Casa dei Tessuti
Via de' Pecori 20–24r.
Map 1 C5 (6 D2).
Tel *055 21 59 61.*

Dolce & Gabbana
Via degli Strozzi 12–18r.
Map 1 C5 (5 C3).
Tel *055 28 10 03.*

Emilio Pucci
Via de' Tornabuoni 22r.
Map 1 C5 (5 C3).
Tel *055 265 80 82.*

Eredi Chiarini
Via Roma 16r.
Map 3 C1 (6 D2).
Tel *055 28 44 78.*

Ferragamo
Via de' Tornabuoni 14r.
Map 1 C5 (5 C2).
Tel *055 29 21 23.*

Gioel
Via Porta Rossa 43r.
Map 3 C1 (6 D3).
Tel *055 28 79 19.*

Gucci
Via de' Tornabuoni 73r.
Map 1 C5 (5 C2).
Tel *055 26 40 11.*

Hermès
Piazza Antinori 6r.
Map 1 C5 (5 C2).
Tel *055 238 10 04.*

Intimissimi
Via dei Calzaiuoli 99r.
Map 3 C1 (6 D3).
Tel *055 230 26 09.*

Louis Vuitton
Piazza degli Strozzi 1.
Map 3 C1.
Tel *055 26 69 81.*

Luisa Via Roma
Via Roma 19r-21r.
Map 3 C1 (6 D2).
Tel *055 21 78 26.*

The Mall
Via Europa 8, Leccio Reggello.
Tel *055 865 77 75.*

Mariella Burani
Via della Vigna Nuova 32r
Map 3 B1 (5 B3).
Tel *055 21 30 14.*

Matucci
Via del Corso 71r.
Map 3 C1 (6 D3).
Tel *055 239 64 20.*

La Perla
Via della Vigna Nuova 17-19.
Map 3 B1 (5 B3).
Tel *055 21 70 70.*

Prada
Via de' Tornabuoni 67r.
Map 1 C5 (5 C2).
Tel *055 28 34 39.*

Raspini
Via Roma 25r-29r.
Map 3 C1 (6 D2).
Tel *055 21 30 77.*

Roberto Cavalli
Via de' Tornabuoni 83r.
Map 1 C5 (5 C3).
Tel *055 239 62 26.*

Taf
Via Por Santa Maria 17r.
Map 3 C1 (6 D4).
Tel *055 239 60 37.*

Valentino
Via dei Tosinghi 52r.
Map 1 C5 (6 D2).
Tel *055 29 31 42.*

Versace
Via de' Tornabuoni 13-15r.
Map 1 C5 (5 C2).
Tel *055 28 26 38.*

Yves Saint Laurent
Via de' Tornabuoni 29r.
Map 1 C5 (5 C2).
Tel *055 28 40 40.*

SHOES

Divarese
Piazza del Duomo 47r.
Map 3 C1 (6 D2).
Tel *055 230 28 95.*

Francesco
Via di Santo Spirito 62r.
Map 3 B1 (5 A4).
Tel *055 21 24 28.*

Peluso
Via del Corso 5-6r.
Map 3 C1 (6 D3).
Tel *055 26 82 83.*

Quercioli
Via Calzaiuoli 18/20r.
Map 3 C1 (6 D2).
Tel *055 21 39 41.*

Romano
Via Porta Rossa 14r.
Map 1 C5 (5 C3).
Tel *055 28 96 88.*

LEATHER GOODS

Beltrami
Via della Vigna Nuova 70r.
Map 1 C5 (5 C2).
Tel *055 28 77 79.*

Il Bisonte
Via del Parione 31r.
Map 3 C1 (5 C3).
Tel *055 21 57 22.*

Bojola
Via de' Rondinelli 25r.
Map 1 C5 (5 C2).
Tel *055 21 11 55.*

Coccinelle
Via Por S. Maria 49r
Map 3 C1 (6 D4).
Tel *055 239 87 82.*

Furla
Via de' Calzaiuoli 47r
Map 3 C1 (6 D3).
Tel *055 238 28 83.*

Madova
Via dei Giucciardini 1r.
Map 3 C2 (5 C4).
Tel *055 239 65 26.*

Peruzzi
Borgo de' Greci 8–20r.
Map 4 D1 (6 E4).
Tel *055 28 90 39.*

Scuola del Cuoio
Piazza di Santa Croce 16.
Map 4 E1 (6 F4).
Tel *055 24 45 33.*

DIRECTORY

TOILETRIES

Aline
Via dei Calzaiuoli 53r.
Map 3 C1 (6 D3).
Tel *055 21 54 36.*

Erboristeria Inglese
Via de' Tornabuoni 19.
Map 1 C5 (5 C2).
Tel *055 21 06 28.*

Erboristeria di Palazzo Vecchio
Via Vacchereccia 9r.
Map 3 C1 (6 D3).
Tel *055 239 60 55.*

Farmacia di Santa Maria Novella
Via della Scala 16.
Map 1 A4 (5 A1).
Tel *055 21 62 76.*

Profumeria Inglese
Piazza dell'Olio 4.
Map 3 C1 (6 D2).
Tel *055 260 88 01.*

Le Vanità
Via Porta Rossa 55r.
Map 1 C5 (5 C3).
Tel *055 29 01 67.*

JEWELLERY

Aprosio & Co.
Via di Santo Spirito 11.
Map 3 B1 (5 B4).
Tel *055 29 05 34*

Bulgari
Via de' Tornabuoni 61r.
Map 1 C5 (5 C3).
Tel *055 239 67 86.*

Parenti
Via de' Tornabuoni 93r.
Map 1 C5 (5 C2).
Tel *055 21 44 38.*

Pommellato
Via de' Tornabuoni 89r–91r.
Map 1 C5 (5 C2).
Tel *055 28 85 30.*

Torrini
Piazza del Duomo 10r.
Map 2 D5 (6 D2).
Tel *055 230 24 01.*

ART AND ANTIQUES

Armando Poggi
Via dei Calzaiuoli 103–116r. **Map** 6 D3.
Tel *055 21 17 19.*

Arredamenti Castorina
Via di Santo Spirito 15r.
Map 3 B1 (5 A4).
Tel *055 21 28 85.*

Cei
Via dei Fossi 17.
Map 1 B5 (5 B3).
Tel *055 239 60 39.*

Ducci
Lungarno Corsini 24r.
Map 3 B1 (5 B3).
Tel *055 21 91 37.*

Galleria Tornabuoni
Borgo San Jacopo 53r.
Map 3 C1 (5 C4).
Tel *055 28 47 20.*

Mirabili
Lungarno Giucciardini 24r.
Map 3 B1 (5 A4).
Tel *055 294 257.*

Mosaico di Pitti
Piazza de' Pitti 23r.
Map 3 B2 (5 B5).
Tel *055 28 21 27.*

Neri
Via dei Fossi 55–57r.
Map 1 B5 (5 B3).
Tel *055 29 21 36.*

Romanelli
Lungarno degli Acciaiuoli 74r. **Map** 3 C1 (5 C4).
Tel *055 239 66 62.*

Ugo Poggi
Via degli Strozzi 26r.
Map 1 C5 (5 C3).
Tel *055 21 67 41.*

Ugolini
Lungarno degli Acciaiuoli 66–70r.
Map 3 C1 (5 C4).
Tel *055 28 49 69.*

GIFTS

La Bottega dei Cristalli
Via dei Benci 51r
Map 4 D1 (6 F4).
Tel *055 234 48 91.*

Lisa Corti Home Textile Emporium
Piazza Ghiberti 33r.
Map 4 F1.
Tel *055 200 18 60.*

Mandragora
Piazza del Duomo 9.
Map 2 D5 (6 D2).
Tel *055 29 25 59.*

Passamaneria Valmar
Via Porta Rossa 53r.
Map 1 C5 (5 C3).
Tel *055 28 44 93.*

Pineider
Piazza della Signoria 13r.
Map 4 D1 (6 D3).
Tel *055 28 46 55.*

Sbigoli Terracotte
Via Sant'Egidio 4r.
Map 6 F2.
Tel *055 247 97 13.*

Signum
Borgo dei Greci 40r.
Map 3 C1 (6 E4).
Tel *055 28 06 21.*

BOOKS AND PAPER

Edison
Piazza della Repubblica 27r.
Map 1 C5 (6 D3).
Tel *055 21 31 10.*

Feltrinelli International
Via Cavour 12–20r.
Map 2 D4.
Tel *055 21 95 24.*

Giulio Giannini
Piazza de' Pitti 37r.
Map 3 B2 (5 B5).
Tel *055 21 26 21.*

Paperback Exchange
Via delle Oche 4r.
Map 2 D5 (6 E2).
Tel *055 29 34 60.*

Il Papiro
Piazza del Duomo 24r.
Map 2 D5 (6 D4).
Tel *055 28 16 28.*

Il Torchio
Via de' Bardi 17.
Map 3 C2 (6 D5) (6 D4). ***Tel*** *055 234 28 62.*

FOOD AND WINE

Alessi
Via delle Oche 27r.
Map 3 C1 (6 D2).
Tel *055 21 49 66.*

Bottega dell'Olio
Piazza del Limbo 2r.
Map 3 C1 (5 C4).
Tel *055 267 04 68.*

Dolceforte
Via della Scala 21.
Map 1 B5 (5 B2).
Tel *055 21 91 16.*

Old England Stores
Via de' Vecchietti 28r.
Map 1 C5 (5 C2).
Tel *055 21 19 83.*

Pegna
Via dello Studio 26r.
Map 6 E2.
Tel *055 28 27 01.*

Procacci
Via de' Tornabuoni 64r.
Map 1 C5 (5 C2).
Tel *055 21 16 56.*

Zanobini
Via Sant'Antonino 47r.
Map 1 C5 (5 C1).
Tel *055 239 68 50.*

FLORENCE'S MARKETS

Mercato Centrale
Via dell' Ariento 10–14
Map 1 C4 (5 C1).

Mercato Nuovo
See p112.
Map 3 C1 (6 D3).
Open 9am–7pm daily (Nov–Mar: Tue–Sat).

Mercato delle Piante
Via Pellicceria.
Map 6 D3.
Open Thu am.

Mercato delle Pulci
Piazza dei Ciompi.
Map 4 E1.
Open 9am–7:30pm daily (Nov–Mar: Tue–Sun).

Mercato di San Lorenzo
Piazza di San Lorenzo.
Map 1 C5 (6 D1).
Open 9am–7:30pm (closed Mon in winter).

Mercato di Sant'Ambrogio
Piazza Sant'Ambriogio.
Map 4 F1.
Open 7am–2pm Mon–Sat.

Parco delle Cascine
Piazza Vittorio Veneto.
Open 8am–2pm Tue.

Piazza Santo Spirito
Map 3 B2 (5 B5).
Open 8am–12:30pm Mon–Fri. Antiques market 2nd Sun of month.

Shopping in Tuscany

Small towns throughout Tuscany have a multitude of shops selling a range of handicrafts, foods and some of the best wine in Italy. These are invariably displayed in small shops or at the frequent markets, seasonal fairs and local celebrations *(see pp34–9)*, which are such an integral part of Tuscan rural life.

Display of local pottery

GIFTS AND SOUVENIRS

Characteristic ceramics are found throughout the region, from the famed raw terracotta of Impruneta to the decorated glazed pottery of Montelupo and Siena. In San Gimignano, look out for shops selling artistic ceramics *(see p30)* and hand-woven fabrics.

The best in marble can be found in Pietrasanta and Carrara *(see p172)*. The famous white marble of the Alpi Apuane still serves local craftsmen, who make busts and replicas of sculpted works of art, as in Michelangelo's day.

The Etruscans mastered the art of working alabaster, and today the tradition lives on in Volterra, where many shops sell a range of souvenirs *(see p166)*. The Etruscans also had knowledge of the minerals and precious stones typical of the volcanic Colline Metallifere, Maremma and Elba, the latter famous for its quartz and opals *(see pp234–5)*.

For textiles, Lucca lays claim to a rich tradition of silk manufacture, as well as embroidery and hand-woven fabrics, reflecting the strong rural craft tradition of the nearby Garfagnana area. Rustic crafts are common in the Mugello and Casentino.

FOOD AND WINE

Excursions into Tuscany should be accompanied by visits to a local vineyard where wine is sold directly from the cellars. The Chianti region is studded with farms producing their own wines *(see p229)*. Greve has several good wine outlets, and during the third week of September there is the annual wine festival, the Rassegna del Chianti Classico *(see p38)*.

The excellent Vernaccia, a white wine, is typical of the San Gimignano area. The vineyards around Montalcino produce some of the best wine in Italy *(see p224)*.

Tuscany's rich gastronomic tradition is reflected in the profusion of local products. The main streets of towns such as Greve, Montalcino, San Gimignano and Pienza have a range of food shops.

Sheep's cheese *(pecorino)*, produced around the area of Crete, can be bought directly from the farm or from shops in local towns. In Pienza, shop shelves are laden with local cheeses *(see p226)*, cured meats, wines and grappas. In Grosseto you will find truffles.

A Tuscan delicatessen

Siena is renowned for its *panforte*, a dark cake spiced with cloves and cinnamon, which has been produced since the Middle Ages. Biscuits include *cavallucci* (ground walnuts and aniseed) and *ricciarelli*, made from almonds, orange peel and honey.

MARKETS IN TUSCANY

Markets are aplenty throughout the region. Particularly famous is the Mercato dell'Antiquariato, which sells goods from antique furniture to bric-à-brac. It takes place in Arezzo on the Piazza Grande on the first weekend of each month, in Pisa on the Ponte di Mezzo on the second weekend, and in Lucca in Piazza San Martino on the third weekend.

The Mercato dell'Antiquariato on the Piazza Grande in Arezzo

ENTERTAINMENT

There is plenty going on in Florence and Tuscany by way of entertainment throughout the year. The warm summer months see a concentration of events from traditional festivals, classical concerts and dance performances to open-air films and live music in alfresco bars. The areas of Santo Spirito in the Oltrarno and Santa Croce are home to lively bars and restaurants, while clubs tend to be situated on the edge of town. Opera lovers will not be disappointed; Florence's Teatro del Maggio, one of Italy's best, hosts some fine operas and concerts, while Tuscany plays host to the celebrated Puccini Opera Festival.

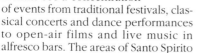

Puccini Opera Festival poster

PRACTICAL INFORMATION

Local newspapers, such as *La Nazione* and the Florence section of *La Repubblica*, carry entertainment listings. The monthly magazine *Firenze Spettacolo*, with a short section in English, lists local events, entertainment venues and places to eat and drink. Look out too for the free, bi-lingual, *Concierge Information*, which is a useful source of listings, and the twice-weekly English newspaper *The Florentine*. Websites detailing events in the region include www.firenze.net, www.comune.firenze.it, and www.turismo.toscana.it.

BOOKING TICKETS

Box Office is a ticket agency for concerts, opera and ballet nationwide. Tickets for performances at the **Teatro del Maggio** can also be purchased at their box office and online. It is advisable to buy tickets for opera in advance, but for other events, tickets are generally available on the door.

FACILITIES FOR THE DISABLED

Most major concert halls and music venues in Tuscany are now fully wheelchair accessible. However, churches, villas and gardens, which hold occasional performances, are unlikely to be so well equipped. If in doubt, always check in advance. There is a booklet published by the Province of Florence available at tourist offices, which details the accessibility of many outdoor venues in the area.

OPERA AND CLASSICAL MUSIC

The most important musical event in Tuscany is the annual Maggio Musicale festival *(see p32)*, held at **Teatro del Maggio** in Florence between late April and late June, and features opera, concerts and ballet. The theatre also puts on a year-round programme, while Orchestra della Toscana gives several concerts a month at its base in **Teatro Verdi**. From October to April the wonderful 18th-century **Teatro della Pergola** in Florence hosts world-class chamber music concerts. **Estate Fiesolana** organizes opera, dance and music events from July to August in Fiesole's atmospheric amphitheatre.

The rest of Tuscany also celebrates the arts. Puccini's lakeside villa on the shores of Lago di Massaciuccoli makes a spectacular setting for the **Puccini Opera Festival**, held every July to August. The Opera Barga festival showcases little-known works in the restored **Teatro dei Differenti** *(see p174)*. In July and August, Siena hosts the **Estate Musicale Chigiana** in the magnificent abbeys of San Galgano, Monte Oliveto Maggiore and Sant' Antimo. The **Incontri in Terra di Siena** festival is known for its excellent chamber music, and the **Tuscan Sun Festival**, based in Cortona, has an exciting music and arts programme.

FILM, THEATRE AND DANCE

Films in English are shown three times a week at the **Odeon Original Sound** in Florence, and several other Tuscan towns now cater for the huge number of foreign visitors by screening English-language films.

Theatre has a long and distinguished history in Tuscany, but performances in

Fiesole's Roman amphitheatre is the setting for opera and dance events

Contemporary dance performance

English are rare, and as such, the genre attracts few non-Italian speaking visitors. However, Tuscany's 300 local theatres – many of them now restored – are worth a visit.

Dance is popular throughout the region and several festivals, including the Florence Dance Festival, feature classical and contemporary dance.

JAZZ, BLUES AND ROCK

Florence will not disappoint jazz fans. A great season of progressive jazz concerts, often featuring international names, is staged in the **Sala Vanni**, while several bars regularly hold live jazz sessions.

Big-name rock concerts are mostly held at the 7,000-seater **Nelson Mandela Forum** or at the city's football stadium. For smaller, more intimate venues go to clubs such as **Auditorium Flog**, **Tenax** or **Saschall**. *Firenze Spettacolo* has a detailed list of bars and clubs hosting live music.

In summer, Florence's piazzas and gardens become the venues for alfresco bars and live music. Summertime also sees open-air jazz and rock concerts taking place all over the region.

Blues fans should look out for **Pistoia Blues**, a mid-July weekend jamboree of open-air blues concerts, which attracts well-known names.

OPEN-AIR ENTERTAINMENT

Unique to Tuscany are the many traditional festivals celebrated through the year, the most famous being the Palio in Siena *(see p222)*. The others range from large events attended by thousands of spectators to tiny little village sagre. Commonly defined by food, drink and music, these events are a great way to see the Tuscans at play.

CHILDREN'S ENTERTAINMENT

While Florence and Tuscany are extremely child-friendly, child-orientated entertainment is lacking so parents need to be inventive. As far as museums are concerned, only the Museo dei Ragazzi in Palazzo Vecchio *(see pp78–9)* has a specific programme for children, but several other museums, such as Museo di Storia della Scienza *(see p74)* and Museo "La Specola" *(see p119)*, are fun too. For children below ten years, **Mondobimbo Inflatables Parterre** has bouncy castles and **Giardino di Boboli** is good for a run-around.

Outside Florence, there's a small zoo in Pistoia *(see p187)* and **Parco Preistorico**, with its gigantic model dinosaurs, is near Pisa. **Pinocchio Park** at Collodi *(see 183)*, is dedicated to one of Tuscany's most loved characters, and **Parco Giochi Cavallino Matto** is a huge funfair with plenty of rides to keep the kids amused.

DIRECTORY

OPERA AND CLASSICAL MUSIC

Box Office
Via Alamanni 39. **Map** 1 B4. *Tel 055 210 804.* **www**.boxol.it

Estate Fiesolana
Tel 055 597 83 08. **www**.estatefiesolana.it

Estate Musicale Chigiana
Via di Città 89, Chigiana. *Tel 057 722 091.* **www**.chigiana.it

Incontri in Terra di Siena
La Foce, Chianciano Terme. *Tel 057 869 101.* **www**.lafoce.com

Puccini Opera Festival
Torre del Lago. *Tel 0584 35 93 22.* **www**.puccinifestival.it

Teatro dei Differenti
Piazza Angelio 8, Barga. *Tel 0583 72 32 50.*

Teatro del Maggio
Corso Italia 16. **Map** 1 A5. **www**.maggio fiorentino.com

Teatro della Pergola
Via della Pergola 12–32. **Map** 2 E5. *Tel 055 226 43 16.* **www**.pergola. firenze.it

Teatro Verdi
Via Ghibellina 99. **Map** 4 D1. *Tel 055 21 23 20.* **www**.teatroverdifirenze.it

Tuscan Sun Festival
www.tuscansun festival.com

FILM, THEATRE AND DANCE

Florence Dance Festival
Borgo Stella 23r. **Map** 3 B1. *Tel 055 28 92 76.*

Odeon Original Sound
Piazza Strozzi. **Map** 5 C3. *Tel 055 21 40 68.*

JAZZ, BLUES AND ROCK

Auditorium Flog
Via Michele Mercati 24B. *Tel 055 48 71 45.*

Nelson Mandela Forum
Viale Malta 4. *Tel 055 678 841.*

Pistoia Blues
Tel 057 321 622. **www**.pistoiablues.com

Sala Vanni
Piazza del Carmine 14. **Map** 3 A1. *Tel 055 287 347.*

Saschall
Lungarno Aldo Moro 3. *Tel 055 650 41 12.*

Tenax
Via Pratese 46. *Tel 055 308 160.*

CHILDREN'S ENTERTAINMENT

Giardino di Boboli
Piazza de' Pitti. **Map** 3 B2. *Tel 055 29 48 83.*

Mondobimbo Inflatables Parterre
Piazza della Libertà. **Map** 2 E2. *Tel 055 553 29 46.*

Parco Giochi Cavallino Matto
Via Po 1, Marina di Castagneto Donoratico. *Tel 0565 74 57 20.*

Parco Preistorico
Via Cappuccini 20, Peccioli. *Tel 0587 63 60 30.*

Pinocchio Park
Collodi. *Tel 0572 42 93 42.* **www**.pinocchio.it

SPECIALIST HOLIDAYS AND OUTDOOR ACTIVITIES

Nowhere is the Italian motto for good living, *la dolce vita*, more in evidence than in Tuscany. Sitting outside a café in a Tuscan village you can glimpse original Renaissance art or take in the sight of well-tended olive groves and vineyards terraced into the steep hillsides. No wonder the gentle pace of an activity holiday here, which in many cases means painting the stunning countryside or sipping vintage wines, is so appealing. For those more interested in energetic pursuits the region has plenty of sporting activities on offer, from horse riding to water sports. For educational courses see p298.

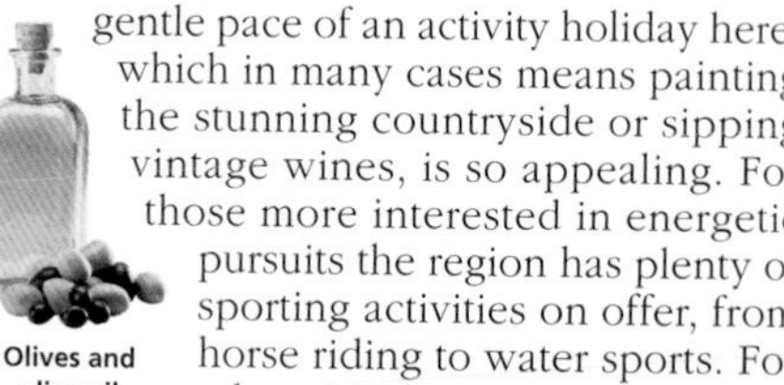

Olives and olive oil

ART

Those of an artistic persuasion can enrol at art school and try their hand at sculpture, art restoration or painting the beautiful countryside. **Centro d'Arte Verrocchio**, a residential art school in the hilltop village of Casole d'Elsa offers courses in drawing, painting and sculpture. Students can work on the terrace in stunning surroundings. For city-based courses try **Lorenzo de' Medici Art Institute of Florence**. The semester and summer school programmes include sketching, watercolour, fine art, painting, print-making, restoration and art history.

COOKERY AND WINE TASTING

Tuscany offers many gastronomic delights from pecorino cheese to porcini mushrooms. The regional cuisine values quality of ingredients rather than complex technique, and recipes are handed down from one generation to the next.

There are plenty of cookery courses where you can learn Italian food traditions – some of which are listed on **Nonna Lina's Kitchen** website.

Originally a medieval Benedictine abbey, **Badia a Coltibuono** *(see p229)* is a prestigious Chianti wine-producing estate. Courses on offer here range from brief wine and olive oil tastings, to five-day residential cookery courses with tours of the vineyards, olive mills and wine-making cellars at Monti in Chianti.

Apicius Culinary Institute in Florence is affiliated to Lorenzo de' Medici Art Institute. The duration of the cookery courses range from one-week to year-long diplomas.

La Cucina del Garga cookery school and restaurant, also in Florence, teaches recipes with a modern flourish. It holds one-day classes in the city and four to eight-day gastronomic excursions in Tuscany.

Vineyards offer wine tastings by appointment. **Chianti Classico** promotes stays at vineyards in the Chianti Classico region, while **Consorzio del Vino Brunello di Montalcino** has information on visits to the Brunello region. Specialist *enoteca* (wine bars) and shops, including **Millesimi** near Santa Spirito, also arrange wine tastings by appointment.

Students learning Italian recipies

Painting the beautiful Tuscan countryside

WALKING, CYCLING AND HORSE RIDING

Tuscany's scenery can be best enjoyed at walking pace. Several holiday companies offer walking itineraries, some through the landscape of forested hills and olive groves, while others wend their way through the medieval hilltop towns, taking in cultural landmarks along the way. **Ramblers Holidays** and **Sherpa Expeditions** are two such companies, and **Club Alpino Italiano** runs guided mountain treks.

Another great way to see the Tuscan countryside is by bike. For cycling holidays contact **Cicloposse**, which deals in both guided and self-guided bike tours.

The Maremma in southern Tuscany is famous for its wild horses and *butteri* (cowboys), and there are plenty of riding schools in the region. **Vallebona** in Pontassieve organizes trekking holidays and guided tours on horseback and **Rendola Riding Stables** at Montevarchi offers riding lessons.

SPA HOLIDAYS

Spa holidays are enjoying a renaissance with many hotels offering a pool, gym and massage treatments, but Tuscany has the real thing. Try the thermal pools at **Terme di Saturnia** in the Maremma, or bathe in the warm sulphurated waters of Cascate del Gorello *(see p238)* close by. You can purchase a day pass to experience the therapeutic waters of **Montecatini Terme** *(see pp184–5)*, with its nine spas. A vast array of health and beauty treatments is also available.

WATER SPORTS

Tourists on the Ponte Vecchio *(see pp106–7)* can watch canoes gliding through the inky waters of the River Arno. **Societa Canottieri Firenze** offers keen rowers visitor membership for a nominal sum.

In summer, many locals travel to the coast to escape the city heat. Those who can't head for one of the open air swimming pools. **Costoli** is open summer and winter, and **Piscina Bellariva** has indoor and outdoor pools.

For the more adventurous there is diving off the coast of Elba *(see pp234–5)* through **Spiro Sub Diving Club**.

MOUNTAIN SPORTS

Skiing in the Appennines is a possible day trip from Florence because, rather than being isolated in Alpine resorts, the slopes at **Abetone** near Pistoia are only 80 km (50 miles) away. Weekly as well as daily ski passes are available.

Ufficio Guides organise summer mountaineering courses, but single-minded climbers can go rock climbing independently at **Le Cave di Maiano** at Fiesole.

GOLF

Combine a few rounds of golf at **Ugolino Golf Course** with sightseeing in Florence, or enjoy a golfing holiday at **Punta Ala Golf Club** overlooking the coast, at Grosseto *(see p238)*, an hour from Pisa airport.

DIRECTORY

ART

Centro d'Arte Verrocchio
Casole d'Elsa.
www.verrocchio.co.uk

Lorenzo de' Medici Art Institute of Florence
Via dell'Alloro 17r.
Map 1 C5 (5 C1).
Tel *055 28 31 42.*

COOKERY AND WINE TASTING

Apicius Culinary Institute
Via Guelfa 85.
Map 1 C4.
Tel *055 265 81 35.*
www.apicius.it

Badia a Coltibuono
Gaiole in Chianti.
Tel *0577 74 48 32.*
www.coltibuono.com

Chianti Classico
Via Scopeti 155, San Casciano, Val di Pesa.
Tel *055 822 85.*
www.chianticlassico.com

Consorzio del Vino Brunello di Montalcino
Costa del Municipio 1, Montalcino.
Tel *0577 84 82 46.*
www.consorziobrunellodimontalcino.it

La Cucina del Garga
Via delle Belle Donne 3.
Map 1 C5 (5 C2).
Tel *055 21 13 96.*
www.garga.it

Millesimi
Borgo Tegolaio 35r.
Map 5 B5.
Tel *055 265 46 75.*
www.millesimi.it

Nonna Lina's Kitchen
www.nonnalinaskitchen.com

WALKING, CYCLING AND HORSE RIDING

Club Alpino Italiano
Via del Mezzetta 2.
Tel *055 612 04 67.*
www.caifirenze.it

Cicloposse
Via I Maggio 27, Pienza.
Tel *0578 749 983.*
www.cicloposse.com

Ramblers Holidays
Tel *01707 33 11 33.*
www.ramblersholidays.co.uk

Rendola Riding Stables
Montevarchi.
Tel *055 970 70 45.*
www.rendolariding.freeweb.org

Sherpa Expeditions
Tel *020 857 7 27 17.*
www.sherpa-walking-holidays.co.uk

Vallebona
Via di Grignano 32, Pontassieve.
Tel *055 839 72 46.*

SPA HOLIDAYS

Terme di Saturnia
Saturnia (Grosseto).
Tel *0564 60 01 11.*
www.terme-di-saturnia.info

Montecatini Terme
Viale Verdi 41, Montecatini Terme.
Tel *0572 7781.*
www.termemontecatini.it

WATER SPORTS

Costoli
Viale Paoli, Florence.
Tel *055 623 60 27.*

Piscina Bellariva
Lungarno Aldo Moro 6, Florence.
Tel *055 677 521.*

Societa Canottieri Firenze
Lungarno Luisa dei Medici 8. **Map** 6 D4.
Tel *055 28 21 30.*
www.canottierifirenze.it

Spiro Sub Diving Club
La Foce 27, Marina di Campo, Elba.
Tel *0565 97 61 02.*
www.spirosub.isoladelba.it

MOUNTAIN SPORTS

Abetone
Tel *0573 602 31 (tourist info).*
Tel *0573 600 01 (ski info).*

Le Cave di Maiano
Via delle Cave 16, Fiesole.
Tel *055 59 133.*

Ufficio Guide
Libreria Stella Alpina, Via Corridoni 14b/r.
Tel *055 41 16 88.*
www.ufficioguide.it

GOLF

Punta Ala Golf Club
Punta Ala, Grosseto.
Tel *0564 92 21 21.*
www.puntaala.net/golf

Ugolino Golf Course
Via Chiantigiana 3, Grassina.
Tel *055 230 10 09.*
www.golfugolino.it

SURVIVAL GUIDE

PRACTICAL INFORMATION

Visitors have been coming to Tuscany for centuries, drawn by its slendid art and architecture, landscape and cuisine. These may all seem overwhelming at first, so plan carefully to make the most of this beautiful region. Start your day early and take time over lunch: most sights and shops close for several hours and reopen in the late afternoon.

ITALIA
ENTE NAZIONALE ITALIANO PER IL TURISMO

Tourist board logo

Try to have a relaxed attitude to your sightseeing – opening hours can be erratic and may vary depending on the season. Most Italians take their holiday in August, so some places may be shut. If your stay in Florence is limited, you could take a city tour. For a longer stay, consider a study course, offered throughout the year by colleges and language schools.

WHEN TO GO

Tuscany is great to visit year-round and has four distinct seasons. There is a pleasant long spring, making April and May the best months to visit. September and October are generally warm. July and August tend to be very hot and crowded, especially in Florence. It rains a lot in winter, with cooler temperatures, but the region is much less crowded. Coastal areas are best visited from May to September; the mountains are good for snow sports in December through to March. In winter, many towns at high altitudes may be hard to reach without snow tyres.

VISAS AND PASSPORTS

All visitors need a valid passport. European Union (EU) residents and visitors from the US, Canada, Australia and New Zealand do not need visas for stays of up to three months. A visa is required for longer stays; apply at your local embassy or consulate. All visitors to Italy must by law register with police within three days of arrival. Most hotels will register visitors when they check in. For a longer stay you are responsible for registering yourself in person at the **Questura**. If in doubt, contact the local police department or the Questura.

CUSTOMS INFORMATION

Duty-free allowances are as follows: non-EU residents can bring in either 200 cigarettes, 50 cigars, 100 cigarillos or 250 grams of tobacco; 1 litre of alcohol above 22% vol; 4 litres of wine; 50 grams of perfume. Allowances for EU residents are almost unlimited, providing that the goods are for personal use only. Beware that random checks are often made to guard against drugs traffickers.

Non-EU residents who spend €160 in a single establishment that displays a tax-free sign are entitled to a partial refund for Valued Added Tax, known as IVA *(see p284)*. Ask the cashier to fill out the form for you, and when departing the country take the goods and receipts in your carry-on luggage for approval at the airport office. Ask for credit to be added to your credit card for faster processing.

TOURIST INFORMATION

Florence, Pisa and Siena have several **Uffici Informazioni Turistiche** (tourist offices) offering information about tourist sights and authorized guides throughout the region. The "Tourist Rights Protection" desk in the main tourist office in Florence is specifically for making serious, written complaints against service providers. Tourist offices in small towns tend to give details only on their particular town. Travel agents, such as **CTS Viaggi**, can provide information on tours and rail and coach travel in Italy, as well as tickets *(see pp308–11)*.

Tourist information office on a Florence street

ENTERTAINMENT INFORMATION

The best guide for entertainment is the monthly magazine *Firenze Spettacolo*, which has restaurant and café guides, as well as comprehensive details of concerts, exhibitions, museums and sporting events. For select event and exhibition listings, pick up a free copy of *The Florentine* English-language newspaper. Tourist offices have leaflets on local entertainment and events. During summer evenings, fêtes with local bands are held throughout Tuscany, all listed at www.saimicadove.it.

ETIQUETTE AND SMOKING

Italians act conservatively in public: they do not sit on the ground or eat while walking, and they tend to drink in moderation with meals. Smoking, though banned in indoor public spaces, is still common and you will see many people smoking on the streets.

It is traditional to greet and thank shop staff when entering and exiting stores; if you enter a small store say *buon giorno* (good morning), then *grazie* when you leave.

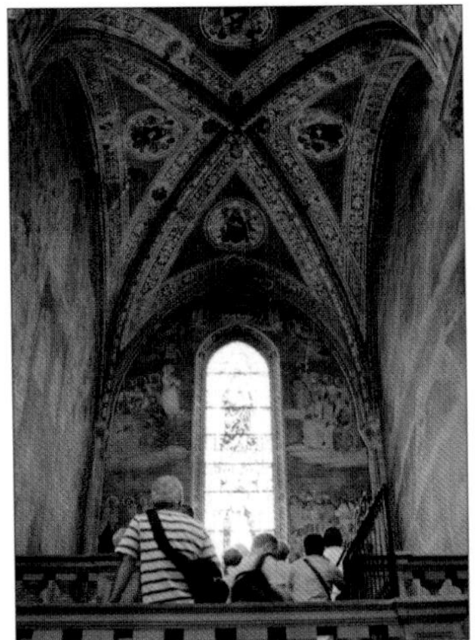

Visitors in Santa Maria Novella, Florence

VISITING CHURCHES

Churches enforce a strict dress code: knees and shoulders must be covered when entering any church. Women should carry a shawl to cover up, while men should avoid wearing shorts. Hemlines at the knee or below are usually fine.

LANGUAGE

Italian is the only official language in Italy, though English is taught in schools. Young people and those in the tourist industry all speak some English, while the elderly and those in small towns will be less likely to know other languages. Effort to speak a few words of Italian is always appreciated.

OPENING HOURS

Opening times tend to vary widely, though in general most museums are closed on Mondays. There are three main museum types: state, city and private, and each has its own opening hours. Plan your time carefully.

Generally, state museums such as the Uffizi, Galleria dell' Accademia and Palazzo Pitti tend to open Tue–Sun, 8:15am–6:50pm. Others such as the Bargello and San Marco are open mornings only, with occasional Monday openings. City museums are open 9am–7pm daily and private museum hours vary. In the country, most diocese museums (next to each town's *duomo*) close at noon and reopen late afternoon.

ADMISSION PRICES

Admission costs for museums average €6–10. Some churches also charge a small entrance fee. Booking in advance is advisable for the **Accademia** and **Uffizi** via the official website or by phone *(see p299)*. **Amici dei Musei** offers an annual pass for state museums, and there are ongoing plans to introduce a city-wide museum pass.

PUBLIC CONVENIENCES

Gabinetto means public toilet, though signs often say WC. Availability is improving throughout Tuscany, although standards vary. There are toilets at almost all museums and cafés. In a bar it is polite to make a small purchase before using their facilities.

A small fee may be charged at the Duomo and train stations, but elsewhere toilets are usually free. Small towns often have a toilet near the main parking area. Carrying tissue paper and hand sanitizer is recommended.

TAXES AND TIPPING

A 20% tax is included in the price of goods and services. In restaurants there is usually a €1–3 *coperto* (cover charge), so leave extra only for superb service. It is not necessary to tip a taxi driver, although they often expect the fare to be rounded up to the next euro.

TRAVELLERS WITH SPECIAL NEEDS

Facilities for the disabled traveller in Tuscany are limited. Pavements are often narrow and difficult to navigate with a wheelchair. Always request an accessible hotel room in advance. Package tour representatives can arrange assistance at airports and hotels. **Accessible Italy** is a specialized non-profit organization that can help you plan your trip and arrange the help you need on-site.

Trenitalia provides passenger assistance for all trains. Many Italian stations have a *Sala Blu* (Blue Hall), which is an assistance point for disabled travellers – there is one in Florence Santa Maria Novella Station *(see p308)*. You may reserve services in advance by email or phone.

Tourists and buskers outside the Uffizi

TRAVELLING WITH CHILDREN

Italians love children, and while hotels and restaurants may not be completely equipped for young visitors, they will be happy to accommodate them. Most restaurants have high chairs and will serve children basic meals such as pasta with olive oil or tomato sauce.

It's best to request cribs or cots at your hotel in advance. Most hotels do not have a kettle or other food preparation facilities for newborns; short-let apartments *(see p246)* are an excellent solution if you need kitchen access. Negotiating narrow pavements can be difficult with pushchairs. Buses in cities have a reserved seating area for people with pushchairs; enter the bus by the wide centre doors. Most sights offer a discounted entry rate for children.

SENIOR TRAVELLERS

Special services or discounts for seniors are few in Tuscany. EU citizens over 65 can get into state museums for free and receive a 25% discount on entry fees to city museums (valid photo ID must be shown), but seniors from outside the EU are not eligible. There is no discount on bus tickets. A train ticket discount of 15% is given to holders of the *Carta Argento*, an annual card you can apply for at train stations. It costs €30 for over 60s, so is only worthwhile if you're planning a lengthy stay in Tuscany. It is free for over 75s.

GAY AND LESBIAN TRAVELLERS

Certain areas of Tuscany are particularly favoured by GLBT travellers, although the scene remains discreet. Most popular are the seaside resorts of Viareggio and Torre del Lago, which have many gay bars, and certain beaches in Torre del Lago and Maremma. There are numerous gay-friendly B&Bs in Tuscany, especially in Florence. The oldest gay bar (men only) in Italy is Tabasco in Florence's Piazza della Signoria. There are few organized venues for women, but Florence's Piccolo Café on Borgo Santa Croce is open to both men and women.

Florence hosts the Queer Festival, dedicated to the arts and film, each November (www.florencequeerfestival.it) and Pitti Immagine fashion events also attract a large gay crowd. The **Arcigay** and **Ireos** associations provide further information (in Italian).

STUDENT AND BUDGET TRAVELLERS

Travellers on a budget will find reasonably priced lodging and meal options throughout Tuscany, but there are very few free activities. Some small churches may be free to visit, and students with International Student Identity Cards (ISIC) are usually able to claim a discount on admission fees at museums and other attractions. The ISIC card also gives access to a 24-hour telephone helpline that provides general advice and information.

The national travel organization, **CTS Viaggi**, has branches throughout Italy and Europe. CTS can issue student cards and offers reasonably priced car hire. They are also able to organize holidays, excursions and courses.

Some traditional *trattorie* have inexpensive set menus, and lunchtime menus tend to be cheaper. There are numerous hostels and budget hotels in Florence and around Tuscany. Camp sites on the outskirts of some towns *(see p247)* are a good option, while those looking for something a little different could opt to stay in a convent. Bear in mind that convents are likely to have curfews and rules about unmarried couples staying together. Facilities vary from basic to luxurious, with corresponding cost.

EDUCATIONAL COURSES

There are many language and art schools in Tuscany. The **British Institute in Florence** is one of the better known, and **The Learning Center of Tuscany** offers TEFL certificate courses. The **Palazzo Spinelli Istituto per l'Arte e il Restauro** offers courses on art, drawing, ceramics and painting. The **Centro Internazionale Dante Alighieri** or the **Università per Stranieri** in Siena have courses on Italian culture, history and cooking. A list of schools in Tuscany is available from the Uffici Informazioni Turistche.

TUSCAN TIME

Tuscany is 1 hour ahead of Greenwich Mean Time (GMT). The time difference between Tuscany and other cities is as follows: London: -1 hour; New York: -6 hours; Perth: +7 hours; Auckland: +11 hours; Tokyo: +8 hours. These figures may vary for brief periods in the summer with local changes. For all official purposes the Italians use the 24-hour clock (eg 10pm = 22.00 hrs).

Student relaxing in the sun in Gaiole in Chianti

ELECTRICAL ADAPTORS

Electrical current in Italy is 220V AC, with two-pin, round-pronged plugs. It is probably better to buy an adaptor before leaving for Italy. Most hotels with three stars and above have electrical points for shavers, and provide hairdryers in all bedrooms.

RESPONSIBLE TOURISM

There are many ways to travel more sustainably in Tuscany thanks to the region's respect for tradition. In the countryside, consider staying at an *agritourismo* *(see p246)* and learn about what they produce, or visit local organic farms and wine producers. Tasty local food produce can be purchased at markets in both towns and cities; small-town markets are often bi-weekly so ask your host for dates. Buy your souvenirs at local artisan workshops. Tuscany is known for hand-decorated paper, ceramics and leather. In Florence, **Context Travel** offers an Oltrarno Artisan tour to meet and learn about these craftspeople.

Local market produce

CONVERSION TABLE

Imperial to Metric
1 inch = 2.54 centimetres
1 foot = 30 centimetres
1 mile = 1.6 kilometres
1 ounce = 28 grams
1 pound = 454 grams
1 pint = 0.6 litres
1 gallon = 4.6 litres

Metric to Imperial
1 centimetre = 0.4 inches
1 metre = 3 feet, 3 inches
1 kilometre = 0.6 miles
1 gram = 0.04 ounces
1 kilogram = 2.2 pounds
1 litre = 1.8 pints

DIRECTORY

IMMIGRATION INFORMATION

Questura
Via Zara 2 (police office), Florence.
Map 2 D3.
Via della Fortezza, 17 (immigration office), Florence.
Map 1 C3.
Tel *0554 97 76 02.*
Via del Castoro, Siena.
Tel *0577 20 11 11.*
Via Lalli 4, Pisa.
Tel *050 58 35 11.*
http://questure.poliziadistato.it/

EMBASSIES AND CONSULATES

Australia
Via Antonio Bosio 5, Rome.
Tel *06 85 27 21.*
www.italy.embassy.gov.au

New Zealand
Via Clitunno 44, Rome.
Tel *06 853 7501.*
www.nzembassy.com

UK
Lungarno Corsini 2, Florence. **Map** 3 B1 (5 B3). ***Tel*** *055 28 41 33.*
http://ukinitaly.fco.gov.uk

USA
Lungarno Amerigo Vespucci 38, Florence.
Map 1 A5 (5 A2).
Tel *055 26 69 51.*
www.florence.usconsulate.gov

TOURIST INFORMATION & AGENCIES

CTS Viaggi
Borgo La Croce 42/r, Florence.
Tel *055 28 95 70.*
Via Bandini 21, Siena.
Tel *0577 28 50 08.*
www.cts.it

Uffici Informazioni Turistiche
Via Cavour 1r, Florence.
Map 2 D4 (6 D1).
Tel *055 290 832.*
www.firenzeturismo.it
Piazza del Campo 56, Siena.
Tel *0577 28 05 51.*
www.terresiena.it
Piazza del Duomo, Pisa.
Tel *050 56 04 64.*
www.pisaunicaterra.it

ADVANCE BOOKING

Amici dei Musei
www.amicideimuseifiorentini.it

Booking Line (Uffize and Accademia)
Tel *055 294883.*

Firenze Musei
Tel *055 29 48 83 (tickets).*
www.firenzemusei.it
www.museicivicifiorentini.it

TRAVELLERS WITH SPECIAL NEEDS

Accessible Italy
Tel *+378 94 11 11.*
www.accessibleitaly.com

Trenitalia
Tel *199 30 30 60.*
www.trenitalia.com

GAY TRAVELLERS

www.arcigay.it
www.ireos.org

STUDENT & BUDGET TRAVELLERS

Accommodation
www.ostellofirenze.it
www.monasterystays.com

CTS Viaggi
Borgo La Croce 42/r, Florence. ***Tel*** *055 28 95 70.*
Via Bandini 21, Siena. ***Tel*** *0577 28 50 08.*
www.cts.it

EDUCATIONAL COURSES

Centro Internazionale Dante Alighieri
Via Tommaso Pendola 36, 53100 Siena.
Tel *0577 495 33.*

The British Institute
Lungarno Guicciardini 9, 50125 Florence. **Map** 3 B1 (5 B3). ***Tel*** *055 267 78 270.* **www**.britishinstitute.it

The Learning Center of Tuscany
Viale Corsica 15c, 50134 Florence. ***Tel*** *055 051 50 35.* **www**.learningcentertuscany.com

Palazzo Spinelli Istituto per l'Arte e il Restauro
Borgo Santa Croce 10, 50122 Florence. **Map** 4 E1 (6 F4). ***Tel*** *055 24 60 01.* **www**.spinelli.it

Università per Stranieri
Via Pantaneto 45, 53100 Siena. ***Tel*** *0577 24 01 11.* **www**.unistrasi.it

RESPONSIBLE TOURISM

Context Travel
Via Baccina 40, Rome. ***Tel*** *06 97 62 52 04.*
www.contexttravel.com

Personal Security and Health

Tuscany and its cities are generally safe as long as common-sense precautions are taken. Reports of serious crimes are rare, but petty theft and pickpocketing are common problems in the crowded tourist areas of Florence and Pisa. Ensure that you have adequate travel insurance before leaving for Italy, as it is very difficult to obtain once you are in the country.

POLICE

The *vigili urbani*, or municipal police *(see p313)*, wear blue uniforms in winter and white during summer. They are most often seen in the streets regulating traffic. The *carabinieri* are the military police. They dress in black trousers with a red stripe on the leg and deal with a variety of offences from theft to speeding. *La polizia* (the state police) wear grey trousers with a magenta stripe. They specialize in serious crimes. While uniforms differ, in an emergency the first officer on the scene is responsible and will help you.

A team of *carabinieri* on duty in Florence

WHAT TO BE AWARE OF

When looking after your personal safety, use common sense as you would in any large city. Pickpocketing takes place on public transport and in crowded piazzas, markets and queues. Italian women tend to keep one hand on the closure of their handbag at all times (zip closures are best), while men put a hand over the pocket in which they keep their wallet. Young women may occasionally be subjected to harassment from whistling men on the street.

Women should not walk home alone late at night. Always use official taxis which clearly display their licence number. When you call for a taxi you will be given the car number, for example Napoli 37, which will be visible on a sticker on the side of the taxi.

IN AN EMERGENCY

The telephone number for medical emergency services is **118** and the operator should be able to assist you. Report all serious crime to the police, through dialling **112**.

LOST AND STOLEN PROPERTY

Avoid being a victim of theft in Tuscany in the same way as you would at home: lock doors, keep valuables in a safe and never leave anything in plain view inside a car. In the case of robbery, you must report the theft to the police within 24 hours and obtain a statement *(denuncia)* in order to make an insurance claim. Ask your hotel reception for assistance in doing this.

Lost property may be difficult to recover. Lost items on trains can sometimes be located by asking customer services. In some stations, lost bags will be put in a safe deposit box and you will have to pay to collect them.

MINOR HAZARDS

Inoculations are not necessary for Tuscany. Mosquitoes are an irritation. Equip yourself with mosquito repellent as these insects are common, especially in the centre of Florence, and screens on windows are rare. Alternatively, use an electrical device (referred to as *vape* from the brand name), which works by heating mosquito repellent in tablet or liquid form. *Vape* can repel mosquitoes for up to 12 hours. These small devices are available in grocery stores and houseware shops *(mesticheria)*. For a longer stay you might prefer to use a temporary window net or to place a mosquito net over your bed. Both are available from a *mesticheria*.

Do not underestimate the strength of the sun – drink plenty of water and use a high factor sunscreen. Although Italians prefer the taste of bottled water, tap water is perfectly safe in the cities. Many rural homes use water from a well – visitors may prefer to drink bottled water.

HOSPITALS AND PHARMACIES

If you are in need of urgent medical attention, you should go at once to the *Pronto Soccorso* (outpatients/emergency) department of the nearest main hospital.

If you have a medical problem during the night or at the weekend, but it is not an emergency, the **Guardia Medica** service in Florence is a fast and easy solution, similar to a walk-in medical clinic. It is open through the night and at weekends, and may charge a small fee for treatment.

In the summer, major tourist areas (including Florence and Siena) set up a Tourist Medical Centre, which operates during daytime hours.

In Florence and Siena, the **Associazione Volontari Ospedalieri** has interpreters who can help with medical

Outside a typical pharmacy *(farmacia)* in Florence

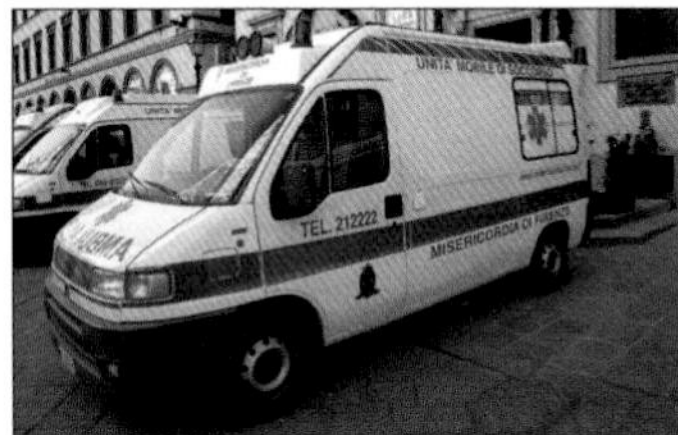

Fleet of ambulances run by the Misericordia at a Florence hospital

Police car patrolling the Campo dei Miracoli in Pisa ***(see pp156–63)***

matters. The service is free and available in English, French, German and Spanish.

If you need a dentist during your stay in Tuscany, ask for a recommendation at your hotel or look for an English-speaking dentist in the English yellow pages (www.insidersabroad.com/english yellowpages).

Pharmacies in Tuscany have a night and weekend rota *(servizio notturno)* posted on their doors. The **Farmacia Comunale 13** at Florence's Santa Maria Novella station is open 24 hours a day, as is the **Farmacia Molteni** in Via dei Calzaiuoli. Pharmacies do not usually accept prescriptions from other countries.

The Misericordia is one of the world's oldest charitable lay institutions and arranges many ambulance services in Tuscany. Most of the staff are volunteers, but there is also a fully qualified medical team. The traditional black cassock is for formal parade only; volunteers do not wear it during medical emergencies.

TRAVEL AND HEALTH INSURANCE

Visitors from the EU are officially entitled to reciprocal state medical care in Italy. Before you travel, pick up a European Health Insurance Card (EHIC), which covers emergency medical treatment. It is available online (www.dh.gov.uk) or at the post office. The EHIC does not cover repatriation costs or additional expenses, such as accommodation or flights for anyone travelling with you. Purchasing additional travel insurance before leaving home is recommended.

Visitors from outside the EU should take out a comprehensive travel insurance policy before travelling.

DIRECTORY

EMERGENCY NUMBERS

Ambulance
Tel *118.*

Automobile Club d'Italia
Tel *116.*
www.aci.it

Fire
Tel *115.*

General SOS
Tel *113.*

Medical Emergencies
Tel *118.*

Police (Carabinieri)
Tel *112.*

Tourist Medical Centre
Via Lorenzo Il Magnifico 59, Florence. **Map** 2 D2.
Tel *055 47 54 11.*

Traffic Police
Florence ***Tel*** *055 227 69.*
Pisa ***Tel*** *050 31 39 21.*
Siena ***Tel*** *0577 24 62 11.*

QUESTURA (POLICE OFFICES)

Via Zara 2, Florence.
Map 2 D3.
Tel *0554 97 76 02.*
Via del Castoro, Siena.
Tel *0577 20 11 11.*
Via Lalli 4, Pisa.
Tel *050 58 35 11.*

24-HOUR PHARMACIES

Farmacia Comunale 13
Santa Maria Novella station, Florence.
Map 1 B4 (5 B1).
Tel *055 21 67 61.*

Farmacia Molteni
Via dei Calzaiuoli 7r, Florence.
Map 6 D3.
Tel *055 28 94 90.*

HOSPITALS

Arcispedale di Santa Maria Nuova
Piazza di Santa Maria Nuova 1.
Map 6 F2.
Tel *055 275 81.*

Associazione Volontari Ospedalieri
Florence
Tel *055 234 45 67.*
Siena
Tel *0577 24 78 69.*

Azienda Ospedaliero-Universitaria Careggi
Via delle Oblate 1, Florence.
Tel *055 794 111.*

Guardia Medica
Piazza Del Duomo 20, Florence.
Tel *055 28 77 88.*
Via Sant Agostino 6, Oltrarno.
Tel *055 21 56 16.*

Meyer Children's Hospital
Via Luca Giordano 13.
Map 2 F2.
Tel *055 566 21.*

Pisa Hospital
Ospedale di Santa Chiara, Via Roma 67.
Tel *050 99 21 11.*

Siena Hospital
Policlinico Le Scotte, Viale Bracci 16.
Tel *0577 58 61 11.*

LOST CREDIT CARDS

American Express
Tel *06 722 82.*

Diners Club
Tel *800 86 40 64 (freephone).*

VISA
Tel *800 87 72 32 (freephone).*

LOST TRAVELLER'S CHEQUES

American Express
Tel *800 87 20 00 (freephone).*

Thomas Cook
Tel *800 87 20 50 (freephone).*

VISA
Tel *800 87 41 55 (freephone).*

Banking and Currency

Visitors to Tuscany have a number of options available to them for changing money. Banks and ATMs tend to give more favourable rates than bureaux de change, hotels and travel agents, but the paperwork when using a bank is usually more time consuming. When changing money you will need to show some form of identification, such as a passport. Alternatively, credit cards can be used for purchasing goods. Traveller's cheques are no longer frequently used.

A typical ATM point in the centre of Florence

Entering and leaving a bank through an electronic double door

BANKS AND BUREAUX DE CHANGE

Banks usually open between 8:30am and 1:20pm Mon–Fri. Most branches also open for an hour or so in the afternoon from about 2:45pm till 4pm. They close at weekends and on public holidays *(see p37)*. Exchange offices stay open longer, but in general the rates are less favourable.

In Florence, the exchange office behind the railway station is open from 8am till late evening, depending on the season. In Pisa, the exchange offices in Piazza del Duomo and at the railway station are open until the evening and at weekends.

To change money at a bank, bring your passport and be prepared to fill out numerous forms. As procedures vary from branch to branch, it may be worth asking staff for help.

For security reasons, most Italian banks have electronic double doors. Press the button to open the outer door, then wait for it to close behind you. The inner door then opens automatically. Metal objects may set off emergency detectors as you enter. You may be asked to deposit your belongings in lockers outside the secured area.

ATMS

The most convenient way to access your cash in Italy is to make withdrawals using an ATM. To avoid complications, check which cards the ATM accepts before inserting your card. Travelling with more than one debit (and credit) card is recommended in case one is not accepted. Most ATM machines accept VISA or MasterCard for cash advances, but be aware that interest is payable as soon as the money is withdrawn.

Italian ATMs dispense a maximum daily amount (approximately €300), so if you need to make a larger cash payment you should plan ahead and make withdrawals from cash machines over more than one day.

Before your trip, be sure to tell your bank that you are travelling to Italy. They should remove any flags or limits on your bank and credit cards to avoid having them blocked. Ask your bank if you need a different PIN number for use in Italy: if you have a 6-digit PIN it may not work, as Italian ATMs usually accept 4- or 5-digit PINs only.

A branch of Banca Toscana, seen widely across the region

CREDIT CARDS AND TRAVELLER'S CHEQUES

Credit cards are widely accepted throughout Italy, and it is worth bringing one, or more, with you. VISA and MasterCard are the most popular, while American Express and Diners Card are rarely accepted. To avoid problems using your card during a trip you should inform your credit card company before travelling.

Some restaurants, cafés and shops may require a minimum expenditure to accept credit card payment. Be aware that petrol stations do not accept credit cards, only cash. Always make sure you have some cash in case your credit card is not accepted.

Traveller's cheques are no longer in common use. Few stores will accept them (or even know what they are) although hotels may accept them for payment or exchange. If a bureau de change does accept traveller's cheques, be aware that there is a minimum commission charge, which may make changing small sums of money uneconomical.

THE EURO

The euro (€) is the common currency of the European Union. It went into general circulation on 1 January 2002, initially for 12 participating countries. Italy was one of those 12 countries, and the lira was phased out in February 2002. EU members using the euro as their sole official currency are known as the Eurozone. Several EU members have opted out of joining this common currency.

Euro notes are identical throughout the Eurozone, each one including designs of fictional architectural structures and monuments. The coins, however, have one side identical (the value side), and one side with an image unique to each country. Both notes and coins are exchangeable in each participating country.

Euro Bank Notes
Euro bank notes have seven denominations. The €5 note (grey in colour) is the smallest, followed by the €10 note (pink), €20 note (blue), €50 note (orange), €100 note (green), €200 note (yellow) and €500 note (purple).

5 euros

10 euros

20 euros

100 euros

200 euros

500 euros

2 euros

1 euro

50 cents

20 cents

10 cents

Coins
The euro has eight coin denominations: €1 and €2; 50 cents, 20 cents, 10 cents, 5 cents, 2 cents and 1 cent. The €2 and €1 coins are both silver and gold in colour. The 50-, 20- and 10-cent coins are gold. The 5-, 2- and 1-cent coins are bronze.

5 cents

2 cents

1 cent

Communications and Media

Sign outside a *tabacchi* shop

Payphones are few and far between in Italy, as access to Internet services and the use of mobile phones have increased. Pre-paid long-distance telephone cards are also now increasingly used by visitors. The postal service in Italy, once dogged by slow service, is much improved and also offers relatively fast courier services. Italians produce a lot of magazines (though fewer newspapers), and international and foreign-language print material can be found in areas catering to large numbers of tourists.

INTERNATIONAL AND LOCAL TELEPHONE CALLS

The growing use of mobile phones in Italy has caused a cutback in public telephone services. Telecom Italia no longer has telephone offices, although there are some privately operated calling centres offering international phone services. Payphones are rare on the street, although there should be working payphones at train stations and airports. To use a public payphone you need to purchase a Telecom Italia *scheda telefonica* card at any *tabacchi* or newsagent. Insert the card before making a call. You can also use a pre-paid long-distance calling card in public payphones (without using a Telecom *scheda*), also available from *tabacchi*. These have an 800 number on the back and a scratch-off code.

Public payphone sign

When dialling locally, city landline numbers start with a 0. To make a long-distance call, dial 00, followed by the country code and area code, before dialling the number. If using a long-distance calling card, use the 800 number provided, dial the country and area codes (without the 00 prefix), and then dial the number.

You can usually make landline phone calls from your hotel, although these are expensive – ask for a price list if it is not displayed. You can also use long-distance calling cards with hotel phones – it should be free to connect. Most private apartment rentals and *agriturismos* do not have phones in guest rooms. Faxes can be sent from post offices, copy centres, *cartolerie* (paper/office stores) and Internet points.

Telephone company logo

MOBILE PHONES

The cost of mobile phones and services has reduced to such an extent that it can now make sense to buy a mobile phone in Italy if you are visiting the country for more than one week and intend to use your phone a lot. The two major providers, **Tim** and **Vodafone**, sell basic phones for around €30, including a SIM card with €5 credit. You can purchase additional credit from any *tabbachi*, newsagent or mobile phone store (be sure to specify the carrier name). To buy a mobile phone, you will need to bring a copy of your passport. When you purchase a new SIM card, you need to make a 1 minute call to a landline or other mobile phone in order to activate it, which can take up to 24 hours. However, it is possible to buy an unlocked Italian mobile phone and SIM online if you wish to get set up before your trip. The SIM usually expires one year from your last top up.

If you have an unlocked phone from the UK or Europe, you can purchase an Italian SIM and use it in your phone. Alternatively, set up a roaming agreement with your provider. If using a roaming plan, be sure to top up your credit before leaving home.

If you are travelling from North America, Australia or New Zealand, a tri-band/GSM phone should, technically, work in Italy. Check with your phone operator about roaming charges.

When using an Italian mobile phone, note that calls between phones using the same provider may cost less than calls to mobile phones serviced by other providers, depending on the package you signed up to. Long-distance rates are usually high but you can use a long-distance calling card with your mobile phone – calls will still cost more than from a landline, however.

INTERNET AND WI-FI

Increasing numbers of hotels and businesses are providing free or paid Internet services to their customers, and some Italian cities plan to offer free Wi-Fi for residents and tourists. You will be required to complete a brief registration process to use any Internet service in Italy. If your hotel Internet service is fast, Skype calls via your laptop will be perfectly viable; calls to landlines will require a small cash credit. Skype also allows you to

REACHING THE RIGHT NUMBER

- City dialling codes are: Florence 055; Siena 0577; Pisa 050; Viareggio 0584; Arezzo 0575; Lucca 0583; Pistoia 0573.
- Mobile dialling codes begin with 3 (no 0).
- International operator assistance is on 170. You can place reverse charge and credit card calls on this number.
- *See also* Emergency Numbers, *p301*.

make calls to toll free numbers in the US and UK (convenient if you need to contact your bank or credit card company), though you will be charged at the standard rate for these calls.

For those without a laptop, there are also many privately operated Internet points in Tuscany. In small towns these may be located at the back of a store or bar. **Internet Train** (www.internettrain.it) has 25 stores in Tuscany (with eight in Florence); you simply buy a charged magnetic card which can be used across their network.

POSTAL SERVICES

To send letters or postcards, purchase stamps *(francobolli)* at any *tabbachi*. There is usually a red mailbox right outside. Mailboxes have two slots: the one designated *per la città* is only for destinations within the city; *altri destinazioni* is for everywhere else.

For oversized letters or packages, go to the post office. Sub-post office hours are usually 8:30am–2pm Mon–Sat. Main offices stay open until 8pm. Post offices also provide banking services, so for the postal desk you must follow the correct procedure. Take a number from the yellow machine with the green envelope symbol by the entrance. The letter "P" combined with your number will be called out.

Priority mail *(posta prioritarià)* now designates regular airmail. Delivery time is somewhat variable, ranging from four days to six weeks worldwide. However, the post office also offers a well-priced international and national courier service *(paccocelere)* for tracked, on-time mail. Fedex and UPS are the main consumer courier services. Check www.fedex.com and www.ups.com for offices in Tuscany. **Mailboxes Etc.** also ships mail using either courier; they have five stores in Florence and one in each of Siena, Arezzo and Pisa.

Newspaper kiosk stocking all major newspapers and magazines

ADDRESSES

Florence has a confusing dual address system. Each street has a double set of numbers: a red number indicates a shop, restaurant or business, while a blue or black number refers to a hotel or domestic residence. When writing to a business, insert an "r" after the number to distinguish it from a residential address. Each set of numbers has its own sequence, so business premises at, say, No. 10r may well be next to a residential address at No. 23.

Busy main hall at Florence's central post office

NEWSPAPERS AND MAGAZINES

Most Italian newspapers such as *La Repubblica* and *La Nazione,* publish supplements with a regional focus. European and American newspapers such as *USA Today*, the *International Herald Tribune* and the *Financial Times* are available on the day of issue at stations, hotels and major newsagents.

TELEVISION

There are a dozen Italian TV channels including two music channels (MTV and DeeJay). Many hotels have satellite TV with BBC and CNN news in English, as well as German and French channels.

DIRECTORY

MOBILE PHONES

TIM
Via dei Lamberti 12, Firenze.
Via Salicotto 11, Siena.
www.tim.it

Vodafone
Via de' Martelli 31, Firenze.
Via del Paradiso 30, Siena.
www.vodafone.it

MAIN POST OFFICES

Pellicceria 3, Florence. **Map** 6 D3.
Tel *055 273 61.*
Piazza Matteotti 37, Siena.
Tel *0577 21 42 95.*
Piazza Vittorio Emanuele II, Pisa.
Tel *050 51 95 14.*

COURIERS

Mailboxes Etc.
Florence: Via San Gallo 61r; Corso Tintori 39r. **www**.mbe.it

TRAVEL INFORMATION

Tuscany is easily reached by air, with airports in both Florence and Pisa. Amerigo Vespucci (Peretola) airport in Florence offers connections with all major European cities, although it does not accommodate long-haul flights. Pisa airport (Galileo Galilei) receives low-cost and scheduled flights, including a direct international New York JFK–Pisa flight daily in summer.

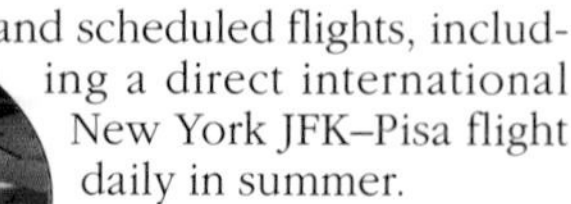

Alitalia aircraft

The city of Florence is also well connected by train and coach from most European cities. Train and coach travel, although slower and not necessarily cheaper, is a greener alternative to flying or driving.

Check-in area at Florence airport

GREEN TRAVEL

Getting to Tuscany from mainland Europe without flying is possible due to Italy's excellent train network, which serves major towns and cities including Florence, Pisa and Arezzo. Small discounts are available if travelling by train in a group of 10 or more. For information on train travel *see pp308–9*.

For those areas of Tuscany which are badly served by train, such as Siena and the coast, you may need to rent a car – look for economical diesel-engine models that use less fuel. If you want to explore the rolling hills of Tuscany without a car, two options are worth considering: **ATAF** *(see p315)* offers an inexpensive coach tour of the Chianti area, while a tourist steam train *(see p309)* runs occasional scenic day trips to seasonal fairs. Most towns and cities, can be explored on foot or using local buses *(see pp314–15)*.

ARRIVING BY AIR

There are numerous daily arrivals at both Florence and Pisa airports from all major airlines, including **Alitalia** and **British Airways**. Some of the low-cost airlines also serve the region. **Ryanair** flies from London Stansted and Dublin to Pisa, **EasyJet** flies Gatwick–Pisa, and **Meridiana** flies Gatwick–Florence.

As there are few direct intercontinental flights to Tuscany, consider flying to Rome and taking the train up to Florence. The journey is approximately 1 hour 25 mins. Alternatively, you could hire a car in Rome and drive to Tuscany. Alitalia flies direct to Rome from Los Angeles, Chicago, Montreal, Toronto, Perth and Melbourne, and many other airlines offer good worldwide connections via Rome and other European capitals.

FLORENCE AIRPORT (FLR)

Florence's Amerigo Vespucci airport, often known as Peretola, is small, with relatively few shops and bars. The "Vola in Bus" goes to and from the airport every 30 minutes 6am–8pm and hourly 9–11pm. The bus to the city centre leaves from in front of the airport building, while the bus to the airport departs from Florence's Santa Maria Novella train station. The evening buses (from 9pm) leave from Piazza dell'Unità. The journey takes 20 minutes and tickets may be purchased from the driver. Line 2 of the tramway system will link the airport to Santa Maria Novella train station and Piazza Libertà once it is complete.

Only take a taxi from the official taxi rank. Drivers will charge a supplement for coming from the airport plus a supplement for any luggage. There is also an extra charge on Sundays and holidays. Fares start at €20 for the journey to/from the airport. Check that the meter is switched on at departure.

Modern exterior of Florence's Amerigo Vespucci airport

Entrance to Pisa's Galileo Galilei airport

PISA AIRPORT (PSA)

Pisa airport has several shops, bars and restaurants. There are no money-changing facilities in the baggage hall so take some euros with you in order to hire a trolley.

There is a taxi rank at the front of the airport and good public transport links. Trains run directly from Pisa's Galileo Galilei airport to Florence's Santa Maria Novella station. To reach the trains, turn left as you leave the airport arrivals hall. Train tickets can be bought from the information kiosk at the airport. The journey to Florence takes 1 hour and the service generally runs once an hour, but is less regular in the early morning and evening. There is also an infrequent train serving Lucca and Montecatini. The train to Florence stops at Pisa Centrale and Empoli, where you can change on to the local line serving Siena.

The No. 3 bus runs from Pisa airport to the town centre. Buy tickets before you get on the bus from the airport information kiosk. There is also a frequent coach service to Santa Maria Novella station in Florence.

On the platform at Pisa airport's train station

AIR TICKETS AND FARES

It is worth shopping around for the lowest air fares online or with a travel agent such as **CIT Viaggi**. There is no rule as to when the best prices may come up; if fares seem high when you start looking, try a few days later and you may be pleasantly surprised. A good way to start is by comparing online prices at Expedia and Travelocity, and looking at the airlines' own websites. Signing up for email alerts or special offers is another way of getting a good deal.

PACKAGE HOLIDAYS

Package holidays incorporating a stay in Florence with nights in Rome and Venice are often available. Compare prices online and look at websites for major hotel resellers, such as Expedia. Whilst convenient, package deals are not always a cheaper option. Through contacting a hotel directly, it may be possible to negotiate a lower rate than those found online. This is also a good way to support local hoteliers, as they will receive payment direct from the customer.

CAR RENTAL

All the major car rental firms have rental offices at both Florence and Pisa airports. However, it is cheaper to make rental arrangements before your departure *(see p313)*.

Leaving Pisa airport by car, it is straightforward to get on to the dual carriageway linking Pisa and Florence. At Florence airport, turn right to get on to the A1 highway (Rome–Bologna). It is not advisable to drive into the centre of Florence *(see p312)*.

DIRECTORY

AIRLINE INFORMATION

Alitalia
Tel *06 22 22.*
www.alitalia.it

British Airways
Tel *199 71 22 66.*
www.britishairways.com

EasyJet
www.easyjet.com

Meridiana
Tel *892928.*
www.meridiana.it

Ryanair
Tel *050 50 37 70* or *899 67 89 10.*
www.ryanair.com

AIRPORT INFORMATION

Florence
Tel *055 306 13 00.*
www.aeroporto.firenze.it

Pisa
Tel *050 84 93 00* & *050 84 91 11.*
www.pisa-airport.com

TICKETS AND FARES

CIT Viaggi
Florence ***Tel*** *055 28 41 45.*
London ***Tel*** *020 8686 0677.*
Sydney ***Tel*** *(02) 9267 12 55.*

AIRPORT CAR RENTAL

Avis
Florence Airport
Tel *055 31 55 88.*
Pisa Airport ***Tel*** *050 420 28.*

Hertz
Florence Airport
Tel *055 30 73 70.*
Pisa Airport ***Tel*** *050 491 87.*

Maggiore
Florence Airport
Tel *055 31 12 56.*
Pisa Airport
Tel *050 425 74.*

Travelling by Train

Travelling overland can be a pleasurable way of getting to and travelling around Tuscany. Italy's state railway (Ferrovie dello Stato, or FS) has a train for every type of journey, from the quaintly slow *regionale* (local trains) through various levels of rapid intercity service to the luxurious, super-fast *freccia rossa*, which rushes between Italian cities at a speed to match its ticket price. The network between large cities is good, but journeys to towns on branch lines may be quicker by coach *(see p310)*.

Freccia rossa **(red arrow) train at Santa Maria Novella station**

ARRIVING BY TRAIN

Florence is a major arrival point for trains from Europe. The Galilei from Paris and the Italia Express from Frankfurt travel direct to Florence. Passengers from London have to change in Paris or Lille. From Florence, there is a direct train link with Pisa's airport *(see p307)*.

Trains from all over Italy arrive at and depart from Pisa Centrale and Florence's Santa Maria Novella stations. The high-speed *freccia rossa* train stops at Santa Maria Novella, connecting to Bologna and Milan in one direction, Rome and Naples in the other.

Some intercity and regional trains stop at Florence's other two (smaller) stations; from here you can take a regional train to Santa Maria Novella for free, or it may be quicker to take a local bus to your final destination *(see p314)*.

SANTA MARIA NOVELLA STATION, FLORENCE

Santa Maria Novella *(see p113)* is Florence's central railway station. It is always crowded and attracts some unsavoury characters, so you need to be vigilant and take care of your belongings. There is a taxi rank in front, and local buses *(see p314)* depart from the side of the building.

Facilities include a left luggage office, a pharmacy, a *sala blu* (for disabled traveller assistance), a hotel-booking service, and newspaper kiosks which also sell city bus tickets. The nearest tourist information office is at Piazza della Stazione 4, across the street. Florence also has two other smaller train stations – Campo de Marte and Rifredi – running some regional trains and intercity night trains.

SIENA STATION

Siena's train station is situated outside the city walls on Piazzale Carlo Roselli. It is quite small and about a 20-minute walk from the centre. Any bus from opposite the station goes to the city centre. The TRA-IN bus company *(see p315)* runs coaches to Montepulciano, Montalcino and Buonconvento. These depart from the front of the station. Tickets must be bought from the bus ticket window or self-service machines before you board.

PISA CENTRALE

Pisa's central station is quite large, with facilities including a restaurant and bar, newspaper kiosks selling bus tickets, a currency exchange booth and left luggage office.

Tourist information is at the front of the station. Most local buses, including to the Campo dei Miracoli *(see pp158–9)* and to the airport, stop in front of the station. A bus information and ticket office are close by. Pisa also has another train station at the airport *(see p307)*.

TICKETS AND FARES

Fares vary by train type (the slowest trains cost the least) and class (first and second). Fares and timetables are listed online (www.trenitalia.it). Fast trains have obligatory seat booking, while regional trains do not have reserved seats.

There are often special offers online for certain trains or destinations, as well as online price variations for fast trains (Eurostar and *freccia rossa*). You can get a 15–30 per cent discount on advance bookings for the *freccia rossa*, but such tickets come with limited flexibility if you need to change your booking later; you can also pay a 20 per cent surcharge in order to have total flexibility.

Trenitalia offers a Travelcard for one week, two weeks, or a month on the route and train type of your choice, offering 1,000 km (620 miles) of travel during the specified period. Travelcards can be purchased online or at train stations.

Logo on an intercity train

BUYING TICKETS

Always buy a ticket before you travel, otherwise you will be charged the price of a full-fare ticket plus a €50 fine. If the ticket office is busy, try one of the self-service ticket machines found at most stations. You must validate your ticket before every trip by stamping it in one of the yellow machines situated at the entrance to most platforms. If you forget to stamp your ticket, write the time and date on the edge of the ticket and explain your error to the inspector in order to avoid paying a fine.

To purchase tickets online you must first register at www.trenitalia.com. American Express is not accepted. You can download and print your ticket in PDF form or show the reservation number to the agent on the train. Tickets bought online do not need to be validated. When booking tickets online, make sure you are aware of any limitations on flexibility – most tickets purchased online can only be amended online, and sometimes a penalty will be incurred. If you think you may want to change your ticket later, wait to purchase it at the train station once you are in Italy. In most cases, a few days' advance purchase will be sufficient to get the train of your choice, except on or around major holidays.

Some regional trains allow you to bring a bicycle on board; these are indicated by a bicycle symbol on the train timetable. Tickets for bicycles (valid for all trips within a 24-hour period) can only be purchased at the train station; stamp both sides before boarding and attach half to the bicycle itself.

RAIL PASSES

Europe-wide train passes, such as EurRail (US) or InterRail for those under 26 (Europe), are accepted on the FS network – supplements are payable on fast trains and there are restrictions on private lines. A senior railcard, offering a 15% fare reduction, is available *(see p298)*.

TOURIST TRAINS

Ferrovie Turistiche offers day trips on historic steam trains for tourists. A popular trip is to Marradi, a small mountain town bordering Tuscany and Emilia-Romagna which hosts a chestnut festival in November and a Christmas fair in December.

DIRECTORY

BOOKING AGENTS

CIT Viaggi
Piazza della Stazione 51r, Florence.
Map 1 B5 (5 B1).
Tel *055 28 41 45.*

Ferrovie Turistiche
www.ferrovieturistiche.it

Palio Viaggi
Piazza Gramsci, Siena.
Tel *0577 28 08 28.*

MACHINES FOR FS RAIL TICKETS

Ticket machines at main stations have a multi-language touch screen and accept credit and bank cards as well as cash. Regional stations may be unmanned and often have rather basic ticket machines which take cash only and do not issue change. If you put in too much cash, you will be issued with a paper receipt – you need to take this to the nearest main station for a refund.

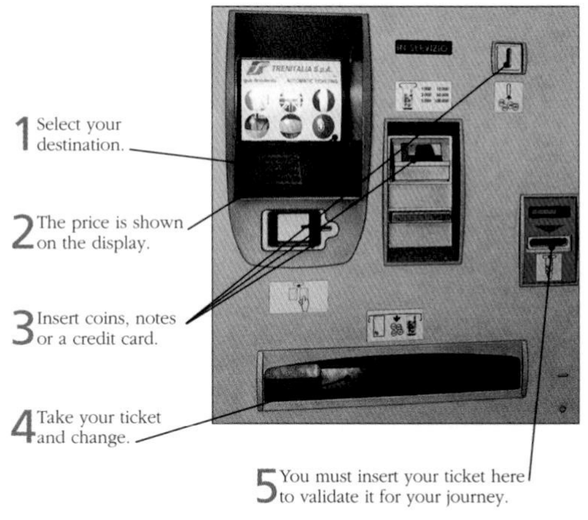

1 Select your destination.

2 The price is shown on the display.

3 Insert coins, notes or a credit card.

4 Take your ticket and change.

5 You must insert your ticket here to validate it for your journey.

ITALY'S PRINCIPAL FS NETWORK

The Italian State Rail Network operates various types of service. Check fares and timetables at www.trenitalia.com. All trains have facilities for disabled travellers *(see p297)*.

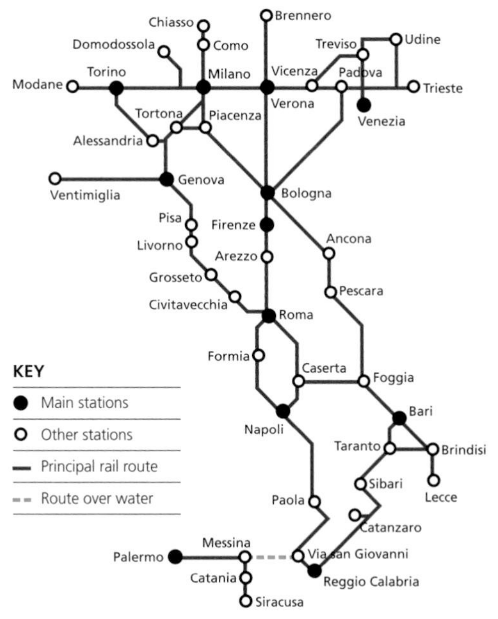

Travelling by Bus and Coach

Florence is linked by coach to most major European cities, and local companies operate an extensive network of services within Tuscany. Coaches are considered to be quicker where there is no direct train link, particularly in the countryside. Although the train is faster for long journeys, the coach may be a cheaper option. The coach companies' main offices, usually situated near city railway stations, stock timetables and route maps to help you plan your journey. This information is also provided online, but due to the complexity of schedules it is usually more helpful to consult a local travel agent.

ARRIVING BY COACH

Santa Maria Novella railway station in Florence is Tuscany's main arrival and departure point for all long-distance coach journeys, and the hub of the extensive local coach network. The **Lazzi** company runs coach services to major European cities from Florence and sells tickets for Eurolines coaches. Tickets can be booked at their office by Santa Maria Novella station. There are express services from Florence to Rome, run by Lazzi, and from Florence to Siena run by **TRA-IN** or **SITA**.

THE NETWORK

Florence has four main coach companies. Lazzi serves the region north and west of Florence and SITA serves the southern and eastern regions (including Siena, San Gimignano and Volterra). The **COPIT** bus company connects the city with the Abetone/ Pistoia, region and **CAP** links it to the Mugello area north of the city. All of these companies have ticket and information offices near Santa Maria Novella railway station.

Siena's main bus and coach company is TRA-IN, which runs local and regional services. Local services leave from Piazza Antonio Gramsci and regional buses from Piazza San Domenico. There is a ticket office in both squares. TRA-IN runs buses to most of Tuscany, including a direct coach to Rome twice daily.

In Pisa, the city bus company **CPT** serves the surrounding area, including the towns of Volterra, Livorno, San Miniato and Pontedera. These buses leave from Piazza Sant'Antonio. Lazzi runs a service to Viareggio, Lucca and Florence from Pisa, departing from Piazza Vittorio Emanuele II, where there is a Lazzi ticket office. Arezzo's **La Ferroviaria Italiana** bus lines connect to all the small towns nearby including Cortona.

TICKETS AND RESERVATIONS

Coach tickets must be purchased at an authorized ticket reseller or at the bus company's office. It's worth discussing your requirements with a travel agent who can help you understand the complex schedules and routes. On most routes, reserved seating is not available. Passengers need to line up before the bus departure time in order to get a seat. Expect a long wait around the holidays.

A SITA coach, serving southern and eastern Tuscany

A ticket office in Pisa, selling Lazzi and CPT tickets

DIRECTORY

FLORENCE

CAP & COPIT
Largo Fratelli Alinari 9. **Map** 1 C4 (5 B1). ***Tel*** *055 21 46 37.* **www**.capautolinee.it

COPIT of Pistoia
Via Filippo Pacini 47. ***Tel*** *0573 36 30.*

Lazzi
Piazza della Stazione. **Map** 1 B5 (5 B2). ***Tel*** *055 21 51 55.* **www**.lazzi.it

SITA
Via di Santa Caterina da Siena 15r. **Map** 1 B5 (5 A1). ***Tel*** *800 37 37 60 (Tuscany); 055 29 49 55 (national).* **www**.sitabus.it

SIENA

TRA-IN
Piazza Antonio Gramsci. ***Tel*** *0577 20 42 46* or *0577 20 41 11.* **www**.trainspa.it

PISA

CPT
Piazza Sant'Antonio 1. ***Tel*** *050 50 55 11.* **www**.cpt.pisa.it

Lazzi
Piazza Vittorio Emanuele II. ***Tel*** *050 462 88.* **www**.lazzi.it

AREZZO

La Ferroviaria Italiana
www.lfi.it

Travelling by Ferry and River Boat

Tuscany has a long and beautiful coast that boasts seven islands of which Elba, Giglio, Capraia, and Giannutri are visitable. All are well served by the ferry companies Moby and Toremar, especially during the summer months. The mainland ports are Piombino, Santo Stefano and Livorno (Leghorn). The closest airport is Pisa, from which you can reach Piombino by a combination of bus and train, or by car. For Livorno, bus No. 101 from the airport arrives in Livorno city; from there switch buses for the port.

Portoferraio, the main port on Elba

ARRIVING BY FERRY

Tuscany can be reached by ferry from other regions of Italy. Livorno is connected to Sardinia (port of Cagliari) and Sicily (Palermo); Piombino connects to Sardinia (Olbia) and Corsica (Bastia). Livorno is also the major port for international cruise ships.

PORTS

Tuscany's mainland ports are Livorno, Piombino and Porto Santo Stefano. On the islands, Elba's main port is Portoferraio, along with the smaller Rio Marina and Porto Azzurro. The other islands have only one tourist port.

If you arrive at Stazione Marittima, at the port of Livorno, and wish to take a self-guided day trip to Florence, the train is your best option. It takes 1½ hours and there are trains every hour. Take the shuttle bus (€5 return) from the port to Piazza Grande, in front of the Duomo. From here various city bus lines go to Livorno Centrale train station. Alternatively, Piazza Grande is about 10 minutes' walk from where ferries dock. It will take longer to walk from other parts of the port used by major cruise lines, but taxis are available. From the port, there is also a bus service to Pisa Airport and Pisa train station, which takes around 35 minutes. The train to Pisa runs approximately every 20 minutes and the journey takes 15–20 minutes.

TRAVELLING BY FERRY

When driving to any port, follow signs for *Porto/Imbarchi* and then the sign for your chosen ferry company (**Moby** or **Toremar**).

If you are taking your vehicle on the ferry, you will be directed to line up and turn off your engine in a numbered lot to await the boat. There is also short- and long-term parking available at Livorno and Piombino.

Washrooms are scarce at ports, but services on board are available and reasonably clean. Ferries have both indoor and outdoor seating and a snack bar. There is limited shade outdoors so be sure to wear a hat.

Ferries from Piombino to Elba and Porto Santo Stefano to Isola del Giglio take approximately 1 hour. Livorno to Capraia is nearly 3½ hours on the ferry or 1½ hours on the fast boat (passengers only, no vehicles). Ticket costs vary depending on what vehicle you take and the number of passengers you are travelling with. Toremar tends to be the cheaper option.

TICKETS

Tickets for all ferries can be purchased directly from the ferry company. It's also worth checking their websites, which may have special offers. Avoid resellers who may charge extra. Advance booking is strongly recommended if you are travelling with a vehicle; for travel in August you will need to book a few weeks in advance. Individuals travelling without a vehicle can usually get tickets on the day of travel.

RIVER BOAT TOURS

From June through to September, the **Renaioli Association** in Florence offers inexpensive 1 hour boat tours on the Arno, departing from near Ponte alle Grazie. Boats seat up to 16 people with a minimum of six people per group. It is possible to reserve a tour guide to accompany you on the tour. Price varies by number of guests and use of guide.

DIRECTORY

FERRY OPERATORS

Moby
Tel 02 76 028 132 (from abroad).
Tel 199 30 30 40 (from Italy, toll).
www.moby.it

Toremar
Tel 02 26 302 803 (from abroad).
Tel 892 123 (from Italy, toll).
www.toremar.it

RIVER BOAT TOURS

Renaioli Association (Arno tour) and Tickets
Tel 347 7982 356.
www.renaioli.it
info@renaiolo.it

Driving in Florence and Tuscany

There are certain areas of Tuscany, such as tiny hill towns and authentic *agritourismo* locations, which are best reached by car. However, heavy traffic in some areas and narrow roads in others can make driving difficult, and it is unwise to drive without someone to help navigate. Train and coach travel *(see pp308–10)* are good options for reaching larger towns and cities. It is best to avoid having a car if you intend to stay in the cities of Florence or Siena; both cities restrict car traffic and parking is difficult and expensive.

Country road in the mountainous Garfagnana region of Tuscany

ARRIVING BY CAR

The main *autostrada* (toll highway) that services Tuscany (between Rome and Bologna) is the A1, also known as *Autostrada del Sole*. *Autostrada* signage is green. The Firenze–Mare (A11) goes to Pisa, Lucca and the coast. There are two *superstradas* (four-lane highways): the Firenze–Siena and the "Fi–Pi–Li", short for the cities it serves (Firenze, Pisa and Livorno). *Superstrada* signage is blue. Both types of highway have large service stations with good facilities, including self-service restaurants and large markets selling everything from *prosciutto* to CDs.

Drivers from the UK need a Green Card for insurance purposes, and the vehicle's registration document. EU nationals who intend to stay for more than six months and do not have the standard pink licence will need an Italian translation of their licence (IDP: International Drivers' Permit), available from most motoring organizations and Italian tourist offices.

SOS columns on the road allow instant access to emergency services. In a rental car, call the 800 number provided by the agency. The **ACI (Automobile Club d'Italia)** will tow anyone for free and offers free repairs to members of affiliated associations, such as the AA or RAC in the UK.

RULES OF THE ROAD

Drive on the right, use the left lane only for passing, and give way to the right. Seat belts are compulsory in the front and back. You must carry a warning triangle in case of breakdown and a fluorescent safety vest, which you must wear if you exit the vehicle on the highway. Speed limits for cars are: in town centres 50 km/h (30 mph); on roads outside cities 70 or 90 km/h (43/55 mph); on the *superstrada* 90/110 (55/70 mph) as indicated, and on the *autostrada* 130 km/h (80 mph).

Sign for specified parking times

DRIVING IN TOWNS AND CITIES

City centres are usually fraught with one-way systems, limited traffic zones and moped drivers who weave through traffic. You must be constantly vigilant and aware of other road users in order to avoid accidents. In Lucca, Siena and San Gimignano, only residents and taxis may drive inside the city walls, while Pisa has limited traffic zones around the Arno. Visitors may go in to unload at their hotel but must then park outside the residents' area.

Florence has an extensive pedestrian zone around the Duomo so that not even taxis or buses may use the roads connecting major sights in that area. Inside the *viali* (ring road), there is a strict *zona a traffico limitato* (ZTL), with electronic gates barring traffic when the ZTL sign is red. The fine for an infraction is steep. The light is green only on Sundays and late at night. If you stay in a hotel in the ZTL you will be given a temporary access permit so that you can unload your luggage, but then you must park elsewhere.

PARKING

Street parking in the centre of Florence (and in most of Tuscany) is indicated by blue or white lines on the pavement. White lines indicate residents' parking only. Visitors must park in the designated areas marked by blue lines and pay at the meter. Insert the amount of money for the time you need, and leave the receipt visible on the dashboard.

There are three large underground car parks in central Florence: at Santa Maria Novella station; below the Mercato Centrale; and at the Fortezza da Basso. Slightly further out, and less costly (€1.50 per hour, €18 daily rate), are the Parterre north-east of Piazza della Libertà, and the ultra-modern Alberti car park near Via Aretina. Some hotels offer their own parking while others have agreements for reduced rates with private garages.

In Tuscany, one day a week is set aside for street cleaning, when parking is forbidden. Parking signs show a small symbol (which looks a little like a tractor) with a day and time, indicating when cleaning takes place each week.

If you park illegally, your car could be towed away. If this happens, phone the **Vigili**, the municipal police, to find out where it has been taken.

Road signs in Gaiole in Chianti, central Tuscany

DRIVING IN THE COUNTRYSIDE

Driving on Tuscan country roads offers incredible views and hairpin bends. Sound your horn when approaching a blind bend (flash your lights at night). If using GPS, always check the route on a printed map and avoid impossibly convoluted white roads; they are likely to be poorly paved, narrow and steep. Avoid driving in unfamiliar areas of the countryside at night.

TOLLS AND FUEL

Autostradas are toll highways; you are issued with a ticket on entry, and pay as you exit. At the toll exit, signs above each lane indicate the payment method available – either an attendant who will accept cash or a machine that accepts credit cards. The yellow lane is reserved for electronic "Telepass" holders.

Fuel stations are regularly spaced on *autostradas*, but less so on *superstradas*. In the countryside they can be found in or just outside most towns. Small fuel stations close for a long lunch, but most operate 24 hours with automatic machines – insert banknotes into the machine, select the tank number, then begin pumping fuel. Don't put in more money than is needed to fill your tank, as the machine does not give change. Instead, a receipt is issued which you can use to get change when the fuel station is open. The machines do not take credit cards. Unleaded fuel is *senza piombo*; diesel is *gasolio*.

CAR RENTAL

Car rental in Italy is expensive and, ideally, should be booked online or through a tour operator before travelling. To rent a car you must be over 21, and have held a licence for at least a year. Visitors from outside the EU need an International Drivers' Permit (IDP). Make sure the rental package includes collision damage waiver, breakdown service and insurance against theft *(casco)*.

MOPED AND BIKE RENTAL

Moped (scooter) rental is available across Tuscany. It is not advisable for visitors to ride a moped in cities due to heavy traffic, but touring the countryside is very pleasant. Helmets are mandatory.

Bicycle rental is available in most towns and is a sustainable and inexpensive way to get around. Helmets are mandatory for children.

A moped rider crossing the Arno river in Florence

DIRECTORY

BREAKDOWN

Automobile Club d'Italia
Viale G. Amendola 36, Florence. **Map** 4 F1.
Tel *055 248 61.*
Via Cisanello 168, Pisa.
Tel *050 95 01 11.*
Viale Vittorio Veneto 47, Siena.
Tel *0577 490 01.*
Emergency toll free number:
Tel *803 116.*
www.aci.it

TOWING AWAY

Vigili (Municipal Police)
Florence ***Tel*** *055 78 38 82.*
Pisa ***Tel*** *050 91 03 78.*
Siena ***Tel*** *0577 29 25 54.*

CITY CAR RENTAL

Avis
Borgo Ognissanti 128r, Florence.
Map 1 A5 (5 A2).
Tel *055 21 36 29.*
c/o de Martino Autonoleggi, Via Simone Martini 36, Siena.
Tel *0577 27 03 05.*

Hertz
Via Maso Finiguerra 33r, Florence.
Map 1 B5 (5 A2).
Tel *055 239 82 05.*

Maggiore
Via Maso Finiguerra 31r, Florence.
Map 1 B5 (5 A2).
Tel *055 21 02 38.*

MOPED AND BIKE RENTAL

Automotocicli Perozzi
Via dei Gazzani 16, Siena.
Tel *0577 28 83 87.*
www.perozzi.it

DF Bike
Via Massetana Romana 54, Siena. ***Tel*** *0577 27 19 05.*
www.dfbike.it

Florence by Bike
Via San Zanobi 91r.
Map 2 D3.
Tel *055 48 89 92.*
www.florencebybike.com

Getting Around Towns and Cities in Tuscany

Tuscan cities are compact enough to get around reasonably comfortably on foot, and the city buses are relatively cheap, regular and wide-ranging. A one-way ticket takes you 15 km (10 miles) out of town, making the bus ideal for trips from the city centre to outlying areas of Florence, Pisa or Siena.

WALKING

Sightseeing on foot in Tuscan cities is made all the more pleasurable by the fact that there are plenty of squares in which to rest and watch the world go by, or cool churches to pop into when the heat gets too much. Most towns have pedestrian zones, including the area around Florence's Duomo and almost all of Siena, in which walking is very pleasant. On streets where traffic does have access, pavements tend to be narrow and crowded.

Be sure to cross the street at the white pedestrian crossings, which are sometimes accompanied by traffic lights. Although required to by law, not all drivers will stop voluntarily at crossings so proceed with caution. It helps to make eye contact with drivers and then step out slowly but confidently. Some very large streets have pedestrian underpasses.

Signs for sights and landmarks have brown backgrounds. In Florence, use the Duomo and river as orientation points. A gentle stroll around the main sights of Florence can take just a couple of hours. The main sights in Pisa are all in the same square. Siena is compact but hilly, so be sure to wear comfortable shoes.

The cities can be unbearably hot in summer. Plan your day so that you are inside for the hottest part. Recuperate Italian-style with a leisurely lunch followed by a siesta. Shopping is more pleasant in the early evening, when it is cooler and the streets start to come alive.

Signs showing pedestrian routes to sights and landmarks in Florence

CYCLING

Bicycles can be rented in all towns and cities. Lucca is a great town for cycling as it is flat and has a bike path along the city walls. Florence has some bike paths on the *viali* (tree-lined avenues), but otherwise bikes share the road with other vehicles.

No Pedestrian Access sign

Tour companies, such as **Florence by Bike**, offer bike tours departing from Florence and Siena. They take a pleasant route into the countryside and provide bikes, helmets, water and food.

GUIDED TOURS

Tours and private guides can be arranged through **APT** or a travel agent. For guided walks around the city, contact **ArtViva** or **Context Travel**. **Citysightseeing Firenze** offers a hop-on hop-off bus service (complete with audioguide) to all the major sites in the city. Segway tours of Florence and Pisa are arranged by **Segway Firenze**. The Florence tour is limited to the historic centre due to the number of narrow streets.

One of Florence's ATAF buses in a narrow street

CITY BUSES

Florence's city bus company is called **ATAF**, Pisa's is **CPT**, and Siena's **TRA-IN**. City buses are bright orange. Most lines run frequently until around 9:30pm, after which they tend to run hourly. There are designated night bus lines offering services through the night, but these are very infrequent.

Florence does not have a main terminus, but most buses can be picked up alongside Santa Maria Novella station or in Piazza San Marco. Buses run near most major sights: normal bus routes indicated by numbers and names are supplemented by electric minibuses, indicated by letters C1, C2, C3 through to D, that serve the narrow streets in the very centre of town.

Pisa's buses also serve the main sights. Most buses stop at the railway station and Piazza Vittorio Emanuele II. In Siena the main bus stops are Piazza Antonio Gramsci and Piazza San Domenico. There are bus information kiosks at all these points, but they are not always open. Tourist information offices can usually help, or consult the route maps online.

In all cases, enter the bus at the front or back and get off through the middle doors. The four low seats at the front of the bus are meant for the elderly, the disabled and people with children, although Italian etiquette calls for people to give up their seats for anyone in greater need than themselves.

BUS TICKETS

Tickets for city buses must be bought before travel and validated (stamped) in the machines on the bus. They can be boughts at newsstands, bars displaying the bus company sign (ATAF, APT, TRA-IN) or *tabacchi*, or at the bus terminus. If you are likely to make a few trips, buy multi-trip tickets that offer a slight discount. There are two- and four-trip paper tickets available; in Florence there is also the *Carta Agile* with an electronic chip loaded with €10, €20, or €30. Any of these multi-trip tickets can be used by people travelling together; just validate once for each passenger. Children under 1 metre high travel free.

If you are planning to stay longer in any one town, consider a multi-day ticket or monthly pass, which are non-transferable. Anyone wishing to claim a student discount must first purchase a student photocard.

Ticket-stamping machine

TRAMS IN FLORENCE

There have been plans to run trams through Florence for several years. In 2010, Line 1 finally opened. This connects the suburb Scandicci to Santa Maria Novella train station. Line 2 from Florence airport to Santa Maria Novella train station and Piazza Libertà is under construction. Line 3 is still under debate.

Tickets for the bus are also valid on the tram. Be sure to validate the ticket on whichever transport you use first, by stamping it in the machine found on board.

TAXIS IN TUSCANY

Official taxis found in Tuscan towns and cities are white with a "Taxi" sign on the roof. Only take taxis at official ranks – ignore all offers from touts at the stations. There are supplements for baggage, for rides between 10pm and 7am, on Sundays and on public holidays, and for journeys to and from the airport. If you phone for a taxi, the meter starts to run from the moment you book it, so by the time it arrives you could already owe several euros. Generally, travelling by taxi is rather costly. Taxi drivers are usually honest, but make sure you know what any supplements are for. Italians give very small tips or nothing at all

In Florence, there are ranks at Via Pellicceria, Piazza di Santa Maria Novella (near the station) and Piazza di San Marco. In Siena, taxis can be found in Piazza Matteotti and Piazza della Stazione; and in Pisa at the Piazza del Duomo, Piazza Garibaldi and Piazza della Stazione.

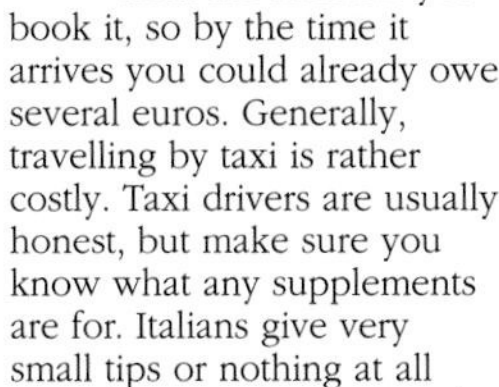

Taxi waiting for a fare at an official rank in Florence

DIRECTORY

CYCLE RENTAL

DF Bike
Via Massetana Romana 54, Siena.
Tel *0577 27 19 05.*

Due Ruote Rent
Borgo Ognissanti 153r, Florence.
Map 1 A5. ***Tel*** *055 239 96 96.*
www.dueruoterent.com

Florence by Bike (tours and rentals)
Via San Zanobi 91r, Florence.
Map 2 D3. ***Tel*** *055 48 89 92.*
www.florencebybike.com

I Bike Italy (tours)
Via de' Lamberti, 1, Florence.
Map 6 D3.***Tel*** *055 0123994.*
www.ibikeitaly.com

GUIDED TOURS

APT
Via Alessandro Manzone 16, Florence. **Map** 2 F5. ***Tel*** *055 23 32 0.* **www**.firenzeturismo.it

ArtViva
Via Sassetti 1, Florence.
Tel *055 29 26 20.*

Citysightseeing Firenze
Piazza Stazione 1, Florence. **Map** 1 B5 (5 B1). ***Tel*** *055 29 04 51.*

Context Travel
Via Baccina 40, Rome.
Tel *06 97 62 52 04.*

Segway Firenze
www.segwayfirenze.com

CITY BUSES

ATAF
Ufficio Informazioni & Abbonamenti, Piazza Stazione, Florence. **Map** 1 B5 (5 B1). ***Tel*** *800 424 500.* **www**.ataf.net

CPT
Ufficio Informazioni, Piazza Sant'Antonio 1, Pisa. ***Tel*** *050 505 511.* **www**.cpt.pisa.it

TRA-IN
Piazza Antonio Gramsci, Siena.
Tel *0577 20 42 46.*

TAXIS

Florence Radiotaxi
Tel *055 47 98* or *055 42 42.*

Pisa Radiotaxi
Tel *050 54 16 00* or *050 56 18 78.*

Siena Radiotaxi
Tel *0577 492 22.*

General Index

Page numbers in **bold** type refer to main entries

A

B

C

D

G

M

U

V

Acknowledgments

Dorling Kindersley would like to thank the following people whose contributions and help have made the preparation of this book possible.

Main Contributor
Christopher Catling has been visiting Florence and Tuscany since his first archaeological dig there as a student at Cambridge University 25 years ago. He is the author of several guide books on the city and region.

Additional Photography
Jane Burton, Philip Dowell, Neil Fletcher, Steve Gorton, Michelle Grant, Frank Greenaway, Alexandra Korey, Neil Mersh, Rebecca Milner, David Murray, Ian O'Leary, Poppy, Rough Guides/James McConnachie, Clive Streeter, Christine Webb, Linda Whitwam.

Additional Illustrations
Gillie Newman, Chris Dorr, Sue Sharples, Ann Winterbotham, John Woodcock, Martin Woodward.

Cartography
Uma Bhattacharya; Colourmap Scannning Limited; Contour Publishing; Cosmographics; European Map Graphics; Suresh Kumar; Kunal Singh. Street Finder maps: ERA Maptech Ltd (Dublin), adapted with permission from original survey and mapping by Shobunsha (Japan).

Cartographic Research
Caroline Bowie, Peter Winfield, Claudine Zante.

Design and Editorial Assistance
Louise Abbott, Beverley Ager, Gaye Allen, Douglas Amrine, Sam Atkinson, Rosemary Bailey, Claire Baranowski, Marta Bescos, Tessa Bindloss, Hilary Bird, Julie Bond, Lucia Bronzin, Ann-Marie Bulat, Carolyn Burdet, Julia Burdet, Jacob Cameron, Cooling Brown, Vanessa Courtier, Michelle Crane, Felicity Crowe, Nicola Erdpresser, Joy FitzSimmons, Anna Freiberger, Natalie Godwin, Jackie Gordon, Katie Greenaway, Vinod Harish, Jacky Jackson, Annette Jacobs, Claire Jones, Emma Jones, Roberta Kedzierski, Steve Knowlden, Alexandra Korey, David Lamb, Neil Lockley, Siri Lowe, Georgina Matthews, Rebecca Milner, Kamin Mohammadi, Catherine Palmi, Helen Partington, Alice Peebles, Marianne Petrou, Pamposh Raina, Ellen Root, Sands Publishing Solutions, Baishakhee Sengupta, Shailesh Sharma, Asavari Singh, Kate Singleton, Ellie Smith, Meredith Smith, Nicky Swallow, Rachel Symons, Andrew Szudek, Dawn Terrey, Tracy Timson, Alka Thakur, Daphne Trotter, Nick Turpin, Glenda Tyrrell, Janis Utton, Conrad van Dyk, Alastair Wardle, Lynda Warrington, Fiona Wild, Stewart J. Wild.

Special Assistance
Antonio Carluccio; Sam Cole; Giuseppe de Micheli and Moira Barbacovi at the Museo dell'Opera di Santa Croce; Julian Fox, University of East London; Simon Groom; Signor Tucci at the Ministero dei Beni Culturali e Ambientali; Museo dell'Opificio delle Pietre Dure; Signora Pelliconi at the Soprintendenza per i Beni Artistici e Storici delle Province di Firenze e Pistoia; Prof. Francesco Villari, Direttore, Istituto Italiano di Cultura, London.

For special assistance in supplying the computer-generated image of the Gozzoli frescoes in the Palazzo Medici Riccardi: Dr Cristina Acidini, Head of Restoration, and the restorers at Consorzio Pegasus, Firenze; Ancilla Antonini of Index, Firenze; and Galileo Siscam SpA, Firenze, producers of the CAD Orthomap graphic programme.

Photographic Reference
Camisa I & Son, Carluccio's, Gucci Ltd.

Photography Permissions
Dorling Kindersley would like to thank the following for their permission to photograph:

Florence: Badia Fiorentina; Biblioteca Mediceo-Laurenziana; Biblioteca Riccardiana; Centro Mostra di Firenze; Comune di Firenze; Duomo; Hotel Continentale; Hotel Hermitage; Hotel Villa Belvedere; Le Fonticine; Museo Bardini; Museo di Firenze com'era; Museo Horne; Museo Marino Marini; Museo dell'Opera del Duomo di Firenze; Ognissanti; Palazzo Vecchio; Pensione Bencistà; Rebus; Santi Apostoli; Santa Croce; San Lorenzo; Santa Maria Novella; Santa Trinità; Soprintendenza per i Beni Ambientali e Architettonici delle Province di Firenze e Pistoia; Tempio Israelitico; Trattoria Angiolino; Ufficio Occupazioni Suolo Pubblico di Firenze; Villa La Massa; Villa Villoresi. **Tuscany:** Campo dei Miracoli, Pisa; Collegiata, San Gimignano; Comune di Empoli; Comune di San Gimignano; Comune di Vinci; Duomo, Siena; Duomo, Volterra; Museo della Collegiata di Sant'Andrea, Empoli; Museo Diocesano di Cortona; Museo Etrusco Guarnacci, Volterra; Museo Leonardiano, Vinci; Museo dell'Opera del Duomo, Pisa; Museo dell'Opera del Duomo, Siena; Museo delle Sinopie, Pisa; Opera della Metropolitana di Siena; Opera Primaziale Pisana, Pisa; Soprintendenza per i Beni Ambientali e Architettonici di Siena; Soprintendenza per i Beni Artistici e Storici di Siena; Soprintendenza per i Beni Ambientali, Architettonici, Artistici e Storici di Pisa.

Picture Credits
t = top; tl = top left; tc = top centre; tr = top right; cla = centre left above; ca = centre above; cra = centre right above; cl = centre left; c = centre; cr = centre right; clb = centre left below; cb = centre below; crb = centre right below; bl = bottom left; b = bottom; bc = bottom centre; br = bottom right; (d) = detail.

Every effort has been made to trace the copyright holders and we apologize in advance for any unintentional omissions. We would be pleased to insert the appropriate acknowledgments in any subsequent edition of this publication.

Works of art have been reproduced with the permission of the following copyright holders: *Cavaliere* (1943) Marino Marini © DACS, London 2006 104t.

The publisher would like to thank the following individuals, companies and picture libraries for permission to reproduce their photographs:

dF Aeroporto di Firenze S.p.A.: 306br, 306cla; Agenzia per il Turismo, Firenze: 72tr; Alamy Images: Gary Cook 267t; CuboImages srl/Nico Tondini 135t; Stock Italia 302bl; Alitalia: 306t; Archivi Alinari, Firenze: 104b; The Ancient Art and Architecture Collection: 77tl; Archivio Fotografico Enciclopedico, Roma: Giuseppe Carfagna 38t, 39b, 203t, 203c; Luciano Casadei 38b; Cellai/Focus Team 38c; Claudio Cerquetti 33bl; B. Kortenhorst/K & B News Foto 21t; B. Mariotti 39c; S. Paderno 23t, 39t; G. Veggi 34c. The Bridgeman Art Library, London: Archivo dello Stato, Siena 47clb; Bargello, Firenze 68t, 69t; Biblioteca di San Marco, Firenze/K & BNews Foto 97t; Biblioteca Marciana, Venezia 44br; Galleria dell'Accademia, Firenze 94b; Galleria degli Uffizi, Firenze 27br, 45b, 47cla, 80b, 81tl, 81tr, 83t, 83b; Musée du Louvre, Paris/Lauros-Giraudon, 105t; Museo di San Marco, Firenze 52tl, 53t, 97cb; Museo Civico, Prato 188t; Palazzo Pitti, Firenze 121tr; Sant'Apollonia, Firenze 89t (d), 92c (d); Santa Croce, Firenze 72b; Santa Maria del Carmine, Firenze 127bl (d); Santa Maria Novella, Firenze 111cr; © The British Museum: 42b. Foto Carfagna & Associati: 285cl, 286tr, 290tc; Casa Dei Tessuti: 285br; Bruce Coleman: N. G. Blake 33br, Hans Reinhard 33cla, 33cra; Corbis: Ric Ergenbright 267c; Eye Ubiquitous/Paul Seheult 134bc; Owen Franken 266cla; Massimo Listri 285tc; Joe Cornish: 32–33, 36t, 37, 129t, 205, 227t; Giancarlo Costa, Milano: 34t, 45t, 55clb, 56ca, 56bl, 149 (inset), 268tl. Il Dagherrotipo: Salvatore Barba 135b, 137b; Marco Cerruti 136cla; Maurizio Leoni 136b; Paolo Marini 11t, 134tl; Giovanni Rinadli 137t. Mary Evans Picture Library: 46t, 48b, 50bl (Explorer), 55b, 56br, 74c, 179c, 196c. Ferrovie Dello Stato S.p.A.: 308cr, 308tl; Florence Dance Festival: Rambert Dance Company/ Swamp 291tl; Four Seasons Hotel Firenze: 249crb. Jackie Gordon: 57cb, 286tl, 309. Robert Harding Picture Library: 58–9; Alison Harris: Museo dell'Opera del Duomo, Firenze 27bl, 67t, 67c; Palazzo Vecchio, Firenze/Comune di Roma/Direzione dei Musei 4t, 52cb (Sala di Gigli), 53clb, 79t; San Lorenzo, Firenze/Soprintendenza per i Beni Artistici 91c; Santa Felicità, Firenze 119t (d); Santo Spirito, Firenze 118b; 116; Hotel Porta Rossa, Firenze: 183b; Hotel Torre di Bellosguardo: 248bl; Pippa Hurst: 183cr. The Image Bank: 60t; C. Place 100, 108t; Guido Alberto Rossi 11t, 11b; Impact Photos: Piers Cavendish 5b; Brian Harris 19b; Index, Firenze: 186t (d), 186b, 186c (d), 187t; Biblioteca Nazionale, Firenze 9 (inset); Biblioteca Riccardiana, Firenze 59 (inset), 243 (inset) 295 (inset); Galileo Siscam, S.p.A, Firenze 56–7; P. Tosi, 66cr; Gaetano Zumbo 10tr; Istituto e Museo di Storia della Scienza di Firenze: 74b, 75t; www.italiancookerycourse.com: 222cra. www.landscapepainting.com: Daria Insalaco 292b; Frank Lane Picture Agency: R. Wilmshurst 33crb; Lungarno Hotels: 246tl. The Mansell Collection: 47b; Misericordia Ambulance Service: 301tl; Museo dell'Opificio delle Pietre Dure, Firenze: 95c. Marka: F Pizzochero 31cla. Grazia Neri, Milano: R. Bettini 36b; Carlo Lannutti 57b; Peter Noble: 5t, 18, 172b, 222tr, 222cra, 300c. Obika Mozzarella Bar/Osteria Tornabuoni: 265cl; Osteria le Logge: 265b; Oxford Scientific Films: Stan Osolinski 236tr. Palazzo Vecchiette: 249bl; Roger Phillips: 202cra, 202crb; Photolibrary: Bertrand Gardel 313bl; Andrea Pistolesi, Firenze: 224b, 290b; Poste italiane: 305bl; Emilio Pucci S.R.L, Firenze: 57cla. Retrograph Archive, London: © Martin Breese 173c, 184b, 247t, 269bl; Restaurant Il Pozzo: Mario Palma 265t; Royal Collection: © Her Majesty Queen Elizabeth II: 55t (d). SAT Societa Aeroporto toscano SpA./Pisa Airport: 307tl; Scala, Firenze: Abbazia, Monte Oliveto Maggiore 211t; Galleria dell'Accademia, Firenze 92b, 94t, 95t; Badia, Fiesole 49clb; Badia, Firenze 70b; Bargello, Firenze 41t, 43bl, 46b, 49cla, 49b, 51cr, 54br, 66tr, 68b, 69cla, 69cra, 69clb, 108c; Battistero, Pisa 158b; Biblioteca Laurenziana, Firenze 90c; Camposanto, Pisa 156b; Cappella dei Principi, Firenze 50tl, 90t; Cappelle Medicee, Firenze 53crb, 91t; Casa del Vasari, Arezzo 199t (d); Chiesa del Carmine, Firenze 126–7, (126t, 126b, 127br all details); Cimitero, Monterchi 28c; Collegiata, San Gimignano 212cb; Corridoio Vasariano, Firenze 106t; Duomo, Lucca 180b; Duomo, Pisa 159t; Duomo, Prato 28t (d), 29t (d), 29c (d), 29b (d), 28–9; Galleria Comunale, Prato 188b; Galleria d'Arte Moderna, Firenze 54cb, 121tl; Galleria Palatina, Firenze 55crb, 122–3; Galleria degli Uffizi, Firenze 19t, 43cla, 43br, 48c, 50c, 50br, 51t, 51cl, 51b, 52cl, 52b (Collezione Giovanna), 80t, 81ca, 81cb, 81b, 82t, 82b, 83c (d); Loggia dei Lanzi, Firenze 77tr; Musée Bonnat, Bayonne 69b; Musei Civici, San Gimignano 40, 213b, 215b; Museo Archeologico, Arezzo 199c; Museo Archeologico, Firenze 42ca, 43clb, 43bl, 93cb, 99t, 99b, 240b; Museo Archeologico, Grosseto 240c; Museo Civico, Bologna 48tr; Museo degli Argenti, Firenze 53b, 54t, 54ca, 120b; Museo dell'Accademia Etrusca, Cortona 43t, 44ca; Museo dell'Opera del Duomo, Firenze 47t, 63t (d); Museo dell'Opera Metropolitana, Siena 26t; Museo di Firenze com'era, Firenze 71t, 125t, 165b; Museo Diocesano, Cortona 204b; Museo Etrusco Guarnacci, Volterra 42t; Museo di San Marco, Firenze 84, 96t (d), 96c, 96b, 97ca, 97b; Museo Mediceo, Firenze 50tr; Museo Nazionale di San Matteo, Pisa 157t; Necropoli, Sovana 241crb; Palazzo Davanzati, Firenze 103c (Sala dei Pappagalli); Palazzo Medici Riccardi, Firenze 2–3; Palazzo Pitti, Firenze 120c, 121bl; Palazzo Pubblico, Siena 46–7, 219t; Palazzo Vecchio, Firenze 52–53 (Sala di Clemente VII), 78t (Sala dei Gigli); Pinacoteca Comunale, Sansepolcro 197b; Pinacoteca Comunale, Volterra 166cr; San Francesco, Arezzo 200–1, (200t, 200b, 201t, 201b, 201cl all details); San Lorenzo, Firenze 27t; Santa Maria Novella, Firenze 26b, 46c (d), 49t (d), 110b; Santa Trinità, Firenze 102t; Santissima Annunziata, Firenze 98b; Tomba del Colle, Chiusi 42cb, 228t; Tribuna di Galileo, Firenze 54–5; Vaticano 41b (Galleria Carte Geographica); SITA bus: 310bl; SuperStock: age fotostock 10cla, 301cl; Sygma: G. Giansanti 222cla, 222crb, 222bl; Keystone 57t. Teatro del Sale/ Cibreo: 264br; Telecom Italia: 304ca; The Travel Library: Philip Enticknap 94cr, 218t.

Map cover
SuperStock: Robert Harding Picture Library.
Jacket
Front - SuperStock: Robert Harding Picture Library. Back - Alamy Images: Art Kowalsky tl; Robin McKelvie clb; Dorling Kindersley: John Heseltine bl; Kim Sayer cla. Spine - SuperStock: Robert Harding Picture Library t.
Front Endpaper
The Image Bank: tl; Scala, Firenze: tr.
All other images © Dorling Kindersley. For further information see **www.dkimages.com**

Phrase Book

In An Emergency

Help!	**Aiuto!**	*eye-**yoo**-toh*
Stop!	**Fermate!**	*fair-**mah**-teh*
Call a. doctor	**Chiama un medico**	*kee-**ah**-mah oon **meh**-dee-koh*
Call an am-ambulance.	**Chiama un' ambulanza**	*kee-**ah**-mah oon boo-**lan**-tsa*
Call the police.	**Chiama la polizia**	*kee-**ah**-mah lah pol-ee- **tsee**-ah*
Call the fire brigade.	**Chiama i pompieri**	*kee-**ah**-mah ee pom-pee-**air**-ee*
Where is the telephone?	**Dov'è il telefono?**	*dov-**eh** eel teh-**leh**-foh-noh?*
The nearest hospital?	**L'ospedale più vicino?**	*loss-peh-**dah**-leh pee-**oo** vee-**chee**-noh?*

Communication Essentials

Yes/No	**Sì/No**	***see/noh***
Please	**Per favore**	*pair fah-**vor**-eh*
Thank you	**Grazie**	***grah**-tsee-eh*
Excuse me	**Mi scusi**	*mee **skoo**-zee*
Hello	**Buon giorno**	*bwon **jor**-noh*
Good bye	**Arrivederci**	*ah-ree-veh-**dair**-chee*
Good evening	**Buona sera**	***bwon**-ah **sair**-ah*
morning	**la mattina**	*lah mah-**tee**-nah*
afternoon	**il pomeriggio**	*eel poh-meh-**ree**-joh*
evening	**la sera**	*lah **sair**-ah*
yesterday	**ieri**	*ee-**air**-ee*
today	**oggi**	***oh**-jee*
tomorrow	**domani**	*doh-**mah**-nee*
here/there	**qui/là**	***kwee/lah***
What?	**Quale?**	***kwah**-leh?*
When?	**Quando?**	***kwan**-doh?*
Why?	**Perchè?**	*pair-**keh**?*
Where?	**Dove?**	***doh**-veh*

Useful Phrases

How are you?	**Come sta?**	***koh**-meh stah?*
Very well, thank you.	**Molto bene, grazie.**	***moll**-toh **beh**-neh **grah**-tsee-eh*
Pleased to meet you.	**Piacere di conoscerla.**	*pee-ah-**chair**-eh dee coh-**noh**-shair-lah*
See you soon.	**A più tardi.**	*ah pee-**oo** **tar**-dee*
That's fine.	**Va bene.**	*va **beh**-neh*
Where is/are …?	**Dov'è/Dove sono …?**	*dov-**eh**/doveh **soh**-noh?*
How long does it take to get to …?	**Quanto tempo ci vuole per andare a …?**	***kwan**-toh **tem**-poh chee voo-**oh**-leh pair an-**dar**-eh ah…?*
How do I ? get to …	**Come faccio per arrivare a …?**	*koh-meh **fah**-choh pair arri-**var**-eh ah…?*
Are you getting off?	**Scende?**	***Shen**-deh?*
Do you speak English?	**Parla inglese?**	***par**-lah een-**gleh**-zeh?*
I don't understand.	**Non capisco.**	*non ka-**pee**-skoh*
Could you speak more slowly, please?	**Può parlare più lentamente, per favore?**	*pwoh par-**lah**-reh pee-**oo**len-ta-**men**-teh pair fah-**vor**-eh*
I'm sorry.	**Mi dispiace.**	*mee dee-spee-**ah**-cheh*

Useful Words

big	**grande**	***gran**-deh*
small	**piccolo**	***pee**-koh-loh*
hot	**caldo**	***kal**-doh*
cold	**freddo**	***fred**-doh*
good	**buono**	***bwoh**-noh*
bad	**cattivo**	*kat-**tee**-voh*
enough	**basta**	***bas**-tah*
open	**aperto**	*ah-**pair**-toh*
closed	**chiuso**	*kee-**oo**-zoh*
left	**a sinistra**	*ah see-**nee**-strah*
right	**a destra**	*ah **dess**-trah*
straight on	**sempre dritto**	***sem**-preh **dree**-toh*
near	**vicino**	*vee-**chee**-noh*
far	**lontano**	*lon-**tah**-noh*
up	**su**	***soo***
down	**giù**	***joo***
early	**presto**	***press**-toh*
late	**tardi**	***tar**-dee*
entrance	**entrata**	*en-**trah**-tah*
exit	**uscita**	*oo-**shee**-ta*
toilet	**il gabinetto**	*eel gah-bee-**net**-toh*
free, unoccupied	**libero**	***lee**-bair-oh*
free, no charge	**gratuito**	*grah-**too**-ee-toh*

Making a Telephone Call

I'd like to place a long-distance call.	**Vorrei fare una interurbana.**	*vor-**ray** **far**-eh oona in-tair-oor-**bah**-nah*
I'd like to make a reverse-charge call.	**Vorrei fare una telefonata a carico del destinatario.**	*vor-**ray** **far**-eh oona teh-leh-fon-**ah**-tah ah **kar**-ee-koh dell dess-tee-nah-**tar**-ree-oh*
I'll try again later.	**Ritelefono più tardi.**	*ree-teh-**leh**-foh-noh pee-oo**tar**-dee*
Can I leave a message?	**Posso lasciare un messaggio?**	***poss**-oh lash-**ah**-reh oon mess-**sah**-joh?*
Hold on.	**Un attimo, per favore**	*oon **ah**-tee-moh, pair fah-**vor**-eh*
Could you speak up a little please?	**Può parlare più forte, per favore?**	*pwoh par-**lah**-reh pee-**oo** **for**-teh, pair fah-**vor**-eh?*
local call	**la telefonata locale**	*lah teh-leh-fon-**ah**-ta loh-**kah**-leh*

Shopping

How much does this cost?	**Quant'è, per favore?**	*kwan-**teh** pair fah-**vor**-eh?*
I would like …	**Vorrei …**	*vor-**ray***
Do you have …?	**Avete …?**	*ah-**veh**-teh… ?*
I'm just looking.	**Sto soltanto guardando.**	*stoh sol-**tan**-toh gwar-**dan**-doh*
Do you take credit cards?	**Accettate carte di credito?**	*ah-chet-**tah**-teh **kar**-teh dee **creh**-dee-toh?*
What time do you open/close?	**A che ora apre/ chiude?**	*ah keh **or**-ah **ah**-preh/kee-**oo**-deh?*
this one	**questo**	***kweh**-stoh*
that one	**quello**	***kwell**-oh*
expensive	**caro**	***kar**-oh*
cheap	**a buon prezzo**	*ah bwon **pret**-soh*
size, clothes	**la taglia**	*lah **tah**-lee-ah*
size, shoes	**il numero**	*eel **noo**-mair-oh*
white	**bianco**	*bee-**ang**-koh*
black	**nero**	***neh**-roh*
red	**rosso**	***ross**-oh*
yellow	**giallo**	***jal**-loh*
green	**verde**	***vair**-deh*
blue	**blu**	*bloo*
brown	**marrone**	*mar-**roh**-neh*

Types of Shop

antique dealer	**l'antiquario**	*lan-tee-**kwah**-ree-oh*
bakery	**la panetteria**	*lah pah-net-tair-**ree**-ah*
bank	**la banca**	*lah **bang**-kah*
bookshop	**la libreria**	*lah lee-breh-**ree**-ah*
butcher's	**la macelleria**	*lah mah-chell-eh-**ree**-ah*
cake shop	**la pasticceria**	*lah pas-tee-chair-**ee**-ah*
chemist's	**la farmacia**	*lah far-mah-**chee**-ah*
delicatessen	**la salumeria**	*lah sah-loo-meh-**ree**-ah*
department store	**il grande magazzino**	*eel **gran**-deh mag-gad-**zee**-noh*
fishmonger's	**la pescheria**	*lah pess-keh-**ree**-ah*
florist	**il fioraio**	*eel fee-or-**eye**-oh*
greengrocer	**il fruttivendolo**	*eel froo-tee-**ven**-doh-loh*
grocery	**alimentari**	*ah-lee-men-**tah**-ree*
hairdresser	**il parrucchiere**	*eel par-oo-kee-**air**-eh*
ice-cream parlour	**la gelateria**	*lah jel-lah-tair-**ree**-ah*
market	**il mercato**	*eel mair-**kah**-toh*
news-stand	**l'edicola**	*leh-**dee**-koh-lah*
post office	**l'ufficio postale**	*loo-**fee**-choh pos-**tah**-leh*
shoe shop	**il negozio di scarpe**	*eel neh-**goh**-tsioh dee **skar**-peh*
supermarket	**il supermercato**	*su-pair-mair-**kah**-toh*
tobacconist	**il tabaccaio**	*eel tah-bak-**eye**-oh*
travel agency	**l'agenzia di viaggi**	*lah-jen-**tsee**-ah dee vee-**ad**-jee*

Sightseeing

art gallery	**la pinacoteca**	*lah peena-koh-**teh**-kah*
bus stop	**la fermata dell'autobus**	*lah fair-**mah**-tah dell **ow**-toh-booss*
church	**la chiesa**	*lah kee-**eh**-zah*
	la basilica	*lah bah-**seel**-i-kah*
closed for the public holiday	**chiuso per la festa**	*kee-**oo**-zoh pair lah **fess**-tah*
garden	**il giardino**	*eel jar-**dee**-no*
library	**la biblioteca**	*lah beeb-lee-oh-**teh**-kah*
museum	**il museo**	*eel moo-**zeh**-oh*
railway station	**la stazione**	*lah stah-tsee-**oh**-neh*
tourist information	**l'ufficio turistico**	*loo-**fee**-choh too-**ree**-stee-koh*

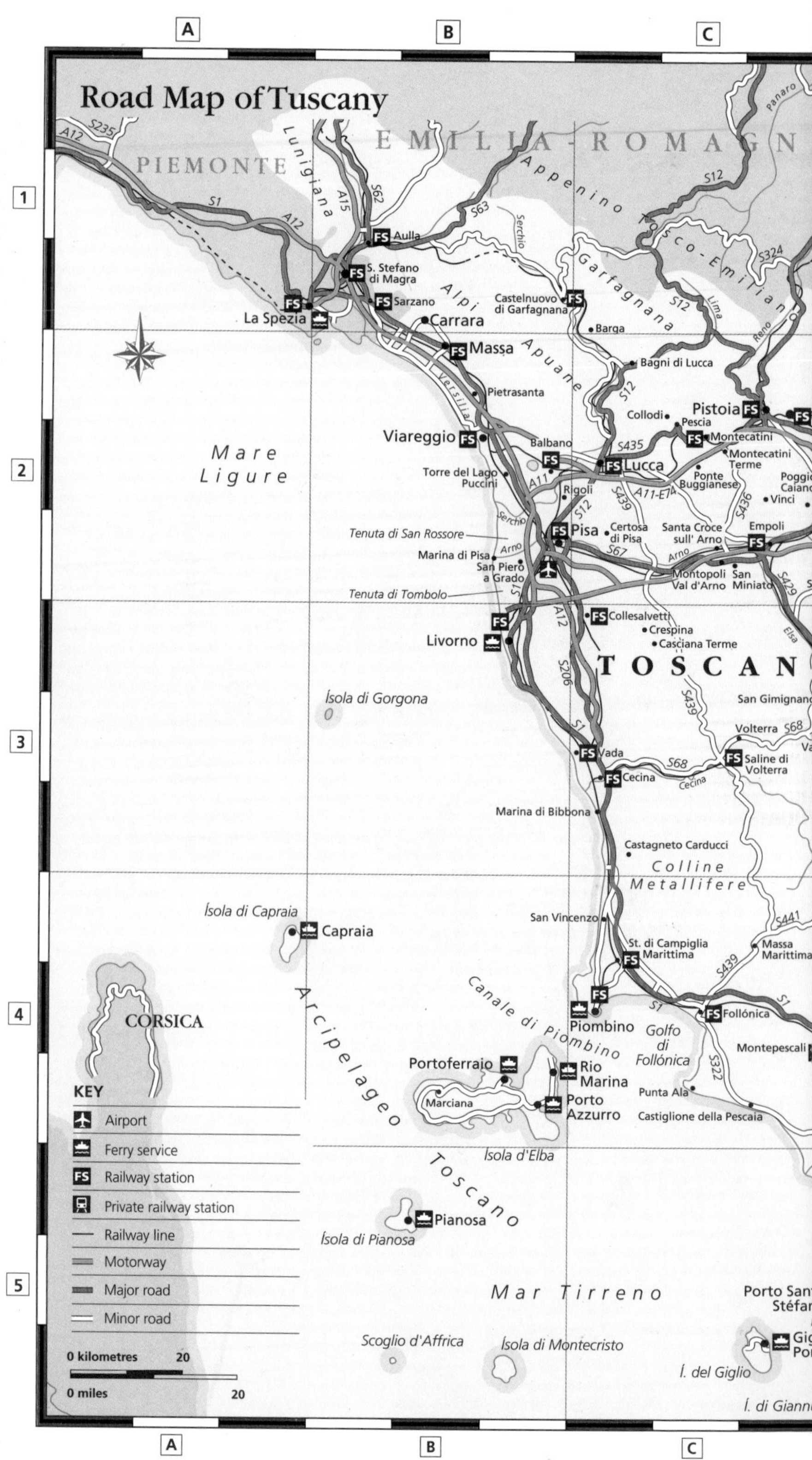
Road Map of Tuscany
A
B
C
1
2
3
4
5
EMILIA-ROMAGN
PIEMONTE
Lunigiana
Appenino Tosco-Emiliano
Garfagnana
Alpi Apuane
Versilia
Mare Ligure
TOSCAN
Colline Metallifere
Canale di Piombino
Arcipelageo Toscano
Mar Tirreno
CORSICA
Aulla
S. Stefano di Magra
Sarzano
La Spezia
Carrara
Massa
Castelnuovo di Garfagnana
Barga
Bagni di Lucca
Pietrasanta
Viareggio
Collodi
Pescia
Pistoia
Montecatini
Montecatini Terme
Balbano
Lucca
Torre del Lago Puccini
Rigoli
Ponte Buggianese
Vinci
Tenuta di San Rossore
Pisa
Certosa di Pisa
Santa Croce sull' Arno
Empoli
Marina di Pisa
San Piero a Grado
Montopoli Val d'Arno
San Miniato
Tenuta di Tombolo
Collesalvetti
Crespina
Casciana Terme
Livorno
Ísola di Gorgona
San Gimignano
Volterra
Vada
Saline di Volterra
Cecina
Marina di Bibbona
Castagneto Carducci
San Vincenzo
St. di Campiglia Marittima
Massa Marittima
Ísola di Capraia
Capraia
Piombino
Golfo di Follónica
Follónica
Montepescali
Portoferraio
Rio Marina
Marciana
Porto Azzurro
Punta Ala
Castiglione della Pescaia
Ísola d'Elba
Pianosa
Ísola di Pianosa
Porto Sant Stéfar
Scoglio d'Affrica
Ísola di Montecristo
Í. del Giglio
Í. di Gianne
KEY
Airport
Ferry service
Railway station
Private railway station
Railway line
Motorway
Major road
Minor road
0 kilometres 20
0 miles 20